# Robert Frost

# Robert Frost
# The Poet as Philosopher

### Peter J. Stanlis

### Introduction by
### Timothy Steele

ISI
BOOKS

*Wilmington, Delaware*

Stanlis, Peter J. (Peter James), 1920–

    Robert Frost : the poet as philosopher / Peter J. Stanlis ; introduction by Timothy Steele. —Wilmington, Del. : ISI Books, c2008.

        p. ; cm.
        ISBN: 978-1-933859-81-4 (pbk.)
        First published in hardcover in 2007.
        Includes bibliographical references and index.

        1. Frost, Robert, 1874–1963—Philosophy. 2. Frost, Robert, 1874–1963—Criticism and interpretation. 3. Dualism in literature. I. Title.

PS3511.R94 Z92543 2008          2008934072
811.52—dc22          0810

Book design by Jennifer M. Connolly

ISI Books
Intercollegiate Studies Institute
3901 Centerville Road
Wilmington, Delaware 19807
www.isibooks.org

Manufactured in the United States of America

# Table of Contents

# Dedication

In gratitude and to the memory of Paul D. Moody, Harry G. Owen, Reginald L. Cook, Victor E. Reichert, and to Frederick Burkhardt.

# Introduction

As much as we may have prized Robert Frost's poems for their technical dexterity, enchanting images, apt tropes, and deft turns of phrase, we have very imperfectly understood the ideas and beliefs that inform his work. This situation is partly of his doing. Unlike such other modern poets as William Butler Yeats, Wallace Stevens, Ezra Pound, William Carlos Williams, and T. S. Eliot, Frost generally refrained from formal self-commentary. He did not produce a significant body of criticism or auto-criticism that invited and facilitated the interpretation of his thought. "I write no prose and am scared blue at any demand on me for prose," he tells John Freeman in an undated letter from the mid-1920s. Likewise in 1962, the year before his death, he declined a request for an article about the Cold War, saying that "articles seem nothing I can undertake. . . . My limit seems to be verse and talk." To be sure, Frost wrote a handful of short essays, but by and large these pieces are occasional—public addresses, prefaces for books, and the like. Although they bristle with wit and insight, they do not elaborate a personal mythology, develop a theory of the imagination, announce a literary movement, advocate a novel prosody, or mine the literary past for materials to energize the poetic present.

Even if Frost had written more prose than he did, it is uncertain whether we would have gained a surer purchase on his ideas since his background and education had encouraged him to be cautious, tactful, and reticent. He adhered to the Yankee code that it is as unwise as it is unmannerly to parade our deepest feelings openly or to force our convictions on others. One suspects that he agreed with the protagonist of "The Generations of Men," who, discussing with a cousin their common ancestors, observes,

> *But don't you think we sometimes make too much*
> *Of the old stock? What counts is the ideals,*
> *And those will bear some keeping still about.*

Frost's intellectual guardedness also reflected his belief that much in life is unknowable and his alarm at people who demand easy answers to complex questions. Like Emily Dickinson and Herman Melville, he felt that nature itself resists assaults on its ultimate secrets. In "For Once, Then, Something," he describes looking down a well and being on the verge of identifying, beneath the water's surface, a shiny object—"a something white, uncertain, / Something more of the depths"—when a droplet strikes and blurs the pool, as if to preserve its modesty and privacy: "Water came to rebuke the too clear water." Similarly, in "A Passing Glimpse," he remarks, "Heaven gives its glimpses only to those / Not in position to look too close." No one welcomed more than Frost perceptive and open-minded curiosity, but he was at pains to distinguish this quality from the grasping, exhaustive scrutiny that endeavors to milk every last drop of meaning from a relationship, an experience, or a poem. "Easy does it," he says of his work while reading it to an audience in Berkeley in 1956. "Don't get any more out of it than you have to. Don't press it. Let it do it to you." And again: "I never want to be thorough with anything as delicate as a poem. Close. I get as close as I can to it. But not thorough."

Frost's reserve is also connected to his view of the function of poetry. As does Aristotle, Frost believes that poetry, though possessing traits that link it to philosophy, history, and science, has its own way of encountering and making sense of the world. For him, the truths poetry communicates are human and comprehensive, not partisan and dogmatic. To use the example he adduces in his preface to Edwin Arlington Robinson's *King Jasper*, poets have less to do with grievances than with grief. And so far as Frost is concerned, the purpose of the individual poem is not to expound fact or doctrine, but to attempt a fluid, existential engagement with experience. "It begins in delight and ends in wisdom," he says in "The Figure a Poem Makes." "Like a piece of ice on a hot stove the poem must ride on its own melting." A poem may ultimately produce, no less than a work of religion, economics, or chemistry, "a clarification of life." But even then, the poetic clarification will be, according to Frost, "not necessarily a great clarification, such as sects and cults are founded on, but . . . a momentary stay against confusion." (It is significant that the only times Frost's muses desert him are when he goes against his Aristotelian principles and native inclination and in such poems as "Build Soil" ventures to be didactic. He had many talents, but his excellent "Lesson for Today" notwithstanding, he was not suited for public satire in the way that, for instance, Martial and Juvenal or John Dryden and Jonathan Swift were.)

A final reason for Frost's circumspection is that, as much as he may have wished to be understood, he felt the natural human disinclination to open up to a world that is not always sympathetic or supportive. As he puts it in the first two stanzas of "Revelation," a lyric from his very first book:

> We make ourselves a place apart
> > Behind light words that tease and flout,
> But oh, the agitated heart
> > Till someone really find us out.
>
> 'Tis pity if the case require
> > (Or so we say) that in the end
> We speak the literal to inspire
> > The understanding of a friend.

Although the feeling Frost describes is virtually universal, it pierced him with special poignancy. The early death of his bright but unstable father and the family's consequent dependence on the charity of his paternal grandparents appear to have created feelings of personal and social insecurity that never entirely left him. Further, if most of us are sometimes loath to "speak the literal to inspire / The understanding of a friend," such a course is doubly problematical for poets, who trade less in the literal than in the metaphoric. Frost was a poet. The furthest he could or would go was to plant his ideas and beliefs in his poems, blending them with image and dramatic context, where they might work quietly and indirectly on the sensitive and unhurried reader.

Yet Frost's poems are wonderfully accessible, and if we misconstrue him, the cause cannot simply be his reluctance to digest for us his aims, ideals, and motives. For a fuller explanation, we must look to another quarter—a quarter Peter J. Stanlis brilliantly illuminates. As Stanlis shows, Frost was a dualist, and a key reason we have misunderstood him is that we have not sufficiently appreciated how deeply this philosophical outlook pervades his writing and thinking. (Dualism, we will remember, refers to the theory that reality is constituted of independent principles, or pairs of independent principles, such as good and evil, spirit and matter, particularity and wholeness. Monism, in contrast, posits that reality is explicable in terms of a single principle, and monism commonly takes one of two forms—idealistic or materialistic—the first holding that mind or spirit is the ultimate principle, the second that matter is the ultimate principle.)

Such is the strength of Stanlis's thesis that many of us will find it compelling even before we peruse the impressive analysis and meticulous documentation with which he supports it. No sooner, that is, do we consider the proposition that Frost is a dualist than we think of all those poems of his involving, to use a phrase he employs in his introduction to Sarah Cleghorn's *Threescore*, "things in pairs ordained to everlasting opposition." We think of "After Apple-Picking" and "Birches," which juxtapose the claims of earth with those of heaven. We think of "The Death of the Hired Man," where the husband Warren argues, in the interest of strict justice, that he and his wife are not obliged to shelter the feckless Silas, while the wife Mary pleads that they should do just that in the name of mercy. We think of "Love and a Question," which contrasts personal desire with charitable self-sacrifice. Or we think of "Mending Wall," in which communal engagement debates protective isolation.

Moreover, such poems are dualistic not only in structure, but in spirit. They do not raise and resolve questions. Instead, they explore problems which most of us must address at one time or another, but for which we will probably never find answers that are true or just under all circumstances. Such poems examine alternatives rather than take sides between them. They dramatize conflicts between opinions or outlooks that are, though sharply opposed, more or less equally valid or comprehensible.

Frost is apparently thinking of this aspect of his work when, in his *Paris Review* interview, he objects to critics who—citing lines from his poetry without referring to the dialectical context in which they may be embedded—mistake provisional statements for expressions of absolute belief. Illustrating this misguided procedure, he speaks of critics who assume that he is anti-New Deal on the basis of things like the bitter definition of home that Warren gives in "The Death of the Hired Man": "Home is the place where, when you have to go there, / They have to take you in." While not gainsaying the legitimacy of Warren's opinion, Frost stresses that it is, in the poem, immediately balanced by Mary's more clement definition: "I should have called it / Something you somehow haven't to deserve." As Frost says of Mary's statement, "That's the New Deal, the feminine way of it. . . . Very few have noticed that second thing; they've always noticed the sarcasm, the hardness of the male one."

We might note as an aside that no statement in Frost's poetry has been more frequently misappropriated from its dualistic context than "Good fences make good neighbors." A recent and striking instance of this was provided by United States Senator Jeff Sessions, who used the statement to advocate the construction of a colossal barrier along the border of Mexico and United States. Admittedly, good fences can promote neighborliness, but one wishes that the senator had given more thought, as the narrator of "Mending Wall" recommends, to what he was proposing to wall in or wall out, not to mention to whom he was like to give offense.

So immediately persuasive is Stanlis's thesis that we may ask ourselves why we have not perceived Frost's dualism more clearly before now. The obvious explanation is that few of us bring philosophical training to our reading of poetry, such training being irrelevant to our appreciation of most of the essential beauties and benefits of fine verse. There is, however, another and deeper answer to the question.

Poetic theory and practice, from the eighteenth century forward, are largely involved with or expressive of monism, and we expect, without necessarily being aware of our expectation, that our poets will be monists. Romantic and modern aesthetics are themselves monistic to the extent that they derive from the transcendental idealism that Immanuel Kant articulated and that writers like Friedrich Wilhelm von Schelling and Samuel Taylor Coleridge developed with special reference to the arts. This tradition infuses the poetry of our nation, which was itself founded in the Romantic era. We receive the tradition in the poetic theory of Ralph Waldo Emerson—whose pantheistic transcendentalism emphasizes the spiritual unity of all creation—and in the poetic practice of Emerson's chief disciple, Walt Whitman. The tradition is subsequently extended, in different ways, in the work of Pound, Eliot, Williams, and (most influentially) Stevens in his Post–*Harmonium* phase. Granted, our literature has produced a trenchant critic of monistic philosophy in general and monistic idealism in particular. This is William James, under whose spell Frost fell while a special student at Harvard in the 1890s and whom Frost described as his "greatest inspiration" there, despite never taking an actual class from him. But on the whole, we have tended to agree with Emerson's assertion in "The Transcendentalist" that our intellectual options are those offered by monism: "As thinkers, mankind have ever divided into two sects, Materialists and Idealists."

This, in any case, is the mindset we have brought to bear on Frost. We have regarded him as either a transcendental (idealist) monist or a materialist monist. For most of his career, he was cast in the former role, largely because his stage presence suggested an avuncular bard who embodied the values of the literary New England of Emerson and Thoreau. Late in Frost's life, this situation changed when many began to recognize what thoughtful readers had all along known: he was more complicated than his public image suggested, and currents of anguish, loneliness, and self-doubt ran beneath the beautiful surfaces of his poems. With this shift, critics refigured Frost as a materialist monist, a poet acquainted with desert places and desolate nights devoid of spiritual presence or transcendence. This reinterpretation was epitomized by Lionel Trilling's famous address at a celebration of the poet's eighty-fifth birthday. "The universe that he conceives," Trilling said on that occasion, "is a terrifying universe. Read the poem called 'Design' and see if you sleep the better for it. Read 'Neither Out Far Nor In Deep,' which often seems to me the most perfect poem of our time, and see if you are warmed by anything in it except the energy with which emptiness is perceived."

As Stanlis explains, Frost tried to counter these monistic interpretations and to affirm his dualism. Although he admired and generously praised Emerson's poems, he believed Emerson's transcendentalism to be ethically naïve. Frost's reservations are evident in his remarks on receiving in 1958 the Emerson-Thoreau Medal from the American Academy of Arts and Sciences. Having affectionately characterized Emerson as "a cheerful Monist, for whom evil does not exist, or if it does exist, needn't last forever," he adds, "A melancholy dualism is the only soundness." And although Frost appreciated that the materialist interpretations of his work were corrective, he did not think they were correct, and he rejected them along with the idealist interpretations. This twin rejection is implicit in a letter he wrote to Lawrance Thompson, his official biographer, in the wake of Trilling's address. Citing a phrase from "Uriel," one of his favorite poems by Emerson, Frost says,

> Did Trilling have something the other night? . . . At least he seemed to see that I am as strong on badness as I am on goodness. Emerson's defect was that he was of the great tradition of Monists. He could see the "good of evil born" but he couldn't bring himself to say the evil of good born. He was an Abominable Snowman of the top-lofty peaks. . . . I couldn't go as far as that because I am a Dualist.

It is sadly characteristic of the misinterpretations that have pursued Frost that Thompson could not or would not absorb the poet's explanation of his philosophical orientation. Re-reading Thompson's biography today, one is struck as much by his misunderstanding of Frost's thought and work as one is by his malice toward Frost himself. Further, reading between the

# Introduction

lines, one sees that Frost and Thompson fell out in the later years of their acquaintance partly because the poet came to realize that the biographer did not grasp his poetry or comprehend his intellectual background and religious beliefs. (Although the picture of Frost that Thompson presents in his biography is too confused and blinkered to characterize easily, it can perhaps be described as a compound of the two monistic interpretations: he appears to see Frost as a transcendentalist driven by moral-psychological disturbances over to the Dark Side.)

Thanks to the work of a number of recent scholars, many of Thompson's misrepresentations of Frost the man have been rectified, and we now have Stanlis's splendid book, which gives us a rich and revelatory analysis of Frost's poetry and thought. Frost says in his address on Emerson, "Emerson's name has gone as a poetic philosopher or as a philosophical poet, my favorite kind of both," and Stanlis, drawing on a lifetime's study of Frost and on his long friendship with him, shows us the poet as a philosopher in the true sense of the word—a lover of wisdom. Here we encounter a Frost who was not only a superb writer, but also a man deeply and intelligently engaged with the larger scientific, social, political, educational, and religious issues of his time.

Stanlis's discussion of Frost's dualism will lay to rest many myths, chief among them the one, generated by Thompson and others, that Frost was politically or socially reactionary. The truth is that Frost simply believed, as a dualist, that evil existed and probably would always exist, and he was therefore skeptical of the utopian movements of the first half of the twentieth century and resisted their calls to commit all our resources, including the arts, to the service of new political or spiritual dispensations. He believed passionately in liberty, and his work contains some of the sharpest and most sympathetic portraits of the working poor in all of modern poetry; but—again, as a dualist—he believed liberty was meaningless or even vicious without the stability and order of statutes and institutions. His politics, which mix liberal and conservative elements, may be best suggested by that stirring passage in the second stanza of Katherine Lee Bates's lovely hymn "America the Beautiful":

*America, America,*
*God mend thine every flaw,*
*Confirm thy soul in self-control,*
*Thy liberty in law.*

In this respect, Frost resembles, as Stanlis indicates, Edmund Burke. Like Burke, Frost was a meliorist in that he thought it possible for us, with effort, to increase our hold on the planet. But also like Burke, he doubted that collective action could ever entirely eradicate the various ills that beset our species, and he was fearful that radical change might make those ills worse. When in 1962 Frost told a gathering at the Kennedy White House, "I've been a Democrat all my life—but I've been a little unhappy since 1896," he was, in a sense, expressing the Old Whig position: one must resist arbitrary power and privilege, but one must remember as well that popular will can turn ugly if manipulated by demagogues and that social engineering and departmentalization sometimes patronize and diminish—and sometimes end up tyrannizing—the people they profess to aid.

In the course of illuminating Frost, Stanlis sheds oblique but revealing light on other American poets, particularly Frost's fellow philosophical poet Wallace Stevens. Like Frost, Stevens was a special student at Harvard in the 1890s and took James's pragmatism as a philosophical stimulus or starting point for his own thinking. Stevens was especially impressed by James's critique of philosophical idealism and of the era's genteel Christianity—a Christianity that confidently and monistically identified God with His Creation even though this identification was rendered doubtful and repellent by the discoveries of the new science and by the appalling conditions under which much of the human race was obliged to live. As Margaret Peterson points out in her *Wallace Stevens and the Idealist Tradition*, Stevens's great first book, *Harmonium*, not only draws on James's ideas, but also contains verbal echoes of James's prose.

Stevens, however, eventually moved back to the idealist camp, endeavoring to substitute a theory of Imagination in place of the Christianity and the traditional God in which he no longer believed. Unfortunately for Stevens, he could never fully believe in the metaphysical efficacy of the Imagination, and in consequence his later work ping-pongs between idealist monism and materialist monism—between assertions of the unifying and ordering power of Imagination (as in "The Idea of Order at Key West") and bleak visions of a wintry universe of non-transcendence (as in "The Course of a Particular"). Stevens's poetry also offers a third species of monism—we can call it "momentary monism"—which denies permanent grounds for idealist faith, but which records intuitions of a Wholeness we can transiently experience. ("The House Was Quiet and the World Was Calm" and "Final Soliloquy of the Interior Paramour" are two poems that treat this state.)

If Frost and Stevens shared an early esteem for James, they diverged in their opinions of James's colleague George Santayana, and this divergence reflects some of the philosophical differences between the poets. Frost's keen interest in and knowledge of science prevented him from imagining it conflicted with the fundamental concerns of religion. He never considered dismissing religion in general or Judeo-Christianity in particular merely because the doctrines and practices of temporal ecclesiastic institutions had grown enfeebled or intellectually bankrupt. For these and other reasons, Frost regarded Santayana's thoroughgoing skepticism as factitious and unpersuasive and, in its relativism, unhelpful as a guide to living. Stevens, in contrast, admired Santayana greatly, and the two men became friends during Stevens's time at Harvard. Santayana's argument that poetry and religion express the same imaginative impulse affected Stevens's ideas on the subject, and Santayana's theory of essences influenced themes Stevens developed in such late poems as "Notes Toward a Supreme Fiction" and "To an Old Philosopher in Rome," his tribute to Santayana. Further, Stevens doubtless recognized that Santayana, who repeatedly expressed attachments to both atheism and the institution of the Catholic Church, embodied a condition he too experienced—a nostalgia for and preoccupation with an abandoned faith.

We cannot know, this side of the grave, whether monism or dualism (or pluralism or some other position) is the best explanation of reality and being, but Stanlis's discussion of Frost supplies a fascinating account of a road less traveled by American artists and thinkers. If Stevens's monism offers a moving picture of some of the dilemmas into which Romantic philosophy and aesthetics have led us, Frost's dualism suggests fruitful avenues of escape.

A related and more specific observation might be made with reference to our nation's poetry. There are no absolute rights and wrongs in aesthetic matters, any more than there are in philosophical ones. But looking at American verse of the last 150 years, we may well feel uneasy that we have so thoroughly (and, often, so unknowingly) committed ourselves to the tradition of Emerson and Whitman and to the Romantic idealism or monism that underlies that tradition. We assume that our poets will sing of themselves, and we trust that their songs—no matter how obscure, slapdash, solipsistic, or windy—will partake of an organic wholeness of things and will, in some vague way, express or fulfill our deepest needs and concerns. We do not have to choose between the poetics of Frost and those of Emerson and Whitman. Yet we need some balance between them for the sake of our literary sanity. Reading Stanlis on Frost's dualism, we may conclude that it would be to our advantage to explore, or at least to admit into discussion, a position that preserves for poetry both reason and instinct, both part and whole, both objectivity and subjectivity, both freedom and constraint, both nature and artifice, both regular meter and personal rhythm.

## Robert Frost: The Poet as Philosopher

Whatever our individual opinions about this matter, we can all enjoy Stanlis's study of Frost for its rewarding discussion of the intellectual adventure of the poet's life. If monists must, in some manner, explain and account for the particulars of our beautiful and bewildering universe, dualists must endeavor to show us how the particulars, and the principles that govern them, are related. Frost was profoundly religious as well as philosophical. From first to last, he thought hard and affectionately about life, nature, and the universe; and as is evident from his late poems, he took seriously the story of the Incarnation and pondered the strange, miraculous coexistence of spirit and flesh, of consciousness and matter. He always tried to harmonize, while respecting equally, the polarities he perceived. As the final stanza of "Two Tramps in Mud Time" indicates, he never lost the sense that, in our attempts to reconcile the conflicting claims we face in our brief lives, we enter into the ultimate and mysterious duality of time and eternity:

> But yield who will to their separation,
> My object in living is to unite
> My avocation and my vocation
> As my two eyes make one in sight.
> Only where love and need are one,
> And the work is play for mortal stakes,
> Is the deed ever really done
> For Heaven and the future's sakes.

*–Timothy Steele*
*Los Angeles, California*
*November 2006*

# Prelude

# The Conversationalist as Poet

From around 1913 until Robert Frost's death in January 1963, almost everyone who knew him personally agreed that he was among the most brilliant, provocative, learned, and original conversationalists of the twentieth century.[1] Two of his English friends during 1912–14, Wilfred Gibson and John W. Haines, have recorded how all his power of colloquial eloquence burst through his pent-up accumulated experience of life and literature, evidencing the splendid conversationalist who later greatly impressed so many persons throughout his life.

During the 1920s, Louis Untermeyer, Raymond Holden, Wilfred E. Davison, and Julius John Lankes, among others, recorded visits with Frost in which his unique greatness as a talker impressed them most forcefully. Reginald L. Cook, a close friend of Frost for thirty-seven years, called him "the master of the riposte, humanly exulting in superior feats of wit" and pronounced him "one of the greatest talkers of his time."[2] Similarly, Louis Mertins, who had many long talks with the poet during the 1930s and 1940s, concluded that "Frost was one of the greatest conversationalists of the twentieth century, as Aristotle was of the Golden Age of Greek culture."[3] My own experience with Frost as a conversationalist, mainly in his cabin at the Homer Noble Farm near Bread Loaf during the summers of 1939–44 and in 1961 and 1962, but also on occasions in Boston, Ann Arbor, and Detroit, convinced me that he was a man of great imagination, wit, and humor, that his intellectual brilliance was beyond dispute, that he possessed immense learning in many subjects, and that he was without peer as a raconteur.[4] After several conversations with Frost at Bread Loaf in August 1941, William Carlos Williams confirmed my view of Frost as a conversationalist: "He's a good talker, witty, loaded with information and well able to take care of himself anywhere, anytime."[5] Very late in the poet's life, after an interview with him, John Ciardi recorded that they had "talked till midnight" and again "the next morning. . . . It was great talk. . . . It always is when Mr. Frost warms to it, for he is certainly one of the master conversationalists of this age."[6] Such abstract testimonies to Frost's powers of conversation could be multiplied many times over, but none of them answers the crucial questions that inevitably arise—how did Frost become such an outstanding conversationalist; how is his conversation related to his conception of poetry and creative practice as a poet; and, finally, how does his talk reveal vital aspects of his philosophical beliefs, centered in his dualism? In answer to these queries, an account of the natural history of his genesis and development as a poet yields some important insights into his nature as a conversationalist.

The earliest evidence that conversation was to be a vital element in Robert Frost's life and art is provided, ironically, not by the poet but by Elinor White, his future wife. In 1892, when she and Frost graduated as co-valedictorians at Lawrence High School in Massachusetts, her valedictory address was titled "Conversation as a Force in Life." Undoubtedly, along with their mutual physical, mental, and emotional attraction and their love of poetry, Elinor and Robert Frost shared a faith in the art of living in and through good conversation.

Whether or not Frost took his cue on the importance of good talk from his wife, there is no doubt that from early manhood until his death the poet believed that next to poetry itself the art of conversation with sophisticated literary friends was the great social, aesthetic, and intellectual passion of his life. During the summers of 1915 and 1916, Morris P. Tilley, a professor of English at the University of Michigan, was Frost's neighbor near Franconia, New Hampshire, and recorded: "He believes that conversation with friends has given him the moments of highest joy, greater than that of books."[7] Fortunately, the dramatic moment of epiphany in Frost's life as a poet is provided by him, when he experienced during a conversation with a preacher friend of his patrons, Susan and Reverend William Hayes Ward—the aesthetic revelation of how, in general, his conversation was related to his early poetry.

Frost's sudden flash of insight and intuitive understanding occurred in 1895, at age twenty-one. It was like a divine revelation to one of God's elect, because it provided him with the essential principle and objective of his whole aesthetic theory and future practice as a poet. It is necessary to quote Frost's whole lengthy passage on this event, reported retrospectively, because it reveals how his response led him to test whether his revolutionary perception was valid, by examining the whole tradition of major English poets with his theory in mind, and also because it illuminates the reason for the enormous difference between *A Boy's Will* (1913) on the one hand and *North of Boston* (1914) and all of Frost's subsequent poetry, with its conscious emphasis upon structured form:

> Perhaps when that preacher friend of Ward's looked me up shortly after my first poem appeared in *The Independent* and talked to me about it, something providential was happening to me. I'm sure the old gentleman didn't have the slightest idea he was having any effect on a very stubborn youngster who thought he knew what he knew. But something he said actually changed the whole course of my writing. It all became purposeful.

> One day as we talked he said to me that when he read my poems it was just like hearing me talk. I didn't know until then what it was I was after. When he said that to me it all became clear. I was after poetry that talked. If my poems were talking poems—if to read one of them you heard a voice—that would be to my liking! So, I went to the great poets, from Chaucer and Shakespeare to Coleridge and Wordsworth. And looked for this very thing in their lines. I will admit, when I have been quoted on the matter I have been made to speak rather mistily. But one thing must always be kept in mind: Whenever I write a line it is because that line has already been spoken clearly by a voice within my mind, an audible voice.

> There has been a great hue and cry raised over what I have had to say regarding voice posturing, or as I have sometimes called it, the sound of sense. When I first began to write poetry—before the illumination of what possibilities there are in the sound of sense came to me—I was writing largely, though not exclusively, after the patterns of the past. For every poet begins that way—following some pattern, or group of patterns. It is only when he has outgrown the pattern and sees clearly for himself his own way that he has really started to become. You may go back to all those early poems of mine in *A Boy's Will*, and some that are left out of it. You will find me there using the traditional clichés. Even "Into

My Own" has an "as't were." In "Stars" there is a line "O'er the tumultuous snow"; while in my very first poem, "My Butterfly," I was even guilty of "theeing" and "thouing," a crime I have not committed since. . . . The young poet is prone to echo all the pleasing sounds he has heard in his scattered reading. He is apt to look on the musical value of the lines, the metrical perfection, as all that matters. He has not listened for the voice within his mind, speaking the lines and giving them the value of sound.

There is another angle to this. It is suggested by a proneness to the unique. It is the value of current words in writing poetry. It has been a long time since I consciously fell into any of the clichés so common in verse. It has been a long time since I used any word not common in everyday speech. For example, I would never think of using the word "casement" for window in general. Whenever I have used that word, which I have occasionally, it was because I was writing about that kind of a window—never for window as such. In this, perhaps, I have unconsciously tried to do just what Chaucer did when the language was young and untried and virile. I have sought only those words I had met up with as a boy in New Hampshire, working on farms during the summer vacations. I listened to the men with whom I worked, and found that I could make out their conversation as they talked together out of ear-shot, even when I had not plainly heard the words they spoke. When I started to carry their conversation over into poetry, I could hear their voices, and the sound posture differentiated between one and the other. It was the sense of sound I have been talking about. In some sort of way like this I have been able to write poetry, where characters talk, and, though not without infinite pains, to make it plain to the reader which character is saying the lines, without having to place his name before it, as is done in the drama.

Because I have been, what some might call, careless about the so-called proper beat and rhythm of my lines, there have been those who think I write free verse. Now, I am not dead set against vers libre; but you know there is no idea you cannot express beautifully and satisfactorily in the iambic pentameter. Much of my verse is written in this form—blank, unrimed verse. I have always maintained that it takes form to properly perform, and free verse has no form, and so its performance is meager. . . . The greatest freedom poetry can attain is having form, a frame, to work in. Free verse is batting a ball into space and wondering why it doesn't return to the batter. Poetry written in form is like batting a ball against the side of a wall and feeling it return to the bat. A picture frame with its four simple lines is necessary to the showing of a picture. Try it and see. The frame thus becomes a part, even, of the picture.[8]

This long passage contains practically all of the essential elements necessary to understand Frost's early development as a poet, including the enormous differences in diction, tone, and forms between the lyric poems in *A Boy's Will* and the narrative-dramatic poems in *North of Boston*. But the discovery in 1895 that what he was consciously after was "poetry that talked" required Frost to become a master conversationalist first, quite apart from his poetry. Over the next twenty years, up to around 1915, he developed simultaneously as a conversationalist and a poet whose control of "voice posturing" by fictional characters in a dramatic setting provided the tone and "sound of sense" in the subtle shades of meaning in his poems.

During Frost's decade in Derry, he had to pursue his theory and practice between good talk and poetry in isolation, because there was no sophisticated literary person with whom he could discuss his aesthetic ideas. Yet he greatly enriched his germinal belief in conversational poetry in a variety of ways. Frost was briefly a friend to John Hall, a local semiliterate farmer whose mother-wit language greatly appealed to him. Lawrance Thompson has noted Hall's influence on Frost's theory of language in poetry:

He became fascinated by Hall's witty, picturesque, back-country way of implying meaning through sly inflections and modulations of voice. They gave color and bite to the sound of sense. As a flattering tribute to Hall and other north-of-Boston farmers, Frost had gradually modified his way of talking. He deliberately imitated the manner in which his neighbors unconsciously slurred words, dropped endings and clipped sentences.[9]

For about a decade Frost continued to perfect his conscious art of talking like a New Hampshire farmer, so that both in his conversation and in his poetry written in Derry he was exploring the various ways of converting colloquial speech into a new art form.

In 1907, after Frost had begun teaching at Pinkerton Academy, he revised the curriculum in English studies, recommending for the improvement of the students "to teach them the satisfaction of superior speech." Since superior speech came close to the essence of drama in poetry, Frost advocated that "expression in oral reading . . . is made the test of appreciation."[10] During the school year 1909–1910, Frost directed his prize students who published the Pinkerton *Critic* to present five plays: Marlowe's *Doctor Faustus*, Milton's *Comus*, Sheridan's *The Rivals*, and Yeats's *The Land of Heart's Desire* and *Cathleen ní Houlihan*. Frost adapted and compressed these plays, deleted what he called "rhetorical passages" and replaced them with "speaking passages," thus stripping them down to their essential form for colloquial presentation on the stage.[11] All of this editing and rewriting strengthened his growing conviction that all writing was good only to the extent that it was dramatic, and that "all the fun's in how you say a thing." To Frost, closet drama, meant only for silent reading with the eye, was totally displaced by drama for speakers on the stage.

More and more during his years in Derry and at Pinkerton Academy, Frost came to harmonize the concept of the poet as conversationalist and the conversationalist as poet. Indeed, he came to believe that good conversation was almost as much an art as poetry itself. If good poetry is practically synonymous with good dramatic talk, so too does good talk acquire the essential character of poetry. Frost once told Louis Mertins that "he had his first experience in listening to genuine conversation when he heard Æ [George Russell] and Yeats talk together in Ireland."[12] Mertins summarized the close reciprocal relationship Frost had come to perceive between poetry and good conversation:

> Whenever Frost in after years had occasion to refer to that visit to Eire [in 1928], it was not of the Irish landscape, or of Irish farming, or of the Irish peasantry, or of the Sinn Feiners, or of the Eire Republic, or of de Valera that he talked. These things scarcely formed a backdrop. It was always of the other-worldly conversation he held with the two Irish mystics—men of the older Ireland—such talk, he said, "as nowhere else on earth have I ever heard the like of. These men took ordinary conversation and lifted it into the realm of pure literature."[13]

Like these Irish poets, Frost himself, during a lifetime of talks with friends, often lifted ordinary conversation into the realm of pure literature. The main difference between dramatic poetry in monologues or dialogues and his conversations with friends was that his poetry was cast in traditional literary structured forms, such as sonnets, odes, lyric stanzas, and blank verse narratives, and in the techniques of meter, rhythm, and rhyme, whereas good conversation was much more loose, whimsical, discursive, and delivered intuitively by speaking spontaneously to the present moment.

Frost was well aware that his years on the Derry farm and as a teacher at Pinkerton Academy were his period of apprenticeship as a poet, a time of fruitful germination and strong development, when he came into his own and consciously acquired his personal voice in poetry. He and his wife, Elinor, knew that he was a true poet, but by 1912, at age thirty-eight, despite strenuous efforts to become known, he had received very little public recognition. He knew that he had to do something decisive and dramatic, to declare himself for a life of poetry, so that he would not be reduced to the ranks of a routine academician teaching English in public education. When he was offered a teaching position at the Normal School in Plymouth, New Hampshire, for the academic year 1911–12, he accepted with the provision that he could resign after one year. In August 1912 he consciously gathered himself together to make "the long deferred forward movement" to fulfill his career as a poet. His grandfather's will and annuity, and the sale of his Derry farm, provided the money needed, and late in the summer Frost and his family left Boston for Glasgow and then settled in Beaconsfield, England, where he began the process of the great harvest he desired for his poetry.

Frost was acutely aware that in going to Britain he was returning, as to a homecoming, to his ancestral roots, both in his family and in his literary life. As a young woman his mother had migrated to Ohio from Scotland, and his father's family were descendants of immigrants to New England from seven generations ago. The literary language of Chaucer, Shakespeare, and Milton and the long and rich tradition of English poetry were deeply rooted in his psyche, so that he experienced joy and satisfaction living near London. In retrospect he once remarked that living in old England made him more aware of New England than ever before. His literary experience in England, in coming to know and be known there by some of the outstanding poets of the pre–World War I era and in having *A Boy's Will* published in April 1913, and *North of Boston* in May 1914, proved absolutely decisive in shaping his entire future life as a poet.

In a letter to Wilbur E. Rowell (July 17, 1913), Frost referred to *A Boy's Will* as a "very personal" collection of poems and stated that "practically all of it" was written "five years ago on the farm in Derry." He repeated this statement in a letter to John Bartlett (November 5, 1919): "the first book . . . was mostly written on the farm before I attended school at Pinkerton."[14] But his discovery in 1895 that he was consciously after "poetry that talked" was not applied in practice in the poems of *A Boy's Will*. Conventional literary rhetoric and archaic usage still dominated these early lyrics. Except for a few poems in this first collection, his revolutionary theory of language as spoken sounds in idiomatic and colloquial talk was first fulfilled in his second book. As he noted in a letter to John Bartlett on December 18, 1913:

> In "North of Boston" you are to see me performing in a language absolutely unliterary. What I would like is to get so I would never use a word or combination of words that I hadn't *heard* used in running speech. I bar words and expressions I have already seen. You do it on your ear. Of course I allow expressions I make myself. War on clichés.[15]

Clearly, the great revolution in Frost's poetry occurred between *A Boy's Will* and *North of Boston*.

Although, as Frost himself said, no poet ever wrote in order to fulfill a theory of writing, it is evident that in the decade or more before he went to England, he was consciously developing his theory of language as a vehicle for "correspondence" between a writer or speaker and his audience. His revolutionary conception of language applied not only to his poetry, but to all spoken and written prose sentences. In a letter to John Bartlett (February 22, 1914), he provided a definition of a sentence based not upon conventional rules of grammar and logic, but upon the meaning in sounds: "A sentence is a sound in itself on which other sounds called words may be strung."[16] On May 18, 1914, Frost wrote to Sidney Cox that "the science of verse" as he perceived it in sentence structure applied to teaching: "The novelty if you didn't miss it was the definition of a sentence which is calculated to revolutionize the teaching of literary composition in the next twenty years."[17] As both a poet and a classroom teacher of composition, Frost believed that "oral reading" through a close attention to the "voice posturing" of speakers and their changes in "voice tones," so natural without inflated literary rhetoric in actual conversation, was the most valid and effective method of conveying meaning in both writing and reading, whether poetry or prose.

Soon after Frost was established and feeling at home in the literary circles of London, in an important letter to John Bartlett, significantly dated "Fourth-of-July" 1913, he noted that his declaration of independence on his "letter head" showed "how far we have come" since he left Pinkerton Academy. His self-conscious personal independence from the common beliefs and practices of established Victorian poets, such as Swinburne and Tennyson, that "the music of words was a matter of harmonized vowels and consonants," is amply underscored in this letter:

> To be perfectly frank with you I am one of the most notable craftsmen of my time. That will transpire presently. I am possibly the only person going who works on any but a worn out theory (principle I had better say) of versification. You see the great successes in recent poetry have been made on the assumption that the music of words was a matter of harmonized vowels and consonants. Both Swinburne and Tennyson arrived largely at effects in assonation. But they were on the wrong track or at any rate on a short track. They went the length of it. Any one else who goes that way must go after them. And that's where most are going. I alone of English writers have consciously set myself to make music out of what I may call the sound of sense. Now it is possible to have sense without the sound of sense (as in much prose that is supposed to pass muster but makes very dull reading) and the sound of sense without sense (as in Alice in Wonderland which makes anything but dull reading). The best place to get the abstract sound of sense is from voices behind a door that cuts off the words. Ask yourself how these sentences would sound without the words in which they are embodied:
>
> *You mean to tell me you can't read?*
> *I said no such thing.*
> *Well read then.*
> *You're not my teacher.*
>
> *He says it's too late.*
> *Oh, say!*
> *Damn an Ingersoll watch anyway.*
>
> *One-two-three—go!*
> *No good! Come back—come back.*
> *Haslam go down there and make those kids*
> *get out of the track.*
>
> Those sounds are summoned by the audile imagination and they must be positive, strong, and definitely and unmistakably indicated by the context. The reader must be at no loss to give

his voice the posture proper to the sentence. The simple declarative sentence used in making a plain statement is one sound. But Lord love ye it mustn't be worked to death. It is against the law of nature that whole poems should be written in it. If they are written they won't be read. The sound of sense, then. You get that. It is the abstract vitality of our speech. It is pure sound—pure form. One who concerns himself with it more than the subject is an artist. But remember we are still talking merely of the raw material of poetry. An ear and an appetite for these sounds of sense is the first qualification of a writer, be it of prose or verse. But if one is to be a poet he must learn to get cadences by skillfully breaking the sounds of sense with all their irregularity of accent across the regular beat of the meter. Verse in which there is nothing but the beat of the meter furnished by the accents of the polysyllabic words we call doggerel. Verse is not that. Neither is it the sound of sense alone. It is the resultant from those two. There are only two or three meters that are worth anything. We depend for variety on the infinite play of accents in the sound of sense. The high possibility of emotional expression all lets in this mingling of sense-sound and word-accent. . . . Never if you can help it write down a sentence in which the voice will not know how to posture *specially*.[18]

It would be a great mistake to conclude from this letter that Frost's theory of "voice posturing," "the sound of sense," and the "audile imagination," and his statement that cadences or tones are created through rhythm breaking across regular meter—that all this is merely concerned with the phonetic techniques of poetry. His theory goes to the heart of his entire aesthetic philosophy and conception of art, and is ultimately a vital part of his great skill and power both as a conversationalist and poet, and in his metaphorical habits of thought as a philosophical dualist. In all of Frost's conversation and thought the "play" between spirit and matter was frequently bridged by his aesthetic theory, centered in the sound of sense.[19]

Frost's letter to Bartlett on July 4, 1913, shows that when he went to England late in 1912 the connections between his theory of language in poetry, his powers of conversation, and his dualistic philosophy were firmly established. This fusion of his art and thought gave him such enormous self-confidence that his theory of language was valid that he did not hesitate to challenge the rival theory held by Robert Bridges, the English Poet

Laureate. In a very revealing letter to Sidney Cox (January 19, 1914), Frost took strong exception to the view propounded by Bridges to Frost when they met in London:

> He rides two hobbies tandem, his theory that syllables in English have fixed quantity that cannot be disregarded in reading verse, and his theory that with forty or fifty or sixty characters he can capture and hold for all time the sounds of speech. One theory is as bad as the other and I think owing to much the same fallacy. The living part of a poem is the intonation entangled somehow in the syntax idiom and meaning of a sentence. It is only there for those who have heard it previously in conversation. It is not for us in any Greek or Latin poem because our ears have not been filled with the tones of Greek and Roman talk. It is the most vola-tile and at the same time important part of poetry. With it go the accents the stresses the delays that are not the property of vowels and syllables but that are shifted at will with the sense. . . . When men no longer know the intonations on which we string our words they will fall back on what I may call the absolute length of our syllables which is the length we would give them in pas-sages that meant nothing. . . . English poetry would then be read as Latin poetry is now read and as of course Latin poetry was never read by Romans. Bridges would like it read so now for the sake of scientific exactness. Because our poetry must sometimes be as dead as our language must, Bridges would like it treated as if it were dead already.
>
> I say you can't read a single good sentence with the salt in it un-less you have previously heard it spoken. Neither can you with the help of all the characters and diacritical marks pronounce a single word unless you have previously heard it actually pro-nounced. Words exist in the mouth not in books. You can't fix them and you don't want to fix them. You want them to adapt their sounds to persons and places and times. . . .
>
> Bridges wants to fix the vocables here and now because he sees signs of their deteriorating. He thinks they exist in print for peo-ple. He thinks they are of the eye. Foolish old man is all I say.[20]

Frost's theory of language clearly included the principle that certain spo-ken cadences are inherent in English words and phrases and are practically innate to those who speak it as their mother tongue. Implicit in his theory is that particular sentence sounds and voice tones are metaphors—ways of conveying subtle shades of thinking or feeling that capture meanings.

During Frost's entire period in England, until World War I forced him to sail for home from Liverpool on February 13, 1915, he spent much of his time refining upon his theory of language, in letters to friends and editors in America and in lively conversations with his English literary friends. In his letters to Thomas B. Mosher (July 17, 1913), to John Bartlett (August 6 and December 8, 1913, and especially February 22, 1914), to Sidney Cox (September 15, 1913, May 18, September 17, and December 1914, and February 2, 1915), and to John Cournos (July 8 and July 27, 1914), Frost elaborated upon his theory and provided specific examples of how it worked in practice through tones, stresses, moods, and what he called "gossip," and of sounds as metaphors.

It is highly significant that the most favorable English reviews of *North of Boston*, by Lascelles Abercrombie, James Cruikshank Smith, and Edward Thomas, were written after Frost had talked with each reviewer about "the sound of sense" in his "poetry that talked." Abercrombie's review in the *Nation* (London, June 13, 1914) was titled "A New Voice." Two weeks before it appeared, Frost wrote to his friend John W. Haines that "the discussions of my technique wouldn't have been what it was if Abercrombie had nothing to go on but the book. He took advantage of certain conversations in which I gave him the key to my method." Frost was quick to add that "'method' is the wrong way to call it," because "certain principles of art" and, he might have added, his philosophical convictions regarding spirit and matter, dictated his method and content in his poetry.[21]

In talks with Smith and Edward Thomas he made these reviewers well aware that the poems in his second volume deliberately performed "in a language absolutely unliterary" and in accordance with "the voice within his mind," within the traditional meter and original rhythms of his flexible and distinctive blank verse. After Frost visited Smith in Scotland, where he had observed with pleasure the stone walls separating meadows and farm land, he sent him some manuscript poems, and his friend responded: "Of course I recognized 'Mending Wall' at once as the poem which had been suggested by our walk at Kingsbarn."[22] When *North of Boston* appeared in print, Smith commented on several poems in a letter to Frost in a manner that showed he was very familiar with Frost's aesthetic theory.[23] But perhaps nowhere is the poet as conversationalist and the conversationalist as poet more evident than in Edward Thomas's three reviews of *North of Boston* in the London *Daily News*, the *New Weekly*, and the *English Review*.

Thomas emphasized the revolutionary nature of Frost's colloquial dramatic poems, noted his "conviction that a man will not easily write better than he speaks when some matter has touched him deeply,"[24] and put his finger unerringly on four of the best poems in Frost's volume: "The Death of the Hired Man," "Home Burial," "The Black Cottage," and "The Woodpile." There can be no doubt that his excellent reviews were the direct result of his long conversations with Frost.[25]

Neither these original English literary critics nor subsequent American critics have come close to a full awareness of how completely and brilliantly Frost's theory of language and passion for good talk were fulfilled in practice in *North of Boston*. In a great variety of ways all sixteen of the poems in this volume reproduce the tones of actual speech by a great range of characters or speakers. In the dramatic monologues and dialogues the "voice posturing" of his characters captures the "sound of sense" so skillfully in their tone and nuances that (as Frost aimed after 1895) he was able "to make it plain to the reader which character is saying the lines, without having to place his name before it, as is done in the drama." In many of the poems, but most notably in "The Generations of Men," whole pages of dialogue occur without the speaker being identified. By their speech, characters reveal their essential nature, temperament, values, and their circumstances and view of life, so that an alert reader can follow their dialogue without having to identify them by name. Many of the poems are narratives launched initially in the first person singular before evolving into monologues or dialogues. Even in passages where an authorial voice provides descriptive exposition as stage directions and connects the spoken passages, Frost captures the appropriate tones of colloquial speech as "poetry that talked."

Frost's literary critics have failed to note the great extent to which he actually worked into the dialogues of his fictional characters his own assumptions and principles on the art of conversation as a civilizing force. In "A Hundred Collars," Lafe, the half-drunk and crude French-Canadian bill collector, and the stuffy Yankee self-conscious academic, Doctor Magoon, are forced to share a hotel room, and the almost impenetrable wall that separates them culturally is breached when Lafe says, "Now we are getting on together—talking." In "Home Burial," the failure of the insensitive husband and his neurotic wife to talk about their dead child intensifies their alienation. When he laments, "A man can't speak of his own child that's dead," his wife counters, "You can't because you don't know how to speak." His vain attempts to soothe her hysterical state provoke her to say, "*You*—oh, you think the talk is all." After he digs their child's grave in their home burial plot and enters their home, her anger is intensified by recalling his inappropriate talk:

> *I can repeat the very words you were saying.*
> *"Three foggy mornings and one rainy day*
> *Will rot the best birch fence a man can build."*
> *Think of it, talk like that at such a time!*

Frost clearly believed that just as "good talk" can create civil harmony, interactions of characters with a deranged psyche or an inability to speak will create cross purposes and a fatal relationship. In "The Generations of Men," at the Stark family's reunion of Yankees filled with "pride of ancestry," a young man and woman meet as "stranger cousins" and establish an intimate rapport by playfully reproducing the imagined voices of their ancestors, particularly Granny Stark. After they note that "Folks in her day were given to plain speaking," they "consult the voices" of their ancestors, and "speak but by the voices" because "the voices give you what you wish to hear," having the power of revelation and the gift of prophecy. The young man even takes his cue from Frost's theory of language, and says to his cousin, "perhaps you have the art of what I mean." Frost's many passages on the power of conversation in the poems of *North of Boston* include even minute details, such as the off-stage lady in "The Black Cottage" who "liked to talk," and the lonely speaker out walking in "Good Hours," who has "no one at all with whom to talk." This final poem is the fitting denouement for the many dramatic poems in *North of Boston*.

While Frost was writing the poems for his second volume, he continued to sharpen his aesthetic and intellectual tools through talks with sophisticated literary people in London, such as Frank Flint, Ezra Pound, Robert Bridges, and T. E. Hulme. But only after he moved to rural Gloucestershire in May 1914 did his conversation take on epic proportions in both method and content. All that had been slowly gestating and developing in his thought and poetry since 1895, for lack of a fit and sympathetic audience to hear his talk, blossomed into mature fulfillment during the last eight months of his life in England. Although poetry and his theory of writing remained the centerpiece in Frost's conversations, as Edward Thomas, John Haines, and Wilfred Gibson noted, there was also a profound social and philosophical dimension to Frost's conversation. Unlike Pound, who never really understood Frost's poetry or aesthetics, his friends in Gloucestershire knew that he was no artless primitive plowboy who wrote simple-minded verse. Haines recorded Frost as a talker "full of anecdotes," and characterized some of his traits:

He talked much and well but liked occasional long silences and especially late at night enjoyed giving long, slow soliloquies on psychological and philosophical subjects. . . . His sense of humour pervaded all his talk and he could be sarcastic if he wanted to, though usually his humour was kindly and he had a great sense of fun.[26]

Although the austerities and the uncertainties created by the war with Germany and the Frost family's strained financial resources prevented their months in the West Country from being an unbroken pastoral idyll, nevertheless this brief period was one of the happiest Frost was ever to know. His two published books in England, and his knowledge that a long-established American publisher had agreed to issue new editions of his books, gave Frost great satisfaction and the needed confidence that his sojourn in England had enabled him to come truly into his own as a poet.

In 1926, Wilfred Gibson wrote a retrospective and nostalgic poem, "The Golden Room," commemorating the literary gathering of Frost and his friends in July 1914 in a rose-latticed cottage called the Old Nailshop. Although the lines are not great poetry, Gibson captured the image of Frost as a dominant conversationalist among his English literary friends:

*Do you remember that still summer evening*
*When, in the cosy cream washed living room*
*Of the Old Nailshop, we all talked and laughed—*
*Our neighbors from The Gallows, Catherine*
*And Lascelles Abercrombie; Rupert Brooke;*
*Eleanor and Robert Frost, living awhile*
*At Little Iddens, who'd brought over with them*
*Helen and Edward Thomas? In the lamplight*
*We talked and laughed; but, for the most part, listened*
*While Robert Frost kept on and on and on,*
*In his slow New England fashion, for our delight,*
*Holding us with shrewd turns and racy quips,*
*And the rare twinkle of his grave blue eyes?*

*We sat there in the lamplight, while the day*
*Died from the rose-latticed casements, and the plovers*
*Called over the low meadows, till the owls*
*Answered them from the elms, we sat and talked—*
*Now, a quick flash from Abercrombie, now*
*A murmured dry half-heard aside from Thomas;*

*Now, a clear laughing word from Brooke; and then*
*Again Frost's rich and ripe philosophy,*
*That had the body and tang of good draught cider*
*And poured as clear a stream. . . .*

Three days after this memorable evening the Archduke Ferdinand was assassinated, and within a month Europe was plunged into World War I, and soon Frost and his friends were scattered forever, Brooke to die of fever and Thomas from enemy gunfire in the war, and Frost and his family to return to America. Yet Frost knew upon his arrival home that his fulfillment as a poet was all but assured if he had the courage to persist in the course he had set for himself. Between 1915 and his death in 1963, Frost added many fresh dimensions to his brilliant achievements both as a poet and conversationalist, but that is another story.

# 1

# Dualism:
## The Basis of Frost's Philosophy

My subject is Robert Frost's philosophy, and my thesis is that dualism provides the whole basis of his total but unsystematic philosophical view of reality. This includes Frost's epistemology, his psychology, his logical and analogical methods of reasoning, his emotional bias and choices regarding ideas and events in conflict, his conception of what is true or false, good or evil, ugly or beautiful—in short, that Frost's dualism accounts for his view of God, man, and nature; that it permeates much that he said about science, religion, art and poetry, society and politics, and education; and, finally, that it provides the characteristic qualities in his brilliant and witty conversation. Dualism as the basis of Frost's philosophy is the foremost single element that scholars and literary critics need to consider in any study of his life and thought, including the themes of his poetry.

Yet up to the present no biographies of Frost and very few studies of his beliefs or critical discussions of his poetry have dealt directly, consciously, and deliberately with his philosophical dualism. The few scholars who have mentioned Frost's dualism have failed to ascertain its particular nature against the context of Western philosophy since the ancient Greeks. They have neglected to deal with his dualism on his own terms, or to acknowledge its supreme importance for an understanding of Frost the man, the poet, and the writer of prose.

Before discussing dualism in Frost's writings and the state of scholarship and literary criticism regarding the poet and dualism, it is useful to define what is meant by philosophical dualism. Considered abstractly, the term "dualism" (sometimes called "pluralism"), first utilized by historians of ideas in the eighteenth century, indicates the belief that reality consists of two distinct, absolute, and all-inclusive elements, most commonly identified as matter and mind, or as Frost preferred, matter and spirit.[1] The opposite philosophy, "monism," contends that reality consists of only one element. The pre-Socratic Greek philosophers who held that reality was earth, air, fire, or water were simple monists. Their successors, Democritus, Epicurus, and especially Lucretius in *De rerum natura*, were far more sophisticated material monists. Plato's belief that all earthly objects are merely illusory shadows or imitations of perfect Forms or Ideas in a transcendent realm of being makes him the archetypal spiritual or idealistic monist. Whether materialist or idealist, all monistic philosophy holds that "existence in all its infinite parts and aspects is absolutely one and indivisible. All realities and processes in existence are organically interconnected, interrelated and interdependent."[2] The great task of monistic philosophy is to harmonize, reconcile, integrate, and synthesize these apparent opposites and to unify them into an organic whole. Monism places great emphasis upon human discursive reason as the instrument for acquiring knowledge, in order to pursue "progress" toward the ultimate social goal of mankind in modern times—to be united into one autonomous world organization.[3] In contrast to both material and spiritual monism stands the dualistic philosophy of Aristotle, in which spirit and matter are both regarded as real and exist together in a complex perpetual relationship in the universe and the existential world of mankind.

In Frost's introduction to *Threescore: The Autobiography of Sarah N. Cleghorn* (1936), a modern Vermont Puritan lady and ardent reformer of the kind he much admired, in spite of their basic philosophical disagreements, he discussed why he disliked another type of monist social reformer—one who was "a raw convert to the latest scheme for saving the soul or the state."[4] Frost objected to the simplicity of such crude reformers, zealots full of fluid inspiration and bursting rapture, whose doctrinaire ideological view of reality ignored the complex contradictions ever present in man's trial by existence. Such a simplistic and dogmatic monism, Frost noted, "ignores so superciliously the strain we may have been under for years trying to decide between God and the Devil, between the rich and the poor (the greed of the one and the greed of the other), between keeping still about our troubles and enlarging on them to the doctor and—oh, *between endless other things in pairs ordained to everlasting opposition.*"[5] Frost believed that in the constant conflict of complex ideas and conditions in the daily life of man, "there must always be a thousand *ex parte* lawyers for one judge, sitting out impartial till sides have all but wiped each other out in encounter and judgment has all but pronounced itself." In such conflicts, neither side is ever totally victorious or totally defeated.

To Frost, the dualist philosopher is like the impartial judge: he must observe both sides of the difficult case life presents and yet retain his impartial independent judgment, regardless of his own bias or preference:

> A philosopher may worry about a tendency that, if run out to its logical conclusion, might ruin all; but he worries only till he can make out in the confusion the particular counter tendency that is going to collide with it to the cancellation of both. Formidable equasions often resolve into no more information than that nothing equals nothing. . . . The philosopher values himself on the inconsistencies he can contain by main force. They are two ends of a strut that keeps his mind from collapsing . . . in having once more remarked the two-endedness of things.[6]

Frost's dualistic philosophy always made him keenly aware of the "two-endedness of things" and the difficulty or impossibility of resolving complex religious, moral, intellectual, and social problems through well-intentioned but simple monistic assumptions, methods, or conclusions.

A summary of Frost's "endless . . . things in pairs ordained to everlasting opposition" could include the following, many of which appear in Frost's poetry, prose, and conversations: matter–spirit, body–soul, God–Devil, good–evil, heaven–hell, Old Testament–New Testament, physical–metaphysical, orthodox–heterodox, justice–mercy, quality–quantity, church–state, sense–essence, bond–free, love–thought, woman–man, feminine–masculine, heart–mind, fire–ice, rich–poor, finite–infinite, eternal–temporal, universal–particular, life–death, comic–tragic, radical–conservative, liberty–slavery, liberty–equality, free will–necessity, rights–duties, civilization–utopia, griefs–grievances, war–peace, heredity–environment, ancient–modern, past–present, youth–age, nature–art, knowledge–ignorance, intelligence–stupidity, reality–illusion, objective–subjective, pessimism–optimism, outer weather–inner weather, day–night, light–dark, hot–cold, beauty–ugliness, truth–error, centrifugal–centripetal, space–time, motion–rest, whole–part, courage–cowardliness, fact–fiction. This short list of dualistic opposites, contradictions, contraries, ambiguities, or paradoxes could go on *ad infinitum*, and every reader can make his own list.

There can be little doubt that the "endless . . . things in pairs ordained in everlasting opposition" was to Frost the universal, God-given condition of man's trial by existence. In a letter to Lawrance Thompson (July 11, 1959), while discussing and rejecting Emerson's monism, Frost identified his philosophical orientation beyond dispute: "I am a dualist."[7] But such an abstract identification tells us nothing about the precise nature of Frost's dualism, nor of its vital place in his poetry, prose, and conversation. Frost has provided his own short list of dualistic oppositions: "democracy-monarchy, puritanism-paganism, form-content, conservatism-radicalism, systole-diastole, rustic-urbane, literary-colloquial, work-play."[8] But since Frost limited the application of these contraries to "the differences that make controversy . . . in one period" or "the next," they reveal very little about his philosophical dualism. Robert Francis has recorded a statement of Frost's that can leave no doubt that his dualism is very evident throughout his poetry: "He talked about religion. He had heard that Yvor Winters was asking whether he were a monist or a dualist. His poetry ought to answer that. There was almost as much about evil in it as about good. Good is the better half of evil. To find out what he believed, one would have to stay around him for a long time. He would himself. And the answer would depend not so much on what he said as on how he acted."[9] We shall return later to the implications in the last three sentences of Francis's report, but an inventory of the most explicit passages or lines in Frost's poetry that reveal his dualism should be highly illuminating.

The first example, from "The Literate Farmer and the Planet Venus," indicates that Frost's dualism is not restricted to separate pairs of antithetical things or concepts, external to man in nature or civil society, but is built into the very spiritual and physical nature of man:

> *You know how cunningly mankind is planned:*
> *We have one loving and one hating hand.*
> *The loving's made to hold each other like,*
> *While with the hating other hand we strike.*

"Quandary" contains an excellent passage on Frost's moral dualism:

> *Never have I been sad or glad*
> *That there was such a thing as bad.*
> *There had to be, I understood,*
> *For there to have been any good.*
> *It was by having been contrasted*
> *That good and bad so long had lasted.*

# Dualism: The Basis of Frost's Philosophy

In "The Wind and the Rain," Frost clearly rejects the optimistic monism and escapist psychology of such writers as Emerson:

> *It were unworthy of the tongue*
> *To let the half of life alone*
> *And play the good without the ill.*

There is an implicit dualism in such lines as the following:

> *I never dared be radical when young*
> *For fear it would make me conservative when old.*
> —"Precaution"

> *Nature within her inmost self divides*
> *To trouble man with having to take sides.*
> —"From Iron, Tools and Weapons"

> *But Islands of the Blessèd, bless you, son,*
> *I never came upon a blessèd one.*
> —"An Answer"

> *We may doubt the just proportion of good to ill*
> —"Our Hold on the Planet"

> *Two souls may be too widely met*
> —"A Missive Missile"

Frost implies that at the time of death, when the soul or spirit is about to leave the body, or when couples or lovers are about to be separated, dualism dissolves into the oneness of monism:

> *So near to paradise all pairing ends:*
> —"A Winter Eden"

> *A heartfelt prayer for the poor of God,*
> *Or for the rich a curse;*
> —"Love and a Question"

Even if we were to multiply these few examples of dualistic contraries in Frost's poetry, they would hardly be a significant step toward a full understanding of his dualistic philosophy.

Frost's dualism is perhaps most obvious in such themes in his poetry as the conflict between justice and mercy, in "The Death of the Hired Man"; in poems that say spirit in terms of matter or matter in terms of spirit, and in the two masques. Since Frost regarded God as "the ever-ready One," a spirit infinitely perfect, and therefore the only one true absolute Monist, it is significant that in his claim to be an orthodox Old Testament, highly original Christian, Frost's only fusion of spirit and matter in all his poetry is in the doctrine of the Incarnation in "Kitty Hawk":

> *But God's own descent*
> *Into flesh was meant*
> *As a demonstration*
> *That the supreme merit*
> *Lay in risking spirit*
> *In substantiation.*

In the passage that followed, Frost made it clear that common human nature, despite its great imperfections, also consisted of a dualistic mixture of spirit and matter, so that all of his poems centered in dramatic conflicts reflect these two basic elements. In this connection a remark by Robert Francis takes on great significance: "His conversation often turns to some antithesis between the two sexes."[10] Probably the most significant personal conflict in Frost's dualism is not in the justice-mercy contradiction, but in the war between the sexes, in the more or fewer differences in perspective, temperament, and values between men and women, as set forth in so many of Frost's dramatic monologues and dialogues. The perennial conflicts between the sexes were probably more frequent, more sustained, and more important in the sum of human happiness or misery than the antithesis between justice and mercy, good and evil, or rich and poor in society at large.

It would be a cardinal error for any scholar or literary critic to assume that Frost's philosophical dualism can be reconstructed or understood through a study of his poetry. The creative product of the poet's aesthetic imagination does indeed reflect facets of his ontology, his epistemology, his methods of perception and angle of vision, and even his normative principles, each of which is an element of reality, but a thorough understanding of Frost's poetry itself depends greatly upon a full comprehension of his dualism, and therefore cannot be correlated with his total perception of a spiritual and material reality consisting of unresolved pairs of conflicting opposites. Even the creation of form in poetry, one of the sustained passions in Frost's life, cannot resolve dualistic opposites into a monistic unity. To Frost, a poem is only "a momentary stay against confusion," not a permanent solution to any things "ordained to everlasting opposition." The unity created by form in a poem does not result in a final or permanent unity in content or theme. This is an important distinction that many literary critics of Frost have failed to understand and that has led them to assume or make unreasonable demands that he should provide a final solution to the metaphysical mysteries of man's life on earth, or even to the perennial social and economic problems that afflict society. Frost believed that the great mysteries of life have no permanent or final answers in the temporal life of man, that something must always be left to God. He also believed that the perennial problems of man in society could at best be ameliorated, that class conflicts between rich and poor, and the rival claims of justice and mercy, could be adjusted to prevent any one extreme from completely triumphing over its opposite, but that no final solutions were possible. His philosophical dualism, nevertheless, provides the key to a sound understanding of Frost's total philosophy.

What then is required for a thorough and valid comprehension of Frost's dualism? Nothing short of a complete natural history of his life and thought from at least the beginnings of his literary career as a schoolboy in Lawrence, Massachusetts; from his first composition of a poem in March 1890 to his death in January 1963. The first faint and imprecise indications of Frost's awareness of dualistic opposites is to be found in the *Lawrence High School Bulletin*, in his editorial on the need of literary critics and each individual to review and reconsider any conventional belief in order to make it personally meaningful, a theme he reiterated in his senior valedictory speech. The first set of conflicting contraries Frost mentioned publicly was in his schoolboy valedictory address: "Aggressive life is two-fold: theory, practice; thought, action: and concretely, poetry, statesmanship; philosophy, socialism—infinitely."[11] In an essay on the opposing claims of science and religion, Frost wrote: "Mind is not so much unlike matter after all. It has the property of inertia."[12] In proposing educational reform in teaching classics and science, he wrote: "Longer recitations then—in the classics for mind, in the sciences for mind and matter—are what we need."[13] Another incipient sign of a simple dualism in Frost's early thought is his distinction between two ways of following customs—either blindly and without reflection, or "not without question, but where it does not conflict with the broader habits of life gained by wanderers among ideas."[14] His valedictory speech in 1892, "A Monument to After-Thought Unveiled," reveals a tragic sense which he later identified with his "melancholy dualism": "We know sorrow to be the same through all time."[15] Perhaps an even more significant anticipation of his mature dualism is in his insistence upon action as the forerunner and added consequence of "after-thought": "Not in the strife of action, is the leader made, nor in the face of crisis, but when all is over, when the mind is swift with keen regret, in the long after-thought. The after-thought of one action is the forethought of the next."[16] In his contrast between the dual opposite realms, the practical versus the theoretical, Frost wrote: "Events influence the first class, the limits of language alone the second."[17] Perhaps most significant, in the light of his future career as a poet, is Frost's application of these distinctions to the poet and to life in general: "The poet's insight is his after-thought. It is of varied heart-beat and converse with nature. And the grandest of his ideas come when the last line is written. . . . Life is an after-thought."[18] These are remarkable statements for a seventeen-year-old schoolboy, and they clearly point toward the mature dualistic philosophy that Frost developed and maintained throughout his life.

It would be presumptuous and premature for me to provide an inventory of *all* the crucial elements that would have to be taken into account for a thorough and valid understanding of Frost's dualism. Indeed, the very process of dealing with each element, both in itself and in its complex relationship with its contrary and other elements, is a process of constant discovery and self-discovery in each subject and in the consciousness of the scholar or critic. As a preliminary to a complete inventory, I would include the following subjects: all of Frost's poetry, prose, correspondence, interviews, and comments during poetry readings; a knowledge of Frost's own extensive readings of writers in both the dualist tradition, such as Aristotle, and the monist tradition, such as Plato and Emerson among ideal monists and material monists such as Lucretius, Hobbes, and Marx. Although Frost was painfully aware that "nothing gold can stay" in a world of imperfections and contradictions, he also knew that many, perhaps most, of the world's most famous philosophers and writers, from the ancient Greeks to his own time, were monists. His own complex critical responses to Plato and Emerson are very revealing of his own dualism. Beyond the usual influences on Frost that scholars have noted, I believe that the role of Swedenborg's works, especially *Heaven and Hell* (1758), is of paramount importance. What Frost accepted and rejected of every kind of writer would need to be ascertained. To fully comprehend Frost's dualism, a scholar would have to know his essential views on science, religion and philosophy, society and politics, art and poetry, and education.

A scholar would have to ascertain the place of dualism in each of Frost's five cardinal beliefs: the self-belief, the love-belief, the national-belief, the art-belief, all of which Frost said were "closely related to the God-belief."[19] The most frequently omitted element in Frost's intellectual makeup, other than dualism itself, is the role of "play" in his thought, talk, and poetry, his play with words and his wit, humor, and sense of comedy. Practically every biographer and literary critic has ignored his dictum that "The way of understanding is partly mirth" ("Not Quite Social"), or has dismissed it cavalierly as trivial or irrelevant. But to understand Frost's dualism it is necessary to take seriously his couplet that "It takes all kinds of in and outdoor schooling / To get adapted to my kind of fooling." This applies especially to his metaphorical uses of language. Frost's hierarchical values—prowess, justice, courage, and knowledge—and their opposites would need to be understood in relation to his dualism for a full measure of his philosophy. These elements are far from being an exhaustive list of things to be considered, but a study of them would go far toward a valid understanding of his dualism.

It is time now to return to Robert Francis's statement regarding how Frost's beliefs are to be understood: "To find out what he believed, one would have to stay around him for a long time. . . . And the answer would depend not so much on *what* he said as on *how* he acted. . . ." If understood metaphorically, the phrases "stay around" and "how he acted" could be taken to mean being thoroughly saturated with Frost's works, since he regarded his poems as deeds, "words that have become deeds." This concept applies not only to the form of a poem, but to its theme. But more literally, Francis's statement refers to having a close and sustained intimate knowledge of the poet through direct personal contacts and frequent conversations.[20] Yet even this privilege does not assure profound understanding. If I may be permitted a personal note on this point, it was only after three summers of many long conversations with Frost, and much reflection, that I came to perceive the central importance of his philosophical dualism, and even then its full implications did not emerge for a long time.

But if anyone should have understood Frost well from all the sources available to him, including many long conversations with the poet, Lawrance Thompson was uniquely favored. Yet all of the vital signs are that there was an almost inverse ratio between the facts of Frost's life, poetry, and talk and Thompson's understanding of them. As William Pritchard, among others, has noted, Frost's biographer was almost unbelievably literal-minded, like a fundamentalist in religion, regarding Frost's metaphorical uses of language, and he certainly never understood that "the way of understanding is partly mirth." The sense of "play" was also beyond Thompson's imagination. But Thompson's unfitness as Frost's biographer goes far deeper than a lack of appreciation of the poet's metaphorical language, humor, and sense of play.

Thompson does occasionally refer to Frost's dualism in terms of his character and skill as a poet: "He still had the power to consist of the inconsistent, the power to hold in unity the ultimate irreconcilables, the power to be a bursting unity of opposites, and the power to make poetry out of these opposites."[21] Such a statement gives the wholly false impression that Thompson understood Frost's dualism, but his biography and literary criticism reveal virtually no ability to follow Frost's trail through the pathless woods of his nature and personality, or to mark the witness trees that would enable him to read the symbolic signs provided by the poet's dualism in pursuit of his thoroughly unsystematic philosophy. Four lines from Frost's poem "Maple" apply well to Thompson's limitations:

> *They hovered for a moment near discovery,*
> *Figurative enough to see the symbol,*
> *But lacking faith in anything to mean*
> *The sense at different times to different people.*

Frost once warned Thompson to beware lest he spooked him, and as it applies to Frost's dualism, Thompson was thoroughly spooked.

In the second volume of his biography of Frost, one might assume from the chapter titled "Things in Pairs Ordained" that it deals with Frost's dualism. But the title is wholly misleading: there is no discussion of dualism. Instead, Thompson is wholly concerned with biographical details from July 1935 to early 1936, and he provides a constant stream of slanted pejorative comments on Frost's politics and supposed ill will toward others. Another chapter, "Speaking of Contraries," discusses "West-Running Brook," and the closest Thompson comes to any awareness of Frost's dualism is his remark that "his religious belief . . . enriched and extended the ulterior meanings of his best metaphors, that it permitted him to talk about at least two worlds simultaneously."[22]

Thompson's failure to grasp the importance of Frost's dualism is evident in its omission from the index of every volume he published on Frost.[23] But perhaps the strongest direct evidence of his failure is in his incredibly obtuse criticism in his review of Frost's *The Masque of Reason* in the *New York Times Book Review* (March 25, 1945), which so infuriated Frost. Perhaps above all others, this work expressed Frost's orthodox Old Testament Christianity concerning good and evil, but Thompson described it as an "unholy play" which, he claimed, satirized traditional Christianity.

# Dualism: The Basis of Frost's Philosophy

When Thompson appealed to Rabbi Victor Reichert to explain why Frost was so angry over his review, Reichert had to spend an entire afternoon patiently analyzing Frost's masque, and Thompson sheepishly had to confess in Reichert's guest book how badly he had botched up Frost's theme in his review. If Thompson had really understood Frost's moral dualism, he would have also understood *The Masque of Reason.*

Literary critics whose beliefs are centered in an optimistic monism invariably fail to comprehend Frost's dualism and often turn to abnormal psychology as their way of responding to it. Thompson leads the way in this regard by treating dualism, or the tragic or negative side of things ordained in everlasting opposition, as a supposed moral aberration in Frost. Thus the subject headings in his index under "Robert Frost" are entirely weighted with negative psychological terms, such as "Badness," "Confusion," "Cowardice," "Death," "Enemies," "Fears," "Hate," "Insanity," "Jealousy," "Sadness," "Self-centeredness," "Suicide," and "Wildness." The dualistic contraries to these subjects are omitted, so that no balance is provided, and Thompson creates a demonology about Frost as a morally depraved neurotic.[24] Perhaps the most frequent error among uncritically-minded readers of Thompson's official biography is to assume that because it includes massive empirical facts that therefore Thompson's value judgments on Frost are necessarily valid.

Studies of Frost have yet to recover from Thompson's deliberate character assassination of the poet. With one exception, even the few critics who have dealt with Frost's dualism directly have taken their cue from Thompson's biography. C. Barry Chabot, in "The 'Melancholy Dualism' of Robert Frost," makes no pretence that he is concerned with Frost's literary or philosophical beliefs and publishes a psycho-biographical speculation on his irrational fears and melancholy paranoid escapist personality, appropriately in the *Review of Existential Psychology and Psychiatry* (1974). Mangalam Nilakantan's article "'Something Beyond Conflict:' A Study of the Dual Vision of Robert Frost," (*Indian Journal of American Studies*, 1969) gives no consideration to Frost's dualism as the basis of his philosophy and poetry, but perceives his "dual vision" as an instrumental means to delve into his psychological and emotional character.

To date, the most deliberate and thorough attempt to deal with Frost's dualism is by Johannes Kjörven, *Robert Frost's Emergent Design: The Truth of the Self In-Between Belief and Unbelief.*[25] Kjörven discusses four of Frost's basic beliefs—"the self-belief," "the love belief," "the art belief," and "the God belief"—and omits "the national belief," but notes that these beliefs cover just about every subject Frost had to deal with. Kjörven believes that Frost's mother taught him the proper spiritual way to approach life through these beliefs, but that his father and wife, being agnostics, countered his mother's influence and created an irreconcilable conflict in Frost, a "crisis of belief and unbelief" that paralyzed his will and left him "without direction" in his philosophy.[26] The "emergent design" in Frost's poetry, Kjörven claims, was as close to self-discovery as Frost ever acquired.

Kjörven very rightly takes sharp issue with the many literary critics of Frost who accuse the poet of "ontological indecisiveness" and a "lack of courage," on the valid grounds that it is unreasonable to expect Frost, just because he is a major poet, to resolve metaphysical conflicts within the framework of order in his poetry and thereby "to order it as coherently as possible within a monistic system."[27] He rightly notes that Frost's whole approach to life and poetry is alien to any monistic system.[28] Kjörven's analysis of Frost's poem "I Will Sing You One-O" is an excellent example of the poet's awareness that it is impossible for human nature to achieve absolute or true monistic reality.[29] There are other excellent particular observations on Frost's dualism throughout this study.

But Kjörven falls into some serious errors, such as in his discussion of the justice-mercy contradiction in Frost's masques. He contends, contrary to Frost, that mercy is prior to justice, and neglects *A Masque of Reason* while emphasizing *A Masque of Mercy*, rather than combining both, and argues that "all the other poems with religious implications are variants" of Paul's final speech in the latter masque.[30] Finally, Kjörven holds that Frost hovers indecisively between religious belief and unbelief, and his study omits to consider Frost's dualism in his views of science, religion, society, politics, art, and education.

Perhaps the chief value of a thorough and valid study of Frost's philosophical dualism may be that it will raise the whole level of understanding of Frost above the superficial studies of the many literary critics who believe that Frost was "a spiritual drifter" or "full of devious evasions," an indecisive equivocator or obfuscator, a cowardly escapist from the "real" problems of society, a man of "guarded epiphanies," the archetypal modern autonomous alienated man. Many such critics are themselves monists whose case against Frost consists of a complaint that he is not a monist, even though they do not explicitly think in terms of monism or dualism. I believe that it is significant that even Kjörven's flawed pioneering study of Frost's dualism contradicts the many critics who have accused Frost of a lack of social compassion, by stressing the role of mercy in his thought. A study of Frost's dualism will not only bring more balance into scholarship on his character, thought, and art, but it will open up dimensions of understanding far more profound than any studies of Frost have yet achieved.

# 2

# The Nature and Role of
# Metaphor in Frost's Dualism

When Frost went to England in August 1912 to create his public image as a poet, he was aware that he wanted to write "a poetry that talked," but his aesthetic theory and conception of artistic creativity were essentially unformed and still rooted in a subjective series of moods and feelings that reflected phases of his own spiritual growth. He was cognizant of his undeveloped beliefs regarding his early poetry, and he observed that in compiling the poems he included in his first collection, *A Boy's Will* (1913), the poems "are intended by the author to possess a certain sequence, and to depict the various stages in the evolution of a young man's outlook upon life."[1] To his friend John T. Bartlett he wrote that *A Boy's Will* "comes pretty near being the story of five years of my life."[2] and he referred to this collection as "the record of a phase of post–adolescence."[3] The lyrical poems clearly reflect an autobiographical dimension and conception of creativity wholly in the tradition of nineteenth-century Romanticism.

Any valid understanding of Frost as a thinker and a mature poet must take into full account the enormous change he experienced philosophically, both about human life on Earth and the art of poetry, during his two and a half years in Britain. The radical alteration in the forms and techniques in Frost's poetry, from the short subjective lyrics in *A Boy's Will* to the long objective narrative and dramatic poems about "a book of people" in *North of Boston* (1914), is also reflected in his letters to friends in America on the phonetic role of colloquial voice tones that convey meanings in sound.[4] These aspects in Frost's theory and practice as a poet have been thoroughly reviewed by literary critics and scholars. But the changes in his art and aesthetics during 1912–15 were merely preliminary to a much more important lifelong transmutation in Frost's total philosophy as a dualist, changes which encompassed his beliefs regarding science, religion, history, the humanities, education, society, and politics. Within a more restricted but important context, these changes redefined Frost's life and role as a poet, his whole conception of the relationship of his art to life, of how readers should understand his art and thought, and the practical necessity of educating the American public about the nature and importance of poetry in the culture and life of the twentieth century.

For more than a decade up to around 1930, Frost struggled to convince his friends, literary critics, and the common readers of poetry that the popular assumption that poetry is merely the subjective self-expression of the poet's psyche, an autobiographical response to life experiences, was a seriously inadequate conception of art. In a letter to Sidney Cox (September 19, 1929), he summarized his longstanding objection to this common delusion: "There is no greater fallacy going than that art is expression—an undertaking to tell all to the last scrapings of the brain pan." As early as March 22, 1915, in a letter to William Braithwaite, a literary critic and anthologist who interviewed Frost and was about to write an article about him, he cautioned: "You will be sure to veil what is too personal." Of course Frost was well aware that a poet experienced events in life, and that his emotions were involved in the creative process, and that these things helped to shape the style of his poems. But far more was involved in being a poet, so that a biographical approach to a poet's work that correlated his life with his poetry destroyed the vital distinction between nature and art. A poet was much more than a journalist or a historian reporting on life. To write poems in English required a thorough mastery in knowledge and understanding of the whole tradition of English and American poetry, including the forms and techniques of poetry. As an art form, poetry included fictions and myths that were concerned with truths about human nature, not merely with empirical facts and logical reason. Poets and readers of poetry had to make what Coleridge called "a willing suspension of disbelief" in facts and perceive truths in terms of symbols and the whole range of metaphorical language beyond literal-minded beliefs. A poet had to possess a creative imagination, fancy, and originality, and above all Frost insisted that a would-be poet had to believe in himself and perfect his art through "tons and tons" of self-discipline, in order to believe a poem into existence. In short, faith and moral courage were even more important than talent in being a poet, and many talented young writers failed as poets because they were lured by life into easier and more remunerative professions. To Frost, in art as in religion, many are called but few are chosen. For all of these reasons and others, he dismissed the claim that simple and direct self-expression was sufficient for the creation of poetry.

Despite all of Frost's efforts to convince his friend Sidney Cox that poetry is not simply a disguised form of autobiography, Cox persisted in his desire to write Frost's life in order to help readers understand his poetry. In exasperation, the poet wrote to Cox on April 19, 1932, and began his letter with a severe admonition: "You are getting out of hand." He objected particularly to Cox's prying into his mind for psychological evidence to identify with Frost's supposed life experiences as the source for passages in his poems:

> I grow surer I don't want to search the poet's mind too seriously.
> . . . I have written to keep the over curious out of the secret places
> of my mind both in my verse and in my letters to such as you.
> A subject has to be held clear outside of me with struts and as it
> were set up for an object. A subject must be an object. . . . The idea
> is the thing with me. It would seem soft for instance to look in
> my life for the sentiments in the Death of the Hired Man. There's
> nothing to it believe me. I should fool you if you took me so. . . .
> The objective idea is all I ever cared about. Most of my ideas oc-
> cur in verse. . . . But I never reckoned with the personalities. I keep
> to a minimum of such stuff in any poet's life and works. Art and
> wisdom with the body heat out of it. . . . To be too subjective with
> what an artist has managed to make objective is to come on him
> presumptuously and to render ungraceful what he in pain of his
> life had faith he had made graceful. . . .[5]

This passage confirms and extends a comment that Frost wrote on March 22, 1915, in a letter to William Braithwaite: "I made the discovery in do-ing 'The Death of the Hired Man' that I was interested in neighbors for more than merely their tones of speech." In an even earlier letter to Cox in December 1914 he had objected to the common facile distinction between the subjective and objective elements in a poem: "We write of things we see and we write in accents we hear. Thus we gather both our material and our technique with the imagination from life and our technique becomes as much material as material itself." In his strong opposition to the belief that a poem is only a subjective projection of the poet's psyche, he con-tended that "the breathless swing" of a poem "is between subject matter and form."[6] These remarks explain why Frost was always severely critical of "confessional poetry," such as that of Edna St. Vincent Millay, whose lyrics are often an autobiographical projection of her psychological feelings.

To combat the autobiographical heresy regarding art, Frost made a point of denigrating the use of the first person singular in his poems. In his essay "On Taking Poetry" (1955), he wrote: "The more I say I the more I always mean somebody else. That's objectivity."[7] Yet literal-minded readers with little or no sense of metaphor, and a limited knowledge of Frost, continued to assume that the theme or idea in a poem was necessarily the personal belief of the poet. To such a reader Frost said: "When I use the word 'I' surely you don't believe that I mean me." The first line in his poem "Iota Subscript" is: "Seek not in me the big I capital." Frost even made a pun on "the perpendicular pronoun" by identifying it with the ego of Ezra Pound, perceived as the basic meter in a poem—the "great I am big." What applied to the explicit first person also was relevant to the impersonal authorial voice in the point of view of a poem. Technique as material itself broke down the facile distinction between subject and object and made the creative process not merely a mechanistic method of describing a subject or dramatic situation, but a dynamic use of the imagination. In a conversation with a friend he noted that Shakespeare is neither Hamlet nor Iago nor any other character in his tragedies or comedies, and he had no patience with literary critics who looked for historical characters to identify with persons in the sonnets. Such critics forget that poetry is as much a form of fiction as is the novel or stage plays.

Early in the 1920s Frost attacked yet another common fallacy in how to "take" his art. In discussions with the sculptors Alfeo Faggi, Aroldo du Chêne, and Lorado Taft, and probably with the painter James Chapin, he was made painfully aware of some serious problems regarding how badly modern audiences responded to the visual arts. His talks with these artists resulted in his writing a closet drama, *In an Art Factory*.[8] This work has been badly neglected by literary critics. The chief protagonist in the play, a sculptor named Tony, is probably a fictional composite of Frost's artist friends, but in voicing their complaints he also identifies some of the most common problems Frost encountered in reader responses to his poems.

Tony observed that "an artist wants a public, the more public the better. But he lives in resentment toward their ways of mistaking him. He resists coarsening to them." By striving to improve upon what a poem, sculpture, or painting says, critics seek to transform a work of art into something other than itself. Tony compares such a viewer standing before a sculpture to "a surgeon with a scalpel," eager to cut away whatever he dislikes. This echoes Frost's view that a reader of a poem should "take it right between the *eyes* just as it is." The misreadings of readers and literary critics involved the poet throughout his life in answering "a long line of alienations." The very title of Frost's play, *In an Art Factory,* implies a mechanization of the human spirit wholly contrary to the creative imagination and taste of the poet. The "devilish cunning of critics" often transforms a work of art into something "Commercialized," "Sentimentalized," or "Nationalized." A poem or painting is thus "flattered out of recognition." Tony defines a belief long held by Frost: "the definition of one of the public [is] a person that doesn't know the right thing to do to an artist." In a tone of desperation filled with anger and pathos, in defiance of such critics by insisting that a work of art should be accepted on its own terms, Tony exclaims: "To hell with your criticism, yours or anyone else's. I make a thing and you take it or leave it." On several occasions, Frost contended that explicating in a prose analysis what a poem means, or how its technique functions, is like explaining a joke to someone who fails to get the punch line. *In an Art Factory* is an early dramatic summary of some of Frost's lifelong complaints on how badly some readers responded to his poems.

Yet even in his play, Frost held that "nothing is irreparable." As a result of his rich experiences in many poetry readings, he contended that the intelligent and literate "common reader," who had acquired a strong sense of taste, was often very capable of understanding the art and thought in a poem. This kind of appreciative reader was often found in a town-and-gown audience that included students and faculty educated in the liberal arts. He trusted and appreciated such common readers of poetry far more than he did ideological academic literary critics who were corrupted by speculative rational systems of abstract theory, such as Marxists, Freudians, feminists, scientific linguists, the "New Critics," and postmodernists. Often such critics were addicted to an ideology, which they mistook for a philosophy, and prided themselves on being "intellectual" and "modernists" by virtue of their assumption that the scientific method and discursive analytical reason and logic were the essential tools for dealing with art objects. In general, Frost's complaint against such critics was the same as that expressed by G. K. Chesterton: "I find that if I make the point of a story stick out like a spike, they carefully go and impale themselves on something else."[9] The worst outrages against poetry, Frost believed, were committed by literal-minded ideologues addicted to a closed system of theory. In his letter to Sidney Cox in December 1914, he expressed his contempt for such closed-minded critics: "There are a lot of completely educated people in the world, and of course they will resent being asked to learn anything new." Some "modernist" critics, who took Ezra Pound and T. S. Eliot as their model for poetry, often mistook Frost's concentrated simplicity for simplemindedness, particularly because he retained traditional forms and utilized colloquial language. Lionel Trilling even dismissed Frost's poetry as lacking in cosmopolitan culture, because unlike New York City residents his pastoral settings and rural characters were unsophisticated.

In November 1930 Frost wrote "Education by Poetry" in which, for the first time and far more explicitly than in any other essay, letter, lecture, or interview, he set forth the nature, method, function, and practical importance of metaphorical language in the thinking process by which human nature could best deal with every important subject. He advanced his theme in the form of what he called "a meditative monologue," so that his method was empirical, anecdotal, associative, and whimsical in moving from one reflection to another, as though he did not wish to be taken as too doctrinaire or dogmatic in his argument. This was consistent with his belief that the great problems that humanity always faced could not be settled absolutely, once and for all time. As he put it, "you can tell where the center of the target is by the number of near misses around the bull's-eye." Yet there should be no doubt that "Education by Poetry" is close to being Frost's most serious testament about how poetry as a literary art form is connected with the most profound philosophical ways that mankind thinks and feels about all of its beliefs.

Frost's essay clarifies the nature and function of metaphorical language in relation to his philosophical dualism and may well be regarded as an early elaboration of his general statement to Lawrance Thompson in a letter on July 11, 1958: "I am a dualist." The word "metaphor," which literally means "to carry over," necessarily includes two things connected for the purpose of illuminating one in terms of another. Early in "Education by Poetry," Frost stated the range of metaphorical thinking in an abstract manner: "Poetry begins in trivial metaphors, pretty metaphors, 'grace' metaphors, and goes on to the profoundest thinking that we have. Poetry provides the one permissible way of saying one thing and meaning another." Although this statement is far too abstract to be meaningful, nevertheless it is a giant step toward clarifying what he meant by identifying himself as a dualist. After several pages of digressions on how metaphors work in "the whole of thinking," in "all thinking except mathematical thinking," but including science and even its theory, as in "the metaphor of evolution," Frost then clarified more specifically what he meant by metaphors in carrying over one thing in terms of another:

Greatest of all attempts to say one thing in terms of another is the philosophical attempt to say matter in terms of spirit, or spirit in terms of matter, to make the final unity. That is the greatest attempt that ever failed. We stop just short there. But it is the height of poetry, the height of all thinking, the height of all poetic thinking, that attempt to say matter in terms of spirit and spirit in terms of matter.

Having thus identified matter and spirit as the two basic elements in his dualistic conception of all reality, Frost then added an important precaution that distinguished between a belief in the existence of matter and being a materialist:

It is wrong to call anybody a materialist simply because he tries to say spirit in terms of matter, as if that were a sin. Materialism is not the attempt to say all in terms of matter. The only materialist—be he poet, teacher, scientist, politician, or statesman—is the man who gets lost in his material without a gathering metaphor to throw it into shape and order. He is the lost soul.[10]

To Frost, only a dualist can have "a gathering metaphor" that says spirit in terms of matter or vice versa. Monists, who separate spirit and matter into isolated and irreconcilable opposites and make them into closed absolutes, are lost souls, lost in their material, and cannot make metaphors that combine spirit and matter in an attempt to make a final unity between them, a unity that must fail to reach an absolute.

It is noteworthy that Frost holds the attempt to say spirit in terms of matter, or vice versa, is a "*philosophical* attempt," not merely literary, because the two elements together comprise the whole of reality, which is the concern of philosophy. In literature, the "play" of the creative mind and imagination, in perceiving how spirit and matter interact upon each other, results in revelations through metaphors by which mankind lives and understands itself and its place in the universe. Education by poetry is education through metaphors that enable readers to leap from sight to insight, from sense to essence, from an awareness of the physical to awareness of the metaphysical dimensions of reality. Unlike discursive expository arguments based upon empirical facts, reason and logic, metaphors work indirectly: only through indirections do poets find directions out. Like God, poets write straight with crooked lines. Frost said that "the zig-zag" of a poet's mind is like the straight crookedness of a walking stick. A conventional inventory of all that Frost included as metaphorical language in the techniques and forms of poetry would include such figures of speech as the following: analogy, comparison, contrast, parallel, allusion, paradox, ambiguity, wit, humor, irony, puns, understatement, hyperbole, parable, plot, myth, symbol, image, banter, simile, and the tones and sounds of meaning that constitute style. Thus meter, rhythm, and rhyme in poetry are forms of metaphor. So too are the very forms of literature, epics, comedy and tragedy, and the verse forms in monologues, dialogues, and authorial voice that provide point of view. Blank verse, rhymed couplets, quatrains, and sonnets are also metaphors. All forms of fiction are metaphors that require readers to make an initial "willing suspension of disbelief" in facts in order to be able to accept the truths that literature can impart. This involves such human qualities of mind and feeling, of temperament, imagination, fancy, memory, and psychological traits that make faith or belief prior to empirical knowledge and logical reason. Art is closer to religion than it is to science, because it is necessary to believe in a subject or situation in order to understand it, and not make rational understanding the basis of belief. In Frost's final public poetry reading, "On Extravagance: A Talk" (November 27, 1962), many of his beliefs regarding metaphors are expounded.

Among all the varieties of metaphors and their rich functions in illuminating human perceptions by saying the unknown in terms of the known, or by drawing the strange and mysterious within the orbit of what is familiar and common knowledge, Frost was particularly attracted to the synecdoche. This figure of speech can suggest the part for the whole, as a flag symbolizes a nation, or as New England, regarded as a particular setting or cultural region stands for these qualities in America as a whole. But a synecdoche can also reverse the order of things compared, identifying what is large with one of its smaller counterparts. Frost was especially fond of the opening quatrain of William Blake's "Auguries of Innocence":

> *To see a world in a grain of sand*
> *And a Heaven in a wild flower,*
> *Hold Infinity in the palm of your hand*
> *And Eternity in an hour.*

A variation of this species of synecdoche is in Shakespeare's lines from *As You Like It* introducing the extended metaphor on the seven ages of man: "All the world's a stage / And all the men and women merely players." When cast in the phonetics of meaningful tones of colloquial talk, such figures of speech can illuminate significant relationships in human nature and the world. Thus poetry, as a form of revelation, is comparable to religion, which also says spirit in terms of matter, and is more inclusive than science, which concerns itself with matter as descriptive phenomena but cannot deal with normative ethics and things of the spirit.

To illustrate this difference between poetry and science, Frost quoted the second quatrain of Shakespeare's Sonnet CXVI:

> *O, no! it is an ever-fixèd mark*
> *That looks on tempests and is never shaken;*
> *It is the star to every wandering bark,*
> *Whose worth's unknown, although his heighth be taken.*

The final line, Frost contended, is one of the triumphs of English poetry. It describes the guiding star in its mystery as value, the star in heaven as seen by lovers and poets; and it qualifies this by perceiving the star in the sky as precisely measured matter in space, as recorded by physicists and astronomers. The line is one of Shakespeare's most profound insights, combining spirit and matter and also separating spirit as value from matter as measurable quantity. Shakespeare understood the limits of science in its power to penetrate and measure matter.

Frost's conception of metaphor as a source of aesthetic revelation or meaning was not limited to figures of speech within a particular poem, but included how all of his poems within a volume were related to each other and how all twelve of his collections of poetry, from *A Boy's Will* (1913) through *In the Clearing* (1962), also possessed a metaphorical continuity. This fact is very important for readers of his complete works who wish to understand the philosophical unity in his dualism and the metaphorical unity in his art. In 1942, when Frost's friend Whit Burnett included him in an anthology of "America's Greatest Living Authors" in *This is My Best*, the poet was asked to write out the reasons for his choice of poems to be included. He stated the continuity in his principle of selection and the basis of division as follows:

> I have made this selection much as I made the one from my first book, *A Boy's Will*, and my second book, *North of Boston*, looking backward over the accumulation of years to see how many poems I could find towards some one meaning it might seem absurd to have had in advance, but it would be all right to accept from fate after the fact. . . . In other words, could anything of larger design, even the roughest, any broken or dotted continuity, or any

fragment of a figure be discerned among the apparently random lesser designs of the several poems?[11]

Frost's concern for unity and continuity within and between his volumes of poetry reached back at least twenty-eight years. It is significant that in a letter to Louis Untermeyer (June 8, 1915), he praised his new friend for the unity in art and thought that Untermeyer revealed in his own volume of poetry: "The beauty of your book is that the poems in it all get together and say something with one accord."[12] Frost's statement to Whit Burnett is one of his most explicit "hints" that each poem is more than "a momentary stay against confusion" and that each poem and collection of poems creates a figure that contributes to some form of unity and continuity in the total design of his art and thought.

In addition to the sequential order and rough unity evident within and between each collection of his poems, Frost's selections of poems in separate selected and collected volumes of his work, in *Selected Poems* (1928 and 1934), in *Collected Poems* (1930), and again in *Complete Poems* (1939), contributed further evidence towards some all-inclusive continuity and unity in the unfolding development in his poetry and philosophical dualistic beliefs. The same development applies to his basic beliefs regarding aesthetics and creativity, religion, science, education, society, and politics as separate subjects and themes forming parts of his world view of human nature and the cosmic order of physical nature and the universe. His afterthoughts on these intellectual developments are contained in his prose essays, in his voluminous correspondence, in comments made during interviews, poetry readings, group discussions, and talks with friends, and in miscellaneous writings. Within his poems and between collections of his poetry, the arrangements that provide unity through metaphors and other means could be logical, analogical, or psychological; or grammatical, associative, or emotional; or tonal through the sound of sense, the last being for Frost of the greatest importance for unity.

Just as the arrangement in a book of poems came much later than the composition of particular poems, so too the understanding of Frost's aesthetic and ethical beliefs can best be understood by regarding each work as an item within the largest context of his whole literary career. To appreciate the cardinal importance of "Education by Poetry," it is essential to view it in the light of all of its predecessors and its successors that deal with aesthetic matters and artistic creativity. Frost's letters from England to his American friends during the period of World War I, and "The Imagining Ear" (1915) and "The Unmade Word" (1918), introduce the themes advanced in "Education by Poetry" (1930). It is significant that Lawrance Thompson, who never really understood Frost's dualism or his religion, nevertheless recognized that the course the poet taught in philosophy at Amherst College, a few years before he wrote "Education by Poetry," dealt with "judgments," that is, with normative principles in ethics and aesthetics, which are beyond the concern or reach of the physical sciences. Thompson concluded that Frost's course in philosophy "might be considered a trial flight for his closely related and more successful 'Education by Poetry.'"[13] The major prose works on poetry after 1930 include Frost's "Introduction to E. A. Robinson's *King Jasper*" (1935), "Poverty and Poetry" (1937), "The Figure a Poem Makes" (1939), "The Doctrine of Excursions" (1939), "The Constant Symbol" (1946), "Poetry and School" (1951), and "On Taking Poetry" (1955). These essays are supplemented by many minor works on the art of poetry, but all of them are simply variations on the themes that involve spirit and matter illuminated through metaphors for a deeper understanding of Frost's philosophical dualism.

It is no accident, and indeed perfectly fitting, that Frost concluded "Education by Poetry" with a summary inventory of what he regarded as his most important beliefs. The connection between belief or faith and the interactions between spirit and matter in his aesthetic philosophy turns upon the differences between religion, philosophy, and art as distinct from science. The former are concerned mainly with spirit, whereas science is centered in the laws and principles that govern matter. Although both require acts of faith or belief, they differ mainly in the concern of religion and philosophy with normative principles in ethics and aesthetics, while science deals with a descriptive and analytical account of physical phenomena. It is noteworthy that Frost's basic beliefs—"self-belief," "love-belief," "art-belief," and "national-belief"—finally "are all closely related to the God-belief, that the belief in God is a relationship you enter with Him to bring about the future."[14] Indeed, all five of his beliefs are concerned with how best to bring about the future. Frost noted the close connection between belief in poetry and in religion: "The person who gets close enough to poetry, he is going to know more about the word *belief* than anybody else knows."[15] A young man's "self-belief" compels him through "foreknowledge" to know that he has "something that is going to believe itself into fulfillment, into acceptance."[16] Love-belief, in another person, believes itself into existence and fulfillment; and a poet believes a poem into existence, not through cunning and rational devices but through "something more felt than known." Frost maintained that the founding fathers of the American republic believed the United States into existence.

These basic beliefs of human nature are best understood from the kind of imperfect knowledge that grows slowly and quietly through experience and self-knowledge, a knowledge that requires no scientific verification, so that it is "a knowledge that you don't want to tell other people about because you cannot prove that you know. You are saying nothing about it till you see."[17] Each of these beliefs is assumed and held in silence as maturity grows, so that an individual "knows it cannot tell; only the outcome can tell." Modesty and moral prudence accompany these beliefs until they are "fulfilled": "We are not talking until we know more, until we have something to show." This conviction led Frost not to call himself a poet until after his readers referred to him as a true poet. The spirit behind all five of Frost's beliefs cannot be understood apart from his philosophical dualism, which is the complete antithesis of the agnosticism of Thomas Henry Huxley. Yet some literary critics have interpreted Frost's line "But the strong are saying nothing until they see" as evidence that Frost was an agnostic. Nothing reveals a more complete misunderstanding of Frost's philosophical beliefs than such an error. It ignores Frost's contention that in every important subject people believe and act ahead of any empirical evidence and mathematical method of analytical reason.

In "Education by Poetry," Frost's belief in the almost universal validity of metaphorical thinking was applied not only to matters of faith or belief in religion, philosophy, and poetry, but also to science. He acknowledged that in late years he wanted "to go further and further in making metaphor the whole of thinking." But he made one important qualification. He held that "all thinking, except mathematical thinking, is metaphorical." In excluding mathematics, he rejected the methodology of Descartes and the abuse of science by modern scientific positivists. He observed that from the time of Pythagoras in the ancient world, when the universe was compared with numbers, to the time of Darwin and Einstein in the modern era, science could be understood in terms of metaphors. He noted that Darwin's "metaphor of evolution" is "a very brilliant metaphor" and "has done all our thinking for us" regarding "the growing plant or . . . the growing thing," but that it has been abused by being extended beyond its scientific validity. Without acknowledging his source, he summarized a principle of the physicist Werner Heisenberg: "The more accurately you state where a thing is, the less accurately you will be able to tell how fast it is moving." He was utterly charmed by one sentence from Einstein: "In the neighborhood of matter space is something like curved." Frost even talked with Niels Bohr, Einstein's rival in physics, regarding freedom of the will versus necessity in the movement of atoms through a screen. In a conversation with a friend,

Frost acknowledged that what is metabolic in the chemical process of living organisms finds its counterpart in the metaphorical processes of poetry. Both involve a change in the position, form, or relationship between two separate things and result in a fresh revelation or discovery. In physics, the vertical lines that promote buoyancy to maintain gravity in a floating object are identified as a motocenter. He objected to physicists who think that "life is a *result* of certain atoms coming together . . . instead of being the *cause* that brings the atoms together." In the relation of mind or spirit and matter, Frost clearly gave a premium to spirit.

In "Education by Poetry," Frost's very positive references to both poetry and science and the nature of belief are too limited to reveal the full richness of his total dualistic philosophy regarding the relationships between spirit and matter. If his positive beliefs are all centered in his dualism, conversely his disbeliefs are found in his criticism of the two forms of monism. Like Arthur O. Lovejoy, Frost was convinced that the modern world was increasingly dominated by science and that a monism of matter had corrupted a valid conception of science into scientific positivism. To Frost, science was best regarded as one of the humanities, not as an absolute end in itself through the worship of matter. In the very year of Frost's death, 1963, Aldous Huxley stated perfectly the great objection that Frost had to scientific positivism:

> For science in its totality, the ultimate goal is the creation of a monistic system in which—on the symbolic level and in terms of the inferred components of invisibly and intangibly fine structures—the world's enormous multiplicity is reduced to something like unity, and the endless succession of unique events of a great many different kinds get tidied and simplified into a single rational order.[18]

To Frost, both forms of monism resulted in a spirit of fanaticism and a belief in absolutism, in which spirit and matter were first separated and then made into irreconcilable contradictions. He criticized each monism as a "monomania—the attempt to say all in terms of only one element." Nowhere was monism more clearly evident than in the dominant forms of totalitarian politics. In the eleven chapters that follow, the contrasts between Frost's philosophy of dualism and the tragic consequences of both forms of monism in the totalitarian politics of the twentieth century will become starkly evident.

## 3

# Frost and Darwin's Theory: "The Metaphor of Evolution"

Robert Frost probably first became aware of Charles Darwin's theory of evolution at age fifteen, in the autumn of 1889, during his sophomore year in high school when his older friend Carl Burell (1864–1938) showed him his volumes of Darwin, Herbert Spencer, Thomas Henry Huxley, Grant Allen, and other Victorian writers on evolution.[1] In 1948, Frost remembered that he had "grinned inside at the time" over Allen's book on the evolution of God,[2] although later it had provoked his ire as an instance of how Darwin's theory was abused by stretching its metaphor beyond the breaking point. Burell was an avid botanist and disciple of Darwin, and he introduced Frost into a lasting love of botany as well as a lifelong interest in evolution and science in general as forms of epical metaphors.

Ironically, both the botanist and Frost's mother, Belle Moodie Frost, possessed copies of Richard Anthony Proctor's *Our Place Among Infinities* (1876), but whereas this book had not prevented Burell from losing his religious faith and accepting Darwin's account of the origin of life and the changes in species, Frost's mother countered the supposed atheistic influence of Burell on her son by appealing to Proctor's book. She noted that, through the study of astronomy, that thinker taught that "our faith must not be hampered by scientific doubts, our science must not be hampered by religious scruples." She also quoted to her son a line from Edward Young's "Night Thoughts": "An undevout astronomer is mad." Clearly, Burell's interpretation of Darwin's theory came into sharp conflict with Frost's religious orientation as derived from his mother's Swedenborgian faith, which he remembered fondly throughout his life for its "purity of spirit."[3] His mother's guiding spirit, moreover, was an important early factor in shaping both his religious and his aesthetic beliefs. Throughout his life, Frost was fascinated by Christian theology and the conception of creativity as "correspondence," so that from the very beginning of his newly acquired interest in Darwinian evolution he was faced with the philosophical problem of how to reconcile the materialism in Darwin's naturalism with the strongly opposed religious beliefs taught by his mother."[4]

Belle Frost considered Darwin's theory on the origins of life and on how changes occurred in species both shocking and blasphemous, and she warned her son against listening to such an avowed atheist as Burell. Apparently, at first Frost agreed with her view that the botanist's belief in Darwin's theory was a form of undevout madness. He even expressed his agreement in a limerick titled "The Rubaiyat of Carl Burell":

> *There was a young fellow, begad,*
> *Who hadn't but wished that he had—*
> *God only knows what,*
> *But he blasphemed a lot*
> *And showed he was generally mad.*

But in talking with his mother, when he referred to himself as "a freethinker" Belle feared that he shared Burell's impiety, and she responded, "Oh don't use that word. It has a dreadful history."[5] Frost reassured his mother that he had not become an atheist, but that he was merely rethinking the whole relationship between his conventional belief in God and the claims of the revolutionary theory propounded by Darwin.

In an editorial essay in his high school paper, the *Bulletin* (May 1892), Frost clarified what he meant by rethinking his beliefs:

> A Custom has its unquestioning followers, its radical enemies, and a class who have generally gone through both these to return to the first in a limited sense,—to follow custom,—not without question, but where it does not conflict with the broader habits of life gained by wanderers among ideas. The second class makes one of the first and third. This is best exemplified in religious thought and controversy.[6]

What is most remarkable about his schoolboy statement is that it is the first recorded instance of what became his lifelong habit of mind regarding how he responded to challenging new ideas. It became characteristic of the poet to listen open-mindedly to whatever anyone had to say in expounding his scientific, religious, aesthetic, political, or educational beliefs and then to judge its truth and personal meaning to him: "I'll accept anybody's . . . premises. I'll let them have their say, and then I take it my way." Thus, in a highly eclectic manner, as a "freethinker" or "wanderer among ideas," Frost responded both to Darwin's theory and to the great range of arguments by both critics and defenders of his theory.

Frost's open-mindedness regarding Darwin's theory functioned within the all-inclusive frame of reference provided by his philosophical dualism of matter and mind or spirit and by his growing conviction that all thinking (except possibly mathematical cognition) was essentially metaphorical. This meant that, unlike spiritual monists, such as religious fundamentalists, he did not reject Darwin's theory out of hand; and in sharp contrast to materialist monists and scientific fundamentalists who defended Darwin's theory and used it as a weapon to attack religious belief, he at once retained his lifelong belief in God and respect for religion while accepting as valid whatever appeared to be true in Darwin's thought. Whether in religion, science, literature, or anything else, fundamentalism was to Frost a state of mind and feeling which treated conceptual ideas and philosophical principles with literal-minded rigidity, and often with a fanaticism that lacked all sense of metaphor.

The trinity of Frost's open-minded eclectic method, his philosophical dualism, and his faith in metaphorical thinking makes his response to Darwin's theory of evolution extremely complex. His deep knowledge of that theory, his positive response to much of it, his important differences with its propounder, and his conflicts with some of its defenders and critics require an accurate and thorough study of the whole controversy over evolution as experienced by him throughout his adult life. Only after making such a study can readers of his poetry make those important distinctions that are necessary to appreciate the nature and extent of the impact that evolutionary theory had on his thought and verse.

Frost was aware that his mother continued to be troubled by Darwin's theory, especially that crucial aspect of it which supposedly traced the origin of man and his descent from a common ancestry with the apes. To counteract that view, she quoted from Genesis 2:7 —"*And the Lord God formed man of the dust of the ground, and breathed into his nostrils the breath of life; and man became a living soul.*"[7] Belle Frost was unaware that in a letter to Thomas Henry Huxley (December 25, 1859), Darwin had candidly admitted that "we know nothing as yet [of] how life originates"[8] and that in *The Origin of Species* (Chapter XV) he had noted "the old belief in the creation of species from the dust of the earth." In response to this expression of his mother's troubled state of mind, Frost had a "ready answer," which he came to regard, in retrospect, as his first memorable witticism: "You say, God made man of mud, and I think God made man of prepared mud."[9] Frost was well read in Emerson, and he may have taken his cue from that thinker's statement: "Man was made of social earth." In fact, he became so fond of his youthful witticism, made in 1892, that he repeated it, with significant variations, many times until his death in 1963.

In a poetry reading at Bread Loaf (June 30, 1955), he provided an addition to his witticism that explicitly harmonized Genesis with Darwin: "It doesn't make any great difference to give up saying that God made [man] out of mud. All you have to say is that God made him out of prepared mud—worked it up from animal life. So it comes to the same thing—it's a Darwinian thing."[10] Metaphorically speaking, as it applies to the origins of life and the evolution of man, it does indeed come to the same thing, whether the appeal is primarily to things of the spirit, as in religion, or to things rooted in matter, as in scientific theory. Frost's philosophical dualism of spirit and matter provided him with different metaphorical ways of explaining the same phenomena. Implicit in his witticism is his general belief that, despite apparent contradictions, there was no real conflict between science and religion, only "contrarieties" that needed to be resolved into a harmonious whole. The basic method of resolving all such contrarieties was through the free play of metaphorical thinking—the exploration of comparisons, contrasts, similarities, differences, analogies, parallels, parables, and so on, which involved saying spirit in terms of matter and matter in terms of spirit.

It is enormously significant that sixty-seven years after Frost first made his witticism, he contended in the "The Future of Man" symposium (1959) that the general public eventually came to reconcile its faith in traditional religion with Darwin's theory by accepting the core idea in his witticism. He imagined what a contemporary scientist would say to the public in defending the radical and disturbing implications that science had created in its recent explorations of outer space, and he then drew a parallel between how the public had come to accept Darwin's theory and how it could respond to the "new novelties" of space exploration: "It seems a shame to come on you with our new novelties when you are hardly up around after what Darwin, Spencer, and Huxley did to you last century. . . . Remember how you were helped by being reminded all you were asked to do was change from your old idea that God made man out of mud to the new idea that God made man of prepared mud."[11] Frost came to have three very distinct and separate views of Darwin, Spencer, and Huxley; but, in considering how science (or matter) and religion (or spirit) are related, he clearly believed that new scientific theories or discoveries, which were always subject to change, did not destroy basic and enduring revealed religious truths, but merely compelled mankind to modify its understanding of them.

For example, in *The Masque of Reason* (1945), Frost has God clarify to Job how the novelty of science, with its constant change, compares with the metaphysics of religion and its enduring moral wisdom:

> *My forte is truth,*
> *Or metaphysics, long the world's reproach*
> *For standing still in one place true forever;*
> *While science goes self-superseding on.*
> *Look at how far we've left the current science*
> *Of Genesis behind. The wisdom there though,*
> *Is just as good as when I uttered it.*
> *Still novelty has doubtless an attraction.*

This vital passage is a summary of what Frost had recorded in his notebooks:

> What's wrong with Genesis is the science in it. Let science be called to answer for it, not religion. . . . The science is what is defective in the Old Testament, not the religion. . . . Let religion enter into combination with the science of its time, for it will whether we let it or not. . . . The science that religion takes over today religion will sooner or later drop. The science changes. The religion persists. The religious part of religion has been nearly the same 5,000 years at least.[12]

Clearly, for Frost no scientific theory was ever cast in stone. He believed that any assumed conflict in doctrines and perspectives between science and religion was not an irreconcilable contradiction which forced individuals to choose sides; rather, he saw such conflicts as opportunities to explore whatever elements of truth were to be found in each set of beliefs.

Frost's poem "Sitting by a Bush in Broad Sunlight" (in *West-Running Brook*, 1928), takes its archetypal metaphor from the biblical account of the burning bush and exemplifies how the central point in his original witticism regarding the origins of man is found in both religion and in Darwin's theory of evolution:

*When I spread out my hand here today,*
*I catch no more than a ray*
*To feel of between thumb and fingers;*
*No lasting effect of it lingers.*

*There was one time and only the one*
*When dust really took in the sun;*
*And from that one intake of fire*
*All creatures still warmly suspire.*

*And if men have watched a long time*
*And never seen sun-smitten slime*
*Again come to life and crawl off,*
*We must not be too ready to scoff.*

*God once declared he was true*
*And then took the veil and withdrew,*
*And remember how final a hush*
*Then descended of old on the bush.*

*God once spoke to people by name.*
*The sun once imparted its flame.*
*One impulse persists as our breath;*
*The other persists as our faith.* [13]

Frost had neither gnostic hatred of matter nor denial of spiritual revelation. To him, the truths regarding matter as revealed by science and the truths of spirit as contained in religion are among the great metaphors by which mankind lives and finds meaning in life. Their complex interrelationships are best understood not by treating each as a separate, absolute, autonomous, and wholly self-sufficient reality, as in materialistic and spiritual monism, but as vital contributions to the enduring culture of civilized life, within a philosophical dualism of both matter and spirit.

It took Frost the better part of his adult lifetime to develop fully his dualistic belief that all science, including Darwin's materialist theory of evolution, was compatible with the vital element of mind or spirit, as contained in the humanities, arts, and religion. While he was a student at Harvard University, from autumn 1897 to spring 1899, his knowledge and understanding of Darwin's theory was greatly enriched and extended. Moreover, through his studies of the classics at Harvard, he intensified his faith in the power of metaphorical thinking through literature and thereby strengthened his incipient dualistic philosophy. Indeed, it would be hard to overestimate the importance of Harvard in shaping Frost's intellectual life, both for the development of his views on evolution and for his future as a poet.

Lawrance Thompson's account of Frost's experience as a student at Harvard,[14] largely centered in the influence of William James, whose courses he never attended, is wholly inadequate because it does not clarify what his teachers there contributed toward his greater understanding of Darwin's theory. Moreover, Frost never attended the courses of Asa Gray (1810–88), who, in the years prior to Frost's arrival at Harvard, had converted many of the faculty, including the poet's teachers, to his understanding of Darwin's theory. Gray's comprehensive *Manual of the Botany of the Northern United States* (1848), so greatly admired by Frost, had led Darwin to begin a correspondence with the Harvard botanist, who was privileged to read a manuscript outline of *The Origin of Species* before its publication. His three articles, "Darwin and His Reviewers," in the *Atlantic Monthly* (1860) introduced the Victorian conflict over evolutionary theory to the American public. As editor of the *American Journal of Science*, Gray defended Darwin's theory in the March 1860 number as compatible with theism and belief in a divine mind, will, and personality. His anthology, *Darwiniana: Essays and Reviews Pertaining to Darwinism*, which went into a second edition in 1876, greatly extended knowledge of Darwin's thought among Americans.

But the pertinence of Gray's interpretation of Darwin to Frost's own mature views of evolution is most evident in his two lectures to the Yale Divinity School, "Natural Science and Religion" (1880). Like Frost, Gray was a philosophical dualist and conceived of human nature as compounded of both spirit and matter: "Man, while on the one side a wholly exceptional being, is on the other an object of natural history,—a part of the animal kingdom. . . . Man, in short, is a partaker of the natural as well as the spiritual."[15] Gray quoted Genesis on the origins of life out of dust, and in defense of evolution asked: "Is there any warrant for affirming that these processes were instantaneous?"[16] Frost himself recorded the same question in his notebook. In light of Frost's rejection of monism and of his intense dislike for the word "agnostic," Gray's comment on both is highly significant: "The Darwinian Naturalist," he wrote, is "not the monistic and agnostic philosopher,—from whom . . . we have kept as clear as has Mr. Darwin in every volume and every line."[17] Like Frost in his later years, he took issue with "the assurance with which monistic evolutionists press their answer" to the great mysteries of man's origins and ends.[18] Gray's strong opposition to evolutionary monists anticipates Frost's own belief: "With all life goes duality. There is the matter, and there is the life. . . . The duality runs through the whole. You cannot reasonably give over any part of the field to the monist, and retain the rest."[19]

Gray also discussed at length the vital problem of design in a way that anticipated Frost's poem on that subject. He noted that although Darwin's theory seems "to yield only a crop of accidents," still it was possible "to harmonize our ineradicable belief in design with the fundamental scientific belief of continuity in nature, now extended to organic as well as inorganic forms. . . ."[20] He concluded that "the true issue as regards design is not between Darwinism and direct Creationism, but between design and fortuity, between any intention or intellectual cause and no intention nor predictable first cause."[21] Furthermore, he noted that mind, will, and intention are part of God's design and that "our wills, in their limited degree, modify the course of nature,"[22] two beliefs that Frost came to hold. In his poem "Accidentally on Purpose," he wrote: "Grant me intention, purpose, and design— / That's near enough for me to the Divine," and on several occasions he made it clear that to a certain extent man's reason and will could direct the course of evolutionary change.

As Jon H. Roberts has shown in *Darwinism and the Divine in America* (1988), Asa Gray was Darwin's foremost American apologist in the United States between 1859 and 1888. For forty-six years he was Harvard's most famous professor of botany, and he imbued many of the faculty with his belief that Darwin's theory was wholly compatible with the orthodoxy of Christian theism. In his insistence that the human mind and will were vital factors in evolution, Gray was a precursor of William James's psychology in *The Will to Believe* (1897), which Frost had probably read in magazines in 1895 and which had inspired him to go to Harvard. Following Asa Gray's work, as early as 1868 James had absorbed a positive intellectual response to Darwin: "The more I think of Darwin's ideas the more weighty they appear to me."[23] During his sophomore year, Frost strengthened his dualistic philosophy of mind or spirit and matter, and his insights into both religion and science, through reading James's textbook, *Psychology: The Briefer Course*, a text that he used in teaching at Plymouth in 1912. Like Gray, James presented an open-minded and favorable view of Darwinian evolution that included mind and spirit.[24]

James expounded upon Darwin's famous phrase "the survival of the fittest," which the evolutionist had adopted from Herbert Spencer, as superior to "natural selection" in describing how changes occur in the perpetuation or the extinction of species. James argued that a modicum of selfishness was necessary for anyone to survive and to fulfill himself. Thompson mistakenly believed that Frost adopted this principle in order to justify the sacrifices he had to make to be a poet and concluded that his selfishness made Frost a social Darwinist both in his personal life and in his social philosophy. But there is ample evidence that Frost rejected Spencer's philosophy and that he distinguished between a legitimate self-interest and ruthless selfishness. Frost did not reject common ethical norms in human relationships. Thompson also ignored the fact that James had qualified "survival of the fittest" for minds "altogether apart from any interest in the pure ego which they also possess." But contrary to Thompson, the exact nature and full extent of James's influence on Frost can best be appreciated by noting how much that philosopher owed to Asa Gray's exposition of Darwinian evolution.

Two other teachers of Frost at Harvard, Josiah Royce in philosophy and Nathaniel Southgate Shaler in geology, also enriched his understanding of Darwin's theory by their attempts to reconcile it with their own personal brand of philosophical idealism. Two chapters in Royce's *The Spirit of Modern Philosophy* (1892) explore Darwin's theory: "The Rise of the Doctrine of Evolution" and "Nature and Evolution, The Outer World and Its Paradoxes." Royce was steeped in the tradition of English empiricism, but he was essentially a Platonist. He defended idealism because "it maintains that the world is . . . a world of mind or of spirit." He approved of George Berkeley's idealism, with its stress on the power and reality of the mind: "The world, then, is such stuff as ideas are made of. Thought possesses all things." After paying tribute to the importance of Darwin's *Origin of Species*, Royce noted that Herbert Spencer had anticipated Darwin, and he claimed that Spencer was the dominant power in evolutionary thought after the *Origin of Species*. Royce noted that Spencer was in the tradition of Thomas Hobbes and that his object was to unify all science and thought into a materialist monism. To Frost, who denied that he was a Platonist, Royce's own nonmaterialist monism was not a satisfactory response to Darwin's theory. Nevertheless, Royce made him aware that the dimension of mind or spirit was omitted from Darwin's theory, so that it was seriously inadequate if regarded as a total philosophy of life. As Jay Parini has noted, it is quite likely that the philosophical problems raised by Royce regarding Darwin's theory resulted in Frost's writing "The Demiurge's Laugh" and "Design."[25]

Lawrance Thompson has recorded the general importance of Professor Shaler's course in "Historical Geology" in Frost's intellectual life: "Here was science which interlocked also with his early passion for astronomy and with his later concern for the Darwinian concept of evolution."[26] Shaler was in his twenties when *The Origin of Species* appeared, and years later he recalled that "to be caught" reading Darwin "was as it is for the faithful to be detected in a careful study of heresy."[27] But Shaler was deeply influenced by Asa Gray and was a disciple of Sir Charles Lyell, whose many editions of *Principles of Geology* (1830–33) dominated geological studies during the Victorian era. Lyell believed that mind and will were paramount in man, so he was very reluctant to accept Darwin's theory, and he became a "convert" only by retaining much of his belief in idealistic philosophy. Like Gray and Lyell, Shaler held fast to his religious faith and harmonized it with his understanding of geology. In his poem "Directive," Frost utilized geological imagery (". . . lines ruled southeast northwest, / The chisel work of an enormous glacier"), and the concept of raw power in nature, in a geologically primitive setting, is clearly evident in "The Most of It." Frost's sense of geological time is also evident in other poems, such as "I Could Give All to Time." Undoubtedly, far more than Thompson realized, and in ways that included both spirit and matter, Shaler's course did much to deepen Frost's awareness of the geological basis of Darwin's theory within the framework of his philosophical dualism.

In 1898 Frost took a course in philosophy with George Santayana. The basic textbook, Alfred Weber's *History of Philosophy* (1896), covered all of European philosophy from the pre-Socratic Greeks to the end of the nineteenth century. He presented all of European philosophy in terms of the two great opposed traditions of thought—pluralism or dualism versus monism. Pluralists and dualists perceived reality as composed of two distinct but closely related elements, matter and spirit. Monists held that reality was either all matter or all spirit, or a unified blending of both into one harmonious whole, as in pantheism. Weber made it clear that in the perennial conflict between the claims of the One and the Many, neither a monistic nor a dualistic system of thought exists in any absolute sense: "Even the most decided monists advance a relative dualism," and "conversely . . . the most characteristic pluralistic system acknowledges the relative truth of monism."[28]

Aldous Huxley has noted the extent to which science and scientific theory is centered in a philosophical monism: "For science in its totality, the ultimate goal is the creation of a monistic system in which . . . the world's enormous multiplicity is reduced to something like unity. . . ."[29] Frost was always skeptical of any system of this kind; he utterly rejected any schema that posited a rational order aimed at total unity, whether in science, religion, or politics, because such a closed system invariably excluded everything that contradicted its premises, logic, and ultimate end. His dualism set great value on the separation of the parts within any unified order, and he was skeptical of systematic ideological theories. Frost responded very favorably to Weber's argument that no system of thought is ever an axiomatic absolute beyond dispute. He valued Weber's textbook so much that it became a permanent part of his personal library, and he brought it with him for many summers after 1938, when he went to his farm in Ripton, Vermont.

A section of one chapter in Weber's text was titled "Darwinism and Contemporary Monism," in which the evolutionist's theory was identified as a completely materialistic system among contemporary monisms. But Darwin had not limited his theory to matter alone. In *The Origin of Species,* he had made "natural selection" the chief but not the sole method of changes in species for their survival or extinction. In *The Descent of Man* (1871), he had given "sexual selection" the central role in human evolution. This meant that man's will, reason, passion, and creativeness were factors in making evolutionary changes. Weber made Frost aware that, although Darwin's theory was essentially materialist, it was best understood not as an unqualified monistic philosophy as "found among the pure materialists," and certainly not "in the camp of the spiritualists," but somewhere "between the two camps."[30] Weber's interpretation of Darwin was consistent with Frost's incipient dualistic philosophy and probably did much to confirm him in his belief that reality consisted of both spirit and matter.

Frost clearly agreed with Weber's statement that the mechanistic explanation of finality regarding origins and ends "in Darwin, does not exclude the idea of creation," as was claimed both by materialist monists who defended his theory and by spiritual monists who attacked it. Like Weber, he was highly critical of those who converted Darwin's theory into social Darwinism, while denying that there are "interior, superior, and immaterial" causes in man's constant "struggle for existence."[31] Much more than Darwin, Frost stressed the uniquely creative powers in the mind and spirit of man, so that he differed from his predecessor's rejection of "the view that there is an insurpassable gulf between animals and man, matter and mind."[32] Throughout his adult life, he believed that there was a difference in kind, not merely in degree, between man and other animals. Apart from this vital difference, Frost was in general agreement with Darwin's belief that evolution involved not merely "natural selection," but dual or multiple principles of change in species.[33]

Indeed, Darwin himself provided Frost with the best case for a dualist or pluralist approach to his theory by insisting that natural selection was

not the sole method of making changes in species. In his final edition of
*The Origin of Species* (1872), Darwin set aside his lifelong bland and genial
temperament and in anger strongly criticized those who persisted in mis-
representing his basic principle as an exclusive absolute:

> As my conclusions have lately been much misrepresented, and it
> has been stated that I attribute the modification of species exclu-
> sively to natural selection, I may be permitted to remark that in
> the first edition of this work, and subsequently, I placed in a most
> conspicuous position—namely at the close of the Introduction—
> the following words: "I am convinced that natural selection has
> been the main but not the exclusive means of modification." This
> has been to no avail. Great is the power of steady misrepresenta-
> tion; but the history of science shows that fortunately this power
> does not long endure.[34]

Darwin's basic principle was misrepresented not only by religious monists, such as literal-minded biblical fundamentalists who condemned his
theory as a denial of Genesis and all revealed religion, but also by social
Darwinists, such as Herbert Spencer, and by pseudo-Darwinists, scientific
materialist monists such as Thomas Henry Huxley who praised and defended his theory while digressing radically from its central principle of
natural selection. To Frost, religious monists and scientific monists had
far more in common with each other, although they despised each other,
than they had with pluralists or dualists whose thought was essentially
metaphorical, and who included several principles within the framework
of spirit or mind and matter. A common fundamentalist mentality and
literal-mindedness characterized both religious and scientific materialist
monists and often led to a rigidity and dogmatic fanaticism that Frost despised. His dualism and his sense of metaphor, in total contrast with the
literal-minded monism of religious and scientific fundamentalism, were
centered in a constant intellectual "play" that required careful mediation
between the separate but related claims of mind or spirit and matter.

Frost's dualistic and metaphorical approach to evolution led him to re-
tain a highly favorable view of Darwin and to be very critical of Spencer
and Huxley. Among modern scholars on evolution, Frost's approach to
Darwin is very similar to Stephen Jay Gould's interpretation of his theory.
Gould, a Harvard University scientist, was very much in the tradition of
Frost's teachers there. In "Evolution: The Pleasures of Pluralism" (*The New
York Review of Books*, June 26, 1997), Gould, like Frost, assumes Darwin's

complex metaphorical view of evolution. He notes that "Darwin began the last paragraph of *The Origin of Species* (1859), with a famous metaphor about life's diversity and ecological complexity," in which the evolutionist described how different species of life are so "dependent on each other in so complex a manner . . . produced by laws acting around us." Gould then draws the sharp contrast between how "fundamentalist" scientific monists and metaphorical pluralists understand Darwin's theory:

> The "fundamentalists" among evolutionary theorists revel in the belief that one overarching law—Darwin's central principle of natural selection—can render the full complexity of outcomes (by working in conjunction with auxiliary principles, like sexual reproduction, that enhance its rate and power).

> The "pluralists," on the other hand—a long line of thinkers including Darwin himself, however ironic this may seem since the fundamentalists use the cloak of his name for their distortion of his position—accept natural selection as a paramount principle (truly *primus inter pares*), but then argue that a set of additional laws, as well as a large role for history's unpredictable contingencies, must also be invoked to explain the basic patterns and regularities of the evolutionary pathways of life. Both sides locate the "grandeur" of "this view of life" in the explanation of complex and particular outcomes by general principles, but ultra-Darwinian fundamentalists pursue one true way, while pluralists seek to identify a set of interacting explanatory modes, all fully intelligible, although not reducible to a single grand principle like natural selection.[35]

Frost accepted not only the evolutionist's grand principle of natural selection, but in what he called "passionate preference" he also accepted Darwin's principle of "sexual selection." Finally, like Darwin, he held that in the mysterious and unpredictable course of human history, mind, will, creative power, and memory of man were valid elements in evolution.

By the time Frost left Harvard in 1899, through the indirect influence of Asa Gray, his readings in William James and Alfred Weber's text, and the direct influence of Royce and Shaler, his knowledge and understanding of Darwin's theory, and the whole Victorian controversy over evolution, were essentially established. During the years on the Derry farm, and in those he spent teaching at Pinkerton Academy and in Plymouth, New Hampshire,

1900–12, Frost read voraciously in many subjects and further consolidated his knowledge and understanding of Darwin's thought beyond the principle of natural selection. Frost knew well the evolutionist's *The Voyage of the Beagle* (1839), *On the Origin of Species* (1859), and *The Descent of Man* (1871). Soon after its publication in 1911, he read *The Life and Letters of Charles Darwin, Including an Autobiographical Chapter* (1911), edited by his son, Francis. He probably also knew Darwin's *The Expression of the Emotions in Men and Animals* (1895), and in 1925 he was given a copy of Darwin's *Journal of Researches*.[36] On several occasions, Frost remarked that Defoe's *Robinson Crusoe*, Thoreau's *Walden*, and Darwin's *The Voyage of the Beagle* were among the books he most esteemed: "I set those three on a special shelf of mine."[37] It is significant that all of these works are centered in man's struggle to survive, one of the central themes in evolutionary theory, and one consistent with Frost's lifelong belief that man's life on earth is a constant trial by existence.

Frost was well aware that to scientists and the general public Darwin's *Origin of Species* was of paramount importance in his theory, but he took sharp issue with those who ranked it among the world's best one hundred books (as distinct from most influential) while omitting *The Voyage of the Beagle*:

> People who think they're making a list of the hundred best books . . . put in Darwin's *On the Origin of Species*. This other one— *Voyage of the Beagle*—this is where he thought of it (natural selection) on that enterprise. That's the beauty of it. A beautiful story—people and things and animals and observations, great world travel. It's one of the wonder books.[38]

The term "wonder books" was one of Frost's ways of identifying outstanding works in the tradition of the arts and the humanities. In sharp contrast, *The Origin of Species*, as Darwin himself admitted, was a highly compressed abstract, an empirically factual and metaphorically speculative work that demanded a close reading of its descriptive and analytical propositions. But it had no redeeming art to make it aesthetically attractive or emotionally satisfying.

*The Voyage of the Beagle*, however, was a masterpiece that combined clear scientific observations of plants, animals, and geological formations in a natural and humanized landscape. Moreover, its appeal included those qualities Frost cherished most: literary sensibility and deep appreciation of metaphorical thinking. Small wonder that he called it a "book of the worthies and unworthies through the ages" and considered it one of the four best works of prose written during the nineteenth century. During his life on the Derry farm, Frost delighted in reading portions of *The Voyage of the Beagle* to his children. To him it was a prime example of how science at its best was a vital part of the humanities in Western civilization.

Although *The Voyage of the Beagle* confirmed his appreciation of Darwin's theory, Frost was probably in error in assuming that the evolutionist first thought of his basic principle of natural selection during his almost five years as the official naturalist on the *Beagle*, from December 17, 1831, to October 2, 1836. Darwin's statement that the voyage on the *Beagle* was by far the most important event in his life as a scientist, and that it determined his whole career, may have led the poet astray. Frost's error is readily understandable. He knew that Darwin had taken Charles Lyell's *Principles of Geology* (1830) with him on the *Beagle*. He had correlated fossil specimens through geological ages with living "animals of all classes," and with the botany and zoology of South America and all of the islands in the Pacific Ocean where the *Beagle* had landed.

But as Darwin recorded, he did not open his notebooks until July 1837, nine months after his return to England. As he said in his *Autobiography*, he then had worked for over a year "on true Baconian principles, and without any theory collected facts on a wholesale scale." According to the evolutionist, for many months his theory of how natural selection could be applied to organisms living in a state of nature remained a mystery to him. Ironically, his germinal concept of how evolutionary changes occurred, derived from his reading in October 1838 of Thomas Malthus's ideological and speculative *Essay on the Principle of Population* (1798). From that treatise he "had at last got a theory by which to work." By June 1842, he had written "a brief abstract" of thirty-five pages on his theory. He enlarged it to 230 pages in 1844. Twelve years later, in 1856, he completed his manuscript but continued the process of revision. He would have continued to revise his theory, but unexpectedly his "plans were overthrown . . . in the summer of 1858," when he received an article by Alfred Russell Wallace that "contained exactly the same theory" as his own. Thus, twenty-three years after he had gathered his "harvest of facts" during his voyage on the *Beagle*, Darwin was pressured into publishing *The Origin of Species* in November 1859.[39]

Many things in Darwin's personal character and temperament and in his careful and thorough methods as a scientist appealed deeply to Frost. The poet believed that the evolutionist was courageous. Moreover, he did not agree with those who charged that Darwin's long delay in publishing his theory derived from a fear of criticism. Frost knew that the evolutionist had said that he had learned "never to trust in science to the principle of exclusion," which made him very cautious in his theoretical speculations about empirical facts. The poet also knew that Darwin was well aware that his theory had some serious weaknesses, especially regarding large gaps in the geological record and the ignorance of scientists regarding the laws of genetics. In fact, Darwin's mind was not doctrinaire, dogmatic, and closed; it was open to revisions in his theory through further discoveries. This attitude was consistent with Frost's belief expressed in "The White-Tailed Hornet": "Won't almost any theory bear revision?" Darwin hated controversy and never engaged in public debates about his theory. Moreover, he was content to let his "converts" plead his cause, even when they did not agree with him on some basic principles.

Darwin also took great pains not to antagonize the religious sensibilities of those who disagreed with him, and he expressed deep respect for "the judgment of the many able men who have fully believed in God." But he admitted that for him "the whole subject is beyond the scope of man's intellect; but man can do his duty." In chapter 15 of *The Origin of Species* he wrote: "I see no good reason why the views in this volume should shock the religious feelings of any one." Like Frost, Darwin believed that religion and science involved two very different ways of understanding reality; he declared that "theology and science should each run its own course."

Darwin's principle that all species of life are involved in a constant struggle to survive was especially appealing to Frost, and it was consistent with his belief that man's life on earth was an eternal "trial by existence." The poet knew that, unlike Spencer and Huxley and many other ardent Victorian disciples, Darwin had some reservations about his theory being the basis for a belief in the idea of "progress" that would lead mankind to a future utopian state. Nor did he hold that his theory should be extended beyond biology, botany, and zoology into every branch of human concerns. But above all, Darwin's metaphorical way of presenting many aspects of his theory was particularly attractive to Frost. The poet appreciated the great pains he had taken to stay within the valid bounds of evolution as a scientific metaphor, as well as his care not to extend his theory into social, political, economic, and religious matters.

It is important to note that during the years that Frost was initially most concerned with Darwin's theory, in the last decade of the nineteenth century and during the first several decades of the twentieth century, many scientists, theologians, belletrists, and the public at large had become so critical of his theory that it appeared destined for the dustbin of history.

Darwin himself had contributed something toward his demise by admitting that, in the literal sense, "natural selection is a false term," a concession that raised questions about his central principle. In fact, the metaphorical ambiguities and difficulties inherent in the concept of natural selection continued to trouble him until his death. Even before publishing *The Origin of Species*, in a letter to Asa Gray in 1857, he admitted that "multiform difficulties will occur to every one, with respect to this theory."[40] As Robert M. Young has observed, the phrase "natural selection" had caused so much trouble by 1866 that Wallace wrote a friendly letter urging Darwin to drop it altogether:

> I have been so repeatedly struck by the utter inability of numbers of intelligent persons to see clearly, or at all, the self-acting and necessary effects of Natural Selection, that I am led to conclude that the term itself, and your mode of illustrating it, however clear and beautiful to many of us, are yet not the best adapted to impress it on the general naturalist public.[41]

Ultimately, Darwin was persuaded to substitute "survival of the fittest" for natural selection. But this concession gave credence to those who converted his theory into social Darwinism, thereby further weakening support for his theory, since it appeared to attack the traditional Judaeo-Christian ethics of Western civilization. Other serious problems combined with the steady attacks launched by literary critics undermined almost completely the public's belief in Darwin's conception of evolution.[42]

Robert Frost was well read in the extensive literature surrounding Darwin's theory during the late Victorian era, and he was therefore keenly aware of the vast range of conflicting views that obtained regarding evolution among scientists, theologians, and literary writers. Since he absorbed some of the ideas set forth by both critics and defenders of Darwin's theory, a summary review of the literature on evolution helps to clarify his own later convictions about that corpus of thought. Frost knew that between 1859 and 1870 Darwin's theory had been widely embraced because of the favorable reviews, articles, and public lectures indited by the British scientific establishment, which included such men as T. H. Huxley, Joseph Dalton Hooker, Charles Lyell, W. B. Carpenter, Herbert Spencer, Alfred

Russell Wallace, Grant Allen, Ray Lankester, John Tyndall, and George J. Romanes. A similarly well-disposed cadre existed on the Continent, led by Ernst Haeckel in Germany.

But beginning in 1871, when St. George Jackson Mivart (1828–1900) published *Genesis of Spirit*, there developed a steady crescendo of serious criticism of Darwin's theory, directed mainly against his chief principle of natural selection, but also against the determinism and materialism implicit in his thought. This criticism was so compelling that by 1904, as Peter J. Bowler observed, "there was no longer any need to pay even lip service to the theory of natural selection."[43] The initiator of the onslaught, Mivart, a Catholic convert, was a former student of Huxley, a friend of Darwin, and a strong believer in evolution. His acknowledged competence as a scientist made his powerful set of critical strictures against Darwin's thought more troublesome to the great evolutionist than those of any other critic.[44] Indeed, Mivart provided the chief weapons against Darwin's theory among both scientists and the public for the last three decades of the nineteenth century. Ironically, it was Darwin's chief defender, Thomas Henry Huxley, who made that antagonist aware of the great difficulty in believing in natural selection.

Mivart quoted a long passage from *The Origin of Species* in which Darwin had admitted that he had exaggerated the importance of natural selection. He then struck at the heart of the evolutionist's theory: "To admit any such constant operation of any such unknown natural cause is to deny the purely Darwinian theory which relies upon the survival of the fittest by means of minute fortuitous indefinite variations."[45] He argued that this wholly naturalistic conception, based upon adaptive changes of species in reacting mainly to physical environment, was negated by the records of fossils and also by the actual observed conditions of living species.

In place of evolution by chance, Mivart posited a non-Darwinian theory of growth through directed change, an innate, inner-directed source for changes in species, involving the mind, will, and emotions of man, which he contended formed "harmonious self-consistent wholes." In addition to physical environment, as applied to man, such changes, he held, could be made through genetics, the creative powers in man, or a God-given directive. Without insisting upon an overall theistic plan or design, Mivart's criticism of Darwin gave precedence to man's mind or spirit as elements inherent in organic matter and in the evolutionary process. In effect, he provided a scientific rather than a vague theistic interpretation of the theme in Robert Chambers's *Vestiges of the Natural History of Creation* (1844) and thereby advanced a non-Darwinian model of evolution based upon changes in species through separate and independent lines of development, rather than through related forms of species descended from a common ancestor.

Mivart's stress upon the power of mind and moral sense in man conceived of human cognition as different in kind, not merely in degree, from that of other animals. He was a philosophical dualist, and when Darwin's successor, George Romanes, defended the materialist theory in an article, "Mind and Monism," he wrote a rebuttal, affirming that man's cognition directed matter, not the reverse. It was to refute Mivart's criticism and case for creative evolution that Darwin added a new chapter in the final edition of *The Origin of Species*. [46] This concession was naturally noted by subsequent critics of that work.

As the first important critic of Darwin, Mivart was to make the case for what eventually came to be called "creative evolution." His dualistic concept of the evolutionary process combined two diametrically opposed elements: on the one hand, the unique role of mind, including will, reason, and creativity; on the other, changes in species induced by determinism and centered in matter. This formulation of Mivart's, developed by such successors as Samuel Butler, William James, and Henri Bergson, profoundly influenced Frost's reaction to Darwin's thought. To understand the full complexity of Frost's mature response to the revisions in Darwin's theory, it is necessary to consider his convictions regarding evolution as they developed within an historical context that embraced the late Victorian period and the early decades of the twentieth century. During this period a new range of interpretations of Darwin's theory was conceived.

As already noted, from 1897 to 1899, Frost absorbed some important elements of creative evolution through his Harvard studies. His reading in William James and in Alfred Weber's *History of Philosophy* made him aware that no monistic system based upon matter was ever absolute, that "even the most decided monists advance a relative dualism." The relative dualism in Darwin was most evident in his use of metaphorical language to describe the evolutionary process and in his strong case for "sexual selection" in *The Descent of Man*, wherein he conceded that human will, reason, and creativity were factors in the evolutionary process. Moreover, toward the conclusion of his *Autobiography*, Darwin stated that he found it hard to believe that the order and beauty he perceived in the universe were the result of pure chance. This was a large concession to the argument for design and theism, and it ran contrary to the earlier main thrust of his theory.

Thus there were enough ambiguities and paradoxes in Darwin's early theory to create serious problems of interpretation for both his critics and his defenders. Indeed, in the history of ideas there are perhaps no ironical contradictions to compare with those that involved the commentators on Darwin's theory of evolution. A strong case can be made that those who argued in favor of creative evolution and who were regarded as Darwin's most severe critics were actually far closer to his theory than those who defended him, such as Huxley, who assumed a wholly mechanistic process of evolution based wholly upon materialistic monism. No writer exemplifies this apparent contradiction more completely than Samuel Butler (1835–1902). Although Frost mentioned Butler during discussions of evolution with me at Bread Loaf, he did not identify which of that writer's works he had read. But the large number of similar and identical beliefs Frost came to hold in common with him regarding evolution is highly significant for any estimate of the poet's understanding of Darwin's theory.

Frost's only recorded notice of Butler was in an important retrospective passage in a letter to Louis Untermeyer (November 25, 1936), in which he noted that against the rival metaphor of the state as head of a peaceful and ideal family, as propounded by Karl Marx, Butler's own view of evolution retained Darwin's basic metaphor of conflict and survival:

> Isn't it a poetical strangeness that while the world was going full blast on the Darwinian metaphors of evolution, survival values, and the Devil take the hindmost, a polemical Jew in exile was working up the metaphor of the state's being like a family to displace them from mind and give us a new figure to live by? Marx had the strength not to be overawed by the metaphor in vogue. Life is like battle. But so is it like shelter. The model is the family at its best. At the height of the Darwinian metaphor, writers like Shaw and Butler were found to go to the length of saying even the family within was strife, and perhaps the worst strife of all. We are all toadies to the fashionable metaphor of the hour. Great is he who imposes the metaphor. From each according to his ability to each according to his needs. Except ye become as little children under a good father and mother.[47]

Undoubtedly, Frost had read Butler's *The Way of All Flesh* (1903), his autobiographical novel on the terrible conflicts between Ernest Pontifex (Butler) and Theobald and Christina Pontifex (his parents). Moreover, Frost was certainly aware of what Darwin himself called "The Darwin-Butler Controversy," which raged through Victorian society before and during the years that Frost was most concerned with the great evolutionist's thought.[48]

Following Lawrance Thompson, it has become a commonplace among scholars and literary critics of Frost that William James and Henri Bergson had a profound influence upon his thinking regarding evolution.[49] But the far more important similarities and identical beliefs that the poet held in common with Mivart and Butler, especially as revealed in the latter's criticism of Darwin and Huxley, have been entirely ignored. Even before comparing Butler and Frost, however, it is worth noting how close Butler was to both James and Bergson in philosophical beliefs. Cyril E. M. Joad, Butler's biographer, has noted the dualistic assumptions common to all three writers, and their intellectual affinities: "There is no evidence that he [Butler] had read William James . . . but there is plenty of evidence to show that, had he read him, he would have found in him a philosopher after his own heart. . . . The conclusions of Butler and James were in many ways identical."[50] Moreover, Joad noted, "Butler is anticipating Bergson. There is, indeed, so strong a likeness between the thought of the two men that Butler may well have been one of the undetected sources of Bergson's philosophy."[51] Indeed, Bergson's *Matter and Memory* (1896) is so close in its dualistic assumptions, argument, and spirit to Butler's *Unconscious Memory* (1880) and to sections of *Luck or Cunning* (1887) that a plausible case could be made that Bergson may have plagiarized portions of Butler's two works.

Butler's original relationship with Darwin began as that of an enthusiastic disciple. He had personal connections with the evolutionist through family ties: his grandfather was headmaster of the Shrewsbury School, which Darwin had attended, and Butler's father and Darwin were contemporaries at Cambridge University. Like Darwin, he abandoned his Anglican faith and became a "freethinker." He escaped to New Zealand, and while there during 1859–64 he read Darwin's *Origin of Species*. A friend, E. R. Chudleigh, pronounced Butler "an ultra-Darwinian." He published "Darwin on the Origin of Species: A Dialogue" (1862), in which he reconciled Darwin's theory and Christianity. A character speaks lines that Frost himself could have written: "I believe in Christianity, and I believe in Darwin. The two appear irreconcilable. . . . Both being undoubtedly true, the one must be reconcilable with the other, and . . . the impossibility of reconciling them must be only apparent and temporary, not real." Butler sent a copy of his article to Darwin, who commended it as "remarkable for its spirit and from giving so clear and accurate a view of [my] theory."[52] After Butler returned to England in 1864, he visited Darwin twice at his home in Down and became a lifelong friend of his son Francis.

After Butler had read Mivart's *Genesis of Spirit,* he perceived clearly the determinism and materialism in Darwin's theory that led him to evolve into the evolutionist's most savage and troublesome critic. Because of a serious misunderstanding entertained by Butler over the publication of a biography of Erasmus Darwin in 1879, prefaced by an article in a German journal, *Kosmos,* to which Darwin had contributed, Butler became convinced that Darwin had plagiarized a portion of his *Evolution Old and New* (1879) and had secretly attacked him. Darwin's refusal to prove his innocence merely intensified Butler's antagonism; and for the next twenty-three years he poured forth a steady stream of criticism against the evolutionist. In four editions of *Evolution Old and New,* in *Unconscious Memory* (1880), which was an extension of the thesis advanced in *Life and Habit* (1871), and in *Luck or Cunning* (1887), Butler contrasted creative evolution with the weaknesses he perceived in the determinism and materialism that characterized the thought of those who defended Darwin's theory. Unfortunately, Butler seldom made any distinction between Darwin and his defenders. His culminating criticism, "The Deadlock in Darwinism," consisted of three essays in *Universal Review* (April–June 1890), republished in *Essays on Life, Art and Science* (1904). In his posthumous *Notebooks,* Butler attacked the abuse of science that transmuted it into scientific positivism.

At the core of Butler's arguments in favor of creative evolution was his philosophical dualism, which combined mind or spirit and matter as the basis of reality. In *Evolution Old and New* he approved of Mivart's statement that "The material universe is always and everywhere sustained and directed, by an infinite cause, for which to us the word mind is the least inadequate and misleading symbol."[53] This stance caused Huxley to write to Darwin (February 4, 1880): "I am astounded at Butler . . . has Mivart bitten him and given him Darwinphobia?"[54] In the introduction to *Luck or Cunning,* Butler charged that Darwin's defenders were "pitchforking mind out of the universe."[55] Similarly, he asserted that Huxley was "trying to expel consciousness and sentience from any causative action in the working of the universe."[56] Among "men like Huxley," he noted, "was a craving after a monistic conception of the universe."[57]

Like Asa Gray, Butler believed that there could be no compromise between a dualism of matter and mind or spirit and any form of monism. Regarding "body and mind," he wrote, "they are two, not one; if, then we are to have our monistic conception . . . one of these must yield to the other; which, therefore, is it to be?"[58] According to his assessment, Darwin's theory, as presented by Huxley and his colleagues, was "an essentially mechanical, mindless conception of the universe," in which "animals are automata," and human nature differs only in degree from other forms of animal life.[59] But, as a philosophical dualist, Butler argued regarding "mind and matter," or "body and soul," that "the two become a body en-souled and a soul embodied."[60] Like Frost, he believed that there was a quali-tative difference between man and other animals, so that their common dualism resulted in a conception of evolution that was creative rather than merely mechanical.

At the time of Darwin's death, Butler admitted that he had been from the beginning a very reluctant critic and that he had found it hard to sepa-rate the evolutionist from Huxley and such camp followers as Grant Al-len, Ray Lankester, and George Romanes, all of whom attacked him, while Darwin himself never answered his criticism. His sharpest criticism was directed against Huxley, who, he noted, had made himself the official pub-lic spokesman for the great evolutionist: "Professor Huxley is the man of all others who foisted Mr. Darwin upon us."[61] Even while in New Zealand, after first reading *The Origin of Species*, Butler had stated that "mind is the controller of evolutionary direction," so that when Huxley's essay "Physical Basis of Mind" appeared, he replied: "There is no life but protoplasm, and Huxley is its prophet."[62] Again, in the *Fortnightly Review* (November 1874), he condemned that polemicist for preaching "mindless designless luck as the main means of organic modification" and charged that his view of evo-lution rid the world of "thought and feeling."[63] He extended his criticism of Huxley in his essay "Mental Evolution," which appeared in the *Athenaeum* (January–June 1884).

Butler correctly sensed that Darwin's theory was based far less on a materialistic monist assumption than it appeared to be in Huxley's exposi-tion of it. Although during his voyage on the *Beagle*, the future evolution-ist had lost his faith in revealed religion, he still retained respect for the theistic beliefs of others; and he denied that his theory violated anyone's religious faith. Butler noted that, shortly before Darwin died, he had rein-troduced design into nature in a circumspect manner, although he had opposed it for many years; and he further observed that this implied the teleological belief that nature had a final purpose. In his *Autobiography*, Darwin confirmed this surmise of Butler's by identifying himself as a the-ist. No such spiritual element was to be found in Huxley's views on nature or on evolution.

It is significant that Francis Darwin remained sympathetic toward But-ler and sought to reconcile his views on evolution with those of his father. There were good grounds for such a reconciliation. Peter J. Bowler, a mod-ern scholar on Darwin's theory, has observed, "But it is by no means clear that Butler's position was as fundamentally anti-Darwinian as he thought. He still accepted that the organisms' efforts to adapt to changes in their environment comprise the driving force of evolution." This meant that Butler was "much closer to the spirit of Darwinism" than he supposed, since he admitted that not only the mind or spirit of man but also external forces could drive the evolutionary process.[64] In short, despite his harshness, Butler's criticism of Darwin's theory merely qualified it, but did not destroy it. Such an interpretation of the controversy between the great evolutionist and his principal belletristic critic requires a thorough revision of the conventional Victorian views of Darwin's theory as well as Frost's position regarding evolution. There was an element of Lamarck's theory of evolution in Darwin's thought, which Mivart and Butler expanded in their criticism of his theory.

As both Mivart and Butler complained, Darwin was far too sensitive regarding personal criticism of his theory. Moreover, he was so eager to secure "converts" to his conception of evolution and so willing to have Huxley and his colleagues defend him that he ignored or was unaware of how far those epigoni differed in thought from his basic principles or how much the views of his severe critics coincided with his own. His personal dislike of Mivart; his avoidance of all public controversy, including a possible battle with Butler; his almost total dependence upon Huxley for advice and support; and his own serious weakness in philosophy combined to give him an initial strong advantage in having his theory accepted almost as an unquestionable dogma. His enthusiastic backing of Huxley reinforced the enthusiastic devotion that polemicist accorded to him.

Led by Huxley, the numerous and stentorian camp of Darwinians dominated the chief sources of public opinion regarding science. They first marginalized critics of the evolutionist; they then systematically demolished the public reputation of writers such as Mivart and Butler. Huxley took great pains to ruin the former's career as a scientist; the latter was dismissed as a radical iconoclast who was emotionally unstable and unqualified to pass judgment on scientific theory. Frost was well aware of this campaign of vilification. In his notebooks, he wrote: "Don't forget how the Christian world hated Darwin for threatening their belief and how the Darwinians hated Lamarck to the point of destroying him by discrediting him for threatening their belief."[65]

But towards the end of the nineteenth century, as the weaknesses in Darwin's theory became increasingly apparent, and as Huxley's materialistic monism came to be seriously questioned, the Lamarckian arguments advanced by Mivart and Butler in favor of creative evolution took on a new life. Design, mind, and purpose were once more evident in the universe. As George Bernard Shaw wrote in 1921: "We are turning in weary disgust and disillusion from Neo-Darwinism and mechanism to vitalism and creative evolution."[66] He praised Butler lavishly in *Back to Methuselah* (1921); moreover, in his private correspondence, he hailed him as "the most profound philosophical literary genius of the last half of the nineteenth century."[67] The recipient of all this adulation insisted that the mind of man was an important factor in scientific studies of matter, a contention that gradually became a basic element in modern theories of physics.

Shaw noted that in the period that followed the First World War, the Victorian tables were reversed: that "now . . . Butler's eminence is unchallenged," and "the bankruptcy of Darwinism" was evident.[68] According to Shaw, "ever since the reaction against Darwin set in at the beginning of the present century, all scientific opinion worth counting has been converging rapidly upon *Creative Evolution*."[69] Moreover, he contended that "creative evolution is already a religion, and is indeed now unmistakably the religion of the twentieth century. . . . It is . . . a religion that has its intellectual roots in philosophy and science just as medieval Christianity had its intellectual roots in Aristotle."[70]

Frost was keenly aware that the great battle was between adherents of Darwin's theory as set forth by T. H. Huxley and his camp followers and those writers and scientists within the Christian and humanistic tradition who were defending creative evolution as an important variant of Darwin's theory. By 1920 Frost had clearly allied himself with the latter group and was becoming a severe critic of the Huxley tradition regarding evolution. The poet had read Butler, and he knew Shaw's arguments in favor of creative evolution. He had read that writer's *Arms and the Man* while in Plymouth, New Hampshire, in 1912; he had seen Shaw's *Fanny's First Play* in London in the same year; and he heard Shaw lecture in London in 1913. In his letter to Louis Untermeyer (November 25, 1936), he had linked Shaw with Butler as two writers who still accepted the basic Darwinian principle that conflict was at the heart of evolutionary changes in species. But he also noted a basic flaw in Shaw's socialist politics in applying Darwin's principle regarding evolutionary conflicts: "Shaw thinks better knowledge as between nations will bring them together in peace and yet he thinks families from knowing too much of themselves are nests of hate and must be broken up."[71]

Frost's acceptance of creative evolution included Darwin's basic principle that conflict between and within species is always present. In his notebooks he compared Darwin and Marx and rejected Marx's belief that "our rivalries could be ameliorated or done away with." [72] He stated this in a couplet: "And Marx has found a way for us to cease / From doing one another harm in peace." He then discussed at length the conflict for survival between the American Indians and their European rivals. He cited the bravery, nobility, and respectable culture of the Indians, and concluded: "You have to be secretly sorry for their fate because you are a good Darwinian." To Frost, victory in war meant "responsibility for the future." Throughout his life he sympathized with the Indians, yet as a Darwinian he accepted the historical fact of the triumph of European culture in the Western Hemisphere. This too was a part of creative evolution.

Lesley Francis was perfectly accurate regarding Frost's very enthusiastic response to Henri Bergson's *Creative Evolution* (1911). She noted that her grandfather approved of that philosopher because his "dualistic approach to science and religion appealed to him."[73] This meant that, in accepting creative evolution, Frost did not reject Darwin's theory, but only modified and supplemented it by including Bergson's *élan vital*, which provided what was most lacking in Darwin.[74] Frost was aware that Bergson's criticism was directed mainly against the sterile, rigid, mechanistic, and deterministic conception of the material universe as perceived and popularized by Herbert Spencer and Thomas Henry Huxley. Like Mivart, Butler, and William James before him, but unlike Frost, Bergson's neo-Platonic idealism did not distinguish sharply between Darwin's qualified materialism and the materialistic monism of his defenders. His book was not for Frost an original pioneering study, as Thompson and many other scholars have so often assumed. Rather, it was the culmination of all that the poet had learned about evolution from his experience at Harvard, from his reading of James, and from his extensive knowledge of the public controversies over Darwin during the final decades of the Victorian era.

Lesley Francis was right to stress Frost's dualism in discussing both science and religion. Because of his dualism, Frost perceived Darwin's theory as an epical metaphor, combining matter and spirit. Therefore, the evolutionist's materialism did not trouble him, since matter was a vital part of his own philosophy. "Materialism," he wrote, "is not the attempt to say all in terms of matter. The only materialist—be he poet, teacher, scientist, politician, or statesman—is the man who gets lost in his material without a gathering metaphor to throw it into shape and order. He is the lost soul."[75] Yet in setting the neo-Darwinian conception of evolution which was centered in matter alone, against creative evolution which was centered in mind or spirit, Frost recognized that there was a danger of falling into a monism of mind or of spirit. He satirized such a monism in his poem "Etherealizing." Unlike the writers in the tradition of creative evolution, Frost distinguished sharply between Darwin and his principal defenders, such "lost souls" as Spencer and Huxley. His dualism and metaphorical method of reasoning enabled him to retain both matter and spirit or mind as contraries to be reconciled. To Frost creative evolution was much more than simply a matter of adding mind to matter in the discussion of Darwin's theory.

To the poet, evolution as a concept is not merely a fabricated construct of man's theoretical reason working upon empirical observation. That was the facile method that abused science into scientism and that dogmatized evolution into a systematic and absolute philosophy. Frost was aware that the abuse of the metaphor of evolution could lead men into monomania, the excessive fondness for explaining all aspects of life through a single analogy. Herbert Spencer was most guilty of that error. In strong contrast to such a method, Frost's view that evolution was an open-ended process, like artistic creativity, meant that it involved all of the generative powers and the sensual imagination of man, which he called "passionate preference."

Frost held that the self-conscious creative powers in man combine emotion, reason, intuition, the senses, imagination, conscious and unconscious memory, free will, and courage—all of which he summarized in the term *mens animi*. This comprehensive power raised man qualitatively above all other forms of animal life. Moreover, as he conceived it, *mens animi* was as much a "thought-felt thing" as applied to evolution as it was to the creation of a poem. It transcends Butler's belief that "mind is the troller of evolutionary direction"[76] and includes more than Bergson's *élan vital* and Pascal's reason of the heart.[77] To Frost, creative evolution ultimately involves the active and productive achievements of individuals and the human species that give shape and direction to culture and enduring civilization.

During the period of World War I, Frost's acceptance of creative evolution as an improved variant of Darwin's theory is evident in several of his statements written to Louis Untermeyer. On May 24, 1916, he wrote: "Evolution is like walking on a rolling barrel. The walker isn't so much interested in where the barrel is going as he is in keeping on top of it."[78] On January 1, 1917, the poet commented to Untermeyer on the practical value of Bergson and of J. Henri Fabre for his method of combating the formulated arguments and claims of the defenders of mechanistic evolution. After noting that he was "fond of seeing our theories knocked into cocked hats," he wrote: "What I like about Bergson and Fabre is that they have bothered our evolutionism so much with the cases of instinct they have brought up." He then added: "You get more credit for thinking if you re-state formulae or cite cases that fall easily under formulae, but all the fun is outside saying things that suggest formulae that won't formulate—that almost but don't quite formulate."[79]

Early in 1919, when Untermeyer boasted that his socialism, and therefore by implication his socialist friends, were of a higher order than the free enterprise economic system that Frost defended, the poet turned his friend's claim into delicious humor in an evolutionary joke: "When I think of all the human pains that went to uplifting *Pithecanthropus Erectus* into the Piltdown man and the Piltdown man into the Neanderthal and the Neanderthal into the Heidelberg and him into the likes of me and Woodrow Wilson . . . why by osteopathetic manipulation . . . couldn't you for instance effect the next great change of me into Max Eastman or Jack Reed."[80] Frost liked to say that he was never more serious than when he was joking, so that in deliberately violating the geological chronology of prehistoric man, in placing the Piltdown man ahead of the Neanderthal, he made his mock-serious bantering tone doubly effective in his deprecatory retort to Untermeyer. An added touch of humor lies in his rather low opinion of Woodrow Wilson's politics. His witty *reductio ad absurdum* joke is based upon his serious belief that the process of creative evolution gives man the power and right to hold fast to a given position. This was Frost's conviction in 1919; and in an interview on September 29, 1959, he reiterated this belief.[81]

Frost's response to an important article by Theodore Baird, a colleague at Amherst College, provides good evidence that he continued to think well of Darwin long after he had accepted creative evolution. Baird sent a copy of his article "Darwin and the Tangled Bank"[82] to Frost, who was pleased to have confirmed his long-held belief that the evolutionist's theory was in essence a great contribution to Western man's metaphorical inheritance and that his view was also held by Darwin himself:

> I find it hard to decide which to put your essay into (*The Voyage of the Beagle* or *Origin of Species*). . . . We are considering one of the three best prose books of the nineteenth century. . . . I am away over on the side of Darwin as you depict him. My accusation that he was only adding to our metaphorical heritage falls to the ground when you make me realize that he said so first himself. My accusation becomes a citation for bravery. You make him even more what I like to think he was.

The poet then concluded his letter by distinguishing Darwin's theory from that of the literal-minded "lost souls" with no sense of metaphor, whose defense of Darwin separated science from the humanities in order to make evolution into a self-contained, absolute, closed system of materialistic monism:

> Those straight-laced humanists had better be careful about whom they read out of the party. I got a dose of them in Cincinnati last week—bush leaguers. It takes too long to dawn on them that science is merely one of the humanities.[83]

Frost's very favorable view of Darwin rested upon his belief that, in presenting his theory, unlike many of the defenders of his views, he did not exceed the empirical evidence he had acquired by stretching his metaphor of evolution beyond the breaking point. Alfred North Whitehead held exactly the same view: "Darwin's own writings are for all time a model of refusal to go beyond the direct evidence, and of careful retention of every possible hypothesis." Whitehead then added the same important distinction with which Frost had ended his letter to Baird: "But those virtues were not so conspicuous in his followers, and still less in his camp-followers."[84] During the last four decades of his life, much that Frost had to say about evolution, Darwinian and non-Darwinian alike, turned upon his belief "that science is merely one of the humanities."

But the theory of evolution that engaged Frost from around 1920 to his death in 1963 was radically different from the one that had concerned him up to the period of World War I. At the end of the nineteenth century, the prophecies of Butler, Shaw, and other writers that Darwin's theory would soon be extinct proved to be wholly wrong. Ironically, at exactly the time that it was being relegated to the dustbin of history, a revival of his theory began. That rejuvenation eventually rehabilitated Darwin's theory in a highly strengthened form.

One of the greatest weaknesses in Darwin's case for natural selection was his ignorance of genetics. He had tried to explain genetic phenomena through what he called "pangenesis," but his argument had been ably refuted by Francis Galton. Although the laws of genetics had been discovered by the Austrian botanist and monk Gregor Mendel (1822–84), his experiments were published by the obscure provincial Society for the Study of Natural Science in 1866, so that neither Darwin nor the scientific community of Europe in general knew anything of his work. But in 1900, Hugo De Vries (1848–1935), a Dutch botanist, discovered Mendel's work, and his publication of *The Mutation Theory* (1900–03) began to revitalize Darwin's theory through valid principles of genetics and heredity.[85] His studies and those of other scientists revolutionized biological theory as much as the quantum theory later revolutionized physics. It provided a new basis for Darwin's principle of natural selection that explained changes in species through heredity rather than merely through the interaction of the organism and the physical environment. The culmination of this development is effectively described by Ronald Fisher in *The Genetic Theory of Natural Selection* (1930).

The revival of Darwin's theory was also reinforced by new discoveries in the geological records of extinct species and by the synthesis of genetics and biological studies with botany, chemistry, and the physical sciences. As Julian Huxley showed in *Evolution: The Modern Synthesis* (1942), these developments took about forty years. Frost was well aware of this congeries of scientific advances; they shaped his views on Darwinian and non-Darwinian evolution for the last forty years of his life, ideas formulated with particular attention to what he called "three generations of Huxleys." From around 1920 to 1963, in poetry and prose, Frost's philosophical dualism, his faith in metaphorical thinking, and his acceptance of creative evolution as a vital variant of Darwin's theory provided the essential basis for both his affirmative statements on evolution and his critical views on social Darwinism and the scientific positivism of those three generations of Huxleys.

## 4

# *Frost and the*
# *Three Generations of Huxleys*

In July 1941, during a conversation with Frost in his cabin on the Homer Noble Farm near Bread Loaf, Vermont, I raised the question of the role, extent, and abuse of science and technology in human affairs during the twentieth century. Frost responded that this enormously complex and important subject deserved a separate talk session, and he invited me to return early in August for some "good talk" about the dominance of the physical sciences in modern life and culture. He suggested that I could prepare myself for our talk by reading an anthology by Henrietta Huxley, the widow of Thomas Henry Huxley (1825–95), *Aphorisms and Reflections from the Works of T. H. Huxley* (1907); and Leonard Huxley's two-volume edition of his father's biography, *Life and Letters of Thomas Henry Huxley* (1913). The full import of the poet's suggestion, and much that he said in our talk that followed, was gradually revealed to me during the remaining years of Frost's life, during poetry readings and in events in which the poet participated.

On July 28, 1955, after a poetry reading at Bread Loaf, Frost commented upon abuses of Darwin's theory of evolution in answer to the question: "What about Sir James Frazer and *The Golden Bough?*"

> Those are minor people. They're down in the bush leagues. That kind of stuff all comes under the Darwinian thing. And one of them wrote a book on the evolution of God—where it started from. . . . Another on the idea of the evolution of love.[1]

Three years later, on June 30, 1958, from the same podium, Frost returned to his theme on the abuses of evolution as a theory:

> I was thinking the other day how sick I was of the word evolu-
> tion. I have to report that it's subsiding somewhat—you don't
> hear it as much as you used to. I never was satisfied with the evo-
> lution talk in all the years by the Huxleys—the three generations
> of Huxleys: I never was satisfied that there wasn't a terrible gap
> still between animal life and human . . . Still unsatisfied.[2]

In his talk in August 1941, Frost referred to "the three generations of
Huxleys," and he made it very clear that he did not limit that pithy phrase
to Thomas Henry Huxley, his wife Henrietta and his son Leonard, and his
grandsons Julian and Aldous Huxley. Although Frost regarded Thomas
Henry Huxley as the fountainhead of the whole Huxley tradition in the
modern world, "the three generations of Huxleys" was best understood not
literally but metaphorically.[3] In his Bread Loaf talk in June 1958 he referred
to "a whole string of these people like Huxley." The "evolutionary talk"
that never satisfied Frost, both from scientists and from the less informed
laity, extended over several generations of Victorian and twentieth-century
adherents to the views expressed by Thomas Henry Huxley on evolution,
science, philosophy, education, religion, the arts and humanities, and human nature itself—in short, to the entire modern culture of Western civilization.

Among persons that Frost included in his epical gathering metaphor
were such lifelong friends of T. H. Huxley as John Tyndall and Herbert
Spencer, H. G. Wells, Huxley's student and disciple, was the most representative figure among the second generation of Huxleys; he later collaborated
with Julian Huxley in several scientific projects. The three generations encompassed both scientists and laymen, those who Frost said engaged in
"the facile spieling in our day" about evolution, or who abused appeals
to science as a golden calf to be worshiped. Believers in "progress," such
as Frost encountered during the 1920s at the University of Michigan, and
ignorant champions and critics of evolution, such as Clarence Darrow and
William Jennings Bryan during the "monkey trial" in Dayton, Tennessee,
were among those he criticized most severely. Frost believed that the separation of science from the humanities divided Western civilization into the
"two cultures" described by C. P. Snow in *The Two Cultures and the Scientific Revolution* (1959). According to Frost, the tragic separation of the two
cultures was greatly facilitated by the three generations of Huxleys, beginning with T. H. Huxley. His critical involvement with the Huxley tradition
reached its culmination in 1959, in his confrontation with Julian Huxley in
"The Future of Man" symposium.[4]

In August 1941, Frost first observed that Henrietta Huxley's anthology—the distilled essence of T. H. Huxley's nine volumes of essays—and Leonard Huxley's biography were both "sanitized versions" of Huxley's basic beliefs about science, religion, education, and philosophy. Both collections almost totally omitted Huxley's many vitriolic attacks upon institutional religion, particularly Judaism and Christianity, which had caused such bitter controversies with his Victorian contemporaries. Both collections also toned down his denigration of the inherited system of education in Britain and throughout Europe, centered in the ancient Greek and Latin classics and the trivium and quadrivium in the humanities. Frost noted that Henrietta Huxley's anthology concluded with her incredibly crude original poem, "An Agnostic Hymn," which he called "nausiating." When asked was it the atrocious verse or the agnostic theme that so repelled him, he replied: "Both, but particularly the agnosticism."

Both works featured what a few years later Julian Huxley called his grandfather's "almost fanatical devotion to scientific truth and its pursuit."[5] Frost's remarks concentrated upon T. H. Huxley's total devotion to science, its methods and objectives, and what it signified to the modern world. He referred to a passage in Leonard Huxley's *Life and Letters of Thomas Henry Huxley* that underscored how much his father perceived that the Victorian era was permeated by the belief in the methods and spirit of science:

> The leading characteristic of the nineteenth century has been the rapid growth of the scientific methods of investigation to all the problems with which the human mind is concerned, and the correlative rejection of traditional beliefs which have proved their incompetence to bear such investigation. . . . The activity of the scientific spirit has been manifested in every region of speculation and of practice.[6]

Frost commented that throughout his adult life Huxley was among the foremost Victorians to extend constantly the assumptions, methods, and objectives of the physical sciences to every branch of human learning, including education, religion, the creative arts, and the humanities and society.

Frost argued that it was important to note that Huxley was not content simply to advance the cause of science, which in itself was praiseworthy. There was a destructive side in Huxley's case for science, in his belief that when the activities of science were applied to non-scientific subjects and these areas of human concern "proved their incompetence to bear such investigation," these traditional beliefs should be rejected. Implicit in this assumption was Huxley's belief that science was the only valid source for verifiable knowledge and truth—in short, that science was all in all. That belief was itself based upon Huxley's philosophical monism centered wholly in matter. What Julian Huxley praised as an "almost fanatical devotion to scientific truth and its pursuit," Frost condemned as "monomania or mono-metaphor," which he defined as an "excessive fondness for explaining all aspects of life through a single analogy."[7] Frost's philosophical dualism, centered in both spirit and matter and in the dynamic and complex interaction or "play" of both realms upon each other, was clearly a world removed from T. H. Huxley's science based upon matter.

Frost believed that the physical sciences were important and that they had a vital role in giving shape to modern life, but he insisted that they were best regarded as part of the humanities. He referred to the humanities as "the great book of the worthies" regarding human nature and the vast range of human concerns from the ancient world to modern times.[8] The humanities were a far more valid source for understanding human nature than were the physical sciences. Huxley's notion that science, abstracted from all other disciplines, should sit in judgment of the humanities and of education, religion, and the creative arts, was to Frost a highly dangerous illusion, fraught with consequences catastrophic to the culture of civilization. It presupposed that a civilized order could be built through science upon a monism of matter alone. In contrast to Huxley's view, Frost believed that science could provide a valid descriptive account of physical phenomena, and it could harness such knowledge into practical uses through technology, but it could not create sound normative principles in ethics, aesthetics, and the personal and social values of human nature. Such cultural concerns involved the mind and spirit of mankind and could not be adequately satisfied through a mastery over physical nature by science.

Frost was convinced that the real differences between Darwin and Huxley were not over the mechanism by which evolutionary changes in species occurred, such as natural selection. Huxley did indeed reject natural selection because it was not yet proved, as so many scholars have noted. But his positive response to evolution as a metaphor was that it provided him with an ideal instrumental means to expand the domain of the physical sciences. Frost noted that several years before Darwin's *Origin of Species* appeared in November 1859, even before Huxley assumed the role of being Darwin's "general agent," he was eager to extend the methods and aims of science to every branch of human learning. Evolution was merely helpful in pursuit of his ambition to make science supreme everywhere. As Leonard Huxley recorded: "Huxley warned Darwin, 'I will stop at no point so long as clear reasoning will carry me further.'"[9] In carrying analytical and logical reason through science as far as it would go, Huxley contended that "the man of science is the sworn interpreter of nature in the high court of reason."[10] This meant that he considered the methods of science not only universally valid, and practically infallible, but worthy of the highest esteem. He advised: "Cherish her, venerate her, follow her methods faithfully and implicitly in their application to all branches of human thought."[11] To Frost, Huxley's conception of science converted it into an object of idolatry, a golden calf or god to be worshipped, before which all other objects of belief were regarded as false gods.

Although agnosticism was the great cardinal principle in Huxley's intellectual armory, he recognized that his claims for the godlike sovereignty of science, his conviction that human reason "constitutes the sole trustworthy foundation" for "absolute validity" in arriving at universal truth through science, was finally based upon an act of faith:

> The one act of faith in the convert to science, is the confession of the universality of order and of the absolute validity in all times and under all circumstances, of the law of causation. This confession is an act of faith, because, by the nature of the case, the truth of such propositions is not blind, but reasonable, because it is invariably confirmed by experience, and constitutes the sole trustworthy foundation for all action.[12]

In short, science was to Huxley a religion, a self-contained, autonomous system, wholly based upon matter, which he believed should provide the basis for a new culture for modern civilization. That culture, together with a new political world order, assumed what Aldous Huxley identified as a unified monistic system: "For science in its totality, the ultimate goal is the creation of a monistic system in which the world's enormous multiplicity is reduced to something like unity."[13] Frost's strong opposition to Huxley's views on science as a religion can best be understood in terms of his philosophical dualism of spirit and matter, in which the religious, educational, artistic, political, and social multiplicity in the world is preserved. The whole direction of Huxley's future comments on evolution as the chief vehicle for scientific progress was initiated and greatly accelerated on December 26, 1859, in his review of Darwin's *Origin of Species* in the *Times* of London.[14] He prophesied that the theory of evolution would extend itself into "the domain of sciences over regions of thought into which she has, as yet, hardly penetrated." To his friend Joseph Hooker he admitted that "as a scientific review the thing is worth nothing."[15] What mattered was that science itself would evolve and triumph: it would absorb "psychology, politics . . . political economy . . . civil history . . . and sociology" into "the province of biology," because mankind would recognize that "the physical organization and structure of man is entirely biological."[16] This extension of biological science into all regions of thought was precisely what Frost later called "scientism," which he regarded as not valid science but the abuse of science.

According to Frost, the abuse of science was clearly evident in the Victorian belief in "progress" as a law of history. The first stage of "progress" was a mastery by mankind of physical nature through science, inventions, and technology. The later stages would involve the scientific control of man in civil society and the whole direction of human history. By eliminating all of the ills that flesh is heir to, the final temporal destiny of man's future was conceived as a worldwide social order of universal peace and prosperity. This was Huxley's visionary conception of the historical role and development of evolutionary science, and over sixty years later Frost encountered it in full flower in Julian Huxley, in the symposium on "The Future of Man."

T. H. Huxley believed that science, in its role as a revolutionary movement, was originally rooted in the religious and cultural conflicts of the sixteenth century, if not earlier rebellions against the long-established traditional authority in church and state, and that science in modern times, during and beyond the Victorian era, pointed toward a glorious future world order:

> We are in the midst of a gigantic movement greater than that which preceded and produced the Reformation, and really only the continuation of that movement. But there is nothing new in the ideas which lie at the bottom of the movement, nor is any reconciliation possible between free thought and traditional authority. One or other will have to succumb after a struggle of unknown duration, which will have as side issues vast political and social troubles. I have no doubt that free thought will win in the long run. . . . or that this free thought will organize itself into a coherent system, embracing human life and the world as one harmonious whole. But this organization will be the work of generations of men, and those who foster it most will be those who teach men to rest in no lie, and to rest in no verbal delusions. [17]

Frost took his historical cue from an even longer period of time than Huxley and came to a diametrically opposite conclusion regarding "progress" in human affairs:

> All ages of the world are bad—a great deal worse anyway than heaven. . . . One can safely say after some six to thirty thousand years of experience that the evident design is a situation here in which it will always be about equally hard to save your soul. Whatever progress may be taken to mean, it can't mean making the world an easier place in which to save your soul . . . your decency, your integrity.[18]

However understood, "progress" did nothing to improve the moral nature of man; the power it created was limited to matter, to physical phenomena, and could be used as easily to destroy as to improve society. That was why Frost believed that one age is like another for the soul and that there was no evidence science was moving society toward a harmonious and unified utopian world.

Huxley's assumption that "the modern knows that the only source of real knowledge lies in the application of scientific methods of enquiry to the ascertainment of the facts of existence,"[19] which included the whole realm of spirit as well as matter, frequently called forth Frost's wrath. He considered Huxley's premises based upon a monistic illusion; his methods were sheer arrogance, and his objectives were a menace to the very survival of the humanities, religion, and the creative arts. He denied that science had any right to dominate the realm of man's spirit. Reginald L. Cook has well summarized Frost's objections to the beliefs of the three generations of Huxleys: "What he resents is the intrusion of science into things that aren't science."[20] During the first half century after Huxley's death in 1895, Frost was increasingly aware that the scientific and materialistic philosophy of Huxley came more and more to dominate the whole culture of Western civilization. In an interview with Inez Robb (December 14, 1949), Frost stated that "he would hate a brave new world" such as that proposed by the Huxley tradition, and he criticized one of its current American disciples: "A scientist like Vannevar Bush must be full of a feeling of progress, but a man who feels deeply about humanity must feel we are back in ancient Egypt."[21] In his talks with me at Bread Loaf, Frost contended that Huxley's delusion was that he believed that the measurable and quantitative dimensions of matter as phenomena, with which science was legitimately concerned, could be extended to the immeasurable and qualitative elements in things of the spirit, such as religion, education, and the arts and humanities. It was very disturbing to Frost that Huxley's program was being accepted by so many of his countrymen. Shortly before the poet's death, his friend Louis Untermeyer summarized Frost's many decades of frustration: "He is still disillusioned about Progress; distrustful of Science, which has taken man deeper and deeper into matter, further into space, and further away from the spirit. . . . He is still against One World, World Federation, Universal Brotherhood, unity, conformity, the breaking down of barriers in the interest of Oneness; he is unalterably against One Anything."[22] It is significant that without identifying Frost's dualism, Untermeyer recognized the poet's intense opposition to the monism of matter that characterized the philosophy of the three generations of Huxleys.

In 1917, at age forty-four, Frost fell briefly into a happy delusion regarding "progress," but in a letter to Charles Lowell Young he immediately retracted this lapse in understanding: "Now I get my punishment for letting myself believe even for the least division of an hour that there is any such thing as progress."[23] From that date forward, for the rest of his life, the poet was most vehement in his strong condemnation of the dangerous illusion that progress existed through evolution and the methods of science applied to human affairs. In his notebooks, he wrote: "Much confusion comes from confusing progress with evolution."[24] During the late 1920s, Wade Van Dore, Frost's "handy-man," recorded in his journal: "Though he was very interested in science, he mistrusted what he called growth or progress."[25] Reginald L. Cook recalled that at his first meeting with Frost, on July 15, 1925, at Bread Loaf, "Frost immediately began to talk about the idea of progress," and that he spent several hours, with his "vigorous thrust of ideas," condemning every aspect of the concept of progress.[26] Frost told me at Bread Loaf in 1939 that the idea of Progress as understood by some historians and sociologists, of mankind moving toward a Utopian state, was pure illusion.[27] In another talk with me in 1948, the poet noted that one of the most ardent believers in progress leading to Utopia was Huxley's disciple, H. G. Wells, but that in his last book, *Mind at the End of Its Tether* (1945), Wells went from illusion to complete disillusion and predicted the extinction of humanity.

In these talks about "progress," Frost denied that evolution and the scientific method and technology altered the moral, intellectual, aesthetic, or social nature of man. The traditional deadly sins, pride, envy, avarice, lust, sloth, gluttony, and anger, which marked human depravity and spread crime through society, were as rampant in modern civilization as they had been in past ages. Only those who confused knowledge with intelligence fell into the belief in "progress," but there was no evidence that modern man in general was intellectually superior to his ancestors, nor that contemporary thinkers were intellectually greater than such giants of the past as Aristotle, Aquinas, or Kant. Mankind was not moving toward superman, and modern man was in a "terminal" state. Bad taste in art, degenerate forms of entertainment, and general ignorance were common in modern civilization. The ancient forms of political despotism still flourished in modern totalitarian systems and made domestic tyranny and international wars more destructive than ever. None of these spiritual evils in human nature and society were mitigated, much less eliminated, through scientific improvements in matter. The conditions of human life in society were altered by improvements in transportation, communication, the mass production of goods in industry, etc., and in the expansion of man's lifespan through medicine, but changes in the problems of old age and the mortal nature of man did not translate into a future Utopia.

Frost's serious witticism, which he repeated on several occasions, that "the opposite of Utopia is not hell, but civilization," was a direct rebuttal of Huxley's belief that in some distant future mankind "shall touch the Happy Isles."[28] The poet's much more savage answer to Utopian thinking, filled with an understated tone of quiet condescension and satirical contempt, is in his couplet "An Answer":

> *But Islands of the Blessèd, bless you, son,*
> *I never came upon a blessèd one.*

But the poet's negative views regarding "progress" are most significantly understood in terms of his dualism of spirit and matter, which provides the basis of his favorable response to Darwin's theory, and his strong criticism of Huxley's monism centered in matter alone.

In his *Autobiography*, Darwin acknowledged that when he wrote *The Origin of Species* although he had lost his faith in biblical revelation, his theistic belief was still strong. Years later his troubled metaphysics led him to adopt Huxley's principle of "agnosticism." But his dormant theism combined with his belief in the struggle for survival led him to a modified version of the argument regarding design: "I cannot look at the universe as the result of blind chance, yet I can see no evidence of beneficent design, or indeed of design of any kind, in the details."[29] Darwin's statement could have provided Frost with the theme of his sonnet "Design," which included a design for darkness. Regarding the idea of progress, Frost perceived a vital distinction between Darwin's stand on progress and how such defenders of his theory as Huxley regarded the concept. Although Darwin once expressed his belief that mankind "in the distant future will be a far more perfect creature than he is now,"[30] this remark was more a pious hope than a commitment to belief in progress. To his friend Joseph Hooker, he stated his far more basic belief that the physical universe contains no evidence of a principle of moral benevolence. Peter J. Bowler, an excellent scholar on evolution, has recorded the essential reason why Darwin's theory excluded the idea of progress: "Darwin's theory made it impossible to see the human race as the predestined goal of progress, since the metaphor of the evolutionary tree is incompatible with the belief that we stand at the head of a ladder of evolutionary progress."[31] Partisan politics, Bowler observed, created "the Darwinians' assumption that evolution could be used as a model for the liberal view of progress."[32] Frost utilized Darwin's metaphor of the evolutionary tree during his talk in the symposium on "The Future of Man" to reject the idea of progress.

Darwin himself has provided the best evidence why his theory did not sanction a belief in progress as a law of history. After he authorized Clemence-Auguste Royer to translate *The Origin of Species* into French (1862), he was appalled to discover in her fifty-page introduction her rhapsodic statements of faith in mankind's "progress" through evolutionary changes, leading to an eventual wholly secular Utopian society: "The doctrine of M. Darwin is the rational revelation of progress, putting itself in its logical antagonism with the irrational revelation of the Fall."[33] In her faith in science and abstract discursive logic and reason, and in her antagonism against Christianity, Royer was really a belated child of the French Enlightenment, in the tradition of Descartes, Voltaire, and the *philosophes*. Huxley's biographer, Adrian Desmond, noted: "Darwin was nonplussed to find himself the culmination of Cartesian philosophy,"[34] the very philosophy so warmly espoused by Huxley himself. David L. Hull, in "Darwinism and Historiography," has well summarized the dilemma he faced regarding Royer's thesis:

> Darwin got more than he bargained for. . . . Royer turned out to be an enthusiastic evolutionist, but, for her, evolution was progressive. Not only did she preface her translation with an anticlerical diatribe, an indulgence that Darwin carefully denied himself in his public utterances, but she also gave her translation a title that emphasized the progressive nature of evolution, a notion that Darwin questioned increasingly as the years went by.

But, even in his earliest publications, Darwin did not emphasize the progressive nature of evolution.[35]

Darwin was so disturbed by Royer's introduction and translation that he authorized a new translation by Jean-Jacques Moulinie, which appeared in 1873. What is noteworthy, however, is that Frost perceived that like Royer, in the process of explicating Darwin's theory as progress through evolution, Huxley, Herbert Spencer, H. G. Wells, and others among the modern three generations of Huxleys engaged in the same "anticlerical diatribes" as Royer. Their appeals to "progress" were an abuse of Darwin's theory, just as "scientism" was an abuse of valid science, and this distinction enabled Frost to admire Darwin while remaining highly critical of the three generations of Huxleys.

Huxley's cardinal belief that the assumptions, methods, and objectives of physical science should be applied to every subject, combined with his perception of evolution as a metaphor for improvements in species, contributed not only to the idea of "progress," but also to the development of modern sociology and to creating the misnomer "social Darwinism."[36] Athough the term "sociology" was invented by Auguste Comte, within the English-speaking world Huxley's friend and colleague Herbert Spencer (1820–1903) is credited with being the father of sociology. Belief in evolution, progress, and Spencer's sociology became so intricately intertwined that their fusion into "social Darwinism" often made it difficult to distinguish between causes and effects in these combined beliefs. But Darwin was not a social Darwinist,[37] and the concept deserved to be better understood as an important element in Spencer's sociology. Although inadvertently Huxley contributed to the ideas of both progress and of so-called social Darwinism, Spencer played a far greater role in combining evolutionary theory with sociology, politics, and the economics of "social Darwinism."[38]

"Social Darwinism" assumed that Malthus's theory of population was valid—that population increases at a geometrical ratio, while available food supplies expand at merely an arithmetical rate. It included Spencer's famous phrase "the survival of the fittest," which he coined in 1852, seven years before Darwin's *Origin of Species*. Social Darwinists interpreted the phrase in terms of an extreme version of the principle of laissez faire in Adam Smith's economic theory—that no limits should be set upon total individual and corporate freedom in the economic enterprises of capitalism. Individualism in the so-called "Protestant ethic" probably contributed to this conviction. According to this concept, competition and conflicts in society, like those among animals in a state of nature, are the normal struggle for survival, and in society market forces alone, without any interference by the state, should be allowed to determine conflicts. Social Darwinism assumed that an unbridled social structure would reflect the struggle for survival in nature, without reference to the traditional ethical norms in human social relationships. The political and legal basis of social Darwinism was supported by a liberal democratic theory that protected property rights and class interests. A philosophical monism of matter was assumed, as was the belief that partial evil resulted in universal good and a belief in the progress of mankind toward better ages to come. Such a collection of beliefs clearly worked for the advantage of those entrenched in power, at the expense of the poor and weak, and led to sanctioning inhumane conditions of labor for women, children, and independent manual laborers. Their suffering was treated with total indifference.

Huxley and Spencer were essentially of one mind in wishing to extend the sciences to all of civil society through an ethics based upon nature. Huxley asserted: "There is such a thing as a science of social life."[39] In "Science and Culture," he argued that in studying man in corporate society, "this knowledge is only to be obtained by the application of the methods of investigation adopted in physical researches to the investigation of the phenomena of society." In this pursuit, Huxley held, there is no valid distinction between the phenomena of matter in the universe and the life of mankind in civil society: "Nature . . . denotes the sum of the phenomenal world, . . . and society, like art, is therefore part of nature."[40] On this basis, Huxley, like Spencer and other adherents of "social Darwinism," obliterated any meaningful qualitative difference between the behavior of animals in the jungle of nature and actions by men in society, whose code of ethics derived from normative laws, customs, and religious and cultural beliefs. It was wholly in keeping with Huxley's monism of matter that he referred to the laws of government in society as "customs of matter."[41] In his essay "The Struggle for Existence and Its Bearing Upon Man," he argued that the law of the jungle, of nature "red in tooth and claw," applied to man in civilized institutions. In such a world, "the weakest and stupidest went to the wall; while the toughest and shrewdest . . . survived. Life was a continuous free fight . . . the Hobbesian war of each against all was the normal state of existence."[42] These beliefs are clearly in harmony with "social Darwinism."

Huxley was acutely aware that his view of life in society involved his conception of the moral nature of man, both natural and acquired. He prefaced his account of the moral nature of man by first separating ethics from evolution: "The notion that the doctrine of evolution can furnish a foundation for morals seems to me to be an illusion. . . ." He then defined his conception of man's universal natural depravity as traditionally set forth in Calvinist theology:

> The doctrines of predestination, of original sin, of the innate de-
> pravity of man and the evil fate of the greater part of the race,
> of the primacy of Satan in this world, of the essential vileness of
> matter, of a malevolent Demiurgus subordinate to a benevolent
> Almighty, who has only lately revealed himself, faulty as they are,
> appear to me to be vastly nearer the truth than the "liberal" pop-
> ular illusions that babies are all born good, and that the example
> of a corrupt society is responsible for their failure to remain so;
> that it is given to everybody to reach the ethical ideal if he will
> only try; that all partial evil is universal good, and other optimis-
> tic figments, such as that which represents "Providence" under
> the guise of a paternal philanthropist, and bids us believe that
> everything will come right (according to our notions) at last.[43]

Huxley combined his belief in the natural depravity of man (except for God's elect, whether as Calvinists or believers in science as man's redeem-er) with his full acceptance of Thomas Malthus's doctrine on population: "The so-called Malthusian doctrine . . . is a truth which, to my mind, is as plain as the general proposition that a quantity which constantly increases will, some time or other, exceed any greater quantity the amount of which is fixed."[44] In practice this belief contributed much toward justifying so-cial Darwinism: "In spite of ourselves, we are in reality engaged in an in-ternecine struggle for existence with our presumably no less peaceful and well-meaning neighbors. . . . [The] non-moral nature [of man] proclaims and acts upon that fine old Scottish family motto, 'Thou shalt starve ere I want.'"[45] According to the natural ethics of physical nature, such behav-ior is acceptable as normal; only in institutional society, with its idealis-tic ethical principles, are such natural acts stigmatized as evil: "Civilized man brands all these ape and tiger promptings with the name of sins; he punishes many of the acts which flow from them as crimes."[46] Despite his objections to Spencer's libertarian individualism regarding laissez-faire economics, and his belief that government should play an important role in regulating economic affairs, Huxley was no less committed to the basic principles of social Darwinism than was Spencer.[47]

Darwin's essentially negative response to the character and sociological beliefs of Herbert Spencer provides some insights into why he was dubious about extending biological science beyond the realm of matter into areas that included religion, the arts, humanities, and social theories. Soon after its publication, he sent a copy of *The Origin of Species* to Spencer, and in return received the sociologist's *First Principles* (1860–62). Their mutually negative reactions to each other's work set the direction of their long-range views of their vital differences. In his *Autobiography,* Spencer dismissed *Origin* because it contradicted his own Lamarckian belief that environment largely modifies species. Upon first reading Spencer, Darwin felt an "enthusiastic admiration for his transcendent talents," but soon became convinced that his work rested upon "unfounded speculation," and he noted that "his deductive manner of every subject is wholly opposed to my frame of mind." He also was repelled by Spencer's convoluted abstract definitions and admitted that "his style is too hard work for me," so that "his conclusions never convince me."[48] After Darwin perceived how ignorant Spencer was of biology, he lost any respect for him as a theorist on man in society. Spencer never persuaded Darwin that evolution as a metaphor and the scientific method would lead man progressively to a utopian future.[49]

Darwin limited his theory almost entirely to the realm of physical nature and was not eager to extend it beyond matter into areas of the spirit as traditionally understood by his contemporaries. His own philosophical orientation was largely centered in matter, but he never entirely lost his original theism, even after he declared himself an agnostic, and he always retained respect for those who held fast to orthodox religious beliefs. He was frequently troubled by those who invoked him and his theory in order to sanction their own reworking of his theory, or such a principle as natural selection, into contexts radically different from his beliefs, and with results that were far removed from his work. His most forcefully expressed concerns were against some of his French and German supporters, but also against all speculative theories of social progress. Darwin once expressed his concern that the possibility existed that the sun could burn itself out and the universe could cease to exist, a concept that made belief in progress wholly irrelevant.

From his reading of Darwin, Spencer, and Huxley, Frost clearly believed that there was a vital difference between the great evolutionist and many of his English disciples. His humane, prudent, and bland temperament set him apart from them, so that his views on man in society differed from their beliefs regarding "progress" and the so-called "social Darwinism" of many of their contemporaries. Darwin was a lifelong firm abolitionist regarding slavery. His active role as landed gentry and country squire in the charity work of his parish church in Downe, which kept him a nonbelieving, nominal Anglican and believer in temporal salvation through good works, militated against the moral sensibility of the social Darwinists. His later agnosticism differed in spirit from Huxley's aggressive monomania and from Spencer's militant atheism. When he eventually adopted Spencer's famous phrase "the survival of the fittest," he acknowledged that raw violence ruled in nature, but he recognized far more than Huxley or Spencer that the moral laws and civil customs of society condemned the whole concept of "social Darwinism." Darwin's differences from his disciples were sufficient for Frost to think favorably of him, while he remained critical of both Huxley and Spencer.

One of the most serious and enduring misconceptions regarding Frost's character was the direct result of his dualistic beliefs, which led his biographer to identify his views of man in society as identical with social Darwinism. This accusation was a particular extension of the far more general and serious image of Frost as a moral monster. Undoubtedly, for many reasons, Thompson failed to understand that Frost's essential beliefs derived from his dualism; first among them was his inability as a firmly committed monist to comprehend Frost's complex views of the conflicting elements in social beliefs embodied in the dualism of spirit and matter. The poet believed that conflicts in society were inevitable, because his dualism included the practical principle that "everything has its opposite to furnish it with opposition."[50] In total contrast, Thompson's monism led him to believe that social conflicts could and should be eliminated by cooperation between contending interests. Thus, whereas Frost believed as an "Old Testament Christian" that justice preceded mercy in human affairs, Thompson as a secularized New Testament sentimentalist interpreted the poet's view as lacking in charity to the poor. When Frost said favorable things about religion and things of the spirit, to Thompson this meant that he merely "continued his warfare against science—particularly against Darwinian evolutionary theories." When Frost admitted that evil existed as well as good, Thompson's monism, centered in the belief that evil is merely the absence of Good as an absolute, led him to conclude that the poet was an evil man. Two chapters in his biography dealt explicitly with Frost's dualism. In "Speaking of Contraries," Thompson's ineptness in discussing dualism is clearly evident, and he drifted off into biographical matters that had nothing to do with Frost's philosophical beliefs. In "Things in Pairs Ordained," Thompson's main purpose was to attack Frost's supposed "prejudices." Throughout his biography, whenever Frost said anything positive about matters relating to spirit, Thompson assumed that this negated or excluded what appeared to be its contradictory opposite rooted in matter.

# Robert Frost: The Poet as Philosopher

Perhaps nowhere are the polar opposites and stark differences between Frost's dualism and Thompson's monism more evident than in their conflicting conceptions of the nature and appropriate function of human reason in the study of human affairs and in physical nature. Frost had assimilated the whole vast range of traditions of rational thought in Western civilization. These included the ancient pagan Greek and Roman philosophers, Aristotle, Plato, Cicero, and the Stoics; and medieval Christian theologians such as St. Thomas Aquinas who promulgated belief in the "right reason" of moral natural law. The intellectual nature of man included a normative and intuitional conception of reason closely connected with ethics, art, the humanities, and corporate society. Right reason comprehended all that was common and unique in human nature that set it apart qualitatively from other species of animal life—a high moral imagination or sense of good and evil; intuition; conscience and consciousness; individual and corporate experience lodged in memory; belief in free will; and the emotional elements in religion, above all in love, which were so essential in aesthetic creativity; and in the belief that man is by nature a civil and social animal. Right reason was the instrumental means of comprehending the basic principles in moral natural law, which enabled all uncorrupted human beings to distinguish between good and evil in the uses of power, in actions involving life, liberty, and property. The concept of right reason was an essential assumption in the dualism of Frost. It was at the core of his conception of mind or spirit by which he perceived that human nature was more than a biological form of animal life, more than animated matter.

In sharp contrast to Frost's generic view of right reason, Thompson perceived reason as an abstract absolute, rooted in empirical observations of physical phenomena, a logically discursive, analytical, and mathematically deterministic process by which to arrive at scientifically verifiable truths. Thompson's conception of reason is practically identical with that of Descartes and with his Victorian disciple Thomas Henry Huxley, and it assumes a monism of matter as the ultimate reality and that the mind of man is derived from matter. Although Descartes speculated on theological problems, his methodology was purely intellectual, not ethical, and his great concern was not with good and evil in human nature but with what was true or false in physical phenomena. The appropriate domain of Cartesian rationalism was in physics, not in ethics; it was the essential tool of science, and it came to dominate scientific methodology for several centuries, into the modern era. Frost accepted both types of reason, each in its own appropriate sphere of competence, whereas Thompson treated "right reason" as an unwarranted limitation on Cartesian rationalism, and accused Frost of being "anti-intellectual." He even made that false assumption the basis of his accusation that the poet's conception of laissez faire made him a social Darwinist:

> RF, having first learned the doctrine of right reason from his mother's teachings, permitted it to shape many of his attitudes toward the limitations of human reason. He also used this doctrine for purposes of buttressing his version of laissez faire.[51]

When perceived within the context of Frost's all-inclusive philosophical dualism of good and evil and the full range of his understanding of various concepts of human reason, Thompson's statement reveals a number of serious crude errors. First, as a boy the poet may indeed have first learned the simple facts about "right reason" from his mother, but his mature understanding of that vital concept involved a complex philosophical and historical grasp of its significance in Western civilization far beyond Thompson's comprehension. To Frost, "right reason" was not an end in itself, nor did it set limits upon discursive and analytical reason when applied in the realm of matter. As the instrumental means of apprehending moral natural law, it set limits to human freedom, and therefore to laissez faire in economics, within the moral norms of natural law ethics and also within the legal norms of constitutional law. Thompson not only failed to understand Frost's distinction between normative right reason and descriptive discursive reasoning as a process, concepts which supplemented each other, but he did not perceive that right reason placed moral limits upon freedom in economics and was the reverse of laissez faire as understood by social Darwinists. This led him to the false conclusion that Frost was a moral monster.

Historically, from the seventeenth century to the modern era, the important differences between Frost and Thompson regarding the range of meanings and appropriate applications of reason in human affairs and in physical phenomena find an exact parallel in the conflicts over human nature and reason between Blaise Pascal (1623–62) and René Descartes (1596–1650). Like Frost, Pascal was an Augustinian in his Christian theology and a dualist in his philosophy. Both men were highly skeptical of Descartes' so-called dualism. As a scientist Pascal was more than a match for Descartes. His brilliant achievements in mathematics and physics, his *Essai pour les coniques* (1640) on the projective geometry of the cone (known as "Pascal's theorem"), his explication of probability theory in calculus, and his treatise on hydrostatics and work on the barometer won him early and enduring fame among scientists. Although Descartes in the *Meditations on First Philosophy* (1641) attempted to put a positive interpretation upon religious doubts, he made mathematical reason and analytical logic so dominant, even in affirming his belief in God and in religious discourse, that only mathematically demonstrative knowledge was considered valid. Pascal rejected Descartes' methodology as contrary to religious revelation and the primacy of faith over discursive logical reason, yet compatible with normative reason. Pascal's theology is very close to Frost's own religious experience and faith, which form the capstone of his "four beliefs" in the final paragraphs of "Education by Poetry."

In comparing Frost and Pascal, it is noteworthy that both men put a premium upon the creative and spiritual dimensions in human nature, while respecting the scientific, material, and deterministic elements in man as a biological animal. In his *Pensées* (1670), Pascal wrote: "For it is impossible that our rational part should be other than spiritual; and if any one maintain that we are simply corporeal, this would far more exclude us from the knowledge of things, there being nothing so inconceivable as to say that matter knows itself. It is impossible to imagine how it should know itself."[52] Frost's distinction between the intuitive reason or imagination of creativity and the mechanistic and logical reason of geometrical discourse, so central in his aesthetics and in his essay "The Figure a Poem Makes," finds its exact equivalent in Pascal's difference between *l'esprit de finesse* and *l'esprit géométrique*.[53] What Pascal called "intuition" and Frost referred to as "the better wildness of logic," which he said is best understood "backward in retrospect" rather than forward in prophecy, is common and central in the moral and aesthetic imagination of both men. Both Pascal and Frost ranked such intuition far above logical reason.

In contrast with both men, Descartes, like Leibniz after him, made geometrical certitude the model for certitude in every branch of human knowledge, including religion and the arts. Thomas Henry Huxley and the three generations of Huxleys, including Thompson, refined upon Descartes and made a complete antithesis between science and religion. In opposition to Descartes, Pascal contended that geometrical certitude exists only in matter and does not extend to the range between the mysteries and the infinities.[54] Frost was in total agreement with Pascal on this point. It is also significant that Pascal distinguished between "contradictions" and what he called "contrarieties," between real and only apparent antinomies, a distinction that Frost frequently maintained in conversations with friends.[55] Despite their many external differences of time and place, the religious and philosophical beliefs of Pascal and Frost are so similar that their views of human nature and conception of reason sets them in strong opposition to the whole rational tradition of Descartes and his nineteenth-century disciples in the three generations of Huxleys. The serious problems and flaws in Thompson's biography of Frost are best perceived not merely as conflicts in personality, but in the light of Thompson's adherence to the philosophical and scientific traditions of Descartes and Thomas Henry Huxley and his disciples.

Thompson's monistic assumptions often led him to make a false antithesis between the dualistic elements in such matters as good and evil, or justice and mercy, in the beliefs of Frost, and invariably he put the most unfavorable construction on his interpretations. A case in point is how he handled one of the poet's greatest and recurrent concerns throughout his life, what Frost called "the justice-mercy contradiction." This complex subject and theme is central in *The Death of the Hired Man*, presented within a secular and social world, and in *A Masque of Reason* and *A Masque of Mercy*, within a biblical context. As a dualist, Frost believed it was possible to combine and reconcile justice and mercy. In religion he held that every person hopes that on the day of judgment God's mercy will be greater than His justice. In the practical politics of temporal society, parties differ about which deserves priority. Frost believed that in American politics the Democratic Party favored mercy for the masses, and the Republican Party stressed justice to individuals. Although he identified himself as a Democrat, he believed that in temporal affairs justice should precede mercy, because it was necessary for society to allow freedom to produce wealth before the government could distribute benefits to the poor. Frost was highly critical of Franklin D. Roosevelt's "New Deal" because he believed that the president was too power hungry and too eager to consolidate political power in a centralized federal government. Nevertheless, his letter to Louis Untermeyer on November 25, 1936, on Roosevelt's reelection during the dark years of the Great Depression, reveals that he was not a social Darwinist regarding economics and human suffering: "I don't feel it is humanity not to feel the suffering of others. The last election would confute me if I did. I judged that half the people that voted for his Rosiness were those glad to be on the receiving end of his benevolence and half were those over glad to be on the giving end. The national mood is humanitarian. Nobly so—I wouldn't take it away from them."[56]

Also in 1936, Frost wrote an introduction to Sarah Cleghorn's *Threescore*, the autobiography of a Puritan Vermont lady described by Thompson as a "rabid New Dealer, the humanitarian socialist-reformer-poet in Vermont." Frost referred to Cleghorn as "a saint and a reformer" and cited her famous quatrain:

> *The golf links lie so near the mill*
> *That almost every day,*
> *The laboring children at their work*
> *Can see the men at play.*

He praised her poem for its "high explosive for righteousness" against child labor, and his approval of her social consciousness is a world removed from any interpretation of laissez faire that would justify social Darwinism. Yet Thompson treated Frost's tribute to Cleghorn as satire. He thought that he discovered "subdued ironies and sarcasms in his tribute to the reforming zeal of this woman. . . . He would have spoiled what was genuine in his tribute to his friend if he had openly stated his own doctrine of laissez faire, and his own belief that justice should always take precedence over mercy."[57] As a monist, Thompson set justice as an absolute against mercy, and assumed that when Frost gave a priority to justice he transformed it into an absolute that excluded it from any relationship with mercy. In short, the presence of justice necessarily meant the total absence of mercy.

During the 1950s, Frost became increasingly aware that Thompson as a monist had no understanding of his dualism. After twenty years as his official biographer, Frost's conception of reality as "endless . . . things in pairs ordained to everlasting opposition" was perceived by Thompson in monistic terms, by his assumption that the presence of one element in every pair of dualistic opposites precluded the existence of its opposite. Frost believed that during man's "trial by existence" on earth, both elements in every dualistic conflict always had to be taken fully into account. For example, the conflict between good and evil in human nature, and in society, was a perennial and constantly recurring war that had no final and absolute conclusion. To Thompson, the existence of good as an absolute (God) precluded the presence of evil (the devil) or vice versa. This meant that nothing is either good or evil but thinking or feeling makes it so. Reality is not a matter of philosophical understanding, but depends wholly upon a person's psychological attitude. To Thompson, Frost's belief that evil existed in human nature and in the world was sufficient proof that he was a moral monster. During many years of his close relationship with Frost, Thompson made his subjective psychology rather than philosophical principles the basis of his understanding the poet. In a well-researched and excellent article, "The Poet as Neurotic: The Official Biography of Robert Frost," Donald G. Sheehy has shown that Thompson's entire orientation was in a neo-Freudian psychoanalytic theory put forth by Karen Horney and that he even rewrote chapters in the biography to make them conform to her theory of neurosis.[58] In 1978, in a literary memoir, I noted how exclusively weighted Thompson's biography was with negative emotional and psychological terms, such as "badness," "confusion," "cowardice," "death," "enemies," "fears," "hate," "insanity," "jealousy," "sadness," "self-centeredness," and "suicide."[59] But every opposite human character portrait was totally omitted. Thus the public image of Frost as a psychologically complex but morally normal man, with an attractive social personality, was replaced by Thompson's image of him as a moral monster.

Between 1952 and his death in January 1963, Frost made several attempts to instruct Thompson in how to understand his moral dualism. On May 1, 1952, in a letter on Thompson's book on Herman Melville, he discussed the problem of evil in *Billy Budd*. A subtle tone of whimsy runs through much of Frost's letter. He assumed that an indirect approach to Thompson's monism, which did not injure his sensibility, was best achieved through a critique of Melville's harsh treatment of God. Although Frost's criticism was directed against Melville, indirectly it applied as well to Thompson's optimistic monism, in which evil was perceived as the absence of good. He noted that Melville's treatment of good and evil was flawed, because he attributed to God what he should have directed against His opposite, the devil. Frost observed that literary critics of Thompson's thesis seemed "favorable to you, though not quite able to go the whole length with you in your belief that Herman (sic), hated god. . . . Of course Melville hated God every step of the way in doing Billy in. You did a great chapter there. Melville hated evil for the rather personal reason that Emerson's God included evil as just some more good and Melville couldn't stomach Emerson." Frost believed that Melville loathed Emerson's optimistic monism, that he perceived Emerson as "the confidence man" who taught that there were only higher degrees and lesser degrees of absolute good, but that no such thing as evil existed.[60]

Frost's most direct criticism of Melville includes how Thompson treated the problem of evil: "I must confess you do take away from Melville's stature a little in making him bother to believe in a God he hates. How could he have failed to see he had got round by a series of insensible cog-slips to where he should have changed God's name to devil. He seems rather weak on the brain side." Frost's ironical delicacy was that Melville was guilty of bad theology, which applied as well to Thompson, but the poet hastened to add that this in no way should distract his readers from admiring his great talents as a writer: "We may admire him more wrong than almost anybody but Hawthorne right." Frost's aesthetic principle was that a writer's good or bad philosophy, his "wisdom" hardly matters, as compared with his skill as an artist in the mastery of form and technique. Frost concluded his letter with a whimsical broad appeal to St. Augustine and St. Thomas Aquinas, the two Christian theologians who had discussed the problem of good and evil, of God and the devil, most profoundly. He noted that in Graham Greene's fiction a "formula for an entertaining salvation is to have sinned deeply and repented greatly. Always lots of nonsense abroad. He must be thinking of St. Augustine more than St. Thomas Aquinas." Frost believed that Greene abused St. Augustine's theology in his novels by stressing the saint's pagan, sinful life before his religious conversion. In contrast, Frost noted, "Thomas was a good boy from first to last." Even though Frost preferred the theology of St. Augustine, he approved of St. Thomas's doctrine of *felix culpa*, the happy fall from grace at the heart of Christian theology. But the main thrust of his criticism of Melville's harsh response to Emerson's optimistic monism was simply too subtle for his biographer. He knew that Thompson was very sympathetic to Emerson and the whole tradition of Platonic idealism. Thompson, like Descartes, was simultaneously both a material monist and a spiritual monist, but not a dualist. His materialist monism made a complete antithesis between science and religion, and his spiritual monism enabled him to condemn Frost on moral grounds for not creating an absolute monism that merged the spiritual and material realms into one reality. Thompson once noted that Frost's poetry "permitted him to talk about at least two worlds simultaneously," but art was the realm of fiction, and no such division between spirit and matter existed for Thompson in the mundane world of ordinary experience.[61]

Frost's letter to Thompson on May 1, 1952, is best perceived as a prelude to another letter on July 11, 1959, in which once again he attempted to instruct Thompson about his dualism. In this letter there is no playful irony; the language is personal, direct, and conciliatory, and prudently diplomatic, but a note of concerned desperation is evident in Frost's urgent plea to Thompson for a better understanding of his dualism:

> It won't be long before you see me again to assert your right to get me right or wrong in our long continuum. It's odd we've managed each other so well in a situation that has its perils. It does us both credit. . . . I've meant to give you all the advantages, supply you with all the facts, and keep nothing back, save nothing out for my own use in case I ever should write my own story. And I have left entirely to your judgment the summing up and the significance. You've had a long time to turn me over in your mind looking for some special phrase or poem to get me by. By now

you may think you have plucked the heart out of my secret and I don't care if you have. All is easy between us. We have sized each other up without disillusionment. . . . I trust my philosophy still bothers you a little. It bothers me. You should have heard me talking the other night about the Uriel your class in American Literature wouldn't let you talk to them about. One or other of us will fathom me sooner or later. Did Trilling have something the other night? . . . At least he seemed to see that I am as strong on badness as I am on goodness. Emerson's defect was that he was of the great tradition of Monists. He could see the "good of evil born" but he couldn't bring himself to say the evil of good born. He was an Abominable Snowman of the top-lofty peaks. But what a poet he was in prose and verse. Such phrases. Arnold thought him a voice oracular. ("A Voice oracular has pealed to-day.") I couldn't go as far as that because I am a Dualist and I don't see how Mathew Arnold could because he was a Dualist too. He was probably carried away by the great poetry.[62]

Together with his letter of May 1, 1952, this letter goes far toward illuminating the poet's final sustained attempts to explain his philosophical beliefs to his biographer. The relationship between his dualism of good and evil and his moral character is further underscored in his essay "On Emerson" and in his concluding remarks in "The Future of Man" symposium, both delivered in 1959.

Frost soon realized that his many pleas to Thompson had fallen upon deaf ears. His biographer's inability to understand him, so amply revealed in 1945 in his review of *A Masque of Reason* in the *New York Times*, was so deeply ingrained that nothing could dislodge it. His almost total neglect of Frost's poetry was the natural consequence of his belief that when the poet used metaphorical language in conversations with him he was merely telling "lies" about himself. Thompson's amateurish speculative psychoanalysis of Frost concentrated almost all of his attention upon the poet's supposed or real neurotic inner psyche. Frost had good reasons to fear that the method revealed in Thompson's book on *Melville's Quarrel with God* (1952) was a prelude to how he would handle Frost as an evil man. Finally, in desperation, the poet called out to Stanley Burnshaw, his last editor at Holt, "I'm counting on you to protect me from Larry." Burnshaw responded with his book *Robert Frost Himself* (New York, 1986). It was no accident that in his attempt to redeem Frost from Thompson's portrait of him as a moral monster, Burnshaw began his book with a concise summary, "To the Reader":

Denis Donoghue meets Lawrance Thompson, 1957. "Evidence
that the (official) biography would be a work of riddance." Frost,
America's "best loved poet," dies (1963). In August 1970 portrayed
as "a monster." Lack of published protests. Frost to Burnshaw, "I'm
counting on you to protect me from Larry" (1959).

Burnshaw clearly recognized that a whole generation of Frost's readers
and literary critics, who lacked the factual knowledge to judge the accu-
racy of Thompson's thesis, had been corrupted into accepting his public
image of the poet as a psychotic and depraved man. Several prominent
reviewers who took Thompson largely at face value confirmed his portrait
of Frost. Denis Donoghue, normally a learned and sound literary critic,
met Thompson and was brainwashed into accepting his claim that Frost
was a social Darwinist.

Later, Donoghue modified his views. But the general public and many
teachers of literature continued to accept the negative image of Frost. Burnshaw's two chapters, "The Fabrication of the 'Monster' Myth," and "Toward
the 'Knowable' Frost," demolished the myth created by Thompson and set
the stage for a revitalized understanding of the poet. Good literary critics
rose above biographical concerns of character and temperament and wisely
concentrated on Frost's poems. Richard Poirier, in *Robert Frost: The Work of
Knowing* (1977), provided an excellent critical model for a renewal of Frost
as a poet. Yet Thompson's harsh negative biography continued to haunt
Frost studies, because a writer and his work cannot be wholly separated, so
that his biography has been a continuous impediment to an understanding
of Frost, both as a man and a poet, despite Burnshaw's work.

But a valid knowledge and understanding of Frost requires much more
than nullifying a flawed biography. Frost's reference to the three generations of Huxleys includes those of his contemporaries whose philosophical
orientation he believed was flawed. Their views on the nature and relationships of science, religion, art, the humanities, and education came to
dominate the culture and values of the twentieth century, including the
place of poetry as an art form. To understand Frost both as a man and a
poet, it is necessary to take into full account the central place of his philosophical dualism. This requires knowledge of how his beliefs differ from
the two types of monism which have been in revolt against dualism since
the seventeenth century. That is the subject and theme of the next chapter
and a preliminary to the chapters that follow it.

# *Frost and Creative Evolution*

In order to understand precisely what Robert Frost meant by "creative evolution," it is first necessary to consider the history of that notion in general, to examine it not merely as an original concept of the idealistic Victorian and modern critics of Darwin, but as a theory that existed side by side with the mechanistic theory that was centered in matter and biology since the ancient Greeks. In the opening two paragraphs of Henry Fairfield Osborn's important and largely denigrated article "Aristogenesis, the Creative Principle in *The Origin of Species*"(1934), he made it clear that both Darwin and his critics, in their respective conceptions of evolution, were anticipated by the Greeks. The very title of Osborn's article indicates that Darwin's great work included elements of the creative principle:

> As the title of his epoch-making work Darwin chose "The Origin of Species" (1859) because, as conceived by Linnaeus (1735), "species" was the ultimate unit of Creation in the animal and plant world. *Nullae speciae novae* was the battle cry of the conservatives of pre-Darwin days, but what Darwin devoted his life to was *the origin of adaptations, not of species.* Species are simply the by-products of adaptations.

> Adaptation and the origin of fitness carries us back with a gigantic leap over time to Democritus (450 B.C.), the opponent of the intelligent creative design of Anaxagoras (500–428 B.C.) and the proponent of fixed natural laws in a purely mechanical system. . . . In truth mechanical adaptation was the oriflamme from Empedocles (495–435 B.C.), the father of the evolution idea, through

Anaxagoras, Aeschylus, Aristotle and Plato. The Greeks led the way in forming what may be called the proto-Darwinian "chance hypothesis," the proto-Lamarckian "inheritance of acquired adaptations" hypothesis, and finally the "entelechistic" doctrine of natural law tending to perfection. The progressive improvement or retrogressive degeneration of human and animal mechanisms were the guideposts to the use and disuse inheritance speculations from the naturalists of Greece and Rome to Erasmus Darwin and Lamarck . . .[1]

As Osborn summarily noted, the ancient Greeks anticipated "every phase of modern speculation, amplified but not radically altered by our 'neo-Darwinians,' 'neo-Lamarckians,' 'mutationists' and 'geneticists,' 'entelechists' and 'vitalists,' all of whom feel the magnetism of the eternally baffling problem of the origins of adaptations."[2] In short, from the ancient Greeks to the time of Frost, there were several theories of evolution besides that of Darwin, and the basic conflicts over evolution were between those who adhered to the "chance hypothesis" based upon "fixed natural laws in a purely mechanical system," such as was held in its most extreme form by Ernst Haeckel and Thomas Henry Huxley, and those who believed in the "inheritance of acquired adaptations" hypothesis, a belief in "intelligent creative design," such as was advanced by Jean-Baptiste Lamarck and refined by Mivart, Butler, and Bergson. But since creative evolution in general allowed for great variations, both in basic principles and in the elements included in creativity, and since Frost's conception of creativity was highly original, his version differed in important ways from those of his predecessors.

What were the vital factors that distinguished Frost's creative evolution from that of Darwin's Victorian critics in the same tradition? The poet's eclectic habit of mind, his willingness to "accept anybody's . . . premises . . . let them have their say, and then . . . take it my way," meant that his philosophical dualism of mind or spirit and matter, combined with his thinking in metaphorical terms, enabled him to be far more original than any of his predecessors regarding the concept. His dualism was well balanced between the respective claims of matter and spirit, so that unlike Butler and Bergson he did not stress spirit to the almost total exclusion of matter but continued to accept Darwin's biological and botanical basis of life. Although Frost continued to be highly critical of Huxley's interpretation of Darwin's theory, eventually it appeared to him that Butler and Bergson opposed Huxley's material monism, not as dualists, but as spiritual monists.

No monistic view of evolution, or of anything else, could ever satisfy Frost. In his notebooks, he recorded the difference between his dualism and the two kinds of monism, the mechanistic one centered wholly in matter and the idealistic or spiritual one. Regarding evolution in man as a species, he rejected both of them:

> Mechanism and Idealism: What's the difference? By any name all monisms come to the same thing. If all is good or all is bad we were still secure in monism. But we find in experience that there is a division between good and bad. We get both permanently so far as we have gone.[3]

The whole tenor of Frost's dualistic philosophical orientation in rejecting both forms of monism remained firmly fixed, rooted in his experience that good and bad, true and false, in all of their respective complexities, were constant factors of mind or spirit and matter throughout human history. His conception of creative evolution was deeply grounded in his philosophical dualism, which respected matter and biology, but which construed mind or spirit as the most vital active element in generating changes in man as a species.

Sir Isaiah Berlin's famous adoption of Archilochus's distinction between two basic types of human thinkers—the fox and the hedgehog—may be fruitfully applied when considering the contrast between Frost's dualism and the two monisms regarding evolution. After noting that "the fox knows many things, but the hedgehog knows one big thing," Berlin compares the monism of the hedgehog with the dualism or pluralism of the fox:

> For there exists a great chasm between those, on one side, who relate everything to a single central vision, one system, less or more coherent or articulate, in terms of which they understand, think and feel—a single, universal, organising principle in terms of which alone all that they are and say has significance—and, on the other, those who pursue many ends, often unrelated and even contradictory, connected, if at all, only in some de facto way, for some psychological or physiological cause, related to no moral or aesthetic principle.[4]

In terms of Berlin's analogy, Frost was clearly a fox, not a hedgehog, but in one important respect he differed from Berlin: he included a moral and aesthetic principle in his pluralistic conception of creative evolution. As a fox, Frost was always skeptical of ideological system-builders, whether in science, religion, politics, or anything else.

Berlin's analogy is no less applicable to thinkers concerned with physical nature than to those engaged in fields such as politics and ethics, so that Frost was well aware that there were two very different types of naturalists. In talks with students at Bread Loaf during the summers of 1939 and 1940, he identified Henry David Thoreau and Charles Darwin as naturalists who were almost polar opposites, although he readily admitted that he could admire both of them, each in his own way. Thoreau's *Walden* was for Frost the best single-word title borne by any book. It underscored the place as the dramatic setting for Thoreau's observations and narratives about nature. "All poetry begins with geography," Frost said, and much in *Walden* is poetry in prose. Thoreau, a Harvard man who wore his classical education very lightly, invariably applied his value system in the humanities when describing events or places in nature. He was also a very keen observer of the natural world; in that respect he even excelled James Thomson, whose descriptive powers in *The Seasons* are proverbial. Moreover, Thoreau was not interested in reducing his empirical observations to any system or ideology. He found infinite resources within himself, in his aesthetic imagination and moral sense, so that like Saint Francis of Assisi he perceived something divine in every aspect of physical nature. Whether at Walden Pond or during a week on the Concord and Merrimack rivers, he transmuted every walk or trip in nature into a revelation about life and an episode of self-discovery.

In comparing Frost's responses to Thoreau and Darwin, it is good to remember his assertion that among the works he most cherished were *Walden* and Darwin's *Voyage of the Beagle*.[5] Both books were to Frost perfect examples of how naturalists could explore the external world as empirical and rational observers while subordinating science to the discipline and value system of the humanities. During the almost five years' voyage on the *Beagle*, from December 27, 1831, to October 2, 1836, Darwin surveyed Brazil, Patagonia, Tierra del Fuego, Chile, Peru, and various islands in the Pacific, including the Galapagos Archipelago, Tahiti, New Zealand, and Australia. Although he was only twenty-two years old when he embarked on the *Beagle*, he was already an experienced naturalist, with an amazing knowledge of plants, animals, birds, reptiles, insects, fossils, and geological formations. The facility with which he described in scientific terms the organisms and specimens he collected is striking proof of his maturity as a scientist. Yet his intimate personal, chronological narrative and his clear and concise prose style and sense of metaphor make his book at once a classic of science and a masterpiece of literature. Undoubtedly, Frost's very favorable response to Darwin's account of the voyage of the *Beagle* carried over into his acceptance of *Origin of Species*. Like Whitman, who "contained multitudes," Frost's dualism enabled him to perceive Darwin's theory as an epic metaphor, despite its being so heavily weighted by matter. But Darwin's theory of how changes occur in species through natural selection was wholly mechanistic, a world removed from a perception of science as one of the humanities. How did Frost account for the great differences between Darwin's *Voyage of the Beagle* and *Origin of Species*?

In his conversations with students at Bread Loaf, Frost made it clear that Thoreau as a naturalist provided the best explanation of what had happened to Darwin after the great evolutionist returned to England and became totally immersed in his scientific projects. Six years before Darwin had published *Origin of Species*, Thoreau wrote in his journal (March 9, 1853) on the great danger in studying nature without reference to the spirit of man, which transcended a direct view of physical nature:

> Man cannot afford to be a naturalist, to look at nature directly, but only with the side of his eye. He must look through her and beyond her. To look at her is as fatal as to look at the head of Medusa. It turns the man of science to stone.[6]

Frost agreed with Thoreau, and on several occasions he spoke vehemently and at length about passages in Darwin's *Autobiography* that revealed the evolutionist's gradual and eventually total loss of aesthetic sensibility regarding literature, music, painting, and the arts. During his voyage on the *Beagle*, Darwin recorded his former enthusiasm and taste for good literature. Later, in his autobiography he lamented his loss of such aesthetic sensibility:

> I was fond of reading various books, and I used to sit for hours reading the historical plays of Shakespeare . . . , I read also other poetry, such as Thomson's "Seasons" and the recently published poems of Byron and Scott. . . . I mention this because later in life I wholly lost, to my great regret, all pleasure from poetry of any kind, including Shakespeare.[7]

> I took much delight in Wordsworth's and Coleridge's poetry; and can boast that I read the "Excursion" twice through. Formerly, Milton's "Paradise Lost" had been my chief favourite, and in my

excursions during the voyage of the *Beagle*, when I could take only a single small volume, I always chose Milton.[8]

Up to the age of thirty, or beyond it, poetry of many kinds, such as the works of Milton, Gray, Byron, Wordsworth, Coleridge, and Shelley, gave me great pleasure; and even as a schoolboy I took intense delight in Shakespeare, especially in the historical plays. I have also said that formerly pictures gave me considerable, and music very great delight. But now for many years I cannot endure to read a line of poetry: I have tried lately to read Shakespeare, and found it so intolerably dull that it nauseated me. I have also almost lost any taste for pictures or music.[9]

Darwin regretted "this curious and lamentable loss of the higher aesthetic tastes," because it resulted in "the atrophy of that part of the brain . . . on which the higher tastes depend." He concluded by describing his state of mind and feeling and by identifying the cause of his great loss: "My mind seems to have become a kind of machine for grinding laws out of large collections of facts. It sometimes makes me hate science."[10] In a moment of great candor, two years before he published *Origin of Species*, in a letter to Thomas Henry Huxley (July 9, 1857) he confessed that he consciously and deliberately sought to depersonalize his desires and emotions in order to achieve greater objectivity in his work: "Alas: A scientific man ought to have no wishes, no affections—a mere heart of stone."[11] Two years after his monumental book had appeared, Darwin retrospectively identified a major cause of his loss of emotional and intellectual sensitivity. In a letter to H. W. Bates (December 3, 1861), he wrote: "I have long thought that too much systematic work [and] description somehow blunts the faculties."[12] At the time that Darwin wrote *Origin of Species*, he was both emotionally and intellectually at the opposite pole from Frost when the poet formulated his conception of creative evolution.

Frost thought that it was remarkable that, given Darwin's enervated condition, he still retained enough of the sensibility he had had during his voyage on the *Beagle* to make good use of metaphorical language in explaining the principles of his theory. Darwin as a naturalist continued to fascinate Frost for the rest of his life. As he saw it, the evolutionist was the archetypal case of how a normal and superior mind could become aesthetically desensitized by being too immersed in the mechanical processes of its work. But the poet denied that science as such was the cause of Darwin's deprivation of aesthetic sensibility. The real cause was excessive specialization of any kind, the subversion of one's humanity in one's professionalism. Frost always believed that specialization destroyed the creative powers in man. He stated on several occasions that acquiring a vast quantity of factual knowledge beyond what could be usefully employed by the imagination, intuition, reason, consciousness, will, and memory injured the human psyche. Darwin was particularly vulnerable to the loss of his aesthetic sense because, as he acknowledged, his education in the humanities was to him "simply a blank."[13] In addition to this severe self-depreciation, Frost noted that during his voyage on the *Beagle* Darwin experienced a loss of faith in revealed religion. There was therefore nothing to set bounds to the scientific descriptions and quantitative measurements of facts in his research, no impediment centered in the value system of the humanities.

Despite his reservations about any scientific theory treated as an abstract absolute, Frost continued to think well of Darwin throughout his adult life. When the poet was seventy-five years old, during an interview on November 17, 1949, he made a tantalizing analogy regarding himself and Darwin: "If a writer were to say he planned a long poem dealing with Darwin and evolution, we would be tempted to say it's going to be terrible. And yet you remember Lucretius. He admired Epicurus as I admired, say, Darwin. And he wrote a great poem.[14] It is doubtful whether Frost ever seriously intended to write a long poem about Darwin and evolution, but he was clearly concerned about the naturalist's theory, both in his poetry and prose. Eventually that concern dilated upon how far it fell short of his own conception of creative evolution. As a dualist, Frost had the perennial problem of how to reconcile Darwin's apparent monism, centered in a mechanistic view of nature as pure matter, even in biology, with the contrary monism of such idealists as Thoreau, whose view of nature was more centered in mind or spirit. His belief that science is merely one of the humanities and his metaphorical treatment of both science and religion as two very different but not contradictory ways of understanding reality went far to humanize the differences between the two types of naturalists. Thoreau's type of humanistic naturalism is captured in Frost's poem "Two Look at Two," (1923), and Darwin's scientific naturalism is well illustrated in "The Most of It" (1942).[15]

The originality of Frost's conception of creative evolution cannot be perceived if it is assumed that he simply followed the traditional formulations of such critics of Darwin's theory as Butler and Bergson. Lawrance Thompson's account of Frost's enthusiastic response to Bergson's *Creative Evolution* (1911) has often misled a whole generation of scholars and literary critics to assume that the poet was a close follower of that philosopher.[16] Thompson's initial error was his failure to distinguish sharply between dualism and monism in Frost's philosophical orientation. Indeed, on several occasions he even implied that the poet was committed to a monistic view of man and nature.[17] As a result of this imprecise treatment of Frost's philosophical perspective, many literary critics have assumed that his imagery and conception of nature, particularly in "West-Running Brook," are indebted largely to Bergson. The culminating error in Thompson's contention lay in his belief that "for Frost, and perhaps for Bergson . . . 'creative evolution' was of ultimate importance because it could be used to preach the gospel of triumph over death."[18] This utterly simplistic misinterpretation of both Bergson and Frost was justified by Thompson's dubious claim that they were philosophically and religiously related by way of Lucretius and Saint Paul, which he thought was evident in Frost's poem "West-Running Brook."[19]

John F. Sears in "William James, Henri Bergson and the Poetics of Robert Frost" (1995) relied heavily upon Thompson's account of Frost's relationship with Bergson. In describing that thinker's psychology regarding "the mysteries of time, creation, and process," Sears raised the important question: "Bergson asked how does evolution express spirit?" To answer his query, he turned to Emerson's transcendental belief in the superiority of mind or spirit over matter and concluded: "Our experience of the material world is thus effortlessly incorporated into our mental activity."[20] Thus Frost's dualism of matter and mind was subsumed by Sears into the very Emersonian monism that the poet expressly rejected. A few years after Frost read Bergson, he came to perceive the French philosopher as in the tradition of Emerson and Butler, a spiritual monist rather than the dualist he had first thought him to be. As Dorothy Judd Hall noted in "An Old Testament Christian," Frost's "initial enthusiasm" for Bergson "eventually waned," but she offered no explanation of why or how the poet came to modify his views on that philosopher's conception of creative evolution.[21]

Frost's doubts about Bergson's philosophical orientation probably began shortly after he had read the French thinker's version of creative evolution. In 1939 at Bread Loaf, in a retrospective conversation with me, Frost stated that George Santayana's critique of Bergson was essentially valid. Santayana's fifty-page analysis of Bergson's *Creative Evolution*, in "The Philosophy of Henri Bergson," appeared in *Winds of Doctrine* (1913), just two years after Frost had read Bergson.[22] Santayana attacked Bergson's highly optimistic idealism and psychology, based upon his central principle, *élan vital*, which was his circumlocution for God, and according to Santayana was very similar to "the will of Schopenhauer or the unknowable force" of Herbert Spencer.[23] He also noted that Bergson "has a horror of mechanical physics" and that "reason and science make him deeply uncomfortable."[24]

Since Frost respected the whole range of the biological and physical sciences as part of the humanities, far from having a horror of physics, he accepted it as wholly consistent with his belief in matter as a basic constituent of his dualistic philosophy.

But apart from religion and science, as applied to aesthetics and art, Bergson, like Jean-Jacques Rousseau, made spontaneous emotion and self-expression paramount in creativity. He said nothing about the need of self-discipline to provide both direction and purpose in the creation of artistic design. This separation of emotion from reason, moral imagination, and the creation of form, lay at the heart of Bergson's psychology and aesthetics. His conception of creativity violated Frost's belief that "a poem is a thought-felt thing," a harmony of mind and passion, which required "tons and tons of discipline" in order to master technique and provide the means of creating form out of the raw materials of life. Finally, in sharp contrast to Frost, Bergson's creative evolution also contained an implicit belief in progress as applied to human nature itself. In 1940, Santayana repeated this criticism, writing sarcastically of "a Bergsonian vision of a miraculous human evolution."[25] In rejecting Bergson's view of "progress" by the period of World War I, Frost had come to believe that human nature was "terminal" and was not evolving into superman, a belief that he held for the rest of his life.

Frost had no access to Santayana's most explicit criticism of Bergson's view of reality, which is set forth in a "Note on Bergson" deposited in the Manuscript Collection of Columbia University in 1969 and written on notebook sheets. The Spanish philosopher's own materialism is evident in his critique of Bergson's separation of matter and spirit: "The inertia of matter he calls matter, the energy of matter he calls life." He then charged that Bergson absorbed matter into a monism of spirit:

> Matter turns out to have no other substance than spirit itself . . .
> In a pure monism it would make no real difference whether we
> called the one reality God or Nature, mind or matter, water or
> fire or will, since in any case this substance must be the seat and
> source of every kind of distant existence. . . . The great stream of
> "life" is said to run through matter . . .[26]

In his "Note on Bergson," Santayana made explicit what had been implicit throughout his criticism of him in "The Philosophy of Henri Bergson" in 1913.

Whether through Santayana or on his own initiative, or both, Frost came to doubt that Bergson shared his own dualistic view of reality. As a result of his skepticism, the poet's conception of creative evolution was qualitatively different from that of Bergson. Nevertheless, he continued to praise Bergson, not as an enthusiastic admirer but as a challenger of the established scientific orthodoxy of materialistic monists regarding evolution. Thus on January 1, 1917, he wrote to Louis Untermeyer: "What I like about Bergson and Fabre is that they have bothered our evolutionists so much. . . ."[27] Yet over the next several decades, in his further pursuit of Santayana, Frost discovered that apart from their agreement regarding Bergson, in his basic philosophy he thoroughly disagreed with his former Harvard teacher.

Frost's highly diverse but essentially critical response to Santayana as a man of letters and as a philosopher extended over six decades, and it illuminates basic elements in his own conception of creative evolution. In 1960, during Frost's interview for the *Paris Review*, he was asked whether Santayana interested him while he was the Spaniard's student at Harvard in 1898, and he responded:

> No, not particularly. Well, yes. I always wondered what he really meant, where he was headed, what it all came to. Followed that for years. I never knew him personally. . . . But I admired him. It was a golden utterance—he was something to listen to, just like his written style. But I wondered what he really meant. I found years afterward somewhere in his words that all was illusion, of two kinds, true and false.[28]

Lawrance Thompson claimed that Frost's initial response to Santayana was rage and hatred against his teacher's satirical and cynical condemnation of all idealistic thinking as naïve self-deception.[29] But Frost's own words indicate that his first reaction was far more ambiguous and complex. He admired the philosopher's "golden utterance," his patrician grace as a speaker, and the subtle cadences and concise simplicity of his polished prose style, with its crisp epigrams and luminous personal insights that so often conveyed a magisterial profundity. But Santayana's literary brilliance obscured his basic philosophical principles, so that Frost "wondered what he really meant" and "where he was headed." Only after he had followed his former teacher for many years did he discover that Santayana believed that all religions and philosophies were merely forms of true or false illusions, myths that only credulous people accepted as true.[30] Through further reading in Santayana, Frost came to realize that this conviction was the logical outcome of the philosopher's materialism, naturalism, and agnosticism, all of which were incompatible with Frost's dualistic philosophy.[31]

Frost's dualism of mind and matter always maintained a balance in their respective claims, but with a bias in favor of mind or spirit. Santayana's whole philosophy was permeated with the opposite conviction, that "the realm of matter . . . is the true matrix of mind."[32] The superiority of matter over mind was not limited to science, but applied to every aspect of human thought and action. Santayana even asserted that the sonnets he wrote at Harvard as an undergraduate assumed the sovereignty of matter over mind: They "pointed out well enough where a mature solution might be found: in obedience to matter for the sake of freedom of mind."[33] Matter or physical nature sets the standard for both empirical facts and for values in art and religion: "Our senses, no less than our poetry and myth, clothe in human images, the manifold processes of matter."[34] Unlike Frost, Santayana admired both Herbert Spencer and Bertrand Russell, because in their comments on ethics, aesthetics, and every acceptable form of idealistic thought they perceived mind as rooted in material nature and the biological nature of man.

Santayana found no difficulty in reconciling his belief in the primacy of matter with his religious inheritance as a Roman Catholic: "The Latin and Catholic is hopelessly materialistic even in his religion. . . ."[35] This belief is the basis of his lifelong intellectual Epicureanism and pious reverence for Catholicism, which he denied was in any way contradictory: "Being at once a beast and a spirit doesn't seem to me a contradiction. On the contrary, it is necessary to be a beast if one is ever to be a spirit."[36] Unlike the dualism in Frost's philosophy, which involved construing spirit in terms of matter and matter in terms of spirit, Santayana was simultaneously an absolute material monist and a strict spiritual monist, with each theory mutually exclusive on its own terms, without interactions between them. But whenever this equivocal and ambiguous relationship between matter and spirit appeared headed toward a dissolution, Santayana resolved the problem in favor of materialism: "My whole description of the spiritual life is . . . an extension of my materialism and a consequence of it."[37] In "A General Confession," he admitted that his Catholicism "is a matter of sympathy and traditional allegiance, not of philosophy," which enabled him "to love the Christian epic, and all those doctrines and observances which bring it down into daily life."[38] In his belief that every philosophy and religion was either a good or bad illusion, Santayana clearly perceived Catholicism as a good and valid illusion. It is small wonder that William James, his colleague at Harvard, characterized his views on matter and spirit as "moribund Latinity."

Since Santayana's philosophy was so wholly at odds with Frost's, including his conception of creativity and creative evolution, the poet's critical negative response to Santayana's condemnation of New England Puritanism is an important dimension of his intellectual life. In contrast to Catholicism as a good form of religious illusion, Santayana believed that Calvinism was a false and evil illusion, which warranted his strong condemnation. Calvinist Puritanism liked its biblical religion pure, without any contamination from pagan philosophy, sensual art, or Roman Catholic superstitions. In 1940, Santayana recalled that when he was a young instructor in philosophy, his Harvard colleague "Royce felt how much I hated the worship of a Calvinistic God."[39] He acknowledged that his Spanish origins and early religious orientation made him strongly opposed to New England Puritanism and modern America: "My Catholic background and Latin mind placed me in conscious and sometimes violent contrast with old Boston, and with the new America that has grown up for the most part after my day."[40] His hatred of New England Puritanism and its influence upon modern America is a major theme in many of his publications during the four decades after Frost had been his student at Harvard. Since Frost's whole background was in the tradition of Protestant Dissenters, and because he held very positive views of America, Santayana's criticism was directed at some of Frost's most cherished and essential beliefs.

During the early decades of the twentieth century, perhaps as part of his critical reaction to Santayana, Frost developed his own unique conception of New England Puritanism. He also became a strong defender of American society against such critics. Yet he seldom made a public issue of his positive beliefs regarding Puritanism and America. But when Santayana published *The Last Puritan: A Memoir in the Form of a Novel* (1936), Frost felt compelled to respond publicly to its savage indictment of New England and Puritanism. His particularly strong reaction was due to the book's long run as a best seller, which he believed would popularize a fallacious interpretation of Puritanism, New England, and creativity.

*The Last Puritan* is a fictional autobiography of a retired professor of philosophy who describes and comments fully on all aspects of the Yankee descendents of the colonists of Massachusetts. The setting is Boston, a city converted by its Calvinist origins into "a moral and intellectual nursery, always applying first principles to trifles." To underscore his theme, Santayana elaborated it in a prologue and an epilogue. The prologue elucidates: "Puritanism self-condemned." The chief protagonist, Oliver Alden, is the last Puritan because "in Oliver Puritanism worked itself out to its logical end. He convinced himself, on Puritan grounds, that it was wrong to be a Puritan, yet "he remained a Puritan notwithstanding."[41]

Oliver Alden is a latter-day Boston Brahmin, "a self-inhibited Puritan" at war with "the living forces of nature," who is incapable of having any spontaneous feelings of enjoyment; his self-control makes him admit that he hates all pleasures and what is called "having a good time." He is obsessed by an "absolute conscience," which imposes duties on him based upon rigid social conventions. In short, he is the embodiment of Santayana's earlier nonfictional accounts of "the genteel tradition."[42] He is the genteel tradition at bay. In total contrast to the Calvinist "thin-spun race" represented by Oliver is his Catholic cousin, Mario Van de Weyer. He is a complete cultural Epicurean: a carefree, irresponsible but lovable rascal; a kindhearted rogue; a romantic Don Juan favored by women. His outward happy paganism hides an inward religious grace; he embodies the rich and sensual charm of the Mediterranean world.[43]

Frost not only thoroughly digested this fictional account, he paid special attention to the epilogue, which presented the final tragedy of the last Puritan: "A moral nature burdened and over-strong, and a critical faculty fearless but helplessly subjective—isn't that the true tragedy of your ultimate Puritan?" The novel's final sentence made a strong lasting impression on Frost: "After life is over and the world has gone up in smoke, what realities might the spirit in us still call its own without illusion save the form of those very illusions which have made up our story?" The poet's immediate criticism of Santayana's account of Puritanism and New England, of the philosopher's religious and historical inadequacies, was merely a prelude to his ultimate rejection of that thinker's whole philosophy, which culminated in the belief that every form of idealism was an illusion. In a letter to Lawrance Thompson (June 12, 1948), Frost wrote: "The last pop of poppycock was for Santayana to say 'true illusion and false illusion that is all there is to choose between.'"

The enormous differences between Santayana and Frost regarding Puritanism, America, and creativity in the arts and evolution can be explained to some extent by their early lives, in their family background, particularly their religious upbringing. They were both brought to New England as children, Santayana from Spain in 1872, at age nine, with a Catholic inheritance; Frost from California in 1885, at age eleven, with a Protestant inheritance compounded of Presbyterian, Congregational, Unitarian, and Swedenborgian elements. Santayana's whole intellectual and cultural orientation derived from the ancient traditions and lifestyle of

Latin Europe; Frost's entire psychology and value system were centered in the new world, in the promise of America to grow from a raw and primitive colonial society into a great nation. Baker Brownell, Santayana's student during his final year at Harvard, has summarized well those aspects of the philosopher's life that provided Frost with one of his main critical points:

> Though he lived in America forty years from childhood to mid-
> dle age, was educated there in Kindergarten, public school, col-
> lege and university, held the famous Walker travelling fellowship
> from Harvard two years, wrote eleven of his books and earned
> his living there as a teacher of philosophy until he was fifty, San-
> tayana never admits that he was more than an alien in our midst,
> a friendly observer without ties or burdens, an Athenian exiled
> by practical compulsions in Syracuse. He retired from teaching
> in January 1912, left these shores immediately, and, I believe, has
> never returned.[44]

To Frost, Santayana had neither sympathy with, nor understanding of, America. In essence, he resembled such American expatriates as Henry James, Ezra Pound, and T. S. Eliot, whose aesthetic and cultural orientation became predominantly European.

As young men, both Santayana and Frost were aware that throughout New England orthodox Calvinism had long been replaced in many Congregational churches by the far more liberal and secularized theology of Unitarianism. Salvation was no longer restricted exclusively to the small minority of God's elect, but was available to all of humanity. But whereas Santayana was highly critical of Unitarianism, regarding it as Calvinism turned inside out, an abandonment of Christianity, Frost wholeheartedly accepted the transmutation in Calvinism as a positive improvement in the broad range of Augustinian Christianity. To Santayana, the changes in Puritanism were superficial, as was evident in his severe criticism of Emerson's transcendentalism and William James's pragmatism and psychology, those quintessential formulations by the founders of "the genteel tradition." Frost was well aware that New England Puritanism still retained some of the prime cultural constituents of the old Calvinist tradition. During the brief period that his mother, sister, and he had to stay with his grandparents, after arriving from California, he experienced their sour disposition and harsh disciplinary attitude over trifles that often characterized the Puritan temperament. Moreover, at first, as he readily admitted, he did not like his New England neighbors. But in time he came to appreciate the candor, freshness, and originality in Yankee speech, a basic Puritan trait which became so essential in his poetry. He also learned to admire the enormous courage, discipline, and self-reliance that derived from New England Puritanism, traits that were so vital in both artistic creativity, and in the development of a strong civil-social order as the chief mechanism in creative evolution for man as a species.

Frost's conception of the changes in Puritanism is clearly evident in his poem "The Generations of Men" (1913), which placed him at the farthest pole from Santayana and other critics of New England Puritanism, while it sharpened his beliefs regarding both artistic production and creative evolution. His poem explored the modern Yankee Puritan "pride in ancestry," voiced by a young man and woman, distant cousins who meet by chance during a reunion of the Stark family. Regarding their original Calvinist inheritance, they note: "The life is not yet all gone out of it." They are liberal toward new arrivals in New England: "One mustn't bear too hard on the newcomers." For decades, Frost strongly approved of the waves of immigrants who flocked to America during the nineteenth century and later. In "The Generations of Men," the young couple voice Frost's view of himself as expressed in a letter to Louis Untermeyer (June 30, 1919): "Half of me has been here nine generations, the other half, one generation: which makes me more representative I think than if I was altogether of old stock. I'm an ideal combination of been-here-since-the-beginning and just-come-over." The young man in the poem voices Frost's own latitudinarian conviction on how to regard Puritanism:

> *But don't you think we sometimes make too much*
> *Of the old stock? What counts is the ideals,*
> *And these will bear some keeping still about.*

Restoring a public awareness of the enduring "ideals" of New England Puritanism became an important theme in Frost's intellectual life, particularly during the decade of the 1930s.[45] It also provided an important element in his conception of creative evolution. It would take a substantial study to describe in detail Frost's defense of New England Puritanism. Here it is sufficient to summarize his main thesis regarding the ideals and achievements of New England, to note his rebuttal of those who demonized the Puritans, and to perceive the connection between his view of Puritanism and his conception of artistic creativity and creative evolution.

Frost was in substantial agreement with the portraits of New England Puritans painted by Samuel Eliot Morison in *Builders of the Bay Colony* (1930) and *The Puritan Pronaos* (1936), and especially by Perry Miller in *The New England Mind* (1939). Miller's book shattered the narrow and unhistorical view of Puritans as inhibited by their strict moral code of behavior: "Even in the shadow of their creed the Puritans were not sexually inhibited.... They read secular poetry, played musical instruments, cracked jokes, and imbibed prodigious quantities of alcoholic beverages."[46] According to both Miller and Frost, it was also a serious mistake to regard Calvinism as an original and self-sufficient conception of Christianity. In his first chapter, "The Augustinian Strain of Piety," which established a frame for his entire study, Miller made it clear that Calvinism was merely an extreme modern form of Augustinian Christianity. On this vital point Frost agreed with him. But Frost refined upon Miller and also insisted that Puritanism, in its basic Augustinian theology and piety, was to be found in every religion—not only in the Catholic, Lutheran, and Anglican forms of Christianity, but also in Judaism and even in the pagan mythology of ancient Greece and Rome. To Frost, a Puritan was anyone who was willing to put moral bounds on what he wanted, including not only pleasures of the senses, such as "wine, women, and song," but also such things as political power. A Puritan was essentially an ascetic regarding pleasure and power. He was as much a practitioner of restraint through prudence and temperance as he was a person devoted to recognition of, and abidance by, right moral principles. His opposite, Frost believed, was the self-indulgent hedonist and the undisciplined egocentric.[47]

Frost knew that his highly eclectic and original conception of Puritanism as self-restraint regarding personal pleasure and power was highly remote from how most people understood it. On June 30, 1955, during his poetry reading at the opening session of the Bread Loaf School of English, he threw down a challenge: "I thought if I came up again some evening, I'd like to talk about Puritanism—in Greek, Roman, Early Roman, New England, and Later Roman. . . ." To whet the interest of his audience, he added: "Wait until you hear me on the subject. . . . Come up and I'll really shock you."[48] A month later, on July 28, he returned to Bread Loaf and spoke informally "On Puritanism, Darwin, Marx, Freud, and Einstein." It is noteworthy that he placed Puritanism at the head of these seminal modern thinkers. To those who had the common conventional view of Puritanism, Frost's reflections were undoubtedly a shock.

He first noted that for many years he had thought of the pagan Puritanism of the ancient Greeks and Romans: "Everything about Diana and Minerva had something to do with chastity and all that—and restraint." He remarked that among English poets "the mockery of Chaucer" and "the severity of Langland" were early indications of the rise of modern

Puritanism, which culminated in the sixteenth-century religious explosion of the Protestant Reformation. Milton was to Frost "the great poet of Puritanism," and his "Comus" was the perfect example of a Puritan poem. In politics, Frost contrasted two American presidents in relation to Puritanism: "There were no checks in [Franklin D.] Roosevelt," because "he would have taken the presidency as many times as you would give it to him, in contradiction to George Washington who had checks within himself." Among contemporaries whom he knew personally, Frost designated as "a very puritanical lady" the American Catholic poet Louise Imogene Guiney; the Supreme Court Justice Benjamin Cardozo; the humanist Irving Babbitt; and a Catholic reporter on the *Boston Post*, whom he characterized, as "one of the most learned people, with his Irish wit . . . an old Puritan" who liked to quote Saint Thomas Aquinas's aphorism: "The virtue of all virtues is prudence."

Frost then recalled that in "Comus" Milton "talks like a Socialist . . . that's a kind of Puritanism," and therefore, he contended, "Marx is a Puritan, Karl Marx." If the Protestant Reformation was an Augustinian Puritan revolt, so too, Frost believed, was its Catholic counterpart: "Another thing . . . the Puritans gave us is the great counterrevolution—Loyola and all that. . . . " By logical extension through history, he concluded: "We all may go back to the Roman church in the end. I'm not saying we won't. The tremendous blow Puritanism struck over three or four or five hundred years there in history—that'll be forgotten. . . . Sometimes when I don't think I know any good Puritans in the Protestant church I go see my Catholic Puritans, and they're there." More and more during the 1940s and 1950s, Frost came to believe that among his contemporaries religious Jews and Roman Catholics were far more likely to be Puritans than were Protestants.[49]

Instead of perceiving Puritanism as Frost did, in the ancient pagan Greek and Roman mythology and in Judaism and the whole tradition of Augustinian Catholic and Protestant Christianity, the critics of New England Puritanism "get it all narrowed down to a certain kind of people that came late to America. . . . Plymouth Rock People and the Mayflower people . . . " These narrow-minded critics, lacking in historical and theological perspective, "like to talk about witchcraft and Salem."[50] They ignore the transformations of Calvinism, of "puritanism bursting through its age-long repressions,"[51] the "puritanism [that] didn't repent [but] relented a little and became Unitarianism."[52] As a consequence, such prejudiced critics ignored the vital intellectual, political, and cultural achievements of the best among New England Puritans.

Frost liked to remind his listeners that New England Congregational Puritans were the first to establish many of the academies and universities in America—not only Harvard and Yale, but such excellent colleges as Amherst, Williams, Dartmouth, Bowdoin, Middlebury, and many other schools scattered around New England. These colleges provided the models for American education. Frost noted that "the Puritan movement . . . scattered teachers . . . all over the United States."[53] Puritans were also pioneers in women's education, founding Mt. Holyoke, Smith, and Vassar. Compared with any other city, Frost observed, Boston was "where there were more college-educated people," and New England "was the most collegiate community the world ever saw."[54] Although the primary purpose of the men's colleges initially was to educate their clergy, they admitted the laity, and the curriculum always included not only biblical studies but the extensive requirements in the whole European cultural tradition comprehended by the medieval quadrivium and trivium, albeit purged of its Catholicism. In the Puritan educational system, the liberal arts and humanities, including science, were well preserved and much honored. Puritan education enhanced the cultural life of America, and it thereby made possible the evolutionary development of civil society, contributing in the process to Frost's conception of creative evolution.

Frost was well aware that after America achieved its independence, in the early decades of the American republic, as the course of empire moved westward, the New England Puritan "ideals" that "will bear some keeping still about" mentioned in his poem "The Generations of Men" were diffused throughout the Midwest. Frost knew that when Connecticut became a state in 1786, its leaders had retained a legal claim to the area on the south shore of Lake Erie around Cleveland, Ohio, which they called "the Western Reserve." He also remembered that during several decades before 1825, Congregational pioneers from Connecticut had migrated "in ox-drawn, canvas-covered wagons" over the route marked by the Erie Canal and settled in that area. As John F. Fulton, a biographer of one of their most famous descendants wrote: "Here in the Western Reserve they had finally established what was said to be the largest, strongest, and most characteristic single, compact colony in the West, the last distinct footprint of Puritanism."[55] Frost regarded these pioneers as the early forerunners of those who migrated westward before and after the Civil War. Imbued with this acute sense of American history, Frost began his sustained public attacks on those who, like Santayana, had traduced the whole New England Puritan cultural tradition.

Within a year after Santayana's *The Last Puritan* (1936), on June 8, 1937, Frost delivered the commencement address at Oberlin College, entitled "What Became of New England?" He deliberately chose that school as the place to inaugurate his plan because it had been founded by descendants of New England Puritans. He opened his address with the thematic contention that New England had diffused its "ideals" in education, politics, and culture throughout America: "Friends, graduating class of 1937 and New England—once removed, perhaps, as Western Reserve; twice removed, from Wisconsin; four times removed, like me, from California—but New England."[56] He first disposed of those critics who had described New England as "a decadent and lost society." He noted that as early as 1913 it had "cost me some pain" that critics of *North of Boston* had praised the book for his skill in picturing that region in decline.[57] He objected to Ford Madox Ford's reference to New England independent farmers as a "peasantry" that had "dried up and blown away in three hundred years." Conversely, he praised Van Wyck Brooks's *The Flowering of New England*, except for "a slight suggestion of the Spengler history—indication of decline." Clearly, Frost was painfully aware that many others besides Santayana had a highly negative understanding of New England Puritanism.

One of the major themes in Frost's important address was the vital contribution of New England to the future social and political development of the United States as a constitutional democracy: "What was New England? It was the first little nation that bade fair to be an English speaking nation on this continent . . . with its capital at Boston." He noted that "people in Virginia remarked the rapid development of the little nation there. . . . The little nation that was and was to be gave itself, as Virginia gave herself, westward, into the great nation that she saw coming, and so gave help to America." Long before New York became the chief channel for European migrants to the United States, Frost observed, "New England . . . was the port of entry of our freedom." Regardless of their exclusive theology and conscious religious intention, the Puritans were to Frost part of the large unfolding historical design that ultimately produced in the United States a social and political nation of disparate peoples.

The Calvinist religious "covenant of grace," based upon a fixed compact between the Puritans and God, could not long be restricted to those who regarded themselves as "God's elect." With each new wave of immigrants, the original vision of an Edenic world recovered, an earthly paradise, a "new Jerusalem," a shining city on a hill, yielded increasingly to the idea of an open society, wherein the monolithic Augustinian concept of the city of God was transformed into the multiple secular city of man. In time, the Calvinist theocracy evolved into the expanded and secularized "Commonwealth of Massachusetts," based upon a social contract theory that anticipated the postrevolutionary constitutional democracy of the United States. Thus the New England social covenant of a common citizenship of free men changed American social relationships from the medieval concept of fixed status within a hierarchical system into the open status of voluntary contractualism of free individuals with equal civil and legal rights under constitutional law.[58] As all this makes clear, New England was to Frost not merely a geographical region, but a capacious metaphor to live by, an evolving way of American life, in which the Puritan virtues of faith and courage provided the principles, beliefs, and disciplined actions that helped to create a great new nation.[59] The creation and expansion of a just and free civil-social order was a crucial element in Frost's conception of creative evolution.

In saying that like New England, "Virginia gave herself, westward," the very language of Frost's Oberlin College address anticipated his poem "The Gift Outright," which he called his history of the United States in sixteen lines. The shift from a dependent English settlement and colony to an independent American nation, filled with the promise of a great historical destiny, reached its climax in the final lines of that poem:

> *Such as we were we gave ourselves outright*
> *(The deed of gift was many deeds of war)*
> *To the land vaguely realizing westward,*
> *But still unstoried, artless, unenhanced,*
> *Such as she was, such as she would become.*

New England Puritanism provided not only the westward direction of national expansion; its work ethic also helped to shape the cultural character of the American people. In addition, it gave Frost his own political orientation regarding the conflicting claims to legal sovereignty advanced by a regional and central authority. The structure and traditions of the Congregational Church, with its sovereignty vested in the local parish, provided him with the model for his social individualism and for his conception of a geographical, democratic, political sovereignty centered in "states rights," as opposed to a wholly dominant centralized and hierarchical federal authority.

In his Oberlin College address, moreover, Frost assailed those critics who attacked New England Puritanism as deficient in aesthetic sensibility. He complained that "they want to rob the Puritans of art." But "there was Boston," with its simple but "beautiful architecture," and he noted that although the Puritans didn't have a theatre, they did not "mind a play if it was in a book—Cotton Mather had one of the first folios of Shakespeare—and you could read a play in Boston." Moreover, in the domestic arts, "there were ten silversmiths in Boston before there was a single lawyer."[60] But the poet's strongest defense of the Puritans was his recognition of their achievements in literature. At Bread Loaf, Frost noted that from the colonial beginnings to the modern era the list of Puritan writers reads like a roster of America's greatest writers: Anne Bradstreet, Michael Wigglesworth, Philip Freneau, during the early years, and Bryant, Barlow, Franklin, Emerson, Thoreau, Hawthorne, Longfellow, Melville, Whittier, Holmes, Lowell, and Dickinson. In addition to these giant figures from the past, there were such moderns as Robinson and Wallace Stevens, and a whole host of lesser known writers such as Sarah Orne Jewett and Mary Wilkins Freeman. Even an expatriate poet such as T. S. Eliot was in essence a New England Puritan. Clearly, these writers contributed heavily to the formation of America's high culture. Whereas Frederick Jackson Turner believed that "the wilderness masters the colonist," Frost contended that the Puritans transformed the moral and aesthetic character of the "unstoried" and "artless" western lands and "enhanced" them into the civil-social features characteristic of modern America.

One of the most significant interpretations Frost ever made was to link the creative power in literature and the arts with the Puritan modification and renewal of language. This vital connection permeated his whole dualistic philosophy. It also was the basis of his conception of creative evolution, and as such it underscored his criticism of Santayana's philosophy, especially that writer's severe strictures against New England Puritanism. At Oberlin he noted that "the whole function of poetry is the renewal of words, is the making of words mean again what they meant." Later in his address, he connected this statement with the whole Puritan tradition:

And the thing New England gave most to America was the thing I am talking about: a stubborn clinging to meaning; to purify words until they meant again what they should mean. Puritan-

ism had that meaning entirely: a purifying of words and a renewal of words and a renewal of meaning. That's what brought
them to America and that's what kept them believing. . . . They
saw there was a meaning that was not elusive.[61]

The Puritan "renewal of words" and "renewal of meaning" through language is at the aesthetic core of Frost's entire literary enterprise in forming
his plain colloquial style in both poetry and prose. It also constitutes the
pith of his belief in creative evolution as the primary force in the development of civilization. Puritanism provides the nexus between ethics as a
check upon the will and the passions and aesthetic creativity in providing
form in both art and the structured order of civil society.

In Frost's poem "The Generations of Men," the young speakers imagi-
natively "consult the voices" of their Puritan ancestors, and regarding their
great-grandmother Stark, the man recalls that "Folks in her day were given
to plain speaking." This construal of the simplicity, directness, and con-
creteness of Puritan language touches what both Frost and Perry Miller
regarded as perhaps the most important moral and intellectual trait of the
earliest English Puritans. In their religious rebellion against the elaborate
liturgical forms of worship purveyed by Rome and Canterbury, their passion for "plain speaking" based in Scripture characterized their sermons.
Miller devoted an entire chapter to "The Plain Style" of the Puritans, explaining that "for three or four decades before the settlement of New England" the syntax and plain style of Puritan preachers was "prominent in
the intellectual inheritance of New Englanders."[62] Following his English
models, Increase Mather's "low style" and "naked simplicity" in preaching set a standard for many Congregational sermons. Frost's defense of
the linguistic originality in the work of New England Puritans is perhaps
best appreciated when perceived historically, as part of the revolution in
the English prose style achieved by their scientists in the early decades of
the seventeenth century. Thomas Sprat showed in his *History of the Royal
Society* (1667) that the Puritan members of this scientific community were
instrumental in establishing the plain style as the proper vehicle for scientific discourse.[63] Charles Darwin was wholly in the Puritan tradition in
writing his scientific works.

In light of the poet's defense of this linguistic originality, his strong criticism of Santayana at Oberlin takes on enormous significance. It provides a
means of understanding his conception of creative evolution. Frost believed
that Santayana's extremely harsh criticism of both New England Puritanism
and America was based upon his misunderstanding of the original and full

meaning of words. Such phrases as "all men are created free and equal," "a God-fearing man," "divine right," and so on, were treated obtusely by the philosopher; his materialism and rationalism gave him only a superficial and literal-minded discernment of language as a vehicle for comprehending these ideas. It is small wonder that Thompson recorded that Frost said repeatedly that "Santayana is the enemy of my spirit."[64] In 1937 at Oberlin, Frost recalled his first encounter with him almost forty years earlier:

> In 1897 I was sitting in a class in college when I heard a man spend quite the part of an hour making fun of the expression that we were all free and equal. So easy to dismiss.... You can get out a theory that meanings go out of things, you can call it disillusionment. You can get disillusionment of a phrase such as fearing God and equality. And then you can form a religion like George Santayana. He lets you see that there is nothing but illusion, and it can be just as well one kind as another. There is illusion that you are unconscious of, and there is illusion that you become conscious of later.... But you should go right on anyway because there's no proof, all is illusion.... You grow to be a sad person....[65]

Frost concluded his criticism by noting in regard to such heterogeneous subjects as witchcraft, modern industrialism, and the New Deal that "you can make it all illusion with a little help of Santayana. He says right out in his philosophy that there are two kinds of illusion, two kinds of madness: one is normal madness, and the other is abnormal madness."[66] Frost's appreciation of the great irony in Santayana's thought was unique: he alone saw that the philosopher's exaltation of reason and his insistence on the sole reality of matter ended in the woeful sadness of complete illusion, whereas the Puritanism that he so savagely criticized provided a constant renewal of meaning through language in the creative and evolving life of American civil society.

In general, scholars and literary critics have ignored the vital role of Puritanism in Frost's aesthetic theory, in his practice as a poet, and in his conception of creative evolution. He believed that two important elements were necessary for a poet's creativity to produce successful and enduring art. One of these was bold emotion—the passion to "set us on fire" and "set us revolving,"[67] a wild and sensuous Dionysian frenzy that energizes a poet's sensibility, consciousness, memory, and fictional imagination. But in itself such a Rousseauistic discharge of raw impulses and feelings is not enough to produce durable poetry. As Frost objected: "There is no greater fallacy going than that art is expression."[68] A true poet knows how to make his emotions "jet at one outlet only," so that his images and metaphors are compressed and remain focused on his theme and do not "ooze off" and become "turned loose in exclamations." Frost called such raw emotions "sunset raving." In his notebooks he recorded: "Creation is the boldness. How to be with caution bold is the problem."[69] Clearly, the second essential element in creativity involved the Puritan virtue of self-restraint in all its aspects. These included the poet's belief in himself and his art, and his prudence, caution, disciplined will, and courage, which controlled and directed his emotions through "the prism of the intellect." Thus the fusion of mind and passion in Frost's aesthetic theory and conception of creativity was summarized in his phrase *mens animi*. He thought it fitting in the mythology of the ancients that Apollo, not Dionysus, was the god of poetry.

The social, ethical, and aesthetic self-restraint that provided the Apollonian qualities in Frost's Puritan conception of creativity, both in poetry and in the evolution of man in society throughout recorded history, derived from both ancient classical and epic literature and Scripture. To Frost, the perfect example of a Puritan poet who exemplified his conception of creativity was John Milton. He possessed the moral, intellectual, and aesthetic virtues at their fullest development. His courage in overcoming his blindness, his erudition, his serene self-confidence, and his mastery of his craft transformed the chaotic elements in nature and human affairs into the abiding forms of his poetry, thereby enabling him to create the greatest epic in the English language.

In a letter to G. R. Elliott (April 22, 1947), Frost defined his own particular Puritan tradition. He noted that his "approach to the New Testament is rather through Jerewsalem [sic] than through Rome and Canterbury." Thompson's chapter on Frost's Puritanism, "Yes I Suppose I Am a Puritan," is too rooted in the conventional misconceptions of that religio-cultural tradition, too literal-minded in its exposition, too monistic in its philosophical orientation, and too isolated from both the poet's aesthetic theory and his practice. Like many literary critics who follow him, Thompson displays no awareness of the relationship between Frost's Puritanism and his conception of creative evolution.

In 1959, during the symposium on "The Future of Man," in strong opposition to Sir Julian Huxley's belief that changes in the human species were "more or less accidental," Frost contended that the mechanism of evolutionary changes in man, "the best guide of all," is "passionate preference."[70] A few months later, on May 5, 1960, during a Senate hearing in Washington, D.C., when he testified in favor of a proposal to establish a national academy of culture, Frost reiterated his thesis of how mankind has "come up" through evolutionary changes: "I think it's passionate preference. Passionate preference. It's done in all ways—in the arts more than anywhere else."[71] For Frost, the connection between aesthetic production and creative evolution as a vital instrument in human culture included but transcended Darwin's mechanism of change through natural selection. Passionate preference was Frost's chief principle of natural selection. Creative evolution was man's "best guide upward" and included for Frost the initial intention, purpose, and design of God or nature in the universe. His ultimate rebuttal of Sir Julian Huxley is in his poem "Accidentally on Purpose," particularly in the concluding lines:

> *Grant me intention, purpose, and design—*
> *That's near enough for me to the Divine.*
>
> *And yet for all this help of head and brain*
> *How happily instinctive we remain,*
> *Our best guide upward further to the light,*
> *Passionate preference such as love at sight.*

Thus Frost made central to evolutionary changes in man the very aesthetic principle of creativity most lacking in Darwin's theory.

At first sight Frost's appeal to "passionate preference" may seem the equivalent in his conception of evolution to Darwin's strong case for "sexual selection" in the fourth chapter of *The Descent of Man* (1871). Both are in their respective contexts the essential but not exclusive mechanism of evolutionary changes in man. But Darwin's "sexual selection" is wholly based upon biology, whereas Frost identified his principle as "that inexorable thing in us, Biblical thing . . . passionate preference for something we can't help wishing were so." The poet's principle derives from the scriptural injunction for man to "increase and multiply." It involves the profound difference between primitive man's biological lust in a state of nature and historical man's social, moral, and religious conception of love in a divinely ordained institution of marriage. As Frost noted in his "Letter to *The Amherst Student*," his creative evolution transcends Darwin's adaptive principle of a mechanistic natural selection: "In us nature reaches its height of form and through us exceeds itself."[72] Frost's creative evolution goes beyond the scientific explanation of man as a biological creature composed solely of matter; it also includes the aesthetic and religious dimension of man as a creature that possesses spirit.

On several other occasions, Frost confirmed his belief that creative evolution includes far more than can be explained by Darwin's naturalistic theory. The practical concerns and life of man within an historically developed complex society were far more in harmony with the poet's conception of creative evolution than they were with a theory centered wholly in a primitive pre-civil state of nature. Considered metaphorically, both conceptions of evolution provided basic myths by which mankind could live. On March 10, 1961, during an interview with Earl Ubell for the *New York Herald Tribune*, the poet acknowledged his great "attraction to science" and once more repeated his boyhood witticism regarding evolution: "God made man out of prepared mud." Ubell then recorded: "However, he prefers the myth to live by—the Garden of Eden, the fall of man. . . . He prefers it to live by, rather than the story of the descent from an albino monkey."[73] In March 1961, during his state-sponsored visit to Israel, Frost rejected some of the historical accounts by his Arab guide regarding places and events mentioned in the Bible, but then, according to Thompson, he declared: "At least, he said, they offered greater elevation and moral significance than the evolution myths created by Charles Darwin."[74] Frost's preference for the Biblical norms by which to live is expressed negatively in the concluding lines of his poem "The White-Tailed Hornet":

> *Our worship, humor, conscientiousness*
> *Went long since to the dogs under the table.*
> *And served us right for having instituted*
> *Downward comparisons. As long on earth*
> *As our comparisons were stoutly upward*
> *With gods and angels, we were men at least,*
> *But little lower than the gods and angels.*
> *But once comparisons were yielded downward,*
> *Once we began to see our images*
> *Reflected in the mud and even dust,*
> *'Twas disillusion upon disillusion,*
> *We were lost piecemeal to the animals,*
> *Like people thrown out to delay the wolves.*
> *Nothing but fallibility was left us,*
> *And this day's work made even that seem doubtful.*

Frost believed that, along with the heroic tales of epic literature, the biblical account of man's epic story came much closer to the daily life of man, and the record of human experience throughout history, than Darwin's biological account of man in his theory of evolution.

But Frost's creative evolution did not reject Darwin's theory: rather, it supplied a supplementary exposition of how man continued to evolve throughout history, beyond biology. To the poet, art is man's nature, as well as biology. His conception of creative evolution represents the culmination of the long intellectual and cultural tradition that validates Perry Miller's observation that "Puritan theorists sought to unite in one harmonious system both science and religion, reason and faith."[75] This system also embraced many cognitive strains of Frost's total philosophy: his dualism of spirit and matter; his faith in metaphorical thinking; his belief that science is merely one of the humanities and not a separate and self-sufficient subject; his conviction that human nature differs qualitatively from all other forms of animal life in kind, not merely in degree; and, finally, his concept of creative evolution including the constant "renewal of language" and "renewal of meaning," which he identifies with his original notion of Puritanism as a basic element in man's power to produce both art and civilization.

# 6

## *Frost and Lovejoy's*
## *The Great Chain of Being*

In 1933, Arthur O. Lovejoy delivered the William James Lectures at Harvard University, which were published as *The Great Chain of Being* in 1936. Soon after the book appeared, Reginald L. Cook, a very close friend of Robert Frost's, recorded a talk with the poet: "Not only a one-way talker, Frost was an interested inquirer and a patient listener. He would ask what I thought of St. John Perse's *Seamarks*—I hadn't read it—or Arthur O. Lovejoy's *The Great Chain of Being*, which I had read."[1] Like Frost, Cook believed that "Lovejoy's seminal book" was a masterpiece of scholarship in the history of ideas, and they discussed it at length, along with Lovejoy's earlier book, *The Revolt Against Dualism* (1930).

As a result of their lengthy conversations on these books, Cook voiced one of the most sweeping and profound statements that any literary critic or scholar has ever made on the beliefs and art of Frost: "The route through the poetry of Robert Frost leads . . . away from the Great Chain of Being to an exercise of options in an 'open-ended universe.'"[2] This statement encompasses the most essential philosophical and scientific beliefs Frost held regarding the views of the physical universe and external nature described by important thinkers during more than three centuries. It includes the poet's view of the dominant metaphor of the Enlightenment, the great chain of being, and the conception of knowledge which provided its basis, in relation to his dualism. Lovejoy's *The Great Chain of Being*, together with *The Revolt Against Dualism*, describes and analyzes the conflicts between the two types of monism and the "natural dualism" he adhered to in common with the poet, from the time of Descartes (1596–1650) to the era of Einstein (1879–1955). Thus Lovejoy's two books, and Frost's responses to them, clarify the precise nature of the poet's dualism within a complex historical context and help to define his world view and conception of physical nature within the frame provided by Einstein's theory of relativity and the concept of an open-ended universe.

But before launching into this complex comparative account of the philosophical beliefs of Frost and Lovejoy, it is useful to note how the poet regarded scholarship in comparison with poetry and to note the similarities and differences in the educational background and intellectual orientation of the two men. One of the most common and serious misconceptions of some literary critics and scholars is the assumption that because Frost was a poet and not a professional scholar, he was therefore indifferent or even hostile to serious research. He certainly had a low opinion of bad scholarship, the kind of "busy-work" that produced many worthless doctoral theses. During a lecture at Middlebury College, however, on May 27, 1936, Frost said: "Now the great scholarship . . . I venerate it."[3] Eighteen years later at Bread Loaf (July 5, 1954), he repeated and emphasized this assertion: "Now the great, great, greatest scholarship—the greatest scholarship I venerate."[4] On another occasion, he said: "histories are my favorite," especially when they are "true to ideas or to human nature."[5] Scholarship like that of Lovejoy, that articulated the history of ideas, appealed particularly to him because it combined history and philosophy. According to Cook, Frost admired the epic sweep of Lovejoy's two books because they described the dynamics in the scientific and philosophical beliefs of important European and American thinkers from before Descartes to the first three decades of the twentieth century.

Although Frost admired truly significant scholarship, he distinguished sharply between how scholars and poets acquired their knowledge:

> Scholars and artists thrown together are often annoyed at the puzzle of where they differ. Both work from knowledge; but I suspect they differ most importantly in the way their knowledge is come by. Scholars get theirs with conscientious thoroughness along projected lines of logic; poets theirs cavalierly and as it happens in and out of books. They stick to nothing deliberately, but let what will stick to them like burrs where they walk in the fields. No acquirement is on assignment, or even self-assignment. Knowledge of the second kind is much more available in the wild free ways of wit and art.[6]

The differences cited by Frost are clearly evident in any comparison of Lovejoy's scholarship with the poet's beliefs and art, particularly in how they present their thematic ideas. In formulating his arguments about dualism and monism, Lovejoy's scholarship is relentlessly thorough, detailed, logical, analytical, and sometimes even systematic. Yet despite the technical and closely argued language of academic scholarship, his thesis is readily comprehended. The language and method in Frost's poetry and prose is starkly antithetical, far more colloquial, simple, and indirect; his metaphorical ways of thinking in "the wild free ways of wit and art" are a world removed from the logical exposition of Lovejoy. It requires both taste and judgment, and a gift in the imaginative interpretation of the poet's symbols, to deal well with such different methods. In his prose essays and letters, Frost's beliefs are more easily understood. But even in prose his ideas are never systematically developed; they remain isolated and scattered among many unrelated works. These differences make for certain difficulties in comparing Frost and Lovejoy, but they are not insurmountable problems to perceiving their respective philosophical beliefs. Lovejoy was rare among scholars because he was not primarily a rationalist; he considered the entire psychological and aesthetic nature of man, which included the role of basic emotions.

The apparent gap between the scholar and the poet is somewhat narrowed by comparing affinities in their education and family background. Arthur O. Lovejoy (1873–1962) was born five months before Robert Frost (1874–1963), and the poet survived the scholar by fewer than two months, so that they were almost exact contemporaries. Both men had European mothers and American fathers. At an early age they both revealed a deep strain of self-reliance and originality, and a characteristic intellectual independence by emancipating themselves to a great degree from the institutional religions of their families—Lovejoy from the Episcopal Church and Frost from the Congregational Church of his father's family. Yet they both retained a deep sense of piety and a lifelong reverence toward their respective religious inheritances. Lovejoy entered Harvard in the autumn of 1895, as a graduate student in philosophy; Frost in the autumn of 1897, as a special student, but with a decided interest in philosophy. This was the "golden age" of the department of philosophy at Harvard, which boasted such outstanding teachers and thinkers as William James, Josiah Royce, George Santayana, George Herbert Palmer, and Hugo Munsterberg. Although Lovejoy and Frost were almost exact contemporaries at Harvard and studied with the same teachers, the scholar went to Paris in the autumn of 1898 to study comparative religion, whereas the poet abandoned his studies at the university on March 31, 1899. There is no record that they knew each other as students.

Both students came under the spell of William James, and although they venerated the memory of their teacher, as individuals they were both so self-reliant and original that they never became his slavish disciples. Lovejoy knew his mentor well, both as a teacher and a writer, but Frost never had a course with the philosopher and knew him only as a writer. His profound influence on their general patterns of thought endured throughout their lives. He attracted Frost and Lovejoy because he was the first American academic philosopher to explore the close and complex relationships between philosophy and psychology. His writings, centered in the whole human psyche, involved not only abstract reason and logic, but the basic human emotions, desires, consciousness, will, memory, and retrospection. James pioneered research on the differences between subject and object; the distinctions between the knower and the known; in short, between mind or spirit and matter. He is most often thought of as a pragmatist and a relativist who rejected abstract absolutes and systematic theory, and both Lovejoy and Frost perceived him as essentially an epistemological dualist. But his dualism was infused with psychology and a common-sense theory of knowledge based largely upon memory, retrospection, and past empirical experiences; it was wholly distinct from the initial methodological doubt, mathematical logic, and abstract reasoning of René Descartes' philosophy, which has often been categorized as a form of dualism.

Whether from their Harvard education or quite independent of it, Lovejoy and Frost both came to look with profound skepticism at the whole tradition of Platonic idealism in Western thought. That tradition included the various other modified modern forms of idealism, such as the subjectivism of George Berkeley and the optimism of Emerson and the New England Transcendentalists, who largely rejected the reality of evil and human tragedy within their monist philosophy. Josiah Royce championed the Platonic tradition at the Harvard of Lovejoy and Frost, and he expressed his idealistic monism in his view of the absolute unity in Nature in his celebrated aphorism: "The One is in all, and all are in the One." The pluralistic philosophy of William James stood in sharp contrast to the Platonic stance of Royce, and both Frost and Lovejoy, each in his own way, were in basic agreement with him. Their acceptance of his concept of "the will to believe" was a vital element in their highly individualistic view of reality as pluralistic and in their conception of "truth" not as a fixed abstract absolute, but as rooted in principles combined with concrete experiences that included changes in the human condition throughout history. When considered within the framework of the medieval theological conflict between realists and nominalists, both Lovejoy and Frost may be counted in the nominalist camp.

To Lovejoy, James's pragmatism was not a single absolute system or unified philosophy, but a series of protean propositions. In 1908, Lovejoy published *The Thirteen Pragmatisms*, which he called "a baker's dozen of contentions"; therein he discriminated between the many subtle shades of qualified beliefs in his mentor's unsystematic philosophy. Like James, he distinguished between what is regarded as rationally valid or "true" and what is believed on faith. He held that meaning may attach as much to what is believed as to what is factually or empirically true. The question of belief, therefore, is independent of the kind of empirical and analytical verification demanded by atheists and rational agnostics as proof of a proposition, or hypothesis, or theory.

There is no way to verify whether Frost's similar responses to James's pragmatism resulted from reading the philosopher himself, or from studying Lovejoy's *The Thirteen Pragmatisms*; conceivably, he may have arrived at the same conviction regarding empirical truth and belief on faith on his own initiative. But there is no question that Frost was of one mind with James and Lovejoy in assuming that beliefs may flourish in the midst of truths that change over long periods of time. In his poem "The Black Cottage," written at about the same time that Lovejoy published *The Thirteen Pragmatisms*, he expressed the same contention regarding truth and belief:

> *For, dear me, why abandon a belief*
> *Merely because it ceases to be true.*
> *Cling to it long enough, and not a doubt*
> *It will turn true again, for so it goes.*
> *Most of the change we think we see in life*
> *Is due to truths being in and out of favor.*

In addition to their agreement with James on the relativity of truth, both Lovejoy and Frost recognized that his pluralism needed some unifying factor, so that human existence is not reduced to unrelated brute empirical facts in a chaotic universe. They both preferred the word "dualism" to James's "pluralism," because it provided a recognizable frame of reference in mind or spirit as contrasted with matter, thereby encompassing all of reality. Dualism retained a sense of order that avoided both the chaos of pluralism and the dogmatic absolutism of either form of monism.

The dualism of both Lovejoy and Frost included a theism that perceived human nature as qualitatively different from noncognitive forms of animal life and as capable of unique power and freedom in creativity. Lovejoy's first teacher in philosophy, George Holmes Howison, at the University of California, Berkeley, had summarized the basic connection between belief in God and creativity: "the created, as well as the creator, creates."[7] This belief involved truths as revelation. Frost's God-given revelations were expressed in his belief in "the truths we keep coming back and back to," as well as in the God-like power of man's artistic creativity. James also very likely contributed much to the similar beliefs of Frost and Lovejoy regarding the moral nature of man. Because of their theism and their belief in man's power of will and cognition and in aesthetic creativity, Frost and Lovejoy assumed that human nature was qualitatively superior in spirit or mind to all other forms of animal life, regardless of any similarities in their genetics and biological development.

In strong contrast to their convictions on the qualitative superiority of human nature to other forms of animal life were such behavioral psychologists as J. B. Watson and B. F. Skinner, to whom biology and mechanistic physical nature were all in all. They assumed that evolution from a common ancestor made all species of animals only quantitatively different in degree, but not in kind. Their experiments in conditioned behavioral responses to external stimuli were criticized by both Lovejoy and Frost, who did not believe that human behavior could be reduced to a purely mechanistic and deterministic explanation without destroying what was uniquely human in a species of life. Frost expressed his strong objection to such experiments on several occasions, and Lovejoy did likewise, criticizing the assumption that nonhuman, mechanistic processes of thought and knowledge could be validly equated with those of mankind: "One of the most curious developments in the entire history of thought is the invention in our day of what may best be named the Hypodermic Philosophy—the doctrine, resulting from the application to a cognitive animal of the biological concepts found sufficient in the study of animals assumed to be noncognitive, that the organic phenomenon of knowing may be exhaustively described in terms of molecular displacements taking place under the skin."[8] Later, he refined upon this criticism of behaviorism in discussing Bertrand Russell's monism, which was then centered in matter and applied to the thought processes of human nature: "As a variety of the Hyperdermic Philosophy, it is necessarily incapable of giving any account of the distinctive peculiarity of the biological phenomenon of knowing—i.e., of the ability of the cognitive animal in some sense to reach outside his skin."⁹ Both Lovejoy and Frost regarded thinking as a creative act, which was reflected in the moral, intellectual, and aesthetic nature of individuals and also in the social institutions of human nature.

Perhaps the most explicit affinity in the beliefs of Frost and Lovejoy was their strong agreement with the thesis William James expounded in his essay "The Ph.D. Octopus" in *Harvard Monthly* (March 1903). In this work, James objected vigorously to the German tradition of scholarship introduced through Thomas Henry Huxley's influence at The Johns Hopkins University, which resulted in "the increasing hold of the Ph.D. Octopus upon American life." The focus of James's attack was the extension of the scientific method as employed in the physical sciences to graduate school studies in the humanities, culminating in the doctoral degree. He objected to making it the requirement for teaching in a college or university. He noted that the formal requirements for the degree diverted "the attention of aspiring youth from dealing directly with truth to the passing of examinations." Moreover, he held that intellectual brilliance and aesthetic originality in students were sacrificed in favor of adherence to the mechanical, predetermined requirements in programs of pseudoscientific research. To James, the degree was "a tyrannical machine with unforeseen powers of exclusion and corruption" in intellectual matters, which in turn fostered "academic corruption" in the university through "the prestige of certain privileged institutions." He foresaw that Ivy League snobbery would become widely imitated throughout the academy and would do great damage to individuals, whose failure to meet the requirements of the system was regarded as "a sentence of doom that they are not fit" and made many "broken-spirited men thereafter." The doctoral degree did not "guarantee that its possessor will be successful as a teacher" and "in reality it is but a sham, a bauble, a dodge, whereby to decorate the catalogues of schools and colleges." The implications of the subordination of the humanities to the physical sciences and technology manifested themselves throughout the rest of the twentieth century in the triumph of a utilitarian and materialist theory of education and a disastrous decline in the humanities.

When Lovejoy completed his master's degree at Harvard, his vision of freedom and talent in higher education, like that of William James, was centered in an aristocracy of talent that precluded earning a doctorate. When he was hired for his first teaching position, at Stanford University, and was asked why he lacked the degree, he responded: "I am personally very indifferent about it and regard it as unwise for a man to go at all out of the way of his own philosophical interests in order to conform to the requirements of this exercise."¹⁰ He held that truly great teachers do not need advanced degrees. In an essay, "William James as Philosopher," he praised his teacher's "large and ardent personality" and "richly endowed mind," contrasting those attributes to the rigidity of the "system builders."[11] Similarly, Frost believed that originality, initiative, and self-reliance were sufficient qualifications for good teachers: "The older teachers had large minds that reached right out into the clear." Upon this point Reginald L. Cook remarked: "He meant that they had not only intellectual but also spiritual bravery so that they could face the final terror of things."[12] A mastery of the humanities was the educational ideal of both Frost and Lovejoy, because they both believed that a university was a place where universal knowledge should be taught, not merely an instrument for specialized training in a profession.

Despite their common education in the ancient Greek and Roman classics, their common philosophical orientation in dualism and a common-sense perception of knowledge, and their shared views on abuses in higher education, in their respective lives as scholar and poet Lovejoy and Frost were quite different individuals. Although they each maintained a lifelong connection with university life, their differences in temperament were very evident in their respective attitudes toward academic life. Lovejoy was clearly far more comfortable than Frost as a university teacher. In a letter to Louis Untermeyer (May 9, 1936), the poet admitted his strong reservations about structured higher education: "I'm imperfectly academic and no amount of association with the academic will make me perfect." Their differences in temperament were also evident in their political views. They were both strong American patriots, albeit without jingoism, and although they both despised all forms of ideological speculation that justified totalitarian government and were both men of sentiment who disliked sentimentality, in the perennial social conflict between justice and mercy, Frost gave priority to justice to individuals, whereas Lovejoy favored mercy to the masses. This distinction in emphasis made Frost a liberal conservative highly critical of Franklin D. Roosevelt's "New Deal," while Lovejoy was a conservative liberal who supported that radical program. Finally, in their views of man's reason and science they differed; Lovejoy was less skeptical than Frost that the advantages claimed for modern science and technology would result in a higher quality of civilization.

These differences, and others, should not distract attention from the crucial importance of Lovejoy's *The Great Chain of Being* and *The Revolt Against Dualism* in giving substance to Reginald L. Cook's observation that "the route through the poetry of Robert Frost leads . . . away from the Great Chain of Being to an exercise of options in an open-ended universe." Since the poet's intellectual life and beliefs, expressed in both his poetry and prose, were enriched by Lovejoy's two masterpieces of scholarship, it is necessary to summarize the essential ideas that he absorbed from these seminal studies.

It is probably impossible to identify in depth all that Frost learned from his reading of Lovejoy's *The Great Chain of Being.* Prior to reading this book he, of course, knew much of what is commonly categorized as "the Enlightenment," for which "the great chain of being" is the dominant explanatory metaphor. To Lovejoy, the metaphor of God as the clock-maker of a universe as mechanistic as a timepiece was a subordinate element within the great chain of being. Before reading Lovejoy, the poet understood the Enlightenment not as a historian or philosopher, but in terms of important aspects of its thought and culture as revealed in English literature during the seventeenth and eighteenth centuries. He was well-read in the prose of these centuries, and he had retained in memory many poems or passages by such seventeenth-century poets as Donne, Ben Jonson, Shakespeare, Milton, Crashaw, Herbert, Waller, Vaughan, Marvell, Lovelace, Cowley, and Dryden; and such eighteenth-century poets as Pope, Young, Blair, Christopher Smart, Collins, Gray, Goldsmith, Burns, and Blake.[13] Many important aspects of the ideas discussed in Lovejoy's book are found in the work of these writers. But his systematic and historically rooted study presents the metaphor of the great chain of being largely in terms of how scientific perspectives and philosophical beliefs were understood throughout Europe by educated people. His book provided a vital supplement to Frost's own literary knowledge and understanding of this era. It illuminated how the poet's view of "Nature" perceived as the physical cosmos, and how man's place in the natural order, understood through discursive reason and mathematical logic, shaped important elements in Frost's mature philosophy of dualism.

Frost was well aware that the scientific, philosophical, and even cultural life of Europe during the seventeenth century was profoundly influenced by the impact of new discoveries and theories upon the inherited religious beliefs of many centuries. The work of Copernicus, Galileo, Francis Bacon, Descartes, and Isaac Newton, among many others, led many Europeans to modify or abandon much in the medieval worldview. The Enlightenment perceived the physical universe in a new light, as a divinely ordained great chain of being in which every species of life, including man, had its fixed place in a hierarchical order. The new cosmology proposed an orderly, stable, limited, deterministic system, governed by mechanistic natural laws which could be understood rationally far better than they could be through religious revelation.

But this gradual shift from a Ptolemaic to a Copernican view of the universe initially precipitated a very painful and emotionally traumatic religious conflict regarding the origin, nature, and destiny of man. The medieval belief that the earth was the center of the universe, that man was created in the spiritual image of God, though in a fallen state, and that faith in Christ could redeem believers from sin into eternal salvation—all this and more was clearly challenged by the new cosmology. As early as 1611, John Donne's poem "An Anatomie of the World" lamented how the improved science of astronomy had brought great disorder in the heavens and had introduced disturbing doubts and chaos into the spiritual lives of Europeans:

> *The Element of fire is quite put out;*
> *The Sun is lost, and th' earth, and no man's wit*
> *Can well direct him where to look for it,*
> *And freely men confesse that this world's spent,*
> *When in the Planets, and the Firmament*
> *They seeke so many new; they see that this*
> *Is crumbled out again to his atomies.*
> *'Tis all in pieces, all coherence gone*
> *All just supply, and all Relation. . . .*[14]

With "all coherence gone" out of the medieval world view of the physical universe, an upheaval of epic proportions was about to revolutionize mankind's view of itself in relation to the cosmic order. The centuries-long traditional doctrine of Christianity and the more ancient Jewish tradition, which taught that human nature was a duality of body and spirit, was subjected to intense scrutiny. Ironically, instead of emancipating man's mind and spirit, at first the revolutionary cosmology plunged him into deep despair by intensifying the belief that because of human pride and the fall from grace through original sin, which had led to the expulsion from Eden, the whole human race was sinking more and more into moral and physical depravity. Man as a corrupted microcosm reflected the increasing anarchy and corruption of the cosmic order as a macrocosm. This philosophy of despair largely persisted during the first three decades of the seventeenth century; thereafter, both the traditional religious beliefs which exalted man and the revolutionary forces of science opposed to it began to prevail.[15]

Within religion, traditional appeals to the mercy of God counteracted belief in universal natural depravity. Although the assumption that natural man, apart from sanctifying grace, is essentially depraved was by no means eradicated, it was greatly reduced, and both scientists and theologians contributed to the process of natural redemption. Francis Bacon's *Novum Organum* (1620) and *New Atlantis* (1626) criticized "the blind and immoderate zeal" of religious prophets of doom, and both books pointed the way to the possible temporal redemption of mankind. He rejected the habitual blind obedience to the authority of the ancients and pictured contemporary man as a dwarf standing on a giant's shoulders. The cultural war between the defenders of the ancient classics and religion against the modern champions of science and speculative philosophy, which self-consciously began in England in Bacon's time, was to extend itself far beyond the Enlightenment even into the twentieth century. Yet like many of his contemporaries, Bacon did not abandon the whole medieval worldview; he retained the belief that man is at the center of the world. Moreover, he advanced the popular thesis that everything on earth "works together in the service of man." To a large degree, the spirit of the Enlightenment in its domestic programs may be said to consciously begin with Bacon. Lovejoy was well aware of the great importance of Bacon:

> Scholasticism and its methods were, among those who plumed themselves on the "enlightenment," usually objects of contempt and ridicule. The faith in speculative a priori metaphysics was waning, and the Baconian temper (if not precisely the Baconian procedure), the spirit of patient empirical inquiry, continued its triumphant march in science, and was an object of fervent enthusiasm among a large part of the general educated public.[16]

The empirical and inductive "Baconian procedure" was soon largely displaced by the discursive rational logic and mathematical methodology of Descartes, and within a century after Donne's anguished lament in "An Anatomie of the World," the pessimism of his generation was replaced by the rational optimism of the Enlightenment within the cosmic order of the great chain of being.

Among the hundreds of works in prose and poetry which celebrated the great chain of being, none expressed the "enlightened" view of man and physical nature more perfectly than Alexander Pope's *Essay on Man* (1733–34). As a Roman Catholic, Pope retained belief in traditional ethical norms, and in his earlier poem "An Essay on Criticism," (1717), he had applied a normative conception of "Nature" to man's creativity and his aesthetic theories:

*First follow Nature, and your Judgment frame*
*By her just Standard, which is still the same;*
*Unerring Nature, still divinely bright,*
*One clear, unchang'd, and Universal Light,*
*Life, Force, and Beauty, must to all impart,*
*At once the Source, and End, and Test of art.*

In these lines, Nature is practically a synonym for God. In retaining normative principles regarding God and man, while accepting much in the Enlightenment program, Pope revealed the great ambiguity within the Enlightenment's view of the physical universe, an ambiguity shared by many of his contemporaries, even among the *philosophes.* Although the leading lights among those thinkers, such as Diderot and Voltaire, believed that in subjecting the whole inherited Christian civilization of Europe to rational criticism, they were preparing the way for a more "enlightened" civilization in the future, their religious and cultural roots in the past made them closer than they realized to the medieval Schoolmen, whom they despised. As Carl L. Becker noted, "The Philosophes demolished the Heavenly City of St. Augustine only to rebuild it with more up-to-date materials."[17] The new revolutionary order of the great chain of being could not wholly displace the ancient order and normative beliefs of the classical and Christian inheritance of Europe.

The revolutionary thinkers of the Enlightenment were not only conditioned by their cultural and religious inheritance, but they were also hedged in by, and had to function within, the frame of reference provided by the metaphor of the great chain of being. As Lovejoy put it, "For most men of science throughout this period, the theorems implicit in the conception of the Chain of Being continued to constitute essential presuppositions in the framing of scientific hypotheses."[18] How educated mankind perceives itself in any historical era, regarding its origins, nature, and destiny, is largely reflected in the dominant metaphors of its time. Thus the eighteenth century used the great chain of being, just as the last half of the nineteenth century and early twentieth century employed evolution as its central metaphor and the later twentieth century accustomed itself to acceptance of relativity and an open-ended universe. Lovejoy's *The Great Chain of Being* thus provided Frost with his original historical perspective on the complex intellectual changes that determined man's view of nature and the physical universe during the past three centuries.

In Pope's *Essay on Man,* the "vast chain of being, which from God began," was perceived as extending itself through a hierarchy of fixed gradations through all forms of life, including man and also to the whole physical order of nature in the universe: "All are but parts of one stupendous whole, / Whose body Nature is, and God the soul."[19] In this dualism within a cosmic monism, it was assumed that the wholly determined and fixed order of the physical universe applied as well to human nature within civil society: "The gen'ral order, since the whole began, / Is kept in Nature, and is kept in man."[20] The end result of this line of reasoning culminated in a crucial passage:

> All Nature is but Art, unknown to thee;
> All chance, Direction, which thou canst not see;
> All Discord, Harmony, not understood;
> All partial Evil, universal Good;
> And spite of Pride, in erring Reason's spite,
> One truth is clear, whatever is, is right.[21]

Writers as different from each other as Voltaire and Samuel Johnson took strong exception to such optimistic determinism, as did Lovejoy and Frost. The static and deterministic great chain meant that "whatever is, is right." As applied to human affairs, it meant that man's creativity in changing the social environment for the better was denied. If "all partial evil" was "universal good," then human suffering could not be mitigated. The great chain of being provided a shallow answer to the problem of evil.

Lovejoy also summarized how many Enlightenment writers such as Pope were ambiguous regarding mankind. They perceived a far too simple and supposedly rational conception of human nature in solving the great problems of civil society:

> Assuming human nature to be a simple thing, the Enlightenment also assumed political and social problems to be simple, and therefore easy of solution. Rid man's mind of a few ancient errors, purge his beliefs of the artificial complications of metaphysical 'systems' and theological dogmas, restore to his social relations something like the simplicity of the state of nature, and his natural excellence would, it was assumed, be realized, and mankind would live happily ever after.[22]

Such a passage probably provided Frost with some valuable insights regarding the optimistic illusions of revolutionary ideological theories in making drastic changes in society. Lovejoy's chapter "Romanticism and the Principle of Plenitude" revealed how the sensibility in literary Romanticism combined with the developing optimism generated by the advance of science to spread an optimistic growing belief in the natural goodness of man.[23] During the last half of the eighteenth century, the ancient "theological dogma" that natural man is essentially depraved was largely replaced by the opposite doctrine that man in a pre-civil "state of nature" or in simple primitive society was innately good. Primitivism, the logical extension of this belief, postulated that naturally good human beings become corrupted by the complexities and demands placed upon them by "artificial" institutions and oppressive social customs.

The enormous popularity of cultural primitivism during the last half of the eighteenth century became a vital element in the most radical aspects of Enlightenment revolutionary theories that attacked monarchy, aristocracy, and institutional religion in order to establish some form of natural or simple society. Pope had touched briefly on such cultural primitivism in *Essay on Man*, picturing "the poor Indian" seeking and finding an ideal state wholly apart from the corrupt behavior of men in the highly artificial society of Europe:

> Yet simple nature to his hope has given,
> Behind the cloud-topped hill, an humbler heaven;
> Some safer world in depth of woods embraced,
> Some happier island in the watery waste . . .
> Epistle I, 11.103–106

Later, Pope stated a basic belief of cultural primitivism, that "the state of nature was the reign of God":

> Pride then was not; nor arts, that pride to aid;
> Man walked with beast, joint tenant of the shade;
> Epistle III, 11.148 and 151–152

No one was better informed than Lovejoy on the long history of primitivist ideas from their crudest form among the ancient Greeks to Europe in the eighteenth century. Its basic premise was that there existed an antithesis between civilization, perceived as the source of man's corruption from natural goodness, and an idealized, fictional, pre-civil or simple state of nature. Together with George Boas, Lovejoy published a study of this whole complex phenomenon, *Primitivism and Related Ideas in Antiquity* (1935), in which he described, analyzed, and harshly criticized the irrational discontent of civilized persons who yearned to return to an idealized Eden-like primitive state wholly removed from civilized society.[24]

Although no written record exists that Frost read the studies on primitivism by Lovejoy and Boas, his philosophical dualism, his realistic view on the moral nature of man, and his belief in the redemptive power of organized civil society all indicate that his view of cultural primitivism was consonant with their thesis. What was said by Lovejoy, Boas, and their disciple Lois Whitney in hundreds of pages of profound scholarship on cultural primitivism was poured forth by Frost into a few highly concentrated lines of poetry. In one intense, satirical couplet, filled with calm, understated irony, amused scorn, and condescending contempt, he dismissed the mindless sentimentality that leads men to believe literally in the fictional illusions of a past golden age or idyllic primitive Utopian society. Even the title of his couplet, "An Answer" (1940), has a finality enough to wither the very concept of cultural primitivism: "But Islands of the Blessèd, bless you, son, / I never came upon a blessèd one." Frost was well aware that modern cultural primitivists did not restrict their yearning for a utopian simple society to a past lost Eden; he knew that they also looked for future perfection in human affairs through science, technological inventions, and "progressive" political ideologies.[25] Such primitivist theorists believed as revolutionaries that before mankind could be redeemed as perfected human beings, the long-established societies which were corrupt beyond redemption had to be destroyed. His well-known witticism that "the opposite of Utopia is not hell, but civilization" is clearly a satirical attack on cultural primitivism. In "A Case for Jefferson" (1936), Frost satirized a modern American progressive primitivist:

> *Harrison loves my country too,*
> *But wants it all made over new.*
> *He's Freudian Viennese by night.*
> *By day he's Marxian Muscovite.*
> *It isn't because he's Russian Jew,*
> *He's Puritan Yankee through and through.*
> *He dotes on Saturday pork and beans.*
> *But his mind is hardly out of his teens:*
> *With him the love of country means*
> *Blowing it all to smithereens*
> *And having it all made over new.*

To Frost, the social and political implications of cultural primitivism are elements in twentieth-century revolutionary and totalitarian systems.

Lovejoy's *The Great Chain of Being* enriched Frost's perception of the long history of primitivism so that he understood modern revolutionary systems and totalitarian ideologies within the historical context of earlier periods of history.

The concluding chapter of *The Great Chain of Being*, "The Outcome of the History and Its Moral," is an excellent summary of the weaknesses in Enlightenment rationalism:

> But the history of the idea of the Chain of Being—in so far as that idea presupposed such a complete rational intelligibility of the world—is the history of a failure; more precisely and more justly, it is the record of an experiment in thought carried on for many centuries by many great and lesser minds, which can now be seen to have had an instructive negative outcome. The experiment, taken as a whole, constitutes one of the most grandiose enterprises of the human intellect. But as the consequences of this most persistent and most comprehensive of hypotheses became more and more explicit, the more apparent became its difficulties; and when they are fully drawn out, they show the hypothesis of the absolute rationality of the cosmos to be unbelievable. . . . Rationality, when conceived as complete, as excluding all arbitrariness, becomes itself a kind of irrationality.[26]

The "static and constant" worldview of the great chain of being, based upon an unbounded confidence in discursive human reason, proved to be unsatisfactory. Lovejoy's account of this failure is in harmony with Frost's own lifelong skepticism about man's reason being sufficient to comprehend and solve the great problems in civil society and in the relationship of man's mind or spirit and matter regarding the physical universe. The common charge against Frost that he was "anti-intellectual" was invariably made by those who were still strong adherents to the rationalism of the Enlightenment.

Lovejoy's three late chapters "The Chain of Being and Some Aspects of Eighteenth-Century Biology," "The Temporalizing of the Chain of Being," and "Romanticism and the Principle of Plenitude" summarized the powerful forces that weakened and eventually destroyed "the hypothesis of the absolute rationality of the cosmos. . . ." The pre-Darwinian studies in biology, by J. B. Robinet, Charles Bonnet, and other French theorists, and by James Burnett (Lord Monboddo), Erasmus Darwin, and other British speculators in science, although crude and more dubious than scientific, expanded man's consciousness of time and the age of the earth by many thousands of years, far beyond the age provided in the Bible. Together with the study of fossils by geologists, these pre-Darwinian theories of evolution temporalized the chain of being and pointed toward the study of modern physics and the eventual perception of an open-ended universe. Moreover, the "sensibility" of literary Romanticism further challenged the abstract rational theories of the Enlightenment and was accompanied by the development of a revived Platonic idealistic monism, well expressed by Shelley in "Adonais": "The One remains, the many change and pass, / Heaven's light forever shines, earth's shadows fly. . . ." Such idealistic monism became a widespread belief throughout the nineteenth century, as was evident in the growth of Unitarianism and Emerson's New England Transcendentalism. This idealistic revolt against traditional dualism regarding good and evil ran parallel with a similar revolt, wholly on neutral grounds, generated by a scientific monism centered in matter. Faith in the great chain of being was finally largely extinguished by the combined influences of Romantic idealism, Darwin's theory of evolution, and Einstein's theory of relativity. These developments revolutionized modern man's view of the physical universe and his nature and destiny. Although Lovejoy's *The Revolt Against Dualism* was published before *The Great Chain of Being*, it is really a sequel to the later work. Subsequent discussions will explore the conflicts between dualism and the two monisms that occurred from the era of Descartes to Einstein; they will also clarify the precise nature of Frost's dualism by perceiving it within the historical context of these philosophical and scientific conflicts.

# 7

## *Frost and the Modern Revolt Against Dualism*

When Reginald L. Cook recorded that "Frost's relationship to time was non-Cartesian,"[1] he revealed that in his conversations with him about Lovejoy's *The Revolt Against Dualism* the poet had retained an essential theme in Lovejoy's study that pointed ahead to the modern open-ended conception of the universe, which followed Einstein's theory of relativity. Cook's statement also indicates that the precise nature of Frost's dualism stands in sharp contrast to the supposed dualism of René Descartes (1596–1650) and the whole tradition of the scientists and philosophers who adopted his metaphysics up to the modern era. Lovejoy's negative thesis was that the entire Cartesian strain of thought was in revolt against "natural dualism," sometimes in the name of dualism, but more often in confusion between a monism of matter and a monism of spirit that could not reconcile the mind-matter problem that Descartes had bequeathed to posterity.

But before examining Lovejoy's *The Revolt Against Dualism* and Frost's response to it, it is useful to refine upon Cook's observation and to note that Frost's conception of reason, as well as of time, "was non-Cartesian." To Descartes, man's reason was the power of abstract discursive logic, both inductive and deductive, pursued analytically according to geometrical analysis, a quantitative and deterministic type of reason most suitable for scientific argument or speculative theory in studies of physical nature. Frost believed that this type of scientific reason was valid regarding matter, but that it violated such non-material dimensions in human nature as were found in religion, the arts, and the humanities. For him the corporate life of man in civil society required qualitative rational norms in ethics and aesthetics, and in legal and political prescriptive principles so that anarchy could be prevented and social order could be maintained. He thought that the creative power in man, so evident in the enduring forms of art, far transcended Cartesian rationalism and that the reason and spirit of man included the will to believe, imagination, intuition, and the whole psychological and social nature of the individual beyond physical nature. Frost's definition of a poem as "a thought-felt thing" could not be encompassed by the rationalism of Descartes. Indeed, in Western civilization the spiritual qualities in human nature were held in such high esteem, as distinct from matter alone, that idealistic thinkers in the rational tradition of Plato, such as Berkeley, constructed a spiritual monism in opposition to Cartesian rationalism and a monism of matter. But as is evident throughout this study, Frost rejected both forms of monism and adhered throughout his adult life to a philosophical dualism.

To understand the precise nature of Frost's dualism, a reader could not do better than to compare his statements on "the two-ness of things" with Lovejoy's study of the conflicts between both forms of monism and "natural dualism" in *The Revolt Against Dualism*. The epical structure of his book covers the whole complex pattern of conflicting views of dualism and the two monisms, within an historical context of the past three centuries. Despite its complexity, its brilliant execution distinguishes clearly the brand of dualism held in common by Lovejoy and Frost from other metaphysical systems involving both monisms and dualism.

In his first long chapter, "Cartesian Dualism and Natural Dualism," Lovejoy plunges into the heart of his subject and theme, contrasting in great detail the so-called "dualism" of Descartes with what he calls "natural dualism." He identifies himself as "an unflappable dualist." Then for six chapters he appears to digress in descriptions and close analysis of the monistic and dualistic confusions of such thinkers as Descartes, Locke, Berkeley, Whitehead, and Bertrand Russell. Finally, in his last two chapters, Lovejoy returns to the theme of his first chapter, with a critique of the method of Descartes in his approach to the problem of knowledge. He indicates how the theory of knowledge in "natural dualism" is based upon the "common sense" of human experience, memory, and retrospection. In what follows emphasis will be placed upon Lovejoy's first and final two chapters, because they have the most direct and strongest bearing upon Frost's dualism and his theory of knowledge, which, as will become apparent, harmonizes with Einstein's theory of relativity and the modern conception of an open-ended universe.

In the preface to *The Revolt Against Dualism,* Lovejoy stated that his study was "an examination into the logical course of the debate over the two kinds of dualism," which he identified as "Cartesian Dualism and Natural Dualism." In philosophical terminology, natural dualism is called "epistemological dualism," and the Cartesian species is called "psychophysical dualism." The latter "conceives empirical reality to fall asunder into a world of mind and a world of matter mutually exclusive and utterly antithetical." Descartes thus created a "cleavage of the universe into two realms having almost no attributes in common," which amounted to a "divorce between experience and nature, the isolation of the mental from the physical order."[2] In effect, Descartes created not a dualism but two separate and irreconcilable monisms. It would be a grave error to identify Frost's dualism with Descartes' philosophy.

In sharp contrast to Descartes and the entire tradition among scientists and philosophers, the natural or epistemological dualism to which both Lovejoy and Frost adhered did not separate the realm of mind or spirit from that of matter and therefore avoided the supposed antithesis or contradiction between religion and human nature, on the one hand, and the physical sciences on the other hand. Frost's adherence to natural dualism thus clarifies why he did not perceive religion and science to contradict each other. His constant "play" of metaphors between spirit and matter, not only in his poetry but in every form of discourse, enabled him to perceive each realm in a close reciprocal relationship with the other, as different ways of explaining the same phenomena. Lovejoy noted that the important philosophical and historical conflicts precipitated (but not originated) by Descartes have persisted well into the twentieth century. The revolt against dualism "has been the attempt to escape from that double dualism." This whole problem of the relationship between mind or spirit and matter "has enlisted the greatest and most various philosophical talents" from Descartes to and beyond Einstein. Lovejoy's study is therefore essential for anyone who wishes to understand the precise philosophical orientation of Frost's dualism.

Lovejoy makes it clear that the ultimate conflict between his natural dualism and Descartes' so-called dualism originated in their radically different theories of knowledge and methodology. Unlike speculative rational philosophers such as Descartes, most people acquire their knowledge through ordinary "common sense" experience. From infancy to maturity, a person first witnesses external things, events, or other persons through his senses; the impressions he receives register in the mind and emotions as normal accumulated experiences, which eventually develop into habits in the unconscious mind. They reside there as unvoiced premises for future experiences. Through retrospection and social discourse and communication their experiences become rooted in memory, and this enables each individual to anticipate how to respond to future similar events or things or persons. Thus an individual's knowledge of the world and of himself grows by connecting past experiences with present awareness and possible future events. From such accumulated past experiences the memory of an individual does not allow him to approach each new experience as with a blank mind, but with some already assumed knowledge. A theory of knowledge based upon memory and retrospection on past experience is not restricted to direct and immediate sense perception, because it assumes a "theory of representative perception." According to Lovejoy, this is how "natural dualism" works in both theory and practice. Most people in their common-sense approach to knowledge are therefore natural or epistemological dualists. This goes far toward explaining why Frost's poetry resonates so directly with the common reader, while at the same time having philosophical dimensions and implications beyond ordinary human experience.

Far otherwise is the approach to knowledge of Descartes and speculative thinkers in the tradition of psychophysical dualism. Lovejoy contrasts their method with that of natural dualism:

> Philosophers . . . have begun by provisionally assuming that they know nothing whatever except the passing immediate datum, and have then sought to determine, by reflecting upon the nature or implications of this, how much knowledge of existents which are not immediate data they must, or may, suppose themselves to possess. This was, of course, essentially the method of Descartes, though he applied it confusedly and inconsistently. But it is not the natural road to epistemological dualism. That road starts from the position of natural realism—from the assumption that we already have certain information about realities which are not merely our immediate, private, and momentary data; and it leads to the discovery, or supposed discovery, that this very assumption forbids us to believe that our acquaintance with these realities is at first hand. The time, place, context, or qualities which we have ascribed to them prove inconsistent with these which belong to the data. Not only is this the natural approach to the dualism of datum and *cognoscendum*, but it is also the only approach which is at all likely to be persuasive to those averse to that theory.[3]

Much of his first chapter is an extensive and unremitting contrast between the two radically different theories of knowledge.

Since Lovejoy's principle of arrangement in *The Revolt Against Dualism* is inductive, in the best tradition of Francis Bacon, he did not arrive at his most explicit and strongest objections to the methodology and philosophy of Descartes until his final chapter, "The Nature of Knowing as a Natural Event." To appreciate the full force of his thesis against Descartes requires a reading of his entire study: here it is sufficient to note his stress upon the antithesis between the method of Descartes and the theory of knowledge based upon common sense experience, memory, and introspection:

> If Descartes had been as critical and methodical in rebuilding his world as he was in shattering it, he would have seen that the existential proposition which in his reconstruction, should have immediately followed the *cogito ergo sum* [I think, therefore I am] was *memini ergo fui* [I remember, therefore I have been]. He could not, strictly speaking, have justified it by reasoning; but he could, by simply keeping his attention fixed upon his own consciousness, have, so to say, seen cogito transforming itself into memini before his eyes. Small as this step might have seemed, it would have altered the direction of Descartes' subsequent course of reasoning; and if he had taken it, the history of modern philosophy might well have been widely different from what it has been, and less involved in confusion. For any belief in the possibility of true remembrance is not only a step out of subjectivism, it is also a step into epistemological dualism.[4]

According to Lovejoy's interpretation of Descartes, instead of modifying *cogito ergo sum* with *memini ergo fui*, the French philosopher simply assumed his private version of Berkeley's later formula for idealism, *esse est percipi* (to be is to be perceived). Descartes thereby avoided an epistemological dualism and instead created two monisms, one of matter and one of spirit, thereby forming an ambiguous and incongruously related unity. The influence of Descartes upon scientific theory permeated the rationalism of the Enlightenment and reached to the twentieth century. Many scientists attempted to engraft idealism upon their materialism, but without success. But Descartes' method of doubt and skepticism remained dominant among scientists, who invariably assumed a monism of matter. As Lovejoy observed: "the primary, and almost conclusive, objection to dualism . . . for many men of science, is simply that it is dualistic."[5] The methodology of Descartes was well suited for scientific experiments, but it was woefully inadequate, and indeed destructive, for religion, the arts, and the humanities.

Since Lovejoy's harsh criticism of Descartes has enormous implications for a valid understanding of Frost's theory of knowledge, it is useful to examine his case against that thinker's radically different epistemological theory. Lovejoy shows how the "nature of knowing as a natural event" discredits Descartes' unnatural initial total doubt and the rational assertion out of his consciousness that he exists. He notes that it is the "common sense" of all mankind to believe in their experiences as retained in memory and organized through retrospection. As opposed to Descartes' formulation, Lovejoy's theory of knowledge as memory and thoughtful retrospection does not initially posit the assumption that the mind of man is ever a blank blackboard, or *tabula rasa*, upon which arbitrary and disconnected sense impressions can write whatever chances to occur. Descartes' epistemological theory tends to obliterate both personal biographies and the history of the whole human race. Lovejoy insists that "the primary mode of knowing is . . . retrospection, or more specifically, remembrance."[6] To assume otherwise, that direct immediate sense impressions are the only or primary source of knowledge, is to act as though one is constantly being reborn at each present moment. On the contrary, "all that we call empirical knowledge consists primarily of memories. . . . "[7] Knowledge as memory includes the past, present, and possible future. Thus understood, memory has "the power to bring past and future within the scope of the present consciousness," so that "knowing is a psychological phenomenon."[8]

The belief that knowledge is primarily memory has practical consequences; one of the most important is the recognition that most of what man knows he apprehends indirectly, since it is embodied in such devices as linguistic symbols and figures of speech, like the metaphors of poetry. As Lovejoy put it, "merely to remember is to be aware of a contrast between the image presented and the event recalled."[9] When refined through retrospection, things remembered become "a mode of representative knowledge," so that "Whatever knowledge of real objects you know is indirect or representative."[10] Symbolic knowledge is "a step into epistemological dualism," because "retrospection is . . . a case in which the duality of the datum and the thing known is immediately manifest."[11]

Another important consequence of knowledge as memory is that men become aware that much "belief . . . outruns empirical evidence," so that often we believe and "know by faith."[12] Indirect knowledge through symbols and belief has "the dualistic implication" that results in "foreknowledge or expectation" in the future. Men therefore can believe in something in order to understand it, and not, like Descartes and some agnostics, make their rational understanding the measure of their belief. This principle is common in religious belief and in Coleridge's aesthetic principle that readers of fiction must make "a willing suspension of disbelief" in order to understand a novel or a poem or a play. The whole thrust of Lovejoy's theory of knowledge as memory either rejects or questions every form of doubt and skepticism based upon Cartesian rationalism, which may well end in agnosticism or disbelief.

There is overwhelming evidence in Frost's poetry, prose, and conversations that he was convinced that man's knowledge and understanding of basic beliefs derive largely from memory and retrospection. His mother's religious teaching probably was the earliest source of his views on knowledge and beliefs in religion and aesthetics, which were subsequently extended into other subjects. Lovejoy's *The Revolt Against Dualism* merely confirmed many of the poet's long-held convictions about knowledge and placed them within the historical and philosophical context of the conflicting theories that prevailed from the time of Descartes to the modern era. Lovejoy's thesis about the "common sense" conception of knowledge as memory, which culminated in what he called "natural dualism," was congenial to Frost. Sidney Cox recorded that more than a decade before the poet read Lovejoy, his own brand of dualism was based upon "common sense" and a rejection of monism: "He won't give up common sense." He further noted that Frost's memory of the great diversity of things in nature and of events in history prevented him from accepting any simple monistic view of reality: "The man who remembers, Robert said, can't name one equivalent for all. . . . He insists, repeatedly, that we cannot harmonize all of reality."[13] To Frost, as to Lovejoy, common sense, memory, retrospection, and the rich diversity of experience are all intertwined within natural dualism. These provide a conception of the world far removed from the doubt, subconsciousness, and rationalism in the pseudo-dualism of Descartes. Frost's theory of knowledge permeates all of his thinking about human nature in its relationship with every important subject. Perhaps the greatest current need of scholarship on the poet is a book-length study of his conception of knowledge as revealed in his art and philosophy. Here it will only be possible to cite a few examples of how his view of knowledge is the antithesis of Descartes' theory and method.

Perhaps the earliest important example in Frost's poetry of the metaphysical foundations of his views on knowledge is in "The Trial by Existence" (1913). This poem is a metaphysical fable, probably based upon the myth of Er in Plato's *Republic*, but with the addition of the theme and spirit employed by William James in *The Will to Believe*. In Frost's poem, man's knowledge of his previous life in a transcendent realm is forgotten, lodged in his subconscious mind, yet interwoven with free will, determinism, courage, faith, and revelation as basic traits in the earthly intellectual life of human nature. The oneness of transcendence is contrasted with the multifariousness of things on earth. The poem depicts the courageous choice of souls in heaven who willingly journey to earth to be born and to endure their trial by existence, with all of its joys and sorrows. "The gathering of the souls for birth" is hushed in forgetfulness; otherwise, "the woe were not earthly woe / To which you give the assenting voice."[14] A residual power of recollection is implanted in the bravest souls, so that a remembrance of their divine origins, as creatures with souls, makes them aware of how spirit is linked to matter: "The mystic link to bind and hold / Spirit to matter till death come." The spirit of remembrance in "The Trial by Existence" permeates many of Frost's other poems, especially the monologues and dialogues, but perhaps nowhere more poignantly than in the pathos of "The Lovely Shall be Choosers," a poem on the tragic life of the poet's mother.

Frost's perception of knowledge as recollection is identical to the approach employed by Wordsworth in "Ode on Intimations of Immortality from Recollections of Early Childhood." The most famous lines in that poem perfectly anticipate Frost's plot in "The Trial by Existence":

> *Our birth is but a sleep and a forgetting;*
> *The soul that rises with us, our life's star,*
> *Hath had elsewhere its sitting,*
> *And cometh from afar;*
> *Not in entire forgetfulness,*
> *And not in utter nakedness,*
> *But trailing clouds of glory do we come*
> *From God, who is our home:*

Every point that Lovejoy made about knowledge as memory and retrospection is found very clearly in Frost's religious beliefs and in his aesthetics, including the Augustinian principle that men must first believe in something in order to understand it, because belief as habit normally precedes and outruns any direct knowledge through immediate empirical evidence.

Frost was wholly repelled by Descartes' principle and method that total initial doubt was the best way to establish any indisputable truth acceptable to a hypothetical universal reason. Sidney Cox has recorded the poet's wrath against that thinker's theory as applied to education:

> Education . . . declines to make a shut-eye assumption that there is "any universal reason" in man's possession. . . . Robert Frost indignantly denounced college teaching that "frisks Freshmen of their principles." At Bread Loaf in 1925 he declared that a boy with all his beliefs drawn out of him is in no condition to learn. Or even to live. Everybody needs some beliefs as unquestionable as the axioms of geometry. No postulates deliberately adopted could ever have the force. We have to have unarguable, unde-monstrable, unmistakable axioms, just three or four. And if we didn't abuse our minds we should surely have them.[15]

The worst abuse of Descartes' method was to be found amongst teachers who assumed that because science is true, religion is therefore false, a mere superstition that needs to be eradicated so that the student's mind can be made a blank blackboard upon which to inscribe scientific verities. Teachers then invariably justified such a course of action by claiming that it provided the student with the requisite freedom for "progress" to occur. Cox noted that the poet rejected the idea of progress, arguing instead that "something in school should save us from the fatal credulity of progress prophets."[16]

In Frost's early academic teaching post at Amherst College, he came into sharp conflict with President Alexander Meiklejohn's "progressive" policy in education, which was justified as "freedom for taste and intel-lect." Frost responded to this claim:

> Freedom from what? Freedom from every prejudice in favor of state, home, church, morality, etc. I am too much a creature of prejudice to stay and listen to such stuff. Not only in favor of morality am I prejudiced, but in favor of an immorality I could name as against other immoralities. I'd no more set out in pur-suit of the truth than I would in a living unless mounted on my prejudices.[17]

Clearly, to Frost memory and retrospection of past experience create prejudgments based upon normative moral principles and habits of mind and feeling that have become beliefs "as unquestionable as the axioms of geometry." By "prejudice," Frost did not mean any pejorative understand-ing of that word; he meant that the moral virtues should precede and not be separated from the intellectual virtues.[18] Thus understood, prejudice is so deeply imbedded in both the subconscious and conscious mind that it functions as habit, an unvoiced premise in response to every new experience. Prejudice is part of every person's entailed cultural inheritance. In sharp contrast with Lawrance Thompson's interpretation of Frost's "prejudice" as pejorative, Sidney Cox perceived the psychological complexities in prejudices about human nature. In his commentary on Frost's poem "The Vanishing Red," he noted how easily it could be misinterpreted as showing the poet's supposed lack of sympathy toward the fate of the American Indians, because of the "quiet way of surpassing the prejudices that we all get to thinking of as boldly free from prejudice."[19]

A variation on the same theme regarding prejudice is in Frost's poem "The Black Cottage," in which he touched upon the relationship between belief and truth as relative things: ". . . why abandon a belief / Merely because it ceases to be true. / Cling to it long enough, and not a doubt / It will turn true again, for so it goes. / Most of the change we think we see in life / Is due to truths being in and out of favor." In a letter to Louis Untermeyer (May 3, 1926), he alluded to this passage and spoke of the "truths that we keep coming back and back to." Undoubtedly, he had in mind the three or four beliefs that he held to be as unquestionable as the axioms of geometry. Frost never identified these basic beliefs, but probably they would include the Ten Commandments; the common-sense belief that the universe continues to exist even when no one perceives it, as during sleep; that all men are morally equal in the sight of God as their creator and that they therefore should be treated equally before the law; that man's life on earth is often filled with unmerited tragedy; and that the "two-endedness of things," as in dualism, persists throughout human history.

To Frost, beliefs may be firmly held, but they need something like a witness tree that marks the boundaries of truths lodged in memory. In the emblematic poem "Beech," which provides a guide to readers of *A Witness Tree*, he connected memory as knowledge with concrete reality in order to show how boundaries establish truths and overcome Cartesian doubts:

> *One tree, by being deeply wounded,*
> *Has been impressed as Witness Tree*
> *And made commit to memory*
> *My proof of being not unbounded.*
> *Thus truth's established and borne out,*
> *Though circumstanced with dark and doubt—*
> *Though by a world of doubt surrounded.*

It is clear that Frost appeals to memory as containing a world of knowledge beyond the agnostic world of rational doubt. Where Descartes made doubt the best starting point in the pursuit of truth, Frost placed memory, reflection, and belief: "Belief is better than anything else," he wrote, "and it is best when rapt, above paying its respects to anybody's doubt."[20] Not only is belief prior and superior to knowledge acquired through direct empirical experience, but such knowledge itself needs to be tested by the norms of memory. As Frost said in "A Concept Self-Conceived," "Great is the reassurance of recall." Similarly, in "At Woodward Gardens" he wrote: "The already known had once more been confirmed." So too in "Misgiving" he spoke of being free to pursue "knowledge beyond the bounds of life," which combines empiricism with knowledge rooted in memory, retrospection, and the creative imagination. In particular, whenever time and space are factors in any poem by Frost, readers who understand his conception of knowledge as memory have an added dimension of critical understanding.

Frost's theory of knowledge as memory clearly placed an enormous stress upon the past as experience. He emphasized this point strikingly in "Carpe Diem":

> *But bid life seize the present?*
> *It lives less in the present*
> *Than in the future always,*
> *And less in both together*
> *Than in the past.*

The hierarchy of man's concerns within time reverses Descartes' conception of knowledge as conscious self-awareness in the present. Except for persons who live largely on a nonhuman animal level, by their immediate senses and without moral imagination, even the long, long thoughts of youth are more concerned with the future than with the present. Aesthetic and moral imagination and the "correspondence" which occurs between individuals in their emotional rapport are far more vital to him than the senses and abstract reason. The most perfect example of this aspect of Frost's conception of knowledge is in "All Revelation." The creative imagination perceives knowledge of past experience as necessarily indirect, and therefore best represented in the symbolic forms of art. Among other reasons, this is what makes the arts of such psychological importance to the civilized life of mankind.

In poetry as an art form, symbols result by putting things together within enduring forms. The whole complex arsenal of symbolic tools is contained in figurative language—analogies, parables, images, myths, comparisons, contrasts, similarities, antitheses, ambiguities, puns, rhymes, auditory tones, irony, assonance, dissonance, connotations, personification, alliteration, and so on, but perhaps above all in metaphors and the forms of poetry. As has already been pointed out, symbols are vehicles that convey knowledge and insight indirectly. Frost often identified himself as "a confirmed symbolist." As a poet he acknowledged that "we like to talk in parables and in hints and in indirections."[21] In a detailed examination of him as a symbolic poet, Reginald Cook concluded: "Frost is a symbolist of the physical world of space and time."[22] Ultimately, by uniting the "play" or interaction of mind and matter, symbolic knowledge and understanding includes the "natural dualism" and conception of knowledge held in common by him and Lovejoy.

Frost's theory of knowledge as memory and retrospection is clearly evident in his method of composition. As Reginald Cook observed: "He draws his knowledge instinctively from its roots."[23] Moreover, later he made it clear that the poet's roots are not merely on the level of direct and immediate sense experiences; "his world of reality is not a transcription of things directly observed; it is an imaginative transmutation."[24] Needless to say, "transmutation" occurs out of a world remembered; the creative imagination "makes play" with things already known and brings into existence a poem with a fresh revelation and renewed understanding of some enduring truth. To Frost, the setting of a dramatic situation in a poem was among the things rooted in memory: "I often start from some remembered spot."[25] More generally, Frost held that all poetry begins with geography, a sense of place and a sense of time. But in all of the elements in a poem, the composition is in large part an "unconscious activity," in which intuitive insight draws knowledge from memory to the conscious level. As Frost put it: "I summon something I almost didn't know I had."[26] In "The Figure a Poem Makes," he expressly identified memory as the origin of his poems: "For me the initial delight is in the surprise of remembering something I didn't know I knew. I am in a place, in a situation, as if I had materialized from a cloud or risen out of the ground. There is a glad recognition of the long lost and the rest follows."[27]

What applies to the poet in the act of composition also applies to the reader afterwards: poetry is understood as "making play of things we [poets] can trust you largely to know."[28] In writing a poem, "the logic is backward, in retrospect"; reading it draws upon indirect knowledge remembered to form a new revelation of knowledge remembered. Frost often told his audiences during a poetry reading that they should not look for something wholly new, but only for something they knew but had forgotten. Similarly, Cook recorded that through symbols and metaphors, the poet wrote about "things we trust you already know."[29] Between the poet and his reader a "correspondence" is created, because of their shared "common sense" knowledge in memory and retrospection, a world far removed from the doubt, skepticism, and rational logic of Descartes.

Although the main purpose of Lovejoy's *The Revolt Against Dualism* was to describe and analyze the philosophical and scientific conflicts over dualism and the two forms of monism, from Descartes to well into the twentieth century, his book was also an excellent transition for Frost to Einstein's celebrated theory of relativity and the concept of an open-ended universe. Fourteen separate references to the great cosmologist and his theory run intermittently like a golden thread of unity through Lovejoy's study.[30] His description of Einstein's theory provides the basis for his comparisons between the scientist and his predecessors and contemporaries in science and philosophy, and for how his theory functions in an open-ended universe:

> The theory by its implications, though not by its initial postulates, transfers space, time and motion from the physical to the mental world, and by doing so excludes the supposition that the physical world may "be interpreted by analogy with visual sensa and their relations to our visual fields." The theory is supposed to achieve this result by showing that the positions, velocities and shapes of perceived objects, and the dates of perceived events or the duration of processes, are "relative to the standpoint of observers."[31]

Throughout his book, Lovejoy described how Einstein differed both in the methodology of his science and in his philosophical orientation from such contemporaries as Alfred North Whitehead and Bertrand Russell, among many other scientists and philosophers.

Although the modern "cosmology of Einstein" was shared by his materialist monist contemporaries in science, Lovejoy noted that unlike many of them, "so far as philosophers are concerned, the general result of the work of Einstein is simply a vindication of dualism." According to Lovejoy, Einstein was a natural dualist in his philosophy because his theory of knowledge transcended the empirical assumptions and methods of his predecessors and contemporaries. Many of his fellow scientists were still rooted in the empirical-rational tradition of Descartes, Locke, and the

Enlightenment conception of knowledge, and in the Euclidean geometry of Newton's *Philosophiae Naturalis Principia Mathematica* (1687), which Einstein found inadequate for the study of curve-space in the universe. His theory was not the culmination of the scientific tradition of Descartes and Newton, as so many of his scientific contemporaries believed. On the contrary, Lovejoy showed, Einstein's theory was the negation of Cartesian science and methodology; it replaced the cosmology of Newton and the great chain of being of the Enlightenment with a new conception of the universe. To come full circle with Reginald Cook's profound observation that Frost's poetry "leads away from the Great Chain of Being to an exercise of options in an open-ended universe," it is necessary to understand Frost's own original responses to and uses of Einstein's theory, in addition to but also quite apart from what he may have learned from Lovejoy. That is the purpose of the discussion that immediately follows.

# 8

## Frost, Einstein's Relativity, and the Open-Ended Universe

To understand and appreciate the full significance of Reginald L. Cook's statement that "the route through the poetry of Robert Frost leads . . . away from the Great Chain of Being to an exercise in options in an open-ended universe," it is necessary to review the poet's responses to Albert Einstein (1879–1955) and his theory of relativity. It would be an error to assume at the beginning that Einstein's theory imposed itself upon Frost's thinking and thereby determined the route of his poetry. On the contrary, something like the reverse was far closer to what happened. Frost himself, on his own initiative, chose the route of his poetry, and in the World War I period he encountered Einstein's theory and found it so much like his own conception of knowledge that he absorbed it and made it a vital and more complete part of his own understanding of physical nature and the cosmic order in relation to the mind of man. As we shall see, Einstein's theory confirmed and enriched Frost's own philosophical dualism.

During the decade of the 1920s, Frost's own as yet unformed theory of knowledge, still unconscious and incomplete, preceded his encounter with Einstein's theory of relativity, which in turn came before he had read Lovejoy's account of Einstein's theory in *The Revolt Against Dualism* (1930). Einstein's theory sharpened for the poet the modern world's changing view of the universe, just as Lovejoy's two books clarified the historical context within which the philosophical and scientific changes had occurred. In the summer of 1943, I noted that Frost's bookshelf in his cabin at the Homer Noble Farm included Einstein's *Relativity: The Special and General Theory* (1916); Einstein and Leopold Infeld's *The Evolution of Physics from Early Concepts to Relativity and Quanta* (1938); and Hans Reichenbach's recent study, *From Copernicus to Einstein* (1942). These three works, together with Frost's comments on Bernard Cohen's "An Interview with Einstein" in *Scientific American* (July 1955) and some remarks by Frost during conversations with me, form the basis of this chapter on Frost and Einstein.

But before examining Frost's own responses to Einstein and his theory and the poet's use of the scientist's ideas and metaphors regarding time and curved-space in some of his poems, it is useful to summarize the effect of relativity upon the general culture of the twentieth century. Perhaps the best brief account of Einstein's influence beyond scientific theory is in Gerald Holton's *Einstein, History, and Other Passions* (1995).[1] Holton is considered "a world authority on the genesis of relativity,"[2] and his book includes a chapter entitled "Einstein's Influence on the Culture of Our Time." Holton noted that the widespread awareness of "the elements of relativity or quantum physics" began in London on November 6, 1919, when the British eclipse expeditions confirmed Einstein's general theory of relativity.[3] From that date forward, Einstein's fame and influence as the foremost theoretical physicist of the twentieth century penetrated even the popular culture of Europe and America.

It was not long before persons wholly outside of the physical sciences, in religion, the visual arts, and literature, wished to know how Einstein's revolutionary conception of time and space regarding the universe affected human affairs and their own fields of thought and action. In June 1921, Randall Davidson, the Archbishop of Canterbury, asked Einstein what effect the theory of relativity would have on ethics and religion. As Holton noted, Einstein replied: "None. Relativity is a purely scientific matter and has nothing to do with religion."[4] Einstein denied that relativity in physics led to relativity in ethics. Yet his theory released many dubious speculations on the relationship of physics to metaphysics. In light of Einstein's stress upon the importance of the mind of the observer in measuring physical phenomena, the longstanding philosophical differences between dualism and the two monisms had to be reviewed. As Holton observed, the scientific journal *Nature* "felt it necessary to print opposing articles on whether 'Einstein's space-time is the death knell of materialism.'"[5] Einstein regarded himself as "a continuist," not an iconoclast or revolutionary against traditional ethical, religious, or aesthetic values. During several decades after his theory was widely accepted, he often protested against such claims. He denied that cubism in painting, and radical experiments about time consciousness in music or literature, had anything to do with relativity. As Holton noted, such speculations simply resulted in "philosophical misunderstandings."

It is important to distinguish between Frost and Holton's inventory of writers who made use of Einstein's theory in their work, mainly in techniques such as stream of consciousness. Holton's list includes William Carlos Williams, Archibald MacLeish, e. e. cummings, Ezra Pound, and T. S. Eliot in poetry; and such novelists as Thomas Mann, Lawrence Durrell, Hermann Brach, and especially William Faulkner in *The Sound and the Fury* (1929). These writers, and others in drama and literary criticism, often reflected "impressionistic popularizations" of Einstein's theory. Holton mentioned that Robert Frost was among modern poets who "referred directly to Einstein and his work,"[6] but he did not distinguish how Frost differed from other writers. But an explication of Frost's responses to Einstein will make clear that his understanding of Einstein's theory far transcended mere "impressionistic popularizations."[7]

It is noteworthy, as Roger Highfield and Paul Carter observed, that "Einstein always maintained that a general overview of physics could be more valuable than specialized knowledge."[8] This was made clear as early as 1923, when Niels Bohr gave two lectures on the atomic aspects of modern physics at Amherst College. After the Danish physicist's lectures, at a dinner in his honor, Frost asked him far more penetrating questions than were asked by the professional scientists at the dinner.[9] Almost forty years later, in 1962, the Harvard physicist Harvey Brooks told me that from his conversations with Frost he believed that the poet understood Einstein's general theory more profoundly than many of his scientific colleagues in physics did. They had a stronger specialized scientific knowledge of Einstein's theory, but they often lacked the deeper philosophical understanding provided by Frost's dualism.

One of Einstein's young scientific friends, with whom he corresponded, was Hans Reichenbach (1891–1953), whose book *From Copernicus to Einstein* (1942) confirms much that Lovejoy and Frost had to say about Einstein's science.[10] Reichenbach illuminated the changing problems of space, time, and cosmic bodies in motion in scientific theory from Copernicus to Einstein. He appreciated Einstein's achievement as the synthesis of all previous discoveries in astronomy, physics, and mathematics, from Copernicus, Tycho Brahe, Johannes Kepler, Galileo, and Descartes, followed by Olaf Roemer's discovery of time intervals in the movement of light, culminating in Newton's particle theory of light. Although these developments changed man's ancient worldview of the universe, throughout the Enlightenment the cosmic system was still regarded as a closed physical order created by God.

Like Lovejoy and Frost, Reichenbach noted that Einstein's personal qualities of character and temperament had much to do with his success in developing his theory. His mentor and friend, he observed, had "an instinct for the hidden intentions of nature," indeed, "Einstein possesses this instinct to the highest degree."[11] Instinct is not quite the correct word for illuminating Einstein's character and temperament; it is more physiological than psychological and cerebral, and Einstein himself, as we shall see, preferred other terms in describing himself. Reichenbach recognized the scientific dimensions of Einstein's thought, but he fell short of defining his philosophical insights. He did note that Einstein was able to transcend his scientific predecessors and contemporaries because he perceived connections between their separate discoveries that they failed to notice or explicate. Thus he was able to synthesize what for other scientists remained apart.[12] In the grand abstract, Reichenbach did indeed recognize that in Einstein's "method of dealing with the problem of space . . . Einstein's theory represents a new form of philosophical thinking,"[13] but he did not attempt to specify its nature. He appeared unaware of Lovejoy's belief that Einstein held a "common sense" theory of knowledge centered in memory, retrospection, and intuition, which provided the basis of his imaginative creativity in forming his theory. Unlike Lovejoy, Reichenbach showed no awareness that Einstein's philosophical orientation was in "natural dualism."

Frost read Einstein's *Relativity: The Special and General Theory* (1920)[14] and was made aware of much that was encompassed in the complex development of Einstein both as a man and as a highly original and creative physicist. The eclecticism and modesty of Einstein appealed strongly to Frost. The scientist freely acknowledged his indebtedness to many of his predecessors, from Sir Isaac Newton to Karl Frederich Gauss (1777–1855), James Clerk Maxwell (1831–79), Ernst Mach (1838–1916), Hendrick Lorentz (1858–1928), Hermann Minkowski (1864–1909), Arthur Stanley Eddington (1882–1944), and Niels Hendrik Bohr (1885–1962), among many others. From Marcel Grossmann he learned non-Euclidean geometry, which enabled him to deal with curved space-time, and in which "parallel lines do not exist and the three angles of a triangle do not add up to 180 degrees."[15] Frost understood the evolution of Einstein's theory from its early stages to its mature fulfillment. In *Relativity: The Special and General Theory*, Einstein reviewed the development of "classical mechanics" from Galileo to his own era and contrasted the assumptions, methods, physics, mathematics, and view of the universe of Descartes and Newton with those of modern physicists, such as Lorentz, Minkowski, and Mach, whose work was the point of departure for his own gestation of the special and general theories of relativity.

It is essential to understand the complex stages through which Einstein's theory developed from 1905–06, when he projected the special theory, to its culmination in the general theory during 1915–17. One of the best summaries of this process is by Roger Highfield and Paul Carter:

> The year of 1905 was to be Einstein's *annus mirabilis*, in which he produced three separate articles that shook the foundations of science. The papers were sent off at intervals of less than two months, and it is often remarked that they seem to cover dazzingly disparate subjects. But several scholars have pointed out that common threads exist. Professor Jurgen Renn stresses that each is based on a "particulate" view of the world, understanding phenomena in terms of minute bodies: atoms, molecules, electrons and chunks of energy. Each of the papers also marks the final consequence of a long chain of work by masters of classical physics—Boltzmann, Planck and Lorentz. From his letters, it is clear that Einstein avidly devoured their ideas. However, he had sufficient distance from their way of thinking to interpret their research from a new perspective— and to appreciate its revolutionary implications. Their work was like delicious fruit that was ripe for picking.
>
> Einstein's papers share a cavalier artistry that was quite alien to conventional scientific discourse, with its plodding progression from experimental results to explanatory theory. Einstein preferred to begin by voicing his dissatisfaction with conventional wisdom, pointing to ideas that were inelegant or out of harmony. As Gerald Holton has put it, his objections were ones that others might dismiss as being of a predominantly aesthetic nature. He then proposes a principle of great generality. He shows that it helps remove, as one of the deduced consequences, his initial dissatisfaction. And at the end of each paper, he proposes a small number of predictions that should be experimentally verifiable, although the test may be difficult. It was an approach quite different from that of any other scientist of his day, and the rewards it earned him were breathtaking.[16]

The essential element in Einstein's radically different approach to modern theoretical physics, which digressed from the tradition of Cartesian and Enlightenment rationalism, was the aesthetic and creative dimension, with all that it implied in forming a different conception of knowledge, and ultimately in a view of the physical universe very different from that of Newton and the great chain of being. Whether through Einstein himself or through Lovejoy, or both, Frost was made acutely aware that the conception of a closed universe had been replaced by the theory of relativity and an open-ended infinite universe.

Frost could not help but be aware that in a vital passage in Appendix III in *Relativity: The Special and General Theory*, Einstein emphatically rejected as inadequate the methodology and theory of knowledge of Descartes' rationalism and Locke's empiricism in developing scientific theory:

> From a systematic theoretical point of view, we may imagine the process of evolution of an empirical science to be a continuous process of induction. Theories are evolved, and are expressed in short compass as statements of a large number of individual observations in the form of empirical laws, from which the general laws can be ascertained by comparison. Regarded in this way, the development of a science bears some resemblance to the compilation of a classified catalogue. It is, as it were, a purely empirical enterprise.
>
> But this point of view by no means embraces the whole of the actual process; for it slurs over the important part played by intuition and deductive thought in the development of an exact science. As soon as a science has emerged from its initial stages, theoretical advances are no longer achieved merely by a process of arrangement. Guided by empirical data, the investigator rather develops a system of thought which, in general, is built up logically from a small number of fundamental assumptions, the so-called axioms. We call such a system of thought a theory. The theory finds its justification for its existence in the fact that it correlates a large number of single observations and it is just here that the "truth" of the theory lies.[17]

Einstein's key phrase, "the important part played by intuition and deductive thought," provides the philosophical dimension he possessed which distinguished him from so many excellent scientists in his time. When Frost referred to Einstein as a philosopher among outstanding scientists, he recognized in Einstein a willingness to trust his intuition and imagination through deductions from intuited perceptions which transcended the conventional assumptions and methods of his contemporaries. Because of his philosophical assumptions that included mind or spirit as creative powers beyond empiricism, Einstein was able to correlate the "large numbers of single observations" of his contemporary scientists and thus to create his theory.

One of the major themes in Einstein's *Relativity: The Special and General Theory* was the contrast between the "co-ordinates" by which cosmic phenomena were measured by Newton as compared with those in his theory. Einstein could not have arrived at his basic formula, $E=mc^2$, that energy equals mass times the velocity of light squared, if he had followed the empirical-rational theory of knowledge and the coordinates in the method of Newton. As he observed: "the laws of the mechanics of Galileo-Newton can be regarded as valid only for a Galileian system of co-ordinates."[18] The coordinates of Galileo and Newton assumed that space and time were fixed absolutes, that the universe is finite and has a center, and that Euclidean geometry is sufficient to deal with cosmic phenomena. In sharp contrast to the world of Newton, Einstein assumed that the world is "a four-dimensional space-time continuum," that "in gravitational fields there are no such things as rigid bodies with Euclidean properties," and that "as regards space and time the universe is infinite."[19] In view of these and other important differences, Einstein concluded: "the method of Cartesian co-ordinates must . . . be discarded, and replaced by another which does not assume the validity of Euclidean geometry and rigid bodies."[20] It is clear that Einstein abandoned as inadequate the scientific and philosophical tradition of Descartes and Newton, and with it the methodology and empirical-rational theory of knowledge that was sufficient for the Enlightenment.

What are the basic philosophical elements and character traits included in Einstein's "intuition and deductive thought"? Einstein referred to intuition as "holism" through "free creations"; it was the power to leap from sight to insight regarding how "fundamental assumptions" are perceived in a larger and original context. For Einstein, intuition was the equivalent for a scientist of what the aesthetic and creative imagination was for the poet. Combined with his eclectic mind, filled with the rich knowledge of the achievements and experience of his predecessors, Einstein's intuition included what Lovejoy identified as "memory." Einstein's "deductive thought" is the equivalent of what Lovejoy called "retrospection." Lovejoy could have written the scientist's statement: "we formulate the general laws of nature as they are obtained from experience."[21] Locke's principle of a *tabula rasa* was totally abandoned by Einstein in favor of a theory of knowledge based upon experience, memory, and deductive retrospection. Add to this the character trait of courage, the willingness to digress from conventional methods and beliefs, and it becomes evident that Einstein's creative imagination enabled him to believe his theory of relativity into existence just as Frost believed a poem into existence.

An important matter in the intellectual and cultural character of Einstein was his views on religion, which determined for him the perennial question of the relationship between science and metaphysics. By birth to Jewish parents in southern Germany, he was acutely aware of the Ashkenazic tradition in Judaism, but like his parents he treated his spiritual inheritance as a cultural and racial phenomenon, rather than as a revealed religion to which he owed allegiance. Neither the Orthodox nor the Reformed institutional forms of Judaism, nor the later Conservative movement, commanded Einstein's loyalty. However, he favored the Zionist movement and an independent state of Israel, provided the civil rights of the Muslim population were observed. As regards Christianity, in his boyhood he briefly attended a Catholic school in Bavaria, and he did not object when his first wife, the Serbian Mileva Marié, had their two sons, Hans Albert and Eduard, baptized in the Orthodox Church. But Einstein maintained a lifelong independence from all established institutional religions. It would be a serious error, however, to conclude that, like so many of his fellow scientists, he was absorbed into what Oswald Spengler called "scientific irreligion." Einstein possessed a deep sense of piety, and in his metaphysics he was neither a deist nor a monistic pantheist, but a convinced theist whose sense of awe and reverence toward the universe was rooted in an aesthetic and creative belief in God and a realistic view of the moral nature of man.

On March 30, 1952, in a letter to his friend Maurice Solovine, who had expressed wonder about Einstein's supposed departure from the monistic materialism of so many scientists, he made it clear that his sense of awe and aesthetic reverence regarding the physical universe did indeed include a theistic view of reality quite distinct from that of many physicists:

> And here lies the weak point for the positivists and the professional atheists, who are feeling happy through the consciousness of having successfully made the world not only God-free, but even "wonder free." The nice thing is that we must be content with the acknowledgement of the "wonder," without there being a legitimate way beyond it. I feel I must add this explicitly, so you wouldn't think that I—weakened by age—have become a victim of the clergy.[22]

Thus Einstein at once acknowledged his belief in God and distinguished himself from both positivists and atheists and from allegiance to any form of institutional religion. He not only did not set science against religious belief, but admitted that his own "cosmic religious feeling" was for him the source for the "strongest and noblest motive for scientific research."[23] Indeed, to Einstein the eternal incomprehensibility of the universe was deepened with each new scientific discovery, which strengthened his religious sense of awe and wonder. Far from assuming a contradiction between religion and science, he believed that they constantly reinforced each other by expanding man's rational and aesthetic understanding of the universe. As Holton observed: "Einstein's God [is] a God whose laws of nature are both the testimony of His presence in the universe and the proof of its saving rationality."[24] He was highly critical of the "half-understood analogies" of many modern scientists and writers who, he said, do not "advance to an honest understanding of the rational structure of that modern world picture."[25]

Einstein was not content to relegate his theism to an abstract concept, to a remote corner of his mind, as a passive belief; he often applied it concretely to important practical human concerns as a vital part of his personal feelings. For example, he wrote to his friend Queen Elizabeth of Belgium, on the occasion of the death of her husband and sister-in-law, that the renewal of life in nature every spring reminded him of "something eternal that lies beyond the reach of the hand of fate and of all human delusions."[26] A conscious sensitivity to common events in natural phenomena provided Einstein with insights into the ultimate meaning of reality for human nature. Scientists who excluded God from their sensibility were to him deficient human beings. After spending a long vacation with his fellow scientist Marie Curie, he summarized her inability to rise above the mechanistic determinism of pure matter: "Madame Curie never heard the birds sing."[27] To his young friend Esther Salaman he confessed: "I want my peace. I want to know how God created the world."[28] This remark should not be understood as a utilitarian psychological basis for religious faith. Einstein did not believe in God in order to have peace of mind, but peace or psychological well-being was the natural consequence of his God-centered faith. The will to believe was probably as important to him as the substance of what he believed, and it intensified the spiritual euphoria created by the awe and reverence he felt with each revelation about the universe. Belief in God also gave strength to Einstein in facing the great tragedies in temporal life. Will Herberg has well summarized Einstein's type of personal religious orientation: "Religion is a spiritual anodyne designed to allay the pains and vexations of existence."[29] Einstein's most frequently quoted appeal to God occurred in 1926, after several decades of fruitless endeavors to reconcile his differences with Werner Heisenberg and Niels Bohr over the quantum theory, when in exasperation he said to Max Born: "God does not throw dice."[30] His skepticism and lifelong doubts about the quantum theory are not to be taken lightly; he had studied it carefully for over two decades before he made his famous remark to Born. Scientists and scholars have been too quick and facile in dismissing Einstein's negative views on quantum physics as a supposed deficiency in his understanding of the universe.

In his final chapter, "Quanta," in *The Evolution of Physics* (1938), Einstein confirmed the analysis of both Lovejoy and Holton that his basic orientation in science and view of the universe was ultimately centered in a dualism of mind and matter, which subordinated physics to philosophy: "Science," he said, "is not just a collection of laws, a catalogue of unrelated facts. It is a creation of the human mind, with its freely invented ideas and concepts." He then applied this conviction to the quantum theory:

> There is no doubt that quantum physics explained a very rich variety of facts, achieving, for the most part, splendid agreement between theory and observation. The new quantum physics removes us still further from the old mechanical view, and a retreat to the former position seems, more than ever, unlikely. But there is also no doubt that quantum physics must still be based on the two concepts: matter and field. It is in this sense a dualistic theory and does not bring our old problem of reducing everything to the field concept even one step nearer realization.[31]

Einstein believed that the worldview of science toward the physical universe was not wholly separated from the moral and aesthetic nature of man in the formation of modern civilization. This was an important assumption in his view of the quantum theory as distinct from relativity, pointing toward a more open-ended universe. But quantum theory was only one of several possible future developments of physics. Einstein raised the question of how the unknown future might proceed.

Will the further development be along the line chosen in quantum physics, or is it more likely that new revolutionary ideas will be introduced into physics? Will the road of advance again make a sharp turn, as it has so often done in the past? During the last few years all the difficulties of quantum physics have been concentrated around a few principal points. Physics awaits their solution impatiently. But there is no way of foreseeing when and where the clarification of these difficulties will be brought about.[32]

Einstein's refusal to follow the challenge of quantum physics to its logical conclusion was not a blind limitation of his physics, as so many scientists and scholars have contended. It is better perceived as his unwillingness to separate the physical sciences from philosophy, religion, the humanities, and modern culture. He retained his prior belief in a unified field theory, which implied that the physical universe was a rational projection of the mind and will of God. This led him to assume that the uncertainty principle in quantum physics was more a technical problem within physical nature than a fact of nature.[33] This was at the heart of his differences with Werner Heisenberg and Niels Bohr. Einstein conceded that "the quantum theory . . . created new and essential features of our reality. Discontinuity replaced continuity. Instead of laws governing individuals, probability laws appeared."[34] But these essential facts of quantum theory, he believed, functioned within the dualism of the unified field theory of relativity.

But since the future developments in physics derived largely from quantum theory, and Einstein's conception of relativity began to appear increasingly obsolete, his resistance to quantum physics made him appear to be an obfuscationist regarding scientific developments. Robert Frost's conversations with Bohr at Amherst College led him to assert to me that much as he admired Einstein, both as a man and scientist, he believed that the great scientist was wrong to cast doubts upon the quantum theory. In adopting Bohr's view of quantum physics, Frost largely ignored the theory of knowledge assumed by Einstein, which Lovejoy had perceived as basic to a dualistic philosophy which transcended the positivist view of physics as centered in matter alone. Although Frost regarded Einstein as "a great philosopher among great scientists,"[35] he did not make the necessary connection between Einstein's philosophy, his theory of knowledge, and his dualism.

When Lovejoy had stated that "so far as philosophers are concerned, the general result of the work of Einstein is simply a vindication of dualism,"[36] he understood the vital connection between the physicist's theory of knowledge and his achievements in and beyond science. In 1995, sixty-five years after Lovejoy, Holton provided the biographical basis for Einstein's youthful awareness of how vital was the connection between his epistemology and his science:

> Indeed, from his earliest student days, Einstein was deeply interested in the theory of knowledge (epistemology). He wrote, "The reciprocal relationship of epistemology and science is of a noteworthy kind. They are dependent upon each other. Epistemology without contact with science becomes an empty scheme. Science without epistemology is—insofar as it is thinkable at all—primitive and muddled."[37]

In Holton's chapter, "What, Precisely, Is 'Thinking'? Einstein's Answer," he noted that for Einstein "the courage to think" and "thinking in images," as elements in "thought experiments" in science, resulted from "the free play with concepts," which was precisely how Frost regarded the creative process in art and poetry. Far more than intellectual capability, exceptional skill in mathematics, and a thorough knowledge of the achievements of past and contemporary scientists went into the formation of Einstein's special and general theories of relativity. Such character traits as courage, the will to believe, a moral and aesthetic imagination, and faith in the original creative power of the human mind were among the things that made Einstein a philosopher among scientists.

Holton both confirmed and qualified Lovejoy's interpretation of Einstein's philosophy as centered in dualism. He noted that in addition to combining mind or spirit as a creative power with interactions with matter, in Einstein's Herbert Spencer Lecture in 1933, the physicist contended that the "fundamentals of scientific theory" are initially "free inventions of the human mind," so that his conception of curved space-time was the death knell of materialist monism. Holton concluded: "We are left with a thoroughly dualistic method of doing science. On the one hand, Einstein says, 'the structure of the system is the work of reason'; on the other hand 'the empirical contents, and their mutual relation must find their representation in the conclusions of the theory.' Indeed, virtually all of Einstein's commentators have followed him in stressing this dualism—and have left it at that. It is a view of science of which there are many variants." Holton added in his chapter "Einstein and the Goal of Science" that the great physicist held that "the dualistic view is modified" by treating the "fundamentals of scientific theory" as of a "purely fictitious character."[38] Frost understood the aesthetic dimension in Einstein's method in scientific theory and regarded it as a positive factor in his theory of relativity. Einstein's "free play with concepts" was identical with Frost's appeals to "play" in the interactions between mind and matter in creating the metaphors in poetry.

Historical and biographical factors in Einstein's life also contributed to the development of his orientation in philosophy. As a young student in late nineteenth-century Germany, Einstein's available philosophical options were conditioned by the prevailing dominant culture. He was as yet unaware of the centuries of conflicts between some forms of idealistic or materialistic monism in opposition to a multifaceted dualism. In time he became convinced that the moral and aesthetic basis of a civilized social order required the subordination of the physical sciences to the humanities. But as Holton noted, in the Germany of Einstein's youth the dominant philosophy was centered in a materialistic monism:

> At the end of the nineteenth century, in the Germany of Einstein's youth, the pursuit of a unified world picture as the scientist's highest task had become almost a cult activity. . . . Einstein himself could not easily have escaped notice of these drives toward unification even as a young person. For example, we know that as a boy he was given Ludwig Büchner's widely popular book *Kraft und Stoff* ("Energy and Matter") [1855], a work Einstein recollected having read with great interest. The little volume does talk about energy and matter; but chiefly it is a late-Enlightenment polemic. Büchner comes out explicitly and enthusiastically in favor of an empirical, almost Lucretian scientific materialism, which Büchner calls a "materialistic world view." Through this world view, he declares, one can attain "the unity of energy and matter, and thereby banish forever the old dualism."[39]

Büchner's thesis was strongly reinforced by Einstein's reading of two positivist works on science, Ernst Mach's *Theory of Heat* and *Science of Mechanics*. Holton observed that the idea of a monistic unified worldview based upon physical science was intensified early in the twentieth century by "a veritable flood of publications" in Germany calling for a revolutionary comprehensive *Weltanschauung*, and that as young men both Einstein and Sigmund Freud signed a manifesto that endorsed such a monistic objective. [40]

In the process of refining his "special theory" into his "general theory" of relativity, a monism of matter in physics appeared justified to Einstein. He showed that electric and magnetic fields had a common basis, that time and space are not separate, that energy and mass are fused—in short, that many aspects of matter that had previously been thought to be separate were connected. This implied that a future wholly unified physics was possible. But Einstein discovered that each new discovery in science increased his sense of awe and wonder about the universe and all that remained unknown, so that even in science total unity was not possible. For the mature Einstein, a supposedly monistic view of physical reality did not constitute a valid basis for a monistic view of all reality, including the life of mankind in civil society. The concept of a materialistic worldview was a dangerous illusion.

Einstein's independent and original character, and his eclectic habit of absorbing a vast range of other thinkers' beliefs—not only in science but in the humanities, arts, and religion, which he turned to original account in his creativity—made it psychologically impossible for him to accept any single form of philosophy. As Holton observed: "Einstein thought the way to escape illusion was by avoiding being captive of any one school of philosophy."[41] Like Frost, Einstein was a lifelong autodidact; he believed that self-education and lively conversations with friends about new ideas were far more valuable than knowledge acquired formally in school. His mental processes included whatever he found valid in diverse beliefs, so that his mature philosophy was an original fusion of eclectic thought. Einstein's own summary of his eclecticism in pursuit of scientific theory is worthy of note:

> [He] must appear to the systematic epistemologist as a type of unscrupulous opportunist: he appears as a realist insofar as he seeks to describe the world independent of the acts of perception; as idealist insofar as he looks upon the concepts and theories as the free inventions of the human spirit (not logically derivable from what is empirically given); as positivist insofar as he considers his concepts and theories justified only to the extent to which they furnish a logical representation of relations among sensory experience. He may even appear as Platonist or Pythagorean insofar as he considers the viewpoint of logical simplicity as an indispensable and effective tool of research.[42]

It is not surprising that Einstein never identified himself in terms of any category of thought, as Frost once did in reaction to Emerson's monism: "I am a dualist." But there is strong empirical evidence that, both as a scientist and humanist, Einstein rejected both forms of monism.

Einstein's critical response to all of the nineteenth-century forces that combined to give shape and direction to twentieth-century monism would require a substantial article. Here it is sufficient to summarize those monistic developments in Germany that commanded his early attention. As a schoolboy, he read and was so captivated by Ludwig Büchner's *Kraft und Stoff* that, as he stated in his *Autobiographical Notes*, it inspired him to make science his life's work. Büchner was among the first of many writers to picture a world civilization wholly based upon the scientific conquest of matter. His thesis was strongly underscored in Germany and other nations during the last four decades of the nineteenth century and reached a culmination in Wilhelm Ostward's *Monism as the Goal of Civilization* (1913). As Holton noted: "The publications of the monistic movement show that it hoped every aspect of culture, life and society would be guided by monistic ideas, from the education of children to the economy of nations, and of course within the research programs of science itself."[43] The popular nineteenth-century belief in "progress," leading to a worldwide utopian society of peace and prosperity, can best be understood as the fulfillment of a monist materialist philosophy.

One of the foremost champions of a monistic philosophy based upon science was Ernst Haeckel (1834–1919), a founder and longtime president of the German Monist League, which "had branches in forty-one cities" and "organized public mass demonstrations against the church."[44] The chief aim of Haeckel was to make science replace religion as the basis and moral guide in modern civilization. As the foremost German apologist for Darwin's theory of evolution, he contended that since all species of life as "a single original element" could be traced back to matter, therefore "politics is applied biology." On this basis he claimed that the Teutonic race was the ultimate genetic development of biological evolution, and thereby he justified a universal social Darwinism under German political ideology. He was wholly consumed by German nationalism, by Nordic mythology within German Romanticism, by Frederick the Great's Prussian militarism—all of which had contributed toward the unification of Germany under Bismarck in 1870. Haeckel envisioned the triumph of Germany over all European nations during the twentieth century. When he died in 1919, his German Monist League had set in place the monistic ideology that led the post–World War I triumph of totalitarianism in Germany—One nation, One *Volk*, One superior race, One party, and One leader.[45] Both before and after World War I, the scientific, cultural, and political developments in Germany were a cause of great distress to Einstein.

Even as a schoolboy, he was so repelled by so much in German society and education that he rebelled against the patriotic nationalism, militarism, and slave mentality of his teachers and fellow students. As a young man he abandoned his German citizenship and became a Swiss citizen. During World War I he was one of only four scientists in Germany to sign an antiwar petition. His intense hatred of Prussian militarism led him to become a dedicated pacifist.[46] His hatred of the passive obedience of his fellow scientists to the totalitarian politics that emerged in Germany led him to hope that "at the end of the war, with God's benevolent help, they will largely kill each other off."[47] Undoubtedly, his unorthodox personal conception of God was a vital factor in his strong opposition to the monists who made science into an absolute belief that excluded religion. Einstein held that "science without religion is lame; religion without science is blind."[48] The pursuit of a unified world picture through the triumph of physical science was to Einstein an illusion with disastrous consequences, a conviction shared by Frost.

Belief in an absolute materialist monism was far from limited to Germany. In Soviet Russia, as Holton noted, Lenin's *Materialism and Emperio-Criticism* (1908) claimed that Marxism was based upon science, but this was proved to be mere propaganda, "not least by the faulty analysis of [Marxist] philosophy in Lenin's own book, and by the widespread mistreatment which Soviet scientists experienced when their theories did not please their government."[49] Yet the triumph of Marxism in Russia and elsewhere contributed much toward making the twentieth century dominated by monism.[50] In the United States, following the World's Columbia Exposition in Chicago in 1893, faith in a monism of matter through science and technology came to dominate the culture of American life. The fundamental doctrine of the French Enlightenment, that scientific knowledge would be the temporal salvation of mankind, was widely accepted throughout America. In *Modern Monism*, Paul Carus, a latter-day deist almost as anticlerical as Haeckel, led the way in advocating "progress" through "one grand unification program" aimed at establishing one world government. The culmination of this belief came in Vannevar Bush's *Science, The Endless Frontier* (1945), which Frost attacked during an interview on December 14, 1949: "A scientist like Vannevar Bush must be full of a feeling of progress," he said, "but a man who feels deeply about humanity must feel we are back in ancient Egypt."[51] The variations on the themes of Haeckel, Marxism, and American scientism and materialism were uniformly denounced by Frost as "monomania" or "Monometaphor," and in this he was of one mind with Einstein.

The monistic separation of religion from science, with the belief that science alone could provide spiritual understanding, was as much a serious delusion for Frost as for Einstein:

> Desert religion for science, clean out the holes and corners of the residual unknown, and there will be no more need of religion. (Religion is merely consolation for what we don't know.) But suppose there was some mistake, and the evil stood siege, the war didn't end, and something remained unknowable. Our having disarmed would make our case worse than it had ever been before.[52]

But the poet's most vital agreement with the scientist was in their common philosophical rejection of a materialist monism that aimed at dominating world affairs. Louis Untermeyer's summary of the poet's intense feelings on this point is decisive: "He is still against One World, World Federation, Universal Brotherhood, unity, conformity, the breaking down of barriers in the interest of Oneness; he is unalterably against One Anything."[53] Frost defended individual differences and divisions as essential to liberty, and these were best defended under sovereign nations that adhered to moral and constitutional law.

Frost's belief that science was one of the humanities, and not a self-sufficient and independent enterprise, led him to regard Einstein as an ideal example of what a scientist should be. The great physicist united his work in matter with adherence to the humanities, to the fictional aesthetics of art, and even to a belief in God. All of these mental and spiritual concerns functioned within the philosophical framework of a pluralistic or dualistic conception of the physical universe. In light of this complex fusion of spirit and matter, even Einstein's lifelong addiction to playing the violin took on significance in Frost's judgment that Einstein was "a great philosopher among great scientists." Their common faith in what Lovejoy called "natural dualism" as opposed to "Cartesian dualism," most evident in their theory of knowledge, was perhaps the most vital factor in Frost's attraction to Einstein. They both believed that knowledge was indirect, conveyed through metaphors or symbols that included but greatly transcended the Enlightenment assumption that knowledge is direct through empirical experience and refined through discursive or analytical logical reason. They both exalted intuition, retrospection, and deduction from their eclectic adaptations of long-established or new knowledge, all of which, stored in memory, provided the rich source for their original and imaginative creativity. Einstein's mathematical symbols served the same function in his science that metaphors and images served Frost in his poetry. Frost believed that metaphors had to be both "sensational and valid," new and true, just as Einstein believed that the final test of what was original in his thought had to be confirmed by what was valid in his theory.

In light of all that the poet and scientist held in common in their epistemology and creative methodology, it is significant that they were of one mind regarding the psychological theory of Sigmund Freud. Roger Highfield and Paul Carter have summarized Einstein's view of Freud:

> He told Eduard (his younger son) that he had read Freud's writings but was unconverted, and believed his methods dubious— even fraudulent. Einstein had met Freud in Berlin, and corresponded with him on peace and disarmament. In 1936, however, Freud would remark to him, "I always knew that you admired me only 'out of politeness' and that you are convinced by very few of my assertions."[54]

Frost believed that Freud's theory of human psychology regarding the subconscious sexual life of men, women, and children was sensational, but not likely valid. In referring to the theorist, he once made a deliberate slip of the tongue and called him "Sigmund Fraud." In a conversation with me he asserted that there was more valid psychology in the plays of Shakespeare than in Freud's theory. For several decades after around 1920, when it was most fashionable to be a Freudian literary critic, Frost expressed his skepticism of the sexual connections found in images and metaphors, and was condemned as being "anti-intellectual." He responded to the mental illness of his sister Jeannie and his daughter Irma by placing them under conventional institutional care. When his son Carol showed signs of emotional illness, on a personal rather than a professional basis he consulted his friend Merrill Moore, both a poet and psychiatrist, but neither was able to prevent Carol's suicide. Einstein also showed his distrust of psychoanalysis when his son Eduard plunged deeper and deeper into mental illness,[55] and he too looked to conventional institutions as the best available solution. In his basic methodology, Freud was essentially a belated child of the Enlightenment, and since neither Einstein nor Frost considered its methodology adequate in establishing scientific truths, they were both naturally skeptical of his theory.[56]

A chronological review of Frost's comments on Einstein, from the late 1920s through 1959, is highly illuminating, not only for his sustained high regard for the scientist, but for Einstein's philosophical views and his character as a man as well. Frost made use of the central metaphors regarding time and space in several of his poems, and he noted the points he and Einstein held in common in their beliefs regarding creativity. The poet was convinced that scientific theories were as much a product of the creative imagination and sense of form as were poetry and the arts. Bernard Cohen has recorded Einstein's similar belief regarding creativity: "Einstein said he had always believed that the invention of scientific concepts and the building of theories upon them was one of the great creative properties of the human mind."[57] Frost's "wild free ways of wit and art" described Einstein's originality in science and explained how his concept of curved time-space digressed from the conventional beliefs of his fellow scientists.[58]

In 1928, after a conversation with Frost, Genevieve Taggert recorded that "Frost when confronted in conversation with new marvels of science . . . said: 'Isn't science just an extended metaphor: its aim is to describe the unknown in terms of the known? Isn't it a kind of poetry, to be treated as plausible material, not as cold fact?'" When reminded of Einstein's theory of relativity he is quoted as saying: "Wonderful, yes, wonderful but no better as a metaphor than you or I might make for ourselves before five o'clock."[59] Through metaphors science reveals "the unknown in terms of the known" regarding matter, just as poetry does regarding spirit. Both are beyond the "cold fact" of discursive reasoning through empiricism. There was nothing derogatory in Frost's calling Einstein's theory "wonderful" and valid, despite regarding it as not particularly remarkable as a metaphor. Yet his biographer, Thompson, responded to Taggert's statement: "RF never tired of making remarks like these for the purpose of trying to denigrate modern science." Although he criticized abuses made in the name of science, Frost did not denigrate science. In "The Future of Man" symposium he voiced what was his most persistent positive belief regarding science: "It is man's greatest enterprise. It is the charge of the ethereal into the material. It is our substantiation of our meaning. It can't go too far or deep for me."[60] Thompson's criticism raises the question whether any monist, with a literal view of reality, is capable of understanding Frost's complex dualism of spirit and matter and his belief in metaphorical thinking.

In "Education by Poetry" (1930), Frost remarked that "in late years" he wanted "to go further and further in making metaphor the whole of thinking," so that to illustrate metaphorical thinking in science he included examples from Einstein's *Relativity: The Special and General Theory.*[61] Without mentioning Einstein by name, or identifying his book, he drew from two chapters, "The Relativity of Simultaneity" and "The Lorentz Transformation," and commented upon the principle "that the more accurately you state where a thing is, the less accurately you will be able to tell how fast it is moving." He observed that Einstein had identified a moving thing with an event:

> And, of course, everything is moving. Everything is an event now. Another metaphor. A thing, they say, is an event. Do you believe it is? Not quite, I believe it is almost an event. But I like the comparison of a thing with an event.[62]

A recurrent image and metaphor in Einstein's book involved the proximity of stars and planets to each other perceived as curved-space: "As seen from the earth, certain fixed stars appear to be in the neighborhood of the sun." And again: "The stars in the neighborhood of the sun are photographed during a solar eclipse. I am sure the reader will appreciate with sufficient clearness what I mean here by 'neighboring' . . . (if he is not too pedantic)."[63] Stars "in the neighborhood of the sun" are variously described in terms of "curved-space," "curvature" of cosmic bodies, "curvature of light rays," "curvature of space," and "curvilinear motion." Einstein defined "path-curve" as "a curve along which the body moves."[64] Frost was captivated by this cluster of image-metaphors and responded enthusiastically:

> I notice another [metaphor] from the same quarter. "In the neighborhood of matter space is something like curved." Isn't that a good one! It seems to me that is simply and utterly charming—to say that space is something like curved in the neighborhood of matter. "Something like."[65]

Frost was so enamored by Einstein's metaphor that he repeated it with his own variations for years afterward.

In *A Masque of Reason* (1945), Frost pictured biblical time as similar to time in Einstein's theory, so that when Job said to God that his wife, Thyatira (a fictional character not found in the Bible), "now felt younger by a thousand years / Than the day she was born," God responds in terms of Einstein's theory:

> That's about right,
> I should have said. You got your age reversed
> When time was found to be a space dimension
> That could, like any space, be turned around in?

The irony in this dramatic exchange is that the phenomena of time-space, like all of the laws of nature governing the physical universe, were presumably created by God, but "found" by scientists such as Einstein. As an agent of God's revelations in the realm of matter, Einstein and his theory served a religious purpose.

Two years after *A Masque of Reason*, in a letter to Louis Untermeyer (January 9, 1947), Frost domesticated Einstein's curved-space metaphor by identifying it as a principle governing objects in motion on earth: "No line can be straight on a curved world moving in circles." Later in the same letter, he lifted the metaphor beyond an abstract concept of science and applied it to the power in human nature to modify the laws of physical nature in practical matters: "some of the curves we make must offset the curvature of space."[66] Frost's statements strongly imply that the creative mind and will of Einstein not only discovered the laws of relativity in physical nature, but by providing modern man with a new metaphor to live by, his theory modified the strict determinism in the laws governing matter. Frost apparently recognized that by introducing the creative principle of mind into physical nature, Einstein's theory took strong issue with evolutionists such as Thomas Henry Huxley and his German colleague Ernst Haeckel, whose determinism was based upon a monism of matter.

On August 11, 1950, Frost included in a letter to Untermeyer a discursive, soliloquizing fragment of a poem called "Mist, Smoke, and Haze." Amid speculations about characters who wonder who they are and where they are occurs a passage which clearly reflects Frost's reading of Einstein's metaphor on curved-space. Without naming Einstein, it describes one of many past "philosophers / Who came a-visiting their universe":

> *One of these had found reason to conclude*
> *The motion of the earth around the sun*
> *Was nothing but the ultimate adjustment*
> *It had to make itself among the adjustments*
> *Everything else in space was making for it*
> *So it could be the one thing standing still;*
> *And men were not mistaken in their sense*
> *Of being stationary and not whirled*
> *And twisted through a dozen curves at once.*
> *But being made the one fixed point there is*
> *Seems more amusing to them than convincing.*[67]

The central scientific concept that everything in the universe, including man on the planet earth, has to "make adjustments" amidst the whirl of everything through space, makes man unique as "the one fixed point" and "one thing standing still" in the universe. The significance of this fact is best understood by examining a poem in which Frost made a unique use of Einstein's image of "curved-space."

That poem, "The Master Speed," appeared in *A Further Range* (1930), fourteen years before the fragment he sent to Untermeyer. The master speed is Frost's term for the curved-space movement of planets and stars through the solar system. The power of mankind to stand still on earth, beyond historical time, is described in the first nine lines of the poem:

> *No speed of wind or water rushing by*
> *But you have speed far greater. You may climb*
> *Back up a stream of radiance to the sky,*
> *And back through history up the stream of time.*
> *And you were given this swiftness, not for haste*
> *Nor chiefly that you may go where you will,*
> *But in the rush of everything to waste,*
> *That you may have the power of standing still—*
> *Off any still or moving thing you say.*

Since Frost never lost sight of his belief that science is one of the humanities, it was characteristic of him not to rest content with an abstract statement of a scientific theory, but to connect it dramatically to human experience and man's deepest personal concerns. In this characteristic, Frost was of one mind and spirit with Einstein, whose social consciousness made him deeply concerned with how the power over nature created by science and technology influenced human affairs in society. Science as truth was an end in itself, a form of revelation regarding matter just as art and religion were revelations regarding the spirit of man. But the practical consequences of science involved the normative principles and values of the humanities and religion. The final five lines of "The Master Speed" contrasted Einstein's scientific axioms regarding the movement of speeding planets through time-space with the power and choice of earth-bound lovers to stand still forever through the enduring unity of their love:

> *Two such as you with such a master speed*
> *Cannot be parted nor be swept away*
> *From one another once you are agreed*

*That life is only life forevermore*
*Together wing to wing and oar to oar.*

It is most fitting that these lines are carved in stone and form the emblematic theme on the tomb of Elinor Frost in Bennington, Vermont. Probably readers of these lines will not connect them with Einstein's theory of relativity, which appears to be so remote from a love lyric on the fixed eternal unity of true love. But in making such original use of science, Frost is in the tradition of John Donne's metaphysical conceits and John Milton's reconciliation of the depersonalized conceptions of science with the personal beliefs and values of human nature.

On June 30, 1955, Frost lectured at Bread Loaf, ostensibly on how to understand or "take" poetry, yet much of his talk was on his response to I. Bernard Cohen's "An Interview with Einstein," which had already appeared in *Scientific American* (July 1955).[68] Implicit in his indirect method of dealing with Einstein was his assumption that the same difficulties readers had in understanding how to "take" his poetry applied to how to best understand Einstein. Cohen's interview took place two weeks before Einstein's death, so that a spirit of reverence was mixed into Frost's opening remarks:

> I suppose a poem is a kind of fooling. I've just been reading in a sermon by a great Unitarian friend of mine about "the foolishness of God": the foolishness of God. God's foolish, you know, and God's fooling. And I've just been reading about the last days of Einstein, the old man, by somebody who knows his science and who knew his philosophy because he was a great philosopher among great scientists. And the thing about him was that every few minutes it was a burst of laughter about something philosophical or something—God, relativity, or something about Newton. He got a great laugh over his little quarrel with Newton. He once said something in print, something we've seen: "Forgive me, Newton. Forgive me, Newton." Of course, if the height of everything is fooling—God's foolishness—then poetry mounts somewhere into a kind of fooling. It's something hard to get. It's what you spend a good deal of education on—just getting it right.[69]

Frost clearly perceived that if "the height of everything is fooling," if even God is a humorist, that laughter is a vital element in understanding not only poetry, but Einstein's serious nature and scientific thought.

Throughout his lecture Frost paid particular attention to Cohen's statements on Einstein's "rich sense of humor." The contrast between his soft speech and his ringing laughter was enormous. He enjoyed making jokes; every time he made a point that he liked, or heard something that appealed to him, he would burst into booming laughter that echoed from the walls.[70] Throughout the interview, Einstein's humor was intricately intertwined with his personal character and temperament, and with his serious comments on his scientific and philosophical beliefs.

Frost's positive response to Einstein's raucous humor can best be understood in the light of that part of his own aesthetic theory and creative practice that perceives how comedy and tragedy are closely related and how all art is connected with man's philosophical understanding of human nature and life. Laughter and tears have great philosophical significance; between the polarities of comedy and tragedy the "play" of man's creative mind makes the metaphors that "attempt to say matter in terms of spirit, or spirit in terms of matter, to make the final unity." Laughter helps to illuminate the unknown in terms of the known, as much in science as in poetry. Laughter provides an emotional catharsis and is a metaphor by which to judge even the tragic dimensions in the world.

A few of Frost's numerous comments on the role of comedy will suffice to show the vital role of humor or wit or irony he perceived in all serious discourse. His early biographer, Robert Newdick, recorded that "one of Frost's theses is that a man can go no further seriously than he can go in fun."[71] In 1941, while instructing a friend in methods of composition, he said that if a composition has obvious outer seriousness it should also have a subtle core of inner humor; and outer humor or wit should always have a serious inner theme.[72] During private conversations with friends, and in poetry readings, he said that he was never more serious than when he was joking. To Untermeyer, who shared Frost's wide-ranging humor, he wrote that "Banter struck me as one of the best words ever used to explain me," but he added a note of caution: "at bottom the world isn't a joke."[73] In his poetry, he sometimes dropped explicit hints on how readers should interpret him. In "Not Quite Social," he wrote: "The way of understanding is partly mirth." "In the Clearing" features the couplet: "It takes all sorts of in and outdoor schooling / To get adapted to my kind of fooling." In "The Mountain" he reminded readers: "But all the fun's in how you say a thing." To a friend he said: "Never forget the fun of play in reading."[74] From these few examples, it should be evident that Frost perceived Einstein's laughter in response to serious concerns as a sign that the great scientist had a firm grasp of all reality, the whole range of the comic and the tragic and all of the polarities of real and apparent contradictions between spirit and matter that fall within a philosophy of dualism.

On the strictly serious side of life, Frost was deeply moved by Cohen's account of how Einstein had responded to the brazen and humorless attempt of some scientists to suppress the publication of Immanuel Velikovsky's book *Worlds in Collision* (1950), because they regarded his science as utter nonsense. To his Bread Loaf audience he made clear his own hatred of censorship, against those who "wanted to burn that book," and that he approved of the subtle, calm, indirect manner of Einstein in condemning such censorship:

> Old Einstein just happened to speak of it casually, you know, and he didn't name the book, but you could tell what it was from the description of it. He didn't name the publishing house. He didn't name the suppressors. He just said what a charmingly crazy book it was. I've got some on the shelf of my library. Just as charming as Ignatius Donnelly's *Lost Atlantis*. That's another wonderful book. And the books about Shakespeare who didn't write Shakespeare. What's all this severity about, back over these years? The old man Einstein made a laugh about it,—that crazy book. How charming: And terrible—with passion, he said: "How terrible suppressing any book: That's too much for me." Well, I'll leave that. But you can almost judge yourself by how deep you go into things. It's what you call compassion. But think this is more than compassion—this magnanimity.[75]

During his poetry readings, Frost almost never revealed a *cri de coeur*, but Einstein's method, and his passionate understatement in condemning censorship, had moved the poet almost to tears. Like Einstein, he understood that every creative work of literature, on any subject, expressed something of the human spirit, and that no matter how deficient it was in factual knowledge, it deserved to exist. Humor helped in knowing how to "take" it, and time was the best censor; it would screen out the ephemeral from the worthwhile works of man.

One of the most significant statements in Cohen's interview to which Frost responded positively concerned not science but Einstein's philosophy: "Einstein said that at the beginning of the century only a few scientists had been philosophically minded, but today physicists are almost all philosophers, although 'they are apt to be bad philosophers.' He pointed as an example to logical positivism, which he felt was a kind of philosophy that came out of physics."[76] Since Frost regarded positivism as the chief source of the abuse of science into scientism, Einstein's statement prompted him to remark that Einstein was "a great philosopher among great scientists."[77] But precisely what was Einstein's own philosophy?

It is probably impossible to state Einstein's philosophy in terms of an abstract category. It is clearly far easier to state what he rejected as bad philosophy, such as that of "logical positivism" out of physics and similar views derived from a monism of matter alone. In contending that moving bodies in space-time are perceived "relative to the standpoint of observers," he made mind or spirit in man an essential factor in the perception of all reality. Since he believed in God, he was a theist and not an atheist or agnostic. Like Frost, he believed that men act out of faith or insufficient foreknowledge and do not demand prior empirical evidence as proof of something before they believe in it. He had faith in the validity of his theory of relativity long before there was empirical evidence to confirm it. Even before the British scientists observed the eclipse that verified his general theory, Einstein stated his belief that the theory verified the empirical observation more than the verification proved the theory: "Now, I am fully satisfied, and I do not doubt any more the correctness of the whole system, may the observation of the eclipse succeed or not. The sense of the thing is too evident."[78] Einstein held that there was no such thing as an objective physical universe as recorded through sensory experience; there was only a conceptual mental world perceived through the "free play" of the mind through conceptual ideas working upon the raw materials provided by the senses. Thus, he rejected any form of Platonic idealism, including Berkeley's subjective spiritual monism, which assumed a monism of pure spirit.

Neither was Einstein satisfied with the many modern attempts, like those of Bertrand Russell, to hold simultaneously a monism of matter and a monism of mind, each held separately. This type of error led Philipp Frank to contend that "Einstein's theories could be used equally well as propaganda for materialism or against it."[79] It is far more accurate to say that Einstein rejected both a monism of matter and a monism of spirit. Frank's error, like that of scientists who retained the Cartesian "bifurcation of nature," as Lovejoy has shown, resulted in a "vague, confused and aberrant form of dualism," the pseudo-dualism of Descartes. In *Relativity: The Special and General Theory*, Einstein rejected as inadequate the Enlightenment theory of knowledge assumed by Locke and Newton and held to an epistemology that led to what Lovejoy called "natural Dualism."[80] By something like a process of elimination, in rejecting both forms of monism, Einstein's philosophy as revealed in his theory was in Lovejoy's words "simply a vindication of dualism." Frost's own dualistic philosophy helps to explain his very positive response and emotional empathy with practically every point made by Einstein in his interview with Cohen. As a scientist and man, Einstein was to Frost an ideal example of how science can best be regarded as one of the humanities.[81]

Many specific particulars in Cohen's interview, and in Einstein's *The Evolution of Physics* (1938), were very similar, or even almost identical, to beliefs held by Frost. For example, the scientist stated that in all creative work involving the mind, "the use of intuition is dangerous but necessary."[82] Similarly, since the poet identified the mind with intuition, during an interview with Harvey Breit in the *New York Times* (November 27, 1949), his comment on the same subject takes on great significance: "Poetry must include the mind as well as the emotions. Too many poets delude themselves by thinking the mind is dangerous and must be left out. Well, the mind is dangerous and must be left in."[83] The resonance of Einstein's ideas and feelings echoed so vibrantly with Frost's own beliefs and psychology not least of all because they shared a close underlying affinity in philosophical dualism.

In light of Frost's strong favorable responses and basic agreement with the history of ideas in the scholarship of Lovejoy and the scientific theory of Einstein, Reginald Cook's fertile insight that "the route through the poetry of Robert Frost leads away from the Great Chain of Being to an exercise of options in an open-ended universe" takes on enormous significance for literary critics and scholars dealing with his poetry and beliefs. But the "options in an open-ended universe" need to be understood on their own grounds before being applied to Frost's thought and poetry. A good beginning toward this end is provided by Philipp Frank:

> The Abbé Lemaitre, a Belgian Catholic priest, had found that Einstein's equations of the gravitational field in universal space were also consistent with a distribution of matter in the universe which did not always remain the same on the average. Hence, the Abbé could assume that the various galaxies move farther and farther away from one another. He thus founded the theory of the expanding universe, which had been adumbrated in connection with Einstein's theories. . . . [84]

Lemaitre's theory is supported by the astronomical discoveries of more powerful telescopes, leading to Hubble's law—that resulting from the expansion of the universe, space and time are measured by the linear relationship between the distance of a galaxy from the observer and its motion away from the observer. No less a scientist than Arthur Eddington supported Lemaitre's theory.

In response to the concept of an open-ended universe, Frost's poem "Any Size We Please" is rich in ironical implications:

> *No one was looking at his lonely case,*
> *So like a half-mad outpost sentinel,*
> *Indulging an absurd dramatic spell,*
> *Albeit not without some shame of face,*
> *He stretched his arms out to the dark of space*
> *And held them absolutely parallel*
> *In infinite appeal. Then saying, "Hell"*
> *He drew them in for warmth of self-embrace.*
> *He thought if he could have his space all curved*
> *Wrapped in around itself and self-befriended,*
> *His science needn't get him so unnerved.*
> *He had been too all out, too much extended.*
> *He slapped his breast to verify his purse*
> *And hugged himself for all his universe.*

Frost's conception of knowledge and understanding as metaphor placed the theory of an open-ended universe within the historical context of all previous theories that determined the worldview of mankind in various epochs. Frost's metaphorical thought is in keeping with a statement by Holton: "Einstein did not prove the work of Newton wrong; he provided a larger setting within which some limitations, contradictions, and asymmetries in the earlier physics disappeared."[85] Just as Newton's physics displaced the physics of Aristotle and the Ptolemaic conception of the universe with the Copernican theory, and Einstein's theory of relativity displaced Newton only to be modified by quantum physics and further refinements in science, so too the concept of an open-ended universe was best regarded as a metaphor for modern man's view of the universe. Metaphorical thought has the great virtue of avoiding the common error of assuming that each new discovery or theory of science proves all previous theories or beliefs to have been wrong. The idea of progress does not apply to scientific theories. Theories provide the dominant metaphor by which each era of history perceives itself in relation to the universe.[86] Cook's observation that a fresh exercise of options exists for all readers of Frost in the light of the poet's understanding of the open-ended universe is facilitated by taking fully into account the poet's responses to Lovejoy's *The Great Chain of Being* and *The Revolt Against Dualism* and to Einstein's theory of relativity and later developments in scientific theories. Frost's understanding of Lovejoy's two masterful works of scholarship, and his reading of Einstein's theory, clearly provide a vital dimension in the poet's dualist philosophy.

# 9

## Frost and Religion: The Two Masques

Robert Frost has frequently been described by both his critics and his admirers as the most American of modern American poets. The first writer to comment on Frost's uniquely American traits was Ezra Pound. In London, right after he had read the galley sheets of Frost's first book of poems, *A Boy's Will*, in March 1913 and even before the book had appeared, Pound wrote to his friend Alice C. Henderson that his new friend was "vurry Amur'k'n, with I think, the seeds of grace." Pound's remark was most perceptive, because "the seeds of grace" that made Frost an unusually original and gifted poet were planted and had sprung from a soil and national sensibility that was indeed uniquely American. In July 1962, at Bread Loaf, Frost confirmed Pound's insight in an aphorism: "All literature begins with geography."[1] The subjects of the thirty-one brief lyrics in *A Boy's Will* were mainly from American and particularly from New England rural scenes and contained Frost's sensory observations, feelings, and reflections as an idealistic young American, on the seasons, stars, storms, the wind, flowers, and other common objects of nature and rural life, together with a few of the poet's convictions concerning God, love, science, and other such related subjects.

In addition to his subjects and themes, Frost's early poems were in their language and speech rhythms American adaptations of the forms, techniques, and conventions of Romantic and Victorian poetry. The colloquial idiom and simple diction of Frost's first poems were decidedly in the American grain, more in the spirit of Whitman than of Wordsworth. Several critics have remarked on the essentially American character of Frost's use of English, not only in his early poems but throughout his literary career.

Lawrance Thompson has noted that "Frost's entire work is deeply rooted in the American, even in the most vital Puritan, idiom. It is 'native to the grain,' and yet thoroughly original."[2] Louis Untermeyer also considered Frost "the most American of poets" because of his "characteristically plain utterance" and "the conversational tone of speech" in his poetry.[3]

The pastorals and eclogues of Frost's second book, *North of Boston* (1914), were so strongly stamped in their subjects, themes, language, and rhythms of speech with Frost's regional and national temper that Ezra Pound, in his review in *Poetry* (December 1914), called them "American Georgics." Frost's originality in adapting and assimilating the classical eclogues and pastorals of Theocritus, Horace, and Virgil to his personal New England–American idiom in effect created a new genre for modern poetry, in which blank verse, used for description and dialogue, was combined with the narrative ease and discursiveness of prose fiction and with the concise dramatic power of the stage to create an intense psychological human drama.

The native American tradition in subjects, themes, forms, techniques, and language, so evident in Frost's first two books of poetry, was enormously enriched and extended by the five volumes of poetry he published between *North of Boston* and his two masques, published in 1945 and 1947. During these three decades Frost adapted a great variety of poetic forms to his American character and sensibility. Frost once remarked that "the most American trait is Americanniness,"[4] which even in its playful wit suggests that improvised shrewdness and conscious Yankee humor provided the poet with a regional-universal perspective toward life most appropriate for dealing with unreconciled oppositions, for double-edged dramatic ironies, for saying the whole of a theme in terms of a part contained in an image, for harmonizing the eternal "two-endedness of things," such as the conflicting claims of justice and mercy. Frost's "Americanniness" consisted of his skill in handling the complex contraries of life in such a simple and apparently artless style that his poetry became widely read by discriminating intellectuals and uncritical common readers alike. It took the sophisticated Freudian undiscriminating intellectuals a whole generation to discover the "real" Frost, but Americans who were not myopic symbol hunters appreciated Frost, each according to his lights, almost immediately. In 1957 Frost admitted to "having become . . . an almost national poet."[5] Undoubtedly, as some critics have claimed, Frost's wide popularity was a reflection of certain common American traits shaping the national character: "Frost is important as a kind of American culture hero, as an index of certain persistent American characteristics."[6] Lionel Trilling has said the same thing in terms of the main tradition of American literature: "Robert Frost is doing in his poems what [D. H.] Lawrence says the great writers of the classic American tradition did."[7]

Frost's *A Masque of Reason* (1945) and *A Masque of Mercy* (1947) mark yet another leap in his refinements of earlier subjects, themes, techniques, language, and form. Of the three great all-inclusive subjects treated by poets—God, man, and nature—Frost's central subject is always man. A human perspective and human values always provide Frost's point of view toward his subject. In his philosophy he is more a humanist than a theologian or a naturalist, although his humanism in any given poem may incline either way. In *A Boy's Will* Frost was primarily concerned with man's relationship to external nature; and in *North of Boston*, subtitled *A Book of People*, his central concern was man's relationship to man. The five volumes that followed were all devoted to further explorations of these two complex sets of relationships. But in his two masques, for the first time in his life as a writer Frost dealt extensively and exclusively with man's relationship with God. The bulk of this chapter will explore the various aspects of Frost's themes, techniques, and language in the masques, but before analyzing these elements it will be useful to consider briefly the masque as a form of poetic drama, and what Frost did with it.

How do Frost's masques compare with the masque as a conscious literary and dramatic form in English literature? Clearly, they are a world apart from the somewhat profligate popular court masques introduced as *Twelfth Night* for Henry VIII in 1512, with their masked dancers, carnival amusements, and revels with the audience. Nor are Frost's plays related to the mummery pantomimes or folk masques, since his characters wear no masks and speak much dialogue. Also, in their simplicity Frost's plays are the antithesis of the elaborate and lavish spectacle plays put on by Ben Jonson (1572–1637) and Inigo Jones (1573–1652) during the early years of James I's reign. Like the first Jonson-Jones collaboration, *Of Blacknesse* (1605), Frost's two masques have for their setting a fixed scene in perspective, with no procession of actors. The irreverent wit and humor in Frost's *A Masque of Reason* has its earliest analogue in Ben Jonson's antimasque in *The Masque of Queenes* (1609), whose comic interlude parodied the main plot and theme. But unlike Jonson's, Frost's wit and humor are integrated within the dialogue and are an organic part of the main plot and theme rather than mere commentaries on them. In his dialogue, Frost has the epigrammatic conciseness of Jonson. Unlike the figures in most English masques, the characters in Frost's two plays are not mythological; they are stark prototypes of human or spiritual personalities, symbolic of established moral ideals, whose set speeches, like those by characters in medieval morality plays, subordinate the dramatic conflict and action wholly to an allegorical dialogue of ideas. Like Milton's *Comus* (acted 1634, published 1637), which is more a pastoral drama than a masque, Frost's two plays depend more on poetry than on spectacle, and like Milton his main purpose is to state a serious theological and moral principle about an important religious or philosophical problem.[8] But all things considered, Frost's masques owe less to his English sources than to his own resources in the classic American tradition of literature; his masques are uniquely modern adaptations of a poetic-dramatic form that had been almost entirely discarded since the middle of the seventeenth century.[9] Although Frost had a brief "juvenile dream of Broadway" for *A Masque of Reason*, he was in the end "content . . . with the pair of masques as poems,"[10] and it is as closet drama that they should be considered.

## A Masque of Reason (1945)

Frost's *A Masque of Reason* is a dramatic explication of Old Testament justice, contained in the forty-two chapters of the Book of Job, as understood by modern man in a modern setting. At the end of the masque, Frost wrote: "Here endeth chapter forty-three of Job." This is Frost's bland and ironic way of saying that no one can understand his masque without a complete knowledge of the Book of Job, and also, in light of his theme, that his masque is a prophetic-like satire on modern man's excessive confidence in his own reason.

In the opening scene ("A fair oasis in the purest desert"), Job and his wife, Thyatira, awake to find God caught in the branches of the Burning Bush (the Christmas Tree), which, ironically, gives not a light of Old Testament revelation, but "a strange light" of New Testament Christianity, of spirit entangled in matter, or religion organized and refined by art, so that "the Tree is troubled" by God's being "caught in the branches."[11] Job's comment on the Christmas tree ornaments extends this point through a parody of Yeats's rhetoric in "Sailing to Byzantium" and through a probable allusion to T. S. Eliot's "Sweeney Among the Nightingales":

> *The ornaments the Greek artificers*
> *Made for the Emperor Alexius,*
> *The Star of Bethlehem, the pomegranates,*
> *The birds, seem all on fire with Paradise.*

> *And hark, the gold enameled nightingales*
> *Are singing.*

In *A Masque of Mercy*, Frost again criticized Yeats through a long speech by Paul, condemning Yeats for having

> *Once charged the Nazarene with having brought*
> *A darkness out of Asia that had crossed*
> *Old Attic grace and Spartan discipline*
> *With violence.*

Frost then defends Christ against Yeats's charge by noting that Christ introduced "The mercy on the Sin against the Sermon," whose "origin was love."[12] But in *A Masque of Reason*, Frost omitted consideration of mercy in the conflict between justice and mercy.

When God finally gets disentangled from the Christmas tree, Job's wife remarks: "It's God. I'd know Him by Blake's picture anywhere," to which, later, God responds: "The best, I'm told, I ever have had taken." God sets up a plywood, flat, prefabricated throne (obviously a parody on conventional notions of the throne of God, as held by pious literalists, and also in keeping with modern efficiency in construction), and Job's wife guesses the throne is "for an Olympic Tournament, / Or Court of Love," but which Job assumes is for Judgment Day. Job looks for a forthcoming verdict on himself, and being a student of English literature, he bids his wife: "Suffer yourself to be admired, my love / As Waller says." All these biblical, classical, and courtly love allusions, linked by historical and literary anachronisms and verbal buffooneries, immediately establish the mixed comic-tragic ingredients and tone of the whole masque. It is obvious from the very beginning of the masque that Frost's method involves an ironical, mocking, comic treatment of the serious and tragic theme of Job's suffering of injustice. Throughout the masque the whimsical situational comedy, the witty quips, playful puns, and double entendres, indulged in by Job, his wife, and even by God, underscore Frost's mock-serious treatment of the biblical characters, who think and talk like modern Americans and give an externally light tone to the serious internal discourse at the heart of the theme.

There are many things in both the manner and the matter of Frost's masque deliberately calculated to raise the temperature of sincere and conventional religious believers who are hopelessly humorless and, even more, that of sincere and militantly devout agnostics or freethinking atheists who have an undoubting confidence in man's self-sufficient reason.

Unfortunately for Frost, his comic and satirical technique has been the chief source of misunderstanding of his masques. Too many readers have ignored Frost's dictum that in good writing "the way of understanding is partly mirth," and that when writing "is with outer humor, it must be with inner seriousness." Frost's statement in the amended preface to E. A. Robinson's *King Jasper*, that "the style is the way a man takes himself," best explains the function of comic wit and irony in his masques. The terrible tragedies that overwhelmed his family—the early deaths of his parents and several of his children, the mental affliction of his sister, the suicide of his son Carol, and other sorrows that pursued him into late life—were enough to make him the modern living embodiment of Job. On August 9, 1947, when his daughter Irma was about to be confined in a mental institution, Frost wrote to Louis Untermeyer: "Cast your eye back over my family luck and perhaps you will wonder if I haven't had pretty near enough." Then he added: "That is for the angels to say."[13]

Frost's implicit religious faith included both evil and good, and therefore both the tragic and comic sense toward life. This belief required him to assume a God-like, cosmic, stoical detachment toward all of life, even in matters in which he was most personally involved and intensely committed, so that he could grasp the tragic as tragic but also in terms of the comic, and understand sorrow in terms of laughter and irony. In this way of taking himself Frost was unique. Louis Untermeyer wrote of this trait in Frost: "His was a high stoicism which could mask unhappiness in playfulness, which could even delight in darkness." Frost was "one who could tease and be tortured, renounce and be reconciled."[14] Certainly, Frost never lost his balance between the tragic and the comic. Although the theme of his masque is centered in the serious tragedy and unhappiness of Job, Frost's method is playful, like the casual, bantering, whimsical, frolicsome, tongue-in-cheek teasing of one who has a lover's quarrel with the world. His masque is ironical in tone, with levity-gravity and light-somber qualities that at once intensify God's arbitrary injustice to Job and balance it off with the perverse relief of laughter. To Frost, God is a comic wit who cares for man, at once detached and concerned. He is not only the source of revelation but also the master of revels.

Most critics of *A Masque of Reason* have failed to perceive the function of the comic elements and have dismissed the masque as a serious artistic lapse. According to Randall Jarrell, "*A Masque of Reason* . . . is a frivolous, trivial, and bewilderingly corny affair, full of jokes inexplicable except as the contemptuous patter of an old magician certain that he can get away with anything in the world."[15] This singularly obtuse criticism is typical of many critics who cannot understand how comedy, even low comedy, can heighten the sense of high tragedy in Job's affliction. Yvor Winters stated that Frost's comic "details . . . are offered merely for the shock of cleverness; the details are irrelevant to any theme discernible in the poem," and he concluded that the masque is among Frost's "feeblest and least serious efforts."[16] It is ironical that critics who fall far short of Frost's all-inclusive comic / tragic view of the tragedy of man's temporal life should insist from the one-dimensional base of their high seriousness that his wit and humor and comic view of man are sadly misplaced in the masque.[17]

A more valid criticism of Frost's use of comedy in the masque is that it is not always well integrated with the dialogue and dramatic action of the serious theme. This is partly the result of Frost's indiscriminate mixing of things sacred and profane, which has been questioned as bad taste—a sacrilege against the religious sensibility of Christians and Jews. Even here a distinction needs to be made. Frost's comedy is not directed against traditional religious orthodoxy regarding the justice or mercy of God, but against the conventional social respectability of devout but humorless prudes. But it is even more sharply directed against antireligious or nonreligious rationalists. Those readers whose rigid religious faith does not permit spoofing, bantering, and raillery between man and God fail to understand that it is the very intimacy of Job and his wife with God that allows them such liberties in speech. Their dialogue is like gossip, like the fierce spontaneous give-and-take of a domestic quarrel, where an assumed and intense love allows for great liberties in the expression of resentments or demands. There is nothing unctious or reserved about the faith of Job and his wife. If God is a real person, He should be spoken to as a real person, not as a remote and bloodless abstraction.

The whole question in comic relief is whether it fulfills its dramatic purpose artistically. Since most of the comedy is provided by Thyatira, Job's shrewd and sharp-tongued wife, in her remarks to Job, God, and Satan, an examination of her function in the play will clarify Frost's skill in comedy. Clearly, Job's wife is a blood descendant of Mother Eve, by way of the shrew in medieval and Tudor drama. She is proud to acknowledge that the Witch of Endor was a friend of hers. She has the advanced and militant social consciousness of a pre–World War I Bloomer girl or a Women's Liberation advocate. In the modern setting of Frost's masque, Job's wife is an emancipated and sophisticated American woman, the prototype of the most ardent member of the League of Women Voters. But she is also a tangled skein of contradictions. She is convinced that God (being male) has it in for women, and asks Him if it stands to reason (her reason, not God's)

> *That women prophets should be burned as witches,*
> *Whereas men prophets are received with honor.*

Her complaint against this injustice is particularly ludicrous because it follows immediately after God's long speech to Job on why men have to endure injustices they can't explain, for reasons God does not have to give. Thyatira's complaint is the comic equivalent of Job's serious case against God.

But it turns out she wasn't really listening to the exchange between Job and God, because philosophical discourse doesn't interest her. In a tone of disdainful superiority Thyatira says: "You don't catch women trying to be Plato." Job confirms this to God:

> *And she's a woman: she's not interested*
> *In general ideas and principles.*

Thyatira's interests are "Witch-women's rights," so that the moment Satan appears, "like a sapphire wasp / That flickers mica wings," she promptly sits up and says:

> *Well, if we aren't all here,*
> *Including me, the only Dramatis*
> *Personae needed to enact the problem.*

After so many eons of time, as Eve's undoubted and unrepentant daughter, she still feels a deep kinship with Old Nick. When Satan first speaks she responds:

> *That strain again! Give me excess of it!*
> *As dulcet as a pagan temple gong!*

Although this is said in light mock-seriousness, Job's wife is in truth a perverse feminine Romantic to the bittersweet end, and says of Satan:

> *He's very real to me*
> *And always will be. Please don't go. Stay, stay*
> *But to the evensong, and having played*
> *Together we will go with you along.*
> *There are who won't have had enough of you*
> *If you go now. . . .*

Romantic love and sensual delight are supreme for Job's wife. In her rapport with Satan and her emotive anxiety to receive with honor the prince of evil wizards, she has forgotten completely her intellectual concern about witch women's rights and the differences between men and women prophets. Could anything be more charming and disarming than Frost's portrait of Job's wife? Other than a modern naïve intellectual critic, would any male—secular or religious—claim that the comedy she provides has no place in the drama of the masque?

Job's wife supplies the comic subplot for the serious theme centered in the dialogue between Job and God. Her comic role adds an ironical dimension to the main theme. It is ironical that Job, the rational and philosophical male, is less virulent in asking God for explanations that satisfy his reason than Thyatira, the nonphilosophical and emotional female, who is quick to insist "to know the reason why" God allows irrational and unjust events to happen:

> All You can seem to do is lose Your temper
> When reason-hungry mortals ask for reasons.
> Of course, in the abstract high singular
> There isn't any universal reason;
> And no one but a man would think there was.
> You don't catch women trying to be Plato.
> Still there must be lots of unsystematic
> Stray scraps of palliative reason
> It wouldn't hurt You to vouchsafe the faithful.

Job's wife is in a profound sense more reasonable and more religious in rejecting hope or belief in an "abstract" or "universal" reason than men philosophers whose very attempt to find a universal reason is itself a kind of irrational madness.

Frost's serious theme in the masque can best be understood by reference to the Book of Job, the most disturbing book to Judaic orthodoxy in the Old Testament. Its challenge to the Mosaic law contained in the first five books (the Pentateuch), through Deuteronomy, puzzled and disturbed the pious among the orthodox. In Deuteronomy, God is angry at men who are incredulous and disobedient against His commandments. But in the Book of Job much discontent against God is expressed by Job, who has been true to God's law yet has suffered many terrible and apparently meaningless afflictions. But in his acceptance of God's injustice Job helped to change God's old relationship to man. Frost has God acknowledge this to Job:

> *I have no doubt*
> *You realize by now the part you played*
> *To stultify the Deuteronomist*
> *And change the tenor of religious thought.*

In a long speech by God, which contains much that is essential to that part of the theme that is concerned with justifying God's ways to man, and reveals the essence of Frost's own "Old Testament Christianity," Job is made to realize how he stultified the Deuteronomist:

> *I've had you on my mind a thousand years*
> *To thank you someday for the way you helped me*
> *Establish once for all the principle*
> *There's no connection man can reason out*
> *Between his just deserts and what he gets.*
> *Virtue may fail and wickedness succeed.*
> *'Twas a great demonstration we put on.*
>
> *Too long I've owed you this apology*
> *For the apparently unmeaning sorrow*
> *You were afflicted with in those old days.*
> *But it was of the essence of the trial*
> *You shouldn't understand it at the time.*
> *It had to seem unmeaning to have meaning.*
>
> *My thanks are to you for releasing me*
> *From moral bondage to the human race.*
> *The only free will there at first was man's,*
> *Who could do good or evil as he chose.*
> *I had no choice but I must follow him*
> *With forfeits and rewards he understood—*
> *Unless I liked to suffer loss of worship.*
> *I had to prosper good and punish evil.*
> *You changed all that. You set me free to reign.*

Yvor Winters's comment on this vital passage sets it in its correct (religious) historical perspective: "So far as the ideas in this passage are concerned, the passage belongs to the fideistic tradition of New England Calvinism; the ideas can be found in more than one passage in Jonathan Edwards, as well as elsewhere."[18]

In that part of his theme that justifies the mysterious and irrational ways of God to man, Frost added little beyond Scripture or Milton's treatment in *Paradise Lost*. Job's endurance of an apparently meaningless evil which released God from the end of adhering to strict poetic justice was not original with Frost. God's reply to Job's insistence to know "plainly and unequivocally" why God hurt him so is sifted through many delays and witty equivocations, before God gives His shocking reason: "I was just showing off to the Devil." But this aesthetic shock, which is something both more and less than Job can understand, is finally shown to be based on the less shocking idea that "the Devil's . . . God's best inspiration," which in turn rests upon the platitude that God and man cannot exist in a meaningful moral relationship without both good and evil, including evils inexplicable by human finite reason. For mankind this means that spiritual salvation can come only through a perpetual trial by existence, a struggle to endure even unreasonable afflictions and to triumph over them through a personal implicit faith in God.[19] This defense of the ancient ways of God to man comes close to an orthodoxy that is common to both Judaism and historical Christianity.

If Frost's main object had been merely to justify the ways of God's justice to man it would have been more appropriate to call his play *A Masque of Justice*. One excellent critic, Marion Montgomery, has noted that the main thrust of Frost's theme is a criticism of the human error of reading man's own rational nature into God. He asks: "Is man's reason sufficient to overcome the wall between himself and God?" His answer is, not without God's help, which is the traditional answer of Judaism and Christianity in their doctrines of grace. He concludes: "The theme of the poem, then, is that understanding is dependent not only upon reason, but upon faith as well, a faith which helps the finite mind accept the mystery its reason will not completely explain."[20] So far as it goes this is excellent criticism, because it interprets the masque as centered in man's reason rather than in God's justice. But it falls short of a full statement of Frost's theme, which is not merely that man should add faith to his reason, but that modern man's excessive faith in his own reason, his lack of doubt or intellectual skepticism toward his reason, leaves little or no room for any religious faith and ends in the cardinal sin of pride. Frost called his play *A Masque of Reason* not only because he rejected man's finite reason as insufficient to understand and accept the mystery of God's justice, but even more because in essence his masque was a satire on faith in reason as such, a severe condemnation of modern man's proud and delusive Faustian ways toward God.

Frost certainly recognized that there are rational and creative powers in man that give form and meaning through science and art to Nature, and that these probes into the infinite in search of truth are among the chief glories of human nature. In "Neither Out Far Nor In Deep," in man's search for "wherever the truth may be—," Frost had written:

> *They cannot look out far.*
> *They cannot look in deep.*
> *But when was that ever a bar*
> *To any watch they keep?*

Compared to the infinite perfection of God's power and knowledge the rational and creative powers of man are very limited, though the recognition of his limitations does not prevent man from persisting in his search for truth. The satire in *A Masque of Reason* is directed against modern man's failure to recognize the severe limitations of his finite reason.

In light of this interpretation of Frost's main theme, one of the most crucial passages in his masque is this speech by God:

> *Job and I together*
> *Found out the discipline man needed most*
> *Was to learn his submission to unreason;*
> *And that for man's own sake as well as mine . . .*

There is nothing in man's "submission to unreason" contrary to Frost's lifelong belief that man should strive to find "truth" wherever it is by all the power of his limited reason. Job finally comes to understand this paradox when he replies to God:

> *Yet I suppose what seems to us confusion*
> *Is not confusion, but the form of forms,*
> *The serpent's tail stuck down the serpent's throat,*
> *Which is the symbol of eternity,*
> *And also of the way all things come round,*
> *Or of how rays return upon themselves,*
> *To quote the greatest Western poem yet.*

The only critic who has interpreted Frost's masque with reference to Emerson, Reuben A. Brower,[21] has made no use of the allusion to Emerson's poem "Uriel" beyond comparing parallel images. Yet this passage and the lines in "Uriel" to which they allude ("In vain produced, all rays return; /

Evil will bless, and ice will burn . . .") are crucial to an understanding of Frost's satirical theme.

Several critics have noted that Frost's philosophy has many important points in common with Emerson,[22] particularly his love of seeking truth in "a world of conflicts, clear to the limit," and his ability to contain vast inconsistencies within himself, to perceive "how rays return upon themselves" and finally harmonize in "the form of forms." But much as Frost agreed with Emerson's philosophy and admired his skill with words, there was one very crucial difference between them concerning the problem of good and evil. In "Uriel," Emerson had written that "The bounds of good and ill were rent" and that "Uriel's voice" shamed the evil Angels' "veiling wings . . . out of the good of evil born." In a letter to Lawrance Thompson (July 11, 1959), Frost referred directly to these lines and stated concisely how radically he differed from Emerson's optimistic view of good and evil: "Emerson's defect was that he was of the great tradition of Monists. He could see the 'good of evil born' but he couldn't bring himself to say the evil of good born. He was an Abominable Snowman of the top-lofty peaks . . . Arnold thought him a voice oracular. ('A voice oracular has pealed to-day.') I couldn't go as far as that because I am a Dualist. . . ."[23] Frost's ethical dualism included a view of reality in which good and evil were both real, so that evil was born of good as well as good of evil. Emerson's ethical monism made good (God) the only reality to man, and he explained evil not as real in itself but only as the absence of good, so that in the end Emerson explained evil by explaining it away altogether. In Frost's masque God, Job, and Job's wife all refer to evil (the devil) as real, though Satan has a very small part in the play.

Frost's contention that Satan's "originality" in doing evil is "God's best inspiration" implies that great evil provokes God to create an opposing complementary good. In this sense Satan is not only God's great antagonist but also His collaborator in making good and evil meaningful to man.[24] In Judaic and Christian religion Satan's originality, in first defying God, was built upon the false premise that his will and reason were superior to God's and should prevail. This is precisely the same premise upon which the modern rationalist builds his faith in progress through physical science. The evil that comes of good for modern man is his Faustian pride, which is the result of his originality and inventiveness and great success in advancing his knowledge and his power over the laws and processes of physical nature, until he imagines that he can eliminate all temporal evil and achieve salvation through his own self-sufficient reason, without God. This is what from Frost's point of view so frequently underlies modern man's facile optimism, his denial of original sin, that is, of the natural limitations inherent in his finite and fallible nature, and his boundless faith that his private reason is sufficient to create a heaven on earth. Although in religion Frost referred to himself as "an old dissenter"[25] and wrote, "I believe I am safely secular till the last go down,"[26] he was sharply critical of modern secular rationalists whose dissent made their own private reason a substitute for religion. In a letter written a few days before his death, Frost alluded to the combined themes of his two masques and denied emphatically that man's salvation can come of man: "Why will the quidnuncs always be hoping for a salvation man will never have from anyone but God? I was just saying today how Christ posed Himself the whole problem and died for it. How can we be just in a world that needs mercy and merciful in a world that needs justice."[27]

In *A Masque of Reason*, Frost's Old Testament religious orthodoxy is voiced most explicitly by God, who makes it plain that in any conflict between the old, unchanging moral wisdom of Genesis and the claims of modern science, with its novelty and current change, the ethical norms of traditional revelation are still the fountain of wisdom:

> *My forte is truth,*
> *Or metaphysics, long the world's reproach*
> *For standing still in one place true forever;*
> *While science goes self-superseding on.*
> *Look at how far we've left the current science*
> *Of Genesis behind. The wisdom there, though,*
> *Is just as good as when I uttered it.*
> *Still, novelty has doubtless an attraction.*

Frost wrote this passage on the flyleaf of a student's book in 1945 and then added below it: "Really Robert Frost's though by him ascribed to someone higher up."[28] Although Job and even Job's wife express some of Frost's deepest personal convictions, the ideas, viewpoint, and tone of God in the masque are practically identical with Frost's philosophy of dualism.

Perhaps nothing could be more antithetical than the philosophy of modern secular man, with his faith in reason, and Frost's satire on reason based upon a theology that derives from Old Testament religious orthodoxy. Where the modern rationalist makes man's reason supreme and simply eliminates God as irrelevant to his temporal or spiritual salvation, Frost exalts the omnipotence of God's arbitrary justice and makes man's reason appear peevish and impotent by comparison. To those moderns who are infatuated with the dynamics of an ever-changing society and believe in the idea of scientific progress through education, politics, and technology, including ethical "progress" for man, Frost's Old Testament theology and insistence that the world is always a hard place in which to save man's soul must appear as an unforgivable heresy against modern man's faith in himself. Perhaps this explains why so many modern critics have gotten so little out of Frost's masque.

Frost accepted completely the superiority of God's mysterious ways and the limitations and fallibility of man's reason. His hard principles are so well fitted to the voices and exploratory dialogue of his characters in the masque that they appear natural and easy in delivery, perhaps even too easy. This is probably what is behind the charge of some critics that Frost is "smug"; he accepts unflinchingly the fact that there are terrible evils in the world about which man can do little. But the charge of smugness can cut both ways; perhaps the critics themselves are smug in assuming that modern man is God and can remove all unreasonable evils from the world. Only a critic victimized by his pride in his own reason would accuse Frost of dramatizing a philosophy of irrational despair. In *A Masque of Reason*, Frost's explicit theme is Job's quarrel with God for afflicting him with undeserved evils. But implicit throughout the masque is Frost's own lovers' quarrel with smug modern man for not remembering original sin and his fallen state, and for presumptuously assuming the supreme position in the universe. Implicit in Frost's satire against man's presumptuous reason is God's soul-shattering question to Job in chapter 38: "Where wast thou when I laid the foundations of the earth?" In this light the humor and comedy in the masque may well be taken as Frost's amusement that men who forget their own finiteness and limitations should at once deny or question the infinite wisdom of God and yet expect heavenly miracles on earth from the manipulation of their social machinery, from their programs of education, science, and government. Far from being frivolous and irresponsible, as so many critics have charged, *A Masque of Reason* is the purest example in the whole of Frost's writings of his serious case against modern man's fondest delusions about himself. In this masque Frost's intellectual skepticism toward man's reason as an instrument adequate to explain the moral mystery at the core of life is as rigorous and profound, within its dramatic medium, as anything found in the philosophical poems of Donne and Dryden and the prose of Swift and Dr. Johnson. Indeed, *A Masque of Reason* places Frost squarely in the great tradition of Pyrrhonism in English thought and literature.

In 1956, as if in sharp answer to the plot, theme, and method of Frost's *A Masque of Reason*, Archibald MacLeish wrote *J.B.*, also a philosophical drama in verse based on a modern adaptation of the Book of Job. In MacLeish's play, two broken-down actors, Zuss and Nickles, are reduced to being vendors in a circus. They find themselves after closing time on an empty sideshow stage, where a drama on Job, God, and Satan has been performed. They put on the masks and begin to read the parts, Zuss speaking for God and Nickles for Satan. Much of the play consists of their comments on offstage or side-stage flashback scenes centered in J.B., the main character. He is shown first as a devoted husband of Sarah and father of five children, a wealthy banker, a virtuous and admired man, who in a series of tragic scenes loses everything except his embittered wife and is reduced to rags and sores. J.B. becomes the modern prototype of Job, a symbol of suffering humanity in a meaningless universe.

The differences in theme and technique between MacLeish's play and Frost's masque clarify by contrast the Bible-centered orthodoxy of Frost's argument from one that rests upon faith in modern man's reason. MacLeish's play is psychological, naturalistic, and humanitarian, and stresses that a deep sense of guilt distinguishes man from other forms of animal life. Frost's masque is theological, theistic, and humanistic, and the problem of guilt is subsumed by the larger problem of justifying the ways of God to man and by the satire on man's pride and reason. There is no humor in MacLeish's play. In contrast to Job's wife in Frost's masque, J.B.'s wife is an almost desperately serious woman, deeply concerned with her husband's suffering and misfortunes and morally outraged by the idea that God is just. When she says to J.B. of their dead children,

> They are
> Dead and they were innocent: I will not
> Let you sacrifice their deaths
> To make injustice justice and God good![29]

she summarizes the case of the modern secular skeptic against God's ultimate justice. Her skepticism is reinforced by the sarcastic remarks of Nickles on the worsening fate of J.B., who persists like Job in keeping faith in God. Nickles's sarcasm is as close as MacLeish comes to wit as a vehicle for sharpening the theme.

J.B. differs from Frost's Job in seeing all the evils he suffers as a matter of pure chance, rather than as direct or indirect expressions of the divine will. J.B. believes he should love God, but he rejects the injustices of the world as a trial by existence of man's courage and faith in God's inexplicable will or His ultimate mercy to man—which are precisely the themes advanced in

Frost's masques. MacLeish appeals to man's natural reason and finally to love between men; Frost to man's courage and to supernatural faith. MacLeish inspires confidence to endure through knowledge and understanding, even in a meaningless universe; Frost reveals skepticism that man's natural reason is capable of piercing through the design of God's plan. The grand theme of *J.B.* is identical with Matthew Arnold's "Dover Beach." When Sarah says to J.B., "You wanted justice and there was none / Only love,"[30] MacLeish makes it clear that this does not include love from God to man: "He does not love. He is."[31] Most concisely, MacLeish's theme is that only human love redeems man from God's injustice. In contrast, Frost's theme exalts in man a redemptive reverence for God's unknown will and possible love even in the face of terrible and unmerited tragedy. But it is in *A Masque of Mercy* that Frost makes God's love for man the ultimate basis of hope and faith in life.

## A Masque of Mercy (1947)

In a letter to G. R. Elliott (April 22, 1947), written right after he had completed *A Masque of Mercy*, Frost wrote a significant passage that combines the central motifs of both his masques, his "two New England Biblicals," and applied them to himself in his trial by existence since the First World War:

> Two world wars and a few private catastrophes have made a man
> of me who doesn't mind blame. Neither for my sins of omission
> nor commission am I afraid of being punished. All that is past
> like a vision of Dante or Gustave Doré. My fear of God has settled
> down into a deep inward fear that my best offering may not prove
> acceptable in his sight. My approach to the New Testament is rath-
> er through Jerewsalem than through Rome and Canterbury.[32]

This passage is a perfect transition from Frost's exploration of Old Testament justice in *A Masque of Reason* to the other side of the same theological coin, the claims of New Testament mercy as set forth in *A Masque of Mercy*. As a "masque" it is that rarest of literary forms, a city eclogue engrafted upon a dramatic fantasy.

The setting of *A Masque of Mercy* is a bookstore late at night in New York City. There are four characters, all innocent, but each is harassed by a personal spiritual problem involving love and faith toward God or man within the justice-mercy contradiction.[33] The first speaker, Jesse Bel, proprietress of the bookstore, is somewhat like Job's wife in *A Masque of Reason*, a shrewd, hardheaded, bored, slightly alcoholic woman, under psychiatric care because she can't love God, her husband, or her psychiatrist. Her husband is My Brother's Keeper, called "Keeper," a modern pagan-religious man who says he would "rather be lost in the woods / Than found in church." The third character is Paul the Apostle, whom Keeper calls "the Exegete"—"the fellow who theologized / Christ almost out of Christianity." Finally, there is Jonas Dove or Jonah, whom Paul identifies as "the universal fugitive" running away from God's "mercy-justice contradiction." Keeper and Paul divide the serious debate between them, and each at various times expresses Frost's own convictions on justice and mercy. Jonah, like Job, appears as a man unjustly treated by God, and his case provides the essential drama in *A Masque of Mercy*.

The Book of Jonah contains the first notable instance in the Old Testament of God's mercy to sinful man: God spared the wicked city of Nineveh because the people repented and because the city contained many innocent women and children—"More than sixscore thousand persons that cannot discern between their right hand and their left hand." But God's mercy raised a serious moral problem. His ultimate forgiveness of wicked men is as great a mystery as His temporal afflictions upon the innocent. His mercy, that forgiveness which derives from His love, violates the strict logic of poetic justice in favor of man. If Job's punishment despite his obedience to the moral law makes God appear unjust, God's mercy in forgiving sinners who break His law also appears as a violation of strict justice, even if done in order to spare the innocent. In essence this is the viewpoint of Jonas in the early part of the masque.

The occasion for the drama is provided by Jonah's refusal to act as a chosen prophet to the God of the Old Testament, a wrathful God of strict justice, because Jonah fears that God has become softened into a New Testament God of mercy. Jonah has lost his faith in God because he cannot trust God to be strictly just, that is, unmerciful to the wicked. Jonah has refused seven times to prophesy the destruction of Nineveh and has fled from God, because he fears that God will sacrifice his public reputation as His prophet rather than be unmerciful and punish the wicked:

> I've lost my faith in God to carry out
> The threats He makes against the city evil.
> I can't trust God to be unmerciful.

When Paul asks Jonah, "What would you have God if not merciful?" Jonah replies: "Just." After noting that not trusting God to be unmerciful is "the beginning of all wisdom," Paul confronts Jonah with the New Testament case against God's temporal justice:

> *I'm going to make you see*
> *How relatively little justice matters.*

Paul opens his argument by noting that "after doing Justice justice," first "the Gospels" and then later Milton's pentameters go on to say,

> *But Mercy first and last shall brightest shine—*
> *Not only last, but first, you will observe . . .*

But before Paul can bring Jonah to realize that no man in his right senses would demand God's justice for himself when he could have His mercy, there is some dramatic give-and-take between Keeper and Paul on the claims of justice and mercy in the practical affairs of modern man.

In its subsidiary theme, *A Masque of Mercy* makes it clear that Frost believed the main problem of modern man is not commutative justice in the courts of equity, between one individual and another, but a conflict over social distributive justice and the various means by which it is brought about. In a long soliloquy, Paul draws out the range of possibilities for the redistribution of wealth in the modern world:

> *The rich in seeing nothing but injustice*
> *In their impoverishment by revolution*
> *Are right. But 'twas intentional injustice.*
> *It was their justice being mercy-crossed.*

This is the kind of revolution favored by Keeper, whose political views are a summary of the leveling social legislation of Franklin D. Roosevelt's New Deal:

> *The revolution Keeper's bringing on*
> *Is nothing but an outbreak of mass mercy,*
> *Too long pent up in rigorous convention—*
> *A holy impulse towards redistribution.*
> *To set out to homogenize mankind*
> *So that the cream could never rise again*
> *Required someone who laughingly could play*
> *With the idea of justice in the courts,*

> *Could mock at riches in the right it claims*
> *To count on justice to be merely just.*

The main question in bringing about distributive justice "is the form /
Of outrage—violence—that breaks across it." In violent total revolutions,
such as communism, justice is "evil-crossed." Paul concludes:

> *And if you've got to see your justice crossed*
> *(And you've got to) which will you prefer*
> *To see it, evil-crossed or mercy-crossed?*

Although Keeper somewhat flippantly offers a third alternative, to have
justice "star-crossed," in fact Keeper and Paul meet on common grounds
in their politics by both favoring a distributive justice that is "mercy-
crossed."[34] Keeper rejects an "evil-crossed" total revolution:

> *No revolution I brought on would aim*
> *At anything but change of personnel.*

Similarly, Keeper sees the religious basis of Paul's politics in having justice
"mercy-crossed" as originating in the basic law of the New Testament. After Paul has said,

> *Christ came to introduce a break with logic*
> *That made all Other outrage seem as child's play:*
> *The Mercy on the Sin against the Sermon.*

Keeper summarizes how justice in the temporal order of man's practical
affairs is seen from the viewpoint of New Testament Christianity:

> *Paul's constant theme. The Sermon on the Mount*
> *Is just a frame-up to insure the failure*
> *Of all of us, so all of us will be*
> *Thrown prostrate at the Mercy Seat for Mercy.*

Paul in effect concedes that Keeper's summary is valid when he says:

> *Mercy is only to the undeserving.*
> *But such we all are made in the sight of God.*

This long and involved digression into the justice-mercy contradiction in modern politics seems at first very remote from the spiritual problem first posed by Jonah. But it is in fact a concrete illustration of the essential problem of the masque, applied to historical conditions and circumstances that are familiar to modern man.

The religious-political discussion between Paul and Keeper is not a violent difference in principle, but a mild difference in degree from a difference in method. As Keeper says:

> *Our disagreement when we disagree, Paul,*
> *Lies in our different approach to Christ,*
> *Yours more through Rome, mine more through Palestine.*

From this passage, with reference to Frost's letter to G. R. Elliott, it would seem that Keeper speaks more for Frost than Paul. But the characters are not always consistent with themselves as dramatic vehicles for expressing Frost's own ideas, which are about equally divided between Keeper and Paul.[35]

Apparently Jonah, who says little after the opening scenes, has listened intently to the discussion between Paul and Keeper, because in the midst of it he says:

> *I think my trouble's with the crises*
> *Where mercy-crossed to me seemed evil-crossed.*

As their discussion proceeds, Jonah remarks further: "My trouble has been with my sense of justice"; and then near the end of the action, he adds, "I think I may have got God wrong entirely." After Paul convinces Jonah that God's tempering justice with mercy is in harmony with His omnipotence and love, Jonah has the whole justice-mercy mystery applied to him in his favor by Paul's ironical prayerful appeal: "Mercy on him for having asked for justice."

Jonah's complete change in viewpoint concerning justice and mercy finds an exact parallel in Keeper, but within a secular rather than a Scriptural frame of reference. Jesse Bel had chided Jonah early in the play for his lack of faith in God's justice:

> *Your courage failed. The saddest thing in life*
> *Is that the best thing in it should be courage.*

Keeper also laughs at Jonah, but in the end he discovers that he too has lacked courage and faith, not regarding God's justice but His mercy:

> *My failure is no different from Jonah's.*
> *We both have lacked the courage in the heart*
> *To overcome the fear within the soul*
> *And go ahead to any accomplishment.*
> *Courage is what it takes and takes the more of*
> *Because the deeper fear is so eternal.*

Keeper's distinction between the pagan virtue, physical courage, and the Christian virtue, spiritual fear, exalts fear above courage:

> *Courage is of the heart by derivation,*
> *And great it is. But fear is of the soul.*

"The deeper fear" that "is so eternal" is not so much the fear that the trial by existence which is man's life on earth has no final meaning as that it does have meaning but that men as individuals will fail to measure up to what God expects of them.

In what is probably the most vital passage in the masque, Paul defines God's mercy not as the forgiveness of sins or failure,[36] but as His acceptance as a free gift of the best sacrifice man has to offer:

> *Yes, there you have it at the root of things.*
> *We have to stay afraid deep in our souls*
> *Our sacrifice—the best we have to offer,*
> *And not our worst nor second best, our best,*
> *Our very best, our lives laid down like Jonah's,*
> *Our lives laid down in war and peace—may not*
> *Be found acceptable in Heaven's sight.*
> *And that they may be is the only prayer*
> *Worth praying. May my sacrifice*
> *Be found acceptable in Heaven's sight.*[37]

Because of the uncertainty of God's ultimate justice or mercy, man is compelled throughout his life "to stay afraid" deep in his soul, a fear that goes beyond the necessary elemental pagan virtue of courage. As a basis for humility and maximum effort in an absolute commitment to life, this passage is in essence Christian and Hebraic, and it reconciles the justice of the Old Testament with the mercy of the New Testament. In the masque this reconciliation is summarized in the final line, spoken by Keeper: "Nothing can make injustice just but mercy." The religious orthodoxy at the end of *A Masque of Mercy* is at once more subtle and more obvious than in *A Masque of Reason*: more subtle because of Frost's originality in what God's mercy means, and more obvious because the theme of the masque is more congenial to modern man's New Testament emphasis upon a God of love. Yet both masques make the same stress on the limitations of man's knowledge regarding God's ultimate purposes and the need for implicit faith in God. To Frost, God always remains an invisible reality of the ideal spiritual perfection toward which man aspires, with courage and daring and a full, free commitment, and with the softer virtues of love, faith, and humility. Frost's *A Masque of Mercy* has no systematic theology or creed or dogma or revealed path to personal salvation. Instead, it reaffirms from a New Testament viewpoint the same austere sense of right-mindedness and courage found in *A Masque of Reason*. Its drama is verbal debate and quite didactic. It advocates living the trial by existence with daring and faith, on the highest level that man is capable, and in the assurance that when this is done the rest belongs to heaven.

The masques are unique among Frost's poems because they are the culmination in form, technique, and theme of much that Frost had written. James M. Cox has noted the climactic position of the masques in form: "Frost has clearly moved toward comedy and wit—from lyric through narrative toward satire, and finally, to masque."[38] Readers who wish to understand the truly significant place of the masques in the themes of Frost's poetry would have to compare them with many of his earlier poems. "The Trial by Existence" is in many ways an early anticipation of elements in the theme of the masques. The theme of love's contrarieties in "The Death of the Hired Man" is centered in the same conflicting claims between justice and mercy. The contrarieties between transcendent and immanent love in "West-Running Brook" bear comparison with aspects of the masques. The voice tones and patterns of imagery and arguments of the poet-philosopher in "New Hampshire" and "The Lesson for Today" also throw light on the masques. Frost's views toward the ambiguities in traditional religion and modern science could be fruitfully explored by comparing the masques with such poems as "The Demiurge's Laugh," "Neither Out Far Nor In Deep," "All Revelation," "For Once, Then, Something," "Desert Places," and "Design." Indeed, all of Frost's poems on science should be read in the light of Lawrance Thompson's suggestive insight: "Also echoed throughout the masque is the related Bergsonian concept of a continuously creative process which develops the universe."[39] Only after many such comparisons in form, technique, imagery, and theme would we see the full extent to which Frost's masques are in the classic tradition of American literature.

# Frost's Philosophy of Education: The Poet as Teacher

## Frost's Philosophy of Education

No Frost scholar or literary critic has explored the close affinity, at times amounting to identity, between Frost's theory of language and his philosophy of education; between his method as a poet and his practice as a classroom teacher. Since his sole ambition was to be a poet, he never seriously considered teaching as a vocation. Yet, having failed as a farmer and having earned very little by his verse, he found it expedient to teach school. It provided a sufficient means to support his family while often affording some time to write poetry.

The public image of Frost is so completely centered on his role as a poet that it requires a strong shift in perspective to perceive him primarily as a teacher, with a uniquely original philosophy of education and pedagogical method. The poet himself once noted that "the three strands of my life" were "writing, teaching, and farming,"[1] All three strands were intimately interrelated, and in time Frost himself became aware that a special identity little short of absolute existed between his poetry and his teaching: "It slowly dawned on me that my poetry and my teaching were one, and if you know my poetry at all well, you'd see that."[2] If Frost's poems are perceived as parables in metaphorical language and structured form, and as intimate dialogues between the poet as speaker and his readers, they can indeed be regarded as instrumental means to a pedagogical end.

In his essay "Education by Poetry" (1931), Frost made it clear that the essence of both poetry and education is to teach readers and students how to think validly in metaphor and to acquire a sense of form regarding structured physical and spiritual reality: "Unless you are at home in the metaphor, unless you have had your proper poetical education in the metaphor, you are not safe anywhere. Because you are not at ease with figurative values: you don't know the metaphor in its strength and its weakness. You don't know how far you may expect to ride it and where it may break down. . . . You are not safe in science; you are not safe in history."[3] As he increasingly came to believe that all sound thinking was essentially metaphorical, that "all things still pair in metaphor" involving comparisons, contrasts, parallels, conflicts, contradictions, ambiguities, and so forth, within the vast range of interactions between matter and spirit, the great ends of poetry and education became identical means for knowledge, revelation, insight, and understanding. Both Frost's theory of poetry and his philosophy of education were based upon his dualistic view of reality, and this provided the inexorable bond of unity between his poetry and his teaching.

To understand Frost's philosophy of education, it is essential to take fully into account the historical and philosophical origins of the cultural traditions of Western civilization as embodied in the humanities and liberal arts. Although he believed "there's no such thing as progress," he did contend that there were golden eras in the westward historical course of empire:

> There are flowering times—Greece, Rome, Byzantium, Spain, France, England, and so on. . . . Rome wasn't so good as Greece, by general consent . . . and before that, too, of course, Babylon, Assyria, Phoenicia, Egypt. . . . But for a little golden time—the Periclean Age—a great flowering with philosophers and artists, and the general color and glow. Washington was one of ours. He made his form with people and large social forces. That was our flowering time. . . .[4]

In 1937, Lawrance Thompson enlarged upon Frost's belief regarding the course of Western civilization:

> The Western approach, Frost held, had been an attempt to blend materialism and spirituality to the greatest possible extent. The "run" of civilzation, for Frost, had been west-northwest, from the Tigris and Euphrates valleys, from Israel and Asia Minor, up and

across the corner of the Mediterranean to Greece and Rome, up across Europe and England to the United States: west-northwest all the time. He saw America as the high point of civilization. . . .[5]

According to Frost, American democracy also had its ultimate origins in the ancient political traditions of the Greek polis: "Ours is a very ancient political growth, beginning at one end of the Mediterranean Sea and coming westward—tried in Athens, tried in Italy, tried in England, tried in France, coming westward all the way to us."[6] The westward course of civilization included the extension and refinement of the philosophy, art, literature, religion, government, laws, and science of the ancient classical world, combined with and embodied in the world order of Christianity during the Middle Ages, and transmitted after the discoveries of Columbus to the Western Hemisphere. Frost was well aware of how science evolved out of the rationalism of scholastic thought late in the Middle Ages and during the Renaissance and how it became increasingly important in providing the worldview of Europeans and Americans regarding the place of mankind in the universe. Science, he held, was not limited to physical nature; its methods came more and more to be applied to every branch of knowledge. Yet to Frost science always remained a part of the humanities. He contrasted the dynamic duality and interactions between matter and spirit, so characteristic in Western civilization and culture, with Oriental Civilization, which he thought was too rooted in a spiritual passivity, without much science.

To Frost, a person was well-educated to the extent that he possessed knowledge and insightful understanding of the essential facts and principles that gave substance and spirit to all of the enormously complex historical and philosophical elements that had formed Western civilization. Both his positive principles and methods in education, and his harsh negative strictures on all that he perceived to be wrong with modern American education, from high school through college and graduate studies, reflected his belief that Western culture provided the norms for a valid system of education. At the heart of Western culture were the humanities, which Frost on several occasions called "the book of the worthies."

For centuries the classical and Christian-oriented system of education had remained virtually intact throughout Europe and America, up to modern times. In June 1939, in conversation with students at the Bread Loaf School of English, Frost indicated his awareness that a revolutionary change in education had occurred during the Victorian era. This was the very period in which Frost grew into maturity as a student and teacher.

The Victorian conflict was precipitated by Thomas Henry Huxley, among others, who advocated that science and technology, as independent and self-sufficient subjects, should displace the ancient classical curriculum in British education. His chief opponents were Matthew Arnold and John Henry Cardinal Newman, who defended the long established humanities tradition of education. Frost was highly emphatic in making it clear that his sympathies were entirely with Arnold and Newman, particularly because Huxley's educational program in an accelerated form slowly but surely was becoming dominant in the twentieth century.

Matthew Arnold was himself the product of his father's philosophy of education, as summarized by Gordon A. Craig:

> In the first half of the nineteenth century, the curriculum of Rugby School in England was dominated, as was true of other public schools, by instruction in Greek and Latin. In addition . . . all students from the first to the sixth grade read history, both ancient and modern, which was interlarded with generous portions of Herodotus, Thucydides, Xenophon, and Livy. Dr. Thomas Arnold, the famous headmaster of Rugby, once gave the rationale for this by saying, "The history of Greece and Rome is not an idle inquiry about remote ages and forgotten institutions but a living picture of things present, fitted not so much for the curiosity of the scholar, as for the instruction of the statesman and citizen."[7]

Matthew Arnold strongly rejected Huxley's crusade to replace the ancient Greek and Latin languages and classics, taught at Cambridge and Oxford, with modern science and technology, centered in a utilitarian curriculum and pragmatic courses in mechanics, industry, business, and commerce. In "Literature and Science," he had disapproved of Huxley's criticism of the liberal arts as too remote from life and therefore useless, or at best an ornamental appendage in human nature. Frost told the students at Bread Loaf that Arnold's line from "Dover Beach," "where ignorant armies clash by night," inspired much of his negative view on modern education. His awareness of the whole course of modern education was a refinement of Arnold's thesis against Huxley, but it was reinforced by his own experience of American education. He feared that the blend of matter and spirit which had characterized Western culture for centuries would increasingly be subordinated to a monistic materialism based upon science. Both in high school and college, Frost had studied Greek and Latin languages and literature, so that when he stated to the Bread Loaf students that the degeneration and corruption of modern American education began when Greek and Latin were dropped from the high school curriculum, he meant far more than the loss of a knowledge of these ancient languages.[8] It meant that the literature, art, philosophy, and culture of the ancient classical world was largely abandoned, with the result that students were rendered incognizant of a great deal of what had made Western civilization the greatest achievement of mankind.

Frost found much to admire in Newman's educational philosophy in *The Idea of a University* (1852). Like Frost, Newman was a philosophical dualist,[9] and neither found any contradiction between science and religion. Both also shared an essentially Aristotelian rather than a Platonic view of reality and the arts. Despite all of their differences in time, place, and religion, the broad premises and the view of human nature that they held in common eventuated in their having remarkably similar conceptions of education. Their most important difference was between Newman's belief that theology was central in higher education and Frost's belief that the power of artistic creativity and originality in ideas was most crucial in the educational process."[10] Yet even in this vital difference they had something in common: Frost's four "beliefs," culminating in belief in God, are very similar to Newman's "Discourse III, on the Bearing of Theology on Other Knowledge." Also, Newman's argument that studies which "exercise the faculty of judgment . . . are the true basis of education for the active and inventive powers"[11] is close to Frost's emphasis on aesthetic creativity as basic in education.

Both Newman and Frost believed that the humanities went far beyond Bacon's scientific dictum that "knowledge is power"; they held that moral and aesthetic wisdom were greater traits of human character. Frost agreed with Newman's belief that the chief object of education was to develop the total nature of a student by acquiring the essential principles of universal knowledge through a cultivation of the intellectual virtues. As Newman put it: "general culture of mind is the best aid to professional and scientific study; and educated men can do what illiterate cannot."[12] Both held that good judgment and a cultivated taste were among the great values of liberal education, because the humanities form a habit of mind that endures for a lifetime.

Frost found many of Newman's particular points very close to his own beliefs. He certainly agreed with Newman's criticism of John Locke's attack upon the learning of Latin, which the philosopher held to be a useless language.[13] Then too, his attitude towards formal instruction coincided with Newman's, whose unqualified endorsement of independent studies echoed

Frost's frequent advice to students to abandon their university studies to pursue their own genius: "Self-education in any shape . . . is preferable to a system of teaching which, professing so much really does so little for the mind. . . . How much better . . . is it for the active and thoughtful intellect . . . to eschew the college and university altogether, than to submit to a drudgery so ignoble."[14] Newman's belief that "knowledge is its own end" and opposition to narrow specialization in education, and several other important points, were close in substance and spirit to Frost's philosophy of education.

In an interview with Janet Mabie published in *The Christian Science Monitor* (December 24, 1925), Frost stated what was probably his most important positive conviction about education. It was based upon his entire previous experience as a student and teacher, but more directly upon what he underwent as a member of the faculty and poet-in-residence at Amherst College and the University of Michigan. He called his basic method "education by presence." It was his alternative to the standardized academic assumptions and methods in American colleges. In essence, "education by presence" was Frost's adoption and original refinement of the tutorial method of instruction practiced at Oxford and Cambridge universities, as he applied it broadly in the more democratic and informal conditions of American colleges. He noted that "students get most from professors who have marked wide horizons," because they pay close attention to teachers with a reputation beyond the local campus.

Education by presence led Frost to state that "the business of the teacher is . . . to challenge the student's purpose" beyond any occupational objectives. The most effective method in challenging a student's purpose was not through formal contact in the classroom; that is, through a structured course of lectures and the routine of a fixed curriculum for majors, which includes tests, keeping notebooks, research assignments, prescribed papers, busy work, and the whole formulated apparatus of colleges, through subjects divided into specialized departments—all aimed at a final grade. Even academic committees were pure anathema to Frost. He once remarked that if he were president of a college he would abolish all committees except one—a committee to abolish all committees. He did not believe that the primary objective of a college was to stock the student's mind with all sorts of detailed knowledge, much of it beyond his capability to utilize in any purposeful and creative activity. He held that students responded best not to "putting the screws" on them, but to placing them in "an atmosphere of expectations." He acknowledged that his greatest inspiration as a student at Harvard was from William James, "a man whose classes I have never attended," and that "the book that influenced me most was Piers the Plowman, yet I never read it." In both of these instances Frost's creative imagination was released in ways that inspired him to pursue his own life's work in thought and poetry. Although education by presence was the most essential element in Frost's philosophy of education, it assumed the necessity of acquiring a set of prerequisites that included the ancient classics and an understanding of the history, philosophy, literature, religion, and science of Western civilization.

Of the three basic ways of teaching—by formal contact through lectures in the classroom, by informal social contact, and by virtually no contact between teacher and student—Frost favored the last as first in importance. Even in "formal classroom teaching," he contended, "it is the essence of symposium I'm after. Heaps of ideas and the subject matter of books purely incidental." The give-and-take of good talk between two individuals came the closest to "the wild free ways of wit and art" which led to superior "prowess and performance" in studies, in art, and in life. A conversation between a teacher and student was to Frost a "seminar of the elect," which allowed talent and genius to develop ambitions without the restraints of system.[15] Informal contacts between independent and original teachers could draw out the best in students by creating "an atmosphere of expectations." In 1924, at Amherst, he urged the administration to bring a famous painter to campus, so that students could have the experience of a studio apprenticeship. He believed that the presence of great artists, scientists, and scholars would benefit everyone on campus and that the whole cultural life of the community would be enhanced, thus minimizing the materialism that threatened to subordinate or even to destroy the humanities in education.[16]

At the New School of Social Research in New York City, Harry Hansen recorded in 1930 how Alvin Johnson practiced Frost's concept of education by presence in a small seminar: "Alvin Johnson used to place Frost in a circle of students and give him free rein to do as he would. It wasn't long, he says, before the room was surcharged with a spirit—a feeling of common understanding superinduced by the elemental and profound wisdom of the teacher."[17] Clearly, Frost's breadth and depth of knowledge in many fields, and his brilliance as a conversationalist, were the key ingredients for success through education by presence. In such a seminar, a run-of-the-mill teacher could easily be a disaster. Yet Frost advocated that "every teacher should have his time arranged to permit freer informal contacts with students. Art, the various sciences, research, lend themselves to this treatment. . . . Courses should be a means of introduction, to give students a claim on me, so that they may come to me at any time, outside of class periods." Such an informal system of education required students who were genuinely interested in learning and in developing their talents. Frost called such students "self-starters" and said of them: "I favor the student who will convert my claim on him into his claim on me. . . . Give me the high-spirited kind that hate an order to do what they were about to do of their own accord." Like Matthew Arnold's "saving remnant," such students were what Frost called "the free-born," who wished to develop their intellectual, moral, aesthetic, social, and physical nature as an end in itself, apart from any regard for professional objectives.

It would be a mistake to conclude that Frost's education by presence made his philosophy of education too elitist for American society. In contrast to the "free-born" students were "the slaves," those who accepted uncritically the whole conventional system of structured institutional training. Frost stated his preference unequivocally, but made it clear that he would also provide for the slaves: "I am for the wide-open educational system for the free-born. The slaves are another question. I will not refuse to treat them as slaves wherever found. 'Those who will, may,' would be my first motto: but a close second, 'Those who won't must.' That is to say, I shouldn't disdain to provide for the slaves, if slaves they insisted on being. I shouldn't anyway unless I were too busy with the free-born."[18] He was well aware that in American democratic society it was necessary and good to accept and support the general compulsory system of free public education which prevailed from kindergarten through high school.

In an interview in South Shaftsbury, Vermont (August 18, 1936), he acknowledged that in American education "we have generally made it possible for most anyone to go as far in any direction as he seemed willing and capable." He agreed that students should "get as much general education over as wide a field as possible," without regard to distinctions based upon special ability and interests. He would "let the sheep and the goats run together for a good long while," confident that because of the range in ability and cultural interests students "eventually . . . separate themselves." On this occasion the one caution he adopted was to advocate "the extension of general education and the postponement of specialization until later years." To Louis Untermeyer, he confided that he was for people learning as well as learned people: "I'm for educated humanity all the time—except in any undiscriminating way."[19] Although Frost's philosophy of education laid great stress on superior intellectual and creative ability and the possession of cultural interests, it did not preclude instruction for the less qualified members of the general public.

## *Frost as Critic of Modern Education*

Although Frost called himself a "radical" in education, he also insisted that he was not a "rebel." In his defense of the ancient classical tradition in education, centered as it was in the humanities and liberal arts, he was in fact a traditionalist; his radicalism consisted of an attack on the leaders in American education, those who had betrayed that tradition and had established a science-oriented and materialist system of instruction. Frost believed that the great failure in American education was in the high schools. In 1958, while he was Consultant in Poetry at the Library of Congress, he answered questions from teachers, students, and would-be writers, and delivered himself on the state of education in high schools, on which, half spoofingly, he declared himself to be "the greatest living expert":

> I have long thought that our high schools should be improved. Nobody should come into our high schools without examination—not aptitude tests, but on reading, 'riting, and 'rithmetic. And that goes for black or white. . . . A lot of people are being scared by the Russian Sputnik into wanting to harden up our education or speed it up. I am interested in toning it up, at the high school level. . . . If they want to Spartanize the country, let them. I would rather perish as Athens than prevail as Sparta. The tone is Athens.[20]

By toning up high school education as Athens, Frost meant two things: disciplining the students and retaining the highest possible standards in a curriculum centered in the classics and humanities. During an interview on December 1, 1961, he made it clear what he meant by toning up high school education: "I'm at large, and I'm a civilized man, but school is for discipline. A student is an orange pip between my fingers: if I pinch him he'll go far. I'm not violent, but I'm going for the whole damn system. Discipline. Tightness. Firmness. Crispness. Sternness, and sternness in our lives. Life is tons of discipline."[21] A high-minded puritan element was clearly part of Frost's libertarian philosophy of education.

Probably the greatest error ever made regarding Frost's views on education was committed by Jeffrey Meyers when he claimed that the poet was an "advocate" of and a "strong believer in progressive education."[22] Nothing could have been further from the truth. Meyers committed the common fallacy of the false single alternative. He assumed that because Frost and John Dewey's disciples were both highly critical of the established system of schools, their views must be identical. In fact, Frost regarded the reforms initiated and popularized by Dewey in Columbia University as the worst possible solution for what was wrong with American secondary education. To Sidney Cox, who knew Frost well for almost forty years and regarded him as his mentor, and who modeled his teaching style on that of the poet, he wrote: "Something in school should save us from the fatal credulity of progress prophets."[23] He reminded Cox that in America "progress is our chief native simile."[24] As Cox noted, Frost's antithetical philosophy of education was formed independently, years before Dewey's theory became public:

> Before anyone had heard of John Dewey outside the University of Chicago and Columbia, Robert Frost was mocking at the rigidities and unrealities of formal education, turning his back on them, and then, as teacher, inconspicuously sabotaging them in the academy and normal school. But by the time that all the quick catchers-on were practicing the new progressive stereotypes, Robert Frost was saying school was a place for drill, rote learning, the three R's; literature and experience were too delicate and too much alive for school. Let school deal with numbers and letters. Let it not mechanically meddle with imagination, insight, taste.[25]

Cox observed that one of the most important differences between Frost and "progressive" educators was in their conceptions of freedom: "He was no early Dewey. Freedom from rote learning was not his point; there was need for that. It was not freedom from direction. . . . It was not freedom from lecturing. . . . It wasn't freedom to say 'No, no, no' to the teacher's 'Yes, yes, yes.'"[26] Whereas Frost wished to tighten student discipline, progressive theorists loosened the reins of control and introduced the child-centered school.

But the differences between Frost's views and those of Dewey went far beyond their respective conceptions of freedom. Even as a high school student, Frost defended tradition and social custom. He wrote that he would "follow custom—not without question, but where it does not conflict with the broader habits of life gained by wanderers among ideas." This, he added, was in sharp contrast with the "radical enemies of custom," who would establish "an inquisition to compel liberality."[27] To Frost, progressive education was a closed system that would "compel liberality." Like Rousseau, it would force students to be free, not merely from self-discipline, but from social traditions and normative beliefs. As Louis Mertins has recorded, the qualities of disciplined character that Frost cherished were the opposite of those fostered by progressive education:

> In a world trembling toward progressive education—he is stressing rules of hard learning. . . . Frost wanted, always, for himself and for his students, complete freedom of thinking and acting. . . . He wanted the student to be a free agent, untrammeled by the teaching system. But he went against the "new" theories that "readin,'" "writin,'" and "rithmetic" were expendables and unimportant. How many times he has excoriated some lazy pupil for handing in a dirty school "project" full of slovenly spelling and impossible grammar! . . . For the slovenly teacher who said case didn't matter, he had many scornful words.[28]

To Frost, the progressive theory of the child-centered school was false. Its worst feature was to encourage immature and uneducated students to have a decisive voice in determining the curriculum. Frost's response was to declare, "There is such a thing as not being old enough to understand."[29] He always insisted that youth must go to school to age and to be educated in the humanities. His views had ample room for "self-starters," students who were "daft on education," like the college boy in "The Death of the Hired Man," who "studied Latin, like the violin, because he liked it." Such a boy was truly a wanderer among ideas, destined to live "the broader habits of life," regardless of his professional objectives.

Two things in progressive educators provoked Frost's particular rage— their abandonment of the ancient Greek and Roman classics and their attempts to apply the scientific method in teaching. The latter separated form or technique from genuine content. On February 8, 1917, he wrote to Untermeyer on "the latest thing in the schools": "Damn these separations of the form from the substance. I don't know how long I could stand them." Twenty years later, on January 5, 1937, he again wrote to Untermeyer on the same theme, noting that in his view the president of the University of Chicago advocated the progressive theory in studying languages:

> I see where President Hutchins doesn't believe in learning languages ancient or modern. Only grammar (from the Chinese glamour) logic mathematics and rhetoric. Of all the god dam— . . . Some more of this form-without-content guff. Ain't we had almost enough of it pro tem? Kick me under the table if I'm out of

order. The best way to learn to swim is out of water, pivoted on a skewer. I was taught all the motions of a screw driver before I saw my first screw. Very expensive Montessori education at Madam Zitsker's in San Francisco circa 1880. . . . [30]

To Frost, teaching technique without reference to the content in subjects resulted in ignorance and avoided the complex experience of creativity—"the breathless swing between matter and form,"[31] which only the free and creative mind could experience. In his view, teaching was an art, not a science, and the scientific method was out of place in classroom teaching.

The teacher training methods of John Dewey's theory came in for some of Frost's harshest criticism, yet his censure was qualified by an awareness that some teachers do need help:

> The beautiful bare text for me. Teachers who don't know what to do with it, let them perish and lose their jobs. I don't allow for the existence of teachers who depend on "teachers' helps." But I dunno! There are more people on earth than are provided for in my philosophy—latitudinarian though I try to be. . . . If there are teachers in quantity who need your help you must help them. Only do it as little as you can and withdrawingly so as to throw them finally on their own resources.[32]

When Frost accepted a one-year appointment in 1911–12 to teach at the Plymouth Normal School in New Hampshire, the first thing he did was to discard the textbook, Monroe's *History of Education*. He replaced it with William James's *Talk to Teachers on Psychology* and *Psychology: The Briefer Course*, and such primary fictional works of literature as Mark Twain's "The Celebrated Jumping Frog of Calaveras County." In teaching the James texts, he deliberately sabotaged the assumption of progressive educators that psychology is a science and that it could provide the key to better teaching: "I went up there to disabuse the Teacher's College of the idea that there is any immediate connection between any psychology and their classroom work, disabuse them of the notion that they could mesmerize a class if they knew enough psychology. That's what they thought."[33]

Frost also rejected the social objective of progressive education—to indoctrinate students in favor of egalitarian democracy. He always favored education that would allow "the cream to rise to the top." He believed that in secondary education the progressive theory stressed emotion too much, whereas graduate studies were too centered in abstract reason: "I know there is a crowd of 'emotionalists' who threw all to the winds except emotion. I think they're perhaps worse than the 'intellectualists,' who are the other extreme. But a happy mixture, that's it."[34] To Frost, sound education involved all of human nature.

Frost was very fond of Mark Twain's short story "The Celebrated Jumping Frog of Calaveras County," both for its lyrical qualities as a prose narrative and for its essential theme. He interpreted the story as "a great parable in education."[35] When the frog was trained and sensitized to jump with only a feather-like prod in his rear, he out-jumped all rival frogs set against him. But when the city slicker, who bet against his owner, secretly slipped a handful of buckshot pellets into the champion frog, even strong and persistent prods could not budge him, and very ordinary frogs were able to out-jump him. Frost explained that before the frog was filled with buckshot he was "like a poet . . . a free spirit" who had assimilated only as much knowledge as was needed to give him strength to jump far. But after swallowing the buckshot pellets the frog "became a scholar . . . weighted down and ponderous with useless knowledge, and unable to jump." Frost's own prototype of a ponderous professor was Dr. Magoon in "A Hundred Collars," a satirical portrait of a deadly introverted nervous academic who was rather too fond of calling himself "Doctor." When he is forced to share a hotel room with a half-literate French-Canadian bill collector, named "Lafe," who mistakes him for a medical doctor, Magoon corrects him by saying, "Well, a teacher." Frost was favorably oriented to sound scholarship, but he despised academic affectation.

Perhaps nothing reveals more about Frost's philosophy of education than his conflict over first principles with Alexander Meiklejohn, president of Amherst College from 1912 to 1923. In 1916, Meiklejohn began his program to build an unusual faculty by appointing Frost to teach at Amherst, beginning in January 1917, even though the poet had no degree. Frost approved of Meiklejohn's opposition to the elective system, which had been propounded by President Eliot at Harvard, and also his apparent endorsement of the core curriculum centered in the ancient classics and humanities, called "The Amherst Idea," so that initially he and the president got along well.

But when Meiklejohn hired and gave preferential promotions to young faculty members in courses in sociology and economics, many of whom were ideological theorists and believers in the idea of progress, Frost became skeptical of his leadership. His skepticism was confirmed when the president invited radical visiting lecturers to Amherst, such as the Marxist-anarchist Emma Goldman. Sidney Cox recorded Frost's response to the new faculty who assumed that science and religion were incompatible, and who therefore thought it their right and duty to disabuse students of their traditional religious beliefs in favor of science and radical partisan politics: "Robert Frost indignantly denounced college teaching that 'frisks freshmen of their principles,' because 'a boy with all of his beliefs drawn out of him is in no condition to learn.'"[36] Meiklejohn's special interest was logic, and unlike Frost he believed that it was possible to translate logic through speculative discursive reasoning and argument into solutions to life's practical problems.

To Frost, Meiklejohn's conception of academic freedom was merely a collegiate adaptation of Dewey's progressive education in the form of doctrinaire compulsory liberalism, centered in social problems rather than in psychology. Meiklejohn's educational reforms were in the spirit of what Frost called "the guild of social planners," men who assumed that abstract reason and logic were sufficient to solve the world's great perennial problems. After meeting with some of Meiklejohn's young faculty appointees, Dwight Morrow, an Amherst trustee, described them to a friend as "bumptious young men . . . who insisted that nobody thought or studied at Amherst until they came."[37] Frost's similar criticism of the whole experimental method introduced by Meiklejohn was centered in its effect upon the students, giving them the happy illusion that, despite their ignorance of the humanities, they were profound thinkers:

> The boys had been made uncommonly interesting to themselves by Meiklejohn. They fancied themselves thinkers. At Amherst you *thought*, while at other colleges you merely *learned*. . . . I found that by thinking they meant stocking up with radical ideas, by learning they meant stocking up with conservative ideas—a harmless distinction, bless their simple hearts. I really liked them. It got so I called them the young intelligences—without offense. We got on like a set of cogwheels in a clock. They had picked up the idea somewhere that the time was now past for the teacher to teach the pupil. From now on it was the thing for the pupil to teach himself using, as he saw fit, the teacher as an instrument. The understanding was that my leg was always on the table for anyone to seize me by that thought he could swing me as an instrument to teach himself with. So we had an amusing year. . . . I sat there patiently waiting, waiting for the youth to take education into their own hands and start the new world. Sometimes I laughed and sometimes I cried a little internally. I gave one course in reading and

one course in philosophy, but they both came to the same thing. I was determined to have it out with my youngers and betters as to what thinking really was. We reached an agreement that most of what they had regarded as thinking, their own and other peoples, was nothing but voting—taking sides on an issue they had nothing to do with laying down.[38]

Frost then made it clear that unless students had original ideas based upon essential knowledge in the humanities, ideas that they could put forth in terms of metaphors, analogies, comparisons, and so forth, they could not rightly claim to be "thinkers":

Many were ready to give up beaten and own themselves no thinkers in my sense of the word. They never set up to be original. They never pretended to put this and that together for themselves. Never had a metaphor, never made an analogy. But they had. I knew. So I put them on the operating table and proceeded to take ideas they didn't know they had out of them as a prestidigitator takes rabbits and pigeons you have declared yourself innocent of out of your pockets, trouserlegs and even mouth. Only a few resented being thus shown up and caught with the goods on them.[39]

As Frost saw the matter, the Meiklejohn program merely converted faculty and students alike into social meddlers: "Shakespeare says it is the right virtue of the meddler to be rotten before it is ripe. Overdevelop the social conscience and make us all meddlers."[40] In general, Frost disliked reformers and considered many of them to be mindless activists.

The hubris of their young teachers deluded egotistical students to imagine that through their rational discussions they could find easy and valid solutions to the complex problems of society. Frost's poem "An Empty Threat" (1923) concludes in a satire aimed at this type of rationalism: ". . . life's victories of doubt / That need endless talk-talk / To make them out." If Meiklejohn's rationalism would come to prevail in American education, Frost believed it was only a matter of time before the so-called "social sciences" would replace literature; psychology would replace philosophy; and modern languages would replace Greek and Latin, and in turn be replaced by philology.

In pursuit of his educational objectives, Meiklejohn perceived himself as an avant-garde pioneer preparing the way for an enlightened future America. In his inaugural address, he hoped to give students "that zest, that delight in things intellectual" that would make them "men of intellectual culture." His course in logic created disciples among his students, who regarded him as a brilliant, witty, socially charming, and eloquent teacher and man of ideas. His charismatic talks in chapel inspired his devoted students with an enthusiasm to go out and conquer the world. Years after he was forced to resign, largely for financial mismanagement, Phyllis Bottome defended him in the *New Republic*: "President Meiklejohn was adored by the undergraduates, and the attention of America was sympathetically focused upon his great experiment."[41]

Although Meiklejohn's progressive ideas provoked strong opposition among the faculty, his difficulties at Amherst were more the result of his administrative decisions and policies. He dismissed faculty members who failed to meet his requirements and forced retirement at age sixty-five. Above the objections of the faculty committee on promotions, he advanced one instructor to associate professor. He dismissed five associate professors whom he regarded as "deadwood," and when the faculty objected to their bad treatment he confronted them with charges of disloyalty. Among the long-established faculty, Professor George Bosworth Churchill in the Department of English became Meiklejohn's chief adversary. By 1920 the Amherst faculty was divided into two strongly opposed factions, pro- or anti-Meiklejohn, and Frost was clearly on the side of the traditionalists in education.[42] To the poet, the system of education introduced by Meiklejohn was simply the American version of Julien Benda's *trahison des clercs*, teachers who abandoned the quest for philosophical truths based upon the Western tradition of humanities and instead engaged in political squabbles. Frost was aware that Meiklejohn held him in contempt as an "anti-intellectual." In his view, the president was a Pied Piper of Hamelin, luring innocent students by his siren song to their destruction. Their differences became so unbearable to Frost that he resigned from Amherst in 1920 and returned to his farm in Franconia, New Hampshire. In a letter to an Amherst alumni group who had invited him to speak to them, he rejected their invitation and wrote that he had resigned because he was "too much out of sympathy with what the present administration seems bent on doing with this old New England College."

In retrospect, it appeared to Frost that Meiklejohn had subverted his own original "Amherst Idea" that had first attracted the poet to the college, in favor of the illusions of the idea of progress. On May 15, 1920, he wrote to Wilbur L. Cross at Yale on why he had left his first academic teaching post:

I discovered what the Amherst Idea was that is so much talked of, and I got amicably out. The Amherst Idea as I had it in so many words from the high custodian is this: "Freedom for taste and intellect." Freedom from what? Freedom from every prejudice in favor of state, home, church, morality, etc. I am too much a creature of prejudice to stay and listen to such stuff. Not only in favor of morality am I prejudiced, but in favor of an immorality I could name as against other immoralities. I'd no more set out in pursuit of the truth than I would in pursuit of a living unless mounted on my prejudices.[43]

It is clear that, like Edmund Burke, whom the poet greatly admired, by "prejudice" he simply meant moral habit beyond reflection built into human nature from infancy in favor of home, church, and state. Frost was convinced that Meiklejohn's "freedom for taste and intellect" was destructive of the norms in the basic institutions of civil society and involved a drastic separation of the intellectual virtues from the moral virtues.

In 1924, Frost accepted President George Olds's invitation to return to Amherst College as poet-in-residence and stated that he was eager to "help show the world the difference between the right kind of liberal college and the wrong kind."[44] His connection with Amherst continued with occasional interruptions for several decades, and in the long run his influence on the college was far greater than that of Meiklejohn. An ironical conclusion to this complex story was made in 1954 by Charles Cole as president of Amherst: "Alexander Meiklejohn's great contribution to Amherst was Robert Frost."[45] The poet's "education by presence" had become a legend, not only at Amherst, but in the collegiate institutions of the surrounding region: Mount Holyoke, Smith, and the University of Massachusetts.

### *The Poet as Teacher*

One of the supreme ironies in Frost's life, particularly as a teacher, was the common charge by educators such as Meiklejohn that he was an "anti-intellectual." This charge often resulted from the poet's skepticism of certain ideas propounded by academic specialists, whose affectation, vanity, or pride led them to parade their erudition. He once responded to the charge by asking, "Does anyone go around calling himself 'pro-intellectual'?" Frost's favorite phrase for self-styled "intellectuals," not only in academia but in the arts and poetry, was "pseudo-intellectual." He applied the phrase to the esoteric style and poetry of allusion characteristic of works by Ezra Pound and T. S. Eliot and warned against their partisan literary critics, who loved to explicate their methods and symbolism to uninitiated students: "You want to watch for those people who seem to enjoy what they don't understand."[46] Frost distinguished between obscurity and profundity, and held that it was arrogant to equate specialized knowledge with intellectual superiority and to treat with condescension the nonacademic world or to treat the general reader as stupid or ignorant.

Frost's own range and depth of knowledge and understanding, so evident in his teaching, was far greater than that of many of his critics. Sidney Cox recorded of the poet's intelligence: "I . . . think him the wisest man, and one of the two deepest and most honest thinkers I know."[47] According to G. A. Craig, Frost's colleague at Amherst, the poet's knowledge "was astonishingly ample and exact" with "an almost photographic knowledge of a great many poetic, philosophic, and historic texts."[48] Rabbi Victor Reichert, himself a highly educated and intellectually sophisticated scholar, recorded: "Frost with . . . not too much experience in the scientific literature connected with the Bible, would grasp things—deeply too—with greater penetration than many of the so-called great scholars who were committed to that kind of work."[49] Reichert also noted: "Robert Frost was probably the most formidable intellect I'd ever encountered in my life."[50] He was also frequently amazed at the unexpected depths of knowledge Frost revealed in many fields: "More than once he absolutely astonished me by the treasures it [Frost's mind] contained and upon which he could draw as from a bottomless well with effortless ease. . . . Frost could amazingly sit on top of endless facts. He held in his grasp a university of learning in all branches of literature, philosophy and science."[51] Frost's astonishing memory made him a walking encyclopedia of knowledge in literature, history, and philosophy. Professor Hewette Joyce of Dartmouth College once asked Frost to teach his class impromptu for an hour on Milton's "Lycidas" and discovered that he knew the whole poem by heart. His brilliant and loving comments on the poem electrified the teacher and awestruck the students. In my eight summers of conversations with Frost at Bread Loaf (1939–44 and 1961–62), I discovered that he knew to memory thousands of lines of poetry, not only from the whole tradition of English and American poetry, but also Greek and Latin poets, especially Homer, Virgil, Lucretius, and Horace. Frost took the whole history and culture of Western civilization as his field of knowledge as a teacher, but he wore his learning without ostentation and without claiming to be an intellectual.

Frost's career as a teacher extended from the spring of 1893 almost to his death in 1963. It included teaching in a one-room country school in New England and in the most complex and prestigious ivy-covered gothic-structured colleges and universities. His first instruction was to "twelve barefooted children in the neck of the woods in South Salem, New Hampshire," in the rudiments of English, Latin, and algebra.[52] In an interview in 1961, Frost said, "I've taught every darn year from kindergarten to graduate school, Latin, English, mathematics, history, algebra, philosophy, and one year psychology."[53] He held a great variety of academic positions, beginning with Pinkerton Academy in Derry, New Hampshire (1905–11); in the Normal School in Plymouth, New Hampshire (1911–12); at Amherst College (1917–20); at the University of Michigan (1922–23 and 1925–26); again at Amherst (1923–25, 1926–38, and 1949–63). In addition to these positions, he delivered the Norton Lectures at Harvard (1936) and was the Ralph Waldo Emerson Fellow in Poetry at Harvard in 1942–43, concluding his career as George Ticknor Fellow in the Humanities at Dartmouth College. Lawrance Thompson has noted Frost's "unusually extensive participation in the teaching activities at Bread Loaf,"[54] which included sessions with the summer school graduate students and in the poetry clinics at the Writers' Conference between 1920–62 at the school, and after 1926 at the conference. Some schools invited Frost back time and time again, such as Wesleyan University in Middletown, Connecticut; the New School for Social Research; Agnes Scott College in Decatur, Georgia; Kenyon College in Gambier, Ohio; Vanderbilt University; and Pierson College, Yale University. In December 1956, during a television interview on *Meet the Press*, Frost said, "I think the best audience the world ever had, probably, is the little town-and-gown audience that we get in the little college towns in the U.S.A.—two thousand towns."[55] As C. P. Snow observed of Frost: "No professional writer has ever spent so much time in contact with academic life."[56]

It may seem paradoxical that Frost spent so much of his adult life as a teacher or poet-in-residence in academia, yet was constantly severely critical of colleges and universities. The paradox is partly resolved by observing that while he despised the methodology, institutional requirements, and excessively structured bureaucratic hierarchy in higher education, he nevertheless thoroughly enjoyed close relationships with many faculty members and students, some of whom became lifelong friends. In a letter to Louis Undermeyer (May 9, 1936) commenting on how his series of Charles Eliot Norton Lectures were well-received by an enthusiastic town-and-gown audience, he revealed his doubts about the response of the Harvard administration and some faculty:

I don't feel I made too big a hit with the dignitaries and authorities. . . . There was a moment in March when I thought that perhaps they were giving me back my father's Harvard. But probably I was fooling myself. I'm imperfectly academic and no amount of association with the academic will make me perfect. It's too bad, for I like the academic in my way, and up to a certain point the academic likes me. Its patronage proves as much. I may be wrong in my suspicion that I haven't pleased Harvard as much as I have the encompassing barbarians. My whole impression may have come from the Pound-Eliot-Richards gang in Eliot House here.[57]

Time and time again, Frost spoke of being "always at it against colleges in a vain attempt to reconcile myself with them." But his severe negative strictures need to be understood as only a part of the strong ambiguity he always felt about institutional education, which was a factor in his role as a teacher: "I've been a teacher all my life . . . but I've been a dissatisfied teacher. I can't leave it alone. I'm like some monkeys Darwin tells about. Somebody showed them some snakes, and they screamed and ran away, but they kept coming back. I'm that way about education."[58] C. P. Snow was probably right in holding that while Frost's "literary originality" differed sharply from "academic literary thinking," nevertheless "in his subtle and labile temperament, he was much more academically inclined than he pretended, or liked, to think."[59] For over four decades, Frost haunted the academic scene, partly because it provided him with a steady income and a variety of literary prestige, but also because, as a teacher, the caliber of people he knew in colleges, and their cultural concerns, were of a much higher order than what was to be found anywhere else. He loved to wage a fine scholastic contention with academically oriented and sophisticated people.

A more personal reason also continued to link him with higher education. He admitted that his continuity with colleges was in part his gratitude for their positive response to his poetry: "What has brought me back in and partly disarmed me is the kindness the colleges have shown my poetry. I find myself even anxious to be useful to them in requital."[60] Frost was especially grateful for the many honorary degrees conferred on him by American and British colleges and universities. To Louis Mertins, he admitted how deeply he valued his many connections with the academic world: "One can't take a home, or a companion, or a college out of his heart without leaving a great void, great empty place."[61] In "Build Soil," Frost ranked colleges in his hierarchy of social values right behind friendship, the nation, and the family: "Don't join too many gangs. Join few if any. Join the United States and join the family—But not much in between unless a college." To Louis Untermeyer he wrote on June 26, 1939: "I wonder at myself for still hanging around education after all these years: but I suppose what keeps me is the reasonable doubt that the college belongs entirely to the scholars."[62] Frost clearly believed that the college belonged far more to the teacher and student than to the scholar, and least of all to the administration.

As much as he deplored the excessive machinery of administration, modeled upon the rigid and impersonal methods of industry and business, he also objected to the analytical methods employed by many teachers, particularly in literary criticism. Much as he despised scientific scholarship for the sake of erudition, he objected to any literary criticism which assumed that the scientific method was a valid instrument in the discussion of literature. Untermeyer recorded Frost's strong disapproval to pages and pages of detailed analytical criticism of "Stopping by Woods on a Snowy Evening":

> The trouble with this sort of criticism, he said, is that it analyzes itself—and the poem—to death. It first depersonalizes the idea, then it dehumanizes the emotion, finally it destroys whatever poetry is left in the poem. It assumes that criticism is not only an art but also a science; it acts as though poetry were written in order to be dissected and that its chief value is in offering a field-day for ambiguity-hunters. You've often heard me say . . . that poetry is what is lost in translation. It is also what is lost in interpretation. That little poem means just what it says and it says what it means, nothing less but nothing more.[63]

Frost was aware that the great danger for the common, literal-minded, inexperienced reader of poetry is that much that is vital in the poem will be missed—its form, technique, and content; its tone and mood in the emotional, phonetic, and imaginative use of metaphorical language. But he thought that the opposite danger often seduced the professional literary critic and classroom teacher—the use of the poem as a springboard for analytical speculations and the reading of far more into the content of a poem than is warranted. Such readers assumed that the aesthetic imagination is no more than reason and that a poem could be read the same way as discursive prose argument appears in a scholarly article. But to Frost a poem was "a felt-thought thing," to be read on its own terms, and it involved the total nature of the reader, not merely abstract reason. In his notebooks, Frost asked: "What can you do with a poem besides read it to yourself or someone else?"[64] He listed forty-one things that can be done with a poem, such as memorizing it, or applying it to everyday experience, but he was adamant in rejecting analytical criticism as a valid response to literature.

In a letter to Sidney Cox (January 2, 1915), even before he became a regular teacher in academia, Frost expressed his skepticism and dislike toward academic scholarship and literary criticism and the failure to appreciate literature as an aesthetic art form:

> I see you really doing something in the next few years to break into the worst system of teaching that ever endangered a nation's literature. You speak of Columbia. That reminds me of the article on American literature by a Columbian, George Woodbury [Woodberry], in the *Encyclopedia Britannica*. I wish you would read it or the last part of it just to see that we are not alone in thinking that nothing literary can come from the present ways of the professionally literary in American universities. . . . Everything is research for the sake of erudition. No one is taught to value himself for nice perception and cultivated taste. Knowledge knowledge. Why literature is the next thing to religion in which as you know or believe an ounce of faith is worth all the theology ever written. Sight and insight, give us those. I like the good old English way of muddling along in these things that we can't reduce to a science anyway such as literature, love, religion and friendship. People make their great strides in understanding literature at most unexpected times. I never caught another man's emotion in it more than when someone drew his finger over some seven lines of blank verse—beginning carefully and ending carefully—and saying simply "From there to—there." He knew and I knew. We said no more. I don't see how you are going to teach the stuff except with some such light touch. And you can't afford to treat it all alike, I mean with equal German thoroughness and reverence if thoroughness is reverence. It is only a moment here and a moment there that the greatest writing has. Some cognizance of the fact must be taken in your teaching.[65]

Frost clearly agreed with William Wordsworth's dictum, "We murder to dissect," so that as a teacher he believed that nothing was more fatal to the humanities and liberal arts than the application of analytical reason and the scientific method. Things of the spirit, such as religion and the arts, could not be understood in the descriptive and quantitative terms of the physical sciences.

In an interview in February 1916, Frost was vehement in his criticism of academic education: "I hate academic ways. I fight everything academic. The time we waste in trying to learn academically—the talent we starve with academic teaching."[66] As a student, Frost had "walked out of two colleges like nothing at all" rather than put up with all that he found wrong with their academic methods and requirements.[67] At the Unterberg Poetry Center of the 92nd Street YMHA in New York in 1958, Frost warned students against being drowned in a sea of irrelevant and unassimilated knowledge: "My great complaint of education is that it is so loaded with material you never move in the spirit again. You've got to get into it but no more than you can swing and sing."[68] He believed that far too many students, even at the Ivy League schools, become corrupted and overwhelmed by excessive materials required by the faculty. To Untermeyer, Frost expressed this conviction in a stark simile on August 8, 1921: "You remember that beautiful line of Wilkie Collins in *The Woman in White*: 'Her son was drowned at Oxford at the age of eighteen.' Eighteen is just about the age at which most of them get drowned at Harvard and Yale."[69]

Probably the most recurrent theme in Frost's criticism of "academic rigidity and myopia" was that "excessive planning deadened innovation" and creativity and depersonalized the whole process of learning. He asked: "Why did everything have to be programmed?" It was folly to institutionalize "what should remain free and adventurous" like a love affair.[70] Students and faculty who accepted "laid-on" education often lacked any sense of play, of fancy and imagination, and became deadened by scholastic methodology. Frost's lifelong ambition as a teacher was "to make school as unschoollike as possible."[71] Academic learning was especially fatal in developing skills in good writing: "That's the trouble with graduate studies—graduate schools. They think you command what is in your notebook. You can't command it. You've got to be so familiar with it you can throw the notes away. . . . Theses from graduate school are hard to sell."[72] For Frost, mere factual erudition not only did not help to make good writing, it could be a positive hindrance. In a letter to Untermeyer (January 9, 1947), Frost translated Joseph Scaliger's *Erudita inscitia est* as "Erudition is a form of ignorance," and added: "The learned Duns Scotus, patron saint of scholars, was so full of things not worth knowing that his name has come down to us spelled Dunce: '*Sapientiae pars est quaedam aequo animo nescire velle.'"* (There is a kind of wisdom in calmly choosing not to know.) To Frost, an intelligent, widely-read nonacademic writer who had assimilated knowledge over many years of interest in a subject was often a far better and more vital writer than scholars trained in graduate schools. With some reservations, he instanced James Truslow Adams as a case in point: "Adams . . . is a better scholar because a livelier, a less deadened by school, than any of the academics. He has the freedom of the real as you never get it in the teacher-taught. He has come to learning as you come to the table, not the conference round table, but the dinner table." No one knew better than Frost how much the scientific method and the "German thoroughness," introduced into American higher education at Johns Hopkins University, had reduced the humanities to mere raw materials for dead doctoral dissertations.[73]

To the end of his life, Frost believed that the arts and humanities should be at the center of education. But under the system that had come to prevail in American education, they received short shrift, and their neglect resulted in a vulgarized national culture in which values were largely materialistic. When MIT added a humanities program to its scientific curriculum, Frost criticized it because it was introduced "like an ingredient" in bread; it wasn't, as it should be, the essential part of education. Through the humanities, "the past," he asserted, "is the great book of worthies,"[74] which provided the basis of Western civilization in its history, literature, philosophy, religion, science, law, and politics. Frost believed that both in the personal lives of individuals and in the cultural life of a nation, "the denouement tells the story," and however much individuals were well trained to excess in a profession, to the extent that they were deficient in the arts and humanities, they were not truly educated.[75]

## 11

# The Individual and Society

*We're always too much out or too much in.*
*At present from a cosmical dilation*
*We're so much out that the odds are against*
*Our ever getting inside in again.*
*But inside in is where we've got to get.*
*My friends all know I'm interpersonal.*
*But long before I'm interpersonal*
*Away 'way down inside I'm personal.*
*Just so before we're international*
*We're national and act as nationals.*

*Frost, Build Soil—A Political Pastoral*

Like Aristotle in the *Politics* and like Edmund Burke throughout his political philosophy, Robert Frost believed that man is by his innate nature a
social animal.[1] The membership of men in civil society is not a matter of
personal choice nor a voluntary and revocable contractual relationship; it
is rather a biological and moral necessity and the result of a complex and
extended historical inheritance. Men are born into society without their
choice, and the essential elements in their continued relationship with the
social order are also beyond voluntary choices.

Frost was always intensely aware that there is a continuous and unresolved ambiguity between the necessary claims of society upon each individual, for duties to be performed, and the contrary claims of each indi-

vidual upon his society, to be as free and independent as possible within the laws and customs of society. This continuous conflict between society and the individual, which exists wherever moral or legal authority external to the individual existed, was fully accepted and even enjoyed by Frost: "I like all this uncertainty that we live in, between being members and being individuals. That's the daily problem: how much am I a member; how much am I an individual; how comfortable am I in my memberships?"[2] Despite the continuous conflict between the individual and society, Frost believed that there is a natural identity of self-interest and social benevolence in both individuals and society, which keeps men together in society. But the relationship between the claims of self-interest and social benevolence, like that of authority and freedom, is subject to continuous adjustments.

This idea of the simultaneous separateness and unity of each individual in society is the central theme in Frost's early poem "The Tuft of Flowers," and it remained a firm personal conviction throughout Frost's life. In this dramatic monologue, the speaker, who has come to mow a field, begins by stating his belief that like a previous, off-stage, invisible mower, who had worked and "gone his way," he too must work and be alone:

*"As all must be," I said within my heart,*
*"Whether they work together or apart."*

But at the conclusion of the poem, after the speaker has shared in the aesthetic experience of his predecessor, in enjoying the beauty of the tuft of flowers that had been deliberately left standing, "from sheer morning gladness at the brim," the mower has reversed his belief about the individual's relationship to others in society:

*"Men work together," I told him from the heart,*
*"Whether they work together or apart."*

Many of Frost's other poems, such as "The Vantage Point,"[3] "Mending Wall," and even "Stopping by Woods on a Snowy Evening," affirm the same theme in a variety of ways. His own prose statements over many years, in letters, interviews, and conversations, leave no doubt that he always believed the individual and society could transcend their conflicts and achieve harmony and that this process of reconciling differences was part of his larger belief that man is by his innate nature a social animal.

The relationship between the individual and civil society was more natural, and more important to Frost, than the relationship between human nature and external physical "nature" itself. A line in "New Hampshire"—"Nothing not built with hands of course is sacred"—summarizes his belief that in the order of priorities and values the proper study of mankind is man himself, with external "nature" decidedly subordinated. If full weight is given to this important point, it fully justifies rejecting the common false stereotype of Frost as a "nature poet." In his poems, physical "nature" is most often merely the background setting for a human drama, rather than the subject. On this vital point, he himself said, "I guess I'm not a nature poet. I have only written two poems without a human being in them."[4] Unlike Wordsworth, Frost never posited an antithesis between human society as something "artificial" and physical phenomena such as mountains, forests, skies, and oceans as "natural." To him, human society, with its institutions and structured social relationships, is perfectly "natural" to man. It is as normatively natural for men to live together in society as it is for nonhuman forms of life to live in a state of physical nature. Theories of a social contract based upon a supposed pre-civil "state of nature," such as those of Hobbes, Locke, and Rousseau, had no place in Frost's conception of the individual in civil society.

## Frost on Rural and Urban Society

Many of the most serious misinterpretations of Frost as a reflective poet and philosopher, which charge him with being indifferent to modern urbanized society and its human problems, stem from a gross failure to understand his complete subordination of external physical nature to society. Such critics invariably dismiss Frost as a mere "nature poet," content to present pictorial scenery. They invariably assume that he made an absolute antithesis between rural and urban life, in favor of the former. But the distinctions Frost made between rural and urban man fall within his grand conception of man as a social animal. Although he always preferred the rural to the urban life, he never set them against each other by identifying the former with external nature: "I'm very much a country man, and I don't like to see city against country."[5] In considering the relationship between the individual and civil society it is not necessary to include his views on external physical nature except as the setting for his view of social man in his rural life.

The complex relationships between each individual and his society are very evident in Frost's distinction between the lifestyles of rural and urban society. To him, country and city life were two different aspects of general civil society; they were distinct but not antithetical, and each contained advantages to human nature which the other lacked, and thus they supplemented each other. The common problem of all men in both of these basic ways of life was how to reconcile their privacy and integrity as individuals with the public demands made upon them by other men and by their memberships in social institutions. This was the same ancient problem that Plato had raised in the *Republic*: how can a man be both a good man, true to his highest moral self, and also a good citizen, true to the legitimate claims of his political society?

One aspect of this basic question could be stated in terms of economic personal freedom and dependency upon society: to what extent should a man be economically self-reliant as an individual, even to enduring poverty or to amassing wealth beyond his personal needs; to what extent should he be dependent upon society, whose urbanized economy rested largely upon the researches of science, the interdependence of technology, assembly-line industrialization, the division of labor, credit, monetary exchange, and commerce and finance? As an objective to be realized, whether through withdrawal for self-reliance or through involvement in social interdependence, or some combination of both, Frost's answer to this vital question was plain and clear: "What we want is the largest possible number of citizens who can take care of themselves. What we need is character."[6] Where in modern society was self-reliant human "character" to be found at its best?

There was no question in Frost's mind that, in the initial stages of man's life, the greatest degree of self-reliance, love of individual freedom, reflective leisure, and integrity and character was to be found in the life of the country. The simplicity of such life fostered these human qualities much more than their opposite traits, which were more common in urban centers. In particular, during the early period of life, the cultivation of personal character, defined as the moral and intellectual virtues, could take place best in the country. The country also provided the basis for an aesthetic appreciation of external nature, although the aesthetics of art and special talents in most arts flourished best in the city. Frost believed that to develop as a total human being, a man had first to depend upon his own inner resources, and he learned to do this best through life on a farm: "The farm is a base of operations—a stronghold. You can withdraw in yourself there."[7] Solitude for reflection is an essential ingredient in self-development: "I think a person has to be withdrawn into himself to gather inspiration so that he is somebody when he comes out again among folks—when he 'comes to market' with himself. He learns that he's got to be almost wastefully alone."[8] He

*The Poet, Philosopher, and Educator in his Study in Franconia, 1914*

*Robert Frost with his wife, Elinor at Rockford College Library, 1936*

*Photgraph taken by Frederick G. Welcher, courtesy of Rockford College*

*Standing on the Porch of
the Little Theater at Bread
Loaf, Robert Frost in 1940*

*photo taken by Peter J. Stanlis*

*Robert Frost at bat during a baseball game at Bread Loaf, August 1941.
Peter Stanlis (center) is watching in the background*

Photograph courtesy of Middlebury College News Bureau

*Frost during a poetry
reading at Bread Loaf in the Little Theater, 1943*

Photograph courtesy of Middlebury College News Bureau

*Frost with Eamon de Valera, the Prime Minister of Ireland, after receiving his Honorary Degree from Dublin University, after receiving an Honorary Degree from both Cambridge and Oxford Universities in June 1957.*

*Frost with W.H. Auden at Oxford University, where Frost received an honorary degree, June 1957*

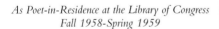

*As Poet-in-Residence at the Library of Congress Fall 1958-Spring 1959*

*Robert Frost with Louis Untermeyer*

*Peter Stanlis and Robert Frost at the University of Detroit*
*November 13, 1962*

*Here, Stanlis showed Frost a copy of* From Snow to Snow,
*which Frost had inscribed to him on New Year's Eve in 1939-1940 in Boston*

*Photograph by Joe Clark, courtesy of the University of Detroit*

*Stanlis discussing the procedures with Frost for the Honorary Degree
Ceremony at the Unviersity of Detroit, November 13, 1962*

*Robert Frost and Peter Stanlis
Marching in the Academic Procession for
Frost's Honorary Doctor's Degree at the
University of Detroit, November 13, 1962.*

*For his tribute to Frost, on this occasion,
see "Afterword-Poetry as Revelation"
pages 345–348*

Photographs courtesy of the University of Detroit

*Over 10,000 were in attendance at Frost's poetry reading at the University of Detroit in November 14, 1962*

*Robert Frost giving a poetry reading in the Memorial Building at the University of Detroit November 14, 1962*

believed that a conscious sense of self-identity through isolation, like that of the speaker in "A Tuft of Flowers," should precede a sense of social relationships with other men.

Frost never believed that an individual should live a rural life in order to escape from the demands of urban society, but rather in order to plunge deeper into his own nature, to explore and find his strengths and weaknesses, to measure his ordinary self against his ideal self, so that when he ventured into urban society he came with the greatness of his intellectual, moral, aesthetic, and social capability already well-developed:

> You associate yourself with your fellows in order that you may be stronger yourself. The individual and the social—I know those two things are always getting something out of each other. But I am mostly interested in solitude and in the preservation of the individual. I want to see people sufficiently drawn into themselves. Most of the iceberg is under water. Most of oneself should be within oneself. A man must do that in order to be somebody when he comes out to market with other folks. He should be a large-proportioned individual before he becomes social. If a man is wastefully alone, he should be better company when he comes out.[9]

Clearly, Frost believed that the reflective isolation of country life when young was the best preparation for a man's later trial by existence in civil society. Although Frost loved both "the quiet of the garden" and "the market place" of urban society[10] and saw them as always closely related but distinct spheres of man's social life, rather than as antithetical, he emphasized the total development of the individual as the great end of living, and civil society (both rural and urban) as merely the necessary instrumental means of human self-fulfillment. In the relationship of the individual to society, the perfection of each individual always remained for Frost the highest purpose of life.

Frost rejected the opposite doctrine that the individual should exist mainly as an instrument for the development of society. In essence, this theory of man was the ideal of all totalitarian ideologies. But there was nothing antisocial in Frost's self-reliant individualism. He believed that when large numbers of individuals became maturely developed as complete human beings, society would indeed receive the benefit of their knowledge, talents, and character and therefore would naturally be improved. The primary development of the individual, cultivating his talents alone in rural life before contributing them as benefits to urban society, for example, applied to poets and to poetry as an art, and to similar activities of the whole human race:

> Poetry is more often of the country than of the city. Poetry is very, very rural—rustic. It stands as a reminder of rural life—as a resource. . . . It might be taken as a symbol of a man, taking its rise from individuality and seclusion—written first for the person that writes and then going out into social appeal and use. Just so the race lives best to itself—first to itself, storing strength in the more individual life of the country, of the farm—then going to market and socializing in the industrial city.[11]

The great purpose of the well-developed individual in "going to market and socializing" was never to merge into the mass of humanity, in its institutional life, but always to become more truly himself: ". . . Remember the paradox that you become more social in order that you may become more of an individual."[12]

Although Frost clearly favored the total development of the independent social individual as the supreme good and regarded rural society as the best means to that end, he also believed that a balance between the country and urban life should be maintained, both within society and within each individual in society: "I should expect life to be back and forward—now more individual on the farm, now more social in the city—striving to get the balance."[13] This ideal of harmony applied to the individual as well: "The balance is between our being members of each other and being individuals."[14] The well-balanced social individual was never too isolated within himself or his rural environment, nor was he too homogenized within urban society:

> One of the most sociable virtues or vices is that you don't want to feel queer. You don't want to be too much like the others, but you don't want to be clear out in nowhere. . . . You are always with your sorrows and cares. What's a poem for if not to share them with others. But I don't like poems that are too crudely personal. . . . We have all sorts of ways to hold people. . . . Hold them and hold them off. Do you know what the sun does with the planets? It holds them and holds them off. The planets don't fall away from the sun, and they don't fall into it. That's one of the marvels: attraction and repulsion. You have that with poetry, and you have that with friendships.[15]

There is much of the classical ideal of the golden mean in Frost's belief that it is better to be a well-balanced social individual than to be excessively personal or too committed to society.

In his poem "Build Soil—A Political Pastoral," Frost made it clear that in modern life there is a serious imbalance between the individual and society, with the former being overwhelmed by his commitments and involvements in social institutions. The two chief characters in the poem, Tityrus, the rural poet, and Meliboeus, the potato man, discuss and draw out the range of the well-balanced individual and the well-balanced society. Tityrus defines the extent to which all human beings, in their relationship with society, are "always too much out or too much in." He says of contemporary man: "We are too much out, and if we don't draw in / We shall be driven in." His plea is to draw in for privacy from too many involvements in society. He advises Meliboeus that men should "Keep off each other and keep each other off," because "We're too unseparate out among each other—" Finally, Tityrus cautions against an individual's becoming too involved with social group action:

> *Don't join too many gangs. Join few if any.*
> *Join the United States and join the family*
> *But not much in between unless a college.*

Meliboeus confirms this theme at the conclusion of the poem:

> *I agree with you*
> *We're too unseparate. And going home*
> *From company means coming to our senses.*

Like his two wise rural characters in the poem, Frost himself believed that the same imbalance which has submerged the individual in institutional society was to be found throughout the world of the twentieth century due to the submergence of the country into the city. Like many contemporary sociologists and economists, he believed that industrialized urban life had absorbed too much of the rural life of the United States. Even during the early decades of the twentieth century, Frost thought the nation was already too far gone in urbanization. But he hoped for a revival of rural life. As the imbalance affected by more and more industrialization continued, his analysis of the general character of Americans, resulting from this imbalance, was clearly voiced in an interview in June 1931:

We are now at a moment when we are getting too far out into the social-industrial and are at the point of drawing back—drawing in to renew ourselves. The country life we are going back to I can't describe in advance, but I am pretty sure it will not be the country life we came out of years ago. Farming, what survives of it, has demeaned itself in an attempt to imitate industrialism. It has lost its self-respect. It has wished itself something other than what it is. That is the only unpardonable sin: to wish you were something you are not, something other people are. It is so in the arts and in everything else. . . .

The farmer has industrialized to his own hurt. He has made himself too social right on the farm. He has entered into the competitive outside life. The strength of his position is that he's got so many things that he doesn't need to go outside for. The country's advantage is that it gives many pleasures and supplies many needs for nothing. The tendency of our day is to throw away all these things and count them worthless. . . .

A person is always being pulled out of himself socially, and it is always in the person, and up to the person, to take corrective measures. He should know when to say, "I am too much out of myself—too overt." The tendency for the preservation of his individuality draws him back, and I would guess that the loss of a people is in its industrialization. They are inclined to draw away from their base which is in the country.[16]

As early as 1919, Frost had savagely denounced "the god damned fools . . . who have made and made such a mess of industrialism."[17] He was sorrowfully aware that the powerful forces of modern industrialism were destroying American rural life, and he was convinced that unless the United States reversed its course to restore a more balanced rural-urban nation, there would be a serious loss of individual freedom throughout the nation.

In the same interview in which Frost expressed his forlorn hope for the revival of rural life in America, he noted that what was happening in the United States by default, through social and economic attrition and abuse of freedom, was being fostered in Soviet Russia deliberately, through its system of collective farming: "They seem to be industrializing the work of the land."[18] Frost was harshly critical of the Soviet five-year plans that eliminated all privately owned farms in Russia. In 1938, he noted that the closest things in the United States to collective farms were the cooperatives and that they couldn't compete economically with private farming. Some members of cooperatives banded together and acted politically to make up their economic deficits through help from the government. Frost noted of this development: "cooperatives having found that they cant compete with individual enterprise have hit on the idea of seizing the government and destroying their rivals by force. Then they are communists."[19]

In sharp contrast to the cooperative farms were the independent farms of New England, which Frost admired. In 1961, looking back at the survival of independent farms through the Great Depression, he underscored the virtues of the independent individualism of the New England farmers, noting: "the New Englander's uncanny ability to get the most from the least that has made him such an independent hardy individual."[20] Even then he found it "deplorable" that some Vermont and New Hampshire farms were giving way to huge combines: "There goes your neighborliness: there goes much of the rugged individuality that has made New England what it is."[21] The shift from rural life to urban life, and the urbanization of rural life itself, was to Frost one of the great social tragedies of twentieth-century America.

## Rural Freedom versus Independence from Society: Thoreau

In reacting against the urban-rural imbalance in modern American society, how far did Frost wish to go in restoring a healthy rural life? In answering this question perhaps a good point of departure might be to note that among Frost's favorite books he especially esteemed Defoe's *Robinson Crusoe*, Darwin's *Voyage of the Beagle*, and Thoreau's *Walden*. These three classics, he said, "have a special shelf in my heart."[22] *Walden* was to Frost "a tale of adventure . . . a declaration of independence and a gospel of wisdom."[23] Frost was very explicit in his reason for approving the central themes of *Robinson Crusoe* and *Walden*:

> What has brought about our ability to "do things"? All our adaptability to circumstances? Go back to *Walden* and *Robinson Crusoe*. These experimenters found themselves, when trial came, able to, and *did*, pit themselves naked against an infinitely unfriendly nature, and they provided some part of, no inconsiderable part of, creature comforts sufficient.

> I should hate to think we had educated all the animal ability out of ourselves. A little quail skips out of the egg on the run, unfolded by surprise, and never stops. Snakes have to look af-

ter themselves from the day they are hatched out, or, in the case of the rattler, after they are born from their mother. They have no coddling. I have always maintained that we coddle human frailties too much. We encourage the dish to run away with the spoon. Just set a man against the elements. Let him battle. If he's worth his salt he'll make it, if not it doesn't much matter. He's got to ride like ice on his own melting. He may make a botch of it, but nothing's irredeemable. I often come back to the woman who in the crowd touched the hem of Christ's garment. It was enough.[24]

The biological self-sufficiency and independence of the animals in a state of nature provided Frost with a norm that, with necessary qualifications, applied as well to men like Crusoe on his island and to Thoreau in his experiment at Walden Pond. But to what extent did such a norm apply to masses of men in the complex system of economic interdependence that characterized modern society?

Frost was well aware that the kind of self-contained freedom forced upon Robinson Crusoe, and freely chosen briefly by Thoreau at Walden Pond, was not man's freedom in society, but merely independence from society:

Thoreau had an impatience with membership and sometimes even citizenship. His theme was freedom in a way, but it was a freedom within freedom; that is to say, an independence that seems to stop short somewhere of Liberty with a capital "L." I called it myself once a one-man revolution. A statue to it would be less stature than one of Liberty in New York Harbor. . . . But he was not interested in the liberty brightest in dungeons and on the scaffold, as much as he was in the daily liberties he could take right under the noses of the high and mighty and the small and petty. . . . We know well enough what we mean by freedom in practical politics, but it is a subject apt to get more confused when gone too far into. It seems to break down into a number of freedoms that conflict. Thoreau was content to settle for something less difficult that I call independence.[25]

It is clear from this passage that at best Thoreau was to Frost an individual corrective against the excessive claims and demands of society upon individuals in their daily lives. But the experiment at Walden Pond did not provide a basis for a free social order in a complex civilization. It was too unsocial for that. Although his experiment was secular, it required a religious self-denial and self-discipline, like the asceticism of a monk in his cell. Thoreau's protest was really against allowing the complexities of social machinery to absorb too much of a man's personal integrity and private life. It was a remonstrance against carrying a heavy mortgage on one's back for thirty years. In making a supreme virtue of simplicity and self-denial, Thoreau showed at Walden Pond how much of political and economic society he could live without.

Frost believed too strongly in the corporate character of man, however, to accept Thoreau's private "independence" in place of civil freedom in society. The moralist's kind of "independence" was what Frost once called "unchartered freedom," and although it provided private freedom against too much structured social restraint, it was inadequate for any form or order in art or in civil society. During the summer of 1940, at Bread Loaf, Vermont, I discussed Thoreau's theme of independence from society with him, and he dismissed Thoreau rather curtly: "Life among the woodchucks is not for me." The moralist's kind of "independence" from society was nihilistic to Frost and inadequate for social freedom.

## The Land

Less nihilistic than Thoreau were those modern agrarians, such as the "Fugitives" and "unreconstructed" Southerners at Vanderbilt University, who during the 1920s and 1930s made a serious plea for a mass exodus from urban life back to the land. Frost sympathized with their objectives but disagreed with their program. He did not believe that modern technology and division of labor, despite all their abuses, should be abandoned or dismissed: "I am not a 'back-to-the-lander.' I am not interested in the Thoreau business. Only a few can do what Thoreau did. We must use the modern tools at our disposal."[26] He noted that there was plenty of empty unclaimed land always available for any individual who wished to return to the country in order to gain more self-reliance and independence than was possible in urban society. In this strictly limited and personal sense he believed in a kind of safety-valve "return to nature":

> The land be your strength and refuge. But at the same time . . . let me utter a word of warning against the land as an affectation. What determines the population of the world is not at all the amount of tillable land it affords: but it is something in the nature of the people themselves that limits the size of the globulate mass they are socially capable of. There is always, there will al-

ways be, a lot, many lots of land left out of the system. I dedicate these lots to the stray souls who from incohesiveness feel rarely the need of the forum for their thoughts or the market for their wares and produce. . . . The land not taken up gives these stay-outers, these loosely connected people, their chance to live to themselves a large proportion of time with the throng. . . . Refuse to be rushed to market or forum. Don't come as a product till you have turned yourself under many times. We don't have to be afraid we won't be social enough. Hell, haven't I written all that in my first book? But the point is the unconsidered land makes the life I like possible. Praise be to the unconsidered land.[27]

Frost's conception of "the land" as individual empty lots, available for those individuals who wished to become or remain more self-sufficient and free from urban society, was the basis of private "independence" as distinct from public social freedom.

But there was another conception of "the land." To him the political and social freedom of Americans as citizens of a great nation depended upon "the land" conceived of as the constitutionally incorporated geographical area lying between the Atlantic and Pacific oceans and between Canada and Mexico. He said: "What gives us our freedom is having a territorial basis, belonging to the land."[28] His phrase "belonging to the land" can best be understood in legal and political terms, not simply as a geographical area. The land comprising the area of the United States was part of the corporate character of Americans as a people and a nation. To him there was no such thing as a "people" apart from its legal-political character. A nation is not merely numbers of individuals told by the head, living within a geographical area. As a nation a "people" is the product of their total historical inheritance, which gives them their essential character. The United States possessed its land legally as part of its political sovereignty under its constitution.

Frost's poem "The Gift Outright," which he called his brief history of the United States from its settlement in colonial times to the present, celebrated the emergence of American self-identity and national consciousness as a fusion of a desire for political freedom and a growing love of the land as something that possessed them as a people. The theme of the poem was developed wholly out of the first line: "The land was ours before we were the land's." There had to be a shift from a sense of possessing the land to being possessed by it before the first settlers could overcome the psychological sense of being colonists belonging legally to England. By the total gift of themselves, by their surrender to the land, the colonists gradually acquired a new identity, that of a politically free American nation. Colonials are not a people (though they possess the land) but a possession of another people. Colonials lack political and legal sovereignty, which are essential to being a nation.

## Freedom, Loyalty, and Sovereignty

From Frost's idea that political and social freedom requires "a territorial basis, belonging to the land," the question of an individual's relationship to his society can be raised in terms of freedom and responsibility under the sovereignty of American constitutional law. What was Frost's conception of political sovereignty? The poet's usual terms for it were "accountability" and "answerability." Sovereignty or "accountability" was moral before it was legal or political; it began for him within the conscience of each individual. Legally, within the American nation, sovereignty was divided between the federal system and the united individual states. He always had a strong bias in favor of local or regional autonomy, and called himself a "sep-a-ra-tist": "I am . . . also a separatist. You can't mix things properly until you have separated them, unscrambled from their original chaotic mixture and held them separate long enough to test their qualities and values."[29] By starting with the individual citizen, he was able to distinguish between the large legally-defined liberty provided by the state in society and the personal free actions of individuals within that social order. The difference, Frost noted, was "between formal liberty, which is a state structure like the Parthenon in all parts consistent with itself, and scot-free impulse which is nothing but what everything comes from and everything is built out of when it cools off a little and hardens enough for the builders to cut and handle it."[30] The proper relationship between the individual and society lay somewhere between the formal liberty provided by the state and scot-free impulse.

If the scot-free impulses of every individual were totally unrestrained, theoretically there would be total private freedom in the nation. But since men are not by nature totally good and wise, that social body in its corporate wisdom has imposed necessary restraints upon men through constitutional and statutory laws, so that they may be free, not in themselves alone, but in society. An individual in society has to find his liberties somewhere in-between those allowed by the "state structure" and those "impulses" of his fellow citizens and himself that are restrained by legal and social prohibitions, since both the wrong uncontrolled impulses of others and the restrictions of the state on his right and prudent impulses can tyrannize over him:

> Between the tyranny of being handled and judged by general laws and statistics at the large end and the tyranny of being handled and judged by gossip and fashion at the small end, there should be room for any real fellow with a little effrontery to take his liberties more or less at ease. . . . Deeds that count are liberties taken with the conventions.[31]

Individual freedom in society is a matter of moral prudence between actions dictated by scot-free impulses on the one hand and by what the laws of the state structure and social conventions allow or require on the other hand.

According to Frost, the same resolution of the conflict between authority and freedom that lies within the relationship of society and the individual is also to be found in the relationship of all the world and a particular nation:

> The question for every man and every nation is to be clear about where the first answerability lies. Are we as individuals to be answerable first only to others or to ourselves and some ideal beyond ourselves? Is the United States to be answerable first to the United Nations or to its own concept of what is right?[32]

Frost was convinced that once the question of "answerability" is settled in favor of personal conscience and normative right, both for individuals and nations, each will be "more self-reliant, more prepared psychologically for the endless struggle for existence."[33]

After satisfying his conscience or appealing to God, Frost believed that an individual's natural relationships to society extended to his family and close friends, then to his hometown or local community, then to his state, province, or region, and finally to his country. These loyalties and affections are matters of gradation and not of contradictions; they also differ in kind between personal and moral loyalties and legal loyalties and between necessary and voluntary actions. The sense of local loyalty, emanating outward from the inner soul of an individual, is part of the strength of Thoreau's appeal to his readers: "Thoreau was the chief advocate since the Old Testament of making the most of the hometown and township. Make of the stones of the place a pillow for your head if you hope to see angels ascending and descending. The opposite doctrine is to desert your country because you do not seem to be accepted in it as a prophet."[34] In keeping with his doctrine of sovereignty based upon conscience and local loyalty, he wrote a tribute to a man from Denver, Colorado, a writer who loved his hometown as the core of his regionalism and nationalism:

> *A man is as tall as his height*
> *Plus the height of his home town.*
> *I know a Denverite*
> *Who, measured from sea to crown,*
> *Is one mile five-foot-ten,*
> *And he swings a commensurate pen.*[35]

Frost was highly critical of those Americans who ignored their local and national loyalties while seeking to include a love for the whole world: "We think the word 'provincial' is a shameful word here in America. But . . . you can't be universal without being provincial, can you? It's like trying to embrace the wind."[36] He would certainly have agreed with Edmund Burke's famous description of the hierarchy of public affections that begins with the individual: "To be attached to the subdivision, to love the little platoon we belong to in society, is the first principle (the germ, as it were) of public affections. It is the first link in the series by which we proceed towards a love to our country and to mankind."[37]

Jonathan Swift carried the principle of personal love and loyalty even further than Frost and Burke did. He so hated the merely theoretical virtue that results from a professed love of abstract absolutes of any kind, as distinct from the real though limited practical virtue that can be attached only to specific persons, that he stated his objections to such abstractions in the strongest hyperbolic language:

> I have ever hated all nations, professions, and communities, and all my love is toward individuals: for instance, I hate the tribe of lawyers, but I love Counsellor Such-a-one, and Judge Such-a-one: so with physicians—I will not speak of my own trade—soldiers, English, Scotch, French, and the rest. But principally I hate and detest that animal called man, although I heartily love John, Peter, Thomas, and so forth.[38]

## Frost's Nationalism

At the furthest point removed from Swift was Jean-Jacques Rousseau, who professed love of all mankind in abstract theory, but frequently hated individuals in concrete practice. Frost differed from Swift and the latter, in that unlike Swift he had strong positive feelings for his country, but unlike Rousseau he was profoundly skeptical that any meaningful or effective love and loyalty could be generated by an individual beyond nationalism for mankind in the abstract. He held that no significant relationship to mankind in the abstract was possible. In his conception of an individual's relationship to society, he therefore stopped short of internationalism and humanity in the abstract.

In March 1950, on the occasion of his seventy-fifth birthday, at a press conference the poet said, "What do I want for my birthday? I want prowess for my country, and by prowess I mean native ability to help in everything its people attempt."[39] In 1959, when an interviewer asked whether he had "any wish for the world and his country," Frost responded: "For the world, no. I'm not large enough for that. For my country? My chief wish is for it to win at every turn in everything it does."[40] The same kind of self-identity and preference that an individual gives to himself, his hometown, and to his state and region, also applies to his country before any other corporate loyalty outside of it: "Most of my thoughts have some reference to the U.S.A. I'm a terrible nationalist."[41] In November 1954 a newspaper reporter recorded: "Mr. Frost seemed a little dubious about worrying over international good will." He then quoted him as saying: "I'm a nationalist, and I expect other people to be."[42] This statement applied to the poet's view of his relationship with his country throughout his life.

In his poem "Hyla Brook," Frost's theme is summarized in the line "We love the things we love for what they are." This conception of an individual's loves and loyalties applied in Frost's life not only to other individual people, and to particular institutions and places, but above all to his country. He had an intense love for the United States simply for what it was, with all of its weaknesses and faults as well as for its many strengths and virtues. This conception of love marked a vital difference between himself and his friend Louis Untermeyer, whose Marxist ideology provided him with a set of economic and political norms as absolutes and made him highly critical of the United States, even though he still maintained his allegiance to it. On this point Frost wrote to him: "You stick to what you stick to in spite of what it is, and I stick to what I stick to because of what it is."[43] He believed that the first obligation of a nation, as of an individual, was to be true to itself, to its best image of itself, in all that it was and wished to be.

To Frost, the one unpardonable sin for an individual was to want to be someone or something else than himself: he should be proud of his national origin, his race, his religion, his culture, and whatever things gave him individual character. By being his best self, he could show the world what a person of his nationality, race, religion, culture, etc., was capable of achieving. As with individuals, so with nations. A nation should be proud of itself and not be guilty of wishing to be like another nation. Frost believed that during the 1930s there were two large groups in the United States that were guilty of this unpardonable sin: Anglophiles and Russophiles. He estimated that about ten percent of the American population wanted the United States to be like England, and another ten percent wanted it to imitate the Soviet Russian system. But he thought that the bulk of Americans, the remaining eighty percent of his fellow countrymen, were basically sound in their nationalism. Whether the nationalism of Americans was the result of thoughtless default or profound reflection made little difference to Frost: in either case they were not corrupted by a yearning for foreign norms or ideology. As he wrote to Untermeyer on August 18, 1917: "We are still surer of nationality than we are of anything else in the world—ninety-nine millions of us as in this country."[44] Nothing in the revolutionary changes that occurred after the First World War and that continued to his death in 1963 caused Frost to change his mind about the primary importance of nationalism.

## Frost on the United States and Internationalism

Frost believed that an American's love of the United States was wholly justified because of the great intrinsic civil virtues and freedoms under constitutional law that had been established by the founders of the American republic: "We've got a good arrangement here. We're minding each other's business a certain amount, and we're minding our own business a certain amount. Those fellows [the Founding Fathers] who started it did a good job. I say anything I damn please here."[45] He always felt personally wholly free and at ease under the constitutional liberties in the United States, and he said that the freedom his country gave him was "like old clothes or old shoes"; it fitted his temperament.[46] He defined this freedom as "feeling easy in your harness."[47] Moreover, in opposition to those Americans who looked beyond the borders of the United States for a more ideal kind of liberty,

Frost said, "I think we're the freest people that ever were free."[48] Indeed, he thought there was almost too much freedom in the United States for its own safety: "Our freedom allows us great extremes of thought, and we almost let our people plot against us."[49] But to Frost, it was the mark of a superior civilization, one at ease in its dispensations from forced public conformity, that it could tolerate such abuses of constitutional freedom: "A great civilization in its greatness can afford to indulge in all sorts of deviations and aberrations: individuality to the extent of eccentricity, thrift to the extent of miserliness, privacy to the extent of secrecy. . . ."[50] Whereas many ideological social and political theorists stressed the right of society to regulate, control, and restrict the individual citizen, Frost as an American nationalist, with deep faith in due process and constitutional law, stressed the right of the private citizen not to be politically directed. "Civilized society is a society that tolerates all sorts of divergences, to the point of eccentricity and to the point, even, of doubtful sanity."[51] His tolerance of a vast range of human differences, including serious weaknesses of mind and spirit, is perfectly consistent with both his individualism and his nationalism. During the 1930s as well as later, the poet had frequent occasion to note that the government of the United States was far more tolerant of dissent and criticism among its citizens than the Soviet Russian regime: "It doesn't seem fair or just that an old dissenter like me should live in such an easy going country and so far from discipline that no Stalin will probably be able to lay hands on me to confess me and shoot me in a cellar by a vat of quick lime before I die a natural death."[52] As he saw it, the American republic was not only superior to Soviet Russia, it was perhaps superior to every other modern system of government, because it was willing to tolerate the whole vast range of human expressions of freedom, including even palpable abuses of its system of liberty.

In making comparisons between free societies and those characterized by social repression, Soviet Russia was Frost's most frequent target. The Russian Communist government's condemnation of Boris Pasternak for his criticism of the Soviet system in *Dr. Zhivago* served him as an example of political tyranny. When the Communists prevented that author from accepting the Nobel Prize in literature, Frost commented on this event in November 1958: "What they're ridiculing him for is from selfishness. They don't want their own thing reflected on—it's treason. We stand all that better than they do."[53] He believed that Pasternak's criticism of Soviet repression and inhumanity was based upon an intense love of Russia and was therefore very close to his own type of patriotic nationalism concerning the United States. On those grounds he refused an interviewer's request to make a personal public protest against the Soviet condemnation of Pasternak:

> I couldn't do that. I understood what it was he wanted. He wanted to be left alone. . . . He had done what he wanted. He's made his criticism. He lived in a little artist's colony outside Moscow, and that was where he wanted to live and be left alone, and I had to respect that. I'm a nationalist myself.[54]

His respect for Pasternak was even stronger than his very harsh convictions about Soviet repression: his refusal to condemn the system is an instance of how his magnanimity and empathy toward individuals was an essential element in his love of freedom.

Throughout his life, Frost maintained his strong faith in the American republic as embodying a system that provided the maximum of personal freedom as against the claims advanced by any collectivist society based upon an ideology. During the Great Depression of the 1930s, when many American ideological intellectuals and theorists were infatuated with the Soviet Russian system and its various five-year plans and were eager to modify radically or even destroy the American free-enterprise system in favor of a Marxist one, Frost often opposed them during his public readings of his poetry. He also wrote a satirical poem, "To a Thinker," published in January 1936, against such of his countrymen. The poem, he said, "was aimed at the heads of our easy despairers of the republic and of parliamentary forms of government. I encounter too many such and my indignation mounts till its overflows in rhyme."[55] To Frost, such Americans were worse than enemies during war.

## International Pacifism and Ideological Social Theory

The strength and virtues in Frost's nationalism may best be perceived if it is set in contrast to two things that Frost despised: sentimental international pacifism and doctrinaire ideological social theory, which fostered economic planning at home and which, through the propagation of communism, sought to establish a utopian world-state abroad. He saw a very close connection between international pacifism, national planned economic systems, and international utopian communism. But before considering how the first two of these are related to international utopian communism, it is essential to examine his criticism of international pacifism and national economic planning.

Frost believed that, beginning with Woodrow Wilson, the modern world became the victim of sentimental international pacifism, based on the belief in the natural goodness of man, which Frost regarded as a very dangerous illusion. His comments on the tragic fate of Wilson, written to his Amherst College friend Otto Manthey-Zorn in the summer of 1928, while on a visit to Paris, are highly revealing of the illusion that he perceived in Woodrow Wilson's international policies.

> It's a sad story—one of the saddest in history. . . . I weaken now at the thought of him fallen with a crash almost Napoleonic. He had caliber, he saw as vastly as anyone that ever lived. He was a great something, if it was only a great mistake. And he wasn't merely his own mistake. He was the whole world's mistake . . . as much the whole world's as was Napoleon or Alexander. Some might think his failure was in missing a mark that someone to come after him will hit, but I suspect it was worse than that: he missed a mark that wasn't there in nature or in human nature.[56]

Frost's skepticism about Wilson's League of Nations persisted after the Second World War and was applied to the United Nations. In a letter to Untermeyer in October 1957, he made it clear that his criticism in both cases was that these fond hopes for international peace violated the free choices of men and nations in the pursuit of their own destinies:

> Life is a choice of decisions; it is based on challenges and risks— no risk, no life. The dominating nations are those that risked everything to dominate. The rest just survive. We've got to be clear about our choice, about our answerability to ourselves as individuals and nations. Is the United States to be answerable to the United Nations or to itself? That's the question that hangs over us, and you know what I think the answer is. Wilson's League of Nations was a pretty dream, but it was based on an absurdity and it was bound to go to pieces. The United Nations is worse. It was formed out of desperation, and desperation never solved anything—it can't solve a situation or make enemies love each other or stop nations from dominating and making war.[57]

The consistency of his skepticism about modern man's efforts to secure international peace is very remarkable; it rests upon his doubt that the moral nature of man is subject primarily to reason, goodwill, and social benevolence, rather than to self-interest.

In 1957, when the United Nations was given a huge rock of solid iron ore by Sweden, and it was decided to build the rock into the U.N. building in New York as a symbol of nature's strength and man's unity, Frost was invited "to write a poem celebrating the ideal of the interdependence of the nations."[58] He rejected the prescribed theme of the invitation, noting ironically that iron could indeed be used to strengthen the U.N. building but that it could also be used for weapons of war, which was historically the way with nature and men. After rejecting the U.N. invitation, Frost wrote a couplet that expressed his own convictions:

> *Nature within her inmost self divides,*
> *To trouble men with having to take sides.*

Later, in 1959, he commented upon his couplet: "I was thinking when I wrote of that lump of iron in the United Nations building, that stands for unity. But, even as you look at it, it seems to split. You think of tools that can be made of it, and you think of weapons. . . ."[59] He rejected both the League of Nations and the United Nations as based upon the same illusion: faith in the natural goodness of mankind as an abstract absolute that could be realized by collective action. He believed that they both failed to take into account the dominant trait of human beings: the strong desire to be free to pursue their own destinies as individuals and independent nations.

Within American domestic politics, Frost's early, intense, and constant criticism of the national economic planning of Franklin D. Roosevelt's New Deal was based upon the same self-reliant individualism that underlay his rejection of the League of Nations and the United Nations. He even dubbed Roosevelt's administration "the New Devil," in Scottish dialect, "the New Deil." In *A Further Range* (1936), he attacked the Roosevelt program in four poems: "A Roadside Stand," "Departmental," "Build Soil," and "To a Thinker." His "Build Soil" is a defense of "personal" identity and independence against the "interpersonal" demands of the New Deal economic program and of the "national" as against the "international." It also contains an attack upon the abuse of freedom in private enterprise through greed and a more extended attack upon compulsory benevolence of economic planners and calculating sentimental politicians. As always, Frost was highly skeptical of abstract blueprints and plans to refashion society according to the theories of a self-styled "brain trust" or elite. On this vital point his nineteenth-century brand of liberalism has much in common with twentieth-century conservatism.

## Robert Frost: The Poet as Philosopher

In "A Roadside Stand," the poet pictured the political motives of sentimental New Deal officials as hypocritical, and he described the social consequences of their economic planning upon American citizens:

> *While greedy good-doers, beneficent beasts of prey,*
> *Swarm over their lives to soothe them out of their wits,*
> *And by teaching them how to sleep the sleep of day,*
> *Destroy their sleeping at night the ancient way.*

These lines contain a grim portrait of the debilitating effects of government relief upon the integrity and energy of those who receive such bounties.

With great courage, Frost flew defiantly in the face of the cant and favorite political slogans of New Deal economists and socialist critics of the American free enterprise system. He particularly despised their Marxist terminology, their habit of seeing people in terms of economic classes, rather than as individuals, each with a distinctive character and a set of personality traits. In 1939, to an audience at the Bread Loaf School of English, he attacked their Marxist view of labor: "What some people call 'exploitation,' I call employment." When New Deal politicians condemned "rugged individualism" and politically unregulated freedom in the economic sector of American society as forms of selfishness and callous indifference to the welfare of the poor, he refined upon the phrase "rugged individualist" and called himself a "ragged individualist," thereby insisting that he valued his personal freedom even if it meant poverty. To live life assertively, with courage, Frost said that men needed some "social insecurity." In reply to Mrs. Roosevelt's humanitarian talk about the need to "abolish" poverty, he said, "When I think of all the good that has come from poverty, I would hesitate to abolish it." Frost once stated at Bread Loaf that because of the psychology of the New Deal, which resulted in egalitarian mediocrity, about the only social activity in which the will to excel still remained strong in America was competitive sports.

In his criticism of the New Deal, Frost particularly deplored what he called "the sweep toward collectivism in our time," and in his poem "A Considerable Speck" (1942), he expressed his intense dislike of such sentimental socialism:

> *I have none of the tenderer-than-thou*
> *Collectivistic regimenting love*
> *With which the modern world is being swept.*

The aspect of the New Deal that he objected to most was its compulsory egalitarianism, its leveling of individual distinctions, its subordination of private freedom, originality, and initiative to mere economic security as the great end of life. Frost believed that Franklin D. Roosevelt wished to create "a homogenized society," in which the cream of human nature would never be allowed to rise to the top. As Frost perceived it, this was the New Deal's utopian dream for the new masses of a future America. The poet set himself resolutely against such an objective. In a letter to Untermeyer on March 11, 1937, he indicated where his sympathies lay: "I have so much sympathy with the middle classes in their hour of being wiped out by the New Republic. . . ."[60] In short, his criticism of the New Deal domestic program for the United States, like his condemnation of international pacifism, was that it violated the freedom of individual citizens and tried to make social benevolence compulsory in order to establish peace and harmony among classes, as pacifism sought to do among nations.

## Utopia and Civilization

To Frost, the ultimate test of a true civilization was that individual freedom under constitutional law and representative government was always maintained. By this test, all forms of utopian collectivism were failures. In August 1944, to an audience at Bread Loaf, he threw out the question: "What is the opposite of Utopia?" After no one answered, he repeated: "What is the opposite of Utopia?" Finally, after a long silence, a timorous voice out of the crowd asked: "Hell?" Without hesitation he replied: "No, not hell— civilization!" Surely, this is one of the most witty and condensed *reductio ad absurdum* rebuttals ever voiced against doctrinaire, speculative utopian theory. And in July 1954, Frost elaborated upon this point:

> The opposite of civilization is not barbarism but Utopia. Utopia can let no man be his own worst enemy, take the risk of going uninsured, gamble on the horses, or on his own future, go to hell in his own way. It has to concern itself more with the connection of the parts than with the separateness of the parts. It has to know where everyone is; it has to bunch us up to keep track of us. It can't protect us unless it directs us.[61]

Such social control and repression of individual freedom existed in all societies that had for their objective a utopian society for men—whether in such limited collectivities as the Brook Farm experiment, or in the Soviet scheme of world-wide compulsory utopia.

In his criticism of Brook Farm, Frost insisted that the free choice of each individual to be independent of the collective commune is still the best answer to such utopian tyranny:

> There you had exhibited all the tyranny of the commune. But in Thoreau's declaration of independence from the modern pace is where I find justification for my own propensities. . . . My intolerance has been for the throng who complain of the modern pace yet strive to keep it. There is the widest choice of companions you will fall into step with, be they living or dead. There is no such thing as a prescribed tempo—at any rate, not in civilization.[62]

In this passage he clearly defends individual freedom and civilization as closely linked; he saw no contradiction between personal freedom and organized society, provided both the individual and society were truly civilized. To Frost, Thoreau's criticism was valid against the commune, not against civilization; it also applied to those individuals who lacked the courage to free themselves from the slavery of the modern pace. In these convictions he was profoundly Aristotelian in his view of the individual and society. He was a world removed from Rousseauistic primitivism, real or supposed, or any antithesis between "art" and "nature" in man. In the twentieth century, what he condemned as "the tyranny of the commune" was most evident in the collectivist society of Soviet Russia, where individual freedom in private property and private enterprise and other areas of life was prohibited. Of the Communist system in Russia, Frost wrote: "I don't look to the time when they're going to throw away their dream of Utopia."[63]

In a brilliant insight, Frost perceived that the absolute contradiction between his view of the free individual in a free and civilized society and the views of international pacifists, New Deal politicians, and Marxist Utopians on the other side (each in its own way), lay in the philosophical metaphors provided to the modern world by Charles Darwin and Karl Marx respectively. Although he clearly favored Darwin, he paid tribute to the greatness of vision and power of Karl Marx, who came right after the evolutionist and successfully challenged the established Darwinism metaphor in the process of human evolution: "the survival of the fittest," as set forth by Herbert Spencer.

... [I]sn't it a poetical strangeness that while the world was going full blast on the Darwinian metaphor of evolution, survival values and the Devil take the hindmost, a polemical Jew in exile was working up the metaphor of the State's being like a family to displace them from mind and give us a new figure to live by? Marx had the strength not to be overawed by the metaphor in vogue. Life is like battle. But so is it like shelter. Apparently we are now going to die fighting to make it a secure shelter. The model is the family at its best. At the height of the Darwinian metaphor, writers like Shaw and Butler were found to go the length of saying even the family within was strife, and perhaps the worst strife of all. We are all toadies to the fashionable metaphor of the hour. Great is he who imposes the metaphor. From each according to his ability to each according to his need. Except ye become as little children under a good father and mother! I'm not going to let the shift from one metaphor to another worry me.[64]

There are at least two very important points to note in this vital passage. First, Frost made it clear in his final sentence—"I'm not going to let the shift from one metaphor to another worry me"—that he rose above Marx's metaphor that society is like a family, just as Marx had risen above Darwin's metaphor of human evolution. Second, he recognized that the Marxists, in elaborating their metaphor that humanity was (or should be, or be made to be) like a family, with the State as the father, had a tremendous psychological advantage over the Darwinians, who pictured society as men struggling against each other, like animals in the jungle of nature, within the competitive life of civil society. The paternalism of the New Deal and the worldwide professed humanitarianism of revolutionary Marxism had in common the idea that life was (or should be) like a shelter, that every man should be every other man's brother, keeper, and comrade. The Marxist metaphor of the family also had support from Christianity, Judaism, and other world religions, even though it was a wholly materialistic philosophy and denied the very existence of spirit in man. Thus through the metaphor of society as a family, Marxists, New Deal politicians, and religious international pacifists made common cause against the idea of individual freedom in society, because that resulted in the constant battle to survive and excel. The alternative to individual freedom was economic security provided by a planned and controlled international society, which it was presumed would result in universal peace on earth. Frost was aware that Aldous Huxley understood that universal peace implied a unified monistic philosophy: "For science in its totality, the ultimate good is the creation of a monistic stystem in which . . . the world's enormous mulitplicity is reduced to something like unity."

Like Dostoevsky in "The Grand Inquisitor," Frost understood the greatest problem of the individual in modern society as essentially a conflict between individual spiritual freedom and economic social security or temporal success. This conflict was symbolized perfectly in the biblical parable of Satan's temptation of Christ in the wilderness, in which Christ was offered all the kingdoms of the world in exchange for his willingness to bow down in worship of Satan. Dostoevsky's story was a modern fictional rendering of this parable. It was also remarkably prophetic of the actual historical development of this theme in the politics of the twentieth century. Dostoevsky had written: "Mankind as a whole has always striven to organize a universal state." In his story, the Russian writer had identified man's constant desire for a universal state, for universal peace, and for economic security under one sovereign power—in short, for utopia—as the appeal of the kingdom of Satan as opposed to that of Christ. This was the theme preached by the Grand Inquisitor and offered as the supreme good to mankind.

To Frost, the New Deal politicians, Christian international pacifists, and Marxian Communists played variations on the theme of Dostoevsky's Grand Inquisitor. New Dealers who were ready and even eager to give up representative government, with its checks and balances and its individual freedom as man's civil end, in favor of a government-controlled economy and society, proclaimed their dream of national economic security as the justification for their program. Christian international pacifists, whose militance was directed against the freedom of individual nations and who favored giving up national sovereignty to the League of Nations or the United Nations, aimed at the same objective on an international level. Like the Grand Inquisitor in Dostoevsky's story, the Christian international pacifists had failed to note Christ's words that His kingdom was not of this world. They wished to establish heaven on earth. In this gnostic heresy their peace objectives were identical with the materialist objectives of Marxist Communists, whose messianic dream of a millennium was to be realized in a remote future. The Marxists offered temporal salvation and economic security in exchange for political freedom; spiritual freedom they dismissed as an opiate of the people. As Frost noted, the Marxists were even prepared to be martyrs and to do battle for their ideal of world family peace, "to die fighting to make it a secure shelter." In practice, this meant they were eager to make Darwinian war upon the capitalist world or on any nationalism or rival ideology that opposed their movement for world peace under one rule. Indeed, their revolutionary parties throughout the world were prepared to use every possible means, including force, to gain their ends. For it was clear that the secure shelter could only materialize by giving complete monopoly of political, economic, and social power to the state under the Communist Party, so that the strife and competition between individuals, classes, and nations might be totally eliminated. At the end of history, as Marx envisioned, there would be universal peace established under a Communist utopia. Staunchly opposed to these three variations on the Grand Inquisitor's theme, Frost's lifelong position in favor of individual freedom remained unshaken to his death.

Finally, another important point in his commentary on the Darwinian and Marxist metaphors is his perception of the very close affinity between Marxism and international pacifism: both aimed at eliminating the Darwinian concept that life is a continuous struggle for survival and increased fitness. This point needs further elaboration. As he wrote in a letter to Untermeyer: "The pacifist holds that we needn't hurt each other in war anymore. The Marxist adds, and we needn't hurt each other in peace anymore."[65] Frost rejected the Marxist metaphor that man's life in society is or should be like a family shelter, not only because it was inimical to individual freedom, but also because he doubted that the theory would be feasible in practice. He moreover suspected the sincerity of Marxists when their criticism included the obvious successes in economic productivity of the capitalist world.

In a sustained passage following his comparison of pacifists and Marxists, Frost elaborated his criticism of communism; he also criticized those Americans who apologized for the successes of private free enterprise and set forth his own reasons for defending the American political-economic system:

> The pacifist holds that we needn't hurt each other in war anymore. The Marxist adds, and we needn't hurt each other in peace anymore. . . . And we needn't if we all settle back into Franciscan farmers satisfied . . . with a table set forth with no more than a sprig of lettuce and a glass of water.

> At every commencement I hear young Americans reproach themselves or their country with the indecency of our success and prosperity. I get sick of it. What are the young (and old) going to do about it? Are the Marxians in earnest in their contempt for American dollars? I wish I didn't suspect them of reasoning

from envy. I'm afraid they won't despise riches so much if they can achieve it. All that makes them different from us is their belief they can do it better with the enterprise of gain all centered in one bureau and even one master mind. They may be right and we may be wrong or vice versa. There is nothing especially noble in the position of either—if nobility is the object of life, I can't be bothered too much to discriminate between them. I was born and brought up to our kind of capitalism and I feel as if I might as well not change it to their form of the same thing. Capitalism is the name for the dollar ahead for security. The only dispute between us is as to who should be the keeper of it, the state at the capital of the country or all sorts and kinds of people scattered from boundary to boundary. I have been taught to think that there is no greater peril than to cultivate no greatness except in politicians and statesmen. I should hate it to have all patronage of the arts come from one source.[66]

In sum, the key to Frost's deep distrust of Marxist internationalism and of international pacifism is to be found in his love of freedom and self-reliance, for individuals and nations, and his hatred of compulsory "togetherness" in war or peace. He feared that under any controlled utopian collectivist society, peace would be imposed only after each individual and nation was reduced to nothing and enslaved.

Frost accepted the Darwinian metaphor that life is a constant struggle for survival and improvement. As noted earlier, he believed that something of value could be learned by men in civil society by observing that many animals have the ability to take care of themselves practically from birth. The value of self-reliance was as great for a nation as for individuals. He noted that it had been very strong in the early era of the American republic. He believed that the true glory of the United States was inherent in the spirit of her original settlers and in the pioneers who moved westward from the Atlantic to the Pacific, as he said, "unrolling the map as they went." The early Americans esteemed their independence and "separateness"; they were daring, resourceful, active, and courageous in taking the risks of life, and they were not always seeking social protection or being dependent on others at the expense of their own private freedom. The poet so stressed such individualism that he was opposed to everything and everybody that made people rely more than was necessary upon anybody or anything other than themselves and their own integrity, courage, and resources. In this sense, the basic Darwinian metaphor always remained valid to Frost.

But the Darwinian metaphor in physical nature, as a law of the jungle, was enormously modified within historically developed civil society. Such things as the customs and laws of civilization, of religion and government, protected the weak, sick, and aged, and they provided a humane basis for each individual's personal relationship with society. Under equitable, civilized laws, distributive justice and mercy could be united. Yet all these things involved change, to which the Darwinian metaphor applied whether in the social or the biological sphere:

> All life is cellular. We live by the breaking down of cells and the building up of new cells. Change is constant and unavoidable. That is the way it is with human beings and with nations, so why deplore it?[67]

Paternalistic governments wish to eliminate the conditions under which such changes normally occur in society and to substitute their complete control in place of them.

In modern society, the social and political pendulum under paternalistic government had swung away from justice to individuals in favor of mercy to the masses. Mass mercy is preferred to mercy toward individuals by revolutionary confiscations of wealth, by the redistribution of capital and income in established societies, and by the elimination of the usual causes of failure. He declared that he was "on the other side" politically from those who wished to take all the risks and hardships out of life: "I'm on the side of adversity."[68] For without adversity there is no freedom, and without freedom there is no growth into responsible citizenship. In April 1961, he noted:

> There's too much government getting into our lives. During the last campaign it seemed to me that all the candidates promised to do was to help put the young people into school or the old people into hospitals. People have got to learn to help themselves and take care of their own wherever possible. I remember getting a letter from a very wise mother not so long ago. She asked me how she could give her son the "hardships" of life which had contributed to making the boy's father a successful man. Parents are afraid to give their children some of the hardships of life so vitally necessary in their ripening into judgment, and becoming responsible citizens.[69]

Both on an individual and on a national level, the desire for security and the denial of risks and hardships is paid for by a loss of freedom: "There is no protection without direction."[70] He despised "togetherness" and protection through social collectiveness: "A family or nation that's always crying for protection isn't worth protecting."[71] In an interview on December 14, 1949, Inez Robb recorded that "Mr. Frost readily admitted he would hate a brave new world in which his security were guaranteed from cradle to grave." He called himself "a natural gambler" who did not want the "uncertainty" taken out of life, and among his fellow countrymen he wished to see "the largest possible number of citizens who could take care of themselves."[72] If this is a truth of life for the individual regarding his country, it is also a truth of life in regard to nations in their relationship with each other. When he visited Soviet Russia in September 1962, he put his conviction on this point into a concise and brilliant aphorism, when he simultaneously attacked the atheism and the pacifism in Premier Krushchev's Marxism by saying to him: "God wants us to contend. The only progress is in conflict."[73]

In a free society, one in which individuals competed with each other, strife and the need to overcome obstacles resulted in victory for some and defeat for others. But that is the price of freedom and individual self-fulfillment. He loved the individuality of people and nations, and he accepted their personal differences as he found them, with no wish to make them over into something else. In this he stood in sharp contrast to the ideological collectivist who would force people into a single, unified, lifeless mold: "We think that if people were all the same, they wouldn't want to hurt each other. But in the arts, we want all the differences we can get. And in society, too . . . we really want people to be different, even if it means a risk of fighting with each other."[74] The highest freedom and individualism to him was freedom of the spirit. He held that it is "no paradox that we gain in freedom on a higher plane by sacrificing agents on the next plane below it. All the way up. That's our freedom. When it says 'the truth will make you free' it means that you get a new enslavement that will free you from all your other enslavements."[75]

What conclusion can be drawn from Frost's view of the relationship of the individual to society? It is clear that he believed the supreme purpose of the social order was the total development of the free, mature, and independent individual and that anything that threatened that purpose, whether through anarchy or tyranny, is an evil to be resisted. His emphasis upon individual freedom was in no sense nihilistic; he rejected the primitivist theory of a "return to nature" as the basis of social freedom because, like Aristotle, he believed that civil society was "natural" for man. He believed in the basic institutions of society, such as the family and the state, and he was a strong nationalist. He emphatically rejected the whole idea of a planned society, whether that of the economic brain trust of the New Deal or that of Marxism, or that of the sentimentality of international pacifism. Each of these planned systems in its own way and in varying degrees violated the freedom of the individual citizen in his society or of the nations in the world. In an interview with Frost in the fall of 1957, James Reston summarized the chief objects of the poet's social criticism: "He is against everything and everybody that want people to rely on somebody else. He is against the United Nations. He is against the welfare state. He is against conformity and easy slogans and Madison Avenue, and he hasn't seen a President he liked since Grover Cleveland."[76] Near the end of Frost's life, in 1959, his lifelong friend since the First World War, Louis Untermeyer, also summarized what Frost most disliked and what he insisted upon:

> He is still against One World, World Federation, Universal Brotherhood, Unity, Conformity, the breaking down of barriers in the interest of Oneness; he is unalterably against One anything. You may quote him to the effect that "Something there is that does not love a wall," but you can be sure that he much prefers the opposed quotation that "good fences make good neighbors." He insists on Nature's divisions and differences; "in art, as in nature, we want all the differences we can get. In society, too. We want people and nations to maintain their differences—even at the risk of trouble, even at the risk of fighting one another."[77]

Robert Frost did more than pay lip service to individual freedom; he loved personal freedom, for himself and other men, with an intense and constant passion, and he never sacrificed any part of it for the promises of security from politicians and ideologues, and his conception of freedom was what determined his conception of the individual's right relationship to society.

## 12

# Politics in Theory and Practice

*How small, of all that human hearts endure,*
*That part which laws or kings can cause or cure!*
                    (Goldsmith, *The Traveller,* 11.429–30)

Me and mine are below the threshold of legislative cognizance.
Beyond participation of politicians and beyond relief of senates
lie our sorrows.
                    (Frost, Letter to Louis Untermeyer, February 23, 1932)

The personal life of Robert Frost was filled with great and frequent tragedies. His father died of tuberculosis at age thirty-four; his mother of
cancer at fifty-six; he lost his infant son Eliot in 1900 and his infant daughter Elinor-Bettina soon after; his sister Jean became insane shortly after
World War I; his beloved daughter Marjorie died young of septicemia fever
in 1934; his wife died of an unexpected heart attack in March 1938; his son
Carol committed suicide in the fall of 1940; and his daughter Irma lost her
mind and was institutionalized in 1947. In addition to these strong billows
of calamity which rolled over his family for decades, the poet himself suffered much illness, and for many years the family endured poverty. These
personal afflictions, together with his reading, observations of life, and reflections on the general human condition throughout history, provided the
basis for the poet's tragic vision of man's life on earth.

    In a letter to his Marxist friend Louis Untermeyer on the confinement
of the poet's daughter Irma, he clearly made the reality of his tragic vision

of man's life paramount, while he subordinated the realities of politics in theory and practice:

> Cast your eye back over my family's luck and perhaps you will wonder if I haven't had pretty near enough. That is for the angels to say. The valkyries and eumenides. My only objection to your communism (socialism for safety) is that realized to perfection it can't come within three strata of the stratosphere of touching the reality of our personal life.[1]

He always believed that the terrible, natural, unavoidable afflictions suffered by men in their daily lives were beyond the help of politics. Such cosmic sorrows implied a great injustice built into the very frame and order of man's trial by existence in his temporal life:

> The chiefest of our sorrows is that the world should go as it does—that thus all moves and that this is the justice that on earth we find. What justice? . . . Why injustice, which we either have to turn on the other fellow with a laugh when it is called comedy or we have to take like a spear-point in both hands to our breast when it is called tragedy. . . . But let what will be be. I am so deeply smitten through my helm that I am almost sad to see infants young any more.[2]

The phrase "let what will be be" underscores the stoicism verging upon fatalism that was among the elements compounded into Frost's tragic view of man's life, elements that were beautifully captured in a passage in his poem "The Wind and the Rain":

> *I sang of death—but had I known*
> *The many deaths one must have died*
> *Before he came to meet his own!*
> *Oh, should a child be left unwarned*
> *That any song in which he mourned*
> *Would be as if he prophesied?*
> *It were unworthy of the tongue*
> *To let the half of life alone*
> *And play the good without the ill.*
> *And yet 'twould seem that what is sung*
> *In happy sadness by the young*
> *Fate has no choice but to fulfill.*

In a quatrain, "A Question," he raised the question of the tragedy in man's life on earth from the viewpoint of God:

*A voice said, Look me in the stars*
*And tell me truly, men of earth,*
*If all the soul-and-body scars*
*Were not too much to pay for birth.*

To him, there was no universal or final answer to the question of whether the terrible price of tragedy was sufficiently compensated by birth and the joys of life. Each man had to answer that question out of his own experience and philosophy.

There was never anything maudlin or sentimentally Romantic about Frost's tragic view of man's life. He always accepted the personal tragedies of poverty, disease, failure, public unrecognition, and death with quiet dignity and stoical courage. When Untermeyer was divorced, he wrote to him that this sorrow "must be kept away down under the surface where the great griefs belong."[3] To him the great "griefs" of mankind were subjects for religion and philosophy and subsisted in a realm of reality beyond the mere "grievances" of politics. His tragic vision of life derived from his religion and philosophy and involved the most profound metaphysical and spiritual problems of human life and death. In contrast, politics dealt with man's merely physical and social temporal problems. Like Samuel Johnson, Frost believed that political solutions of public grievances, however perfectly realized, are merely palliatives of recurring problems and that they cannot cure men's irremedial tragic griefs.

Frost's tragic vision of life made him highly skeptical that revolutionary changes in the form of government or in the structure of an economic system can vitally affect the most important concerns of men. Indeed, such changes could do nothing even in the more limited area of human character and ability. On this point he wrote to Untermeyer in 1934: "I consider politics settled by the conclusion I reached last night amid the many movements of my mind that no change of system could possibly make me a bit better or abler, the only two things of any importance to me personally."[4] A well-based and balanced tragic vision of life is of great practical value in politics, he believed, because it prevents men from having delusions about reality; it dissipates their unrealistic faith in miracles achieved through social systems, political programs, and politicians.

Political ideologies such as Marxism were to Frost among the great intellectual illusions of history, promising a heaven on earth beyond man's capability. Early in his friendship with Untermeyer, the poet invited his friend to join him in his tragic view of life, on a plane of reality above the struggles of mere political good and evil: "Leave the evils that can be remedied or even palliated. You are of an age now to face essential Hell. Cease from the optimism as much that makes good as that sees good. Come with me into the place of tombs and outer darkness."[5] This melodramatic appeal was not successful, and Untermeyer remained an ideological Marxist throughout their decades of friendship until Frost's death in 1963.

Since politics falls far short of redeeming men from the "essential Hell" of human tragedy, Frost knew that as a writer he would never place his ultimate faith in any political optimism. "There's one thing I shan't write in the past, present, or future," he wrote in 1917, "and that is glad mad stuff or mad glad stuff. The conviction closes in on me that I was cast for gloom as the sparks fly upward. . . . I am of deep shadow all compact like onion within onion and the savor of me is oil of tears."[6] His prophecy about himself as a writer proved true: he never abandoned his tragic view of man's life and never adopted any "mad glad" political ideology that promised temporal salvation for mankind. Yet his tragic sense did not plunge him into gloom; within the limitations of temporal life he often experienced an exhilarating joy. Throughout much of his life he was a profoundly pessimistic man with an enormous zest for living, who thoroughly enjoyed talking about politics in theory and practice.

Faith in the power of politics to redress man's temporal injustices rests upon the common belief of modern men that human knowledge acquired through empirical study and scientific methods, and human reason, will, and moral character were competent to solve the great problems of poverty, ignorance, disease, crime, war, and so on, on a regional, national, and even international basis. Frost's tragic vision of life was reinforced by his conviction that even within the temporal order the power of politics was severely restricted by limitations inherent to human nature.

To Frost, one of the most important of human limitations was that man's nature, and especially human intelligence, does not improve much, if at all:

> It all comes down to this: We have ways of knowing that human nature doesn't change much. Maybe it gets worse—maybe not. Only the denouement tells the story, the end. Human intelligence, for all our worship of evolution, stays pretty much the same. We'd be hard put to it to show an intellect in our day the equal of Aristotle's or Immanuel Kant's. These, I take it, appear to be capstones, at least of their periods, maybe of all time.[7]

If "the denouement tells the story," then the scientific idea of progress, as applied to the nature of man, is an illusion: "A scientist like Vannevar Bush must be full of feeling of progress but a man who feels deeply about humanity must feel we are back in ancient Egypt."[8]

An important consequence of man's limited intelligence, as Frost wrote to Untermeyer in 1925, is that general human knowledge is limited: "I might sustain the theme indefinitely that you nor I nor nobody knows as much as he doesn't know. And that isn't all: there is nothing anybody knows, however absolutely, that isn't more or less vitiated as a fact by what he doesn't know."[9] Frost applied to himself his intellectual skepticism against the power of human reason to know anything absolutely, and he therefore refused to translate logic into practical life through speculative argument: "Not for me to argue anything where I don't know."[10] He believed that speculative logical reasoning through induction and deduction is never the basis of reality in life, because in the abstract high singular, there isn't any universal reason. Indeed, strict logic tended to put a man outside of any subject he considers. To Untermeyer he wrote: "The logic of everything lands you outside of it: the logic of poetry outside of poetry . . . ; the logic of religion by nice gradations outside of Catholicism in Protestantism, outside Protestantism in agnosticism, and finally outside agnosticism in Watsonian behaviorism. . . ."[11] In this vital sentence, Frost summarized the historical course of rational secularism in the Western world since the sixteenth century.

Like David Hume, Frost always doubted that human knowledge could ever become absolute and thorough, regardless of how systematically men applied the scientific method in establishing factual and empirical truths and general principles to physical nature as well as to the supposed laws of history. Moreover, there are truths of a mystical kind that science cannot reach, such as those that are the great concerns of the humanities, psychology, the arts, and most especially religion. In practical affairs also, Frost believed, the discipline modern man often needs to learn most is his submission to unreason.

Finally, beyond the limitations of intelligence and knowledge and the illusions of rational ideology, there are the finiteness and fallibility of the human will and the moral weaknesses of character. Even when men have knowledge adequate to their political and social purposes, they often fail for lack of prudence, temperance, moral courage, or through expediencies that comprehend ambition or lust for power. Because of all these intellectual and moral limitations in human nature, Frost was skeptical of the claims of modern social scientists that they could ever bring man's social environment under scientific or rational control and thereby, through politics, determine the course and end of human history. Such a scientifically controlled social order might well result in more evil than good for man. Frost's contempt for sociological and psychological behaviorists, whom he called "the guild of social planners,"[12] remained constant throughout his life and grew as their claims for dominance over society increased.

Although he believed that men simply do not know enough and are not God-like enough to control the course of social history, Frost was convinced that men had to act in society on self-belief, out of their inadequate knowledge and character limitations. He distinguished sharply between social knowledge and self-belief. Despite their uncertain general knowledge, men have to have self-belief, and Frost admired decisiveness in such self-belief: "Belief is better than anything, and it is best when rapt, above paying its respects to anybody's doubt whatsoever."[13] Even at the risk of being dead wrong, he believed, a man should firmly assert his philosophical position about life:

> What I love best in a man is definiteness of position. I don't care what the position is so long as it is definite enough. I mean I don't half care. Take a position and try it out no matter who sets up to call you an unhanged traitor. My God how I adore some people who stand right out in history with distinct meaning.[14]

Undoubtedly, Frost's preference for decisive personal belief over faith in human intelligence, knowledge, and character parallels the crucial position in his total philosophy of his tragic view of life compared to the relatively lowly position he assigned to politics. He was aware that when a leader imposes his beliefs on others, the consequences can be disastrous.

Frost's view of human nature led him to doubt that drastic changes in social machinery, based upon ideological revolution, can solve men's basic economic and social problems. He mocked lightly at Untermeyer's Marxist faith in revolutionary ideology: "Pity me for not knowing what would set everything right."[15] He recognized the irony that it takes superior intellectual power and moral wisdom to reject theories that the revolutionary ideologue accepts because of his excessive faith in his own reason and self-esteem. In practical politics, such a thinker is a doctrinaire fanatic, anything but liberal and tolerant, even when the substance of his politics is called "liberal," because he is prepared to impose his ideological theories upon society as dogmatic "truth." A fervent revolutionary is prepared to use force to bring about immediate and drastic change in society, without regard to the human suffering caused by such a course. Frost particularly disliked the Marxist theory that the violent destruction of existing capitalist society was a necessary and constructive act because it would produce greater good in the future. In his satiric portrait of an American ideological Marxist, "A Case for Jefferson," Frost expressed his dislike of violent total revolution:

> *Harrison loves my country too,*
> *But wants it all made over new.*
> *He's Freudian Viennese by night.*
> *By day he's Marxian Muscovite.*
> *It isn't because he's Russian Jew.*
> *He's Puritan Yankee through and through.*
> *He dotes on Saturday pork and beans.*
> *But his mind is hardly out of his teens:*
> *With him the love of country means*
> *Blowing it all to smithereens*
> *And having it all made over new.*

With bland irony, the poet indicated the kind of social upheaval he favored: "I don't mind a revolution if I start it. The kind of revolution I don't like are those someone else starts."[16] He favored a revolution within the individual that would enrich and improve his intellectual, moral, aesthetic, and social nature, but not one that changes the structural forms of institutions in the use of political power. Frost called this inner change in men "a one-man revolution."[17] It was a revolution which took into account all the individual differences of men, and it did not seek to level out distinctions to produce a homogenized mass society.

Frost believed that perhaps the most constantly recurring modern problem in society was that of distributive justice in economics, and he held that most social changes and revolutionary movements were concerned with securing greater equity between rich and poor. Too great extremes between those strata was very bad for any society. Periodically some equalization between the economic extremes had to take place. He expressed this social need in his poem "An Equalizer":

> *And when we get too far apart in wealth,*
> *'Twas his idea that for the public health,*
> *So that the poor won't have to steal by stealth,*
> *We now and then should take an equalizer.*

Frost's deep concern for securing greater equity in distributive justice in general prompted him to write Untermeyer: "Count on me as in favor of reforming a whole lot of things downward."[18] Frost even entitled one of his poems "On Taking from the Top to Broaden the Base." But a policy of equity in economic justice, aimed at establishing greater equality of condition between classes in society, if carried to an extreme, can mean the destruction of individual freedom and individual differences in more than wealth and poverty. To him, solving the problem of distributive justice in economics did not mean that equality should replace freedom or that representative forms of government should be weakened. To him, within the framework of a free society, such government remains the constant and immediate necessary means, and distributive justice is an imperfect and only occasionally realized remote end. This means that, in envisioning economic change in society, political moderation is central to his philosophical outlook.

Frost's criticism of most social and political reformers was only slightly less severe than his indictment of ideological revolutionaries. In an interview in 1957, the poet confessed that he "didn't like reformers."[19] Too many such innovators are mindless and untalented activists: "I am not for the reformer, who is always active but usually has nothing to give."[20] To him, reformers were too interested in "bending the flame," whereas his interest was more basic—"to keep the candle from going over."[21] He summarized his general prejudice against innovators in a couplet of "To a Thinker":

> *I own I never really warmed*
> *To the reformer or reformed.*

Even in times of crisis, when drastic social changes seemed necessary, Frost favored withholding the full force of such change. He expressed this conviction in his poem "A Semi-Revolution":

> *I advocate a semi-revolution.*
> *The trouble with a total revolution*
> *(Ask any reputable Rosicrucian)*
> *Is that it brings the same class up on top.*
> *Executives of skillful execution*
> *Will therefore plan to go half-way and stop.*
> *Yes, revolutions are the only salves,*
> *But they're one thing that should be done by halves.*

Frost favored gradualism in making necessary changes in society, and he therefore was highly critical of the impatience of those who wished immediate drastic reforms. In his *A Masque of Reason*, the poet has Job voice his criticism of impatient reformers:

> *God needs time just as much as you or I*
> *To get things done. Reformers fail to see that.*

Just as it required time for God to create the universe and to recreate it in its ongoing process, it had also required eons and eons of evolutionary time for mankind to improve itself, until ultimately it produced modern man. In a mock-serious thrust at Untermeyer, Frost wrote: "Think of all the human pains that went to uplifting Pithecanthropus Erectus into the Piltdown man and the Piltdown man into the Neanderthal and the Neanderthal into the Heidelberg and him into the likes of me and Woodrow Wilson. . . ."[22] Extending this idea logically, Frost pretended to believe that modern revolutionaries, by virtue of their claim to have the golden key to the establishment of a perfect society, must hold their superior political wisdom by virtue of their assumed higher place in the evolutionary scale of human beings than that of retrograde skeptics such as he. In a witty *reductio ad absurdum* application of this point to several of Untermeyer's revolutionary friends, he inquired of him, "Why by osteopathetic manipulation . . . couldn't you . . . effect the next great change of me into Max Eastman or Jack Reed."[23] Indeed, he suggested that if modern man were intelligent enough to perceive the truth and value of the evolutionary metaphor in understanding past human development, then for that very reason he should be wise enough to reject unwanted changes in society, as part of that very process. This included the power and right to choose to hold fast to a position: "Since we all agree that we're now smart enough to go on with what we are in an evolutionary way, we ought to be smart enough to stop where we are. And I am in favor of stopping where we are. . . ."[24]

Where are contemporary men in their evolutionary development? According to Frost, they are in a state of "uncertainty . . . between being members and being individuals."[25] He preferred to maintain the ambiguous state of modern men, between the claims of individual freedom and the desire of revolutionaries and radical reformers to force them into fixed social participation. He believed that society would be improved more effectively if the individual remained free; revolutionaries believed that individual freedom has to be sacrificed in favor of a collectivism that would improve society. When modern revolutionaries argued that, through historical necessity, they would eventually triumph, and they therefore invited people to help bring about the supposed inevitable changes more quickly, he turned the tables on them by inquiring that if the social changes they favored were indeed "inevitable," why hurry them along? It made more sense to postpone inevitable changes. He concurred in the sentiments of John Dryden's couplet about the best way to alter society:

> *'Twas not the hasty product of a day,*
> *But the well-ripened fruit of wise delay.*[26]

He did not believe that there were any preordained or inevitable changes, such as ideological revolutionaries heralded. As he saw it, social changes often involved reason and choice. When Frost considered the best relationship of man and society, the constant elements that he stressed were the reason of the individual and his free will. He rejected the metaphor of evolution, which assumes that social changes are determined without reference to man's reason and will and which postulates that they are necessarily improvements.

Frost never wrote a sustained discourse on politics, and he never constructed a systematic political philosophy. But he was unusually consistent in his statements about his political convictions, and from his many impromptu remarks uttered over many years, a set of basic principles about man as a social animal is clearly discernible.

Frost was highly skeptical about politics in theory whenever the speculative thought was separated from practical affairs: "Politics is a joke because it is as speculative as philosophy. I lump them together, politics and philosophy, as things a young fellow might toy with in his salad days."[27] His severe skepticism regarding doctrinaire rational ideologies of any kind impelled him to dismiss them as inconsequential: "I'm against all the isms as being merely ideas in and out of favor. The latest ideologies are formidable equations that resolve themselves into nothing more startling than that nothing equals nothing."[28] The delusive plausibilities of speculative theory had no place in his own political philosophy. To him, as to Aristotle and Burke, politics is a branch of ethics, not of science; it is concerned with the good, not with the true. A political philosophy therefore has to be tested by its practical consequences for men in society. Speculative ideology, which assumes it has the "truth," reverses this, and it is indifferent to the practical consequences of its supposed truth to men in society. On this vital point, in July 1940, at Bread Loaf, Vermont, he put the question to me: "How else can anyone explain Stalin's willingness to 'liquidate' (dread word) millions of Russian farmers in order to establish their collective farms?" His view of the relationship between politics in theory and in practice can perhaps be best understood in terms of the usual political terminology employed to describe the spectrum of categorical positions: "radical," "liberal," "conservative," "revolutionary," "rebel," and "reformer."

Although Frost always refused to pin any of these labels on himself, and always objected when anyone attempted to label him, he had some significant things to say about all of these political terms. In an interview, he once remarked: "Two lines from one of my earlier verses sum up my whole viewpoint":

> *I never dared be radical when young*
> *For fear it would make me conservative when old.*[29]

This statement itself reveals his characteristic political moderation midway between extremes, which enabled him to avoid disillusionment by avoiding illusions. His early political convictions remained with him throughout his life. His famous couplet from "Into My Own,"

> *They would not find me changed from him they knew*
> *Only more sure of all I thought was true.*

applies especially to his politics.

From very early in life, Frost rejected any form of radical socialism. In July 1940 at Bread Loaf, he said to me, "In my boyhood I read the radical works of Edward Bellamy and Henry George, but I have never been a radical." He remarked that upon reading George's theory, he rejected it immediately, "because like all socialism it is bad arithmetic, in which two comes before one." He never believed that politics predicated on compulsory social benevolence was superior to politics based upon freedom to pursue legitimate self-interest.

Another objection that Frost had to political radicalism was that it claimed to be original but was not: "More than once I should have lost my soul to radicalism if it had been the originality it was mistaken for by its young converts."[30] He had great reservations about the common variety, run-of-the-mill young radical, and he even wrote a satirical poem deriding this type of dogmatic ignorance or illusion of youth, called "Young, Sure, and Twenty." He sent a highly incisive comment to Louis Untermeyer about this poem:

It was in mockery of conventional young radicals. I never stand young radicals till I see how long they are going to stay radicals. I hate to see people get over either their radicalism or their conservatism. You are still about as radical by the litmus test as you were that Sunday you met me at the Grand Central and took me down for my first and last visit with Floyd Dell and Max Eastman at the Masses office.[31]

Frost contrasted "conservative" and "radical" as follows: "The most conservative thing in the world is that like produces like. The most radical thing is a certain dissatisfaction that that is so."[32] This aphorism captures perfectly the essence of the radical temperament, as he saw it.

As early as 1920, in a letter to Untermeyer, Frost inverted the conventional viewpoints of conservatives and radicals toward social change, in an effort to see if there was a focal confluence between them. He raised the fascinating and original question: which social changes would conservatives favor and which social changes would radicals be sorry to see occur? Frost's answer to this question, in which he imagined himself both a conservative and a radical, is extremely significant for an understanding of his politics:

In the general rush of change with almost everything going, I should think there would be danger that some things would be carried away that even the wildest revolutionary would be sorry to see carried away. Well then that's where I come in. Delegate me to hold on to those. "Here hold these," you could say. You would find me so serviceable that never again would you hurt my feelings by calling me a conservative. I should count my life not spent in vain if I were permitted to sit and hold in my lap just one thing that conservatives and radicals were alike agreed must be saved from being changed by mistake in the general change of other things. I am interested in what is to stay as it is: you are interested in what is not to stay as it is. We can't split on that difference. We operate in mutually exclusive spheres from which we can only bow across to each other in mutual appreciation. If I am a conservative it is the kind of conservative you want in your pay to take care of what you don't want to take with you. And just so if I am a radical it is the kind you can have no kick against because I let you take with you all you care to load up with. The fact is I am neither a conservative nor a radical and I refuse henceforth to be called either. I am a strainer. I keep back the tea leaves and let the tea flow through.[33]

Some of the specific substantive things that both conservatives and radicals "would be sorry to see carried away" are to be found in Frost's poem "The Black Cottage." At the same time, this passage reveals that he regarded whatever existed in society as the norm, containing the irreducible minimum of enduring and desirable things and that he held the proposers of social change to be under greater necessity to prove their case than are the opposers to prove theirs.

Frost also distinguished sharply between a political radical and a rebel; he had considerable sympathy with rebels: "Being rebels doesn't mean being radical; it means being reckless like Eva Tanguay. It means busting something just when everybody begins to think it so sacred it's safe."[34] To him, a radical was bound to an ideology and a doctrinaire political program, whereas a rebel was a critical spirit, at liberty, free to be critical of all ideologies and political programs, policies, propaganda, and slogans. In this sense, he was himself a freewheeling rebel. His criticism of the established social order in his country derived from love of America; his squabbles were like lovers' quarrels. But in another sense, that of rejecting social institutions as the necessary instrumentalities for men in society, his stance as critic was not that of a rebel. Two lines from "Not Quite Social" summarize his position:

> *The way of understanding is partly mirth.*
> *I would not be taken as ever having rebelled.*

The freedom to rebel from ideology and strong governmental controls was the basis of his rebellious individuality. His originality in politics was best expressed by his skepticism about all forms of social conformity and togetherness, whether radical, conservative, liberal, or revolutionary. As a "rebel" he remained free to choose or reject whatever political "truths" he found in any of these general positions, but he remained uncommitted to any of them.

Although Frost refused to be categorized as a political radical or conservative, he clearly and explicitly rejected twentieth-century "liberalism" as a political ideology. He was quoted by an interviewer to that effect: "He said his definition of a liberal was 'someone who is unhappy because he is not as unhappy as other people.'"[35] The bland neutrality of the uncommitted academic liberal was well summarized by the speaker in his Horatian poem "The Lesson for Today," in distinguishing himself from his aristocratic opponent in debate:

*I'm liberal. You, you aristocrat,*
*Won't know exactly what I mean by that.*
*I mean so altruistically moral*
*I never take my own side in a quarrel.*

To him, the modern political liberal is too often a sophisticated, sentimental, unprincipled humanitarian with no definite or strong convictions
about anything; moreover, he is a person who holds to a position more by
default than by depth of conviction.

In a letter to Untermeyer in 1950, Frost described how he responded to
a group of academic pacifist liberals who indulged themselves in the liberal
cliché that no one ever wins a war:

> The great thing is to win in war and peace. I have no patience with
> the casuistry that will persuade undergraduates that neither side
> wins a war—both sides lose it. Among a lot of liberal Northerners
> who were talking that way I once asked the only Southerner pres-
> ent who won the Civil War between the states. It was a cruel thing
> to do—crueler to the liberals than to the unreconstructed South-
> erner, though it hurt him, too. No sir, never from sophistication
> or anything try to make yourself think meanly of victory.[36]

Such decisive criticism did not endear Frost to political liberals. The poet
was aware that he ruffled the feathers of many of them, and he noted that
their defense against him, more often than not, was simply to dismiss him
as of no political account: "Some liberals don't think I am anything to
worry about. But you know how liberals are. You know how they were
about the Russian Revolution and the German Revolution. You can pack
the Supreme Court for all of them. Nothing is crucial."[37]

Frost believed that one of the practical consequences of the indecisiveness of political liberalism is that it encourages convinced revolutionaries imbued with a totalitarian ideology that nations infused with a liberal
credo will not resist their aggression. This had been a large factor in the
success of Hitler, who had perceived that the liberal governments of France
and Britain would not forcibly oppose him. He noted that the same conviction existed among the leaders of the Soviet Union in their attitude toward
the United States. In September 1962, after Frost's interview with Premier
Krushchev, the poet reported: "Krushchev said he feared for us modern
liberals. He said we were too liberal to fight. I suppose that he thought we'd
stand there for the next hundred years saying, 'on the one hand—but on

the other hand."[38] Frost admired decisiveness and courage in politics, and he preferred to see a man take a wrong position than to remain paralyzed in indecision. Adlai Stevenson was to Frost too indecisive to be a strong leader. He once said to me that between them, Stevenson and his wife together would make a good president. Such liberalism was helpless to resist the revolutionary ideologies of the twentieth century, Frost believed, and the decline of the Liberal Party in Britain was in part the result of the public's recognition of this fact. On a trip to England in May 1957, Frost looked up his old friend Lord Beveridge, who had once been a radical and had fathered the welfare state in Britain, and the poet asked Beveridge where the Liberals had all gone: "When I was here last they were a big party. Now they're just a handful."[39] Such was the fate of those who equivocate in politics during an age of revolutions.

Frost's political philosophy can be understood in part through his comments upon democracy. In general, he held it to be superior to all other forms of government: "Democracy with all its faults is the world's best bet till the people's virtue all leaches out of them." He liked what he called "the liberal ease of democracy." In 1960, he had occasion to compare the Soviet Russian type of so-called "democracy" with the American variety, and in making his comparison the poet traced out his understanding of the historical origins of American democracy:

> The world is being offered a choice between two kinds of democracy. Ours is a very ancient political growth, beginning at one end of the Mediterranean Sea and coming westward—tried in Athens, tried in Italy, tried in England, tried in France, coming westward all the way to us. A very long growth, a growth through trial and error, but always with the idea that there is some sort of wisdom in the mob. Put a marker where the growth begins, at the eastern end of the Mediterranean, and there's never been a glimmer of democracy south of there. Over east, in Asia, there have been interesting ideas, but none bothered by the wisdom of the mob. . . .[40]

In extending his comparison between the Soviet Russian type of "democracy" and American "democracy," he put the differences between them in an analogy centered in food and medicine:

> Our democracy is like our bill of fare. That came westward, too, with wheat and so on, adding foods by trial and error and luck.

I think, when corn comes in good and fresh, what would I have done if Columbus hadn't discovered America. . . . What is this Russian democracy? Ours, I say, is like our bill of fare—kills a few people every year probably, but most of us live with it. The Russian democracy is like a doctor's prescription or a food fad. That's all there is to that. That finished them off. . . . I have pretty strong confidence that our kind of democracy is better than a trumped-up kind. I'm pretty sure we're going to win. I'm on our side, anyway.[41]

In comparing the Russian Soviet system and the American, he noted wryly that "by courtesy, we call them both democracies."[42] Both the Russian totalitarian form of government and the American representative form, as "democracies," meant "a more earnest desire than the world has ever had to take care of everybody. To bestow . . . bread and butter, yes; but that's not the top thing. The top thing to bestow is character."[43] As a form of government that went beyond a concern for distributive justice and that also bestowed character, thereby justifying faith in the political wisdom of ordinary people, he favored the extension of democracy throughout the world: "I am out to see a world full of small-fry democracies even if we have to fill them two deep or even three deep in some places."[44]

One of the most significant of Frost's statements about political democracy was made in August 1917, concerning the newly established Kerensky government in Russia. Just two months before the Bolshevik revolution of October 1917, he engaged in some speculation and guesses about that new regime. He noted that it spoke for the Russian middle class as distinct from both the old Russian aristocracy and the new proletariat, and he expressed the hope that free and constitutional parliamentary government had at long last been established in Russia:

Middle class government, which is to say liberal democratic government, has won a seat in Russia and it is going to keep its seat for the duration of the war and share with us in the end in a solid out-and-out middle class triumph such as the Germans enjoyed when they marched into Paris. The lower class seeing nothing in all this for itself may do its worst to create diversions, but it will fail. This may be the last war between bounded nations in the old fashioned patriotism. The next war may be between class and class. But this one will be to the end what it was in the beginning, a struggle for commercial supremacy between nations. I will not guess further ahead than that. The lower class will kick a little on street corners and where it can find a chance in journalistic corners. But it will be suppressed—more and more brutally suppressed as the middle class gains in confidence and sees its title clearer. We are still surer of nationality than we are of anything else in the world—ninety-nine millions of us are in this country. I don't say this to discourage you—merely to define my position to myself. Live in hope or fear of your revolution. You will see no revolution this time even in Germany until Germany goes down with a perceptible crash, and I'm not so sure you'll see one there even then. Everybody is entitled to three guesses, and this is one of mine.[45]

Like many other men, Frost overestimated the courage, foresight, and will-to-power of the Kerensky government and greatly underestimated these traits in Lenin and the Bolsheviks, whom he disliked for their appeal to mob rule based upon class. He erred in his guess about which party would triumph in Russia, because he hoped for the triumph of democracy, which he conceived of as essentially a middle-class parliamentary government—not a proletarian-based dictatorship masquerading as a democracy. But his prophecy that the First World War was the last war to be based on "old fashioned patriotism" and that future wars may be "between class and class" is a remarkably prophetic insight to make in 1917.

To Frost, the essence of American representative democracy is the many constitutional provisions that gave freedom to the individual, insulating him against the political and legal power of the state; it was decidedly not an egalitarianism that leveled out all individual and class differences. He rejected the egalitarian theory of popular sovereignty, with its modern slogan of "one man, one vote." When Carl Sandburg published what Frost called his "New Deal–Fair Deal" propaganda poem, "The People, Yes," he responded by saying that in his view of American democracy he would say, "The people, yes; and the people, no."[46] His faith in the people under democratic government included an awareness of their weaknesses as well as of their strengths and virtues. In an interview he said:

Someone once asked me if I was for democracy or against it, and I could only say that I am so much of it that I didn't know. I have a touchiness about the subject of democracy, of America. It amounts to a touchiness. I know how much difficulty there is about democracy, and how much fun it is too.[47]

He rejected popular sovereignty as the sole basis of American democracy in favor of three other principles: (1) a concept of territorial democracy; (2) the federal-states constitutional system; and (3) a concept of representative republican government based upon both territory and population.

In commenting on his poem "The Gift Outright," Frost said, "What gives us our freedom is having a territorial basis, belonging to the land."[48] His belief in territorial democracy included a strong emphasis upon the autonomy of state and local governments, but it was also the result of the poet's powerful historical sense concerning the founding of America. He believed that the settling of the country was a unique experience for Western man and that the character of its people was in part created by their eventual awareness of how they belonged to the land and not just how the land belonged to them. Politically, this sense of belonging to the land was most intense on the regional, state, or local level, prior to manifesting itself on the national level. The poet undoubtedly derived this vital element in his view of American democracy from his father, William Prescott Frost Jr., who was convinced that the geographical extent of the United States was too vast for it to remain one nation. He thought that it would ultimately split up into six or seven regional independent nations. He recalled that when he was a boy his father once spread out a map of North America and drew out the approximate boundaries of his hypothetical future nations. Although his father's vision of the future never materialized, his regional concept of sovereignty manifested itself in the poet's adherence to a belief in states' sovereignty. He always believed that, for democracy to be effective, the political unit of society and the state should not be too large. His view on this vital aspect of democracy and sovereignty was not unlike that of Jean-Jacques Rousseau in *The Social Contract*. As a states' rights, free-trade Democrat, he called himself a "sep-a-ra-tist." The poet accepted fully the federalism of the United States, but he interpreted it so as to include a strong emphasis upon territorial democracy, manifested on the state and local level.

His belief in the federal constitutional system was voiced in response to a question put to him on why he believed in American democracy:

> Somebody once asked me why I believed in this wasteful democratic system of government we call a republic. I told 'em it was because it was full of checks and balances. Maybe we've got too many checks in it sometimes—we can't have too many balances. It's a system of power divided against itself, so that nobody can get more than is good of power—I mean more than's good for the rest of us.[49]

The federal constitution provided form and legal structure in American society on a national scale and prevented the anarchy of "unchartered freedom" on anything but an individual or small group level. He had great confidence in the enduring power of the American constitution. "The Constitution," he said, "will keep America American after other countries have all broken down and run together from mutual imitation."[50]

To Frost, one of the most important parts of the constitutional form of the American republic was its electoral system used in putting men in public office; therefore, he resisted any attempt to change it: "The electoral system we have worked under politically for so long has got to be preserved, basically unchanged, only modified somewhat."[51] Since the electoral system included representation on the state level, by units of electoral votes for the presidency, by population districts for the representatives, and by equal representation of each state in the senate, his endorsement of the established electoral system was another indication of how he rejected popular sovereignty as the basis of American democracy. To Frost, the United States was a representative democratic republic; it was not a pure democracy based on direct popular will expressed through numbers. In holding fast to the electoral system, Frost was consistent with his conviction that the protection of individual and minority rights, and not the triumph of simple majority will or unchecked popular power, is at the core of the American system of government. To him, the great objective of the American republic was to maintain individual freedom; it was not to establish equality of economic or social condition.

Throughout his long life, Frost frequently stated that he was born a Democrat, that he always remained a Democrat, and that he would probably die a Democrat. What kind of a Democrat was he? In his poem "Build Soil—A Political Pastoral," the chief character in the poem says:

> . . . I was brought up
> *A state-rights free-trade Democrat. What's that?*
> *An inconsistency. . . .*

When he himself was accused of being politically inconsistent, or "mixed-up," he replied: "No, I'm not mixed up, I'm well mixed. . ." As the poet himself has noted, the political mixture of his partisan politics began at birth: "You know, I inherited my status as a states'-rights Democrat from my father—maybe my grandfather. I've never outgrown it."[52]

Whether mixed-up or well-mixed, Frost was certainly one of the most original and unstereotyped Democrats that the party ever had. The wide-ranging class and nationality groups that comprised the Democratic Party certainly suited his individualism. As a party man, Frost was very much like Will Rogers, another famous nonpolitical Democrat, who once quipped: "I'm a Democrat. I don't belong to any organized party." Similarly, the poet once said, "Being a Democrat is like being a woman: you can always change your mind." He then added: "There are more different ways of being a Democrat than of being a Republican." He made this remark in Cambridge, Massachusetts, to a middle-aged couple, conservative, Republican, Harvard friends of his, and the wife listened intently to the poet's statement, and then responded vehemently: "You're right, Mr. Frost, there's only one kind of Republican," pointing to her husband, "and there he sits!" Frost told this story to a group of the faculty at the Bread Loaf School, during the summer of 1961, in the presence of Donald Davidson, a Southern Jeffersonian Democrat. Davidson then asked Frost: "What kind of Democrat are you? Democrat with a capital 'D,' or with a lower case 'd'?" Frost answered: "I'm a G-D Democrat." The "G-D", Frost went on to say, stood for "Godawful Disgruntled," and he had been a "G-D" Democrat since 1896, when Grover Cleveland's second term of office ended.

Frost identified his party politics by calling himself, at various times, a "Madisonian-Washingtonian-Jeffersonian Democrat," or a "Grover Cleveland Democrat," or a states'-rights Democrat. Certainly he derived his partisan position from the public philosophy of the Founding Fathers, whom he greatly admired. His party politics was also greatly influenced by his conception of the agrarian virtues; he therefore stressed individual freedom on the state level and self-reliance on the individual level. In reference to a conversation with President Eisenhower, he is recorded to have said, "I was talking with Eisenhower in the White House a while ago. He got confidential—no secret, I take it—and told me he supposed he was a Jeffersonian Democrat—not a Jacksonian. I told him I was a Democrat (upper case) by training, a democrat (lower case) by birth."[53]

Robert Frost's first political experience was as a boy of ten in San Francisco, where his father was a Democratic precinct worker and campaign manager and later a candidate for city office. To Untermeyer, the poet wrote in July 1918: "I mewed my infancy among political bosses and in party bigotry."[54] Later, Frost told an interviewer: "My first experience was working with my father for the election of Grover Cleveland. The mugwumps made the difference. Now we call them independent voters."[55] Again, he said, "As a child I did what I could by marching and shouting and burning oil to throw the country to Grover Cleveland in '84. And I lived to vote for Debs!"[56] Looking back over six decades, he noted his reasons for admiring

Cleveland, and it is worth remarking that personal character rather than partisan loyalty took prior claim:

> I keep reading about old Grover, and after sixty years I have to admit there were one or two things that could be said against him; but I concede it reluctantly. As Mencken said, Cleveland got on in politics, not by knuckling to politicians but scorning and defying them. He didn't go around spouting McGuffey Reader slogans or wanting to be liked.[57]

Although his loyalty was to the Democratic Party, he was a bit diffident about party politics when it clashed with his scale of higher values, such as those that concerned human character. He put his diffidence as follows: "I can stand a great deal of change in politics. But what I care about isn't settled by elections. I was brought up a Cleveland Democrat and in an off-hand playful way I've remained that." But since "Yankees are what they always were," he thought of himself as a "politician at odd seasons."[58] At bottom, he as an American valued what he believed was best for his country wholly regardless of party politics; he was therefore often highly critical of the leaders and program of his own party.

As a loyal Democrat, Frost wrote to Untermeyer on November 14, 1916, immediately after the presidential election: "Surely you won't mind my taking a little common ordinary satisfaction in the election of Wilson."[59] But it was not very long after that president's reelection before Frost began to have second thoughts about the Democratic president. The poet had no respect for Colonel House, Wilson's chief advisor and friend; he even wrote a parody of House's work, *Philip Dru, Administrator: A Story of To-morrow.* Some of Frost's contempt for House spilled over on Wilson.[60] The president's main political interest, his international pacifism and proposal for "A League of Nations," called forth Frost's harshest criticism. In a letter to his Amherst College friend George Whicher in 1919, he commented savagely on Wilson's message to Congress regarding the League of Nations:

> Does Wilson at last stand revealed to you in his last message to Congress? . . . It seems he came not to bring peace but a League of Nations. Anyone who could use the word afraid as he does there! He is afraid we won't have to be afraid of European nations for some time yet. Does he mean he's afraid we can't look for them to give us a fight worthy of our steel industry or rather chemical

industry? Is it like Richard the Lion-Hearted he talks. No, I'm afraid he talks like a fraud. Afraid am I?[61]

Frost came to have more and more reservations about Woodrow Wilson, both as a Democrat and as a man. Many years later, when the poet was interviewed in the Woodrow Wilson Room of the Library of Congress, surrounded by that president's personal library, he noted that the library had no works of imaginative literature, that it consisted mainly of legal and political works:

> Look around at the books, and you'll see the limitations. Some-
> one said he was so busy he had no time for frills—that's one way
> of looking at poetry. A noble, conscientious man, but he strained
> himself. We need somebody who is unstrained, who has time to
> read poetry and wear flowers.[62]

From the time of Woodrow Wilson on, through the rest of the twen-tieth century, Frost continued to despair for the Democratic Party, much as a father might despair of a wayward child. On July 23, 1920, right after James Cox was nominated by the Democrats for the fall election, he wrote to his friend Untermeyer: "Catch on to the New Radicalism and vote for Harding."[63] Two months later, in another letter, he clearly stated his oppo-sition to Cox for adopting Wilson's international policies, but he was not quite sure about Harding: "I should like to see [him] elected if only I was surer he was anti-international."[64]

Soon after the election of Franklin D. Roosevelt in 1932, like many other "old-line" Democrats such as Alfred E. Smith, Frost realized that the "States' Rights" Democratic Party he had lived with had been captured by the Democratic socialists whose doctrine of political sovereignty and whole political philosophy was directly contrary to his own. As the poet's friend Louis Mertins has observed: "As a States' Rights Democrat, his soul was burdened by the centralization of power in Washington and all the alphabetical agencies which sprang up almost overnight."[65] Frost perceived the terrible irony of history, that during the Great Depression the defeated Republican Party in reacting against the absolute control of Congress and the presidency by the Democratic Party, due to partisan considerations, was forced to assume a policy that reversed its traditional stance and his-torical position on federal sovereignty: "Funny thing, isn't it, the Republi-cans getting into a lather over states' rights—the thing they fought the civil war over. Now they're on the other side."[66]

Since the political parties had apparently reversed their positions on centralized authority and cognate matters after 1932, why didn't Frost become a Republican? In part, because he simply refused to be driven out of the Democratic Party by its socialist wing, just because they were temporarily in command. In an interview in February 1936, he said: "I'm going to stay a Democrat if I have to push everyone else out of the party but Carter Glass." He then added, significantly: "I'm a pursuitist, not an escapist. And I'd rather cast an idea by implication than cast a ballot."[67] He was probably convinced that he could be more effective as a critic of the socialist heresy within the Democratic Party than he could be if he were driven out of the party and was himself declared politically unorthodox by the New Deal Democrats. After all, had he not always believed there were more different ways of being a Democrat than of being a Republican?

Frost considered the concentration of executive and legislative power and Roosevelt's desire to centralize all authority (through packing the Supreme Court) as aberrations from the true principles of the traditional Democratic Party. The poet's position was one that even a good New Deal Democrat like James Farley finally came to adopt. For him, the New Deal was much too big a step in the direction of the twentieth-century ideological totalitarianisms. The emasculation of American representative government in favor of rule by executive decree could not be justified in his mind by an appeal to solving the problems of the Great Depression and of distributive justice. But the American republic survived the Great Depression, the New Deal, and the Nazi and Japanese challenge with its form of government intact. Shortly after Roosevelt's death, when someone suggested to Frost that the twentieth century needed a political Messiah to solve its economic and social problems, the poet wrote: "How can any one fail to see we have one and of the Messianic race, namely Karl Marx. And I'm not joking. F.D.R. came as near being one as I suspect a Democracy can feel the illusion of. Thrice mayor of London Town. No four times."[68] He believed that the greatest danger to the United States during the 1930s was not its failure to solve the problems of the Depression, nor even the Nazi threat from abroad, but rather the New Deal program, because of its movement towards left-wing collectivism.

Frost's satirical poem on Franklin D. Roosevelt, "To a Thinker," begins:

*The last step taken found your heft*
*Decidedly upon the left.*

A few lines later, after describing the unstable movements of the early New Deal, he wrote:

> *Just now you're off democracy*
> *(With a polite regret to be),*
> *And leaning on dictatorship;*
> *But if you will accept the tip*
> *In less than no time, tongue and pen,*
> *You'll be a democrat again.*

Frost claimed that his satire was not really aimed at Roosevelt personally but only at the recognized leader of those "easy despairers of the republic." The poem had first been printed in the *Saturday Review of Literature* on January 11, 1936, under the title, "To a Thinker in Office." In a letter to Henry Leach, editor of *The Forum,* Frost wrote an explanation of "To a Thinker":

> You will see that it was only by restriction of meaning that it was narrowed down to fit the President. Changing the title from "To a Thinker" to "To a Thinker in Office" helped do the business. . . . As a matter of fact it was written three years ago and was aimed at the heads of our easy despairers of the republic and of parliamentary forms of government. I encounter too many such and my indignation mounts till it overflows in rhyme. I doubt if my native delicacy would have permitted me to use the figure of walking and rocking in connection with a person of the President's personal infirmities. But I am willing to let it go as aimed at him. He must deserve it or people wouldn't be so quick to see him in it.[69]

The political satire in this poem is actually playful and light, not savagely indignant.

There were several other important points that Frost leveled against Roosevelt's New Deal administration. The immediate occasion for his writing "To a Thinker," according to an interview in the *Baltimore Sun* (February 26, 1936), was his intense anger about the New Deal farm policy, which he believed was posited upon a view of American farmers as possessors of what he labeled "submarginal minds." That policy was the result of the supposed intellectually "holier-than-thou" assumptions of Roosevelt's so-called "Brain Trust." He always distrusted any separation of the intellectual virtues from the moral virtues, and he believed the academicians in Roosevelt's "Brain Trust" stressed intellect above ethics to an absurd degree. As he saw it, in place of traditional ethics they had only a social consciousness and sentiment. To him, the New Deal "Brain Trust" advisors were like clever, corrupt shyster lawyers, morally decadent, sententious, self-pitying, like such sentimental English poets of the 1890s as Ernest Dowson. In a letter to Untermeyer (July 6, 1936), he wrote: "Dowson is often in my mind these days of Tugwell and the New Deil. (I told you Tugwell reads him to Mrs. Roosevelt . . . )."[70] In this criticism of the New Deal, Frost was attacking the whole philosophical and moral basis of the Roosevelt administration, as manifested in his anger over its farm policy.

One of Frost's major criticisms of the New Deal was based upon his staunch adherence to the idea of personal freedom in the economic sector against a planned economy. During January 1935, while Frost was living in Key West, Florida, he wrote an account to Untermeyer of how debilitating the New Deal public works economic program was on the people and leaders of the city:

> The only thing at all socially disturbing is the presence in force of Franklin D. Roosevelt FERA [Federal Emergency Relief Administration]. This has been one of the Administration's pet rehabilitation projects. No taxes had been paid on anything. Everybody was riding round in cars without silencers and without licenses. There was talk of transporting seventy five percent of the crowd. But nobody could think of anybody who would want them. So the author of a book called *Compulsory Spending* is here with a staff to put everybody at work on public improvements, some building, some tearing down, and some general cleaning up of filthy vacant lots. We had to get our rent thru them. They are mildly and beneficently dictatorial. Both the Mayor of the Town and the Governor of the State have abdicated in their favor. Their great object they say is to restore the people to their civic virtue. When in history has any power ever achieved that?[71]

About a month later, he again commented upon his impression of Key West: "If I seem irritable it is probably due to the horribleness of having to look on at the redemption of a city that has lost its self-respect to the New Deal."[72] Most of the economic pump-priming attempts of the New Deal met with his caustic criticism.[73]

Another major criticism that Frost leveled against the New Deal was its use of economic appeals in elections: its setting the poor against the rich, and its exploitation of envy and discontent for political purposes. This type of neo-Marxism called forth his sharpest attacks. The very idea of judging a person by his economic condition or status was repellent to him. In 1939, during a reading of his poems to an audience at Bread Loaf, he asked: "Don't you think that the poor are disgusting, and the rich are disgusting—as such?" He then asked, if men are to judge people by their class, why concede anything to the Marxists by using "class" only in its economic sense? Why not judge people by their psychological class? "To which class do you belong," the poet asked, "the neurotic class?"

Frost never wrote poetry for "the welfare minded," although some New Deal political friends approached him hoping that he would. As he noted, their hope was based upon a misunderstanding of what he had written early in his life:

> I don't consider myself to blame for their mistake. Ferner Nuhn (Henry Wallace's ghost writer) is still at me for having led him on with North of Boston to expect better of me than A Further Range. Its his damned party politics. I tried to tell him and his like in The Need of Being Versed in Country Things that my subject was not the sadness of the poor. He puts his finger on The Lockless Door with uncanny shrewdness, but not enough to quite bring him through. He says the rich in their top hats knocked at my cottage door and though having provided no way to keep them out I retired through a back window and left the place to them, it was only to join them mischievously by circling round behind and taking their view of the house I had built. Funny but except for one person . . . all the rich who ever came to my door were the condescending welfare minded and they came under the mistaken impression that what I had built was a house of the poor. I was flattered by their attention and I decided to let them have the house any way they would. I wanted to be honest with them in all gentleness: and I satisfied my conscience with hints at the truth, as in the last part of the poem "New Hampshire" and in "The Need of Being Versed in Country Things." But lately I have been getting cross with their fatuosity. My house may be only a one-room shack but it is not the Poor House: it is the Palace of Art. North of Boston is merely a book of people, not of poor people. They happen to be people of simplicity or simple truth miscalled simplicity. Before I get through I'm go-

ing to drive these social servitors back to the social settlements or to concentration camps where I can starve their sympathies to death. For myself I never sought anyone I wasnt thrown with and I never thought of anyone I was with as a possible subject for literature or charity or the literature of charity.[74]

This vital letter reveals not only how true to his self-reliant politics he was, but also how faithful he was to his own poetic integrity, refusing to make it the vehicle for social or economic propaganda. Poetry was for truth about human nature: it was not a vehicle to be utilized in making propaganda for the advocacy of political solutions of social problems such as poverty. As he noted on another occasion: "It's neither the rich nor the poor that I was writing about. Just about people like us."[75] Clearly, he was consciously and strongly opposed to the utilization of economic class consciousness.

Frost perceived both advantages and disadvantages in being rich and being poor. In listing seven disadvantages that Franklin D. Roosevelt had to overcome in order to rise to the presidency, he included the president's wealth. He then pictured Roosevelt at the pinnacle of his career, beyond wealth, beyond even his presidency, engaged in world politics toward the end of World War II: "there he sits on top of the world along with Stalin and Churchill! That row is forever in my mind."[76] Frost admitted that "sometimes wealth has its bad things and poverty has its bad things and limits to our freedom"; nevertheless, contrary to Mrs. Roosevelt's expressed desire to get rid of poverty, Frost noted something to be said for poverty in terms of men's achievements: "Poverty has done so much good in this way in the world that I should hesitate to abolish it."[77] Besides being a spur to ambition, he observed that it made people realistic about life: "Things belong to the poor by their having to come to grips with things daily. And that's a good one on the poor. They are the only realists."[78] But he was also aware that the poor, in wishing to raise themselves above their poverty, were as vulnerable to the delusions of ideology as anyone else: "If the poor promised themselves no more than vengeance in the oncoming revolution I'd be with them. It's all their nonsense about making a better or even a different world that I can't stand."[79]

But the middle classes always remained for Frost the backbone of a free and democratic nation. He feared for the world if they should ever be destroyed through a Marxist or other kind of ideological revolution. He doubted that such an upheaval could succeed: "Sometime the world will try cutting the middle class out of our middle. But my mind misgives me that the experiment of getting rid of the lowest class by cutting it out and dumping it on distant islands failed. You know how the lowest class renewed itself from somewhere as fast as it was cut out."[80] Regarding those who seek to raise people economically through political power, he agreed with Arthur Balfour that the result would be a leveling downward, that no government can "make people equally rich; it can only make them equally poor."[81]

Frost was acutely aware that the very political virtue he esteemed most—individual freedom—could be indicted as perhaps one of the causes of the most acute problem of distributive justice, the extremes of wealth and poverty. Under the open conditions of a free society, competent, ambitious, and energetic people could take full advantage of their liberty to amass great personal wealth and power. In contrast, as a nation's population increased, large masses of people who lacked the traits of character that would enable them to compete successfully in a free society remained very poor. Freedom meant little to the masses, as compared to economic security. This problem of inequitable distribution of the productivity of society was especially acute during the Great Depression. In light of this conviction, he moderated his criticism of the efforts of the New Deal to secure greater equity between rich and poor. An extended passage in *A Masque of Mercy* (1947) contains the essential position the poet held about egalitarian distributive justice accomplished by political means. The character Paul notes that in a free society success, "by its own logic," comes to concentrate "all wealth and power in too few hands," and then he says:

> *The rich in seeing nothing but injustice*
> *In their impoverishment by revolution*
> *Are right. But 'twas intentional injustice.*
> *It was their justice being mercy-crossed.*
> *The revolution Keeper's bringing on*
> *Is nothing but an outbreak of mass mercy,*
> *Too long pent up in rigorous convention—*
> *A holy impulse towards redistribution.*
> *To set out to homogenize mankind*
> *So that the cream could never rise again,*
> *Required someone who laughingly could play*
> *With the idea of justice in the courts,*
> *Could mock at riches in the right it claims*
> *To count on justice to be merely just . . .*
> *The Thing that really counts though is the form*

*Of outrage—violence—that breaks across it . . .*
*And if you've got to see your justice crossed*
*(And you've got to) which will you prefer*
*To see it, evil-crossed or mercy-crossed?*

He has left no doubt that the character "Keeper" (an abbreviation for "My Brother's Keeper") epitomized Franklin D. Roosevelt, whose New Deal sought to "homogenize mankind." In a comment on egalitarianism in education, he remarked: "The matter of giving a pupil an A or a B whether he deserves it—has earned it—or not, made me say awhile ago to some of my New Deal friends that they are trying to homogenize things so that the cream will never rise to the top again."[82] He believed that justice for the rich had to be qualified by mercy for the poor, and in certain of its social legislation the New Deal achieved this, thereby preventing a complete "evil-crossed" or violent revolution.

Frost believed that the duty of all good government was to foster the general welfare in a great many ways that the private interests of citizens could not. As he noted in a passage of his poem "Build Soil," this meant that in the public sector of society "socialism" was a part of every government:

*Is socialism needed, do you think?*

*We have it now. For socialism is*
*An element in any government.*
*There's no such thing as socialism pure—*
*Except as an abstraction of the mind.*
*There's only democratic socialism,*
*Monarchic socialism—oligarchic,*
*The last being what they seem to have in Russia.*
*You often get it most in monarchy,*
*Least in democracy. In practice, pure,*
*I don't know what it would be. No one knows.*

The essential conflict between Frost and the New Deal centered on the extent to which the government's socialistic welfare programs intruded into the private sector of American life, violating the individual's freedom of action. But just as there was "no such thing as socialism pure," there was also no such thing as pure laissez-faire individualism in an actual society. His conception of human nature in society was corporate; man is by his nature a political and social animal. He therefore rejected both the anarchy of pure laissez faire and the tyranny of pure socialism. His comment on the criticism of the New Deal by the "hard-boiled inhumanitarian" writer Albert Jay Nock indicates that pure laissez faire was not his alternative to excessive socialism:

> What did he think? That the Republican Party would repudiate in its toryism everything from old-age pensions and unemployment insurance to rural free delivery, free public schools and the graduated income tax! Nock is a wonderful idealist of the old school. No least taint of socialism and paternalism for him. Absolutely all enterprise private.[83]

Obviously, Frost was not nearly as severe in his well-considered criticism of Roosevelt and the New Deal as were some of its detractors, such as Henry Mencken.[84]

Partly as a Democrat, partly as a friend of some prominent New Dealers, and partly as an apostle of strong but temperate individualism, his criticism of the New Deal became more qualified than severe. In 1944, an interviewer recorded Frost's view of the last years of the New Deal:

> Despite the present Administration's attempts to do everything for the individual, Frost still supports portions of it, because of a personal friendship with many of the leaders, including Vice President Wallace. Maintaining that the present Administration is more interested in promoting the arts than any previous one has been, the poet declared that most of the programs have been successful. He believes that most of these state-sponsored programs are mere dilettantism and do not tend to produce great artists.[85]

When Wallace broke with the Democratic Party and became the leader of the "progressive" socialists, their friendship ended. In a letter to Untermeyer (August 9, 1947), Frost referred to "my former friend Henry Wallace."

It would be inaccurate to conclude that Frost began as a severe critic of the New Deal and gradually mellowed into greater tolerance toward it. He was always acutely sensitive to the suffering of the poor, and he shared the general compassion of the American people toward the victims of the Great Depression. On November 25, 1936, he commented to Untermeyer on the recent reelection of Roosevelt:

I don't mean it is humanity not to feel the suffering of others. The last election would confute me if I did. I judged that half the people that voted for his Rosiness were glad to be on the receiving end of his benevolence and half were those over glad to be on the giving end. The national mood is humanitarian. Nobly so—I wouldn't take it away from them.[86]

Clearly, his criticism of the New Deal transcended his and the government's common humanitarian sympathies for the poor and the desire to solve the complex and profound problems of the Great Depression.

Frost's lifelong faith in the representative system of the American republic, as the essential basis of individual freedom in a society under law, compelled him to reject the New Deal's radical modifications of that system in favor of greater socialism. He believed that every loss of personal freedom was a loss of individual self-sufficiency, and it was also a corresponding gain for collectivist paternalism and totalitarian government. He regarded a free society, making maximum use of individual initiative and motivation, as a far more economically productive society than one controlled or enslaved. He held that the problem in America was not inadequate productivity but the inequitable distribution of its overabundance. In any conflict between the constitutional freedom of the individual and the unconstitutional uses of power by the state, he was invariably on the side of individual liberty. Moreover, he clearly distrusted political ideology as a speculative science that aimed at establishing theoretical perfection in society, because he regarded politics as a part of practical reason, as the art of the possible. He therefore doubted whether men's greatest social problems—distributive justice versus freedom and order, and poverty, crime, war, and ignorance—ever have final or absolute solutions. At best, through government and other institutions, men applied palliatives and secured partial and temporary solutions to such constant problems. He rejected historical determinism, because he believed that conscious and deliberate human decisions, not a supposed law of historical necessity, determined the course of human events. His conception of freedom and individualism was neither nihilistic nor anarchical; he opposed "unchartered freedom," but his defense of the private person in a society under constitutional law was probably his most essential political principle. Throughout his long life he remained true to his own vision of the ideals of democratic government, as instituted in the American republic, and in both theory and practice he held fast to a politics that provided the maximum of personal liberty against all the claims of the modern totalitarian state. For the ultimate basis of Frost's view of man as a political animal was that, consistent with the need of maintaining order and justice in civil society, each man should be as true to himself as possible, a free and self-reliant individual within his society.

## In the Clearing:
## Continuity and Unity in Frost's Dualism

One of the most significant revelations into Robert Frost's philosophical dualism of mind or spirit and of matter as the basis of all reality is the insight that emerges when his essay "On Emerson" (delivered in 1958) is read in conjunction with his remarks in "The Future of Man" symposium (1959) and when both of these prose works together are perceived as a prelude to the poet's climactic case for dualism in his final volume of poetry, *In the Clearing*. "On Emerson" was published in *Daedalus* (Fall 1959); "The Future of Man" remained in several manuscript forms beyond 1959; and Frost's final collection of poetry was published at age 88, on his birthday, March 26, 1962, by Holt, Rinehart and Winston. Yet it is also noteworthy that the continuity regarding Frost's dualism revealed in these works was advanced almost twenty years earlier in a conversation with some Middlebury College students in the poet's cabin near Bread Loaf, Vermont, in his strong criticism of Emerson's idealistic monism.[1] Indeed, the years 1958–59 and 1962 mark the climactic culmination of Frost's lifelong criticism of both the spiritual form of monism, which denies the reality of matter, and the materialistic form, which denies the reality of the spirit. On the positive side, these years reveal his conscious, strong endorsement of a dualism that recognizes that both spirit and matter are implicated in the perception of all reality. In "On Emerson," he once more rejected the incredibly optimistic idealism in Emerson's monism. In "The Future of Man," he rebuffed Sir Julian Huxley's monism of matter. Finally, in *In the Clearing*, for the first time he extended his dualism by combining it with the uniquely creative power of the human psyche through its interactions with matter, beyond religion and the arts into the physical sciences and the historical development of man through civil society. When read in conjunction, these three works reveal the continuity and unity in Frost's dualism during the final decade of his life.

It is important to note that "On Emerson" was delivered as a speech to the American Academy of Arts and Sciences on the occasion of Frost's receiving the Emerson-Thoreau Medal in 1958, and that he therefore deliberately sought "to make myself as much an Emersonian as I can." Thus his talk begins as an expression of his great admiration of Emerson as a poet whose unique skill captured the tones of voice in actual colloquial speech and whose ideas inspired in Frost "troubled thoughts about freedom." But regarding Emerson's moral philosophy, he identified the New England transcendentalist as "a cheerful Monist, for whom evil does not exist, or if it does exist, needn't last forever." The poet noted also that "Emerson quotes Burns as speaking to the Devil as if he could mend his ways." Frost then concluded: "A melancholy dualism is the only soundness."[2] He also reviewed his own "strange history" regarding his thoughts on good and evil, by way of his mother's changes in religion through Emerson, and he observed: "There is such a thing as getting too transcended. There are limits." These were almost the exact words Frost used to the Middlebury students in his cabin in July 1941.

Frost then stated his explicit dualistic objections to Emerson's idealistic monism: "And probably Emerson was too Platonic about evil. It was a mere "το μη ον," a mere non-existence, "that could be disposed of like the butt of a cigarette." Emerson's line "Unit and universe are round" provoked Frost to say, "Ideally in thought only is a circle round. In practice, in nature, the circle becomes an oval. As a circle it has one center—Good. As an oval it has two centers—Good and Evil. Thence Monism versus Dualism."[3] Frost revered what Emerson called "the higher law of the mind," but to him that did not mean that matter in nature should be denigrated as Evil and that moral idealism should be made into an absolute Good. As idealistic monists, Plato and Emerson (and possibly Bishop George Berkeley) made ethical Good an absolute in theory, but to Frost as a dualist, in practice in the daily life of man in society good and evil were both present, and often mixed together, so that to disregard or minimize evil in human nature, to underestimate its power, could result in allowing it to be triumphant. During the 1920s, that was a vital point made by Sidney Cox in observing Frost's dualism: it was the poet's perception of man in his metaphor as a swinger of birches, between idealism and realism, that "he is constantly bringing himself down to earth." For the poet, dualism was the only practical philosophy for man in society.

At Harvard, Irving Babbitt had espoused a dualism akin to Frost's since the beginning of the century. Babbitt often commented on Emerson and liked some of his thought, including his critique of scientism, but was critical of Emerson's ethereal and Romantic leanings. In his first book, *Literature and the American College* (1908), Babbitt complained about Emerson's "disquieting vagueness and lack of grip in dealing with particulars." For Babbitt, man must, if he is to keep his sanity, "maintain the nicest balance between unity and plurality." Not much later, Babbitt's intellectual ally Paul Elmer More published "Definitions of Dualism," philosophical reflections on the "two elements of our being": a unifying power and the multiplicity of impulse.[4]

Toward the end of his essay "On Emerson," Frost anticipated the main thesis and very language he used in "Kitty Hawk" and his theme of dualism throughout much of *In the Clearing*:

> Emerson was a Unitarian because he was too rational to be superstitious and too little a storyteller and lover of stories to like gossip and pretty scandal. Nothing very religious can be done for people lacking in superstition. They usually end up abominable agnostics. It takes superstition and the prettiest scandal story of all to make a good Trinitarian. It is the first step in the descent of the spirit into the material-human at the risk of the spirit.[5]

According to Frost, only a good Trinitarian could understand and accept the virgin birth of Christ and the doctrine of the Incarnation. Toward the end of his life, although Frost showed an increasing awareness and concern about the conflicts between spirit and matter, he also extended their unity by exploring the harmony between them in religious orthodoxy. In "On Emerson," he defended spirit in supernatural revealed religion against the human rationalism that usually ends up producing "abominable agnostics," and in "The Future of Man" symposium he attacked the self-sufficient rationalism of Sir Julian Huxley for exalting agnosticism or atheism in defense of absolute matter against any belief in spirit. In such poems as "Skeptic," "Astrometaphysical," "Why Wait for Science," and "Some Science Fiction," he expressed his own skepticism about the absolute claims of scientific metaphysics rooted in a monism of matter.

In the first of three recorded or edited versions of "The Future of Man" symposium (1959), Frost accepted the challenge to prophesy about mankind's future destiny within evolutionary and historical time. His response was in terms of what he perceived as human originality and creative power, of what he called the "energy and daring" shown in establishing law and order in the recorded life of mankind. Within temporal history, the great dynastic issues that confront the dominant world political powers in every era, "like the one between Persia and Greece, Rome and Carthage, Christendom and Islam" and in contemporary times between the United States and Soviet Russia, result in some form of resolution. Beyond history, evolution presents a different kind of question. The great unresolved evolutionary problem for the nature of mankind as a biological species is, "are we going to be another kind of people?" Frost denied that there would be an evolutionary development "from us to superman," because "our self-consciousness is terminal—there is nothing beyond us." The evolutionary metaphor, "the tree of life . . . has reached its growth." The poet prophesied that the dualism that has characterized the past evolutionary experience of mankind would continue to be permanent and paramount in the future life of the human species:

> It will go on blossoming and having its seasons—I'd give it another hundred or two hundred million years. Make that anything you please. It'll go on leaving Out and blossoming into successions of the doubleness, I foresee, just like the doubleness of the sexes. There'll be two parties always to it, some way. . . . The tree . . . in itself has all the doubleness I see, good and evil, two sexes. . . .[6]

To Frost, the dualism of spirit and matter, of the two sexes, and of good and evil was built into the evolutionary process. What he called "the challenge . . . between man's originality and his law and order," which determined both historical changes and the course of evolution in man, is rooted in the creative power in the mind or spirit of man as a species, as part of his dualistic nature.

In the second and originally unpublished version of "The Future of Man" symposium, Frost paid special tribute to science as "the most formidable" power in man's future challenges. Then he added a very significant qualification: "But philosophy has been formidable too." He made it clear that the most formidable element in philosophy was dualism. A third force involved in man's future destiny is government, because it has ultimate control over the practical uses of science in the social order and because rulers determine which philosophical beliefs will be applied in practice. The challenge that science poses is what modern government is going to do with the latest discoveries, inventions, technologies, and advances of scientists. Frost observed that the swift progress in scientific knowledge and theory creates serious problems for governments: "It seems a shame to come on you with our new novelties when you are hardly up around after what Darwin, Spencer, and Huxley did to you last century."[7] But the formidable power in dualistic philosophy, in the creativity of the human spirit, and even in that which is centered in the procreative instincts also determines future changes: "People are still pairing for love and money" through "passionate preference." Science is much, Frost conceded, but as he had said on several past occasions, it is only "one of the humanities." Science, he claimed, "is man's greatest enterprise. It is the charge of the ethereal into the material. It is our substantiation of our meaning. It can't go too far or too deep for me."[8] His theme and the very language of religion—"the charge of the ethereal into the material" and "substantiation"— are almost identical to the metaphors in his poems "Cluster of Faith" and "Kitty Hawk" in his final volume. In his poem "Pod of the Milkweed," his comments on "waste" in evolution also anticipated the themes in some of the poems in his final volume. Even though some of the poems were written before the symposium on the future of man, they contribute to a better understanding of the poet's views on science in the light of his philosophical dualism.

The third version of "The Future of Man" symposium, revised and extended by Frost himself, appeared in Edward C. Lathem's *Interviews with Robert Frost* (1966), under the significant title "Of Passionate Preference." It is more specific and detailed than the two earlier versions about the mechanisms of evolutionary changes in the human species and indirectly about dualism in the poet's confrontation with Sir Julian's monism of matter. During the last half of the symposium, when the participants were subjected to questions and comments by three shrewd journalists, mainly regarding Darwin's principle of "natural selection," Frost challenged Huxley to identify the method of evolutionary changes in man. The scientist was clearly ill at ease in his response, because he could not justify a wholly external mechanistic and materialistic force or method to explain how evolutionary changes have lifted man upward. Finally, he intimated that chance had arbitrarily determined evolutionary biological changes in man.

Frost countered by specifying that "passionate preference" was the most vital instrument in human natural selection. Passionate preference clearly included the whole human psyche, centered in the will and reason of man, and all that was involved in man's power of creativity. But then Frost added a new dimension to the evolutionary mix: he identified "passionate preference" as "a Biblical thing." This meant that love—as understood within orthodox revealed religion between God and man and between the two sexes in procreation—rather than chance, biology, and the law of the jungle, was the most vital factor in the poet's conception of natural selection and evolution. The full impact of this belief would become evident in the critical commentaries on Frost's poems in "Cluster of Faith," especially in "Accidentally on Purpose," as a prelude to "Kitty Hawk." But in the symposium, the poet's main criticism of Sir Julian Huxley was directed against the scientist's social theory, prophecy, and extension of the growing modern welfare state into an ideological future utopian social order that he called "the fulfillment society." Huxley's international social theory was the logical extension of his Marxist materialism. He believed that a secular system of education based upon the physical sciences, that assumed a monism of matter and transcended nationalism, would ultimately result in the establishment of one world government. Nothing could be more completely opposed to Frost's philosophical dualism and his view of the social order and politics of free men under constitutional law than Huxley's monistic and materialistic vision of mankind's historical future.

The social and political issues raised during Frost's conflict with Huxley continued to concern the poet for the remaining four years of his life. About six weeks after the symposium, on November 19, 1959, during a poetry reading at the Fountain Street Baptist Church in Grand Rapids, Michigan, between reading poems he interspersed comments on his conflict with Huxley.[9] He recalled some of his most trenchant critical remarks during the symposium—on pure science, on the place of science within the humanities, and on the "double meanings" in the Bible. Although he softened his personal criticism of Huxley, he remained adamantly opposed to the scientist's belief that an international united world government would eventually displace the legal sovereignty of existing independent nations. He condemned the idea of a compulsory social benevolence or political "togetherness" implicit in Huxley's monistic theory; he referred to "the one-sided crowd that think we can have one world, no more nations and all that." He opposed Huxley's monistic world politics with an aphorism that he frequently had applied to poetry and that he had voiced to President John F. Kennedy in defense of a foreign policy centered in national self-interest: "The separateness of the parts is equally important with the connection of the parts." During the summers of 1961 and 1962, Frost repeated in discussions with me at Bread Loaf his statement to Kennedy while recalling his conflict with Huxley during the symposium on the future of man.

But the philosophical, scientific, and political issues raised by Frost's differences with Huxley are most evident in his final volume of poetry. *In the*

*Clearing* was published on Frost's eighty-eighth birthday, March 26, 1962. Because it is consciously and deliberately connected with so many of his most important beliefs held throughout his long life, it can well be regarded as his last poetic will and testament, his confession of faith as a philosophical poet. The word "philosophical" is here obviously not meant to suggest that he wished to be didactic but that he wanted to speak poetically about humanity's central questions. Frost died late in January 1963. The very title of *In the Clearing* hearkens back to "The Pasture" in *A Boy's Will* (1913), especially to the metaphorical line "and wait to watch the water clear." The continuity with the poet's past is also evident in his dedication to his early closest and most devoted friends, John Bartlett, Sidney Cox, and Louis Untermeyer. To them he had first confided his ambition as a boy to come into his own as a great poet. Just as "The Pasture" ends with an invitation, "you come too," to share in his long journey as a poet, so too his final dedication includes an unidentified "you," certainly an echo of his first dedication to his wife, Elinor Frost, but also including friends and the general public. Some commentators have also suggested that the invitation includes his secretary, Kay Morrison. Frost always counted upon those closest to him in spirit to know how to "take" him, both as a man and in his self-belief as a poet, and ultimately in his dualistic philosophy. In "On a Tree Fallen Across the Road," he had refined upon the couplet in "Into My Own" on how in time his friends would understand him, "only more sure of all I thought was true":

> We will not be put off the final goal
> We have it hidden in us to attain.

All that Frost thought was true attained its final refinement in the themes of dualism involving spirit and matter in *In the Clearing*.

There is nothing mechanistic about Frost's extension of his dualistic beliefs, because his eclectic and complex mind was never fixed rigidly upon any one philosophical system, but was always open to consider and absorb whatever he found valid through his experiences of life. The continuity recognizable in his final volume, therefore, is not merely a logical extension of his previous art and thought. It includes fresh developments and intuitional insights in the forms, style, techniques, and content of his poems and in the themes of his beliefs as a dualist. Although his final collection falls short as art when compared with *North of Boston* or *New Hampshire*, it is here that Frost's dualism truly came into its own. Within its great diversity, *In the Clearing* provides a continuity and unity that is the fitting climax of his positive beliefs.

The poet acknowledged that the most important poem in his final book is "Kitty Hawk," and any critical summation or "after-thoughts" on his philosophical dualism must take that poem into full account. But "Kitty Hawk" is itself introduced by five poems, significantly called "Cluster of Faith."[10] The first two poems in this group, which Frost set off as a unit, are clearly an explicit sequel to his differences with Huxley as well as a prelude to "Kitty Hawk." In light of all that he had said previously on science, evolution, God's purposes, and love, the first poem in "Cluster of Faith" is especially significant:

"Accidentally on Purpose"

*The universe is but the Thing of things,*
*The things but balls all going round in rings.*
*Some of them mighty huge, some mighty tiny,*
*All of them radiant and mighty shiny.*

*They mean to tell us all was rolling blind*
*Till accidentally it hit on mind*
*In an albino monkey in a jungle*
*And even then it had to grope and bungle,*

*Till Darwin came to earth upon a year*
*To show the evolution how to steer.*
*They mean to tell us, though, the Omnibus*
*Had no real purpose till it got to us.*

*Never believe it. At the very worst*
*It must have had the purpose from the first*
*To produce purpose as the fitter bred:*
*We were just purpose coming to a head.*

*Whose purpose was it? His or Hers or Its?*
*Let's leave that to the scientific wits.*
*Grant me intention, purpose, and design—*
*That's near enough for me to the Divine.*

*And yet for all this help of head and brain*
*How happily instinctive we remain,*
*Our best guide upward further to the light,*
*Passionate preference such as love at sight.*

Undoubtedly, there is much room for a metaphorical range of interpretations of this poem. But in light of Frost's conflicts with "the three generations of Huxleys," nothing is more evident than that "Accidentally on Purpose" emphatically rejects the whole Victorian ethos regarding evolution as interpreted by Thomas Henry Huxley and his grandson. A close reading of this poem provides some strong hints of Frost's own anti-Huxley alternatives in interpreting Darwin's theory. Among other possibilities, the poem includes not only the poet's conception of "intention, purpose, and design" as God's will and reason, but also the cosmic role of love in giving shape and meaning to the universe.

The first stanza describes the physical cosmos as perceived by physicists. The second and third stanzas summarize Julian Huxley's interpretation of evolution as set forth during "The Future of Man" symposium. Frost was particularly skeptical of Julian Huxley's claim, so often put forth since the time of Thomas Henry Huxley and other Victorian scientists, that through the evolutionary process the mind or spirit of man as a biological species was gradually derived from matter. Such an unproved assumption or belief, the poet contended, meant that the universe had no meaning until Darwin's conception of "natural selection" provided mankind with a biological yet mechanistic basis in matter for belief in a purposeful evolving universe. But even granting Huxley's assumption, Darwin's theory and principle of natural selection provided no empirical or rational evidence for faith in a purposeful universe. Frost's emphatic rejection of Julian Huxley, beginning with the fourth stanza, "never believe it," fills the final three stanzas with some of his alternative views and beliefs regarding man in relation to the physical universe. And beyond the physical universe, Frost perceived meaningful purpose within historical rather than evolutionary time, in the social life of man as distinct from life in the jungle.

Frost believed that among the enduring mysteries of the origin and purpose of the universe, including man as a species, neither science, nor religion, nor philosophy, nor art had yet solved beyond doubt the unresolved questions regarding God, man, and physical nature. Whatever men believed was far more a matter of faith than of knowledge. In *A Masque of Reason* (1945), Job had lamented to God the lack of decisive knowledge in man's attempts to penetrate the great mysteries:

> *We don't know where we are, or who we are,*
> *We don't know one another; don't know You;*
> *Don't know what time it is. . . .*

Job's appeals to God to provide man with rational answers to life's mysteries provoked much equivocation on the part of God; He remained unwilling to satisfy Job's request. The same theme regarding the great unsolved mysteries is repeated with variations seventeen years later in "A Cabin in the Clearing." The human condition is characterized by man's lack of knowledge regarding the mysteries, and this is the source of many bitter conflicts. This theme is central in "Neither Out Far Nor in Deep," yet man's limited knowledge did not lead Frost into despair or cynicism regarding purpose in the universe. Neither did it result in contempt for human nature in its persistent attempts to penetrate the unknown, as was claimed by Lionel Trilling in his shallow analysis of that poem. On the contrary, Frost had a sense of awe and reverence toward human nature for persisting and remaining steadfast in its belief and faith that man's life on earth had a purpose. In "A Cabin in the Clearing," like the positive beliefs expressed in the "Cluster of Faith" poems and in "Kitty Hawk," Frost praised "the sleepers in the house" for clearing the woods back from around the house, even though this knowledge did not solve the great mystery of their nature or orientation in the universe:

> And still I doubt if they know where they are.
> And I begin to fear they never will.

But contrary to Trilling and other literary critics, Frost expressed his positive belief in the faith of mankind beyond its limited knowledge:

> No one—not I—would give them up for lost
> Simply because they don't know where they are.

These lines present the poet's alternative to any dogmatic claims that the universe is without purpose or meaning, without any guide upward further toward the light of knowledge and belief.

In the final stanza of "Accidentally on Purpose," he identified human consciousness and the instinct of passionate love beyond biology as a basis for upward mobility that transcends a merely mechanistic and deterministic conception of evolution through "natural selection." Frost believed that mankind has the power to change both evolutionary and historical developments and thus to provide meaning and direction to both its temporal and spiritual destinies. In place of the conception of evolution offered by the three generations of Huxleys, Frost proposed "passionate preference such as love at sight." In this climactic line, he conflated Walt Whitman's phrase "passionate preference" with a compressed version of Christopher Marlowe's line from "Hero and Leander" (line 176), "whoever loved, that loved not at first sight?" This fusing together of Whitman and Marlowe is one of Frost's most brilliant original acts of creative imagination achieved through literary allusions. In the last line of "Accidentally on Purpose," he snatched a grace beyond the reach of art and made man's conscious purpose, not accident or chance, the essential element in evolution and history. His poem was a triumphant trumpet blast that refuted Julian Huxley and was the prelude to his expanded dualism of spirit and matter in the theme of "Kitty Hawk."

Whereas, as George Santayana had pointed out, Whitman had applied the phrase "passionate preference" to the average American's faith and devotion to democracy as his favored form of government, leading to improvements in human affairs in civil society, Frost extended the phrase to include evolution and history, seen as involving spirit and matter, as the central theme in "Kitty Hawk." By identifying "passionate preference" as "a Biblical thing," the poet expanded its meaning beyond biology and politics to include ethics and the spiritual realm of religion and even the creative power of man that included art, science, and the evolution of civil society from primitivism to modernity. Whereas Whitman had limited "passionate preference" to politics, and Julian Huxley had restricted the procreative instinct in human nature to biology and physical nature—to what Frost called "an albino monkey in a jungle"—the poet elevated the meaning of the term beyond lust in a pre-civil state of physical nature to the level of love between the sexes as directed by a moral code in religion within an evolved historical society. By combining Whitman's phrase with Marlowe's conception of intuitive love, Frost gave love a religious, moral, and aesthetic dimension governed by a code of behavior. His view of the evolutionary and historical development of human nature attributed the formative force not to physical nature but to organized civil society and religion and, above all, the creative power in human nature. Within organized society, which is something very different from the jungle of nature, the union of the sexes in marriage, whether perceived as a social contract or a sacrament, made love a dualistic fusion of spirit and body. As Frost's principle of natural selection, love was far more than a matter of physical necessity. By including spirit in the evolutionary process, he harmonized religion and science and made creative evolution his substitute for how the three generations of Huxleys had interpreted Darwin's theory.

In "Kitty Hawk," Frost acknowledged that love is one of the mysteries that baffle human knowledge: "There's no knowing what / Love is all about." As a factor in genetics, Frost's conception of love included spirit, and therefore it transcended Gregor Mendel's laws of genetics as transmitting dominant or recessive genes according to fixed mathematical and predictable patterns. To the poet, changes in the human species through evolution included biological and physical matters accessible to science but also such elements as aesthetic, moral, religious, and social considerations and laws. The biblical dimension in Frost's account of God's "intention, purpose, and design" was manifested in love, beyond lust; it included God's love for mankind as a species. This element provided what was most lacking in Darwin's theory as understood by so many of his Victorian and modern disciples. Although Darwin knew nothing about Mendel's laws of genetics, Julian Huxley was thoroughly familiar with the Austrian monk's experiments in botany. Yet in Huxley's account of the twentieth-century revival of Darwin's theory through a synthesis of the physical sciences beyond biology, his genetics remained rooted in a monism of matter. The ultimate basis of Frost's quarrel with Huxley in "The Future of Man" symposium was more than a disagreement regarding biology. Their differences were philosophical: Matter was for Frost not physicalistic and mechanistic; it interacted with and was, in a sense, even indistinguishable from spirit. The poet's dualism and Huxley's monism of matter could not be reconciled.

In the second poem in "Cluster of Faith," "A Never Naught Song," the opening couplet summarizes the main theme in Frost's criticism of Julian Huxley in "Accidentally on Purpose": "There was never naught, / There was always thought." The poet assumed that even before the creation of the physical universe, God always existed as a spirit infinitely perfect. He acknowledged the importance of matter, but he placed a premium upon man's mind or spirit as the source of perceptions of all earthly reality as "caught ... by the force of thought." The full import of the dimensions of his theme in "A Never Naught Song" was anticipated in Frost's Horatian poem, "The Lesson for Today," in *A Witness Tree*, in the long passage that begins "Space ails us moderns: we are sick with space" and concludes with "So science and religion really meet." In "A Never Naught Song" Frost acknowledged that undoubtedly a universe consisting of matter had to exist before man as a species of life appeared on earth. This meant that a monism of matter, though hardly of the kind assumed by the Huxleys, existed for God before it could be perceived dualistically by the mind or spirit of man:

> It was in a state
> Of atomic One.
> Matter was begun—

*And in fact complete,*
*One and yet discrete*
*To conflict and pair.*
*Everything was there*
*Every single thing*
*Waiting was to bring,*
*Clear from hydrogen*
*All the way to men.*

Frost concluded this highly speculative poem on the hypothetical physical origins of the universe, and even of man, with what may be a concession to the philosophical idealism and monism of Bishop George Berkeley:

*So the picture's caught*
*Almost next to naught*
*But the force of thought.*

But as Sidney Cox had observed, Frost "is constantly bringing himself down to earth," and "on earth things are dual." This meant that once man was created, or evolved, "the force of thought" in the perception of matter and all things on earth replaced God's original creation of matter as a self-sufficient monism with man's dualistic perception of matter. As Berkeley was to argue: "to be is to be perceived."

The third poem in "Cluster of Faith," "Version," compares God as the creator of the universe to an archer who "shot a shaft / On a new departure." Frost believed that like all acts of original creativity, God's "new departure" involved moral courage and intellectual daring, particularly when man was created. The creation of the universe and man was fraught with risks and dangerous possibilities of potential tragedy, a hazard that needed to be taken, but which was balanced with the spirit of comedy. This meant that as creator of all reality and life, God had to have a profound sense of humor: "Then He must have laughed: / Comedy was in it." By way of analogy, the creative power in human nature also needed to include the potential for both comedy and tragedy. This view was consistent with Frost's contention over many years that all good creative writing needed to include the dualism of "the pleasure of ulteriority," that is, of wit, irony, humor, or ambiguity—essential ways of establishing the dramatic "tone" or sense of "play" even in serious discourse. Perceiving a sense of comedy in God confirms and gives metaphysical substance to Frost's statement that he was never more serious than when he was joking. Like the dynamic interaction of mind or spirit with matter, comedy and tragedy play ambiguously in the dualistic conflicts in the complex life of man on earth. The theme of comedy in "Version" is confirmed and extended from God to man and then made reciprocal, from man to God, in Frost's final, untitled, and often quoted couplet in "Cluster of Faith":

*Forgive, O Lord, my little jokes on Thee*
*And I'll forgive Thy great big one on me.*

Finally, serving as a prelude to "Kitty Hawk," these contentions about comedy and God's sense of humor help to explain, and perhaps to justify, Frost's joke in the whimsical verse form and technique in "Kitty Hawk," his most important serious poem in *In the Clearing*.

The fifth poem in "Cluster of Faith," "A Concept Self-Conceived," expressly rejects the kind of monism (of matter) that is "no more than good old Pantheism." It is at once a rebuttal of monism and a serious prelude to the dualism and comic spirit that permeate "Kitty Hawk." Taken together, all five poems in "Cluster of Faith" prefigure and introduce the serious subject and worldview of "Kitty Hawk" and also its whimsical form, technique, and tone. At the same time, all of the poems in *In the Clearing* illuminate Frost's entire life as a poet and an intellectual, specifically all that he voiced about creativity and dualism in prose and poetry during his poetry readings and in conversations with friends.

Before examining Frost's dualism in "Kitty Hawk," it is useful to take note of the importance that he attached to this poem as well as the most unusual verse form and technique in which it is cast. The history of its composition underscores the great concern that he had for "Kitty Hawk." It was first published in booklet form as his Christmas poem in 1956. It consisted of 128 lines. In November 1957 it appeared in the *Atlantic Monthly*, drastically revised and now in 482 lines. After further minor revisions, it appeared in the *Anthology of Magazine Verse* for 1958.[11] Following an interview with John Ciardi, a new concentrated version of sixty-four lines was published in *The Saturday Review* (March 21, 1959), in which, for the first time, Frost's mature view of science as part of man's original creativity was made explicit. All sixty-four lines were incorporated into the final version of "Kitty Hawk."[12]

The structure, verse form, technique, and light tone in presenting the deeply serious subjects in "Kitty Hawk" have appeared incongruous, or at least aesthetically lacking in harmony, to many literary critics whose conventional assumptions regarding serious poetry are too restrictive. The "in- and outdoor schooling" that Frost said was required to understand and appreciate his sense of humor is not easily mastered. First, it is necessary to set aside the common conventional assumption that serious discourse on such subjects as the nature of man and the universe or on the spiritual destiny of man must necessarily be presented in the form and tone of solemn *gravitas* and with somber demeanor, in an exalted and rhetorical blank verse like "the Chinese wall" of John Milton in *Paradise Lost*.

Frost once asserted that the creation of form, however trivial, "stroked faith the right way." In his adherence to the traditional verse forms and techniques of English poetry, he shared a bond of aesthetic fellowship with poets from past ages. His sense of creative identity with a past tradition of poetry served the same general and psychological function as corporate membership in a church did for religious believers who shared a common faith. Frost's deep reverence for the humanities was an enlarged cultural version of the same thing; it extended his aesthetic and intellectual identity even to the ancient Greek and Latin poets. But unlike Matthew Arnold, Frost never confounded the nature and function of art with that of religion. For him, poetry was never a substitute for faith in the doctrines or liturgy of any institutional religion. While art and religion often supplemented each other in a nation's culture, each remained distinct. But Frost assumed that, as an art form, poetry was capable of much originality, so that the light tones of comedy or the spirit of fables like Mother Goose could be utilized even in serious discourse. Alexander Pope's dictum that in poetry "the sound must seem an echo to the sense" did not mean for Frost that the tone of *gravitas* could not be balanced, or even displaced, by humor, irony, and light comedy.

In "Kitty Hawk" he challenged himself to write in the light form, technique, and tone of comedy a serious poem expressing his dualism, which involved both the spirit of religion and the matter studied by science. This demand upon his aesthetic imagination also applied to his readers, who had to have the ability, willingness, and taste to accept his unconventional verse form. Among his predecessors in such an unusual enterprise in English poetry, he praised John Skelton (1460?–1529), the Tudor poet laureate and teacher of Prince Henry (Henry VIII). Skelton castigated abuses in church and state in a verse form described as "a headlong voluble breathless doggerel . . . rattling and clashing on through quick recurring rhymes."[13] In a similar vein, Frost introduced "Kitty Hawk" as "a skylark . . . in three-beat phrases." During a conversation with me in 1961, he praised the "hyperdithyrambic meters of Ogden Nash"; he insisted that such bantering good humor and wit was a fit vehicle for serious ideas. He noted, furthermore, that William Blake's simple lyrical verse forms in *Songs of Innocence* were also utilized in his far more serious *Songs of Experience*. But in "Kitty Hawk" Frost refined the methods of such contemporaries and predecessors by taking for his touchstone of comedy the parables and metaphors of fairy stories, especially those of Mother Goose.

During his early friendship with Sidney Cox, just before and after World War I, he had engaged often in banter about the serious function of humor and wit as a metaphor in the art of poetry. He told Cox that "you start, say, with a jingle from *Mother Goose*," and then "you spread from a limited range of reference to a wider and wider range."[14] Over the next three decades, during poetry readings he often praised nursery rhymes and referred to the childlike parables and metaphors in Mother Goose as containing a profound wisdom in human experience. In an interview with Robert Penn Warren and Cleanth Brooks, "Conversations on the Craft of Poetry" (1959), he insisted that a dramatic prerequisite for all poetry is "catchiness," "from the ballads you hear on the street to the lines in Shakespeare that stay with you without your trying to remember them."[15] Although he cautioned that in verse technique "doggerel," or the mechanical meter of "sing-song," must be avoided and insisted that the rhythm has "got to ruffle the meter," he stated that the philosophical content of Mother Goose was "very deep" and "meant a lot to me . . . all my life."[16] For Frost, a poem was "a little voyage of discovery," in which the initial mood or tone "foretells the end product." A valid description of all poetry, he said, was in a phrase of the ancient Roman poet Catullus, *mens animi*, interpreted by Frost as "the thoughts of my heart," and this included the lightest forms of comedy as a metaphor. He believed that throughout man's "trial by existence" on earth, the elements of comedy were a necessary dimension in man's tragic struggle to save himself from despair. In short, Frost believed that comedy and tragedy should supplement each other and could be combined within a poem or play. This aesthetic principle was in the best tradition of Shakespeare, a convention that Milton abandoned in favor of pure tragedy in *Paradise Lost*.

To introduce all of the poems in *In the Clearing* he fused together two separate passages from "Kitty Hawk." He sought to create an emblematic theme that served the same general function for his final volume that "The Pasture" had performed for all of his previous books of poetry:

> *But God's own descent*
> *Into flesh was meant*
> *As a demonstration*

*That the supreme merit*
*Lay in risking spirit*
*In substantiation.*

*. . . Spirit enters flesh*
*And for all it's worth*
*Charges into earth*
*In birth after birth*
*Ever fresh and fresh.*
*We may take the view*
*That its derring-do*
*Thought of in the large*
*Was one mighty charge*
*On our human part*
*Of the soul's ethereal*
*Into the material.*

This vital archetypal passage, centered in the Christian doctrine of the In-carnation, extended to all mankind "in birth after birth," raises once more the complex, contentious, and unresolved question of Frost's religion. It presents a view that has proven to be beyond the grasp of any of the schol-arship that has dealt with that subject. Yet it should be clear that the refer-ence to the "mighty charge . . . Of the soul's ethereal / Into the material" involves Frost's perennial concern with the dualism of spirit and matter.

Regarding his religion, forty-five years before his emblematic passage introducing *In the Clearing*, he had written to Louis Untermeyer (October 27, 1917), "Do or say my damndest I can't be other than orthodox in poli-tics, love and religion. I can't escape salvation." But in all of the interven-ing years between 1917 and 1959, he had never made clear precisely which religious beliefs he included in regarding himself as "orthodox." This de-liberate omission characterized his usual public reticence in responding to questions about his religious beliefs. The same prudent reserve and silence marked his constant refusal to explain what he meant by any of his poems. The two omissions may well have something in common: a recognition of the inability of human reason to grasp the ultimate mystery at the core of our dualistic existence. There is no question that throughout his life Frost was some kind of theist. Early in his friendship with Untermeyer, on Janu-ary 1, 1916, he wrote: "If there were no God—but there is one. . . ." But the poet's undoubted lifelong monotheism remained diffuse. Although it excluded atheism, agnosticism, deism, and pantheism, precisely what he meant by God remained elusive, at least in public. To call him a "mystic" does not help matters. To friends he trusted or revered he could be very candid in private about his religious beliefs. During my first acquaintance with Frost, in the summer of 1939 at Bread Loaf, he surprised me on several occasions by the intensity and depth of his religious feelings. Although he was securely rooted in his family's Protestant inheritance, essentially as a Congregationalist, he was fond of discussing theology with Jesuit priests, and he had long discussions on biblical themes with his friend Rabbi Victor Reichert, because, he contended, they had "original ideas" to stimulate his moral imagination. In his "Sermon at Rockdale Avenue Temple" to Reichert's congregation (October 10, 1946), he said, "Religion always seems to me to come round to something beyond wisdom. It's a straining of the spirit forward to a wisdom beyond wisdom."

But in "Kitty Hawk," in refining and extending his dualism of spirit and matter, or body and soul, Frost identified his religious "orthodoxy" as affirmed in the central doctrine of all branches of Christianity—the Incarnation of Christ—the "substantiation" of God's spirit into human flesh. In the second part of the emblematic passage, Frost shifted from God to man, and he extended to human beings, as biological creatures made in the image of God, God's courage and risk, or "derring-do." He extended it metaphorically to human nature, in its power of creativity in all things. Frost left no doubt that his emblematic passage on transubstantiation, a crucial doctrine in orthodox Christianity, corresponded with his own religious beliefs. During a poetry reading of "Kitty Hawk" in 1959, he said, "That's what our religion means. That's what the Christian religion means—God's own descent into flesh in substantiation."[17] In effect, "Kitty Hawk" provided a Christian basis for the seemingly pagan theme in "The Trial by Existence," Frost's first explicitly religious poem.

Frost's closest friend at Amherst College in matters of religion, George Ray Elliott, has recorded some important observations on the poet's religious beliefs late in life. In five unpublished letters to Lawrance Thompson, written between 1947 and 1963, Elliott traced what he considered to be the most significant changes in Frost's theism. On April 11, 1947, he stated that for many years Frost had held to "a sort of theism along with disbelief in the Incarnation, i.e., a historically unique manifestation of God in Christ." On March 25, 1963, in a letter after Frost's death, he wrote that since the death of Elinor Frost in 1938, if not before, "RF has accepted more and more the Divinity of Christ just because RF was a brainy and insightful student of the New Testament—though reticent on that. And he saw that the accounts there, and the affairs in history, were inexplicable unless

Christ were God in human form."[18] In his many years of friendship with Frost, Elliott said that his friend "often talked to me about religion because of my keen interest in it, inherited from Scottish Presbyterian ancestors through my father and mother." To Lawrance Thompson, Elliott identified himself as an "Episcopalian." In light of Frost's comments during a reading of "Kitty Hawk" on "God's own descent into flesh in substantiation" and of Elliott's account of Frost's adoption of the Christian view of the Incarnation after his wife's death, the poems in *In the Clearing* take on a strong religious significance.

It is in this context important to note that the last letter Frost ever wrote, dictated from his deathbed, was to Elliott and his wife. Their closeness in spirit is evident in the poet's last words to his friend:

> Why will the quidnuncs always be hoping for a salvation man will never have from anyone but God? I was just saying today how Christ posed Himself the whole problem and died for it. How can we be just in a world that needs mercy and merciful in a world that needs justice. . . . It seems as if I never wrote these plunges into the depths to anyone but you. . . . If only I get well . . . I'll go deeper into my life with you than I ever have before.[19]

Since Elliott believed that Frost knew that he would not recover from his final illness, these words can well be taken as his last will and testament in matters of religion. One of his earliest and most important dualistic concerns, the perennial conflict between justice and mercy in human affairs, so evident in *The Death of the Hired Man* (1913) and in *A Masque of Reason* (1945) and *A Masque of Mercy* (1947), remained with him to the end of his life.

But Frost's emblematic passage from "Kitty Hawk" applies not only to religion and dualism but to all of life. By using the passage as an introduction to the entire volume of poems in *In the Clearing*, Frost signaled his belief that the penetration of God's spirit into matter encompasses the whole history and development of European and Western civilization. By applying the doctrine of God's incarnation to the temporal affairs of man as a species, Frost indicated that, as creatures who share God's creative power, men and women give shape and direction to the whole temporal order of civil society and to their changing conceptions of physical nature. The central metaphor in "Kitty Hawk" now illuminated not only the arts and the humanities and religion, but science and the formation and evolution of society in all of its enduring achievements. Through much of his life, Frost had assumed that only the creative arts reflected a godlike power in especially gifted and disciplined men and women. Not until 1959 did he consciously begin to attribute such an original power to the physical sciences. As perceived and practiced by most scientists, science assumed a monism of matter, and Frost had long been highly critical of that form of monism as the chief source of the abuse of science in positivistic scientism. His strong disagreements with "the three generations of Huxleys" were centered in his rejection of a monism of matter and in his insistence that science was properly one of the humanities.

Frost's lifelong distinction between science and scientism, between the valid uses of science and its abuses, was well stated in terms of his dualism of spirit and matter: "But in taking us deeper and deeper into matter," he observed, "science has left all of us with this great misgiving, this fear that we won't be able to substantiate the spirit."[20] In 1959, in "The Future of Man" symposium, he had summarized his mixed views about science: "It comes into our lives as domestic science for our hold on the planet, into our deaths with its deadly weapons, bombs, and airplanes, for war, and into our souls as pure science for nothing but glory."[21] It is not surprising, therefore, that Frost originally intended to title his final volume of poetry *The Great Misgiving.* That would have been in keeping with the theme of his first poem on science, "The Demiurge's Laugh." Although that poem was probably written around 1906, it was first published in *A Boy's Will* in 1913.

The Demiurge is a lesser and ominous deity in Greek and Platonic mythology, reputed to be in control of the material world, where science is supreme. The poem is cast in the form of a monologue in which the speaker initially expresses his joy during his obsessive pursuit of the Demiurge, even while admitting that it is "no true god." Only when the light of this illusory belief begins to fail and metaphysical and intellectual darkness sets in does he discover through the Demiurge's derisive laugh that his idealistic faith in science as man's redeemer is an illusion, that while he thought that he was pursuing the Demiurge, he was the one being pursued. Thus the speaker is shocked into an awareness that he does not control science, but science commands him. In essence, this revelation is Frost's warning to the twentieth century that material monism and science are not capable of creating a sound civilization. His poem expresses his distinction between admirable science, which serves the material needs of human nature, and corrupt science, which serves destructive practical ends and sacrifices humanity to a materialist ideology. The abuse of science is most evident in time of war. Positivism, with its unbounded faith in a monism of matter and in a discursive reason pursued along abstract mathematical lines and with its exclusion of the whole realm of spirit, prepares the way for a corrupt and brutal civilization.

Implicit in "The Demiurge's Laugh" is Frost's early satire on the uncritical belief of many modern persons that science is the supreme instrument of man's inevitable "progress" toward an eventual utopian world society. Not only positivists but the public at large—indeed, everyone devoted to merely abstract rationality in the tradition of Descartes and to a view of the universe wholly centered in matter in the Victorian tradition of Thomas Henry Huxley, H. G. Wells, and other material monists—was in revolt against belief in a dualism of spirit and matter. Frost perceived the catastrophe that totalitarian ideology and politics were to inflict upon mankind during the twentieth century in terms of the conflict between his dualism of spirit and matter and the monism of matter that came to dominate the modern world. It was Frost's great misfortune that he chose for his official biographer Lawrance Thompson, who was among those swept up in the revolt against dualism and who therefore presented a wholly garbled picture of the poet's central beliefs in his three-volume biography. He accused Frost of being "against science." Such satirical poems as "Why Wait for Science" and "Some Science Fiction," taken literally rather than metaphorically, seemed to support the biographer's contention that Frost's view of science was wholly negative. Thompson ignored such of Frost's statements on science in "The Future of Man" symposium as the following: "It is man's greatest enterprise. It is the charge of the ethereal into the material. It is our substantiation of our meaning. It can't go too far or deep for me."[22] The biographer also paid no attention to the poet's great admiration for truly superior scientists such as Newton, Darwin in *The Voyage of the Beagle,* and Einstein. So far as these scientists retained a belief in spirit and mind distinct from a wholly mechanistic conception of human nature and the physical universe, Frost believed that they contributed to the knowledge and understanding that are necessary for a civilized social order. In a conversation with me, Frost noted that Einstein initially opposed creating the atomic bomb, which indicated that he distinguished between science and its abuses. But when science put great power into the hands of morally depraved totalitarian rulers, it became necessary for civilized men to oppose their power with greater power. This was one of the terrible dilemmas of science in the modern world. Frost finally rejected the phrase "the great misgiving" as the title of his last book (though the phrase does appear in the book in "Kitty Hawk"), and although he remained fearful of the abuses of science, an important change is evident in his adopting a favorable view of science late in life.

At Bread Loaf in 1959, during a retrospective remembrance, Frost voiced his new or radically modified conviction about the positive role of science in contemporary life:

> It begins with my visit when young . . . to Kitty Hawk, long before the Wright brothers were there. And it ends with its dawning on me that all science . . . is our hold on the planet. . . . But it dawned on me at the point that all, the whole, the great enterprise of our race, is our penetration into matter, deeper and deeper, carrying the spirit deeper into matter. And though it looks like something different out into space, that's just deeper into matter, that's material penetration of the spirit—of the ethereal into the material. Put it that way, and that is our destiny—that is why science is our greatness, it's got to do with our penetration into the material.[23]

Although the first part of "Kitty Hawk" is largely biographical, Frost called part two, which dealt with his lifelong commitment to the dualism of spirit and matter, "the philosophical section" of the poem. He had long claimed for poetry and the creative arts and religion the dualistic interaction between spirit and matter; now, through his celebration of the Wright brothers' invention of the airplane, he extended the creative power of the human mind or spirit to science. This further spiritualization of matter related to what was for modern man "the great enterprise of our race."

Frost believed that the apprehension of dualism in all areas of life, including science, could be attained only with delayed mature experience. Undeveloped youth could not perceive the systematic and universal application of human creativity. Early in his adult life, in his conversations with Sidney Cox, Frost had revealed some highly individualistic character traits that only maturity could harmonize into a general philosophy of life. "Youth . . . I believe should not analyze its enjoyments," he told Cox. "It should live. . . . Criticism is the province of age, not of youth." Cox recorded that in his philosophical thinking Frost did not rely on modern "commentators and systematizers"; instead, he went "always to the original finders and makers: the physicist Bohr for information about the behavior of electrons, Gibbon for his large and daring look and his innocent give-away facts, Mayan explorers, Latin and medieval Latin poets, Darwin in his *Voyage of the Beagle*, Prescott for the conquistadors, Aquinas for a specimen of the way theologians think." Through eclectic knowledge acquired over many years, Frost achieved a kind of intellectual originality that resisted the wholesale adoption of any one philosophy or intellectual movement. He gradually shaped acquired knowledge into elements of a personal philosophy. Cox noted that, according to Frost, "the piecing together comes gradually.... Philosophy that you accept crumbles beneath you when you are exposed to a new situation. It doesn't work then. A truly personal philosophy is a slow growth ... and ... is articulate chiefly in deeds." To Frost, this meant that many isolated strands and facts of knowledge acquired since early in life formed recognizable clusters, as when separate stars perceived at night begin to form patterns. Time is required for unity and continuity to emerge: "Constellations of intention gradually emerge. It is the same for a life as it is for history or for the meaning of a poet's whole work."[24] Just as individual poems and prose statements are recorded piecemeal over many years before they acquire and are perceived to have order and continuity, so too the poet's philosophical beliefs regarding spirit and matter develop until they achieve something like universality. Thus did the organic unity of spirit and matter finally come together in *In the Clearing*. Indeed, even after such a continuity and unity was recorded in complex detail in Frost's final volume, many scholars and literary critics still did not perceive his dualism, much less his extension of it beyond art, the humanities, and religion into the realms of science and social institutions, to the historical evolution of civilization as a whole.

One of Frost's deepest and lifelong convictions was that the whole course of modern civilization began in pre-Christian times in the valley of the Tigris and Euphrates rivers. From there the culture and laws of organized society gradually emerged, moving constantly west and northwest, absorbing the biblical culture of Israel and the classical culture of Greece and Rome, until it included all of Europe, and finally, after the voyage of Columbus, the whole of the western hemisphere. In "Kitty Hawk" he summarized this combined secular and providential view of history:

> *Then for years and years*
> *And for miles and miles*
> *'Cross the Aegean Isles*
> *Athens Rome France Britain*
> *Always West Northwest,*
> *As have I not written,*
> *Till the so-long kept*
> *Purpose was expressed*
> *In the leap we leapt.*

Frost's poetical conception of the history of civilization included, as a single unified event, the discovery of America by Columbus and the invention of the airplane by the Wright brothers. These two separate events consti-tuted an epical leap in man's constant pursuit of his temporal and spiritual destiny.

In one of his poems in *In the Clearing*, "America Is Hard to See," Frost noted the great irony that Columbus himself never understood the true nature and importance of his historical achievement. He then rebuked modern Americans who, even with the advantage of historical hindsight, lacked the imagination and spiritual insight to understand America as part of the epic continuity that connects them both with their ancient social origins and their future destiny. Frost even chided himself that in his youth he had failed to celebrate the godlike gift of Columbus:

> *If I had had my chance when young*
> *I should have had Columbus sung*
> *As a god who had given us*
> *A more than Moses' exodus.*

In his poem "For John F. Kennedy His Inauguration," Frost perceived the Wright brothers as "the Columbuses of the air." He praised "the new world Christopher Columbus found" and explicitly linked it with the future world of space exploration prefigured by the Wright brothers:

> *Everyone knows the glory of the twain*
> *Who gave America the aeroplane*
> *To ride the whirlwind and the hurricane.*

Twenty-two years earlier, in his poem "The Wrights' Biplane" (*A Further Range*, 1937), he had summarized in one line a metaphorical image for mankind's future explorations in space: "This biplane is the shape of hu-man flight." In "Kitty Hawk," Frost fused the historical, religious, scientific, social, and political metaphors that formed his conception of the godlike creativity of human nature that gave shape to Western civilization.

Like Edmund Burke, who saw temporal events guided by man's moral prudence as forming part of "the known march of the ordinary providence of God," Frost regarded truly epical events in history as metaphors of di-vine revelation in the secular affairs of mankind. During a conversation with me at Bread Loaf in 1961, while discussing my book *Edmund Burke and the Natural Law* (1958), Frost said that his agreement with Burke's pol-itics, including his theory of politics, went very deep. He agreed with Burke that historical events that appeared disconnected to many persons really possessed a continuity and ultimate unity in forming Western civilization. To Frost as a dualist, that unity in culture always included a spiritual ordering. He believed that the Wright brothers' invention of the airplane was more than a scientific achievement. It was also an instrument of man's future history. It advanced the new world discovered by Columbus. It extended man's power over physical nature beyond earthly limits into outer space. Thus perceived, science shared with religion and the creative arts the power of the human spirit to penetrate all matter. Perhaps even more than religion and the arts, science was to Frost "the fine point of daring in our time."[25] One of his grand themes in *In the Clearing* was that the original creative power in the mind and spirit of man imitated God. Through the ability of mankind to penetrate and master matter across a broad range of concerns, a vast civil-social order of many civilized nations was created.

Frost's perception of the continuity and unity in historical events came to him through an intuition, or revelation, expressed in "Kitty Hawk": "Then I saw it all." In the final two sections of part two, the "philosophical" part of his poem, "The Holiness of Wholeness" and "The Mixture Mechanic," religion and science are telescoped together in a kind of sacred and secular covenant. Each is perceived metaphorically as a segment united with the other within the whole, much as a particular image or metaphor in a poem suggests the whole. To Frost, man's original creativity, in whatever form, whether consciously or unconsciously, directly or indirectly, shares in the power and purpose of God and therefore is redemptive. Religion, art, science, and all human activities work both separately and together toward the divine and temporal culture that shapes the nature and destiny of mankind throughout history. As the culmination of Frost's articulation of dualism, of the unity of spirit or mind and matter expressed throughout his poetry, prose, correspondence, and conversations with friends, "Kitty Hawk" provides the ultimate continuity and unity, not only in *In the Clearing*, but, in retrospect, in Frost's entire literary career and life.

# Afterword

# Poetry as Revelation

*As a student at Bread Loaf, the author learned the theme of poetry as revelation from Robert Frost. The following remarks were given by the author on November 13, 1962, at the University of Detroit, when Frost received his final honorary degree.*

The cells of the brain, I understand, are about equal in number with the stars in the universe. This analogy of gray matter and star matter suggests to me the nature of poetry as a form of human revelation. This effort of the mind of man to approximate the farthest extent of the universe, this seeking by the terrestrial to reach the celestial, is at the heart of all revelation. All forms of revelation help to personalize the universe for us. In the modern world it is easier for many people to understand revelation in religion, history, or science than in poetry. Perhaps before we consider poetry as revelation, as an imitation of the creative act of God, we might briefly consider the revelations of religion, history, and science. Then we will be in a position to see how poetry differs from these subjects.

As members of the Judaic-Christian tradition, whether Old or New Testament style, or both, whether churched or unchurched, we are familiar with religious revelation and prophecy. All Americans are more or less covenanted; they acknowledge and obey the law of Moses or the law of Christ. Despite the tribulations suffered by religion in the past two thousand years or more, despite the abuses of revelation in Scripture, the core of revealed normative principles remains unimpaired. These principles are the revelations of God to man, which all men of faith and right reason acknowledge. Religion contains the greatest and most inclusive of all revelations, because it involves the ultimate origins, nature, and destiny of man.

History as the temporal course of human events also has its power and value as a source of revelation. History reveals "the known march of the ordinary providence of God." Since we cannot arrive at our moral principles by studying men's actions, but rather use our body of revealed laws to judge the actions of men in history, as revelation history is not a source of principles, but at best it is a preceptor of prudence, teaching men temperance.

Science is Nature's revelation to man, supplementing God's revelations through religion and the record of man's temporal events in history. The revelations of Nature through science include the whole of physical creation, from the vast universe to the minutest record of fossils in the sedimentary rocks of geological ages. Inert physical Nature comes to us readymade. But the endless curiosity of man, which is his greatest intellectual virtue, probes the secrets of physical nature generation after generation. The greatest truths of nature have been revealed to us by our own efforts, through experiments in search of pure or theoretical knowledge. Very little has come to man from science automatically, by default. In our vast universe, to many people, astronomically speaking, man is still the astronomer. In the modern world, science as revelation and prophecy, and practical or domestic science, is so ascendant that it often threatens to usurp the just prerogatives of religion, history, and poetry. A Faustian presumption has often accompanied the attempt of science to lift us above bondage to physical nature. But the achievements of science are still limited to material things.

Poetry in the modern world, as in the ancient and medieval eras, is largely concerned with revealing God, man, and nature to the human race. A finished poem is capable of revealing the deepest insights into the meaning and value of the universe and ourselves. As revelation, a finished poem is so rooted in objective reality that it becomes a new thing, capable of appealing to our senses, our minds, our imaginations and emotions: in short, to our total nature. The revelation is not merely of knowledge, but of love: it involves not recognition only, but response, beginning in ecstatic pleasure and ending in calm wisdom. Between a good poem and a responsive reader there is instant rapport, pure *simpatico*. That is what makes poetry at once undefinable and unmistakable. The value of poetry is like the value of a state of grace—an end in itself. Poetry for its own sake implies that our love of it should be audacious and intrinsic, unmixed by motives of practical utility or the dilettantish knowledge of the culture-vulture.

Poetry as revelation achieves its ends in as great a variety of ways as religion, history, or science. If God writes straight with crooked lines, the poet by indirections finds directions out. One basic way to all poetry is through metaphors which include the whole of reality, in which a part suggests the whole. The opening quatrain of William Blake's "Auguries of Innocence" contains about the best statement I know of how this basic method of poetry works:

> *To see the world in a grain of sand*
> *And a heaven in a wild flower,*
> *Hold infinity in the palm of your hand*
> *And eternity in an hour.*

Until we understand that the revelations of poetry are at least as significant as those of science and history, and quite of an order with the revelations of religion, we shall not do justice to the role or importance of poetry in the modern world.

Sir Philip Sidney, in his *Defense of Poetry* (1595), understood its nature and importance and distinguished poetry sharply from philosophy and history. Philosophy, wrote Sidney, is strong in principles but weak in illustrative examples; history is strong in the concrete examples of human behavior but contains in itself no principles for judging men. But poetry, at its best, is strong both in principles and examples, and it has the further great advantage of being cast in a permanent and unforgettable form.

I would refine upon Sidney's argument as it applies to science. Whereas science *knows* truth, poetry embodies it. Science is like a prism of light cast on a particular point of nature, to reveal its laws and operations; poetry is the sun that shines on all alike, unleashing man's imagination upon the whole creation. That is why it is a mistake to read poetry merely for knowledge, apart from living it.

Like religion and science, poetry depends on faith and belief in its revelations. We must indeed make "a willing suspension of disbelief" if we are to understand the illusions of reality created by the poet. As in religion, we must believe in poetry in order to understand it, and not make our understanding the measure of our belief. Once we as readers make this act of faith, we shall see that the poet has created in his poem a great clarification of life. Poetry, like science, is a way for men to conquer time and space, to draw out the future by believing it into existence, by stretching the lengthened shadow of a man from the beginning of time into eternity.

The ordered beauty of the universe and man, and all that is disordered and tragic, is part of the province of poetry. Man is the chief recipient of Divine creation, and man alone gives meaning to created things. As man existed originally as an idea conceived by God, the universe and everything in it also exists in a meaningful form only to the extent that men grasp its truths through the revelations of religion and science and perceive its forms through poetry, incarnate them in bodies of knowledge or of poems, and transmit them to posterity. In science, the richest accumulation of ages is the laws of physical nature man has discovered and preserved. In poetry our inherited wealth is in the figures of speech, aphorisms and metaphors, contained in our literary traditions.

All honor belongs to those who perfect our forms of revelation—whether theologians, historians, scientists, or poets. The processes of revelation have been with man from the beginning and seem destined to continue till time has stopped. Yet certain mysteries always remain. But it is the glory of human nature that the great mystery of the unknown is constantly being penetrated by life in its most advanced forms. And the further we go into the still unknown the less we can claim for ourselves as individuals. Whatever we contribute belongs to the race. No individual can claim a *personal* ownership in the revelations of religion, science, or poetry. And it is because each of us benefits from all that our inheritance has given us, from each past probe and revelation, that we pay homage to poetry and honor our poets.

# Conclusion

## Part One—Dualism: An Historical Perspective

In 1978, I published "Acceptable in Heaven's Sight: Frost at Bread Loaf, 1939–1941," (in *Frost Centennial Essays*, Volume III), a literary account of 136 pages centered in my first three summers of conversations with Frost at Bread Loaf. I described the events that had brought me to become a student at Middlebury College in 1938, and the help I had received from Paul D. Moody, the president of the college, and from Harry G. Owen, my freshman English teacher, who was also the dean of the Bread Loaf Graduate School of English, help that enabled me to go to Bread Loaf as a student in 1939. My first meeting with Frost, late in June 1939 in Ripton, Vermont, began a friendly relationship that continued through six summers at Bread Loaf and was extended for more than twenty-three years, through many meetings and conversations, until the poet's death in January 1963.

The Bread Loaf School, a branch of Middlebury College, located on a campus in the Green Mountains southeast of Middlebury, has existed since 1920 as a summer school granting a master's degree in English studies. In 1925, the Bread Loaf Writers' Conference was founded and was in session during the last two weeks of August, after the school program was completed. From the time of their founding until his death, Frost was intimately connected with both the school and the writers' conference. Year after year he gave two poetry readings each summer at Bread Loaf, one at the school and another at the writers' conference. After he purchased the Homer Noble Farm in 1939, near the Bread Loaf campus, he spent six or seven months each year on his farm and was deeply involved in the academic and cultural life of Bread Loaf. In time the school and writers' conference came to be so closely identified with Frost, and he with both institutions, that they appeared indistinguishable. As his friend Louis Untermeyer said, "Bread Loaf is the most Frost-bitten place in America." To Frost, Bread Loaf was an ideal cultural community. It combined a magnificent humanized mountain setting with a rich literary tradition and cultural life that was utterly unique in the United States. Frost once referred to Bread Loaf as "our magic mountain," a phrase that came to be widely repeated by the students, teachers, writers, and administrators who shared his affection for Bread Loaf.

As early as the summer of 1939, after several meetings and conversations with Frost, I was made aware in general of his philosophical dualism through his belief in "the two-ness of everything" on earth and his comments on pairs of opposites and his distinction between apparently unresolvable "contradictions" and "contrarieties" that could be harmonized in some degree of unity. Beginning in the summer of 1940, in a series of talks in his cabin on the Homer Noble Farm on poetry, science, religion, education, politics, human nature, and the humanities, Frost's pluralistic or dualistic concept of reality as a combination of spirit and matter perceived as metaphors became clearly evident. By 1944, after six summers of talks, I had gradually come to perceive the extent and complexity of Frost's commitment to a philosophy of dualism. He also made it clear that he had his reasons for rejecting both the Platonic tradition of idealistic monism, which exalted spirit at the expense of matter, and the monism of many modern scientists who made matter the sole basis of reality and rejected the claims of spirit as advanced by religion and the humanities.

After earning an M.A. in English, when I left Bread Loaf in 1944 to attend the University of Michigan, following Frost's advice, I thought that I understood the nature and importance of dualism in Frost's philosophy. But I did not yet know what I did not know of the full range and complexity of Frost's thought. During the five summers of 1940–44, I had noted that the books Frost brought with him each summer to his cabin included Alfred Weber's *History of Philosophy* (1896). Frost had first read this textbook at Harvard in his course with George Santayana in 1898. But the significance of his summer reading of Weber did not dawn on me until years later—that to a great extent Frost's judgments on the outstanding thinkers in Western civilization, in philosophy, theology, science, literature, and history, from the ancient Greeks to his own era, were shaped in terms of the dualist-monist controversies. This applied to his view of the pantheistic Romanticism of Emerson's idealistic monism regarding ethics. It was also evident in his criticism of the monism of matter in the materialism of Hobbes and Marx, and of the methodology of Descartes, as these had been absorbed by Thomas Henry Huxley and transmitted to various Victorian and twentieth-century scientists. From Weber's textbook Frost also learned that in the practical affairs and conflicts of mankind, no philosophical system of thought, including dualism, should ever be treated as an abstract, inflexible, absolute category. His own experience of comedy and tragedy in life, his extensive knowledge of history and literature, his reading and approval of Edmund Burke's politics, and his discussion of religion with friends, including especially with Rabbi Victor Reichert, also confirmed what he had learned from Weber.

Frost's convictions about dualism were clearly confirmed for me in many of his major poems, particularly in his dramatic monologues and dialogues between men and women. His more explicit comments on dualism are also evident in such prose essays as his "Introduction to E. A. Robinson's *King Jasper*" (1935); "The Figure a Poem Makes" (1939); "The Constant Symbol" (1946); and "On Emerson" (1959). The several versions of the "Future of Man" symposium (1959), in Frost's conflict with Julian Huxley's monism of matter, also spelled out his opposed belief in dualism as both spirit and matter. Twenty-three years earlier, in his "Introduction to Sarah Cleghorn's *Threescore*" (1936), he had identified such basic dualistic opposites as "God and the Devil," "the rich and the poor," and "endless other things in pairs ordained to everlasting opposition." These conflicts confirmed his remark in conversation that "everything has its opposite to furnish it with opposition." But in any practical attempt to establish harmony or unity between these dualistic conflicts, none of this wealth of evidence in Frost's poetry or prose contained any instruction on how to resolve, or any warning on how not to resolve, things ordained to everlasting opposition.

A careful rereading of Frost's essay "Education by Poetry" (1930) first made me aware that his dualism and the metaphorical language by which the "play" of the creative mind perceives and mediates between apparently polar opposites never attempts to find or create a final or absolute unity between the dualistic opposites of spirit and matter. Frost's first warning or precaution was centered not in dualism as such, but in the nature of metaphorical thinking, when he noted that "all metaphor breaks down somewhere." Just as metaphors have a breaking point, so too the claims for complete supremacy of either of the elements in a dualistic conflict have a breaking point. A recognition of this fact precludes moral prudence from assuming that one element can or should be triumphant over its antagonist. It is a sign of a superior mind to at once maintain basic principles and conciliate opposed beliefs. The following crucial passage in "Education by Poetry" at once affirms Frost's philosophical dualism and sets a general limit on any attempt to resolve the oppositions between spirit and matter into a final, absolute, unified monistic unity:

> Greatest of all attempts to say one thing in terms of another is the philosophical attempt to say matter in terms of spirit, or spirit in terms of matter, to make the final unity. *That is the greatest attempt that ever failed. We stop just short there.* But it is the height of poetry, the height of all thinking, the height of all poetic thinking, that attempt to say matter in terms of spirit and spirit in terms of matter.

The two italicized sentences have often been ignored, even by literary critics who were well aware of Frost's dualism and sometimes even accepted his dualism.

Precisely what did Frost mean in cautioning that attempts "to make a final unity" in resolving conflicts between spirit and matter must necessarily fail? Why should individuals in their private lives, or leaders in institutions and society, stop short of attempts at final unity? For example, in the perennial conflicts between the contradictions that separate justice from mercy, why shouldn't one prevail totally over the other? As a dualist, Frost believed that it was morally prudent and necessary to mediate between the conflicting claims of justice and mercy, to reach an equitable solution that recognized the legitimate claims of both. A monist would refuse to stop short of aiming at abstract perfection of whatever element he favored. A government dominated by a monistic policy might make such an attempt, but Frost believed that in pursuit of such an object it would create serious civil and economic problems, and that it was doomed to final failure.

Probably the most complex and important pairs of dualistic conflicts occur in the realm of ethics, in the contrarieties of opposed good and evil. Frost's inherited Swedenborgian religion, considerably modified by his reading of William Blake and William James (both educated as Swedenborgians) and by his own personal experience and extensive knowledge of history, had led him to regard good and evil not as abstract opposed fixed categories, but as metaphors that required common sense and moral prudence to reach specific practical resolutions. It was a common mistake of monists, particularly among politicians and theologians, to assume that good and evil are total and irrevocable fixed contradictions. They frequently screened their partisan or sectarian monist premises through national, racial, cultural, or ideological beliefs, and identified absolute good within these frames of reference and absolute evil with things outside of their inheritance. Their melodramatic form of political or idealistic monism was often accompanied with a spirit of fanaticism. This was clearly evident in modern totalitarian ideologies. The propaganda slogans of Nazi Germany—one nation, one folk, one race, one party, one leader—underscored the monistic character of that system of government. The same applied to the materialism and culture of the Soviet Union. In his poem "There Are Roughly Zones," Frost condemned the ideological spirit and absolute dogmatic conception of ethics discussed as politics in the totalitarian regimes, recognizing no bounds, yet he insisted that to preserve civilization basic ethical norms had to be obeyed:

> *What comes over a man, is it soul or mind—*
> *That to no limits and bounds he can stay confined?*
> *You would say his ambition was to extend the reach*
> *Clear to the Arctic of every living kind.*
> *Why is his nature forever so hard to teach*
> *That though there is no fixed line between wrong and right,*
> *There are roughly zones whose laws must be obeyed.*

From personal experience Frost was painfully aware that many persons were addicted to speculations in ideological theories that aim at absolute perfection, perceived in terms of abstract, self-sufficient categories. To Frost, true philosophy was the pursuit of wisdom, but ideology was the corruption of philosophy through sophistry and plausible rational speculations within a monistic set of assumptions. Monism always took a part for the whole, by splitting apart the realms of spirit and matter and then offering simple solutions for the complex problems that dualists perceived in things ordained to everlasting opposition in the problems that afflicted humanity.

Frost distinguished between his own dualism as a philosophy that aimed at preserving and enhancing life, liberty, property, and a humane culture in society within the prescriptive laws and inherited customs of civil society, and the contrary assumptions, beliefs, and objectives of both forms of monism, ideologies that sought universal perfection in human affairs. Idealistic monists made spirit the whole of reality and either denied or denigrated matter. In like manner, as monists scientific positivists made matter their sole reality and either dismissed spirit as a superstition or illusion taught by institutional religion or assumed that it was derived from matter and could be perfected as an intellectual virtue when applied through the methods of the physical sciences to human nature and society.

From his knowledge and understanding of Edmund Burke's political philosophy, Frost was aware that idealistic or "Romantic" monists were modern descendents of the eighteenth-century "man of feeling," whose "sensibility" and primitivism assumed belief in the natural goodness of man. Many ideological idealistic monists were convinced that naturally good human nature could fulfill its potential perfection when bad institutions and tyrannical social conditions were eliminated. Modern monists of matter were also descendents of the Enlightenment, not so much from its Romantic sensibility as from its scientific materialism and Cartesian rationalism. In 1962, in comments on *In the Clearing*, Frost took issue with monists of matter regarding the origins of life. After noting that "I like to mingle science and spirit so deliberately in my new book," he made it clear that unlike monists of matter who preach "the gospel of modern science" and "think that life is a result of certain atoms coming together," he believed that through spirit, life is "the *cause* that brings the atoms together." Although idealistic monists and monists of matter believed that they were at opposite polar extremes, and despised each other, Frost believed that they had far more in common than either of them had with his dualism. They both would "homogenize" mankind into some form of international world order under one political system. They both believed in the idea of "progress" as a law of history, that mankind was moving constantly and necessarily toward a utopian world of universal peace and prosperity, to be realized at the end of historical time. Belief in progress was the chief article of faith not only in both forms of monism, but also in both democratic and totalitarian forms of government. Through socialist policies, democratic government could confuse community life with collectivism quite as readily as a totalitarian regime. In "A Considerable Speck," Frost condemned the sensibility and collectivism in modern society:

> *I have none of the tenderer-than-thou*
> *Collectivistic regimenting love*
> *With which the modern world is being swept.*

Frost's familiarity with Arthur O. Lovejoy's two books made him realize that the revolt against dualism, which evolved during the Enlightenment and was enormously accelerated by Romanticism and scientific materialism during the nineteenth century, had come to dominate civilization during the twentieth century.

*318*

# Conclusion

Viewed within the broad perspective of history and philosophy since the seventeenth century, the conflict between Frost's dualism and the two forms of modern monism is simply an extension of the war between the Ancients and the Moderns over whether religion and humanities or science should be the source of metaphysical beliefs. Since the last half of the seventeenth century, this war had raged with ever increasing ferocity, particularly in France and Britain. Jonathan Swift was a staunch defender of the Ancients, and he had satirized in epical works of fiction and in essays the materialism of Hobbes and deterministic methodology of Descartes, condemning their monistic beliefs and deterministic methods as "the mechanical operation of the spirit." Frost's dualism of spirit and matter makes sharp distinctions between the nature and function of things spiritual and material, so that as metaphors their apparent conflicts could not be resolved in antithetical absolutes, with one or the other being triumphant. To Frost, spirit and matter always supplemented each other. But in contending that the physical sciences are best regarded as a vital part of the humanities, he placed a premium upon spirit over matter. Also, contrary to the assertion of Lawrance Thompson, Frost never opposed science, but only its abuses. As Reginald Cook often observed, "What Frost resented was the intrusion of science into things that aren't science—religion, the arts, and the humanities." In conversations with me, Frost expressed his hope that the modern revolt against dualism would be reversed during the last half of the twentieth century. His hope was merely wishful thinking and was never realized. Twenty years after the poet's death, Roger Sperry published *Science and Moral Priority: Merging Mind, Brain, and Human Values* (1983). His book elaborated the thesis of his Nobel Prize speech in Stockholm in 1981, that the world of humanities, "long rejected by the twentieth-century scientific materialism," must now be "recognized and included within the domain of science." Far from reversing the revolt against dualism, Sperry merged spirit and matter into a holistic unity under the sovereignty of science. In the war between Ancients and the Moderns, this thesis represented the final triumph of the Moderns.

The human desire to find or create some form of monism is so compelling that even the few literary critics who have dealt directly, consciously, or sympathetically with Frost's dualism have revealed their instinctive bias in favor of "the final unity" of spirit and matter in some form of monism. Perhaps the first literary critic to show any public awareness of Frost's dualism was Gorham B. Munson in his essay "Against the World in General," written in 1927 and published in Richard H. Thornton's anthology of essays, *Recognition of Robert Frost* (1937). Munson acknowledged that "in

Frost's poetry we are consistently struck by his acceptance of the dualistic world." Munson assumed that the poet's dualism was based upon his study of the ancient Greek and Roman literary classics at Harvard University that taught him the importance of strict personal discipline and "decorous proportion." From this presumed connection between philosophy and the classicism of ancient culture, Munson leaped to the unwarranted conclusion that Frost was a disciple of Irving Babbitt's "New Humanism." Frost did indeed admire many of the philosophical and literary principles in Babbitt's humanism, but he expressly denied that he was a disciple of Babbitt. Like T. S. Eliot, he did not believe that humanism could be a substitute for religion.

Almost forty years later, Stephen D. Warner published "Robert Frost in the Clearing: The Risk of Spirit in Substantiation" in *Frost Centennial Essays*, volume I (1974). Warner rightly perceived that several poems in Frost's final volume, *In the Clearing* (1962), echoed, refined upon, and were the culmination of such earlier poems on metaphysics as "The Trial by Existence" and "Directive." In particular, "Kitty Hawk" dealt with the penetration of man's spirit into matter in substantiation. Warner observed that although the paradoxes of things in everlasting opposition are not easily resolved, he believed that in the end Frost was able to perceive the whole of life and the universe in its parts through the fusion of spirit and matter, and thus he "saw it all." According to Warner, "Directive" prepared the way for the "risk of spirit in substantiation" in "Kitty Hawk" and other poems in Frost's final volume, so that Frost's metaphysics concluded in a monism of spirit.

Joseph Kau presented a more thorough and historically perceptive essay on Frost's dualism in "Trust . . . to go by Contraries: Incarnation and the Paradox of Belief in the Poetry of Frost," in *Frost Centennial Essays*, volume II (1976). Kau noted the historical and philosophical "dilemma which has plagued the humanist since the birth of the modern era, whether to use religion or science as the guide to metaphysics." More particularly, he wrote that "the dualism of Descartes, the pantheism of Spinoza, and the materialism of Hobbes" were too simple and therefore hard to accept by humanists in the twentieth century. Already Kau is involved in two errors. He accepted the common belief that Descartes is a dualist, whereas Frost rejected this interpretation of Descartes and believed that he was simultaneously a monist of matter in his methodology and a monist of spirit in his theology. To Frost, two monisms did not add up to his dualism. Kau's other error was his assumption that Frost was a secular humanist but not a theist, even though the poet affirmed his theism time and time again.

# Conclusion

Kau divided modern poets into humanists who necessarily split over the differences between religion and science. His neat abstract antithetical categories identified how poets may be classified: "science and religion have divided the loyalties of the modern humanist; on the one hand is the theism of Eliot and on the other the materialism of Stevens." He identified Frost as inhabiting the middle region between Eliot's religious faith and Stevens's atheistic materialism. Kau's category arbitrarily assumes that religion and science are necessarily antithetical and that Frost's position involves him in an "ambivalent" metaphysics. He asserts that this makes Frost a spiritual drifter and at times even an agnostic. Kau is himself so ambivalent about his category that he backs off and first contends that Frost is "not a rigid agnostic" and then asserts that if all "human knowledge is limited to experience, then Frost is hardly agnostic." Finally, he notes that Frost "accepts the spiritual nature of things on faith: he is not at all agnostic."

All of Kau's confused speculative maneuvering could have been avoided simply by accepting Frost's statements that he never doubted a belief in God and that he held agnosticism in great contempt. As a philosophical dualist regarding spirit and matter, he did not set religion and science against each other; instead he could "trust . . . to go by contraries" and mediate through metaphors on ways that could harmonize religion and science, and not create rigid categories that set them against each other. But Kau's addiction to abstract categories and rigid logic reached a climax when he examined Frost's poems called "Cluster of Faith" in *In the Clearing*. He observed that "the incarnation theme" by which spirit enters flesh logically makes spirit and matter "essentially one," and therefore the universe is unitary. On this basis he asserts that Frost "proceeds to dismiss the traditional dualism of spirit and matter" and is a pantheist.

Each of the three ideological explications of Frost's dualistic metaphysics, by Munson, Warner, and Kau, violated the poet's warning in "Education by Poetry" against attempts "to make the final unity" by resolving things ordained to everlasting opposition into a monism. All three critics failed to "stop just short there." They ignored Frost's statement that every metaphor has a breaking point. They persisted in rational speculations that sought a simple monistic answer to the complex conflicts within dualism. When no such answer was forthcoming from Frost, they accused him of being "a spiritual drifter." In short, they lacked the moral prudence, humility, and mature wisdom that can come from historical experience, and they refused to accept Frost's belief that many conflicts between things in opposition that afflict mankind may be ameliorated, but have no final solution in an absolute unity. To Frost, such ideological and monistic thinking as was reflected in the three critics of his dualism was evidence of the sweep toward political and social collectivism in the twentieth century and was the result of the general revolt against dualism so graphically portrayed by Arthur O. Lovejoy. Although the result of the triumph of monism was most evident in the totalitarian systems that brought such tragedy to the twentieth century, the two forms of monism were also evident, though to a lesser degree, in the social and economic thought in the politics of democratic nations in Europe and America.

Frost was aware that many physical scientists aimed at creating a wholly monistic rational world order such as was described by Aldous Huxley: "for science in its totality, the ultimate goal is the creation of a monistic system in which . . . the world's enormous multiplicity is reduced to something like unity, and the endless succession of unique events of a great many different kinds get tidied and simplified into a single rational order." This type of monism was the result of the bifurcation of human nature and physical nature into separate and antagonistic realms of spirit and matter, from the time of Descartes to the modern era. Its aim was the complete mastery over physical nature through science, which would result in "progress" in the conditions of man's life in society that would bring about a utopian world order. But mastery over physical nature had to be extended to total sovereignty over human nature and the course of history, and this could be done only through total control by a political ideology. This, in brief, was Frost's explanation of the rise of modern totalitarian systems such as Nazi Germany and Soviet communist Russia. The imperial ambitions of Japan, and to a certain extent those of Britain, the United States, and other nations, also made some form of monist thinking an element in their politics.

For almost fifty years Frost maintained a close literary friendship with Louis Untermeyer, a convinced Marxist whose sympathies with communist Russia never wavered. Although during the Second World War, when Britain and the United States allied themselves with Russia to defeat Germany, Frost referred to Russia as "our dubious allies." In a postwar letter to Untermeyer on January 9, 1947, the poet reviewed the ambiguous relationship in their friendship: "We start so far apart that it would be a wonder if we ever got together. . . . We'll probably end up all one breed one world and word. . . ." Frost concluded this letter in language that echoed his "Introduction to Sarah Cleghorn's *Threescore*": "The bones and struts that hold things apart are softening or rusting away and the muscles and guy wires are pulling us into a small ball. Our last differences are disappearing in saccharine agreement." By 1947, Frost believed that the revolt against dualism was fast becoming the triumph of monism.

Yet Frost maintained his adherence to a dualist philosophy and was consciously aware that this separated him from Untermeyer's political monism as a Marxist. In a letter to Untermeyer on November 25, 1936, he claimed to distinguish between the various forms of modern totalitarian politics: "I can tell you off-hand the difference between a Communist and a Fascist and even between a Nazi and a Fascist. Much discrimination has made me mad at people I don't side with." In 1940, during a conversation with me in his cabin, Frost defined the differences he perceived between a Nazi, a Fascist, and a Communist. The politics of German Nazis harmonized culturally with ancient Teutonic mythology and combined nineteenth-century German Romanticism with the tough mechanized discipline of Prussian militarism and with a sense of nationalism that assumed the racial superiority of Germans as the highest development of human nature through evolution. The Italian Fascists thought of themselves as in the classical tradition of the Roman Empire. But their militarism was softened by the rituals of their religion and the humanism and art of the Renaissance. These cultural influences made them far less fanatical than the Germans. The ideology of Russian communism was rooted in the antireligious materialism of Marx and aimed at establishing a worldwide utopia through international revolution. Whereas Fascism retained some aspects of dualism, both the Nazi and Communist forms of totalitarian politics rejected spirit in favor of matter and scientific technology and were wholly monist in their philosophical premises. Frost's distinction regarding modern forms of political absolutism was confirmed for me by Daniel Gasman's *The Scientific Origins of National Socialism: Social Darwinism in Ernst Haeckel and the German Monist League* (1971). Yet the poet never succeeded in disabusing Untermeyer of his belief in Soviet Marxism.

### Part Two—Dualism: A Contemporary Perspective

Probably the most important single tragedy in Frost's career as a poet, and in his intellectual life, was that in 1939 he selected Lawrance Thompson to be his so-called "official biographer." He had first met his future biographer in 1925 after a poetry reading at Wesleyan University where Thompson was an undergraduate student. By 1939 Thompson's academic credentials appeared to be very sound, and he had shown some sensitive appreciation of Longfellow as a poet, which met with Frost's approval. Three years after his appointment, his book on Frost's poetry, *Fire and Ice* (1942), revealed an understanding of the forms and techniques in Frost's poetry, but he paid almost no attention to how metaphorical language was related to the poet's philosophical beliefs. This was enough for Frost to express his initial disappointment in Thompson, and in his biography Thompson neglected any serious consideration of Frost's metaphors in dealing with spirit and matter as pairs ordained to everlasting conflicts. When Frost said, "Trust me on the poetry, but don't trust me on my life," he meant not only to have strong reservations about what he said about himself, but also what his biographers, both before and after Thompson, had to say about him. The great deficiency in all of Frost's biographers, and in many of his literary critics, was an inability or refusal to deal with his philosophical dualism and the conflicts contained within his metaphorical thinking.

So much criticism has been written regarding Thompson's reasons for presenting Frost as a moral monster, an egomaniac, a social Darwinist who despised the poor, and a hater of science, among other such deficiencies in character, temperament, and beliefs, that it might appear superfluous to reconsider this subject. But several generations since Thompson's biography appeared, Frost continues to be vilified in the mind of the common reader. Even literary critics and academics still take much in Thompson's judgments on Frost at face value, so that the usual explanations of what went wrong in the Frost-Thompson relationship are clearly deficient.

Perhaps the most common error is in the assumption that since Thompson accumulated a mountain of detailed empirical facts and information about Frost, he knew the poet well and therefore his value judgments are well-founded. But this assumption, like that of value-free descriptive sociology, ignores the truth that false conclusions can be drawn from valid facts. Many intelligent persons knew Frost far longer and better than Thompson and came to radically different conclusions about his character and beliefs. The simple-complex nature of Frost, and his philosophical dualism, involved far more than was understood from empirical data. The ever-increasing animosity between Thompson and Frost was also more complex than their differences in temperament. It has been claimed that Thompson was provoked to revenge because Frost provided biographical materials to Elizabeth Shepley Sergeant and that Thompson's infatuation with neo-Freudian psychiatric theory and analysis was crudely applied in retrospect to Frost. These and other such explanations of Thompson's hatred of Frost touch surface dimensions of the problem but do not penetrate to the heart of the flawed biography.

Perhaps the most pertinent question that readers of Thompson's biography need to ask themselves is how intellectually qualified he was to understand and deal with Frost's dualistic philosophy and with his beliefs regarding the partial resolution of contrarieties through the mediation of metaphorical language. The answer to that question may depend upon determining Thompson's own philosophical orientation and, if he was a monist, whether he or any monist can understand the complexities of Frost's dualism.

To a certain extent the excellent but consciously limited revisionist biographies of William Pritchard and Jay Parini have corrected some of the most serious flaws in Thompson's work. Pritchard noted that Thompson had practically no sense of metaphor and that his literal-mindedness seriously limited his understanding of Frost's poetry and thinking processes. Parini extended Pritchard's criticism and observed that Thompson had almost nothing to say about Frost's poetry. Robert Pack has explored Frost's beliefs and uncertainties in ways that far transcend Thompson's methodology. Other writers such as Lesley Lee Francis, Edward J. Ingebretson, Robert B. Hass, George Monteiro, Lisa Seale, Donald G. Sheehy, and John Evangelist Walsh have corrected particular errors in Thompson's biography. All of these writers have concluded that Frost was neither a saint nor a villain, only that he possessed many of the common strengths and weaknesses in human nature. But the philosophical basis of Frost's character and beliefs, centered in his dualism and metaphorical thinking, was not explored by these writers. This omission has allowed monists to accept Thompson's harsh negative portrait of Frost through several generations of readers to the present.

One of the basic characteristic traits of monists is the literal-mindedness and humorless method of treating conceptual ideas as an abstract and fixed absolute category, held without regard to the specific context of the time, place, or circumstances in which ideas are stated. Thompson's biography of Frost illustrates this monistic trait time and time again. For example, Thompson knew that Frost was harshly critical of some social reforms passed by Franklin D. Roosevelt's New Deal. From this general fact, and from Frost's defense of laissez faire as freedom in economics, he leaped to the conclusion that the poet was a social Darwinist who despised the poor and condemned all social reformers. When Frost praised Sarah Cleghorn as a harsh critic of child labor laws and approved of her program of reforms, Thompson concluded that he was being satirical or hypocritical, that he did not mean what he said.

The same method of reasoning was applied to Frost's introduction to E. A. Robinson's *King Jasper*. Since Frost had said some critical remarks about the poetry of Edgar Lee Masters and Carl Sandburg, Thompson had concluded that Frost envied and despised all contemporary poets as competitors. When Frost praised Robinson as a poet, therefore, he disguised his envy and hatred and was hypocritical. The same fallacious reasoning led him to review Frost's *A Masque of Reason* not as a closet drama consistent with religious orthodoxy, but as a satire on religion. Thompson was baffled to learn that Frost was furious about his review. He went to Bread Loaf and asked Rabbi Victor Reichert to explain why Frost was so angry with him. Reichert told me that he spent an afternoon clarifying Frost's religious beliefs to Thompson, who finally admitted that he had completely misunderstood Frost's play. But because Thompson's lifelong monistic processes of thinking could not easily be altered or eradicated, from Reichert's instruction he learned nothing of permanent value that would provide a better understanding of Frost's philosophical dualism.

What kind of philosophical monist was Lawrance Thompson? His irrationally severe criticisms of Frost reveal that, like Descartes, he held fast to a double monism. He simultaneously but separately adhered to a monism of matter that endorsed modern science—even in its mechanistic logic, methodology, and positivism—and also held to an idealistic monism of spirit in the tradition of Plato and Emerson. This double monism made Thompson a psychological Dr. Jekyll and Mr. Hyde. He could make a false and irreconcilable antithesis between two elements in a conflict of spirit and matter, arbitrarily choose either one, and condemn the other to total exclusion. Frost's adherence to a religious belief could thus be construed *a priori* as a rejection of science. The poet's belief that justice preceded mercy in human affairs was interpreted as a narrow Puritan bias that meant he lacked charity or mercy to the poor, and that therefore he was a moral monster. In many of his judgments on Frost, Thompson shuttled back and forth arbitrarily between his two forms of monism.

Thompson's double monism created a remarkable range of ambivalent views on Frost's dualism and metaphysical beliefs. On the one hand, in his chapter centered in Frost's ethical beliefs, called "Yes, I Suppose I Am a Puritan," he acknowledged Frost's dualism, but he also contended that Frost was inclined toward monism:

> In saying repeatedly that he was a dualist in his thinking and a monist in his wishing, he liked to stress the old truths that man has two natures, physical and spiritual, that there are two mutually antagonistic principles in the universe, good and evil, that the world is ultimately composed of, and explicable in terms of, basic entities such as mind and matter. . . .

After this accurate summary of Frost's dualism, Thompson added: "but . . . he was at least emotionally sympathetic with anyone like Plato who made the leap beyond the dualism of the known to the all-controlling 'One' of the unknown." Immediately following this qualification, he quoted and explicated Frost's "mood poem" called "I Will Sing You One-O."

Thompson misinterpreted Frost's hymn to God's oneness by treating it not as an expression of the poet's faith in monotheism, but as evidence that Frost himself was emotionally a monist. This misinterpretation confuses the whole perception of the universe as understood by God as its creator with the earthbound and limited understanding of the cosmic order by human nature. Thompson begged the whole question of the difference between dualism and monism by assuming that the supposed dichotomy between the poet's mind and emotions catapulted him toward being a monist. Frost himself stated that in creating a poem the product was "a thought-felt thing." This implied that the creative process was dualistic and harmonized rather than separated in the poet's thinking and feeling. A conflict between thinking and feeling would result in a failure to create a poem. But Thompson's explication of Frost's metaphysics involved yet a second error. He ignored the poet's belief that no system of dualism or monism can ever be pure and absolute. Frost had learned this from Alfred Weber's *History of Philosophy*, his textbook at Harvard University. Weber stated that historically there had never been a monistic or pluralistic system in any absolute sense, because even the most convinced monists accept a relative dualism and conversely the most determined dualists acknowledge some claims of monism. This fact of history is quite distinct from Thompson's claim that Frost was emotionally inclined toward monism.

During the summers of 1961 and 1962, when I was on the faculty at the Bread Loaf School of English, I learned in conversations with Frost and Victor Reichert that they had both tried for about a decade to educate Thompson about dualism, but without success. The close fusion of Frost's dualism with his conception of the function of metaphorical thought, and his eclectic habit of harmonizing conflicts, was simply too difficult for Thompson to understand. His biographer's book, *Melville's Quarrel with God* (1952), had provided Frost with a good opportunity to contrast his dualism with the metaphysics of both Emerson and Melville. He wrote to his biographer around May 1, 1952, and noted that evil is not merely the absence of good, as Emerson believed, but was intrinsically real in itself as Melville contended in *Billy Budd*: "Emerson's God included evil as just some more good and Melville couldn't stomach Emerson." Frost tactfully praised some aspects of Thompson's study, but he noted that his biographer interpreted Melville's thesis in *Billy Budd* as being that he believed in a God that he hated. To Frost, this meant that according to Thompson, Melville ended by confounding God and Satan: "How could he have failed to see he had got round by a series of insensible cog-slips to where he should have changed God's name to Devil? He seems rather weak on the brain side." Thompson's interpretation of Melville's theme in *Billy Budd* profoundly disturbed Frost. He became fearful that in his biography Thompson would present him in the same way that he had understood Melville's confusion of God and the devil, a confusion dictated by Thompson's double monism.

With a deep sense of desperation, Frost turned to Stanley Burnshaw, his final editor at Holt, and uttered his pathetic cry of anguish: "I'm counting on you to protect me from Larry. Remember!" Burnshaw's response to this desperate appeal was a book-length study, *Robert Frost Himself* (1986). Unfortunately, it appeared sixteen years after the second volume of Thompson's biography *Robert Frost: The Years of Triumph, 1915–1938*. As an *ex post facto* defense of Frost's character it did little to dispel Thompson's fictitious public image of the poet as a moral monster. Burnshaw's book is an autobiographical account of his long career in publishing and editing and includes much about Frost besides its discussion of the flaws in Thompson's biography. Burnshaw's long chapter "The Fabrication of the 'Monster Myth'" describes accurately and in detail the process of alienation that developed in the Thompson-Frost relationship. Although it clarifies the neurotic contradictions in Thompson's character, and his unbounded faith in psychoanalysis, it does not mention Frost's dualism or Thompson's monism. Thus it omits the philosophical basis of their conflicts that Frost believed was so important in Thompson's failure to understand him.

To receive the most profound insights and enduring revelations in Frost's poetry, readers need to understand his dualistic beliefs regarding the great virtues and severe limitations in both human nature and the universe. Readers also should stop short of expecting any final answers to the natural conflicts built into the physical and moral universe. Frost believed that because of the finite and fallible nature of man, and the moral corruptions that accompany political power and money, ultimate archetypal "contrarieties" have no absolute solutions, at least not on earth. The concluding lines in "Our Hold on the Planet" well express Frost's modest positive view of how human nature relates to the planet earth:

> There is much in nature against us. But we forget:
> Take nature altogether since time began,
> Including human nature, in peace and war,
> And it must be a little more in favor of man,
> Say a fraction of one per cent at the very least,

*Or our number living wouldn't be steadily more,*
*Our hold on the planet wouldn't have so increased.*

Frost's dualistic beliefs never satisfied monists who aimed at perfection in human affairs, in a restored Garden of Eden or future utopia through science, but they were a far more valid statement of reality.

Man's life on earth is the stage for the dualistic drama that plays out the trial by existence for each person, to the final tragedy of death. The indifference or even hostility of nature to man precluded any belief by Frost in Wordsworth's early pantheism; he found no sermons in stones nor good in everything. He rejected the Romantic idealism of Emerson's transcendental ethics. Earth is not a Disney World where the lion and the lamb lie down together in peace. The Christian equivalent of Emerson's fatuous Unitarian optimism and sensibility was in people Frost dubbed "New Testament sapheads." He agreed with Darwin's principle that every species of life, including man, competes fiercely for survival. Earth is a hard place in which to save the soul. Frost once remarked that the earth itself is liable to the fate of meaninglessly being broken off, so that the idea of "progress" through science, leading to utopia, was an impossible dream. In short, he rejected a monism of matter as emphatically as he did a monism of spirit.

As a metaphor, earth provides the physical setting for the human drama of the "trial by existence," but the plot actions of the drama and its themes, both for comedy and tragedy, come from the character of human nature itself. Earth provides the material dimension and orientation for Frost's dualism, but such things as creativity, moral courage, the power of will, rational understanding, and the role of love are the elements in the spirit of human nature that combine with earth as matter in the poet's dualism. Frost's inventory of beliefs—self-belief, love-belief, art-belief, national-belief—are all somehow related to God-belief. Late in life Frost identified love as "passionate preference" as "a Biblical thing," one of the unsolved mysteries that connects mankind with God. To Frost, love was like the theological concept of grace in religion, a free gift of God to man, a power that lifts the deepest instincts and intuitions of human nature above mere lust.

In many of Frost's poems, earth and love together form the dual basis in the spiritual drama of human temporal existence. He insists that "Earth's the right place for love," not some idealistic transcendent realm. An idealistic swinger of birches may aspire toward heaven, but he always returns to earth. True love knows that "we love the things we love for what they are," knowing and accepting them with all of their flaws and imperfections. Frost believed that love is blind to the faults of lovers. He agreed with

Shakespeare that "love is not love / which alters when it alteration finds."
But like every virtue, love can fail or be corrupted. A misplaced love can do
infinite harm to a lover's life. Romantic idealists, who "think with the heart
and feel with the mind," have a burning yearning for the high ineffable,
which Hollywood exploits in sentimental fictions. Frost's epitaph, "I had a
lover's quarrel with the world," is an appropriate climax for his ambiguous
themes on the imperfect dual unity of love and earth.

Perhaps one of the best ways to understand Frost's dualism, and the substantive themes in his poetry, is by a conscious awareness of the role of
love in relation to the setting provided by the planet earth. A comparison
between "Two Look at Two" and "The Most of It" provides the range of
Frost's metaphorical treatment of the love-earth relationship. In "Two Look
at Two," the very title and the line "two had seen two, whichever side you
spoke from" reflects the double dualism of how the human couple as lovers
perceive the doe and then the buck, their metaphorical equivalents in nature, and in turn how they are perceived. The poem opens and closes with
the word "love," so that it illustrates what Frost meant by "Earth's the right
place for love." What unites the human couple is their sharing of experience
with nature apart from conflicts in survival. After a series of increasing revelations regarding nature, from "this is all" to "this, *then*, is all," "this *must* be
all," and finally "it *was* all," the poem concludes with a reciprocal response
from earth, that "in one unlooked-for favor . . . earth returned their love."

In sharp contrast, "The Most of It" begins with an isolated individual in
a primitive setting. The protagonist "thought he kept the universe alone."
He seeks "counter-love, original response," but like Adam before Eve he
finds no human reciprocal relationship. Instead, the stark image of the
powerful buck "pushing the crumbled water up ahead" and upon land-
ing forcing the underbrush, teaches him that the most a universe without
love can provide is a desert place, a wilderness of raw impersonal power,
without meaning. The concluding phrase, "that was all," echoes the very
language of "Two Look at Two," but its meaning is the very opposite. Instead of increasing revelations and significance, the protagonist learns that
without reciprocal love the universe is indifferent and hostile to man, capable of inspiring terror. A variation of the same theme, but in a modern
and supposedly civilized setting, is in "An Old Man's Winter Night."

In private conversations with friends, Frost seldom mentioned his own
poems. But on one occasion in his cabin he suddenly became surprisingly
confidential and stated that among all of his poems "To Earthward" held
a unique place. He compared the theme in this poem with that of William
Blake's two early volumes of poems, *Songs of Innocence* and *Songs of Experi-*

*ence*, and he noted that roughly the same relationship was to be found in comparing his poems in *A Boy's Will* and in *North of Boston*. The subject of "To Earthward" is divided exactly into two parts: the first four stanzas deal with "love at the lips," sensory and sensual youthful love; the final four stanzas, on the "pain / and weariness and fault / of tears, the aftermark / of almost too much love," culminate in tragedy and death. During a poetry reading at Bread Loaf, I observed that when someone asked Frost to read "To Earthward," he was visibly shaken, responded with silence, discreetly ignored the request, and quietly said another poem. "To Earthward" was such an emotionally powerful personal poem that it was too painful for him to say it in public.

In matters of form and technique, particularly in the use of colloquial language, Frost encouraged a comparison of himself with Wordsworth. But in substantive matters such as religion, philosophy, and artistic creativity, there is need of a study comparing Frost with William Blake, for their similarities and differences. Like Frost, Blake was a dualist, as is most explicitly evident in *The Marriage of Heaven and Hell*, in which he explores such dualistic polarities as love and hate, creative energy and reason, and heaven and hell, and in "showing the two contrary states of the human soul." Whereas Blake remained a lifelong Swedenborgian and a full-blown mystic, Frost gave up much of his Swedenborgian faith, yet believed in its mysticism. To inspire his poetry, paintings, and engravings, in probing the mysteries of the universe Blake's cosmology looked to "messages from heaven" that existed beyond "the sea of time and space" toward eternity and infinity. In contrast, Frost was far more secular and scientifically oriented, yet he retained a religious mysticism that he absorbed and infused into the spirit of his poems as piety. Both Blake and Frost believed that human creativity is a form of love, released as a spiritual energy from the God-like power of gifted and courageous men and women. During the 1940s, by way of compensating for what he had abandoned in the Swedenborgian religion, Frost discussed religion with Rabbi Victor Reichert. He came to admire the "Classical" Jewish prophets, beginning with the Book of Amos, and he acquired a fondness for making prophecies about modern life, many of which proved to be wrong. But in identifying himself as "an Old Testament Christian" Frost undoubtedly owed much to Reichert.

In reading Frost's poems, it is not enough to limit oneself to critical considerations of form, technique, and the phonetic tones and semantic patterns in colloquial and metaphorical language. Important as these elements are, they are not ends in themselves, but at best the instrumental means to perceive how a poem is "loaded with ulteriority." In such substantive concerns as meaning, one of the most recurrent themes in Frost's poetry is the perennial conflict between justice and mercy. It is significant that in his first poem on that subject, "Love and a Question," Frost came to no final resolution. The question posed is whether a bridal couple should practice charity and thereby allow a passing stranger to "mar the love of two / by harboring woe in the bridal house." In answer to that question, the poem concludes, "the bridegroom wished he knew." Frost's point, that there is no easy or final solution to such complex and ambiguous contradictions, became the touchstone for many of his poems on such dualistic conflicts. Critics who demand final answers, such as Yvor Winters, may condemn Frost as "a spiritual drifter," but Frost held firmly to his spiritual beliefs and had his solutions without becoming a monistic fanatic.

In "Bond and Free," Frost's most abstract statement on ambiguous conflicts, the question is between the claims of love and thought. Love is identified as the feminine "striving in the world's embrace," firmly anchored on earth, in contrast to the masculine addiction to ideological explorations of the universe. This conflict is also left unresolved. Frost not only distinguished between philosophy as the pursuit of wisdom and its abuse as abstract speculative ideology, but his dualism also enabled him to philosophize concretely about human nature and its problems in the spirit of common sense and the experiences of man's life on earth. To Frost, artistic creativity ranked far above the kind of analytical reason that characterized so much ideological theory. He agreed with Wordsworth in "The Tables Turned" that as creative artists "we murder to dissect." In "Bond and Free" he noted that like Icarus, who flew too high and had his wax wings melted by the sun, the ideologue often returns to earth with the "smell of burning on every plume," or he may plunge to his death. It is significant that "Bond and Free" is directly followed in *Mountain Interval* by "Birches," where Frost proclaims that the "Earth's the right place for love." Earth is also the best setting for both poetry and philosophy. Aristotle recognized this far better than Plato, which was why Frost as an earth-bound dualist always preferred Aristotle to his mentor. In *A Masque of Reason,* the line "You don't catch women trying to be Plato" is a tribute to the innate wisdom of women in clinging to earth and thus avoiding the pseudo-intellectual errors of ideology. In short, Frost was one of the most philosophical and least ideological American poets of the twentieth century.

Apart from "The Lesson for Today" and Frost's other reflective poems in the Horatian vein, his dramatic dialogues and monologues provide the best sources for revelations on his dualism, metaphorical language, and philosophical views of spirit and matter. The differences between men and women regarding their perceptions of the universe, and the nature and degree of their love or lack of love for each other, are recurrent dramatic vehicles for illuminating the range of conflicts and possible partial resolutions of the most basic problems that face human nature.

For example, keeping in mind Frost's dualism and conception of how metaphors function, readers would do well to compare how the couples in "West-Running Brook" and "Home Burial" perceive their conflicts and ultimately resolve them. In "West-Running Brook," the wife is so completely subjective, so highly personal and egocentric, that she identifies herself as metaphorically married to the brook as well as to her husband; philosophically she is essentially a Romantic or idealistic monist. In going by contraries against her pathetic fallacy, her husband is basically a monist of matter. In his metaphysics he perceives the flow of the brook, and all of physical nature, in objective and highly intellectual scientific terms. The bridge that binds them and enables them to define and explore their differences, and finally to harmonize what they both said, is their love and affection for each other. Their final harmony consists of two distinct ways of perceiving the same reality. This was the very same principle that Frost held in his belief that religion and science do not necessarily contradict each other but supplement each other.

In sharp contrast with "West-Running Brook" regarding earth as a setting and love as the best vehicle for harmonizing conflicts is the dramatic situation in "Home Burial." The very title is ambiguous and refers indirectly to the death of the couple's marriage as much as it does directly to the burial of their dead infant. The conflict of the couple is emotional and psychological before it is intellectual and philosophical. The wife's sensibility cannot accept the mortality of human nature that includes the tragedy of early death. Her former idealistic monism has been shattered as an illusion, replaced by a disillusioned cynicism and hysterical neurosis that finds no meaning in life, including her husband. She is outraged by his crude stoical temperament and literal-minded acceptance of mundane matters in daily life, including how he takes the death of their child. His psychology reflects a confused monism of matter. Every phrase they speak, every action they make, is at cross purposes. Their total lack of love creates a psychological impasse and absence of mutual sympathetic understanding that cannot be resolved. Without love they cannot harmonize their differences.

The best way for readers of Frost to understand his beliefs, and to appreciate his art as a poet, is to approach his poems with a conscious awareness of his dualism, and without expectations of finding final or absolute solutions to the major problems faced by mankind. Such an approach to

Frost is long overdue. Because he knew that his dualism was rooted in the common sense of everyone's experience, and that to be understood did not require a highly specialized intellectual methodology or aesthetic theory, he held the common reader of his poetry in high esteem. His pervasive dualism was often assumed and therefore unvoiced. Yet it provided a profound personal mythology about life and human nature that was shared by any intelligent, sensitive, and literate reader.

At the core of many of his poems are the two simple assumptions that earth is the setting for the trial by existence that everyone experiences and that love can be the best means of partly resolving the common conflicts of human nature. Frost's dualism is most explicitly evident in such major works as "The Death of the Hired Man," *A Masque of Reason* combined with *A Masque of Mercy*, and "Two Tramps in Mud Time." But a more quietly assumed and implicit dualism is in such monologues or dialogues as "Snow," "In the Home Stretch," "The Generations of Men," "The Hill Wife," and "A Cabin in the Clearing." There is a dualism even in such lyrics as "Fire and Ice," "All Revelation," and "A Passing Glimpse." Indeed, a great many of Frost's poems are best understood in terms of his dualism.

But one major impediment remains in strong opposition to a dualistic reading of Frost's poetry and philosophy—the persistence of both forms of monism in the assumptions, thinking processes, and aspirations of many people in the modern world regarding reality and human destiny. Frost was well aware of Arthur O. Lovejoy's thesis in *The Revolt Against Dualism* (1930) that the enduring tradition of Romantic idealism as a monism, and especially that the growing dominance of the physical sciences and technology in modern education and culture, militated against belief in a dualist-centered view of human nature and the universe. To counter these idealistic and scientific forces of monism, and their respective monomanias, Frost contended that the physical sciences are best regarded as a part of the humanities. During the summer of 1940 in Bread Loaf, when I put the question to him of how the twentieth century would be best regarded in history, Frost predicted that it would be remembered as having finally determined the proper limits of the physical sciences and the methodology of Descartes, and that science would no longer provide the intellectual norms by which to judge the humanities, the creative arts, and traditional religion. This was Frost's essential solution to the epical conflict between the two cultures in modern civilization.

In June 1961, when I returned to Bread Loaf to teach, I asked Frost whether he still believed in his prophecy of 1940. He commented that in his recent experience with the scientists during the "Future of Man" symposium (1959), they all expressed belief in science and technology as the redeemer of mankind in solving its economic and social problems, and that a one-world government would bring universal peace and security to the world. Such a development would assure the triumph of a monism of matter at the expense of the humanities, the creative arts, and traditional religion. Frost admitted that he had engaged in wishful thinking in 1940 and that there were no signs that his prediction would come true. He feared that the two monisms would combine and continue to dominate the culture of modern civilization. During talks with Frost during the summers of 1961 and 1962, I found that he was still strongly agitated by his conflicts with the scientists on the panel of "The Future of Man." He was long familiar, and somewhat amused, by Bertrand Russell's constant shuttling back and forth in several books between the two monisms, before he finally chose to believe in a monism of matter. He regarded Ashley Montague as a humanist who was simply confused. As a social biologist, Montague had conceded far too much to the value-free descriptive form in the methods of modern sociology. Frost was appalled by Hermann Muller's case for scientific genetics. He believed that such a development would destroy the passionate preference in normal love that was so necessary to at least partly resolve basic human conflicts. But his chief criticism was directed against Sir Julian Huxley's Marxist materialism and belief in one-world government, apparently to be dominated by an atheist metaphysics.

Frost's criticism of the scientists during "The Future of Man" symposium was based upon the same conviction as Aldous Huxley in his satire on a brave new world dominated by science and a totalitarian form of world-government. Such a development would utterly dehumanize the culture and politics of modern civilization. Frost did not live long enough to encounter Roger Sperry's *Science and Moral Priority: Merging Mind, Brain, and Human Value* (1983), with its thesis that the humanities should be wholly subordinated to "the domain of science." But in light of his experience with the scientists during "The Future of Man" panel, Frost would not have been at all surprised.

Certainly, from the years immediately following World War I, Frost was more directly concerned with politics than with science as the most immediate serious threat to the traditional culture of the humanities as the basis of a healthy civilization. The Romantic idealistic form of a monism of spirit advanced a sentimental and collectivist conception of political socialism that ignored the moral and intellectual corruptions that political power so often released in human nature. Historically, Frost was aware of this danger from his knowledge of the French Revolution. In the ideological policy of the radical Jacobins who organized and ran the Reign of Terror, and in the imperial ambitions of Napoleon that followed, Frost detected Rousseau's doctrine of compulsory social benevolence as necessary in order to force nations to be free. In France it took the form of a unicameral form of government in a National Assembly that had no checks or balances, a single legislative body that prohibited any parties other than the Jacobins. In Napoleon's imperial military dictatorship it took the form of a foreign policy that sanctioned war upon all the nations of Europe to compel them to accept the French revolutionary form of democracy. The result was decades of constant total war in Europe. The German and Russian forms of political totalitarianism that emerged after World War I took their essential principles from the French Revolution. The Nazis through military conquest and the Soviet Union through its militant foreign policy to provoke revolutions around the world had in common their respective attempts to dominate the world in accordance with their two conceptions of a universal utopian world order.

In proposing "to make the world safe for democracy" through the League of Nations, Woodrow Wilson first made Frost aware that American democracy could fall prey to the same kind of ideological delusions that had afflicted the French Revolution and modern totalitarian politics aimed at establishing world government. There was to Frost no essential difference between the Soviet Comintern and an American foreign policy that might use military means to force any nation to model itself upon American democracy, assuming that it was the norm for world government. Frost's criticism of the fate of Woodrow Wilson and the League of Nations was his prelude to a lifelong opposition to ideological proposals for a world government:

> It's a sad story—one of the saddest in history. . . . I weaken now at the thought of him fallen with a crash almost Napoleonic. He had caliber, he saw as vastly as anyone that ever lived. He was a great something, if it was only a great mistake. And he wasn't merely his own mistake. He was the whole world's mistake . . . as much the whole world's as was Napoleon or Alexander. Some might think his failure was in missing a mark that someone to come after him will hit, but I suspect that it was worse than that: he missed a mark that wasn't there in nature or in human nature.

After the Second World War, Frost's criticism of Wilson and the League of Nations carried over into his condemnation of the United Nations. In a letter to Louis Untermeyer in October 1957, after defending the freedom and sovereignty of individual nations, Frost wrote:

Wilson's League of Nations was a pretty dream, but it was based on an absurdity and it was bound to go to pieces. The United Nations is worse. It was formed out of desperation, and desperation never solved anything—it can't solve a situation or make enemies love each other or stop nations from dominating and making war.

Frost maintained that there was no such thing as a citizen of the world. What he feared most was that some American president with an ideological vision of democracy would follow a foreign policy to compel other nations to conform to the American model. Such a disaster could come from the leader of either political party. Pursued by military means, such a foreign policy could plunge the United States and many other nations into chaos and self-destruction.

Frost's criticism of what he called "the tenderer-than-thou / collectivistic regimenting love / with which the modern world is being swept" was in essence his condemnation of the politics of a monism of spirit. It gave force and justification for the international politics fostered by a monism of matter sponsored by some physical science thinkers. The monism of spirit was an abuse of religion, just as the monism of matter was an abuse of science. Both monisms exhibited the monomania of fanaticism that characterized modern totalitarian thought. No sound culture or healthy civilization worthy of the name could be built upon either monism, much less on a combination of both monisms. Frost's assessment of the modern revolt against dualism did not lead him into cynicism or despair for human nature. He was essentially a man of faith in all of his beliefs, and as he observed in "Education by Poetry," all of man's beliefs regarding man are somehow related to his belief in God. As he concluded his poem "Good-by and Keep Cold," "But something has to be left to God."

# Some Afterthoughts in the Life, Poetry, and Philosophy of Frost

In Robert Frost's high school valedictory address, "A Monument to After-Thought Unveiled" (1892), he stated that "after the strife of action" is over, "the long after-thought . . . of one action is the forethought of the next"; that "the poet's insight is his after-thought," so that "the greatest of his ideas come when the last line is written." The same belief regarding poetry applies to every serious and insightful work of scholarship, literary criticism, and biography, so that in light of this study of Frost as a poet-philosopher some fresh after-thoughts are possible for future studies of the poet's life, art, and thought. The problem of understanding Frost as a man, a poet, and a philosopher necessarily requires taking into full account his dualism of mind or spirit and matter. Since most of Frost's biographers, scholars, and literary critics were either unaware of his dualism or failed to recognize its nature and importance, recognition and valid understanding of his dualism reveals the great need of a radically new approach to every aspect of his life and poetry. In a letter to Bernard De Voto (October 20, 1938), Frost wrote, "My philosophy, non-Platonic but none-the-less a tenable one, I hold more or less unbroken from youth to age." His lifelong adherence to a philosophical dualism provides the means to a counter-revolution on traditional grounds for new and original studies of Frost.

It is significant that in the twenty-four years between the publication of *A Boy's Will* (1912) and *A Further Range* (1937), practically no attention was paid to Frost's dualism by any biographers or critics of his poetry. The first important collection of critical reviews was Richard H. Thornton's edition of fifty-two essays, *Recognition of Robert Frost* (1937). Only one literary critic in this collection showed any awareness of Frost's dualism. Gorham

B. Munson's essay "Against the World in General" had appeared in a slightly different form in *The Saturday Review of Literature* (March 28, 1925) and was reprinted from his book *Robert Frost: A Study in Sensibility and Common Sense* (1927). In his essay, Munson noted that "in Frost's poetry we are consistently struck by his acceptance of the dualistic world."[1] According to Munson, dualism is the inevitable result of empirical observation:

> The end reached by observation as a method, whether it is a poet or a scientist who employs it, is dualism—that is, a set of axioms and laws founded on distinctions. The distinctions are based on appearances and both they and appearances are treated as reasonably final data . . . but the fundamental truth or error of dualism is not plumbed. At any rate, whether or not the real world is dualistic, the apparent world is.[2]

Munson's conception of dualism is wholly in the tradition of Descartes and involves a tissue of confusions because of a failure to distinguish between the physical realm of spirit in human nature. His "observation as a method" limited to empiricism applies to physical science, but the poet's observations transcend physics, mathematical reason, and logic and include intuition and the creative imagination as well as empirical experience in describing the emotional and intellectual world of men.

The title of Munson's essay, "Against the World in General," was borrowed from two lines in Frost's poem "New Hampshire": "I may as well confess myself the author / Of several books against the world in general." In what sense was Frost opposed to the general condition of the modern world? Munson's answer to that question was that "he was writing books against the world in general because he was trying to be a good Greek in New England." More specifically, Munson referred to Frost's studies of the ancient Greek classics at Harvard and concluded that "This classicism of spirit . . . set him apart form the 'New Poetry' movement that flourished from 1914 to about 1925." He argued that "Frost's classical tendencies" and his "feeling for decorous proportion" and "common sense" resulted in his "several books against the world in general." Munson's explicit thesis was that "the purest classical poet of America today is Robert Frost," that his classicism set him apart from Ezra Pound and T. S. Eliot and the "New Poetry" of the free-verse movement because it was combined with his New England Puritanism and individualism. In the end, Munson identified Frost's dualism with the "New Humanism" of Irving Babbitt and a rational-classical vision of life that is neither Romantic nor religious.

# Some Afterthoughts...

Apart from how badly Munson garbled Frost's understanding of dualism, he made some valid points regarding the poet's admiration of the ancient Greek classical principle of moral prudence or temperance, and the strong case for self-discipline, character, and order by the New Humanists. Although Frost shared these traits with them, he was too independent to be a disciple of Babbitt, and his critical strictures against the modern world in general were not merely literary but personal and philosophical. During the summers of 1940 and 1941, in his cabin on the Homer Nobel Farm near Bread Loaf, on several occasions in talks with me he quoted the opening quatrain of Matthew Arnold's sonnet "Immortality":

*Foil'd by our fellow men, depress'd, outworn,*
*We leave the brutal world to take its way,*
*And, Patience! In another life, we say,*
*The world shall be thrust down, and we up-borne!*

In October 1962 at the National Poetry Festival in Washington, D.C., he repeated these lines.[3] In Frost's many futile attempts to achieve recognition for his poetry, against the neglect he endured from the world in general, Arnold's quatrain summarizes well his patience and his final triumphant success.

But ironically, the title of Munson's essay, "Against the World in General," was far more profound than he knew: it included a philosophical dimension regarding Frost's dualism about which Munson was wholly unaware. During the early decades of the twentieth century, especially following the First World War, Frost adhered to his philosophical dualism of mind or spirit and matter while the modern world in general, as Arthur O. Lovejoy observed in *The Revolt Against Dualism* (1930), was abandoning dualism in favor of the two forms of monism. Although spiritual monism existed in many individuals in the modern world, the far more common forms of monism resulted from "getting science on the brain," which manifested themselves in the "bursting rapture" of a monism of matter in such economic and political systems as Soviet Marxism and German nationalist Nazism. Both of these forms of modern totalitarianism confounded community with collectivism and justified their claims to absolute political power by appeals to sensibility and social consciousness. In "A Considerable Speck," Frost separated himself completely from the fanaticism and collectivism of post–World War I economics and politics:

> *I have none of the tenderer-than-thou*
> *Collectivistic regimenting love*
> *With which the modern world is being swept.*

In talks with friends, Frost maintained that the Constitution of the United States prevented the American republic from following the totalitarian systems of Europe during the crisis of the great economic depression and the Second World War. His criticism of Franklin D. Roosevelt as too power hungry in his "New Deal" programs and in seeking the presidency four times is perhaps best understood in light of his concern to maintain constitutional restraints upon political power even during periods of great crisis. Although Frost once said that the American republic was "a Christian adventure into materialism," he never sanctioned the triumph of a monism of matter, but maintained a dualism in which both spirit and matter prevailed.

Despite Frost's explicit rejection of Babbitt's "New Humanism" and his identification of Emerson as a monist, Gorham Munson persisted in identifying the poet's dualism with Babbitt and Emerson. In his book *Making Poems for America: Robert Frost* (1962), in what was essentially a biographical approach to Frost's poetry, in his chapter "How About Being a Good Greek?" Munson identified Emerson's lines about the human law and the law for things with the New Humanism:

> *There are two laws discrete*
> *Not reconciled,—*
> *Law for man, and law for thing;*
> *The last builds town and fleet,*
> *But it runs wild,*
> *And doth the man unking.*

Munson then explicated Emerson's lines as follows:

The doctrine drawn from these lines is called dualism. Dualism is a twofold view of man and the world. The dualist sees man as made of two elements—a human element and a natural element—spirit and matter. This dualistic doctrine of two laws, one for man and one for thing, had attracted a number of followers, mostly in the universities, who were, as one might say, spoiling for an argument with the leaders of American literature in the 1920s. The New Humanists said that this had been a de-

cade of revolt. They called the leaders of the revolt Romantics
and charged that they followed the law for things.[4]

It is highly ironical that Munson came so close to understanding Frost's
dualism, by being perhaps the first critic to perceive it; yet by intruding
extraneous matters from Emerson and the New Humanism he ended by
garbling the poet's understanding of dualism. To Frost, Emerson's monistic moral idealism and the New Humanists' attacks on Romanticism had
nothing to do with dualism as he understood it.[5] Munson's failure even
to mention the two forms of monism that Frost regarded as contrary to
dualism led him to ignore the poet's conviction that many scientists were
complete materialists who denied the existence of spirit. Their monism of
matter placed them at the opposite extreme from Emerson, whose conception of nature and monism of spirit in its idealistic ethical dimensions
came close to denying the existence of matter.

The inadequacy of Munson's explication of Frost's dualism is most evident in the limitations of his understanding of the depth and range of the
poet's criticism of much that was dominant in the modern world. Frost's
alienation was not limited to a literary conflict with "free verse" and Pound
and Eliot, nor to personal discontent with the world's neglect. It included
that whole range of profound philosophical differences in belief between
his dualism and the practical cultural inadequacies of both spiritual monism and material monism. Frost believed that not merely in poetry, but
in painting, music, and all of the creative arts, monism of the spirit was a
source of aesthetic and ethical corruption through much of the twentieth
century. The destruction of form and the celebration of anarchy, so evident
in "free verse," were found in all of the arts; the false theory of aesthetic
freedom was accompanied by an equally false conception of realism that
often degenerated into what Frost called "sewer-realism." The most extreme corruption of the arts was manifested in the mechanistic and vulgar
forms of art as anarchy in popular entertainment.

To Frost, both religious monists and materialist monists in their
most extreme forms were characterized by what he called "monomania
or monometaphor." Whether as a spiritual monism or a monism of matter, Frost contended, monism was an attempt to explain the whole of life
through a single passion or metaphor. During the early decades of the
twentieth century, in the general revolt against dualism, the absolute fanaticism of monism was most evident when it took the form of politics,
economics, nationalism, social sensibility, and racial theory in totalitarian
movements.

But Munson was only the first of many literary critics and scholars of Frost's poetry and philosophical beliefs to distort and misrepresent the poet's deepest held convictions about human nature and the meaning of life and reality. Five years after Munson's essays "Against the World in General" appeared in Thornton's anthology, Lawrance Thompson published *Fire and Ice* (1942). His study of Frost was divided into three parts: "Poetry in Theory," "Poetry in Practice," and "Attitude Toward Life." In the first section of his book, Thompson described and commented quite accurately on how Frost understood the general nature and function of poetry. This was followed by his account of how the poet practiced his techniques to create form, in such subjects as "the sound of sense," "the function of metaphor," "meter, rhythm, and rhyme," "the sense of humor," and "irony and satire." Thompson's statements were essentially valid but incomplete observations and reflections, such as future literary critics were to develop much more thoroughly in many studies.

But in the final section of *Fire and Ice*, dealing with Frost's normative principles in his beliefs and disbeliefs, the official biographer of Frost revealed an almost incredible philosophical incompetence. His intellectual orientation in a confused monism was clearly at variance with the poet's flexible dualistic view of life and complex view of human nature: a rigid fundamentalist temperament and literal-minded mentality devoid of a sense of metaphor was evident in some explications of Thompson's subjects and themes. Implicit in some passages of *Fire and Ice*, a perceptive reader could surmise, were tiny germs that were to grow into the biographer's final condemnation of the poet as a moral monster. For more than a decade after *Fire and Ice*, Thompson remained on quite good terms with Frost. But increasingly his monistic beliefs, rooted in the Cartesian tradition of reason and science, in Enlightenment assumptions regarding knowledge, in his sympathetic adherence to the secular views of what Frost called "the three generations of Huxleys," and above all in his late infatuation with Karen Horney's *Neurosis and Human Growth* (1950), which convinced him that her account of the neurotic personalities applied perfectly to Frost, resulted in a complete alienation from the poet.

It is significant that in tracing out Frost's youthful basic metaphysical beliefs regarding spirit and matter, and the complex personal problems he encountered, Thompson identified Descartes and Emerson as the two most crucial influences that shaped "the course of his nonaesthetic, or moral, life":

Frost was not fooling himself. The rational parting away which brought Descartes to his major premise finally stopped when the psychological reduction had reached that point where the activity of the emotional desire was stronger than the activity of the rational negation. So it was with Frost, who arrived at an arbitrary major premise which balanced for him the affirmations of the emotion and negations of the reason.[6]

Independent and rebellious against all easy answers, Frost threw his skeptical criticism against any careless affirmations. Like Emerson, he made a principle out of nonconformity in his early days and declared that there was nothing more sacred than the integrity of his own heart and mind. For him no final questions were resolved by viewing the world from the position of religious or philosophical monism or dualism.[7]

In essence, grotesque or ludicrous as it may appear, Thompson explained Frost's early ambiguous philosophical orientation by engrafting Descartes' initial doubts and skepticism and his subsequent discursive geometrical reasoning and logical determinism in arriving at absolute certainty regarding his existence, upon Emerson's nonconforming idealistic individualism. To complete this incongruity, he simultaneously dismissed monism and dualism as irrelevant factors in determining possible answers to the problems of belief regarding spiritual reality or physical phenomena. Finally, he contended that because as a young man Frost could not resolve the conflicts between emotional faith and skeptical reason, he retained "a strong religious faith" and "an equally strong religious agnosticism."[8] It would require many pages of explication to unravel Thompson's tangled web of confusions; a brief summary of a few crucial points will have to suffice.

Whatever unresolved beliefs Frost may have had as an adolescent, as he matured soon after high school graduation he became more and more sure of all that he thought was true regarding his beliefs and disbeliefs on important subjects. This was especially true as applied to his explicit and frequent identification of himself as a dualist, and his rejection of both a monism of matter in the tradition of Descartes and a monism of spirit in the tradition of Emerson. Contrary to a widely held belief, Frost rejected the interpretation of Descartes as a dualist. He believed that Descartes' methodology was valid when applied to the physical sciences, but totally invalid when applied to religion, the arts, education, and the humanities.

The same applied to Descartes' conception of reason: geometrical logic and analytical reason applied well in measuring quantitative physical phenomena, but they were destructive when applied to human values that derived from the spiritual nature of man, in such subjects as art, religion, and the humanities. Frost distinguished between nature and human nature and also between reason as discursive logic and mathematical analysis and reason as part of the creative process of intuition and imagination, a normative conception of reason that dealt with ethical and aesthetic values, with what is good or evil and beautiful and ugly, and not simply with what is descriptively true or false. As Lisa Abshear-Seale has shown in her excellent article "What Catullus Means by *mens animi*: Robert Frost's 'Kitty Hawk,'"[9] Frost's conception of poetry was centered in a fusion of emotion and reason, in how their separate identities supplement each other, not, as Thompson assumed, in their total alienation and contradiction. Frost's dualism enabled him to make clear distinctions between physical phenomena and science as opposed to ethical and aesthetic values. It prevented him from creating an absolute and irreconcilable conflict between such differences as emotion and reason that forced him to choose one and to reject the other, as happened under either form of monism.

Perhaps nothing illuminates the intellectual and moral grounds of Frost's dualism as clearly as his rejection of Descartes' methodology, his conception of logical reasoning as discourse, and his materialistic and mechanistic understanding of human nature. Since all of these Cartesian elements are also found in the philosophy and view of science of Thomas Henry Huxley, Frost's criticism of "the three generations of Huxleys" is best understood as his indirect rejection of the entire Cartesian system of thought as applied outside of science and advanced since the seventeenth century. There can be no doubt that Huxley was a completely devoted disciple of the French mathematician and philosopher. In his address "On Descartes' 'Discourse Touching the Method of Using One's Reason Rightly, and Seeking Scientific Truth,'" delivered to the Cambridge YMCS on March 24, 1870, Huxley expressed his exalted view of the epical importance of Descartes' philosophy in the realm of modern thought:

> There are some men who are counted great because they represent the actuality of their own age, and mirror it as it is. Such a one was Voltaire. . . . But there are others who attain greatness because they embody the potentiality of their own era, and magically reflect the future. They express the thoughts which will be everybody's two or three centuries after them. Such an one was Descartes.[10]

More specifically, Huxley summarized the essential achievement of Descartes: "The memorable service rendered to the cause of sound thinking by Descartes consisted of this: that he laid the foundation of modern philosophical criticism by his inquiry into the nature of certainty."[11] But Frost believed that "the cause of sound thinking" ended when Huxley assumed that "the nature of certainty" acquired through Descartes' methodology through the scientific study of matter carried over into the realm of spirit or mind, in such subjects as religion, ethics, poetry, and the humanities.

Huxley addressed the philosophical basis of Descartes' thought in light of the conflict between the two essential elements—mind or spirit versus matter. Because both mind and matter are involved in any perception of reality or the phenomena of external nature, like many interpreters of Descartes (but unlike Frost), Huxley denied that Descartes was essentially a material monist. In the introduction to Huxley's *Man's Place in Nature* (1906), Oliver Lodge, the editor, accepted Huxley's defense of a broad-based Cartesian philosophy that included idealistic principles. He claimed, therefore, that Huxley "entirely repudiated materialism as a satisfactory or complete philosophical system."[12] Lodge's essential evidence for his interpretation consisted of a passage from Huxley in which he expressed his conditional apparent agreement with Bishop George Berkeley's idealistic criticism of Thomas Hobbes's materialism:

> If the materialist affirms that the universe and all its phenomena are resolvable into matter and motion, Berkeley replies, True, but what you call matter and motion are known to us only as forms of consciousness; their being is to be conceived or known; and the existence of a state of consciousness apart from a thinking mind is a contradiction in terms.

> I conceive that this reasoning is irrefragable. And, therefore, if I were obliged to choose between absolute materialism and absolute idealism, I should feel compelled to accept the latter alternative.[13]

Lodge evidently accepted Huxley's statement as a rejection of a belief in absolute materialism and mechanism. Lodge's conclusion ignored Huxley's conditional phrase, "If I were obliged to choose," and translated Huxley's passage as evidence that he was not an absolute materialist.

Frost's extensive reading in the voluminous publications of Huxley[14] led him to the opposite conclusion. For Frost, no conditional "if" existed in Huxley's hypothetical and fictional view of Berkeley's idealism, because he was wholly and intensely convinced that reality consisted entirely of matter. The poet was actively aware that Huxley was a very skillful propagandist, and that to disarm his opponents in religion and idealistic philosophy he frequently presented a public image that made him appear sympathetic toward aspects of their beliefs. Frost knew Huxley's *Man's Place in Nature* (1863) and his article "On the Physical Basis of Life" (1868), but the evidence for Frost's belief that Huxley, like Descartes, was a material monist was clearly evident in his *Lay Sermons* (1870).

In that work Huxley argued that because "the soul becomes a center of force . . . the distinction between spirit and matter vanishes." On the assumption that mind is derived from matter he went on to write that "Descartes' physiology, like the modern physiology of which it anticipates the spirit, leads straight to materialism." Huxley accepted Descartes' belief that animals are "mere mechanized machines," and he committed himself wholly to this dimension in Descartes' philosophy:

> I hold, with the Materialist, that the human body, like all living bodies, is a machine, all the operations of which will, sooner or later, be explained on physical principles. . . . I am prepared to go with the Materialists wherever the true pursuit of the path of Descartes may lead them.[15]

Huxley's commitment merely confirmed what he had stated seven years earlier, in a letter to Kingsley (May 22, 1863), on how he categorized his metaphysical orientation among "only four possible ontological hypotheses":

| | |
|---|---|
| I. | There is no X = Atheism on Berkeleyan principles |
| II. | There is only one X = Materialism or Pantheism, according as you turn it heads or tails. |
| III. | There are two X's, spirit and matter = Speculators |
| IV. | There are three X's, God, souls, matter = Orthodox theologians |

As an agnostic, Huxley believed that none of these hypotheses was an established fact; "but," he noted, "No. 2 is the one I can work with best. . . . [I]t chimes in better with the rules of the game of nature than any other of the four possibilities."[16] Frost believed that Huxley did not merely prefer No. 2; he made it the cornerstone of his entire philosophy of life.

Frost's critical response to Huxley's agnosticism, and the manner in which many literary critics perceived the poet on this important subject, is central to any valid understanding of his philosophical beliefs. During a lecture at a meeting of the Metaphysical Society, Thomas Henry Huxley invented the word "agnostic" to describe his method and belief in his approach to metaphysical problems. Afterwards he successfully propagandized the public acceptance of this term among the circle of his supporters, a meritocracy of scientists, scholars, and political leaders, a closed society within the larger order of Victorian respectability. But he also precipitated a violent and sustained public controversy among orthodox religious contemporaries, a war that extended to the criticism of agnosticism by Robert Frost. Among the many critical essays of Victorian writers,[17] two in particular reveal remarkable similarities with Frost's criticism of Huxley's agnosticism. R. H. Hutton in "Professor Huxley on Agnosticism" in *The Spectator* (February 9, 1889), and its sequel, "The Great Agnostic," noted that Huxley "gloried in being an agnostic"; that he "made a sort of creedless creed of agnosticism"; that it was his "confession of faith." Hutton quoted Huxley that "skepticism is the highest of duties; blind faith the one unpardonable sin," and that "the man of science has learned to believe in justification, not by faith, but by verification." But the one essay that includes much that Frost said about agnosticism was by William Hurrell Mallock, "'Cowardly Agnosticism': A Word with Professor Huxley," in the *Fortnightly Review* (April 1889). Mallock noted that Huxley's agnosticism is not only a method but a creed, and as such it includes an ethical dimension. In "Science and Culture," Huxley wrote that "the assertion which outstrips evidence is not only a blunder but a crime." As an evolutionist he believed that the actions that most people regard as sinful are merely what is involved in the struggle for existence.

To Frost, "agnostic" was Huxley's "signature word," because its assumptions, methods, and conclusions filled everything that he wrote about science, religion, education, and society. It would be easy to fill many pages with the poet's direct and indirect critical remarks on agnosticism, but a few of his most explicit statements will have to be sufficient:

> My greatest prejudice is against an agnostic. He doesn't believe either way. He's just afraid to believe—afraid to disbelieve and afraid to believe. Just agnostic. I saw somebody whose book ended with an agnostic prayer. It's nauseating.[18]

> The one thing I consider a curse is to be an agnostic. Don't say, "We don't know." We know a hell of a lot.[19]

> Belief is better than anything and it is best when rapt, above paying its respects to anybody's doubt whatsoever.[20]

> The logic of everything lands you outside of it. The logic of religion by nice gradations outside of Catholicism in Protestantism, outside of Protestantism in agnosticism, and finally outside of agnosticism in Watsonian behaviorism.[21]

During a poetry reading at Bread Loaf (June 30, 1958), Frost noted that "my annoyance with some words sets me off . . . and one I've thought a great deal of is my antipathy to the word *agnostic*. I know what's the matter with that. . . . I thought just the other day . . . historically speaking I'm a Congregationalist." To which a lady replied that she was an atheist. "I said: Well, thank God, you're not an agnostic." And she said: "I had a suspicion you'd feel that way about agnostics." Frost refused to "go into that, it would take all the rest of the evening."[22] Frost concluded that through "all the years by the Huxleys—the three generations of Huxleys"—his "antipathy to the word agnostic" remained constant. He knew that Sir Julian Huxley was a declared atheist, not an agnostic like his grandfather, and he was far less harsh in his criticism of Julian Huxley, because an atheist is a believer—he believes there is no God, whereas an agnostic lacks the moral courage to believe in anything except his own doubts.

To Frost agnostic doubts and skepticism had their roots in the premises of Descartes' methodology in the search for certainty in knowledge and truth, and the antithesis of all such doubts was in faith or belief, in the moral courage required to believe events into existence. In his thematic poem "Beech," in *A Witness Tree*, Frost asserted that even in a world dominated by doubt basic truths based upon faith can be ascertained:

> *Thus truth's established and borne out,*
> *Though circumstanced with dark and doubt—*
> *Though by a world of doubt surrounded.*

Frost believed that it was far better to adhere to a belief, even one of dubious merit, destined to defeat, than to be triumphant in an agnostic victory. In the final lines of "An Empty Threat" he expressed this conviction:

*And, "Better defeat almost,*
*If seen clear,*
*Than life's victories of doubt*
*That need endless talk talk*
*To make them out."*

Without mentioning Huxley's agnosticism specifically, these lines are an indirect indictment of his methodology, based upon doubt, and his conviction that nothing should be accepted as true until it is ascertained by empirical and rational verification. To Frost, Huxley's agnosticism was "not the latest creed that has to be believed," but merely "a concept self-conceived." But perhaps Frost's strongest criticism of Huxley's agnosticism was in his rejection of the Victorian scientist's belief that rational deliberation upon thorough knowledge was sufficient to enable mankind to come to valid conclusions on which to act in determining its destiny.

Frost was aware of Huxley's letter to Lady Mary Welby (November 27, 1888), in which he castigated people who acted upon insufficient knowledge and judgments with results that were disastrous:

> Surely no one but a born fool can fail to be aware that we constantly, and in very grave conjunctions, are obliged to act upon extremely bad evidence, and that very often we suffer all sorts of penalties in consequence. And surely one must be something worse than a born fool to pretend that such decision under the pressure of the enigmas of life ought to have the smallest influence in those judgments which are made with due and sufficient deliberation. . . . These considerations go to the root of the whole matter.[23]

To Huxley, "the root of the whole matter" of knowledge and decisive action was to avoid being ignorant fools where knowledgeable agnostics fear to tread. But Frost detected a serious flaw in Huxley's argument. The scientist assumed that abundant knowledge and the intellectual virtues were sufficient in solving the practical social problems of mankind. Huxley's error, like Plato's formula that "Knowledge is virtue," ignored Aristotle's insistence that knowledge and virtuous action are required in practical decisions. Such moral virtues as courage and a disciplined will, combined with belief, are necessary beyond knowledge and the intellectual virtues. As Frost said, "I'm not the kind of man who thinks the world can be saved by knowledge; it can only be saved by daring, bravery, going ahead."[24] Contrary to Huxley's agnosticism, Frost insisted that "You should go ahead on insufficient information"[25] and that "You're always believing ahead of your evidence,"[26] because "what fills up the knowing is believing." What was worse, Frost believed, was that although science cannot deal with ethical principles, Huxley still assumed that no meaningful knowledge existed outside of the methods pursued by the physical sciences.

Although Frost's extremely harsh criticism of T. H. Huxley's initial systematic doubt, which Huxley adopted from the methodology of Descartes and which led to his agnosticism, is clearly evident in Frost's abstract statements condemning agnosticism, the full and intense emotional depth of his hatred of Huxley's central principle is best perceived in the poet's indirect criticism, when agnosticism is a specific element within the context of a tissue of human beliefs and achievements. In July 1941, during an extended conversation on agnosticism with me in his cabin on the Homer Noble Farm, Frost condemned agnosticism as "cowardly equivocation." He then proceeded to praise self-belief, moral courage, and a strong, disciplined will as the most admirable character traits in human nature, and as I noted in 1941, he connected these traits with great enduring achievements:

> According to Frost, Milton's greatness as a man and a poet rested on his faith in himself and in his moral courage. His best poems are his shorter, earlier ones, and *Samson Agonistes*, but in *Paradise Lost* Milton proved his courage to the world.

> Wasn't it a thing to marvel at, Frost remarked, that the two greatest epics in our literature were composed by poets who were blind. What incredible feats of courage Homer and Milton performed. Frost's voice became filled with pathos as he said: "Isn't it a sad world when courage is the supreme virtue in man?" I objected that for a poet talent must be supreme, because without talent all the determination in the world would not get him anywhere. Frost conceded that talent was essential, yet he insisted that the reverse was also true—that talent without courage would not make a poet. Without courage all of our other virtues, including our literary talents, become merely theoretical. Writing a poem is primarily an act of self-faith and courage. And failure in writing is largely the result of a lack of faith and courage. No real agnostic could ever write a true poem, said Frost. Writing the

first line of a poem involves a commitment by the poet, and every line thereafter is an act of disciplined will, of courage and faith that he can run the whole course to the finish line and believe the poem into existence. When young writers quit, is it more often a failure of nerve, not of talent.

Frost extended his argument on courage beyond literature to the whole of life. Men should be firm and courageous in their commitments in everything—in love and marriage, in religion, art, politics, and loyalty to their country and their friends. Agnosticism paralyzes the will and makes men cowards. Better a convinced theist or atheist than an agnostic. I remarked that John Henry Newman compared being an agnostic to standing on one leg forever. Frost responded that was what our political agnostics, the liberals, often did. They couldn't make up their minds and therefore were weak and indecisive as leaders. It was no excuse to say that we didn't know enough yet to take a firm position. It isn't a question of knowing, but of believing and acting. Even the best informed men act from insufficient knowledge; often we can believe our knowledge into existence sufficiently well to take action. Agnosticism is a miserable kind of neutrality about the most crucial questions of life and death.[27]

To Frost, the classic example of how agnosticism paralyzed the moral will, and prevented decisive action in the face of public duty, was the abject failure of George B. McClellan, the federal Civil War general. Even when he outnumbered his enemy forces by more than two-to-one and possessed superior equipment and an advantageous field position, McClellan showed that he was a spiritually hollow man and refused to engage the Confederate army. In total contrast, Frost noted, General Ulysses S. Grant persisted in his attacks on enemy forces and positions even when he was at a great disadvantage, and that kind of courageous decisiveness made him a great military leader.

During several talks with me, without going into particulars, Frost observed that Huxley's monism, materialism, and agnosticism involved him deeply throughout his adult life with "all things German,"[28] but especially in his views on religion, science, and education. To do full justice to his observation would require an independent study. Here it is sufficient to limit Frost's insight to a summary of the scientist's intimate professional involvement with the German biologist Ernst Heinrich Haeckel (1834–1919) and to Huxley's crucial role in making physical science and its methodology paramount in modern higher education.

In a letter of October 28, 1862, Huxley initiated his friendship with Haeckel, a professor of biology nine years his junior, at Jena University. He praised a monograph by Haeckel and sent him some scientific specimens. Over the next five years they corresponded and developed a strong personal and scientific intimacy that grew and endured until Huxley's death in 1895. Although there were some slight differences between Huxley's intense agnosticism and Haeckel's militant atheism, their common philosophical orientation based upon a monism of matter and unbounded belief in the methodology of the physical sciences made the substance and spirit in their polemical writings practically identical. Both men were scientific positivists and regarded the physical sciences as the only source of valid or useful knowledge in every field of study. Haeckel's racial theory assumed that Germans were the supreme development in the evolution of man, and this belief probably made him a far more extreme social Darwinist than Huxley,[29] but both men believed that social "progress" required that European civilization should be placed upon a scientific basis.[30]

Haeckel's massive two-volume work *Generelle Morphologie der Organismus* (1866) confirmed Huxley in his own scientific and philosophical beliefs and converted him into an ardent disciple of his young German friend. His discipleship extended itself beyond science and philosophy into Huxley's views on human nature, religion, education, and culture. He praised Haeckel's "attempt to systematize biology" and agreed with his highly original thesis regarding the mechanism by which changes in species took place within the process of evolution. Huxley expressed his basic agreement with Haeckel and noted how greatly they both differed from other scientists and the world in general: "men . . . like you and I stand pretty much alone, and have a good deal of fighting to do in the external world."[31] Huxley pronounced Haeckel's study one of the greatest scientific works ever published. In his *Lay Sermons, Addresses and Reviews* (1870), he noted that Haeckel's "morphology [is] that which concerns itself with function," and he modeled his own understanding of the process of changes in species far more upon that of his German friend than upon Darwin's principle of "natural selection" which, he contended, remained unproved. Regarding the essential principles of evolution theory, Mario A. di Gregoria observed: "Haeckel was more successful than Darwin in convincing Huxley."[32] Haeckel assumed the same role in Germany as the chief defender of Darwin's theory that Huxley had assumed in Britain, but both men differed radically from Darwin regarding the mechanism for changes in species. But Darwin was highly useful to them in advancing their own agenda that science should dominate all subjects in the modern world, including religion and education.

As Daniel Gasman has noted, in order to encompass the laws that govern physical nature, human nature, history, and culture, Haeckel simply carried over his radical material monism into his version of evolutionary theory and into every area of man's knowledge:

> Through evolution he studied the world and everything in it including man and society as part of an organized and consistent whole. He therefore called his new evolutionary philosophy "Monism," and contrasted it with all of traditional thought, which he rather disdainfully labeled "Dualism," condemning the latter for making distinctions between matter and spirit, and for invidiously separating man from nature.[33]

In contrast with Darwin's statement to Haeckel, "your boldness . . . sometimes makes me tremble," Huxley endorsed the German scientist's monism and condemnation of dualism, and he identified Haeckel's non-Darwinian thesis as "the evolution-hypothesis" he agreed with, "the mechanical or mechanistic, homogeneous or monistic view of the universe: in a word, Monism."[34] The complete antithesis between the dualism of Frost and the monism of matter held by Haeckel and Huxley is as absolute as any such polarities can be, because they exist on a philosophical level. As applied to scientific theory, even on that level of understanding, as several scholars have noted, there is much distortion: "the Germans understood Darwin and Darwinism through the distorted lens of Haeckel. When the Germans refer to Darwin, more often than not they in fact mean, not Darwin, but Haeckel and his monist philosophy."[35] Haeckel's perversion of Darwin applies to some extent to Huxley's defense of Darwin's theory in Britain. A comparison between Haeckel and Huxley regarding the extreme monistic basis of their science goes far in explaining why Frost distinguished so sharply between Darwin and Huxley, and why he criticized Huxley's deep involvement with "all things German." But the poet's criticism of the three generations of Huxleys went far beyond science and included his views on religion, education, and the whole inherited culture of European civilization.

When Huxley stated that foremost among the things he cared about was "the progress of scientific thought,"[36] he found in Haeckel a kindred spirit that had led his friend to act upon that belief in reforming German education on a scientific basis. Perhaps the most important single influence that Haeckel exerted upon Huxley was to convince him that the German system of scientific education was the model he should follow in his aim to make science and technology triumphant in Britain. Soon after his encounter with Haeckel, as Leonard Huxley observed, "Few years passed without some utterance from Huxley on the subject of education, especially scientific education."[37] In sharp contrast with Oxford and Cambridge universities, Huxley asserted that "German universities [are] the most intensely cultivated and most productive corporations the world has ever seen."[38] As a model for England, it followed that "Germany is the starting place of most educational methods."[39] For the final three decades of his father's life, Leonard Huxley stated, he worked unceasingly to reform education in Britain, from grammar school through graduate studies, to introduce physical science into the curriculum: "He came forward as a leader in the struggle for educational reform, seeking not only to perfect his own biological training, but to show, in theory and practice, how scientific training might be introduced into the general system of education."[40] His recurrent theme was that the best education is "scientific and technical."[41] Huxley was confident that once science and technology secured a footing in British education, in time it would make scientific thought dominant everywhere.

Huxley contrasted the medieval university, which "looked backwards" in "old knowledge" and engaged in "dialectic cobweb-spinning," with the modern university, which "looks forward, and is a factory of new knowledge," whose "professors have to be at the top of the wave of progress" because they engage in "research and criticism . . . and do laboratory work."[42] Unlike educators in the past, "the modern knows that the only source of real knowledge lies in the application of scientific methods of enquiry to the ascertainment of the facts of existence." This meant that "the chief business of the teacher is not . . . to make scholars" but "to train pioneers."[43] Huxley expressed great satisfaction that "Manchester, Liverpool, and Newcastle have gone in for technical education on a grand scale," without any literary studies to interfere with technical proficiency.[44]

As Huxley perceived the state of education in Britain, two formidable established forces stood as impediments blocking the triumph of scientific education: the Oxford and Cambridge curriculum centered in the ancient Greek and Latin languages and culture, and the dominance in religion of the Church of England. Since he believed that the only valid education was "instruction of the intellect in the ways of nature," the classical languages provided "mere literary training" and "a sham acquaintance with Latin," which he contended was a waste of time and energy.[45] He dismissed classical scholars as "Levites of culture," and he predicted that they would be "extirpated": ". . . the pretenders of our modern humanists to the possession of the monopoly of culture and to the exclusive inheritance of the spirit of antiquity must be abated, if not abandoned."[46] After Matthew Arnold accused him of being deficient in understanding of the ancient classics, Huxley often professed in public that he had "the greatest respect and love for literature," but in promoting his cause for science he noted that "There is a vast difference between men who have had a purely literary, and those who have had a sound scientific, training."[47] He classified "men of literature" as "the little men," whereas a "man of science" was "a big man," a giant standing on the shoulders of his predecessors.[48]

Huxley's unrelenting criticism of the Church of England is best understood in light of his Calvinist family dissenting inheritance. He passed a sweeping anathema against the very existence of bishops and contended that being made a bishop destroyed a man's courage and integrity.[49] He noted that the influence of the Church of England made British universities "half-clerical seminaries" dominated by the theological faculty, which, he argued, "takes us beyond the range of our faculties." Since analytical reason and discursive logic was Huxley's rational standard for establishing scientific truth, he condemned "Episcopal contamination" of human nature for teaching religious mythology as truth.[50] In a letter to Edward Clodd (December 21, 1879), Huxley wrote: "For the last quarter of a century I have done all that lay in my power to oppose and destroy the idolatrous accretions of Judaism and Christianity."[51] Huxley has left no doubt that by "idolatrous accretions" he meant everything in church tradition, including the symbolic and aesthetic elements in liturgical forms of worship, that was not sanctioned by the Bible.[52] He once advocated the study of the Bible in early public education, not for religion but for cultural reasons as part of an educated student's understanding of history. He believed that the Church of England would be "shivered into fragments by the advancing tide of science," unless it became solely devoted to works of charity for the poor.[53] He assumed a complete antithesis between science based upon a monism of matter and religion in its concern with things of the spirit, so that the triumph of science necessarily required the destruction of religion. "I am not afraid of the priests in the long-run," he wrote. "Scientific method is the white ant which will slowly but surely destroy their fortifications."[54] Based upon this belief, and despite his professed agnosticism about the unknown future, Huxley did not hesitate to assume the role of a prophet regarding religion. He declared: "that . . . Christianity is doomed to fall is, to my mind, beyond a doubt." In Frost's talks with me, the poet noted that Huxley's views on education, both his positive and enthusiastic advocacy of science and his harsh criticism of both the ancient classics and established orthodox religion, were all of one piece—that his monism of matter was the whole basis of his philosophy of education.

In one all-night conversation with me in his cabin near Bread Loaf, Frost spent the better part of our talk session expounding on Huxley's role in extending his beliefs about education in the United States. He drew heavily from Leonard Huxley's account in *Life and Letters of Thomas H. Huxley* of his father's visit to America in 1876: "But the educational campaign which he carried on in England had its counter part in America. . . . He was chosen to open the Johns Hopkins University as the type of a new form of education."[55] Frost said that these words from Leonard Huxley first alerted him to everything that was at stake in Huxley's "An Address on the Occasion of the Opening of The Johns Hopkins University." The invitation to speak on this important occasion came from Newell Martin, a former pupil of Huxley's and a biology teacher at the university who was chairman of the dedication ceremonies committee. Frost commented that Huxley's whole visit to America, before, during, and after his address, was marked by evidence of his materialistic value system, derived from his monism of matter.

Even before Huxley landed in New York, on August 5, 1876, from the deck of the *Germania* at the sight of the Manhattan skyscrapers, he remarked how "American" it was: "in the Old World the first things you see as you approach a great city are steeples; here you see, first, centers of intelligence." He marveled at the tugboats in the harbor and said: "If I were not a man I think I should like to be a tug," because, as Leonard Huxley had observed, "They seemed to him the condensation and complete expression of the energy and force in which he delighted."[56] To Frost, this incident expressed Huxley's mechanistic and materialistic conception of nature and human nature as "automata," and this impression was confirmed when Huxley was interviewed by a journalist, who found him "so little of the 'high-falutin' philosopher" and characterized him as "the commercial or mercantile" type. To Frost, these incidents were a trivial yet symbolic prelude to events in Baltimore.

Huxley accepted the invitation to give the inaugural address on the founding of The Johns Hopkins University on condition that the dedication ceremonies would not include anything religious—no role for the clergy, no reference to God, no prayers, hymns, or music. To Frost, this was a sign that Huxley suffered from a "monomania" centered in a monism of matter. The poet had read Huxley's address in the volume of his *American Addresses* (1893), and he observed that as usual after Matthew Arnold's criticism of his weak understanding of the ancient classics, Huxley paid lip service to the liberal arts. But the curriculum he prescribed for training in medicine clearly reflected his endorsement in "centrifugal education," in a concept of specialization, research, and technology so narrow that it even excluded the physical sciences that were not directly connected with biology.[58] Frost charged that Huxley wished to establish an industrial university centered in professionalism and utilitarian values apart from the humanities. He quoted Huxley's case for specialization: "In order to know a little well, one must be content to be ignorant of a great deal." Frost asked: how far could this conception of specialization be carried before a student loses his humanity in a profession? Although Huxley did not mention the German system of higher education, nor the Ph.D., he clearly took for his model the biological sciences as taught in German universities. "German thoroughness" and specialization, Frost said, often resulted in mastery of one area of knowledge and skills but in a disastrous atrophy in other important areas. Huxley's program clearly was a radical departure from what Frost considered a well-balanced liberal arts education, in which the physical sciences were a part of the humanities, not a separate and self-sufficient enterprise.

Frost did not mention by name any German scientists, so it is probably impossible to know how much he believed that Huxley borrowed from Ernst Haeckel and others in his address in Baltimore, and how much was original with him. But the poet recognized some important differences that set Huxley apart from such German scientists as Haeckel. The latter argued that biology should be studied in the same manner as physics. This was accepted in Germany far more than in Britain, so that, as has been observed, as physics encroached upon the domain of biology, "the benevolent evolutionism of Spencer" gave way to "the mechanistic materialism of Haeckel. Disillusionment and pessimism followed."[59] Although Huxley and Haeckel held many common beliefs regarding science, including a faith in materialism, Haeckel as a militant atheist differed from Huxley as an agnostic, and he had a far deeper sense of disgust about the dimension of spirit in human nature. Unlike Huxley, who retained a humanitarian sensibility regarding the poor, Haeckel was not merely a materialist but a modern Manichaean.[60] Frost remarked that Huxley was saved from Haeckel's political fanaticism by his death in 1895—twenty-four years before Haeckel's death—and ironically by the cultural and religious traditions in Britain that he consistently condemned.

In 1872, four years before Huxley's address at Johns Hopkins, his Irish friend, the physicist John Tyndall, had lectured in America in favor of their common philosophy of education, but without much success. Huxley's eloquence moved his audience of around 2,000 to applaud his lecture with great enthusiasm. Frost's belief that the modern world contained "a whole string of people like Huxley"[61] was soon confirmed when the administrators in the Ivy League universities adopted Huxley's program and established the Ph.D. as the required degree to teach in American colleges and universities. To Frost this was a major catastrophe, because he regarded Huxley as a sophist and believed that the application of the methods of the physical sciences to the humanities would corrupt American higher education. The poet agreed with William James, whose critical strictures in his essay "The Ph.D. Octopus" (March 1903) condemned the Ph.D. as a devouring monster that required a heavy technical apparatus that would corrupt the aesthetic, ethical, and social spirit of many students in studying the humanities. Like Arthur O. Lovejoy and other humanists, Frost defended students who refused to submit to the requirements. Frost's own long connection with American colleges was adversely affected by the intrusion of science into the liberal arts. On May 9, 1936, he wrote to Untermeyer: "I'm imperfectly academic and no amount of association with the academic will make me perfect." In his discussions with friends, a recurrent theme was his vehement protest against the corruption of the liberal arts, including poetry, by the methods of the physical sciences.

But Frost's criticism of Huxley's conception of education was not limited to personal responses regarding academia, but included his criticism "against the world in general." He believed that no humane culture or civilization could be built upon a foundation of materialistic monism. That was what the totalitarian systems of the twentieth century attempted to do, and the results were a disaster. Frost held that *hubris* invariably precedes *nemesis*, that the arrogance and pride that establishes a civilization based upon an ideology in which getting and spending and laying waste the powers of the human spirit in the humanities, arts, and religion would inevitably pay the price in a degraded culture and a ruined civilization. This was the main thrust behind his strong criticism of what he called "the three generations of Huxleys."

Although Frost was acutely aware of the cosmic significance to culture and civilization of applying the methods of the physical sciences to every subject that concerned human nature, his most immediate and frequent concern was how this corruption of science applied to literature. In the summer of 1940, after a conversation in his cabin near Bread Loaf, I recorded how he spoke vehemently against literary critics who followed the linguistic scholarship of I. A. Richards in his *Principles of Literary Criticism*:

> The trouble with Richards, Frost said, was that he believed language and psychology were exact sciences, and that therefore critical theory could provide a rational and scientific foundation for the practical criticism of poetry and all imaginative literature. Ransom's "New Critics" were trying to do to literature what Watson and Pavlov and other sociological behaviorists were trying to do to men in society. Frost rejected the entire enterprise. He prophesized that the twentieth century will be remembered in history of having finally determined the true role of science in human affairs, and that men would find that science will fall far short of exact, absolute, and predictable knowledge, especially when applied to man.[62]

Frost did not live long enough to know whether his prophecy was valid, but before publishing *In the Clearing* in 1962 he had concluded that it was far too negative to regard science as "the great betrayal" of the arts, humanities, and religion. In deciding upon the title *In the Clearing* his positive faith in dualism proved far stronger than his negative criticism of both monism and materialism.

The common belief among many of Frost's contemporaries that science and analytical reason provide a valid basis for literary criticism has characterized the ideological interpretations of poetry by Marxists, Freudians, linguists, the "New Criticism," biographical and sociological theorists, and postmodernists. It is small wonder, therefore, that in general Frost had a very low opinion of literary critics. In his poem "A Fountain, a Bottle, a Donkey's Ears and Some Books," he expressed his quiet contempt for the many forms of abuses of poetry by pseudoscientific ideologues:

> *How had the tender verse escaped, their outrage?*
> *By being invisible for what it was,*
> *Or else by some remoteness that defied them*
> *To find out what to do to hurt a poem.*[63]

Although some of Frost's better literary critics have treated the forms and techniques in his poetry with considerable skill and insight, often his themes and important beliefs have been garbled beyond recognition or understanding. Perhaps nowhere is the failure to comprehend the poet's beliefs more evident than in critics who have ignored or misunderstood his philosophical dualism. Frost's dualism was the basis of his positive beliefs, just as his disbeliefs were his negative responses to a monism of spirit or, more frequently, to a monism of matter. Throughout his adult life, Frost made it abundantly clear that the close interaction of spirit penetrating matter was his most vital philosophical conviction. In his letter to Lawrance Thompson of July 11, 1959, he summarized his essential belief in his explicit statement "I am a dualist." This study of Frost's beliefs is simply an epical enlargement of that statement.

The concept most antithetical to Frost's dualism is Thomas Henry Huxley's methodology or creed summarized in agnosticism. The poet's dualism distinguished between empirical facts and literary fictions, and like Coleridge he was able to make "a willing suspension of disbelief" in order to convey truths through metaphors or parables. Poetry enabled him to believe in the power of belief not only in the fictions of art, but in the facts of life. Thus belief took precedence over doubts or skepticism. That was why he held that men are always "believing ahead of your evidence," whether in self-belief, falling in love, composing a poem, confidence in forming a new nation, or believing in the future—that is, in God. That was why like St. Augustine and other theologians, but unlike modern agnostics, Frost did not make reason and scientific proofs the basis for beliefs in things of the spirit. The poet has left no room for doubt that he detested agnosticism more completely and intensely than any other method or creed: "My greatest prejudice is against an agnostic. He doesn't believe either way. He's just afraid to believe—afraid to disbelieve and afraid to believe. Just agnostic. I saw somebody whose book ended with an agnostic prayer. It's nauseating." The spiritual condition of an agnostic called forth Frost's wrath: "One thing I consider a curse is to be an agnostic." Despite many such statements by Frost, a large number of literary critics have categorized him as an agnostic.

Such critics have usually limited their claim that Frost was an agnostic to the poet's religious beliefs. Hyatt Waggoner identified Frost as "an agnostic in respect to the orthodox Christian creeds."[64] Joseph Warren Beach wrote: "Robert Frost is a refined modern agnostic in religion and philosophy: a clear-headed and fastidious realist."[65] Lawrance Thompson called Beach's statement a "gross misinterpretation of Robert Frost's art and thought,"[66] flatly contradicting what he had said in *Fire and Ice*. In *The Robert Frost Encyclopedia*, H. M. Campbell interprets "Sitting by a Bush in Broad Sunlight" as religious agnosticism, and George Bagby states that the poem achieves "at best a precarious kind of faith." Yvor Winters's claim that Frost was "a spiritual drifter" is merely a variation on the same theme, a charge that Frost himself refuted.[67] Similar statements have been advanced by George W. Nitchie, Margaret Edwards, Robert Faggen, and other literary critics.

Marion Montgomery provides one possible explanation of why so many literary critics categorized Frost as an agnostic: "He does not choose to make any sweeping statements about God," and "this has occasioned the belief among some critics that Frost is at best agnostic."[68] Frost's non-membership in a church has also been taken to mean that he was a freethinker who held religion in contempt. On the contrary, Frost respected corporate religious beliefs, but he did not wish to limit himself to a particular theology. As he said, T. S. Eliot was "more churchy" than he, but he was "more religious." Very likely many literary critics were caught up in what Arthur O. Lovejoy called "the revolt against dualism," which dominated the first half of the twentieth century, so that they could not accept Frost's belief that dualism consisted of the penetration of spirit into matter.

Regarding Frost's philosophical or metaphysical beliefs, a good touchstone is found among his literary critics in how they differ in interpreting his poem "The Strong Are Saying Nothing," particularly the final two lines:

*There may be little or much beyond the grave,*
*But the strong are saying nothing until they see.*

Critics who assume with Thomas Huxley that science, analytic discursive reason, and an assumed monism centered in matter have nullified any valid basis for a belief in a dualistic understanding of reality, including spirit entering into matter, will logically conclude that "the strong" in their skepticism and doubts will say nothing about spiritual beliefs until scientific verification provides a basis for belief. But in sharp contrast, critics who accept Frost's "four beliefs" as explicated in the final seven paragraphs in "Education by Poetry" and know how those beliefs ultimately "are all clearly related to 'the God-belief'" will understand how all beliefs have "got to be fulfilled" before talking about them, that "we are not talking until we know more, until we have something to show." In short, the strong in their "self-belief," their "art-belief," their "love-belief," their "national belief," and especially their "God-belief," know that they cannot tell, "only the outcome can tell." Because of their faith, "the strong are saying nothing until they see."

In the differences in temperament between the "monomania" and fanaticism that Frost perceived in Huxley's agnosticism and the quiet modesty and silence of the man of true religious faith, as Reginald Cook observed, "what is significant is the essential fact of belief."[69] As the young Puritan protagonist in "The Generations of Men" observed: "What counts is the ideals / And those will bear some keeping still about." All of Frost's remarks on the need of the man of faith to "stay unassuming" are summarized in the final lines of "The Fear of God":

> *Beware of coming too much to the surface,*
> *And using for apparel what was meant*
> *To be the curtain of the inmost soul.*

In "The Fear of God," Frost cautioned that if a man succeeds in life he should repeat to himself that he owes it to the mercy of God. This theme led Dorothy Judd Hall to note that as "an Old Testament Christian" Frost's faith was strong because it included something like the Calvinist doctrine of being God's elect.[70] Frost held convictions about ontological matters without the need to explain or justify himself to others, and also without requiring prior verification by science. The same reticence in not announcing to the world that he was a poet applied to his religious beliefs. With poetry as with sainthood and religious salvation, many are called but few are chosen.

In light of Frost's harsh critique of agnosticism his final volume of poems, *In the Clearing*, and especially "Kitty Hawk," may well be regarded as his conscious climactic defense of his dualism of spirit and matter as embodied most perfectly in the Christian doctrine of the Incarnation. The birth of Christ was to Frost an historical event of the most profound religious significance, the result of "the charge of the eternal into the material," which provided "our substantiation of our meaning." It is most remarkable that in Linda W. Wagner's edited anthology of critical reviews, *Robert Frost: The Critical Reception* (1977), not one of the sixteen reviews of *In the Clearing* deals with Frost's dualism, nor with the religious theme in "Kitty Hawk." The reviews deal with many irrelevant matters, while Frost's philosophical beliefs are totally ignored. By far the best published critical discussion of Frost's final volume is Stephen D. Warner's "Robert Frost in the Clearing: The Risk of Spirit in Substantiation" in *Frost Centennial Essays* (1974). Warner was concerned not only with the subjects and forms but also with the themes that characterized Frost's poetry throughout his life. He paid attention to "the epigraph, the frontispiece, and the dedication" as well as to the function of "The Pasture" in illuminating the title *In the Clearing.* Warner acknowledged that "Kitty Hawk" is the central poem in the volume, but then he treated it as merely "the record of Frost's survival on the road through the dark wood." He ended his review by treating Frost's account of man's "penetration into matter" as a mere "aside," a characteristic of Americans in their national concerns. Despite his literary virtues, Warner fell far short of identifying the poet's philosophical dualism as the source and sustained basis of the poet's beliefs regarding science, religion, poetry, and the social order of Western civilization.

It is ironical that some of the most perceptive insights in Frost's intellectual orientation are to be found in some unpublished letters by George Ray Elliott, Frost's closest friend in spirit among his colleagues at Amherst College. In five letters written to Lawrance Thompson, between April 11, 1947, and March 25, 1963, Elliott made some important observations on Frost's religious beliefs. In his letter of April 11, 1947, he stated that Frost held to "a sort of theism along with disbelief in the Incarnation, i.e., a historically unique manifestation of God in Christ." In a letter after Frost's death dated March 25, 1963, Elliott wrote that since Elinor's death (if not before), "RF has accepted more and more the Divinity of Christ just because RF was a brainy and insightful student of the New Testament—though reticent on that. And he saw that the accounts there, and the effects in history, were inexplicable unless Christ were God in human form."[71] Elliott noted that in his friendship with Frost, "he often talked to me about religion because of my keen interest in it, inherited from Scottish Presbyterian ancestors through my father and mother," although he identified himself as "Episcopalian." Frost's last letter, dictated from his deathbed, was written to Elliott and his wife. Their closeness in spirit is very evident in the poet's last words to his friend:

> Why will the quidnuncs always be hoping for a salvation man will never have from anyone but God? I was just saying today how Christ posed Himself the whole problem and died for it. How can we be just in a world that needs mercy and merciful in a world that needs justice. . . . It seems as if I never wrote these plunges into the depths to anyone but you. . . . If only I get well . . . I'll go deeper into my life with you than I ever have before.[72]

The correspondence between Frost and Elliott opens up important areas for future students of Frost to explore.

But in a larger frame, this study of Frost as a philosopher also provides opportunities for scholars and literary critics to explore Frost's art and thought more profoundly. If a critic as acute as Stephen D. Warner falls far short of recognizing and understanding the nature and importance of Frost's dualism, how much more difficult is it for critics in general to know and understand the poet's rejection of the two monisms and his firm and lifelong adherence to dualism? Certainly, an awareness and comprehension of Frost's dualism does not guarantee that a critic will make valid judgments about his beliefs and poetry. However, ignorance or a denial of Frost's philosophical orientation can only result in a very limited and mistaken interpretation of those poems that deal with serious philosophical beliefs. Critics whose perceptions are more or less limited resemble persons on the banks of a river who witness the flow of the water but have no awareness of the source or direction of the stream: they will never properly and fully understand Frost's poetry as a whole. They are, as it were, like Ptolemaic astronomers rooted and wedded to a geocentric and false system who refuse to accept the truth of the Copernican heliocentric system. For an interpretation of Frost's philosophical position based upon the sure evidence of his dualism, and not upon a refusal or misunderstanding of it, it is time for a Copernican revolution in the study of Frost's poetry and philosophy.

# Acknowledgments

This study of Frost as a philosopher-poet has been in gestation for more than fifty years, and its conception and birth owe much to a small army of sources. I am pleased and grateful to acknowledge my indebtedness in knowledge and understanding of Frost as a man, a poet, and a dualist thinker.

The most direct and important source by far is Robert Frost himself—in his poetry, prose essays, correspondence, interviews, and panel discussions, but above all in his conversations at Bread Loaf and in Boston, Ann Arbor, and Detroit over a period of at least twenty-three years. In a great variety of ways he dealt with his belief in a dualistic philosophy. After six consecutive summers at Bread Loaf as a student, on the last day of August 1944, when I was about to leave for the University of Michigan where he had directed me to go, I told Frost that someday I would write the best book about his art and thought that I had it in me to compose. I had no notion of the form or theme or method that such a study would take.

In its general form, the theme of this study was with me soon after my first encounter with Frost, but its slow growth emerged only in gradual stages through an ever deepening awareness of its central significance in the character and belief of Frost. The poet remarked on "the doubleness" of all living things on earth in "The Future of Man" symposium (1959). He insisted there that in comparison with science, "philosophy has been formidable, too." He believed this to be the greatest challenge to man's future, and that belief underscored his philosophical dualism. During the summers of 1961 and 1962, in talks with Frost at Bread Loaf, I found that he was still deeply concerned about the conflicts that had agitated him during "The Future of Man" symposium. His adherence to a dualism of spirit and matter and his rejection of both a monism of spirit and a monism of matter were never more evident than in the final two years of his life.

The earliest and most important indirect help I received in coming to know and understand Frost came from administrators and teachers at Middlebury College. Paul D. Moody, the president of Middlebury College, first urged me to go to Bread Loaf and did much to make that possible. Professor Harry G. Owen, my freshman year teacher of English and also dean of the Bread Loaf School of English, seconded Moody, and specifically referred to meeting Frost as an inducement to attend Bread Loaf. Vernon C. Harrington, my freshman teacher of philosophy and a friend of Frost during the 1920s at Bread Loaf, first taught me the close connection between Frost and William James, and he also encouraged me to pursue my literary interests at Bread Loaf. Reginald L. Cook, professor of American literature at Middlebury, was a close friend of Frost since 1925, and he was vehement in insisting that I should come to know Frost at Bread Loaf. When Cook became dean of the Bread Loaf School, he invited me back to Bread Loaf as a teacher in 1961 and 1962, the last two summers of Frost's life, which proved to be the culmination of over twenty-three years of friendship with Frost. Thus it was that in 1939 I went to Bread Loaf and came to know Frost, and the poet's granting me the Elinor Frost Scholarship to attend Bread Loaf the next summer paved the way for six summers at Bread Loaf and an M.A. degree in August 1944. In 1943, Frost encouraged me to go to the University of Michigan for further graduate studies in English. He had been poet-in-residence at Michigan twice during the 1920s, and he made it possible for me to attend Michigan by securing a graduate fellowship for me.

During my six summers at Bread Loaf, 1939–44, I came to know many teachers and students who enriched my knowledge of Frost in various ways. Perhaps the foremost among all of my Bread Loaf influences was Rabbi Victor E. Reichert, the religious leader of the Jewish community in Cincinnati, Ohio. During the 1940s Reichert was at Bread Loaf, largely because of his friendship with Frost. In conversations with him at Bread Loaf and during two visits to Cincinnati, we discussed Frost at length, especially the poet's philosophical and religious beliefs. Frost's views on justice and mercy, on the Sermon on the Mount in the New Testament, in referring to himself as "an Old Testament Christian," and his writing *A Masque of Reason* and *A Masque of Mercy* were shaped to some extent by his many talks with Reichert. Although Frost knew Louis Untermeyer for twenty-five years more than he knew Reichert, his friendship with Untermeyer remained largely literary, whereas with Reichert it grew into personal affection beyond friendship because it was based upon spirit as well as on matter, in contrast with Untermeyer's Marxism and materialism.

I am pleased to dedicate *Robert Frost: The Poet as Philosopher* to the collective memory of Moody, Owen, Cook, and Reichert, but also to Frederick Burkhardt, the former president of Bennington College and a chief editor of *The Correspondence of Charles Darwin* in over thirty proposed volumes. Burkhardt knew Frost, and his encyclopedic knowledge of the ethos of the Victorian controversy over Darwin's theory of evolution provided me with a valuable dimension to a better understanding of Frost and modern science.

Among the faculty members at the Bread Loaf School of English, I acknowledge with gratitude the following who contributed to my better understanding of Frost. In 1939, Donald Davidson, Hewette Joyce, Perry Miller, Lucia B. Mirrielees, Hortense Moore, Theodore Morrison, George F. Thomas, and James Southall Wilson; in 1940, George K. Anderson, Reuben A. Brower, and John Crowe Ransom; in 1941, Elizabeth Drew and Donald A. Stauffer; in 1942, many of those previously named returned to teach at Bread Loaf; in 1943, William Dighton and Thomas Marc Parrott; in 1944, because of World War II, no new faculty members were added at Bread Loaf, but five of its former members returned. Of particular value to me were the two courses I had with Donald Davidson, one in modern poetry and the other in British and American ballads. Perry Miller added substantially to my understanding of New England Puritanism. My course in writing with Theodore Morrison brought me into direct contact with Frost. From George F. Thomas's course in the Platonic tradition in English literature, I learned how Frost could respect Plato and the whole tradition of moral idealism yet greatly prefer Aristotle. Elizabeth Drew's course in modern poetry treated Frost as subordinate to William Butler Yeats, Ezra Pound, T. S. Eliot, and W. H. Auden, but Reuben A. Brower persuaded her to raise her estimate of Frost. My two courses with John Crowe Ransom in literary criticism were modified by Frost's criticism of rational analysis as an appropriate way of reading poetry. In my final two summers as a student at Bread Loaf (1943–44), William Dighton from Queens University was my outstanding teacher.

When I returned to Bread Loaf as a member of the faculty in 1961 and 1962, my closest colleagues were George K. Anderson, Carlos Baker, John Berryman, and William Meredith. But both as a student and teacher at Bread Loaf, Reginald L. Cook remained the outstanding influence in my academic life and also my closest connection with Robert Frost.

For six consecutive summers, I attended the Bread Loaf Writers' Conference and had talks about Frost with members of the administrative staff and would-be writers who participated in the discussions of poetry, prose fiction, drama, and prose nonfiction. Frost and Louis Untermeyer conducted the "poetry clinics," and I came to know them as a team and Untermeyer as an individual literary critic of Frost's poetry. For two summers I roomed with Richard Ellmann in Gilmore Cottage and came to know the basis of his rather negative criticism of Frost's poetry. The Writers' Conference sessions were administered by Ted Morrison and his wife, Kay, both of whom were very close to Frost at Harvard as well as every summer at Bread Loaf. The Morrisons lived in Frost's cottage on the Homer Noble Farm, while the poet stayed in his cabin.

Among the members of the staff with whom I talked were the following: John Ciardi (later director of the Writers' Conference), Bernard DeVoto, J. P. Marquand, Edith Mirrielees, and Wallace Stegner (both individually and as a team), and Fletcher Pratt. Walter Pritchard Eaton served both with the School of English and the Writers' Conference. For several summers we were croquet partners in our epical battles with James Southall Wilson and his wife. Richard Brown, my teacher in eighteenth-century English literature at Middlebury College, was the assistant to the Morrisons during the Writers' Conferences and was much admired by Frost. Between them, I was steered into eighteenth-century literary studies and especially to the political philosophy of Edmund Burke, which became the basis of several of my books and many articles on the Whig statesman.

Guest lecturers during the Writers' Conferences included Archibald MacLeish, Theodore Roethke, and William Carlos Williams, all of whom had significant things to say about Robert Frost. A student at the School of English who stayed over for the Writers' Conference was Dorothy Judd Hall, who later wrote a book on Frost's religious beliefs. I acknowledge my indebtedness to all of these persons connected with the Bread Loaf Writers' Conference from 1939 through 1944.

I knew that Frost, like William James—the teacher at Harvard whom he never had but who influenced him most—had a very harsh negative view of university graduate studies in the humanities, including especially literature. Both Frost and James objected to scholarship based upon the assumptions, methods, and objectives of the physical sciences as unsuitable for the humanities. When I responded to Frost's question about what I planned to do with my life by saying that I wished to teach literature in a good liberal arts college, and that to do this I needed to acquire a Ph.D. degree, I was not surprised at his vehement critical reaction: "Well, if you must corrupt yourself, go to the University of Michigan!" I did not convince him that I could avoid corruption in graduate school studies.

But as a dualist, it was typical of Frost to soften and modify his harsh criticism of persons and institutional studies. His happy experience at the University of Michigan was also a factor in his urging me to go to Ann Arbor. He then provided me with a list of faculty members to be sure to look up because, as he said, "they are such fine teachers and scholars." These included Roy Cowden, in charge of the Hopwood writing program; Clarence D. Thorpe, teacher in Romanticism; Louis I. Bredvold, one of the outstanding American scholars on the Restoration and eighteenth century; and Carlton Wells, who functioned at Michigan much as Theodore Morrison did at Harvard. Frost also urged me to get acquainted with Mary Cooley, the daughter of Charles Horton Cooley, the outstanding humanities sociologist at Michigan whom Frost admired above most university scholars. Mary Cooley was one of Frost's "three graces," and she was in charge of the Hopwood Room. As a graduate student at Michigan, I came to know all of these friends of Frost, and they provided me with a long-range perspective of their reasons for admiring him as a man and poet.

Years later, while teaching in Detroit, I came to know Dorothy Tyler, another of Frost's three graces, and she further extended my understanding of Frost during the 1920s. My indebtedness to Frost's friends at the University of Michigan supplements all that I learned about him through teachers and students at Middlebury College and Bread Loaf.

An account of all of my indebtedness for a better understanding of Robert Frost includes the following persons listed in alphabetical order: Pat Alger, David Bain, JoAnn Baumgartner, Laura Brooks, Robert Buckeye, David Burnett, Stanley Burnshaw, Roberts H. Burton, Richard J. Calhoun, John P. Chalmers, Joan Clark, Juanita Cook, Robert Cotner, Charles Cotter, Tom Curley, Daria D'Arienzo, Matthew M. Davis, Carl Fernelius, Helen Hartness Flanders, Barbara Fleury, Lesley Francis, Howard Friedman, Lesley Frost, Peter Gilbert, Robert Haas, Jack Hagstrom, J. Jean Hecht, Robin Hudnut, Edward J. Ingebretsen, Walter Jost, Annette Kirk, Russell Kirk, John Lancaster, Margaret Lee, Carson McCullers, George Montiero, George Nash, Lea Newman, Marjorie Nicholson, Jay Parini, Joe Parisi, John Paterson, Max Petersen, Michael Plunkett, William H. Pritchard, Louise F. Reichert, Patrick Reilly, John Ridland, David A. Sanders, David D. Sayre, Frank Schier, Dulci Scott, Lisa Seale, Mark Selko, Don Sheehy, Lee Simonson, George Sullivan, W. D. Taylor, Carole Thompson, John Evangelist Walsh, Richard Wilbur, Earl J. Wilcox, and Lester Wolfson.

Although Frost was primarily a poet and not a philosopher in the sense that Aristotle, Plato, and Kant were philosophers, nevertheless he retained a philosophical dimension in his fundamental beliefs regarding God, man, and physical nature. The poet was a lifelong theist in his belief in God. His well-known admiration for William James was reflected in his dualism of spirit and matter as applied to man and nature. His dualism was reinforced philosophically and enriched historically through his reading of James's student Arthur O. Lovejoy's *The Revolt Against Dualism* (1930) and *The Great Chain of Being* (1936). In the early 1940s, Frost discussed the latter work with Reginald Cook and the earlier study with me. Both the substance and the history-of-ideas method of Lovejoy's scholarship appealed to Frost. Lovejoy made him aware of the historical roots since the time of Descartes of the modern revolt against dualism. Frost was amused by Bertrand Russell's many futile attempts to unify mind and matter (what Eddington called "mind-stuff"), and the poet's resistance to Russell's ambivalence strengthened his own adherence to dualism.

Frost rejected the abuse of science into the absolutism of scientism by Thomas Henry Huxley in Britain and by Ernst Haeckel in Germany. His reading of Lovejoy's two seminal works of scholarship helped him to understand and accept Einstein's theory of relativity, which "transfers space, time, and motion from the physical to the mental world." This vital shift in perspective occurs because it shows that "the positions, velocities, and shapes of perceived objects, and the dates of perceived events or the duration of processes" are "relative to the standpoints of observers." Later, Frost even refined upon Einstein's theory by accepting Heisenberg's "principle of indeterminacy."

I acknowledge my indebtedness for an understanding of Frost's dualism and views of modern theories of physics primarily to three sources: Frost himself, Arthur O. Lovejoy, and Louis I. Bredvold. At the University of Michigan, Bredvold introduced me to an in-depth study of Lovejoy's history-of-ideas method in scholarship, and to the works of Lovejoy on primitivism and the idea of progress through science, far beyond anything that Frost had discussed. Together, Bredvold and Lovejoy enabled me to understand better what Frost had explicated at Bread Loaf, and thus to appreciate the depth of Frost's philosophical dualism.

In my conversations with Frost at Bread Loaf, one important subject we discussed had a wholly unforeseen consequence for my experience at the University of Michigan. Frost mentioned that he greatly admired the politics of Edmund Burke, the Whig statesman who courageously opposed the restrictive policy of the British government against the American colonies.

He approved of the curriculum in many American high schools that included teaching Burke's "Speech on Conciliation with the Colonies" (March 22, 1775). Burke's appeals for conciliation and political reform were ignored, and the American War of Independence followed. Frost had also read Burke's *Reflections on the Revolution in France* (1790), and he observed that the Whig statesman had advanced the same principle of moral prudence for reforming social abuses in France. But the violation of moral prudence was committed not by the government, but by the radical Jacobin revolutionary party, in pursuit of an ideological theory of government aimed at destroying the entire historical inheritance of France and of Europe. Unlike some historians, Frost believed that Burke was wholly consistent and right in justifying the American Revolution and condemning the French Revolution. In a course of eighteenth-century British literature with Professor Louis Bredvold, I became so interested in Burke as a literary and political figure that I wrote my doctoral dissertation on Burke's politics, later published as *Edmund Burke and Natural Law*. In 1962, while I taught at the Bread Loaf School of English, Bredvold visited me, and we had a memorable meeting with Frost in his cabin on the Homer Noble Farm.

I am pleased to acknowledge assistance from the library staff of the following institutions in pursuit of my study of Frost: The Robert Frost Library at Amherst College; the Jones Library in Amherst; the Baker Library at Dartmouth College; the Library of Congress; the University of Detroit Library; the University of Michigan Library; the Starr Library at Middlebury College; the New York Public Library; the New York University Library; the Howard Colman Library of Rockford College; the University of Virginia Library; and the Wayne State University Library.

Since various chapters of this book have appeared in print in some form in different publications, it is with pleasure and gratitude that I acknowledge a number of people who have in various ways aided my efforts with this book.

I give thanks to Jac Tharpe, the original editor of the *Frost Centennial Essays*; to Craig Hill, editor in chief of the University Press of Mississippi; and to Cynthia Foster, his administrative assistant, for permission to republish, in whole or in part, the following published work: "Robert Frost's Masques and the Classic American Tradition," *Frost Centennial Essays*, volume I (1974); "Robert Frost: Politics in Theory and Practice," *Frost Centennial Essays*, volume II (1976); "Acceptable in Heaven's Sight: Robert Frost at Bread Loaf, 1939–1941," *Frost Centennial Essays*, volume III (1978). This literary memoir of 136 pages consists of my first three summers of conversations with Frost at Bread Loaf.

## Robert Frost: The Poet as Philosopher

I give thanks to John Howard, former president of Rockford College, for permission to republish "Robert Frost: The Individual and Society" and "Robert Frost: Politics in Theory and Practice." These chapters were originally given as lectures at Rockford College in 1973. They were modified and published as a pamphlet, *Robert Frost: The Individual and Society* (1973). Later they were further revised in form and substance and republished in *Frost Centennial Essays*, Volume II (1976).

I am grateful to Mary Hansen, Office of the Provost, the University of Texas at Dallas, and to Peggy L. Gough, rights and permissions assistant, for permission of the University of Texas Press to use portions of my essay "Constitutional Liberty in Western civilization: The American Republic." This monograph was originally delivered in 1983 as a part of the Andrew R. Cecil Lectures on Moral Values in a Free Society. It was published in volume five of this series, entitled *The Citizen and His Government*. The lecture was given at the University of Texas at Dallas, the sponsor and publisher of the annual lectures.

I acknowledge my gratitude to Jonathan N. Barron, editor of *The Robert Frost Review*, and its official publisher, the Robert Frost Society, for permission to republish "Dualism: The Basis of Robert Frost's Philosophy," *The Robert Frost Review* (Fall 1994). All of the numbers of *The Robert Frost Review* have been useful in a great variety of ways.

Gratitude is expressed to George Panichas, editor of *Modern Age*, and to the officers of the Intercollegiate Studies Institute, for permission to republish in modified form the following articles which formed the basis for chapters in *Robert Frost: The Poet as Philosopher*: "Robert Frost: The Conversationalist as Poet," *Modern Age* (Fall 1997); "Robert Frost and Darwin's Theory of Evolution," Part One, *Modern Age* (Spring 2000); "Robert Frost and Darwin's Theory of Evolution," Part Two, *Modern Age* (Summer 2000); and "Robert Frost and Creative Evolution," *Modern Age* (Spring 2002).

Thanks also is given to Beverly Jarrett, director of the University of Missouri Press, and to the editors of *Roads Not Taken: Rereading Robert Frost*, Earl J. Wilcox and Jonathan N. Barron, for permission to republish "Robert Frost's Philosophy of Education: The Poet as Teacher," which appeared in that collection of essays by the University of Missouri Press (2000).

Acknowledgment is also given to the editors of *English Literary Studies* and the Department of English of the University of Victoria, B.C., Canada, and to Earl J. Wilcox, editor of *His Incalculable Influence on Others: Essays on Robert Frost in Our Time*, for permission to make use of parts of my essay "Robert Frost and Robert Hillyer: An Enduring Friendship," University of Victoria: *English Literary Studies*, No. 63, RLS Monograph Series (1994).

# Acknowledgments

I thank Claes G. Ryn and Joseph Baldacchino, editor and publisher of *Humanitas*, and the National Humanities Institute, for granting permission to republish my article "In the Clearing: Continuity and Unity in Frost's Dualism," *Humanitas* vol. XVIII, nos. 1 and 2 (2005).

I am grateful to the Lamson Library, Plymouth State College, Plymouth, New Hampshire, for permission to quote from files 67, 68, and 69 on Robert Frost as a teacher; also to the McCain Library at Agnes Scott College, in Decatur, Georgia; and the Watkinson Library at Trinity College, Hartford, Connecticut. I am indebted for the use of the Charles H. Cooley "Notebooks" in the Manuscripts of the University of Michigan Bentley Historical Library, for items from June 6, 1925, to November 4, 1928, on "Manuscripts" no. 23; and to the New York University Library at Washington Square for the Robert Frost Library deposited there. I am also grateful to the Amherst Special Collections on Robert Frost, for items 304, 331, 332, 336, 339, and 341, on deposit in the Robert Frost Library.

My gratitude to Peter Gilbert and the Estate of Robert Frost to cite from the until recently unpublished notebooks of Frost in the Baker Library, Dartmouth College. In 2006, *The Notebooks of Robert Frost*, edited by Robert Faggen, was published by the Belknap Press of Harvard University Press (Cambridge, Massachusetts).

I acknowledge the help of the Clifton Waller Barrett collection of Robert Frost in the Special Collections of the University of Virginia.

I am grateful to the various sources which possess copies of photographs of Frost in the public domain for permission to reproduce them in this study. Wherever possible, I am pleased to acknowledge my indebtedness along with captions that identify the time, place, or occasion of each photograph.

# Selected Bibliography

This bibliography is limited to the primary sources of Robert Frost's writings—poetry, prose, correspondence, notebooks, interviews, and lectures—and to all of the essential printed sources of articles and books about the poet. The sources identified in the notes for each chapter are not all included in this bibliography.

## Primary Sources

Anderson, Margaret B. *Robert Frost and John Bartlett: The Record of a Friendship.* New York: Holt, 1963.

Cook, Reginald L. *Robert Frost: A Living Voice.* Amherst: University of Massachusetts Press, 1974.

———. "Robert Frost's Asides on His Poetry." *American Literature* 19 (1948).

Cox, Hyde and Edward Connery Lathem, eds. *Selected Prose of Robert Frost.* New York: Holt, Rinehart, and Winston, 1966.

Faggen, Robert, ed. *The Notebooks of Robert Frost.* Cambridge: Harvard University Press, 2006.

Frost, Lesley. *New Hampshire's Child: The Derry Journals of Lesley Frost.* Albany: State University of New York Press, 1969.

Grade, Arnold, ed. *The Family Letters of Robert and Elinor Frost.* Albany: State University of New York Press, 1972.

Lathem, Edward Connery, ed. *Interviews with Robert Frost.* New York: Holt, Rinehart, and Winston, 1966.

_____. *The Poetry of Robert Frost*. New York: Holt, Rinehart, and Winston, 1969.

_____. and Lawrance Thompson, eds. *Robert Frost: Poetry and Prose*. New York: Holt, Rinehart, and Winston, 1972.

Plimpton, George, ed. *Writers at Work: The Paris Review Interviews*. Second Series. New York: Viking, 1963.

Thompson, Lawrance, ed. *Selected Letters of Robert Frost*. New York: Holt, Rinehart, and Winston, 1964.

Untermeyer, Louis, ed. *The Letters of Robert Frost to Louis Untermeyer*. New York: Holt, Rinehart, and Winston, 1963.

## Secondary Sources

Abel, Darrel. "The Instinct of a Bard: Robert Frost on Science, Logic, and Poetic Truth." *Essays in Arts and Sciences* 9.1, May 1980.

Abercrombie, Lascelles. "A New Voice." *The Nation*, June 13, 1914.

Adams, Frederick B., Jr. *To Russia with Frost*. Boston: Club of Odd Volumes, 1963.

Allen, Grant. *Evolution of the Idea of God*. 1897.

Anderson, Charles R. "Robert Frost, 1879–1963." *Saturday Review of Literature*, February 23, 1963.

Anderson, George K. *Bread Loaf School of English: The First Fifty Years*. Middlebury, VT: Middlebury College, 1969.

Angyal, Andrew J. "From Swedenborg to William James: The Shaping of Frost's Religious Beliefs." *Robert Frost Review*, Fall 1994.

*Anthology of Magazine Verse*. New York: Schulte's Book Store, 1959.

Auden, W. H. *The Dyer's Hand and Other Essays*. New York: Random House, 1962.

Babbitt, Irving. *Literature and the American College*. Washington, D.C.: National Humanities Institute, 1986. First published in 1908.

Bacon, Helen. "For Girls: From 'Birches' to 'Wild Grapes.'" *Yale Review* 67, 1977.

_____. "In and Outdoor Schooling: Robert Frost and the Classics." *American Scholar* 43, 1974.

Bagby, George F. *Frost and the Book of Nature*. Knoxville: University of Tennessee Press, 1933.

_____. "The Promethean Frost." *Twentieth Century Literature* 38, 1992.

Bain, David H. and Mary S. Duffy, eds. *Whose Woods These Are: A History of the Bread Loaf Writers' Conference, 1926–1992*. Hopewell, NJ: Ecco, 1993.

Baldwin, Robert C. and James A. S. McPeek, eds. *An Introduction to Philosophy Through Literature*. New York: The Ronald Press Co., 1950. Includes Pascal, *Pensées*, trans. by W. F. Trotter.

Barker, John. *Strange Contrarieties: Pascal in England during the Age of Reason.* Montreal: McGill-Queen's University Press, 1975.

Barlow, Nora, ed. *The Autobiography of Charles Darwin: 1809–1882.* New York: 1958.

Barry, Elaine. *Robert Frost on Writing.* New Brunswick, NJ: Rutgers University, 1973.

Bartini, Arnold G. "Robert Frost and Moral Neutrality." *CEA Critic* 38, January 1976.

Baym, Nina. "An Approach to Robert Frost's Nature Poetry." *American Quarterly* 17, 1965.

Beach, Joseph Warren. *The Concept of Nature in Nineteenth-Century English Poetry.* New York: The Macmillan Co., 1936.

———. "Robert Frost." *Yale Review* 43, December 1953.

Becker, Carl L. *The Heavenly City of the Eighteenth-Century Philosophers.* New Haven, CT: Yale University Press, 1932.

Beddall, B. H. "Wallace, Darwin, and the Theory of Natural Selection." *Journal of the History of Biology,* 1968.

Bergmann, Sonja, ed. *Ideas and Opinions.* New York: Crown, 1954.

Bergson, Henri. *Creative Evolution.* Trans. by Arthur Mitchell. New York: 1911. Originally published in Paris, 1907.

———. *Les Deux Sources de la Religion et la Morale.* New York: Henry Holt & Co., 1935.

Bernbaum, Ernest. *Guide Through the Romantic Movement.* New York: Thomas Nelson and Sons, 1938. 5 vols.

Bieganowski, Ronald. "Robert Frost's *A Boy's Will* and Henri Bergson's *Creative Evolution.*" *South Carolina Review* 21.1, 1988.

———. "Sense of Place and Religious Consciousness," in *Robert Frost: Studies of the Poetry.* Kathryn Gibbs Harris, ed. Boston, 1979.

Bishop, Morris. *Pascal: The Life of a Genius.* New York: Reynal and Hitchcock, 1936.

Bloom, Harold, ed. *Robert Frost: Modern Critical Views.* New York: Chelsea House, 1986.

Born, Max. *Die Relativitätstheorie Einsteins.* 1922.

Boroff, Marie. "Robert Frost's New Testament: Language and the Poem." *Modern Philology* 69, August 1971.

Bort, Barry D. "Frost and the Deeper Vision." *Midwest Quarterly* 5, Fall 1963.

Bottome, Phillis. *New Republic,* April 15, 1936. On the Frost-Meiklejohn controversy over education.

Bowler, Peter J. *The Eclipse of Darwinism.* Baltimore, 1983.

———. *The Non-Darwinian Revolution.* Baltimore, 1988.

Breit, Harvey. *The Writer Observed.* New York, 1961.

Brock, Heyward. "Robert Frost's Masques Reconsidered." *Renascence* 30, 1978.

Brodsky, Joseph. "On Grief and Reason." *In Homage to Robert Frost.* Joseph Brodsky, Seamus Heaney, and Derek Walcott. New York: Farrar Strauss and Giroux, 1996.

Brooks, Cleanth and Robert Penn Warren. *Understanding Poetry.* New York: Henry Holt, 1938.

Brooks, Van Wyck. *New England Indian Summer, 1865–1915.* New York: Dutton, 1940.

Brower, Reuben. *The Poetry of Robert Frost: Constellations of Intention.* New York: Holt, Rinehart, and Winston, 1965.

Brown, Terence. "Robert Frost's *In the Clearing.*" *Papers on Language and Literature* 5, Summer Supplement 1969.

Browne, Janet. *Charles Darwin: The Power of Place.* Princeton: Princeton University Press, 2002. 2 vols.

Burnett, Whit, ed. *This Is My Best: America's Greatest Living Authors.* 1942.

Burnshaw, Stanley. *Robert Frost Himself.* New York: George Braziller, 1986.

Burtt, Edwin A. *The Metaphysical Foundations of Modern Physical Science.* New York: Harcourt, Brace, and Co., 1927.

Butler, Samuel. "The Deadlock in Darwinism." *The Universal Review,* April–June 1890.

Sister Catherine Theresa. "New Testament Interpretations of Robert Frost's Poems." *Ball State University Forum* 11, Winter 1970.

Chabot, C. Barry. "The Melancholy Dualism of Robert Frost." *Review of Existential Psychology,* 1974.

Ciardi, John. "Robert Frost: The Way to the Poem." *Saturday Review of Literature* 41, April 12, 1958.

Cleghorn, Sarah N. *Threescore.* New York: Arno Press, 1980 and 1936.

Cohen, I. Bernard. "An Interview with Einstein." *Scientific American,* July 1955.

Cook, Marjorie E. "The Serious Play of Interpretation." *South Carolina Review* Spring 1983.

———. "Detachment, Irony, and Commitment," in *Robert Frost: Studies of the Poetry.* Kathryn Gibbs Harris, ed. Boston, 1979.

Cook, Reginald L. *The Dimensions of Robert Frost.* New York: Rinehart, 1958 (Barnes and Noble, 1968).

———. "Emerson and Frost: A Parallel of Seers." *New England Quarterly* 31, June 1958.

———. *Robert Frost: A Living Voice.* Amherst, MA: University of Massachusetts Press, 1974.

———. "A Parallel of Parablists: Thoreau and Frost." *The Thoreau Centennial.* Walter Harding, ed. Albany, NY: 1964.

———. "Robert Frost's Constellated Sky." *Western Humanities Review* 22, Summer 1968.

———. "Robert Frost: An Equilibrist's Field of Vision." *Massachusetts Review* 15, Summer 1974.

_____. "Robert Frost in Context." *Frost Centennial Essays* III, 1978.

Cox, James M. "Robert Frost and the Edge of the Clearing." *Virginia Quarterly Review* 35, Winter 1959.

_____, ed. *Robert Frost: A Collection of Critical Essays*. Englewood Cliffs, NJ: 1962.

Cox, Sidney. *Robert Frost: Original "Ordinary Man."* New York: Holt, 1929.

_____. "Some Educational Beliefs and Practices of Robert Frost." *Educational Record* 29, October 1949.

_____. *A Swinger of Birches: A Portrait of Robert Frost*. New York: New York University Press, 1957. Republished 1961.

Craig, Gordon A. "The Good, the Bad, and the Bourgeois." *New York Review of Books* vol. 45, no. 13, August 13, 1998.

_____. "Robert Frost at Amherst." Amherst College Archives.

Cramer, Jeffrey S. "Forgotten Frost: A Study of the Uncollected and Unpublished Poetry of Robert Frost." *The Robert Frost Review*. Pt. 1, Fall 1992; Pt. 2, Fall 1993.

_____. *Robert Frost Among His Poems*. Jefferson, NC: McFarland, 1996.

Crane, Joan St. C. "Robert Frost's 'Kitty Hawk.'" *Studies in Bibliography: Papers of the Biographical Society of the University of Virginia* 30, 1977.

_____. *Robert Frost: A Descriptive Catalogue of Books and Manuscripts in the Clifton Waller Barrett Library, University of Virginia*. Charlottesville, VA: University Press of Virginia, 1974.

Crocker, Lester G. *An Age of Crisis*. Baltimore: The Johns Hopkins Press, 1959.

Dabbs, J. McBride. "Robert Frost and the Dark Woods." *Yale Review* 23 (March 1934).

Daiches, David. "Enduring Wisdom from a Poet-Sage." *New York Times Book Review*, May 29, 1949.

Darwin, Charles. *On the Origin of Species*. London: John Murray, 1859.

_____. Frances Darwin, ed. *The Life and Letters of Charles Darwin*. New York, 1911. 3 vols.

_____. *The Voyage of the Beagle*. London, 1839.

_____. *More Letters of Charles Darwin*. London, 1903.

_____. *The Correspondence of Charles Darwin*. Frederick Burkhardt, Duncan Porter, Joy Harvey, and Jonathan Topham, eds. Cambridge University Press (fifteen vols. published by 2005).

_____. *The Descent of Man*. London, 1871.

Davison, Peter. "The Self-Realization of RF, 1911–1912." *New Republic* 30, March 1974. Reproduced in *Robert Frost: Lectures on the Centennial of his Birth*. Washington, D.C.: Library of Congress, 1975.

Desmond, Adrian. *Huxley*. Michael Joseph, Ltd., 1994.

DeVoto, Bernard. "The Critics and Robert Frost." *Saturday Review of Literature* 17, January 1, 1938.

Donoghue, Denis. "Robert Frost." *Connoisseurs of Chaos.* New York, 1965.

Doyle, John R., Jr. *The Poetry of Robert Frost: An Analysis.* New York: Hafner, 1973.

Drinkwater, John. *Discovery.* London: Houghton, 1933.

Duvall, S.P.C. "Robert Frost's 'Directive' Out of Walden." *American Literature* 31, January 1960.

Eberhart, Richard. "Robert Frost: His Personality." *Southern Review* 2, 1966.

Einstein, Albert and Leopold Infeld. *The Evolution of Physics from Early Concepts to Relativity and Quanta.* New York: Simon and Schuster, 1938.

Einstein, Albert. *Relativity: The Special and General Theory.* New York: Henry Holt & Co., 1920.

Elder, John. *Reading the Mountains of Home* (on "Directive"). Cambridge: Harvard University Press, 1998.

Emerson, Ralph Waldo. *Prose Works.* Boston, 1870.

————. *The Complete Works of Ralph Waldo Emerson.* Boston, 1876.

————. *The Essential Writings of Ralph Waldo Emerson.* Brooks Atkinson, ed. New York: The Modern Library, 2000.

Evans, Oliver H. "Deeds That Count: Robert Frost's Sonnets." *Texas Studies in Literature and Language* 23, 1981.

Evans, William R., ed. *Robert Frost and Sidney Cox: Forty Years of Friendship.* Hanover: University Press of New England, 1981.

Fabre, J. Henri. *The Hunting Wasps.* New York, 1915.

Faggen, Robert. *Robert Frost and the Challenge of Darwin.* Ann Arbor: University of Michigan Press, 1997.

Farjeon, Eleanor. *Edward Thomas: The Last Four Years.* Oxford: Oxford University Press, 1958.

Feld, Rose C. "Robert Frost Relieves His Mind." *New York Times Book Review* 21, October 1923.

Flint, F. S. "Review of *A Boy's Will.*" *Poetry and Drama* 1, June 1913.

Francis, Lesley Lee. "Between Poets: Robert Frost and Harriet Monroe." *South Carolina Review* 19, Summer 1987.

————. "A Decade of 'Stirring Times': Robert Frost and Amy Lowell." *New England Quarterly* 59, December 1986.

————. *The Frost Family's Adventures in Poetry: Sheer Morning Gladness at the Brim.* Columbia: University of Missouri Press, 1994.

————. "Robert Frost and the Majesty of Stones upon Stones." *Journal of Modern Literature* 9.1, 1981–1982.

Francis, Robert. *Frost: A Time to Talk.* Amherst, MA, 1972.

Frank, Philipp. *Einstein: His Life and Times.* New York: Alfred A. Knopf, 1947.

Garnett, E. "The New American Poet." *Atlantic Monthly* (August 1915).

Gasman, Daniel. *The Scientific Origins of National Socialism: Social Darwinism in Ernst Haeckel and the German Monist League.* London: MacDonald, 1971.

Gerber, Philip L., ed. *Robert Frost.* New York: Twayne, United States Authors Series, 1966. Revised edition, 1982.

Greenberg, Robert, ed. *Robert Frost: An Introduction, Poems, Criticism.* New York: Holt, Rinehart, and Winston, 1961.

Greiner, Donald J. *Robert Frost: The Poet and His Critics.* Chicago: American Library Association, 1974.

Glick, Thomas F. *The Comparative Reception of Darwinism.* Austin: The University of Texas Press, 1972.

Gould, Stephen Jay. *Evolution: The Pleasures of Pluralism.* In *The New York Review of Books,* June 12, 1997 and June 25, 1997.

Gray, Asa. *Natural Science and Religion.* New York, 1880.

di Gregoria, Mario A. *Thomas Henry Huxley's Place in Natural Science.* New Haven: Yale University Press, 1984.

Gruber, Jacob. *A Conscience of Conflict: The Life of St. George Jackson Mivart.* New York, 1960.

Hadas, Rachel. *Form, Cycle, Infinity: Landscape Imagery in the Poetry of Robert Frost.* Lewisburg, PA: Bucknell University Press, 1985.

Haeckel, Ernst. *Freedom in Science and Teaching.* Thomas Henry Huxley, trans. and ed. New York: D. Appleton, 1879.

Hall, Dorothy Judd. "An Old Testament Christian." *Frost Centennial Essays* III, Jac L. Tharpe, ed. Jackson, Mississippi, 1978.

————. *Contours of Belief: Robert Frost.* Athens, OH: Ohio University Press, 1986.

————. "The Height of Feeling Free: Frost and Bergson." *Texas Quarterly* 19 (Spring 1976).

Harris, Kathryn Gibbs. "Robert Frost's Early Education in Science." *South Carolina Review* 7.1, 1974.

————, ed. *Robert Frost: Studies of the Poetry.* Boston: G. K. Hall, 1979.

Hass, Robert Bernard. *Going by Contraries.* Charlottesville: University Press of Virginia, 2002.

Heaney, Seamus. "Above the Brim." *Homage to Robert Frost.* New York: Farrar, Straus & Giroux, 1996.

Hearn, Thomas K., Jr. "Making Sweetbreads Do: Robert Frost and Moral Empiricism." *New England Quarterly* 49, 1976.

Hewlett, Horace W. *In Other Words: Amherst in Prose and Verse.* Amherst: Amherst College, 1964.

Hiers, John T. "Robert Frost's Quarrel with Science and Technology." *Georgia Review* 25, 1971.

Highfield, Roger and Paul Carter. *The Private Lives of Albert Einstein.* New York: St. Martin's Press, 1993.

Hildegard, Hoeller. "Evolution and Metaphor in Robert Frost's Poetry." *South Carolina Review* 33, Spring 1990.

Himmelfarb, Gertrude. "Varieties of Social Darwinism." *Victorian Minds.* New York: Knopf, 1968.

Holland, Norman N. *The Brain of Robert Frost: A Cognitive Approach to Literature.* New York: Routledge, 1988.

Holton, Gerald. *Einstein, History, and Other Passions.* Woodbury, NY: American Institute of Physics Press, 1995.

Hughes, G. *Imagism and the Imagists.* Biblo and Tannen, 1931 and 1973.

Huxley, Aldous. *Literature and Science.* London: Chatto and Windus, 1963.

Huxley, Henrietta Heathorn, ed. *Aphorisms and Reflections from the Works of T. H. Huxley.*

Huxley, Julian and T. H. Huxley. *Touchstone for Ethics.* New York: Harper & Brothers, 1947.

Huxley, Leonard, ed. *Life and Letters of T. H. Huxley.* London. 2 vols.

Huxley, Thomas Henry. *American Addresses.* New York: 1893.

_____. *Evidence as to Man's Place in Nature.* New York: J. M. Denton & Sons, 1906.

_____. *Lay Sermons.* London, 1870.

_____. "Science and the Bishops." *Nineteenth Century,* November 1887; and "An Episcopal Trilogy," September 1888.

Ingebretsen, Edward. *Robert Frost's Star in a Stone Boat: A Grammar of Belief.* San Francisco: Catholic Scholars Press, 1994.

Irvine, William. *Apes, Angels and Victorians.* New York: McGraw-Hill, 1955.

James, William. *A Pluralistic Universe.* New York: Longmans, Green & Co., 1909.

_____. *Principles of Psychology.* New York: Henry Holt & Co., 1890.

_____. *The Varieties of Religious Experience.* New York: The Modern Library, 1902.

_____. *The Will to Believe.* New York: Dover Publications, 1956. Originally published in 1897.

Jarrell, Randall. "The Other Robert Frost" and "To The Laodiceans." *Poetry and the Age.* New York: Alfred A. Knopf, 1953.

Jones, Henry F. "Charles Darwin and Samuel Butler: A Step Toward Reconciliation." 1911.

Jones, Howard Mumford. "The Cosmic Loneliness of Robert Frost: Belief and Disbelief." *American Literature.* Chicago, 1967.

Jones, Richard Foster. "Science and Criticism in the Neo-Classical Age of English Literature"; "Science and Language in England of the Mid-Seventeenth Century." *The Seventeenth Century.* Palo Alto: Stanford University Press, 1951.

Jost, Walter. *Rhetorical Investigations.* Charlottesville: University of Virginia Press, 2004.

Juhnke, Anna K. "Religion in Robert Frost's Poetry." *American Literature* 36, May 1964.

Kau, Joseph. "'Trust . . . to go by Contraries': Incarnation and the Paradox of Belief in the Poetry of Robert Frost." *Frost Centennial Essays* II (1976).

Kearns, Katherine. *Robert Frost and the Poetics of Appetite.* Cambridge: Cambridge University Press, 1994.

Kemp, John C. *Robert Frost and New England: The Poet as Regionalist.* Princeton: Princeton University Press, 1979.

Kjörven, Johannes. *Robert Frost's Emergent Design: The Truth of the Self In-Between Belief and Unbelief.* Atlantic Highlands, NJ: Humanities Press International, 1987.

Knox, George. "A Backward Motion Toward the Source." *Personalist* 47, Summer 1966.

Krailsheimer, A. J., ed. *Pascal: Penseés.* New York: Penguin Books, 1966.

Kuzma, Greg, ed. "Gone into if Not Explained: Essays on Poems by Robert Frost." *Pebble Magazine* 14 & 15. Crete, Nebraska, 1976.

Lancaster, John. "A Descriptive Catalogue of the Robert Frost Collection." The Parkman Dexter Howe Library, Part VII. Ed. Sidney Ives. Gainesville, FL: University of Florida Press, 1990.

Langbaum, Robert. *The Poetry of Experience: The Dramatic Monologue in Modern Literary Tradition.* London: Chatto and Windus, 1957.

Larson, Mildred R. "Robert Frost as a Teacher." Dissertation. New York University, 1949.

Lathem, Edward Connery, ed. *A Concordance to the Poetry of Robert Frost.* Guilford, CT: Jeffrey Norton Publishers, 1994.

———— and Lawrance Thompson, eds. *Robert Frost: Farm-Poultryman.* Dartmouth, 1963.

———— and Lawrance Thompson. *Robert Frost and the Lawrence, Massachusetts 'High School Bulletin.'* New York: The Grolier Club, 1966.

Lentricchia, Frank. *Robert Frost: Modern Poetics and the Landscapes of Self.* Durham, NC: Duke University Press, 1975.

———— and Melissa Christensen Lentricchia, eds. *Robert Frost: A Bibliography, 1913–1974.* Scarecrow Author Bibliographies, No. 25. Metuchen, NJ: Scarecrow, 1976.

Library of Congress. *Robert Frost: Lectures on the Centennial of his Birth.* Washington, D.C.: Library of Congress, 1975.

Lind, L. R. "Robert Frost: Classicist." *Classical and Modern Literature* 1, Fall 1980.

Lowell, Amy. *Tendencies in Modern American Poetry.* New York: Haskell House Publishers, 1970.

Lovejoy, Arthur O. "Bergson and Romantic Evolutionism." *University of California Chronicle,* vol. 15, no. 438, October 1913.

———— and George Boas. *A Documentary History of Primitivism and Related Ideas.* Baltimore: The Johns Hopkins Press, 1935.

————. *The Great Chain of Being.* Harvard University Press, 1936.

————. *Reflections on Human Nature*. Baltimore: The Johns Hopkins Press, 1961.

————. *The Revolt Against Dualism*. New Brunswick, NJ: Transaction Publishers, 1996. Originally published in Chicago, 1930.

————. "William James as Philosopher." *International Journal of Ethics* 20, 1911.

Lynen, John F. *The Pastoral Art of Robert Frost*. New Haven, CT: Yale Univesity Press, 1960.

Macklem, Michael. *The Anatomy of the World: Relations between Natural and Moral Law from Donne to Pope*. Minneapolis: The University of Minneapolis Press, 1958.

MacLeish, Archibald. *J.B.* Boston: Houghton Mifflin, 1956.

MacLiammoir, M. and E. Boland. *Yeats and His World*. Viking, 1971.

Magill, Frank N., ed. *Masterpieces of World Philosophy*. New York: Harper Collins, 1990.

Marks, Andrew R. *The Rabbi and the Poet*. Alton, NH: Andover Green Book Publishers, 1994. 1.

Mason, Julian. "Frost's Conscious Accommodation of Contraries." *CEA Critic* 37, March 1976.

Mayr, Ernst. *The Growth of Biological Thought*. Cambridge, MA, 1982.

"The Story in the Meiklejohn Files" *Amherst College Archives*, Pt. 1, Fall 1982; Pt. 2, Spring 1983.

Mertins, Louis. *Robert Frost: Life and Talks-Walking*. Norman, OK: University of Oklahoma Press, 1965.

———— and Esther Mertins. *The Intervals of Robert Frost: A Critical Bibliography*. Berkeley: University Press of California, 1947.

Miller, Perry. *Errand into the Wilderness*. Cambridge, MA, 1956. Reprinted in New York, 1964.

————. *The New England Mind*. New York, 1939.

Mivart, St. George Jackson. *Genesis of Spirit*.

Monroe, Harriet. *Poets and Their Art*. New York: Macmillan, 1926.

————. *A Poet's Life: Seventy Years in a Changing World*. New York: Macmillan, 1938.

Monteiro, George. *Robert Frost and the New England Renaissance*. Lexington: University Press of Kentucky, 1988.

————. "Robert Frost's Linked Analogies." *New England Quarterly* 46, 1973.

Montgomery, Marion. "Robert Frost and His Use of Barriers: Man vs. Nature Toward God." *South Atlantic Quarterly* 57, Summer 1958.

Moore, James R. *The Post–Darwinian Controversies*. Cambridge, England: Cambridge University Press, 1979.

More, Paul Elmer. *Shelburne Essays*. Vol. VII. New York: Phaeton Press, 1963. First published in 1913.

Morrison, Kathleen. *Robert Frost: A Pictorial Chronicle*. New York: Holt, 1974.

Morrison, Theodore. "The Agitated Heart." *Atlantic Monthly*, July 1967.

_____. *The Bread Loaf Writers' Conference: The First Thirty Years*. Middlebury, VT: Middlebury College, 1976.

_____. "Frost: Country Poet and Cosmopolitan Poet." *Yale Review* 59, Winter 1970.

Mosse, George L. *The Crisis of German Ideology: Intellectual Origins of the Third Reich*. New York: Grosset and Dunlap, 1954.

Munson, Gorham B. "The Classicism of Robert Frost." *Modern Age* 8, 1964.

_____. *Recognition of Robert Frost*. New York: Henry Holt & Co., 1937.

_____. *Robert Frost: A Study in Sensibility and Good Sense*. New York: Doubleday, 1927. Republished in 1968.

Nelson, Robert J. *Pascal: Adversary and Advocate*. Cambridge: Harvard University Press, 1981.

Newdick, Robert S. *Newdick's Season of Frost: An Interrupted Biography*. William A. Sutton, ed. Albany: State University of New York Press, 1976.

_____. "Robert Frost and the Sound of Sense." *American Literature* 9, 1937.

_____. "Robert Frost and the Dramatic." *New England Quarterly*, June 1937.

Newman, John Henry. *The Idea of a University*. New York: Longmans, Green, 1923.

Nilakantan, Mangalam. "Something Beyond Conflict: A Study of the Dual Vision of Robert Frost." *Indian Journal of American Studies*, 1969.

Nitchie, George W. *Human Values in the Poetry of Robert Frost: A Study of a Poet's Convictions*. Durham, NC: Duke University Press, 1960.

_____. "A Momentary Stay Against Confusion." *Robert Frost: A Collection of Critical Essays*. James M. Cox, ed. Englewood Cliffs, NJ: 1962.

O'Donnell, William G. "Parable in Poetry." *Virginia Quarterly Review* 25, Spring 1949.

_____. "Robert Frost and New England: A Reevaluation." *Yale Review*, Summer 1948.

Ogilvie, John T. "From Woods to Stars: A Pattern of Imagery in Robert Frost's Poetry." *South Atlantic Quarterly* 58, Winter 1959.

Orlov, Paul A. "The World's Disorder and the World's Design in Two Poems by Frost." *Journal of the Midwest Modern Language Association* 19.2, 1986.

Osborn, Henry Fairfield. "Aristogenesis, the Creative Principle in *Origin of Species*." *The American Naturalist*, no. 716, May–June 1934.

_____. *From the Greeks to Darwin*. New York, 1894.

Oster, Judith. *Toward Robert Frost: The Reader and the Poet*. Athens, GA: University of Georgia Press, 1991.

Pack, Robert. *Belief and Uncertainty in the Poetry of Robert Frost*. Hanover, NH: University Press of New England, 2003.

_____. "Robert Frost's 'Enigmatical Reserve': The Poet as Teacher and Preacher." *Robert Frost: Lectures on the Centennial of His Birth*. Washington, D.C.: Library of Congress, 1975.

Parini, Jay. *Robert Frost: A Life*. London: Heinemann, 1998. New York: Henry Holt, 1999.

_____. "Emerson and Frost: The Present Act of Vision." *Sewanee Review* 89.2 (Spring 1981).

Peel, J. D. Y. *Herbert Spencer: The Evolution of a Sociologist*. London, 1871.

Perkins, David. "Robert Frost." *A History of Modern Poetry*. 2 vols. Cambridge, MA: Harvard University Press, 1976.

Perrine, Laurence. "Robert Frost and the Idea of Immortality." *Frost Centennial Essays* II, 1976.

Perry, Ralph Barton. *The Thought and Character of William James*.

Peters, Joan D. "Education by Poetry: Robert Frost's Departure from the Modern Critical Tradition." *South Carolina Review* 21.1, 1988.

Poirier, Richard. "The Art of Poetry II: Robert Frost." *Paris Review* 24, 1960.

_____. *Robert Frost: The Work of Knowing*. New York: Oxford University Press, 1977.

Pope, Alexander. *Essay on Man*. 1733–34.

Potter, James L. *The Robert Frost Handbook*. University Park: Pennsylvania State University Press, 1980.

Pound, Ezra. *The Letters of Ezra Pound*. D. D. Paige, ed. New York: Harcourt, Brace, 1950.

_____. "Modern Georgics." *Poetry* 5, December 1914.

Pritchard, William H. *Frost: A Literary Life Reconsidered*. New York: Oxford University Press, 1984.

*Proceedings: National Poetry Festival*. Washington, D.C.: Library of Congress, 1964.

Rechnitz, Robert M. "The Tragic Vision of Robert Frost." *Frost Centennial Essays*, 1974.

Reeve, Franklin D. *Robert Frost in Russia*. Boston: Little, Brown, 1963.

Reichenbach, Hans. *From Copernicus to Einstein*. Trans. Ralph E. Winn. New York: Dover Publications, 1942.

Reichert, Victor E. "The Faith of Robert Frost." *Frost Centennial Essays*, 1974.

_____. "The Robert Frost I Knew." *Frost Centennial Essays* III, 1978.

Richards, Robert J. *Darwin and the Emergence of Evolutionary Theories of Mind and Behavior*. Chicago: University of Chicago Press 1987.

Richardson, Mark. *The Ordeal of Robert Frost: The Poet and His Poetics*. Urbana: University of Illinois Press, 1997.

_____. "Robert Frost and the Motives of Poetry." *Essays in Literature* 20.2 (1993).

_____. "Robert Frost's Prose Writings: A Comprehensive Annotated Checklist and Introductory Essay." *Resources for American Literary Study* 22.1, 1996.

Ridland, John. "Fourteen Ways of Looking at a Bad Man." *Southwest Review* 71.2, Spring 1986.

*Robert Frost Review, The.* January 1992 to Fall 2005. Published annually by the Robert Frost Society. Department of English, University of Southern Mississippi, Hattiesburg, Mississippi.

Robson, W. W. "The Achievement of Robert Frost." *Southern Review* 2, October 1966.

Rogers, James Allen. "Darwinism and Social Darwinism." *Journal of the History of Ideas* 33, no. 2, 1972.

Romanes, G. J. *Darwin and After Darwin.* 1892–1897.

Rotella, Guy. "Comparing Conception: Frost and Eddington, Heisenberg, and Bohr." *American Literature* 59.2, 1987.

Russell, Bertrand. *The Analysis of the Mind.* 1921.

Salska, Agnieszka. "Knowledge and Experience in the Early Frost." *American Poetry between Tradition and Modernism: 1865–1914.* Roland Hagenbuchle, ed. Regensburg: Pustet, 1984.

Sanders, David. "Words in the Rush of Everything to Waste." *South Carolina Review* 7.1, 1974.

Santayana, George. "Apologica Pro Mente Sua." *The Philosophy of George Santayana.* Ed. Paul Arthur Schilpp. Evanston, IL, 1940.

_____. *The Genteel Tradition at Bay.* 1931.

_____. "The Harvard Yard." *Persons and Places.* New York: Scribner's, 1944.

_____. *The Last Puritan.* New York: Scribner's, 1936.

_____. *Physical Order and Moral Liberty: Previously Unpublished Essays of George Santayana.* John and Shirley Locks, eds. Charlotte, NC: Vanderbilt University Press, 1969.

_____. *The Sense of Beauty.* New York, 1896.

_____. *Winds of Doctrine.* 1905.

Schilpp, Paul Arthur, ed. *Albert Einstein: Philosopher-Scientist.* Evanston, IL: Library of Living Philosophers, Inc., 1949.

Schwartz, Sanford. *The Matrix of Modernism.* Princeton: Princeton University Press, 1985.

Seale, Lisa Abshear. "Robert Frost at the Fountain Street Church. Grand Rapids, Michigan, November 19, 1959." *The Robert Frost Review* 13 (Fall 2003).

_____. "What Catullus Means by *Mens Animi*: Robert Frost's 'Kitty Hawk.'" *Robert Frost Review,* Fall 1993.

Sears, John F. "William James, Henri Bergson and the Poetics of Robert Frost." *New England Quarterly* 48 (1995).

Sergeant, Elizabeth Shepley. *Robert Frost: The Trial by Existence.* New York: Holt, Rinehart, and Winston, 1960.

Shaw, George Bernard. *Back to Methuselah.* New York, 1946. First published in 1921.

_____. *Collected Letters 1898–1910*. ed. Dan H. Lawrence. New York, 1972.

_____. "Darwin Denounced." *Pall Mall Gazette*, May 31, 1887.

Sheehy, Donald G. "The Poet as Neurotic: The Official Biography of Robert Frost." *American Literature* 58, No. 3, October 1986.

_____. "Refiguring Love: Robert Frost in Crisis, 1938–1942." *New England Quarterly*, June 1998.

Sims, G. "Alida Monro and the Poetry Bookshop." *Antiquarian Book Monthly Review*, July 1982.

Sinclair, M. "The Poems of F. S. Flint." *The English Review*, January 1921.

Sisson, C. *English Poetry 1900–1950*. New York: Methuen, 1981.

Smith, Thomas G. "Robert Frost, Stewart Udall, and the 'Last Go Down.'" *New England Quarterly* 70.1, March 1997.

Snow, C. P. "Robert Frost." *Variety of Men*. New York: Charles Scribner's Sons, 1966.

Sokol, B. J. "Bergson, Instinct, and Frost's 'The White-Tailed Hornet.'" *American Literature: A Journal of Literary History, Criticism, and Bibliography* 62.1, 1990.

_____. "What Went Wrong Between RF and Ezra Pound." *New England Quarterly*, December 1976.

Squires, Radcliffe. *The Major Themes of Robert Frost*. Ann Arbor: The University of Michigan Press, 1963.

Stallknecht, Newton. *George Santayana*. Minneapolis, 1971.

Stanlis, Peter J. "Rehabilitating Robert Frost: The Unity of His Literary, Cultural, and Political Thought." *The Intercollegiate Review*, Fall 1985.

_____. "Robert Frost: The Individual and Society" and "Robert Frost: Politics in Theory and Practice." *Robert Frost: The Individual and Society.* Rockford, IL: Rockford College, 1973.

_____. "Robert Frost's Masques and the Classic American Tradition." *Frost Centennial Essays* I. Jac Tharpe, ed. Jackson, MS: 1974.

_____. "Robert Frost: Politics in Theory and Practice." (Revised ed.) *Frost Centennial Essays* II, 1976.

_____. "Acceptable in Heaven's Sight: Frost at Bread Loaf, 1939–1941." *Frost Centennial Essays* III, 1978.

_____. *Robert Frost at Bread Loaf.* Middlebury, VT: 1964.

_____. "Robert Frost: The Conversationalist as Poet." *Modern Age*, Fall 1997.

_____. "Robert Frost and Darwin's Theory of Evolution." Part One, *Modern Age*, Spring 2000.

_____. "Robert Frost and Darwin's Theory of Evolution." Part Two, *Modern Age*, Summer 2000.

_____. "Robert Frost and Creative Evolution." *Modern Age*, Spring 2002.

_____. "Dualism: The Basis of Robert Frost's Philosophy." *The Robert Frost Review*, Fall 1994.

_____. "The Role of Dualism and Metaphor in Robert Frost's Intellectual Life." *The Robert Frost Review*, Fall 2000.

_____. "In the Clearing: Continuity and Unity in Frost's Dualism." *Humanitas*, 2005.

_____. "Robert Frost's Philosophy of Education: The Poet as Teacher." *Roads Not Taken: Rereading Robert Frost*. Eds. Earl J. Wilcox and Jonathan N. Barron. University of Missouri Press, 2000.

Stegner, Wallace. "Robert Frost and Bernard DeVoto." Palo Alto, CA: Association of the Stanford University Libraries, 1974.

Stott, Jon C. *An Outline of the Poetry of Robert Frost*. Toronto: Forum House, 1971.

Sullivan, Bradley. "'Education by Poetry' in Robert Frost's 'Masques.'" *Papers on Language and Literature* 22 (1986).

Swedenborg, Emanuel. *Divine Love and Wisdom*. London: The Swedenborg Society, 1969. Originally published in 1763.

_____. *Heaven and Hell*. London, 1931. Originally published in 1758.

Taylor, Welford Dunaway. *Robert Frost and J. J. Lankes: Riders on Pegasus*. Hanover, NH: Dartmouth College Library, 1996.

Tharpe, Jac L., ed. *Frost Centennial Essays*. 3 vols. Jackson: MS, 1974, 1976, 1978.

Thompson, Lawrance. *Emerson and Frost: Critics of Their Times*. Philadelphia: Philo-Biblon Club, 1940.

_____. *Fire and Ice: The Art and Thought of Robert Frost*. New York: Henry Holt, 1942.

_____. *Robert Frost*. University of Minnesota Pamphlets on American Writers, 2. Minneapolis, 1960.

_____. *Robert Frost: The Early Years, 1874–1915*. New York, 1966.

_____. *Robert Frost: The Years of Triumph, 1915–1938*. New York, 1970.

_____, and R.H. Winnick. *Robert Frost: The Later Years, 1938–1963*. New York, 1976.

_____. *Selected Letters of Robert Frost*. New York, 1964.

Thornton, Richard, ed. *Recognition of Robert Frost: Twenty-fifth Anniversary*. New York: Henry Holt, 1937.

Tilley, Morris P. "Notes from Conversations with Robert Frost. *Inlander*, February 1918.

Trilling, Lionel. "A Speech on Robert Frost: A Cultural Episode." *Partisan Review* 26, Summer 1959.

Udall, Stewart L. "Robert Frost, Kennedy and Khruschev: A Memoir of Poetry and Power." *Shenandoah* 26, Winter 1975.

Untermeyer, Louis. *From Another World*. New York, 1939.

_____. "Edward Thomas." *North American Review*, February 1919.

_____, ed. *Robert Frost: A Backward Look*. Washington, D.C.: Reference Department, The Library of Congress, 1964.

Van Dore, Wade. *Robert Frost and Wade Van Dore: The Life of the Hired Man.* Ed. Thomas H. Wetmore. Wright State University Monograph 6. Dayton, OH 1986.

Van Egmond, Peter, ed. *The Critical Reception of Robert Frost.* Boston, 1974.

Waggoner, Hyatt H. "The Humanistic Idealism of Robert Frost." *American Literature* 12, November 1941.

Wagner, Linda W., ed. *Robert Frost: The Critical Reception.* New York, 1977.

Walsh, John Evangelist. *Into My Own: The English Years of Robert Frost, 1912–1913.* New York, 1988.

Warner, Stephen D. "Robert Frost in the Clearing: The Risk of Spirit in Substantiation." *Frost Centennial Essays,* 1974.

Waton, Harry. *A True Monistic Philosophy.* Vol. I. New York: Spinoza Institute of America, 1947.

Watts, Harold H. "Robert Frost and the Interrupted Dialogue." *American Literature* 27, March 1955.

Weber, Alfred. *History of Philosophy.* 1896.

Werkmeister, W. K. *A History of Philosophical Ideas in America.* New York, 1949.

Whitehead, Alfred North. *Science and the Modern World.* Cambridge, England, 1953.

Whitney, Lois. *Primitivism and the Idea of Progress.* Baltimore, 1934.

Wilcox, Earl J., ed. *His Incalculable Influence on Others: Essays on Robert Frost in Our Time.* Victoria, British Columbia, 1994.

Williams, Ellen. *Harriet Monroe and the Poetry Renaissance: The First Ten Years of Poetry, 1912–1922.* Urbana, IL: 1977.

Wilson, Daniel J. *Arthur O. Lovejoy and the Quest for Intelligibility.* Chapel Hill, NC, 1980.

Wiltshire, David. *The Social and Political Thought of Herbert Spencer.* Oxford, England, 1978.

Winters, Yvor. "Robert Frost: Or, The Spiritual Drifter as Poet." *Sewanee Review* 56, 1948.

Yogi, L. L. "The Scientist in Robert Frost's Poetry." *Rajasthan University Studies in English* 10, 1977.

Young, Robert M. *Darwin's Metaphor.* Cambridge, England, 1985.

# Notes

## Prelude, Frost the Conversationalist as Poet

1. The following bibliographical items on Frost as a conversationalist include records of private talks with the poet, interviews, and comments made by Frost during his poetry readings: John Ciardi, "An Interview with Robert Frost," *Dialogue With an Audience* (Philadelphia: J. B. Lippincott, 1963), and "Robert Frost: Master Conversationalist at Work," *Saturday Review of Literature* (March 21, 1959); Reginald L. Cook, *Robert Frost: A Living Voice* (Amherst: University of Massachusetts Press, 1974), and "Robert Frost in Context," in *Frost Centennial Essays*, vol. 3 (Jackson: University Press of Mississippi, 1978); Rosemary Dean, "The Voices of Robert Frost," *Commonweal* 69, 1959; Robert Francis, *Frost: A Time to Talk: Conversations and Indiscretions* (Amherst: University of Massachusetts Press, 1972); Arthur Harris, "Conversations with Robert Frost" (archives of Amherst College Library); Raymond Holden, "Reminiscences of Robert Frost" (archives of the Baker Library, Dartmouth College); Clifford Lyons, "Walks and Talks with Robert Frost," in *Robert Frost: The Man and the Poet*, Earl J. Wilcox, ed. (Conway, Arkansas: UCA Press, 1990); Edward C. Lathem, ed., *Interviews with Robert Frost* (New York: Holt, Rinehart and Winston, 1966); Louis Mertins, *Robert Frost: Life and Talks-Walking* (Norman: University of Oklahoma Press, 1965); Vrest Orton, *Vermont Afternoons with Robert Frost* (Rutland, Vermont: Charles E. Tuttle Co., 1971); Richard Poirier, "Robert Frost," in *Writers at Work: The Paris Review Interviews: Second Series* (New York: Viking, 1963); Daniel Smythe, *Robert Frost Speaks* (New York: Twayne, 1964); C. P. Snow, *Variety of Men* (New York: Charles Scribner's Sons, 1967); Peter J. Stanlis, "Acceptable in Heaven's Sight: Robert Frost at Bread Loaf, 1939–1941," in *Frost Centennial Essays*, vol.

3; William Sutton, ed., *Newdick's Season of Frost: An Interrupted Biography of Robert Frost* (Albany: State University of New York Press, 1976); Dorothy Tyler, "Robert Frost in Michigan," in *Frost Centennial Essays*, vol. 3; Baird Whitlock, "Conversations with Robert Frost," *Xavier Review* 3 (New Orleans, 1983); Richard Wilbur, "Two Robert Frost Interviews" (archives of Amherst College Library).

For visual and auditory recordings of Frost, see *Voices and Visions*, program 5: Robert Frost (The New York Center for Visual History, 1988); The Annenberg / CPB Collection, distributed by Intellimation, P.O. Box 1922, Santa Barbara, Calif. 93116; *The Author Speaks: Robert Frost: An Evening with Robert Frost*, Audio-Forum #AS20, distributed by On the Green, Guilford, Conn. 06437; Burgess Meredith, *The Afterglow: A Tribute to Robert Frost* (Winterset Productions), distributed by Pyramid Film & Video, 2801 Colorado Avenue, Santa Monica, Calif. 90404. For Robert Frost reading twenty-three of his poems, see Decca Records, DL 9033.

2. Reginald L. Cook, "Robert Frost in Context," *Frost Centennial Essays*, vol. 3, 123; and *Robert Frost: A Living Voice*, 208. See especially Cook's chapter "The Sayer," 208–17.

3. Louis Mertins, *Robert Frost: Life and Talks-Walking*, preface, viii. Mertins's book is filled with concrete evidence of the range and power of Frost's conversation.

4. Peter J. Stanlis, "Acceptable in Heaven's Sight: Robert Frost at Bread Loaf: 1939–1941," in *Frost Centennial Essays*, vol. 3, 179–311. This literary memoir covers the first three summers of talks with Frost.

5. William Carlos Williams and James Laughlin, *Selected Letters*, Hugh Witemeyer, ed. (New York: W. W. Norton, 1989), 40.

6. John Ciardi, *Dialogue With an Audience*, 169.

7. See Edward C. Lathem, ed., *Interviews with Robert Frost*, 24. In July 1939, at Bread Loaf, Frost stated to me that next to poetry he valued and enjoyed "good talk" with his friends above anything.

8. Louis Mertins, *Robert Frost: Life and Talks-Walking*, 197–98.

9. Lawrance Thompson, *Robert Frost: The Early Years*, 371.

10. See Lawrance Thompson, *Robert Frost: The Early Years*, 346–47. Both as a teacher and as a poet, throughout his life Frost had little use for rational critical analysis of poetry or for scholarly attempts by academics to deal with poetry systematically through the scientific method. Poetry was for Frost a dramatic performance, both in its composition and appreciation.

11. Ibid., 360–64. In retrospect Frost remarked that revising and putting on these plays at Pinkerton Academy was his happiest experience as a teacher. When he went to the New Hampshire State Normal School at Plymouth in 1911–12, he continued to explore the dramatic elements in poetry as good talk by reading aloud to his students Synge's *Playboy of the Western World* and Shaw's *Arms and the Man*. He became skillful in imitating the Irish accents in Synge's dialogues.

12. Louis Mertins, *Robert Frost: Life and Talks-Walking*, 188.
13. Ibid., 177.
14. Lawrance Thompson, ed., *Selected Letters of Robert Frost* (New York: Holt, Rinehart and Winston, 1964), 97. Frost's statements were confirmed by his sister Jeannie Frost, in a letter to Wilbur E. Rowell, March 8, 1914, 120.
15. Ibid., 102.
16. Ibid., 110. For Frost's elaboration on "sounds" and how they function through changes in voice tones, see 111–13.
17. Ibid., 122.
18. Ibid., 79–81. Frost italicized *specially*. For a detailed account of what Frost meant by vocal images and "talk-songs," see Reginald L. Cook, "Tones of Voice," in *The Dimensions of Robert Frost* (New York: Rinehart and Company, 1958), 61–66.
19. In his English notebooks Frost wrote: "The mind or spirit is not really active unless it is finding constantly new tones of voice." See John Evangelist Walsh, *Into My Own: The English Years of Robert Frost, 1912–1915* (New York: Grove, 1988), 222.
20. Lawrance Thompson, ed., *Selected Letters of Robert Frost*, 107–08.
21. For Frost's letter to Haines, see Lawrance Thompson, ed., *Selected Letters of Robert Frost*, 127. In December 1914, in a letter to Sidney Cox, Frost made it clear that his "method" regarding the sound of sense and voice tones was far more than a technique in writing, because it included all that was vital in his creative imagination and knowledge of life: "We write of things we see and we write in accents we hear. Thus we gather both our material and our technique with the imagination from life; and our technique becomes as much material as material itself." In Frost's poems the method, structure, and material form a single unified whole through the phonetic pattern, including speech tones, and these reveal through the "play" of the imagination vital aspects of the relationship between spirit and matter.
22. John Evangelist Walsh, *Into My Own*, 138. For an elaborate comment on the American genesis of "Mending Wall," see 139–42.
23. Ibid., 144–45.
24. Ibid., 191. For comments on all three of Thomas's reviews, see 189–93.
25. "What the two [Thomas and Frost] certainly did talk about, and at considerable length, was Frost's sound-of-sense theories of versification . . ." John Evangelist Walsh, *Into My Own*, 192–93.
26. Ibid., 167.

## Chapter 1, Dualism: The Basis of Frost's Philosophy

1. See Joseph R. Strayer, ed., *Dictionary of the Middle Ages*, vol. 4 (New York: Scribner, 1984), 297.

2. Harry Waton, *A True Monistic Philosophy*, vol. 1 (New York: The Spinoza Institute of America, 1947), "Introduction," xv. Waton contended that Spinoza and Hegel are the chief modern monistic philosophers. Frost's understanding of the two monisms differs from Waton's account. Since all of the chapters in this study are based upon Frost's understanding of the conflicts between dualism and monism, it is useful to know how he perceived these conflicts throughout European and American history. In 1898, in his course in philosophy with George Santayana at Harvard University, Frost read Alfred Weber's *History of Philosophy* (1896). This textbook made him aware of the whole range of philosophical conflicts between dualists and monists from the ancient Greeks to the late nineteenth century. From Weber he learned that no category of philosophy was to be regarded in any "absolute sense," because "even the most decided monists advanced a relative dualism," and "conversely, the most characteristic pluralist systems acknowledge the relative truths of monism." Frost's own firmly held but unsystematic dualism, like that of Aristotle, was never treated in a doctrinaire or dogmatic fashion as an absolute category. He retained respect for particular beliefs set forth by such idealistic monists as Plato and Emerson, even while rejecting their basic monism. During conversations with me at Bread Loaf, Frost identified as monists Hegel in philosophy, Whitman in poetry, Unitarianism and Christian Science in religion, and Arnold Toynbee in history. During the summers of 1939–44, I noted that the bookcase in his cabin contained Weber's book, brought up from Boston each summer, a sign of how much he valued it. Among other studies in Frost's cabin on the dualism-monism conflicts throughout history was Alfred North Whitehead's *Science and the Modern World* (1953). Whitehead noted that since the seventeenth century, "modern philosophy . . . has oscillated in a complex manner between three extremes. There are the dualists, who accept matter and mind as on an equal basis, and the two varieties of monists, those who put mind inside matter, and those who put matter inside mind." Whitehead also observed that since the seventeenth century, "the scheme of scientific ideas which have dominated thought . . . involves a fundamental duality, with material on the one hand, and on the other hand mind" (19–20). Frost recognized that the crucial figure in this modern development was René Descartes (1596–1650). His empirical-analytical methodology regarding reliable knowledge through science was assumed by many followers to apply with equal validity to both spirit and matter. Frost took strong exception to this assumption, and to histories of philosophy that identified Descartes as a dualist. The poet believed that the French philosopher and mathematician was a double monist. He questioned whether that thinker's methodology was valid regarding things of the spirit. He perceived Cartesian materialism and mathematical reasoning as the basis of what became modern scientific positivism centered in a monism of matter. This monism could be held simultaneously with a monism of spirit, but it did not constitute a dualism. This understand-

ing by Frost needs to be kept in mind when examining his critical responses to Victorian and twentieth-century theories of science regarding Darwin and Einstein, and when examining his perception of the modern revolt against dualism, as set forth by Arthur O. Lovejoy, and how it shaped Frost's beliefs regarding modern culture and totalitarian politics.

3. If no other evidence existed that Frost emphatically rejected both forms of monism, his harsh criticism of all utopian theories that reflect a desire to establish "the fabled federation of mankind" in a "one world" social order would be sufficient to make clear his own dualistic beliefs.

4. Robert Frost, "Introduction to *Threescore: The Autobiography of Sarah N. Cleghorn*," in *Frost: Collected Poems, Prose, & Plays* (New York: The Library of America, 1995), 749.

5. Ibid., 750. My italics.

6. Ibid., 751-52.

7. Lawrance Thompson, ed., *Selected Letters of Robert Frost* (New York: Holt, Rinehart and Winston, 1964), 584.

8. Lawrance Thompson, *Robert Frost: The Years of Triumph, 1915–1938* (New York: Holt, Rinehart and Winston, 1970), 290.

9. Robert Francis, *Frost: A Time to Talk—Conversations and Indiscretions Recorded by Robert Francis* (Amherst: University of Massachusetts Press, 1972), 31–32. Francis's italics.

10. Ibid., 51.

11. Edward C. Lathem and Lawrance Thompson, eds., *Robert Frost and the Lawrence, Massachusetts, "High School Bulletin,"* (New York: Grolier Club, 1966), 21.

12. Ibid., 18.

13. Ibid.

14. Ibid.

15. Ibid., 21.

16. Ibid.

17. Ibid.

18. Ibid.

19. In *Robert Frost: The Years of Triumph, 1915–1938*, only four "beliefs" are mentioned, but in "Education by Poetry," *Selected Prose of Robert Frost* (1949), a fifth—"the national belief"—is included.

20. The literal meaning of Francis's statement is confirmed in an item in Frost's notebooks: "After a person has said a thing you have to stay around with him a long time and perhaps hear him put it in different ways at different times if you are going to understand him."

21. Lawrance Thompson, *Robert Frost: The Early Years, 1874–1915* (New York: Holt, Rinehart and Winston), 477.

22. *Robert Frost: The Years of Triumph, 1915–1938*, 314.

23. Thompson does include "Justice vs Mercy" and "Opposites" in his subject index, but these subjects are merely particular examples of Frost's moral dualism.

24. For the psychological sources and origins of Thompson's demonology, see Donald G. Sheehy, "The Poet as Neurotic: The Official Biography of Robert Frost," *American Literature*, vol. 58, no. 3 (October 1986).
25. Kjörven's book has also been published by Humanities Press International, Inc., Atlantic Highlands, New Jersey.
26. Johannes Kjörven, *Robert Frost's Emergent Design: The Truth of the Self In-Between Belief and Unbelief* (Oslo, Norway: Solum Forlag A/S, 1987).
27. Ibid., 50.
28. Ibid., 50–51.
29. Ibid., 81–83.
30. Ibid., 149.

## Chapter 2, The Nature and Role of Metaphor in Frost's Dualism

1. Lawrance Thompson, *Robert Frost: The Early Years, 1874–1915* (New York: Holt, Rinehart, and Winston, 1966), 392.
2. Ibid., 409.
3. Ibid., 593.
4. See Frost's letters to John T. Bartlett (July 4, 1913 and February 19, 1914); to Sidney Cox (January 19, 1914 and December 1914); to John Cournos (July 8, 1914); and to William Braithwaite (March 22, 1915). The early letters in the decades of correspondence with Louis Untermeyer also contain statements on colloquial voice tones as metaphors of sound that convey meanings.
5. *Frost: Collected Poems, Prose, & Plays,* 729.
6. Ibid., 712.
7. Ibid., 824.
8. See ibid., 576–88.
9. Joseph Pearce, *Wisdom and Innocence: A Life of G. K. Chesterton* (San Francisco: Ignatius Press, 1996), 366.
10. *Frost: Collected Poems, Prose, & Plays,* 723–24.
11. Whit Burnett, ed., *This Is My Best* (New York: The Dial Press, 1942), 277–78.
12. *The Letters of Robert Frost to Louis Untermeyer,* 9.
13. Lawrance Thompson, *Robert Frost: The Years of Triumph, 1915–1938,* 619. The inability of science to make normative judgments in ethics, according to Frost, was evident in 1925 when he confronted a group of academic scientists at the University of Michigan who were "so sure of themselves in evolution that they haven't taken the trouble to think out their position." Evidently the scientists assumed that the biological or physical bases of evolution carried over into improvements in ethics, which warranted a belief in "progress" in human nature and society. Frost challenged them by asking, "Did they think it was ever going to be any easier to be good?" Like Darwin, Frost did not be-

lieve that evolution sanctioned a belief in "progress." See Thompson, *Robert Frost: The Years* of *Triumph, 1915–1938,* 296–97.

14. *Frost: Collected Poems, Prose* & *Plays,* 726.
15. Ibid. Frost's italics.
16. Ibid.
17. Ibid., 727.
18. Aldous Huxley, *Literature and Science* (London: Chatto and Windus, 1963), 11.

## Chapter 3, Frost and Darwin's Theory: "The Metaphor of Evolution"

1. See Lawrance Thompson, *Robert Frost: The Early Years, 1874–1915,* 89–90. Hereafter cited as Thompson, *The Early Years.*
2. See Lawrance Thompson, ed., *Selected Letters of Robert Frost,* 530. Hereafter cited as Frost, *Selected Letters.*
3. In a letter to Thompson (June 12, 1948) Frost wrote: "I looked on my mother's devoutness and thought it was beautiful. She had purity of spirit." Frost, *Selected Letters,* 530.
4. For the respective influences of Burell and Frost's mother on his interest in science and religion during the crucial years 1889–92, see Thompson, *The Early Years,* 88–92 and 118–20.
5. Ibid., 119.
6. Edward Connerly Lathem and Lawrance Thompson, eds., *Robert Frost and the Lawrence, Massachusetts "High School Bulletin,"* (New York: Grolier Club, 1966), 18.
7. At Bread Loaf in 1942, Frost remembered that his mother also quoted from Genesis 3:19: "For dust thou art, and unto dust thou shalt return." In a conversation with me he extended the creation and end of life out of dust to all other creatures.
8. See Francis Darwin, ed., *The Life and Letters of Charles Darwin,* vol. 2 (New York: D. Appleton and Co., 1911), 45. See also 28 and 146. Hereafter cited as Darwin, *The Life and Letters.*
9. Thompson, *The Early Years,* 119.
10. Reginald L. Cook, ed., *Robert Frost: A Living Voice* (Amherst: University of Massachusetts Press, 1974), 100. See also 83. For another variation on Frost's witticism, see Jac Tharpe, ed., *Frost Centennial Essays,* vol. 3 (Jackson: University Press of Mississippi, 1978), 144. In Frost's notebook number 001275 in the Baker Library at Dartmouth College, he wrote: "When the fact of evolution came up to shake the Church's certainties about creation and the date of it 4004 B.C. I bade myself be not dismayed. The old idea we were asked to give up was that God made man out of mud at one stroke. I saw that the new idea would have to be that God made man out of prepared mud that he had taken his time about working up gradation. I was not much put out or off my own thinking. There was as much of a God in it as ever."

11. See "The Future of Man," Richard Poirier and Mark Richardson, eds., *Frost: Collected Poems, Prose, and Plays* (New York: The Library of America, 1995), 869–70. This is an edited fragment of the symposium.

12. Notebook 001729 in the Baker Library, Dartmouth College.

13. For a full explication of Frost's notes in preparing to write "Sitting by a Bush in Broad Daylight" and his comments on the analogies between Genesis and Darwin's theory, see Lawrance Thompson, *Robert Frost: The Years of Triumph, 1915–1938*, 627–30. Hereafter cited as Thompson, *The Years of Triumph*.

14. For James's influence on Frost at Harvard, see Thompson, *The Early Years*, 238–43. Thompson ignores the influence of Gray.

15. Asa Gray, *Natural Science and Religion* (New York: C. Scribner's Sons, 1880), 54–55.

16. Ibid., 55. For a detailed account of Gray's interpretation of Darwin's theory, see James R. Moore, *The Post–Darwinian Controversies* (New York: Cambridge University Press, 1979), 269–80.

17. Ibid., 82.

18. Ibid., 104.

19. Ibid., 105.

20. Ibid., 85.

21. Ibid., 89.

22. Ibid., 87 and 93.

23. See Ralph Barton Perry, *The Thought and Character of William James*, vol. 1 (Boston: Little, Brown, 1935), 265–66.

24. For mind and will as vital factors in James's view of evolution, see Robert J. Richards, *Darwin and the Emergence of Evolutionary Theories of Mind and Behavior* (Chicago: University of Chicago Press, 1987), 440–50. On this important point Thompson wrote: "One of his strongest reasons for admiring William James was the ability of this particular scientist to make his own approaches 'pluralistic' enough to encompass physics and metaphysics. . . . Like James, Frost wanted to be 'pluralistic' in the sense that he could combine naturalism and idealism, physics and metaphysics, skepticism and mysticism. It was a feat which he managed to maintain throughout the rest of his life. . . ." Thompson, *The Early Years*, 243 and 246. Thompson's last sentence indicates that he rejected Frost's dualism as a form of self-deception. That is why, although he was aware of the dualistic opposites in Frost's philosophy "throughout the rest of his life," he nevertheless almost completely ignored Frost's dualism in discussing the poet's beliefs in science, religion, poetry, education, politics, and art. This error goes a long way toward explaining why Thompson's biography is so badly flawed. His index on Frost omits dualism entirely.

25. Jay Parini, *Robert Frost: A Life* (New York: Henry Holt, 1999), 63.

26. Thompson, *The Early Years*, 247. Shaler also taught "Outlines of the Half Course in Natural History, with reference to Dana's Manual of Geology, and Notes," in which he made use of Darwin's recordings on changes in typog-

raphy (16), and on "atolls . . . found by masses of coral growing on sunken craters of old volcanos" (19). (Pusey Library, Harvard University archives.) Clearly, Frost learned a great deal about Darwin's theory from Shaler.

27. Moore, *Post–Darwinian Controversies*, 88.

28. Alfred Weber, *History of Philosophy* (New York: C. Scribner's Sons, 1896), 596 and 526.

29. Aldous Huxley, *Literature and Science* (London: Chatto & Windus, 1963), 11.

30. Weber, *History of Philosophy*, 597.

31. Ibid., 572.

32. Ibid., 563.

33. Naturally, there were other differences between Frost and Darwin. The poet rejected the evolutionist's belief in a conditional "progress," and in his calling himself an agnostic.

34. See Moore, *The Post–Darwinian Controversies*, 174. Darwin had indeed concluded each introduction to each edition of *The Origin of Species* with this sentence: "I am convinced that Natural Selection has been the main, but not the exclusive, means of modification." The only variant was in the first edition, with "most important" rather than "main."

35. Stephen Jay Gould, "Evolution: The Pleasures of Pluralism," *The New York Review of Books*, June 26, 1997. In another article, "Darwinian Fundamentalism," ibid., June 12, 1997, 34–37, Gould criticized "the general fallacies of ultra-Darwinian fundamentalism."

36. Clarence Cook Little, the president of the University of Michigan, presented Frost with a first English edition of Darwin's *Journal of Researches*. See Thompson, *The Years of Triumph*, 284. During the summers of 1939–44, Frost mentioned all of these works by Darwin in conversations with me.

37. See Cook, *Robert Frost*, 65.

38. Ibid.

39. Darwin, *The Life and Letters*, vol. 1, 56 and 68–69; vol. 2, 110.

40. Robert M. Young, *Darwin's Metaphor* (Cambridge: Cambridge University Press, 1985), 92. See also 78–125.

41. Ibid., 100. For further problems regarding natural selection, see B. H. Beddall, "Wallace, Darwin and the Theory of Natural Selection," *Journal of the History of Biology* I (1968), 261–323.

42. For detailed accounts of the great decline in the acceptance of Darwin's theory, see G. J. Romanes, *Darwin and After Darwin* (Chicago: Open Court, 1892–97); Samuel Butler, "The Deadlock in Darwinism," *The Universal Review* (April–June, 1890), republished in 1904 and 1913; Vernon Kellogg, *Darwinism Today* (Philadelphia: J. E. Potter, 1907); J. T. Dennert, *At the Deathbed of Darwinism* (Burlington, Iowa: German Literary Board, 1904); Peter J. Bowler, *The Eclipse of Darwinism* (Baltimore: Johns Hopkins University Press, 1983); and Peter J. Bowler, *The Non-Darwinian Revolution* (Baltimore: Johns Hopkins University Press, 1988), 92, 98–99, 104, 117, 121, and 184.

43. Bowler, *The Non-Darwinian Revolution*, 103.
44. In his *Autobiography*, Darwin forgave all of the critics of his theory "except Mr. Mivart." See Charles Darwin, *The Autobiography of Charles Darwin: 1809–1882*, Nora Barlow, ed. (New York: Harcourt, Brace, 1958), 125–26.
45. St. George Jackson Mivart, *Genesis of Species* (New York: D. Appleton and Co., 1871), 76.
46. For a detailed account of Mivart's conflict with Darwin's theory, see Richards, *Darwin and the Emergence of Evolutionary Theories*, 353–63. For a study of his life as a scientist, and his religion, see Jacob Gruber, *A Conscience in Conflict: The Life of St. George Jackson Mivart* (New York: Columbia University Press, 1960).
47. *The Letters of Robert Frost to Louis Untermeyer*, 284–85. It is important to note that in his preliminary remarks before this passage, Frost took strong issue with social Darwinism by remarking that in the recent reelection of Franklin D. Roosevelt, because of the economic suffering resulting from the Great Depression, it was "humanity . . . to feel the suffering of others," and that "the national mood is humanitarian. Nobly so." Frost's acceptance of Darwin's principle, the survival of the fittest, did not mean an abandonment of traditional ethics in favor of the kind of laissez-faire that justified social Darwinism, as has been claimed by some critics of Frost.
48. Frost read the early version of Darwin's autobiography, edited by his son Francis. The later complete version, edited by Nora Barlow in 1958, includes "Part Two," a long appendix, "The Darwin-Butler Controversy," 167–219. In cooperation with Francis Darwin, Butler's first biographer, Henry Festing Jones, published a pamphlet, "Charles Darwin and Samuel Butler: A Step toward Reconciliation" (1911).
49. Thompson, *The Early Years*, 231–32, 294–95, 381–82, 536–37, 555, and 579–82. See also Thompson, *The Years of Triumph*, 300–04, 325, 506, 624, 643, 691, and 700. John F. Sears, in "William James, Henri Bergson and the Poetics of Robert Frost," *New England Quarterly* 48 (1975), 341–61, has described how James and Bergson provided a basis for Frost's aesthetic theory, and how Bergson's ideas and imagery are reflected in some of Frost's poems, particularly in "West-Running Brook."
50. Cyril E. M. Joad, *Samuel Butler* (London: L. Parsons, 1924), 107 and 140.
51. Ibid., 142–43.
52. Peter Raby, *Samuel Butler* (Iowa City: University of Iowa Press, 1991), 83 and 88. See also 103, 135, and 138. Although Butler called himself a "free thinker," like Frost he was a theist and held that "God is a spirit," but not in the conventional image of a deity in "a flowing beard." 148–49.
53. Samuel Butler, *Evolution Old and New* (London: Boque, 1882), 351. See also 352 and 326–27.
54. Quoted by Raby, *Samuel Butler*, 310. It is noteworthy that Darwin reproduced Butler's remark in his *Autobiography*.

55. Samuel Butler, *Luck or Cunning* (London: Trübner, 1887), 18.

56. Ibid., 140–41.

57. Ibid., 135.

58. Ibid., 137.

59. Ibid., 140.

60. Ibid., 76.

61. Ibid., 89.

62. Ibid., 121.

63. Butler, *Fortnightly Review* (November 1874), 140.

64. Bowler, *The Non-Darwinian Revolution*, 98.

65. Notebook number 001714 in the Baker Library, Dartmouth College.

66. George Bernard Shaw, *Back to Methuselah: A Metabiological Pentateuch* (New York: Dodd, Mead and Co., 1946), preface, xxxv. First published in 1921.

67. For Shaw's defense and praise of Butler, see *Back to Methuselah*, preface, xiii, xlvii, lii, and lv. In a letter to Archibald Henderson (10 February 1905), he praised Butler's "reaction against the materialism of Marx and Darwin" and recommended that Henderson "must read the works of that man of genius." George Bernard Shaw, *Collected Letters, 1898–1910*, Dan H. Laurence, ed. (New York: Dodd, Mead, and Co., 1972), 511. For other of Shaw's comments on Butler's criticism of Darwin's theory, see 301, 303, 413, 670, 672, and 873.

68. Shaw, *Back to Methuselah*, preface, lii and lxxxv. For Shaw's review of Butler's *Luck or Cunning*, see "Darwin Denounced," *Pall Mall Gazette* (May 31, 1887), 4–5.

69. Ibid., 91.

70. Ibid., preface, xc and 91.

71. Notebook number 001723 in the Baker Library, Dartmouth College.

72. Notebook number 001893 in the Baker Library, Dartmouth College.

73. Lesley Lee Francis, "Robert Frost and Susan Ward," *The Massachusetts Review* (1985), 347.

74. For a thorough review of Frost's complex responses to Bergson, see Thompson, *The Early Years*, 381–82, 386–88, and 579–81; *The Years of Triumph*, 300–04, 325, and 624. See also Hildegard Hoeller, "Evolution and Metaphor in Robert Frost's Poetry," *The South Carolina Review* 23, No. 1 (Spring 1990), 127–34; Jay Parini, *Robert Frost*, 109–11. For Frost's annotations and marginalia comments in his own copy of Bergson's book, see Ronald Bieganowski, "Robert Frost's *A Boy's Will* and Henri Bergson's *Creative Evolution*," *The South Carolina Review* 21 (Fall 1988), 9–16.

75. Robert Frost, "Education by Metaphor," *Frost: Collected Poems, Prose, & Plays*, 717.

76. Samuel Butler, *Luck or Cunning*, 168.

77. For an excellent account of what Frost meant by *mens animi*, see Lisa Abshear-Seale, "What Catullus Means by *mens animi*: Robert Frost's 'Kitty Hawk,'" *The Robert Frost Review* (Fall 1993), 37–46.

78. *The Letters of Robert Frost to Louis Untermeyer*, 34. See also Louis Untermeyer, *From Another World* (New York: Harcourt, Brace and Co., 1939), 220.

79. Ibid., 47. In addition to reading Bergson, who provided him with the basic imagery in "West-Running Brook," Frost had read J. Henri Fabre's *The Hunting Wasps* (New York: Dodd, Mead, and Co., 1915), which gave him his central metaphor in "The White-Tailed Hornet." Fabre was a popular botanist and had corresponded with Darwin and visited him, but remained silent about his conception of evolution.

80. *The Letters of Robert Frost to Louis Untermeyer* (May 6, 1919), 86–87. In 1891–92, Eugene Dubois's discovery of "Java man," named "Pithecanthropus Erectus," stressed the primary importance of man's upright posture long before the supposed separate development of the human brain over that of apes. According to Marcellin Boule, the Neanderthal specimen, discovered in France in 1909–11, was far too crude to be the recent ancestor of modern man. Arthur Smith Woodward claimed to have discovered the Piltdown man in 1912, but doubts about its authenticity were raised by Arthur Keith in 1915. It was proved a hoax in 1953.

81. Edward Connery Lathem, *Interviews with Robert Frost* (1966), 213.

82. Theodore Baird, "Darwin and the Tangled Bank," *The American Scholar* 15, 1946.

83. Quoted by permission of the Robert Frost Library in Amherst College and the Estate of Robert Frost. It is noteworthy that whereas Frost praised Darwin's metaphorical thought, Butler objected that natural selection was "too charged with metaphor for purposes of science." Butler, *Luck or Cunning*, 66. See also 146 and 206.

84. Alfred North Whitehead, *Science and the Modern World*, 140. Although Shaw was one of Darwin's most severe critics, he too praised him for his careful methods of research. In a letter to E. C. Chapman (July 29, 1891), Shaw wrote: "Darwin searched with extraordinary diligence for facts to support his theory of natural selection. . . . Writers like Samuel Butler have had no difficulty in convicting him of gross partiality towards his own theory. And yet you will not easily find a more unquestionably honest investigator than Darwin." George Bernard Shaw, *Collected Letters, 1874–1897*, 301.

85. For a detailed account of how Mendel's laws of genetics were made a vital element in the revival and revisions of Darwin's theory, see Bowler, *The Eclipse of Darwinism*, 182–213.

## Chapter 4, Frost and The Three Generations of Huxleys

1. Reginald L. Cook, ed., *Robert Frost: A Living Voice*, 99. Frost was aware that because Darwin's name was so identified with all discussions of evolution, even

abuses of the theory by such minor people as Frazer came "under the Darwinian thing." As a schoolboy, Frost had read Grant Allen's *Evolution of the Idea of God* (1897), another minor work that abused Darwin's theory.

2. Ibid., 120. Frost's reference to "a terrible gap still between animal life and human" alludes to Thomas Henry Huxley's *Evidence as to Man's Place in Nature* (1863). In his conversation with me, Frost objected to Huxley's restricting human nature to its biological dimensions, while ignoring man's place in civil society. He contended that there is "a qualitative difference" between "animal life" in a jungle and "human life" in organized society. Huxley presented an inadequate conception of the moral and social nature of man. Frost also objected to the manner in which Huxley presented images of the changes in man through evolutionary time, which he contended falsified Darwin's principle of natural selection. Frost's criticism in 1941 was confirmed by Janet Browne, Darwin's chief modern biographer, in 2002: "His *Man's Place in Nature*...showed Huxley at his snarling extreme.... Where Lyell hesitated, he ripped along, cynical and acerbic in turn. But it was a line drawing that actually said it all. On first opening Huxley's book, readers saw exactly what his argument would be. His frontispiece showed five skeletons standing in line, each bony figure leaning slightly forward ready to evolve into the next. From gibbon to orang, chimpanzee, gorilla, and man, the implication could not be plainer. Humans were the result of a series of physical changes from the apish state.... It was inspired visual propaganda." Janet Browne, *Charles Darwin: The Power of Place* (Princeton: Princeton University Press, 2002), 221.

3. Frost excluded Darwin from his category of the three generations of Huxleys. He differed strongly from literary critics who lumped Darwin and Huxley together as common advocates of evolution. Even Reginald L. Cook, who during a friendship of almost forty years knew Frost far better than most literary critics, was greatly puzzled by the poet's "decidedly curious dissatisfaction with the Huxleys (Thomas Henry Huxley and Sir Julian Huxley)." *Robert Frost: A Living Voice*, 121. See also 122.

4. Apart from the Anglo-American representatives in the Huxley tradition, Frost was aware of the equivalent views about science and evolution in Germany, through T. H. Huxley's close association for decades with many German scientists, especially Ernst Haeckel (1834–1919).

5. Thomas Henry Huxley and Julian Huxley, *Touchstone for Ethics* (New York: Harper & Brothers, 1947), 115.

6. Leonard Huxley, ed., *Life and Letters of T. H. Huxley*, vol. 1, 396.

7. Lawrance Thompson, ed., *Selected Letters of Robert Frost*, 460.

8. See Reginald L. Cook, "Robert Frost in Context," *Frost Centennial Essays*, vol. 3, 172.

9. Leonard Huxley, ed., *Life and Letters of T. H. Huxley*, vol. 1, 184. See also 178–87.

10. Ibid. vol. 2, 16.
11. Ibid., 78.
12. Ibid., vol. 1, 553.
13. Aldous Huxley, *Literature and Science*, 11.
14. For a detailed account of all that was involved in Huxley's review of Darwin's *Origin*, see Leonard Huxley, ed., *Life and Letters of T. H. Huxley*, vol. 1, 178–92.
15. Ibid., 190.
16. T. H. Huxley, *American Addresses* (New York: D. Appleton, 1893), 139–44.
17. Henrietta Huxley, ed., *Aphorisms and Reflections from the Works of T. H. Huxley*, 90 and 111. In the cultural wars between the ancients and the moderns, the "Battle of the Books" that raged throughout Europe during the Renaissance and Enlightenment, Huxley's views of history and science clearly placed him as the most ardent Victorian champion of the moderns.
18. Frost, "Letter to *The Amherst Student*" (1935), *Frost: Collected Poems, Prose, & Plays*, 739.
19. Henrietta Huxley, ed., *Aphorisms and Reflections from the Works of T. H. Huxley*, 102.
20. Reginald L. Cook, *The Dimensions of Robert Frost*, 183.
21. Edward C. Lathem, ed., *Interviews With Robert Frost*, 128.
22. *The Letters of Robert Frost to Louis Untermeyer*, 378–79.
23. Quoted by Jeffrey S. Cramer, *Robert Frost Among His Poems* (Jefferson, NC: McFarland & Co., 1996), 32.
24. Notebook 001729 in the Baker Library at Dartmouth College.
25. Wade Van Dore, *The Life of the Hired Man* (Dayton, Ohio: Wright State University, 1986), 34.
26. Reginald L. Cook, *Robert Frost: A Living Voice*, 7–8.
27. Peter J. Stanlis, "Robert Frost at Bread Loaf: 1939–1941," *Frost Centennial Essays*, vol. 3, 221.
28. T. H. Huxley and Julian Huxley, *Touchstone for Ethics*, 94.
29. Charles Darwin, *More Letters of Charles Darwin*, vol. 1 (New York: D. Appleton and Co., 1903), 321.
30. Darwin, *The Life and Letters*, vol. 1, 282.
31. Peter J. Bowler, *Charles Darwin: The Man and His Influence*, 158.
32. Ibid., 150.
33. Quoted by Daniel Gasman, *The Scientific Origins of National Socialism: Social Darwinism in Ernst Haeckel and the German Monist League* (London: MacDonald, 1971), 699.
34. Adrian Desmond, *Huxley* (Reading, MA: Addison-Wesley, 1997), 486.
35. See Thomas F. Glick, ed., *The Comparative Reception of Darwinism* (Austin: The University of Texas Press, 1972), 390.
36. A. I. Hallowell in "Self, Society, and Culture in Phylogenetic Perspective" noted that "it was also under the stimulus of Darwin's ideas as applied to man

that historians, economists, sociologists, linguists, cultural anthropologists, and others began to apply evolutionary ideas to human institutions on a wide scale." *Evolution After Darwin*, Sol Tax, ed., vol. 2, *The Evolution of Man: Man, Culture, and Society* (Chicago: University of Chicago Press, 1960), 310.

37. For the vital differences between Darwin's theory and what Huxley, Spencer, and others did to create social Darwinism, see James Allen Rogers, "Darwinism and Social Darwinism," *Journal of the History of Ideas*, 33, No. 2 (1972), 265–80.

38. For Spencer's role in combining evolution, sociology, politics, and economics into "social Darwinism," see J. D. Y. Peel, *Herbert Spencer: The Evolution of a Sociologist* (London: Heinemann Educational, 1971); and David Wiltshire, *The Social and Political Thought of Herbert Spencer* (New York: Oxford University Press, 1978).

39. Harriet Huxley, ed., *Aphorisms and Reflections*, 104.

40. Ibid., 77.

41. Ibid., 87.

42. Thomas Henry Huxley, "The Struggle for Existence and Its Bearing upon Man," *Nineteenth Century* (February 1888), 165. In Germany, Ernst Haeckel, Huxley's close friend and colleague in science, who believed in the same basic monist philosophy, simply added German Romanticism, nationalism, and claims of racial superiority through evolutionary development, to the mixture of ideas in "social Darwinism."

43. Leonard Huxley, ed., *Life and Letters of Thomas Henry Huxley*, vol 2, 322.

44. Henrietta Huxley, ed., *Aphorisms and Reflections*, 74.

45. Ibid., 79.

46. Ibid., 64.

47. Frost was well aware that social Darwinism was not limited to defenders of free enterprise capitalism. He perceived that when Darwin's theory was applied to social problems, it proved so complex and ambiguous that almost every conceivable personal or social economic and political philosophy could be derived from it. Those who objected to the serious abuses of capitalism against labor—both anarchists, such as Prince Peter Kropotkin, and socialists—wished to substitute social cooperation for the conflicts of competition and thus convert personal selfishness into social benevolence. But they still believed in "progress" through evolutionary change and social science, and developed their own forms of social Darwinism. The variety and range of social Darwinism is revealed in the laissez-faire individualism of Spencer, the mild statism of Huxley, the far more radical national socialism of Ernst Haeckel, and the extreme Marxist collectivism and other modern ideological forms of totalitarianism. Frost believed that they all held in common a monism centered in matter, so that their economic and political philosophy reflected a materialist view of reality. The poet's interpretation of the range of social Darwinism is confirmed by such scholars as Gertrude Himmelfarb,

"Varieties of Social Darwinism," *Victorian Minds* (New York: Knopf, 1968); Peter J. Bowler, "Social Darwinism," in *The Non-Darwinian Revolution*.

48. Charles Darwin, *Autobiography*, 108–09. See also *Life and Letters*, vol. 3, 193–94.

49. It remained for H. G. Wells, a man as ignorant of biology as Spencer, to become the foremost champion of "progress" during the early decades of the twentieth century.

50. Lawrance Thompson, *Robert Frost: The Later Years, 1938–1963* (New York: Holt, Rinehart and Winston, 1976), 99. See also 100. Hereafter referred to as Thompson, *The Later Years*.

51. Thompson, *The Years of Triumph*, 553.

52. Blaise Pascal, *Pensées* 72, translated by W. F. Trotter, in Robert C. Baldwin and James A. S. McPeek, eds., *The Introduction to Philosophy Through Literature* (New York: The Ronald Press Company, 1950), 400.

53. For Pascal's distinctions between intuition and analytical reason, see "Two Types of Mind" and "Mathematical and Intuitive Mind" in A. J. Krailsheimer, ed., *Pascal: Pensées* (New York: Penguin, 1966), 209–10. See also "Freedom and Indifference: Intuition," Lester G. Crocker, *An Age of Crisis* (Baltimore: The Johns Hopkins Press, 1959), 136–60.

54. See Morris Bishop, *Pascal: The Life of Genius* (New York: Reynal and Hitchcock, 1936), 92–95.

55. See John Barker, *Strange Contrarieties: Pascal in England During the Age of Reason* (Montreal: McGill-Queen's University Press, 1975). See also, Robert J. Nelson, *Pascal: Adversary and Advocate* (Cambridge: Harvard University Press, 1981). Pascal's *Lettres Provinciales* (1656–57) took strong issue with the rationalism of the Jesuits, whose Thomistic theology differed so markedly from his Augustinian theology.

56. *Letters of Robert Frost to Louis Untermeyer*, 284–85.

57. Thompson, *The Years of Triumph*, 413–14.

58. Donald G. Sheehy, "The Poet as Neurotic: The Official Biography of Robert Frost," *American Literature*, vol. 58, no. 3, October 1986. It is significant that Merrill Moore, a physician and professional psychiatrist, was a close friend of Frost for thirty years and had an altogether positive perception of the poet. In February 1958, after Moore's death, Frost paid tribute to him in the *Harvard Medical Alumni Bulletin*. He noted that Moore's life was "overflowing with poetic sympathy" and that "he dispensed courage as well as poetry." Moore was both a "serious physician and a serious artist." His personality included "something of the rogue . . . that was a part of his great charm." Frost admired both his poetry and his courage, and observed that "he was a rebuke to the stupid give-it-ups who are willing to have it that heroism is out of date," which was precisely what Thompson believed. To Frost, Moore was "like a troubadour," because "poetry was his rapture." In contrast with his friend, Thompson paid very little attention to his poetry and concentrated upon his

negative psychological personality. See *Frost: Collected Poems, Prose & Plays*, 842–43.

59. See Peter Stanlis, "Acceptable in Heaven's Sight: Frost at Bread Loaf, 1939–1941," *Frost Centennial Essays*, vol. 3, 310–11.

60. In July 1941, during a conversation with students in his cabin at Bread Loaf, Frost expounded at length on Emerson's optimistic monism that evil is merely the absence of good, not a reality in itself. He dismissed Emerson as a philosopher but praised him as a poet.

61. For Frost's letter to Thompson, see Thompson, ed., *Selected Letters of Robert Frost*, 552–54.

62. Ibid., 584.

## Chapter 5, Frost and Creative Evolution

1. Henry Fairfield Osborn, "Aristogenesis, the Creative Principle in Origin of Species," *The American Naturalist* (May–June, 1934), vol. 68, no. 716, 193–94. Forty years earlier, Osborn had published a book, *From the Greeks to Darwin* (New York: Columbia University Press, 1894), which almost a century later was dismissed by Ernst Mayr as "too uncritical to be still useful." See *The Growth of Biological Thought* (Cambridge: Harvard University Press, 1982), 872. However, Mayr did not mention Osborn's later article, which appeared when the modern synthesis of Darwin's theory was nearly completed. Osborn's Latin phrase, *nullae speciae novae*, is probably best translated as "no new species."

2. Ibid., 195. It is noteworthy that Darwin himself admitted that scientists as yet knew nothing about the origins of life.

3. Notebook 001723 in the Baker Library, Dartmouth College.

4. Quoted by Alan Ryan in "Wise Man," a review of Berlin's life and work, *The New York Review of Books*, December 17, 1998, 34.

5. See Peter J. Stanlis, "Robert Frost at Bread Loaf," *Frost Centennial Essays*, vol. 3, 245–46.

6. Henry David Thoreau, *Journals*, vol. 6, 30. Quoted in an essay by Scott Slovic, "An Approach to Thoreau and Eisley," *Weber Studies*, Winter 1992.

7. Nora Barlow, ed., *The Autobiography of Charles Darwin: 1809–1882* (New York: W. W. Norton and Co., 1958), 43–44. Darwin wrote his autobiography in stages between August 1876 and his final illness in 1881.

8. Ibid., 85.

9. Ibid., 138.

10. Ibid., 139. Samuel Butler believed that Darwin's theory was so deeply rooted in matter that it had destroyed his ability to retain the concept of mind in the universe. See William Irvine, *Apes, Angels and Victorians* (New York: McGraw-Hill, 1955), 273–74.

11. *More Letters of Charles Darwin*, vol. 1, 98.

12. Darwin, *The Life and Letters*, vol. 2, 171. For other examples of Darwin's lament over his loss of aesthetic sensitivity, see 189 and 273. See also *More Letters of Charles Darwin*, vol. 1, 324–26.

13. In a letter to Canon Farrar (March 5, 1867), Darwin referred to his schoolboy failure to appreciate the humanities: "I am one of the root and branch men." *More Letters of Charles Darwin*, vol. 2, 441. His self-denigration was exaggerated.

14. Harvey Breit, *The Writer Observed* (New York: Collier Books, 1961), 69. See also Edward C. Lathem, *Interviews with Robert Frost*, 124.

15. Two other of Frost's poems that may be read as variations on the theme of "The Most of It" are "An Old Man's Winter Night" and "Desert Places." Important points of similarity to "Two Look at Two" are to be found in "The Need of Being Versed in Country Things."

16. For a detailed account of Thompson's explication of Frost's response to Bergson, see Thompson, *The Early Years*, 381–83 and 579–81; *The Years of Triumph*, 624–26.

17. Thompson made far too much of Frost's recorded remark "that he was a dualist in his thinking and a monist in his wishing" and that therefore "he was at least emotionally sympathetic with anyone like Plato who made the leap beyond dualism of the known to the all-controlling 'One' of the unknown." Thompson, *The Years of Triumph*, 243–45. Thompson then went on to interpret Frost's poem "I Will Sing You One-O" as a "hymn to Oneness," that is, a commitment to monism. But Frost expressly rejected Plato's philosophy and repeatedly made it clear that he was a philosophical dualist.

18. Thompson, *The Years of Triumph*, 625.

19. Ibid., 624–26.

20. John F. Sears, "William James, Henri Bergson and the Poetics of Robert Frost," *New England Quarterly* 48 (1995), 350. Much that Sears writes about Frost's poetics is wholly valid.

21. Dorothy Judd, "An Old Testament Christian," *Frost Centennial Essays*, vol. 3.

22. It is noteworthy that at the same time that Santayana's criticism of Bergson appeared, Arthur O. Lovejoy published "Bergson and Romantic Evolutionism," *University of California Chronicle*, XV, no. 438 (October 1913). There is no evidence that Frost ever read Lovejoy's article.

23. George Santayana, *Winds of Doctrine* (New York: Charles Scribner's Sons, 1913), 69–70.

24. Ibid., 64.

25. George Santayana, "Apologia Pro Mente Sua," in *The Philosophy of George Santayana*, Paul Arthur Schilpp, ed. (Evanston: Northwestern University Press, 1940), 499.

26. *Physical Order and Moral Liberty: Previously Unpublished Essays of George Santayana*, John and Shirley Locks, eds. (Charlotte, NC: Vanderbilt University Press, 1969), 307–08.

27. *The Letters of Robert Frost to Louis Untermeyer,* 47.
28. Robert Frost, *Collected Poems, Prose & Plays,* 884–85.
29. Thompson, *The Early Years,* 244–45.
30. Santayana's conviction that all beliefs are merely forms of illusion was explicitly stated in *Winds of Doctrine,* 51–52. He repeated this conviction with many variations in his subsequent writings.
31. For explications of Santayana's basic philosophical beliefs see *The Philosophy of George Santayana,* Paul·Arthur Schilpp, ed. The antithesis of Santayana to Frost is most evident in William Ray Dennes, "Santayana's Materialism," 419–43; and Sterling F. Lamprecht, "Naturalism and Agnosticism in Santayana," *Animal Faith and Spiritual Faith,* John Locks, ed. (New York: Appleton-Century-Crofts, 1967), 147–63. C. A. Strong, Santayana's college friend and companion for many years, identified him as an agnostic in "Santayana's Philosophy," *The Philosophy of George Santayana,* 448–49.
32. George Santayana, "The Harvard Yard," *Persons and Places* (New York: Charles Scribner's Sons, 1944), 188. As one scholar has noted: "Through all his work, Santayana offers a recurrent reminder that our life cannot be divorced from its natural environment, within which it must seek its fulfillment." Newton P. Stallknecht, *George Santayana* (Minneapolis: University of Minnesota Press, 1971), 9. Regarding Herbert Spencer, Santayana wrote: "I agreed with his naturalism or materialism, because that is what we all start with." *Persons and Places,* 242. See also 243.
33. George Santayana, "College Studies," *Persons and Places,* 241.
34. Ibid., 240.
35. Ibid., 230.
36. Ibid. See also George Santayana, "A General Confession," *The Philosophy of George Santayana,* 12–13.
37. George Santayana, "Apologia Pro Mente Sua," *The Philosophy of George Santayana,* 504.
38. *The Philosophy of George Santayana,* 7.
39. George Santayana, "Apologia Pro Mente Sua," *The Philosophy of George Santayana,* 498. For a typical example of his criticism of "a Calvinistic God," see *Winds of Doctrine,* 353.
40. Ibid., 531.
41. Santayana, "Prologue," *The Last Puritan,* 6.
42. *The Genteel Tradition at Bay* (1931) is a nonfictional prelude to *The Last Puritan.* Eighteen years earlier, in "The Genteel Tradition in American Philosophy," Santayana wrote: "Calvinism . . . is the expression of the agonized conscience. It is a view of the world which an agonized conscience readily embraces." *Winds of Doctrine,* 189.
43. Santayana's main fictional characters are based upon his student friends at Harvard. Edward Bayley, of an old New England Puritan family, was the model for Oliver. Ward Thoren, a recent Catholic convert, provided the basis for his portrait of Mario. See *Persons and Places,* 184 and 231–34.

44. Baker Brownell, "Santayana, the Man and the Philosopher," *The Philosophy of George Santayana*, 51.

45. In a letter to Richard H. Thornton (October 1, 1930), Frost repeated his belief in the importance of the enduring "ideals" of Puritanism. *Selected Letters of Robert Frost*, 288.

46. Perry Miller, *The New England Mind* (New York: Macmillan Co., 1939), 60.

47. For an account of Frost's conception of Puritanism and his rebuttal of those who criticized it on intellectual and aesthetic grounds, see Peter J. Stanlis, "Acceptable in Heaven's Sight: Robert Frost at Bread Loaf, 1939–1941," *Frost Centennial Essays*, vol. 3, 195–97.

48. Robert Frost, "On Taking Poetry" (June 30, 1955), and "On Puritanism, Darwin, Marx, Freud, and Einstein" (July 28, 1955), Reginald L. Cook, ed., *Robert Frost: A Living Voice*, 75–87 and 88–105.

49. Frost once remarked that his *A Masque of Reason* and *Masque of Mercy* were best understood by Jews and Catholics. "The other, the lesser sects without the law . . . they don't get it. They're too apt to think there's rebellion in them . . . But that isn't in them at all. They're not rebellious. They're very doctrinal, very orthodox, both of them." *"Paris Review* Interview," *Frost: Collected Poems, Prose, & Plays*, 891. In an interview on April 5, 1959, Frost said, "The only Puritans left these days are the Roman Catholics." *Interviews with Robert Frost*, 198.

50. *Robert Frost: A Living Voice*, 93.

51. *The Letters of Robert Frost to Louis Untermeyer*, 218.

52. *Robert Frost: A Living Voice*, 76.

53. Ibid., 941. See also 95.

54. Ibid., 93. For an account of how the Puritans combined biblical studies and the ancient classical literary tradition, see Perry Miller, "The Intellectual Heritage," *The New England Mind*, 89–108.

55. John F. Fulton, *Harvey Crushing: A Biography* (Springfield, IL: Charles C. Thomas, Publishers, 1946), 6.

56. Robert Frost, "What Became of New England?" *Frost: Collected Poems, Prose & Plays*, 755.

57. Frost was especially pained by Amy Lowell's review in *The New Republic* (February 20, 1913), in which she wrote: "Mr. Frost's book reveals a disease which is eating into the vitals of our New England life; at least in its rural communities." Frost believed that, as a direct descendent of a famous New England Puritan family, she should have known better. Like other critics, she confounded the simplicity of Frost's fictional characters with simplemindedness. As Frost noted in a letter to Louis Untermeyer (March 10, 1938), the people in *North of Boston* were not merely poor people but "people of simplicity or simple truth miscalled simplicity." In his poem "New Hampshire" (1923), Frost has Amy Lowell show contempt for the state of New Hampshire: "She said she couldn't stand the people in it"; and when the speaker in the poem "asked to know what ailed the people," she answered: "Go read your own books and find out."

58. During the summer of 1940, Frost urged students at Bread Loaf to read Perry Miller's account of how Puritan theology evolved from a covenant of grace between God and the Elect into a social and political contract that provided a democratic basis for American society. See Perry Miller's two chapters "The Covenant of Grace" and "The Social Covenant," *The New England Mind*, 365–431.

59. It is significant that starting with Frost's second book, *North of Boston*, practically every title of his subsequent books of poetry reflects some aspect of New England geography or physical nature. Yet far from being a "regional poet," Frost's New England was a metaphor for all of America.

60. Robert Frost, "What Became of New England?" *Frost: Collected Poems, Prose & Plays*, 756. The following summer, in June 1939, during a conversation with students at Bread Loaf, Frost again defended the aesthetic character of New England Puritans. See Peter J. Stanlis, "Acceptable in Heaven's Sight: Robert Frost at Bread Loaf, 1939–1941," *Frost Centennial Essays*, vol. 3, 195–97.

61. Ibid., 756 and 757.

62. Perry Miller, *The New England Mind*, 335. See also 341 and 349.

63. For a detailed account of the Puritan revolution in English prose style, as applied to both religion and science, see Richard Foster Jones's four articles "Science and Criticism in the Neo-Classical Age of English Literature," "Science and English Prose Style in the Third Quarter of the Seventeenth Century," "The Attack on Pulpit Eloquence in the Restoration," and "Science and Language in England of the Mid-Seventeenth Century," *The Seventeenth Century* (Stanford: Stanford University Press, 1951), 41–160.

64. Thompson, *The Years of Triumph*, 691. See also 692.

65. Robert Frost, *Frost: Collected Poems, Prose & Plays*, 756 and 758. In his poem "The Black Cottage," Frost alluded to Santayana as a man who denied Jefferson's principle that all men are created equal in the sight of God.

66. Ibid., 758.

67. Robert Frost, "Too Anxious for Rivers," *Frost: Collected Poems, Prose & Plays*.

68. Robert Frost to Sidney Cox, September 19, 1929, in *Selected Letters of Robert Frost*, 361.

69. Notebook 001714, 71, in the Baker Library, Dartmouth College.

70. The term "passionate preference" was not original with Frost. It is highly ironical that he was so enamored of this phrase, which he repeated on several occasions, because it originated in the very man whose philosophy he so despised. In noting Walt Whitman's democratic uniformity in multiplicity in *Leaves of Grass*, George Santayana wrote: "Occasionally the beauties of democracy are presented to us undisguised. The writings of Walt Whitman are a notable example. Never, perhaps, has the charm of uniformity in multiplicity been felt so completely and so exclusively. Everywhere it greets us with a passionate preference." *The Sense of Beauty* (New York: Charles Scribner's Sons, 1896), 112. Whereas Santayana applied "passionate preference" to Whitman's conception

of democracy, Frost applied it to religion and the arts as sources of man's creativity in making evolutionary changes in the culture of society.

71. *Interviews with Robert Frost*, 226. It is significant that Alfred North Whitehead, whose views on science and religion were similar to those of Frost, also connected evolution with aesthetic creativity: "The problem of evolution is the development of enduring harmonies of enduring shapes of value, which emerge into higher attainments of things beyond themselves. Aesthetic attainment is interwoven in the texture of realization." *Science and the Modern World* (New York: Macmillan, 1925), 117.

72. Robert Frost, "Letter to *The Amherst Student*," *Selected Letters of Robert Frost*, 106.

73. *Interviews with Robert Frost*, 256.

74. Thompson, *The Later Years*, 288–89.

75. Perry Miller, *The New England Mind*, 77.

## *Chapter 6, Frost and Lovejoy's* The Great Chain of Being

1. Reginald L. Cook, *Robert Frost: A Living Voice*, 208. See also 209. The close, enduring, and warm friendship between Frost and Cook was an important event in the poet's intellectual and academic life and is worthy of a separate study. They first met during the early 1920s, when Cook was a student at the Bread Loaf Graduate School of English, and Frost came to Bread Loaf to give poetry readings and lectures. After Cook returned from England as a Rhodes Scholar in 1929, he became chairman of the Department of American Literature at Middlebury College, and in 1946 he was appointed dean of the Bread Loaf School. Frost admired Cook as an athlete, scholar, and administrator, and they visited each other in Middlebury and at "the Gully," Frost's home in South Shaftsbury, Vermont. They hiked together on the Long Trail and attended Boston Red Sox games as enthusiastic fans. For sixteen summers, Cook introduced Frost at his poetry readings at Bread Loaf and noted that he had witnessed the poet "as preceptor, paterfamilias, outdoorsman, and performer." He observed that "over a stretch of thirty-five years" he had "several hundred meetings with Frost." Cook published many articles on Frost, in *College English, Accent, Vermont Life, Quarterly Journal of Speech*, and *Yankee*, among others. His two books on Frost, *The Dimensions of Robert Frost* (1959) and *Robert Frost: A Living Voice* (1974), are filled with perceptive insights and original reflections on Frost as a man, thinker, and poet. Much of this chapter on Frost's indebtedness to Lovejoy was made possible by Cook's conversations with me in Middlebury and Bread Loaf.

2. Ibid., 306.

3. Ibid., 243.

4. Ibid., 49.

5. Thompson, *The Later Years*, 199–200. Frost particularly admired J. B. Bury's *History of Greece*, and he regarded Charles H. Cooley, the humanistic sociologist whom he befriended at the University of Michigan, as among the best scholars he had ever read. He appreciated Cooley's fusion of scientific precision and literary brilliance drawn from a lifetime of studies in the whole range of the humanities, from the ancient Greeks and Romans to his own era. Following Lawrance Thompson, many literary critics have made much of Frost's friendship with Edward Thomas but have almost totally ignored the intellectually more extensive friendship with Cooley. In their views regarding society, Frost and Cooley were in such close harmony that the poet once half-seriously joked that he would be satisfied to have Cooley do his thinking for him. Cooley's views on Frost, recorded in his notebooks from June 6, 1925, to November 4, 1928, are in "Manuscripts No. 23, 'Charles Cooley,'" in the University of Michigan Bentley Historical Library. In addition to Cooley, Frost held Perry Miller, the Harvard University authority on Puritanism, in very high esteem.

6. Robert Frost, "The Figure a Poem Makes," in *Selected Prose of Robert Frost*, 20.

7. For a detailed account of Lovejoy's dualism, theism, and belief in the power of creativity, see Daniel J. Wilson, *Arthur O. Lovejoy and the Quest for Intelligibility* (Chapel Hill: University of North Carolina Press, 1980), 85–113.

8. Arthur O. Lovejoy, *The Revolt Against Dualism* (New Brunswick: Transaction Publishers, 1996), 15–16. All references to this work will be to this edition. It is worth noting Lovejoy's criticism of the modern mechanistic processes of thought and knowledge inherent in a monism of matter that were satirized by Jonathan Swift in *The Tale of a Tub*, *The Battle of the Books*, and especially in the "Discourse Concerning the Mechanical Operation of the Spirit" (1694). Swift's satire was directed against both the materialism of Hobbes and the religious fanaticism of the extreme Dissenters.

9. Ibid., 316.

10. See Jonathan B. Imber, "Introduction, " *The Revolt Against Dualism*, ix–x.

11. Arthur O. Lovejoy, "William James as Philosopher," *International Journal of Ethics* 21 (1911), 86–87, 91, and 96.

12. Reginald L. Cook, *The Dimensions of Robert Frost*, 189. For Frost's additional comments on scholarship in contrast with poetry, see "The Figure a Poem Makes," "The Constant Symbol," "Education by Poetry," "Maturity No Object," "Introduction to *King Jasper*," and "The Prerequisites," in *Selected Prose of Robert Frost*.

13. During summer conversations with Frost at his cabin near Bread Loaf, from 1939 through 1944 and 1961–62, I heard the poet say whole poems and long passages from all of these poets, as well as from some little known minor poets. He also knew to memory many English and Scottish ballads.

14. John Donne, "An Anatomie of the World," *The Poems of John Donne*, Herbert J. C. Grierson, ed. (New York: Oxford University Press, 1912), vol. 1, 237, II,

206–14. For a detailed account of the serious problems and changes wrought by the new science, see Michael Macklem, *The Anatomy of the World: Relations between Natural and Moral Law from Donne to Pope* (Minneapolis: The University of Minnesota Press, 1958). It is noteworthy that John Milton retained the Ptolemaic cosmology in *Paradise Lost*, even though he sympathized with the new astronomy. He solved the moral dilemma of man in Book VIII of his epic poem, through the angel Raphael's instruction to Adam to "be lowly wise" regarding the cosmos, because "whether heav'n move or earth," the moral and social duties of man remain the same.

15. For the turning point in modern intellectual history that ushered in the Enlightenment, see Victor Harris, *All Coherence Gone* (Chicago: The University of Chicago Press, 1949).

16. Arthur O. Lovejoy, *The Great Chain of Being*, 183. In science, "the Baconian procedure" was eclipsed by the mathematical and rational methodology of Descartes.

17. Carl L. Becker, *The Heavenly City of the Eighteenth-Century Philosophers* (New Haven: Yale University Press, 1932), 31. Becker's book appeared four years before Lovejoy's study so that its thesis was largely incorporated into *The Great Chain of Being*.

18. Arthur O. Lovejoy, *The Great Chain of Being*, 222.

19. Pope, *Essay on Man*, Epistle I, 11. 267–68.

20. Ibid., 11. 171–72.

21. Ibid., 11. 289–94.

22. Lovejoy, *The Great Chain of Being*, 9. Belief in the natural goodness of man runs like a golden thread through much of the literature of "Romanticism." See Ernest Bernbaum, *Guide Through the Romantic Movement* (New York: Thomas Nelson and Sons, 1938), 5 vols.

23. Shortly before his death, Lovejoy published *Reflections on Human Nature* (The Johns Hopkins Press: Baltimore, 1961), in which he confirmed the extent of modern man's belief in his natural goodness: "In general, it is, I take it, evident beyond the need of argument that in the course of the last century Western mankind grew steadily more self-complacent, more self-confident, and more hopeful about both the near and remote future of the race upon this planet. The belief that man is 'naturally good' became a widely accepted premise alike of politics and pedagogies; the taste for satire largely went out of fashion in literature, and the sense of sin rather largely in religion; and to express a 'low view' of human nature became a kind of odious blasphemy," 7–8.

24. A year before Lovejoy and Boas published their massive study, Lois Whitney, Lovejoy's student, published *Primitivism and the Idea of Progress* (Baltimore: The Johns Hopkins University Press, 1934), to which Lovejoy wrote the foreword. Whitney's book described the origins of primitivist ideas in ancient times, and showed how the moral and aesthetic theories of value during the eighteenth century were permeated with primitivism and a sentimental con-

ception of human nature, culminating in the most radical revolutionary theories of society during the last half of the century.

25. As Lois Whitney noted, primitivists believed in an "improvement upward" in the chain of being: "The doctrine provided a favorable environment for a theory of progress in man apart from any evolutionary idea." *Primitivism and the Idea of Progress*, 145. Lovejoy's study of ancient primitivism is pertinent to Frost's admiration of Lucretius' *De rerum natura*. In his chapter, "Lucretius: Primitivism and the Idea of Progress," Lovejoy analyzed the final 686 lines in Book V of Lucretius' poem, which describes an anti-evolutionary conception of primitive man. See *Primitivism and Related Ideas in Antiquity*, 222–42.

26. Lovejoy, *The Great Chain of Being*, 329 and 331.


## Chapter 7, Frost and the Modern Revolt Against Dualism

1. Reginald L. Cook, *Robert Frost: A Living Voice*, 292.

2. Lovejoy, *The Revolt Against Dualism*, 3. For a detailed analysis of the "dualism" of Descartes, see Albert G. A. Balz, "Dualism in Cartesian Psychology and Epistemology," *Studies in the History of Ideas*, edited by The Department of Philosophy of Columbia University, vol. 2 (Columbia University Press: New York, 1925), 85–157.

3. Ibid., 20. Lovejoy's italics.

4. Ibid., 380–81. For critical comments upon Lovejoy's *The Revolt Against Dualism*, see A . E. Murphy, "Mr. Lovejoy's Counter-Revolution," *Journal of Philosophy* XXVIII (1931). For Lovejoy's reply to Murphy, see "Dualism Good and Bad," *Journal of Philosophy* XXIX (1932).

5. Ibid., 43. Lovejoy noted that the attempts of Descartes and Locke to combine belief in the physical world with a theory of knowledge based upon memory "speedily broke down into the subjective idealism of Berkeley and the scepticism of Hume."

6. Ibid., 380.

7. Ibid., 384.

8. Ibid., 390 and 393.

9. Ibid., 381.

10. Ibid., 384 and 378.

11. Ibid., 381.

12. Ibid., 397–98.

13. Sidney Cox, *A Swinger of Birches: A Portrait of Robert Frost* (New York: New York University Press, 1957), 26–27 and 116.

14. In *A Masque of Reason*, Job's "apparently unmeaning sorrow" in his trial by existence is explained by the same principle of forgetfulness stated in "The Trial by Existence": "But it was of the essence of the trial / You shouldn't understand it at the time. / It had to seem unmeaning to have meaning."

15. Cox, *A Swinger of Birches*, 49–50.
16. Ibid., 50.
17. Lawrance Thompson, ed., *Selected Letters of Robert Frost*, 250.
18. See Thompson, *Robert Frost: The Years of Triumph*, 61, 64, 77, 100, and 103, in which he interprets Frost's remarks on prejudices pejoratively.
19. Cox, *A Swinger of Birches*, 21.
20. *The Letters of Robert Frost to Louis Untermeyer*, 166.
21. Frost, "Education by Poetry," *Selected Prose*, 37.
22. Reginald L. Cook, *The Dimensions of Robert Frost*, 140.
23. Ibid., 6.
24. Ibid., 172.
25. Ibid., 53.
26. Reginald L. Cook, *Robert Frost: A Living Voice*, 222.
27. Frost, "The Figure a Poem Makes," *Selected Prose*, 19.
28. Reginald L. Cook, *Robert Frost: A Living Voice*, 243.
29. Ibid., 48.
30. See Lovejoy, *The Revolt Against Dualism*, 4–5, 25, 34, 82, 100, 105, 111, 162–63, 174–81, 200, 329, 341, and 345–46.
31. Ibid., 181.

## Chapter 8, Frost, Einstein's Relativity, and the Open-Ended Universe

1. See Gerald Holton, *Einstein, History, and Other Passions* (Woodbury, New York: American Institute of Physics Press, 1995), 9–16. For a more detailed study of the impact of Einstein's theory upon twentieth-century culture, see L. Peace Williams, ed., *Relativity Theory: Its Origins and Impact on Modern Thought* (New York: John Wiley and Sons, 1968).
2. Roger Highfield and Paul Carter, The Private Lives of Albert Einstein (New York: St. Martin's Press, 1993), 113.
3. Two British expeditions confirmed Einstein's predictions on "an astronomical puzzle—a variation in the orbit of Mercury around the sun that had perplexed scientists since it was first reported in 1859." *The Private Lives of Albert Einstein*, 174. For a detailed account of the great importance of Einstein's achievement, see 174–75 and 189–90.
4. Holton, op. cit., 6.
5. Ibid.
6. Ibid., 9.
7. Frost was familiar with Einstein's and Leopold Infeld's *The Evolution of Physics from Early Concepts to Relativity and Quanta* (New York: Simon and Schuster, 1938), which presented a valid popular understanding of modern physics and relativity. But the poet's understanding of relativity far exceeded this work and included a philosophical dimension that was often lacking in other literary

figures. Einstein's great ability to explain hard problems in physics with clarity was well appreciated by Frost.

8. *The Private Lives of Albert Einstein*, 97.

9. See Thompson, *The Years of Triumph*, 617. See also 618.

10. Hans Reichenbach, *From Copernicus to Einstein*, Ralph B. Winn, trans. (New York: Dover Publications, 1942).

11. Ibid., 94.

12. Reichenbach's chapter "General Theory of Relativity" is a good survey of the physics and mathematics involved in the expansion from the special theory of relativity to the general theory.

13. Reichenbach, *From Copernicus to Einstein*, 120.

14. The first American edition of Einstein's *Relativity: The Special and General Theory* was published by Henry Holt and Company, Frost's own publisher, in New York in 1920. It was translated by Robert W. Lawson, and reproduced by Dover Publications in 2001. Arthur Lovejoy read it in the original German, in conjunction with an explication of Einstein's theory by Max Born's *Die Relativitätstheorie Einsteins* (1922).

15. *The Private Lives of Einstein*, 152.

16. Ibid., 103–04. For a detailed account of Einstein's early development of his special theory, see 104–08.

17. Einstein, *Relativity: The Special and General Theory*, 148–49. In identifying "intuition and deduction" as fundamental in his method and thought, Einstein clearly was not satisfied with Reichenbach's term "instinct."

18. Ibid., 13.

19. Ibid., 66, 112, 117, and 125.

20. Ibid., 101. Einstein credited Ernst Mach with first advocating that "mechanics must be placed on a new basis" (86), even though Mach never went beyond the conventional assumptions of scientific positivism and a monism centered in matter.

21. Ibid., 70.

22. Holton, *Einstein, History, and Other Passions*, 85.

23. Ibid., 83 and 84.

24. Ibid., 12.

25. Ibid.

26. *The Private Lives of Albert Einstein*, 244.

27. Ibid., 159.

28. Ibid.

29. Will Herberg, *Protestant-Catholic-Jew* (Garden City: Doubleday & Company, 1960), revised edition, 267.

30. See *The Private Lives of Albert Einstein*, 201–02.

31. Einstein and Infeld, *The Evolution of Physics*, 93 and 94.

32. Ibid., 93–94.

33. See *The Private Lives of Albert Einstein*, 201–02.

34. Einstein and Infeld, *The Evolution of Physics*, 196.

35. Reginald L. Cook, *Robert Frost: A Living Voice*, 212.

36. Lovejoy, *The Revolt Against Dualism*, 181. It is noteworthy that whereas Lovejoy perceived the twentieth century as a revolt against dualism, Holton treated it as a movement "Toward a 'Monistic Century.'"

37. Holton, op. cit., 75.

38. Ibid., 6, 18, 26–29, and 75. In 1930, when Lovejoy identified Einstein's basic philosophy of mind and matter as dualistic, many contemporary scientists and philosophers did not accept the distinction because they believed that mind was derived from matter. This important theme in *The Revolt Against Dualism* is explicated in two long chapters entitled "Mr. Bertrand Russell and the Unification of Mind and Matter" I and II. Russell equivocated for years over the mind-matter problem. Although in *The Analysis of Mind* (1921) he seemed to adhere to a dualistic theory of knowledge, he still claimed that man's mind was derived from matter. Lovejoy responded: "The attempt to reduce the mental to the physical, or to membership in a class of 'natural entities' which may be either the one or the other according to circumstances, calls for a painstaking effort of reconstruction" (*The Revolt Against Dualism*, 237). Frost's criticism of Bertrand Russell on this subject took the form of satirizing the British philosopher's inability to make up his mind.

39. Ibid., 37.

40. Ibid., 37–39.

41. Ibid., 80.

42. Paul Arthur Schilpp, ed., *Albert Einstein: Philosopher-Scientist* (Evanston, Ill.: Library of Living Philosophies, Inc., 1949), 19. Einstein's italics.

43. Holton, op. cit., 99.

44. Ibid.

45. The belief that science is supreme in all things led William Montgomery to understate greatly the character and temperament of Haeckel: "Haeckel believed in a materialistically flavored monism." *The Comparative Reception of Darwinism*, Thomas F. Glick, ed. (Austin: University of Texas Press, 1972), 84. A much more accurate analysis was made by Carleton J. H. Hayes: "Haeckel was no mere agnostic. He was as sure of scientific atheism as any theologian was of Christianity, and he was neither tongue-tied nor pen-bound in proclaiming his faith." *A Generation of Materialism, 1871–1900* (New York: Harper and Brothers, 1991), 126. For Haeckel's historical role in the development of the Nazi ideology, see Daniel Gasman, *The Scientific Origins of National Socialism*.

46. In spite of his pacifism, Einstein wrote a letter to President Franklin D. Roosevelt urging the government to develop the atomic bomb.

47. *The Private Lives of Albert Einstein*, 245.

48. Philipp Frank, *Einstein: His Life and Times* (New York: Alfred A. Knopf, 1947), 286. Frank added that "many scientists . . . take it much amiss that Einstein even mentions religion and spirituality in the same breath with science,"

49. Holton, op. cit., 100.
50. For a summary of how science and ideology combined to make a monistic century, see Holton, 37–41 and 97–100. For the persistence of dualism and pluralism, see 41–42 and Lovejoy's *The Revolt Against Dualism.*
51. Edward Connery Lathem, ed., *Interviews with Robert Frost* (1966), 128.
52. Frost, "Introduction to *King Jasper,*" *Selected Prose,* 62–63.
53. *The Letters of Robert Frost to Louis Untermeyer,* 379. Frost was always a vehement critic of both the League of Nations and the United Nations, and he did not believe that any world government organization could establish or maintain peace. Such faith ignored the selfishness and depravity in human nature and the prior commitments of members of international bodies to their national self-interest.
54. *The Private Lives of Albert Einstein,* 233.
55. Ibid., 238 and 240.
56. Einstein's criticism of the assumptions of Enlightenment theories of knowledge and methodology is summarized in his remark that "In error are those theorists who believe theory comes inductively from experience." Holton, op. cit., 79. Einstein also often noted the "eternal antithesis" between the creative rational mind, or intuition, and the empirical elements in man's knowledge. See Sonja Bergmann, ed., *Ideas and Opinions* (New York: Crown, 1954), 301.
57. Bernard Cohen, "An Interview with Einstein," *Scientific American* (July 1955), 72.
58. For Einstein's digressions from the assumptions and methodology of Descartes and Newton, see Lovejoy, *The Revolt Against Dualism,* 122–23, 126, 149–52, and 158. For his differences with his contemporaries, see 120–22.
59. Thompson, *The Years of Triumph,* 648–49. Monists make a false antithesis between spirit and matter and assume that belief in one necessarily denigrates the other. Thus Thompson concluded that Frost denigrated science because of his religious beliefs, whereas Robert Faggen praised Frost's celebration of science while largely ignoring his religious beliefs.
60. See "The Future of Man" (unpublished version), *Frost: Collected Poems, Prose & Plays,* 870.
61. Frost valued Einstein's book so much that during the summers of 1940–44 it was among the books he brought to Bread Loaf for summer reading.
62. Frost, "Education by Poetry," *Frost: Collected Poems, Prose & Plays,* 720.
63. Einstein, *Relativity: The Special and General Theory,* 89, 154, 98–99, 124, 132–33, 152–53, and 10.
64. Ibid., 10.
65. Frost, "Education by Poetry," *Robert Frost: Collected Poems, Prose & Plays,* 720–21.
66. *The Letters of Robert Frost to Louis Untermeyer,* 343.
67. Ibid., 365. This passage was omitted when the poem was included in Frost's last book, *In The Clearing* (1962), under the title "A Cabin in the Clearing."

68. Frost's original lecture was recorded by Reginald L. Cook and published nineteen years later in *Robert Frost: A Living Voice* (1974). Twenty-one years after that it was reproduced in *Frost: Collected Poems, Prose & Plays*, under the title "On Taking Poetry," but without Cook's notes.

69. Cook, *Robert Frost: A Living Voice*, 76. During other poetry readings at Bread Loaf, Cook recorded Frost's many other comments on Einstein and relativity. See *Robert Frost: A Living Voice*, 8, 33, 39–40, 76, 78–79. 88–89, 98–100, 113–14, 212–13, 215, and 245. Frost's comments on Einstein in this chapter include these sources as well as Cohen's interview.

70. I. Bernard Cohen, "An Interview with Einstein," *Scientific American* (July 1955), 69. For other examples of Einstein's humor, see 69–70 and 72.

71. Robert Newdick, *Newdick's Season of Frost*, 282.

72. Peter J. Stanlis, "Acceptable in Heaven's Sight: Frost at Bread Loaf, 1938–1941," *Frost Centennial Essays*, vol. 3, 292–93.

73. *The Letters of Robert Frost to Louis Untermeyer*, 184 and 166. Untermeyer recorded that Frost even applied his sense of humor when he was facing a serious operation: "The pain did not stop his raillery." 319.

74. Peter J. Stanlis, "Acceptable in Heaven's Sight: Frost at Bread Loaf, 1939–1941," *Frost Centennial Essays*, vol. 3, 288.

75. Reginald L. Cook, *Robert Frost: A Living Voice*, 76–79. See also 113–14.

76. Cohen, "An Interview with Einstein," 73.

77. Cook, *Robert Frost: A Living Voice*, 212.

78. Holton, op. cit., 143.

79. Philipp Frank, *Einstein: His Life and Time*, 250.

80. Lovejoy, *The Revolt Against Dualism*, 181.

81. Frost had no way of knowing the licentious personal life of Einstein, which his literary executors, Helen Dukas and Otto Nathan, kept hidden from the public, until Nathan's death in 1987. See *The Private Lives of Albert Einstein*, particularly 206–10. In light of his close and continued friendship with Louis Untermeyer, whose personal life was scandalous, Frost's view of Einstein would not have been changed by any posthumous revelations.

82. Cohn, "An Interview with Einstein," 70. In Einstein's *The Evolution of Physics* he frequently discussed the danger but necessity of using intuition in scientific enquiries.

83. Edward C. Lathem, *Interviews with Robert Frost*, 124.

84. Philipp Frank, *Einstein: His Life and Times*, 240.

85. Holton, op. cit., 133.

86. Frost's view is well explicated by Edwin A. Burtt in *The Metaphysical Foundations of Modern Physical Science* (New York: Harcourt, Brace, and Co., 1927), 237–40.

# Notes

## Chapter 9, Frost and Religion: The Two Masques

1. A conversation between Robert Frost and me, Bread Loaf, Vermont, July 6, 1962.
2. Lawrance Thompson, *Robert Frost* (Minneapolis: University of Minnesota Press, 1959), 41.
3. Louis Untermeyer, *Robert Frost: A Backward Look* (Reference Department: The Library of Congress, 1964), 2.
4. A conversation between Robert Frost and a group of students at Bread Loaf, July 1962.
5. Robert Frost to Louis Untermeyer, April 16, 1957, in *The Letters of Robert Frost to Louis Untermeyer*, 369. See also Frost's letter to Lawrance Thompson, also on April 16, 1957, in *Selected Letters of Robert Frost*, 566 (cited below as *Selected Letters*).
6. G. W. Nitchie, "A Momentary Stay Against Confusion," *Robert Frost: A Collection of Critical Essays*, James M. Cox, ed. (Englewood Cliffs: Prentice-Hall, 1962), 174; see also 175. Hereafter cited as *Frost Ctitical Essays*.
7. Lionel Trilling, "A Speech on Robert Frost: A Cultural Episode," *Frost: Critical Essays*, 156. On a vital aspect of the poet's philosophy, Trilling contends that Frost "admires will in the degree that he suspects mind," and that Frost "stands at the center of American thought about American culture because . . . he expresses the chronic American belief that there exists an opposition between reality and mind and that one must enlist oneself in the party of reality" (*The Liberal Imagination*, Anchor Books, 5, 10).
8. While he was a teacher of English and drama at Pinkerton Academy in Derry, New Hampshire, Frost had his students put on Milton's *Comus*. See *Letters of Robert Frost to Louis Untermeyer*, 357–58.
9. In the twentieth century the only notable masques produced in the United States and England were Percy Mackaye's *Masque of St. Louis*, performed in 1914 in St. Louis, and some early seventeenth-century masques performed in 1916 at Stratford during the tercentenary of Shakespeare.
10. *Letters of Robert Frost to Louis Untermeyer*, 333–34.
11. Frost believed that the embodiment of spirit in matter was the manifestation of true religion, and that the highest reaches of poetry were the attempt to say spirit in terms of matter. In "Kitty Hawk," he expressed this idea in a passage celebrating Christ's Incarnation:

> But God's own descent
> Into flesh was meant
> As a demonstration
> That the supreme merit
> Lay in risking spirit
> In substantiation.

But Frost's theism, like Abraham Lincoln's, was not sectarian; he believed it could be best fulfilled individually, not through institutions. Frost once remarked to me (Bread Loaf, July 1942) that "[T. S.] Eliot is more churchy than I am, but I am more religious than Eliot."

12. One critic, wholly missing the point of Frost's parody and criticism of Yeats, even contends that in *A Masque of Mercy* "Keeper's failure" in courage "is also Frost's; and that failure helps to explain, perhaps, Frost's irritated awareness of Yeats in the masques. . . ." G. W. Nitche, "A Momentary Stay Against Confusion," *Frost Critical Essays*, 167.

13. *The Letters of Robert Frost to Louis Untermeyer*, 346.

14. Ibid., 388.

15. Randall Jarrell, "The Other Frost," *Robert Frost: An Introduction*, Robert A. Greenberg and James G. Hepburn, eds. (New York: Holt, Rinehart and Winston, 1961), 131.

16. Yvor Winters, "Robert Frost: or, the Spiritual Drifter as Poet," *Frost Critical Essays*, 71, 79.

17. See for example Radcliffe Squires, *The Major Themes of Robert Frost* (Ann Arbor: University of Michigan Press, 1963), 80–83.

18. Winters, "Spiritual Drifter," 72–73. The fideistic tradition of theology is also found in some of the works of Donne, Dryden, Swift, and Dr. Johnson.

19. Job's wife speaks a passage that combines ideas expressed in Frost's "The Trial by Existence" and "The Lesson for Today":

> *Job says there's no such thing as Earth's becoming*
> *An easier place for man to save his soul in.*
> *Except as a hard place to save his soul in,*
> *A trial ground where he can try himself*
> *And find out whether he is any good,*
> *It would be meaningless. It might as well*
> *Be Heaven at once and have it over with.*

20. Marion Montgomery, "Robert Frost and His Use of Barriers," *Frost Critical Essays*, 142–43.

21. Reuben A. Brower, *The Poetry of Robert Frost* (New York: Oxford University Press, 1963), 164, 215–18.

22. See for example Reginald L. Cook, "Emerson and Frost: A Parallel of Seers," *New England Quarterly*, XXXI (June 1958), 216–17.

23. Frost, *Selected Letters*, 584.

24. In one of his last poems, "Quandary," Frost amplifies the necessary relationship between good and evil:

> *Never have I been sad or glad*
> *That there was such a thing as bad.*

> There had to be, I understood,
> For there to have been any good.
> It was by having been contrasted
> That good and bad so long had lasted.

25. *Letters of Robert Frost to Louis Untermeyer*, 340.
26. Ibid., 331.
27. Frost to G. R. and Alma Elliott, January 12, 1963, in *Selected Letters*, 596.
28. See Elizabeth S. Sergeant, *Robert Frost: The Trial by Existence* (New York: Holt, Rinehart and Winston, 1960), 372.
29. Archibald MacLeish, *J.B.* (Boston: Houghton Mifflin, 1956), scene 8.
30. Ibid., scene 11.
31. Ibid.
32. Frost, *Selected Letters*, 525–26. See also Frost's letter to Lawrance Thompson, 530.
33. The contradiction between justice and mercy is an old subject for debate in Christianity. See for example Godfrey Goodman, *The Fall of Man* (1616), and the reply by George Hakewill, *An Apologie of the Power and Providence of God* (1627).
34. Frost's own views toward "New Deal" politics were in other poems far harsher than what is expressed in *A Masque of Mercy*, where his secondary theme contradicts the criticism of Malcolm Cowley that Frost had no vision of social justice: "There is little in his work to suggest Christian charity or universal brotherhood under God." "The Case Against Mr. Frost," *Frost: Critical Essays*, 41; see also 40, 42–43.
35. The omission of Geneva as an approach to Christ is significant. In this connection Reuben Brower has said: "Frost has remarked that the people who have best understood the Masques were Roman Catholics and Jews," *Poetry of Frost*, 212.
36. This conventional view of the mercy in God's judgment is Marion Montgomery's interpretation. He sees Frost's God as "that which man is sure cares, and will save him, no matter how many times or how completely he has failed." "Robert Frost and His Use of Barriers," *Frost: Critical Essays*, 150.
37. Frost discovered this ending for *A Masque of Mercy* while preaching on Psalm 19 at the Rockdale Avenue Temple in Cincinnati, Ohio, on October 10, 1946. See *Selected Letters*, 555–56.
38. James M. Cox, "Introduction," *Frost Critical Essays*, 150.
39. Thompson, *Robert Frost*, 31.

## Chapter 10, Frost's Philosophy of Education: The Poet as Teacher

1. Edward C. Lathem, *Interviews with Robert Frost*, 242. Hereafter cited as *Interviews*.
2. Horace W. Hewlett, *In Other Words: Amherst in Prose and Verse* (Amherst College: Amherst, 1964), 176. For an account of Frost as poet-teacher, see Robert

Pack, "Robert Frost's 'Enigmatical Reserve': The Poet as Teacher and Preacher," *Robert Frost: Lectures on the Centennial of His Birth* (Washington, D.C.: Library of Congress, 1975), 43–55.

3. Robert Frost, "Education by Poetry," *Selected Prose of Robert Frost*, 39.

4. Sidney Cox, *A Swinger of Birches*, 121–22.

5. Thompson, *The Later Years*, 226.

6. *Interviews*, 240.

7. Gordon A. Craig, "The Good, the Bad and the Bourgeois," in *The New York Review of Books*, XLV, no. 13 (August 13, 1998), 8. For a brief account of the conflict between Arnold and Huxley, see Lionel Trilling, *Matthew Arnold* (New York: Harcourt, Brace and Jovanovich, 1954), 371–72.

8. On two other occasions Frost stated his conviction that the loss of Latin in the high school curriculum was the beginning of the serious decline of American education. In 1916 to Morris P. Tilley he lamented the replacement of the classics by vocational studies. After a visit to Frost at Bread Loaf on June 3, 1962, Robert Cotner wrote: "He felt the decline in American education began when Latin was made an option and finally removed entirely from the curriculum. He had a plan in mind that he talked extensively about—a 'Chair' system for the public schools similar to that used in the better colleges. 'In this system, a teacher upon his own merit in educational preparation, conscientiousness, and experience, would be appointed to a "Chair" within a department and hold that position for the remainder of his career.'" (Letter from Robert Cotner to Peter Stanlis, June 26, 1998.)

9. See John Henry Cardinal Newman, *The Idea of a University* (New York: Longmans, Green and Co., 1923), 227. All references are to this edition.

10. As Louis Untermeyer observed: "Frost was almost as preoccupied with teaching as he was with creating. As a teacher he dwelt almost entirely upon the creative impulse." *Robert Frost: A Backward Look*, 22.

11. Newman, *The Idea of a University*, 175.

12. Ibid., 165. See also 166–67.

13. Ibid., 158–63.

14. Ibid., 148–49. See also 150. Newman praised George Crabbe's "Tales of the Hall," which celebrates the self-education of a farm boy, a work that Frost also admired.

15. Cox, *A Swinger of Birches*, 49.

16. See *Robert Frost at Bread Loaf* (Middlebury, VT: Middlebury College Press, 1964), 4.

17. Louis Mertins, *Robert Frost: Life and Talks-Walking*, 213.

18. *Interviews*, 67–71.

19. Louis Untermeyer, *Robert Frost: A Backward Look*, 22.

20. Thompson, *Robert Frost: The Later Years*, 263–64.

21. *Interviews*, 270.

22. Jeffrey Meyers, *Robert Frost* (New York: Houghton Mifflin Co., 1996), 212 and 262.

23. Cox, *A Swinger of Birches*, 46.

24. Ibid., 264.

25. Ibid., 40–41.

26. Ibid., 52–53.

27. Thompson, *The Early Years*, 119.

28. Louis Mertins, *Robert Frost: Life and Talks-Walking*, 317. See also 318.

29. Thompson, *The Later Years*, 443.

30. Louis Untermeyer, *The Letters of Robert Frost to Louis Untermeyer*, 287–88.

31. Cox, *A Swinger of Birches*, 26.

32. *The Letters of Robert Frost to Louis Untermeyer*, 183 and 194.

33. "Robert Frost," *Writers at Work: The Paris Review Interviews, Second Series*, 24.

34. *Interviews*, 13.

35. *Interviews*, 98. In 1940 Frost discussed Twain's jumping frog story with me: "Robert Frost at Bread Loaf, 1939–1941," *Frost Centennial Essays*, vol. 3, 237–38.

36. Cox, *A Swinger of Birches*, 45. In 1939 Frost said the same thing in conversation with me: *Frost Centennial Essays*, vol. 3, 207. These conversations are filled with a great variety of Frost's comments on education.

37. "The Story in the Meiklejohn Files, Part II," *Amherst College Archives*, Spring 1983, 57.

38. Ibid., 55. See also *The Letters of Robert Frost to Louis Untermeyer*, 170.

39. Ibid.

40. Robert Frost, "Maturity No Object," in *Selected Prose of Robert Frost*, 49.

41. Phillis Bottome, *The New Republic* (April 15, 1936), 280. For a version of the Frost-Meiklejohn conflict more sympathetic to the president, see Thompson, *The Years of Triumph*, 97–122 and 550–57. In defense of Frost, see Louis Mertins, *Robert Frost: Life and Talks-Walking*, 154–59 and 161.

42. See Elizabeth S. Sergeant, *The Trial by Existence*, 258.

43. Frost, *Selected Letters*, 250.

44. Thompson, *The Years of Triumph*, 229.

45. Mertins, *Robert Frost: Life and Talks-Walking*, 324.

46. *Interviews*, 186.

47. Cox, "Preface," *A Swinger of Birches*, 9.

48. G. A. Craig, "Robert Frost at Amherst," 8, Amherst College archives.

49. Andrew R. Marks, *The Rabbi and the Poet* (Alton, NH: Andover Green Book Publishers, 1994), 1.

50. Ibid.

51. Victor Reichert, "The Robert Frost I Knew," *Frost Centennial Essays*, vol. 3, 117–118.

52. *The Letters of Robert Frost to Louis Untermeyer*, 290. See also 252.

53. *Interviews*, 269.

54. Thompson, *The Later Years*, 51.

55. *Interviews*, 161. Frost repeated this remark in "Maturity No Object."

56. C. P. Snow, "Robert Frost," *Variety of Men*, 192.

57. *The Letters of Robert Frost to Louis Untermeyer*, 277. On another occasion Frost clarified what he meant by "giving me back my father's Harvard": "I was at Harvard while the old education, unaffected by Madison Avenue, was in full swing. There wasn't too much difference between the way I was taught there and the way my father was." Frost noted that his father "was permitted to offer those two books of memorized Latin of Caesar for the whole course. . . . Wouldn't that idea kill the progressives in education." Louis Mertins, op. cit., 338–39.

58. *Interviews*, 269.

59. C. P. Snow, op. cit., 192.

60. Thompson, *The Later Years*, 49. See also 396.

61. Mertins, *Robert Frost: Life and Talks-Walking*, 220.

62. *The Letters of Robert Frost to Louis Untermeyer*, 316–17.

63. Louis Untermeyer, *Robert Frost: A Backward Look*, 18.

64. Notebook 001726 in the Baker Library, Dartmouth College.

65. Lawrance Thompson, *Selected Letters of Robert Frost*, 146.

66. *Interviews*, 12.

67. For Frost's reasons for leaving Dartmouth and Harvard, see Morris P. Tilley, "Notes from Conversations with Robert Frost," *The Inlander* (February 1918) and *The Letters of Robert Frost to Louis Untermeyer*, 353.

68. Elizabeth S. Sergeant, *Robert Frost: The Trial by Existence*, 410.

69. *The Letters of Robert Frost to Louis Untermeyer*, 132.

70. Reginald L. Cook, "Robert Frost in Context," *Frost Centennial Essays*, vol. 3, 139. See also *Interviews*, 13.

71. *The Letters of Robert Frost to Louis Untermeyer*, 180.

72. Mertins, *Robert Frost: Life and Talks-Walking*, 356–57. The best study of Frost as a teacher of writing is by Elaine Barry, in *Robert Frost* (New York: Frederick Ungar Publishing Co., 1973).

73. *Interviews*, 230.

74. Reginald L. Cook, "Robert Frost in Context," *Frost Centennial Essays*, vol. 3, 139.

75. The history of Frost as a teacher reflects his lifelong defense of the humanities in the classroom and on the lecture platform. His outstanding qualities as a teacher derive from his mastery of the humanities. When he taught at Pinkerton Academy, Ernest Silver, principal at Pinkerton, and Henry C. Morrison, superintendent of education in New Hampshire, called Frost the best teacher in New Hampshire. John Bartlett, his best student at Pinkerton, stated that "Frost was a good measure above any other teacher he had ever known" (Margaret Bartlett Anderson, *Robert Frost and John Bartlett*, 15). For other examples of student responses to Frost as a teacher, see Marcia Pushell's unpublished essay in Lamson Library, Plymouth State College, Plymouth, New Hampshire,

file 67. Letters from students at Plymouth in support of her essay are in files 68 and 69. Manuscript essays on Frost's outstanding teaching by P. N. Youts, Gardner Jackson, and G. Armour Craig are recorded in the Robert Frost Library in Amherst College. Warren Bower's essay on Frost as a teacher is in the *New York University Notebook*, vol. 7, no. 3 (February 1964). For student and faculty responses to Frost as a teacher see Dorothy Tyler, "Frost's Last Three Visits to Michigan," *Frost Centennial Essays*, vol. 1, 518–34 and "Robert Frost in Michigan," *Frost Centennial Essays*, vol. 3, 7–69. Tyler's comments are typical of what many students wrote: "an extraordinary richness of influence pervades that first year of Frost's presence in Ann Arbor"; "how astonishingly Frost found his way into the University life of the time"; there was an "unquestionable and lasting influence of Frost upon both faculty and students who knew him." *Frost Centennial Essays*, vol. 3, 14, 26, and 42. For a general estimate of Frost as a teacher, see Thompson, *The Later Years*, 459–60.

## Chapter 11, The Individual and Society

1. Aristotle had written: "The state belongs to a class of objects which exist in nature, and . . . man is by nature a political animal; it is his nature to live in a state." *The Politics*, T. A. Sinclair, trans. (Baltimore: Penguin Books, 1962), 28.
2. Edward C. Lathem, ed., *Interviews with Robert Frost*, 213. This interview occurred on September 29, 1959.
3. In *The Vantage Point* the speaker enjoys the double advantage of being alone and self-sufficient in nature and also in a position to observe civil society. He notes that "If I tired of trees I seek again mankind"; he may do so with ease. The same distinction between the isolated individual and the social individual is reflected in Frost's first two collections of poems. As Frost remarked, *A Boy's Will* (1913) has "something unsocial" in it, whereas *North of Boston* (1914) was subtitled "A Book of People."
4. This statement was made by Frost in a television interview in the fall of 1952. It is quoted by Marion Montgomery in "Robert Frost and His Uses of Barriers: Man vs Nature toward God," *Robert Frost: A Collection of Critical Essays*, James M. Cox, ed. (Englewood Cliffs, NJ: Prentice Hall, 1962), 138.
5. *Interviews*, 84.
6. Ibid., 128.
7. Ibid., 76.
8. Ibid.
9. Ibid., 77–78.
10. Ibid., 248.
11. Ibid., 75–76.
12. Ibid., 78.

13. Ibid., 76.

14. Ibid., 208.

15. Ibid., 245. The theme of attraction and repulsion between the individual and society runs through Frost's poem *Build Soil-A Political Pastoral*.

16. Ibid., 76–77.

17. *The Letters of Robert Frost to Louis Untermeyer*, 80.

18. *Interviews*, 78.

19. *The Letters of Robert Frost to Louis Untermeyer*, 311.

20. *Interviews*, 261.

21. Ibid., 262.

22. *Interviews*, 142. In 1959, Untermeyer noted that Frost had been consistent throughout his life about how an individual should save himself from being compromised by the demands of modern urban life: "He still believes that the only way to be saved is to save yourself; two of his favorite books are Robinson Crusoe, the self-sustaining castaway, and Walden, the document of a man who cast himself away to find himself." *The Letters of Robert Frost to Louis Untermeyer*, 378.

23. *Interviews*, 142.

24. Louis Mertins, *Robert Frost: Life and Talks-Walking*, 62–63.

25. *Interviews*, 145. Later in the interview Frost admitted that he shared Thoreau's preference for "independence" over larger social freedom: "I'm more interested in the liberties I take than in the big thing you call freedom or liberty; the little liberties socially, in poetry, art and little trespasses and excesses in things like that." *Interviews*, 156.

26. Ibid., 78.

27. *The Letters of Robert Frost to Louis Untermeyer*, 222–23. The fullest artistic expression of this theme is in Frost's political pastoral, *Build Soil*. Frost admitted in the same letter to Untermeyer that he accepted the unconsidered land as an asset in his personal life: "We are going to make another big attempt at the almost self-contained farm. Almost. No nonsense. Merely much more self-contained than fools would imagine."

28. *Interviews*, 158. On the occasion of this interview, when Frost made this statement, he recited his poem *The Gift Outright*. Frost's theory that American political freedom depends upon "having a territorial basis" is identical with the central thesis of Orestes A. Brownson in *The American Republic* (1865).

29. *The Letters of Robert Frost to Louis Untermeyer*, 211.

30. Ibid., 56.

31. *Interviews*, 145–46.

32. Ibid., 179.

33. Ibid.

34. Ibid., 143.

35. *The Letters of Robert Frost to Louis Untermeyer*, 211.

36. *Interviews*, 19.

37. Burke, *Reflections on the Revolution in France*, in *The Works of Edmund Burke*, vol. 3 (Boston, 1904), 292.

38. Swift, letter to Alexander Pope, September 29, 1725, in *The Correspondence of Jonathan Swift*, vol. 3, Harold Williams, ed. (Oxford: Clarendon Press, 1963), 103.

39. *Robert Frost: Life and Talks-Walking*, 310.

40. *Interviews*, 197.

41. Ibid., 283.

42. Ibid., 121.

43. *The Letters of Robert Frost to Louis Untermeyer*, 125. Frost believed that love of country was above political party loyalty, and years later he was pleased to hear that after President Eisenhower was out of office and met President Kennedy, they were friendly toward each other. (*Interviews*, 282.)

44. *The Letters of Robert Frost to Louis Untermeyer*, 58.

45. *Interviews*, 266.

46. Ibid., 155.

47. Ibid., 135.

48. Ibid., 157.

49. Ibid., 190.

50. Ibid., 146.

51. Ibid., 208.

52. *The Letters of Robert Frost to Louis Untermeyer*, 340.

53. *Interviews*, 190. In September 1962, during Frost's trip to Russia, the poet was asked whether Russian poets were known in America, and he replied: "The chief one seems to be Pasternak." The reporter of this incident noted: "There was an instant hush. The Russians were shocked and embarrassed. The late Boris Pasternak, one of Russia's foremost poets, is still a name that frightens many Russians. He was hounded by Soviet authorities after his book *Dr. Zhivago* was published in the West. It is highly critical of the Communist regime and has not been published in Russia." (*Interviews*, 289.)

54. Ibid., 241.

55. This poem was first published in *The Saturday Review of Literature* for January 11, 1936, under the title "To a Thinker in Office," and it as widely interpreted as a satire against Franklin D. Roosevelt. See *Interviews*, 86–88.

56. See Thompson, *The Years of Triumph*, 330 and 635.

57. *The Letters of Robert Frost to Louis Untermeyer*, 373. Frost wrote to Louis Mertins: "Once in every so often we've got to establish our nationalism with ourselves. You know I'm not friendly toward things like the U.N. I was the same way with Wilson's League of Nations. A country's got to stand or fall on its own. I remember I once said to somebody a long time ago that Wilson came not to bring peace but a League of Nations. Well, can you trust a nation in the U.N. any better than out?" *Robert Frost: Life and Talks-Walking*, 397.

58. *Interviews*, 178.

59. Ibid., 196.
60. *The Letters of Robert Frost to Louis Untermeyer*, 291.
61. *Interviews*, 146.
62. Ibid., 146–47.
63. Ibid., 189.
64. *The Letters of Robert Frost to Louis Untermeyer*, 285.
65. Ibid., 347.
66. Ibid., 347–48.
67. *Interviews*, 179.
68. Ibid., 156.
69. Ibid., 261.
70. Ibid., 178.
71. *The Letters of Robert Frost to Louis Untermeyer*, 372.
72. *Interviews*, 128.
73. Ibid., 289.
74. Ibid., 196.
75. Ibid., 159.
76. Ibid., 178.
77. *The Letters of Robert Frost to Louis Untermeyer*, 379.

## *Chapter 12, Politics in Theory and Practice*

1. *The Letters of Robert Frost to Louis Untermeyer*, 346.
2. Ibid., 220.
3. Ibid., 191.
4. Ibid., 243.
5. Ibid., 136.
6. Ibid., 59. There was a Gothic strain in Frost's tragic sense of life that made his laughter sardonic: "No man can tell you the sound or the way of my laughter. I have neighed at night in the woods behind the house like vampires. But there are no vampires, there are no ghouls, there are no demons, there is nothing but me."
7. Louis Mertins, *Robert Frost: Life and Talks-Walking*, 62.
8. *Interviews*, 128.
9. *The Letters of Robert Frost to Louis Untermeyer*, 175.
10. Ibid., 178.
11. Ibid., 188.
12. See Frost's poem "The Planners," in *Steeple Bush*.
13. *The Letters of Robert Frost to Louis Untermeyer*, 166.
14. Ibid., 58.
15. Ibid., 86.
16. *Interviews*, 170.
17. See *Build Soil*, line 366.

18. *The Letters of Robert Frost to Louis Untermeyer*, 127.
19. *Interviews*, 169.
20. Ibid., 78.
21. *The Letters of Robert Frost to Louis Untermeyer*, 98.
22. Ibid., 86.
23. Ibid., 87.
24. *Interviews*, 213.
25. Ibid.
26. John Dryden, *Astraea Redux* (1660), 2. 169–70.
27. *The Letters of Robert Frost to Louis Untermeyer*, 70.
28. Ibid., 212.
29. *Interviews*, 85.
30. "The Figure a Poem Makes," in *Selected Prose of Robert Frost*, Hyde Cox and Edward C. Latham, eds., 20.
31. *The Letters of Robert Frost to Louis Untermeyer*, 366.
32. *Interviews*, 283.
33. *The Letters of Robert Frost to Louis Untermeyer*, 97–98.
34. Ibid., May 24, 1916, 32.
35. *Interviews*, May 31, 1957, 170.
36. *The Letters of Robert Frost to Louis Untermeyer*, 363.
37. Ibid., 292.
38. *Interviews*, 291.
39. Ibid., 170.
40. Ibid., 240–41.
41. Ibid., 241. Both in his explanation of the historical origins of American democracy out of ancient Greece and in his firm faith that it is a superior form of government and will prevail against its competitors, Frost again reveals some important points in common with Orestes Brownson's *The American Republic.*
42. Ibid., 289.
43. Ibid.
44. *The Letters of Robert Frost to Louis Untermeyer*, 77.
45. Ibid., August 18, 1917, 57–58.
46. A statement made by Frost to me at Bread Loaf, Vermont, in August 1941.
47. *Interviews*, 124.
48. Ibid., 158.
49. Mertins, op. cit., 310.
50. Ibid., 207.
51. Ibid., 402.
52. Ibid.
53. Ibid., 377.
54. *The Letters of Robert Frost to Louis Untermeyer*, 73.
55. *Interviews*, 118.
56. *The Letters of Robert Frost to Louis Untermeyer*, 45.

57. *Interviews*, 178.
58. Ibid., 87.
59. *The Letters of Robert Frost to Louis Untermeyer*, 45.
60. See *The Letters of Robert Frost to Louis Untermeyer*, 67–69 for Frost's lampoon and burlesque of House's political romance and his dig at Wilson.
61. Frost to George Whicher, May 23, 1919, Amherst College library.
62. *Interviews*, 282.
63. *The Letters of Robert Frost to Louis Untermeyer*, 116.
64. Ibid., 117.
65. Mertins, op. cit., 208.
66. Ibid., 333.
67. *Interviews*, 83.
68. *The Letters of Robert Frost to Louis Untermeyer*, 345.
69. *Interviews*, 87–88.
70. *The Letters of Robert Frost to Louis Untermeyer*, 280.
71. Ibid., 251.
72. Ibid., 258.
73. See for example Frost's comments about a scheme proposed by Edward Bruce, a New Deal official, to encourage poets through granting them pensions rather than by putting them on relief (*The Letters of Robert Frost to Louis Untermeyer*, 258).
74. *The Letters of Robert Frost to Louis Untermeyer*, 304–05.
75. *Interviews*, 108.
76. Ibid., 157.
77. Ibid., 156.
78. *The Letters of Robert Frost to Louis Untermeyer*, 80.
79. Ibid.
80. Ibid., 58.
81. Ibid., 347.
82. Mertins, 369.
83. *The Letters of Robert Frost to Louis Untermeyer*, 282.
84. See *Interviews*, 84. Frost summarized his objections to the New Deal in a pithy phrase: "I can't stand coercion."
85. *Interviews*, 112.
86. *The Letters of Robert Frost to Louis Untermeyer*, 284–85.

### Chapter 13, In the Clearing: Continuity & Unity in Frost's Dualism

1. See Peter J. Stanlis, "Acceptable in Heaven's Sight: Robert Frost at Bread Loaf, 1939–1941," *Frost Centennial Essays*, vol. 3, 287–88.
2. *Frost: Collected Poems, Prose & Plays*, 860.
3. Ibid., 865.
4. Irving Babbitt, *Literature and the American College* (Washington, D.C.: Nation-

al Humanities Institute, 1986; first published in 1908), 84–85, and Paul Elmer More, *Shelburne Essays*, vol. 8 (New York: Phaeton Press, 1963; first published in 1913), 248.

5. *Frost: Collected Poems, Prose & Plays*, 866. Frost did not use "superstition" as a pejorative word.

6. Frost, "The Future of Man," in *Frost: Collected Poems, Prose & Plays*, 868.

7. Ibid., 869.

8. Ibid., 870.

9. For a detailed account of this poetry reading and Frost's interspersed remarks, see Lisa Seal, ed., "Robert Frost at the Fountain Street Church, Grand Rapids, Michigan, November 19, 1959," *The Robert Frost Review* 13 (Fall 2003), 12–33.

10. The poems in "Cluster of Faith" repeat and echo statements made by Frost's friend Rabbi Victor Reichert in talks with me at Bread Loaf during the last two summers of the poet's life. The influence of Reichert's biblical beliefs on Frost's religious thought in "Cluster of Faith," and in *A Masque of Reason* and *A Masque of Mercy*, remains an important, insufficiently explored subject.

11. *Anthology of Magazine Verse* (New York: Schulte's Book Store, 1959).

12. For a complete bibliographical account of "Kitty Hawk," see Jeffrey S. Cramer, *Robert Frost Among His Poems*, 169–71.

13. Sir Paul Harvey, ed., *The Oxford Companion in English Literature* (Oxford: The Clarendon Press, 1967), 760. In "Colin Cloute," Skelton appealed to his readers in much the same way that Frost hoped he would be taken in "Kitty Hawk" regarding his whimsical light verse form: "For though my ryme be ragged / Tattered and Jagged / Rudely rayne beaten / Rusty and moth eaten / If ye take well therein / It hath in it some pyth."

14. Sidney Cox, *A Swinger of Birches*, 59.

15. *Frost: Collected Poems, Prose & Plays*, 853.

16. Ibid., 858–59. During Frost's poetry reading at the University of Detroit (November 14, 1962), he referred to Mother Goose as "a profound philosopher." This statement needs to be understood metaphorically, as part of the comic spirit in serious literature. Prior to "Kitty Hawk," Frost's most notable use of comedy in serious discourse was in *A Masque of Reason*, in the fictional character of Job's wife, Thyatira. She functioned as a satirical and humorous foil or contrast to the serious theological discourse between God and Job. Like many reviewers of *A Masque of Reason*, Lawrance Thompson failed to understand Frost's use of the comic dimension in that serious closet drama. This led Thompson to misread *A Masque of Reason* as a satire against orthodox religion. Frost's extension of the comic spirit beyond character into the verse form of "Kitty Hawk" was simply too much for many literary critics of that poem.

17. See Cramer, *Robert Frost Among His Poems*, 170.

18. See Amherst College Special Collections, #341. Elliott's other unpublished letters are listed as #331, #332, #336, and #339. Frost's final letter to Elliott is listed as #304.

19. See Amherst College Special Collections, #304.
20. See Cramer, *Robert Frost Among His Poems*, 170.
21. *Frost: Collected Poems, Prose & Plays*, 870.
22. Ibid.
23. Cramer, *Robert Frost Among His Poems*, 168. Eighteen years earlier, in 1941, during a conversation with me at Bread Loaf on the creative power of mind in relation to matter, Frost said: "The more powerful the mind, the more it could penetrate into matter and space." Peter J. Stanlis, "Acceptable in Heaven's Sight: Frost at Bread Loaf, 1939–1941," *Frost Centennial Essays*, vol. 3, 287.
24. Sidney Cox, *A Swinger of Birches* (1961 edition), 61–63.
25. See Reginald L. Cook, "Robert Frost in Context," *Frost Centennial Essays*, vol. 3, 172–73.

## Some Afterthoughts . . .

1. Gorham B. Munson, "Against the World in General," *Recognition of Robert Frost*, Richard Thornton, ed. (New York: Henry Holt and Co., 1937), 200.
2. Ibid.
3. See *Proceedings, National Poetry Festival* (Washington, D.C.: Library of Congress, 1964), 243–44 and 252. The poetry festival took place on October 22–24, 1962.
4. Gorham B. Munson, *Making Poems for America: Robert Frost* (Chicago: Encyclopedia Britannica Press, 1962), 152. See also 151–53.
5. A comparison of Emerson's conception of "nature" with that of Frost reveals how irreconcilable the spiritual monism of the New England transcendentalist was with Frost's dualism. In "Nature" Emerson wrote: "every natural process is a version of a moral sentence. The moral law lies at the center of nature and radiates to the circumference. It is the path and marrow of every substance, every relation, and every process." See Brooks Atkinson, ed., *The Essential Writings of Ralph Waldo Emerson* (New York: The Modern Library, 2000), 21–22. See also "Idealism" and "Spirit," 24–34. Emerson's monism, which fused nature as physics with nature as ethics, resulted in optimism wholly at variance with Frost's view of nature. In the concluding lines of Frost's poem "Our Hold on the Planet," regarding "the just proportion of good and ill," he stated his realistic view of nature:

    > *Take nature altogether since time began,*
    > *Including human nature, in peace and war,*
    > *And it must be a little more in favor of man,*
    > *Say a fraction of one per cent at the very least,*
    > *Or our number living wouldn't be steadily more,*
    > *Our hold on the planet wouldn't have so increased.*

Emerson's optimistic fusion of physical nature and the moral law was impossible for Frost to accept. His own observations of external nature, and his agreement that Darwin's view of the survival of species in physical nature was valid, placed him at the furthest extreme from Emerson's optimism.

6. Lawrance Thompson, *Fire and Ice*, 181.

7. Ibid.

8. Ibid., 177.

9. See Lisa Abshear-Seale, "What Catullus Means by *mens animi*: Robert Frost's 'Kitty Hawk,'" *The Robert Frost Review* (Fall 1993), 37–46. Frost's poem "Bond and Free," on the nature and relationship of love and thought, exemplifies how his dualism harmonizes two contrary things without destroying either one in order to achieve a monistic unity.

10. Thomas Henry Huxley, *Aphorisms and Reflections from the Works of T. H. Huxley*, Henrietta Huxley, ed. (London: Macmillan, 1907), 167.

11. Ibid., 26.

12. Thomas Henry Huxley, *Man's Place in Nature and Other Essays*, Oliver Lodge, ed. (New York: J. M. Denton & Sons, 1906), xii–xiv.

13. Ibid., xv.

14. Frost had read many of Huxley's essays in the nine volumes of essays published near the end of his life. He was also familiar with Leonard Huxley's *Life and Letters of Thomas Henry Huxley* in two volumes (1913) and with Henrietta Huxley's *Aphorisms and Reflections from the Works of T. H. Huxley.* He had read Huxley's *English Men of Letters* volumes on Hume (1878). Many of Huxley's publications ran to two or more printings.

15. Thomas Henry Huxley, *Lay Sermons, Addresses, and Reviews* (New York: D. Appleton, 1870), 337–39.

16. Leonard Huxley, ed., *The Life and Letters of Thomas Henry Huxley*, vol. 1 (New York: D. Appleton, 1900), 261–63.

17. At Clark University (Worcester, Massachusetts), "The Huxley File" lists 120 Victorian essays on Thomas Henry Huxley, including his use of the methodology of Descartes, his agnosticism, his materialism, and his conception of science.

18. Reginald L. Cook, ed., *Robert Frost: A Living Voice*, 171. The agnostic prayer was by Henrietta Huxley.

19. *Interviews*, 194.

20. *The Letters of Robert Frost to Louis Untermeyer*, 166.

21. Ibid., 188.

22. Reginald Cook, *Robert Frost: A Living Voice*, 121. See also 127.

23. Leonard Huxley, ed., *The Life and Letters of Thomas Henry Huxley*, vol. 2, 227.

24. *Interviews*, 190. Frost contended that sociology was a pseudo-science, because it piled up mountains of information that could not be safely assimilated and utilized for moral social ends. In "The Lesson for Today" he noted that sociologists "tried to grasp with too much social fact / Too large a situation," and

they made "too much bad statistics" a substitute for ethics. Frost also regarded psychology and psychoanalysis as a "pseudo-science," because it made subjective speculation a substitute for empirical knowledge, and like sociology it also was incapable of dealing with ethics.

25. Ibid., 120.

26. Ibid., 271.

27. Peter J. Stanlis, "Acceptable in Heaven's Sight: Frost at Bread Loaf, 1939–1941," *Frost Centennial Essays*, vol. 3, 282–83.

28. Huxley's German orientation began very early and was far more extensive and intensive than what Frost surmised. In 1847, when Huxley arrived in Sydney, Australia, during his voyage on the scientific exploration ship *The Rattlesnake*, he met Henrietta Anne Heathorn, his future wife, and was strongly attracted to her partly because she had been educated in Germany and was proficient in the German language and literature. In May 1855 she came to England, and they were married for forty years, until Huxley's death in 1895. (See *The Life and Letters of Thomas Henry Huxley*, vol. 1, 38–42 and 138–40.) Through Thomas Carlyle's *Miscellaneous Writings*, Huxley became well read in German literature and philosophy, and he was especially taken by Goethe. (Ibid., 181, 351, and 431.) In 1870, he strongly favored Germany in the Franco-Prussian War. Between 1857 and 1892, Huxley was elected to twelve German scientific societies. (Ibid., vol. 2, 501–02.) All of these German influences, but especially his close and enduring friendship with Ernst Haeckel, had a profound effect upon Huxley's scientific and educational beliefs; these were what concerned Frost throughout his criticism of "the three generations of Huxleys."

29. Haeckel quoted Herbert Spencer's phrase "the survival of the fittest" and identified the fittest as "the picked minority" or "the victory of the best," by which he meant the people of Germany: "The cruel and merciless struggle for existence which rages throughout all living nature, and in the course of nature must rage, this unceasing and inexorable competition of all living creatures, is all incontestable fact; only the picked minority of the qualified 'fittest' is in a position to resist it successfully, while the great majority of the competitors must necessarily perish miserably." Ernst Haeckel, *Freedom in Science and Teaching*, T. H. Huxley, ed. and trans. (New York: D. Appleton, 1879), 93.

30. For details on the personal and ideological closeness of Huxley and Haeckel, see Adrian Desmond, *Huxley*, 354–60.

31. Leonard Huxley, ed., *The Life and Letters of Thomas Henry Huxley*, vol. 2, 309–11.

32. Mario A. di Gregoria, *Thomas Henry Huxley's Place in Natural Science* (New Haven: Yale University Press, 1984), 78. For a detailed account of Haeckel's influence upon Huxley's views on science, see 77–82.

33. Daniel Gasman, *The Scientific Origins of National Socialism: Social Darwinism in Ernst Haeckel and the German Monist League* (London: Macdonald and Co., 1971), 6–7.

34. Ernst Haeckel, *Freedom in Science and Teaching*, T. H. Huxley, ed. and trans., 2. For additional evidence of Huxley's identification with Haeckel's philosophical monism, see 4, 18, 22, 25, 46, 50–54, 60, and 84.

35. Daniel Gasman, op. cit., 161. See also Peter J. Bowler, op. cit., 128–29.

36. Leonard Huxley, *The Life and Letters of Thomas Henry Huxley*, vol. 1, 510. According to Huxley, scientific thought was characterized by "unflinching criticism," which was "the essence of the scientific spirit" (vol. 2, 13).

37. Ibid., vol. 2, 300. See also 301 and vol. I, 299, 362, 366, and 373.

38. Thomas Henry Huxley, *Science and Culture*, 206. See also 510–11 in *The Life and Letters of Thomas Henry Huxley*.

39. Leonard Huxley, *The Life and Letters of Thomas Henry Huxley*, vol. 1, 510–11. As Leonard Huxley noted, not all of the influence flowed from Germany to Huxley, because when his father published *Physiography* in 1880, it was perceived as "a new branch of teaching in natural science, even in Germany," where "it was immediately proposed to bring out an adaptation of the book."

40. Ibid., 347.

41. Ibid., vol. 1, 507–10; vol. 2, 160–62, 165, 190–93, 300, and 340.

42. Ibid., vol. 2, 328. For details on Huxley's theme, see 329–37.

43. *Aphorisms and Reflections*, 102.

44. Leonard Huxley, *The Life and Letters of Thomas Henry Huxley*, vol. 2, 192. At the founding of the Josiah Mason College in Birmingham, Huxley excluded from the proposed curriculum "mere literary training." Leonard Huxley recorded: "The greatest stress was laid on training in the scientific theory and practice on which depend the future of the great manufactures of the North" (vol. 2, 14).

45. Ibid., vol. 2, 14–15, 279, and 339.

46. Thomas Henry Huxley, *Science and Culture*, 46. Huxley believed that science "had created modern civilization," that "although the 'culture' of former periods might be purely literary, that of today must be based, to a great extent, upon natural science." *The Life and Letters of Thomas Henry Huxley*, vol. 2, 14–15.

47. *Aphorisms and Reflections*, 49.

48. Ibid., 84.

49. Leonard Huxley, *The Life and Letters of Thomas Henry Huxley*, vol. 2, p. 421. See also Huxley's essay "Science and the Bishops" in *Nineteenth Century* (November 1887) and "An Episcopal Trilogy" (September 2, 1888) in *Essays*, vol. 5.

50. Ibid., vol. 2, 216.

51. Ibid., vol. 2, 9.

52. While recovering from a debilitating illness in Italy, Huxley wrote to his friend Sir John Donnelly (January 18, 1885) on his response to attending a Catholic Mass in Rome: "We are just back from a great function at St. Peter's. It is the gesta of St. Peter's chair." After describing and satirizing the liturgy, Huxley

identified the historical source and temper of his reaction to the liturgy: "I must have a strong strain of Puritan blood in me somewhere, for I am possessed with a desire to arise and slay the whole brood of idolaters whenever I assist at one of these ceremonies. You will observe that I am decidedly better, and have a capacity for a good hatred still" (*The Life and Letters of Thomas Henry Huxley*, vol. 2, 97).

53. Leonard Huxley, *The Life and Letters of Thomas Henry Huxley*, vol. 1, 238.

54. Ibid., vol. 1, 402. See also *Aphorisms and Reflections*, 104.

55. Ibid., vol. 1, preface to the American edition, vi. Later Leonard Huxley reiterated that "the heart of his message to America [was] his message already delivered to the Old Country." 499.

56. Ibid., vol. 1, 494.

57. Ibid., vol. 1, 496. Later, in articles in the *New York Times* and the *Boston Daily Globe*, two journalists took their cue from Samuel Butler and identified Huxley as "Professor Protoplasm."

58. Huxley stated that he favored lightening "the medical curriculum by culling out of it everything which is unessential," including such admittedly important subjects as botany and zoology, which, he said, interfered with his "ultimate goal." He believed that "a medical school is strictly a technical school." See *American Addresses*, 110–116.

59. W. K. Werkmeister, *A History of Philosophical Ideas in America* (New York: The Ronald Press, 1949), 84.

60. The differences between Huxley and Haeckel regarding materialism are made clear in three works of scholarship published in chronological order: Carlton Hayes, in *A Generation of Materialism* (New York: Harper, 1941), treated their common materialism. George L. Mosse, in *The Crisis of German Ideology: Intellectual Origins of the Third Reich* (New York: Grosset and Dunlop, 1954), noted that Haeckel refined upon his materialism in advancing the German ideology that anticipated the Third Reich. Daniel Gasman, in *The Scientific Origins of National Socialism*, showed how Haeckel's science and materialist monist philosophy combined with German nationalism, Romanticism, and racial theory to facilitate the foundation of the post–World War I growth of the Nazi political movement. Gasman devoted seven chapters to Haeckel's views on science, education, and philosophical monism. His main thesis was that "the social Darwinist ideas of Haeckel and the German Monist League which he founded . . . provided an ideological basis for National Socialism" (preface, xiv).

61. Reginald L. Cook, *Robert Frost: A Living Voice*, 99.

62. Peter J. Stanlis, "Acceptable in Heaven's Sight: Frost at Bread Loaf, 1939–1941," *Frost Centennial Essays*, vol. 3, 258–59. Several years later, after I read Élie Halvey's great work of scholarship *The Growth of Philosophical Radicalism* (1928), I asked Frost what he thought of the preface by A. D. Lindsay: "How deeply the Benthamites were influenced by their belief in the possibilities of applying to the study of man and society the principles and methods of the

physical sciences. That is the clue to some of the most curious aberrations of their thought, and to much of their shortsightedness. The belief is still with us. It is curious how often men are still found to argue in the manner of Bentham that if certain things are admitted to be true, sociology could not be an exact science, and therefore the admissions must not be made." Frost responded that Lindsay's criticism was valid, that sociology, like psychology, was a "pseudo-science," but that Jeremy Bentham and the Victorian utilitarians did not originate his method, but had derived it from scientists such as Huxley.

63. For Frost's positive account of how to read a poem, see "On Taking Poetry" and "The Prerequisites."

64. Hyatt Waggoner, "The Humanistic Idealism of Robert Frost," *American Literature* XII (November 1941), 207–23.

65. Joseph Warren Beach, *The Concept of Nature in Nineteenth-Century English Poetry* (New York: The Macmillan Co., 1936), 551–52. See also *The Yale Review* XLIII (December 1953), 204–17.

66. Lawrance Thompson, *Robert Frost: The Years of Triumph*, 590.

67. See Robert Francis, *Frost: A Time to Talk*, 8 and 31–38.

68. Marion Montgomery, "Robert Frost and His Use of Barriers," *Robert Frost: A Collection of Critical Essays*, James M. Cox, ed., 141.

69. Reginald I. Cook, "Robert Frost in Context," *Frost Centennial Essays*, vol. 3, 162.

70. Dorothy Judd Hall, "An Old Testament Christian," *Frost Centennial Essays*, vol. 3, 318–19. An early account of Frost's belief that the strong should say nothing about their talents or destiny was recorded by Robert Newdick through Sidney Cox. Cox said, "I can remember a talk in Littleton in 1922 . . . in which he used the phrase, 'wait until I see,' making the point that the time for evaluating a man's action was not until his objective had a chance to be accomplished." Robert Newdick, *Newdick's Season of Frost*, 220–21. Peter Davison provides a variation on the same theme: "At the age of 39 he knew himself to be among the notable poets of his time two years before the world would get around to finding out. . . . Though he had for decades been living the life of a poet, now at last he knew himself for one. . . ." Peter Davison, "Toward the Source: The Self-Realization of Robert Frost, 1911–1912," *Robert Frost: Lectures on the Centennial of His Birth*, 38. Clearly Frost's line "The strong are saying nothing until they see" has nothing to do with agnosticism but is rather an expression of his faith in himself. For further evidence of this theme, see Lathem, *Interviews with Robert Frost*, 121 and 136.

71. See Amherst College Special Collections, item #341. Other letters by Elliott are listed as #331, #332, #336, and #339.

72. Amherst College Special Collections, #304.

# Index

# Index

# Index

Gough, Peggy L., 374
Gould, Stephen Jay, 38–39
Grant, Ulysses S., 353
Gray, Asa, 33–34, 35, 36, 39, 43, 48, 400
Gray, Thomas, 86, 117
Greene, Graham, 78
Grossmann, Marcel, 144
Guiney, Louise Imogene, 97

## H

Haas, Robert, 371
Haeckel, Ernst Heinrich, 44, 82, 155, 156, 161, 353–56, 359, 372, 405, 407, 420, 438, 440
Hagstrom, Jack, 371
Haines, John W., xi, xxii, xxiv–xxv
Hall, Dorothy Judd, 88, 364, 370
Hall, John, xv
Hansen, Harry, 201
Hansen, Mary, 374
Harding, Warren, 272
Harrington, Vernon C., 368
Hass, Robert B., 325
Hawthorne, Nathaniel, 77, 101
Hayes, Carleton J. H., 420
Heathorn, Henrietta Anne, *See* Huxley, Henrietta.
Hecht, J. Jean, 371
Hegel, Georg Wilhelm Friedrich, 396
Heisenberg, Werner, 24, 150, 151
Henderson, Alice C., 171
Henderson, Archibald, 403
Henry VIII, King, 297
Herberg, Will, 149–50
Herbert, George, 117
Herodotus, 198
Highfield, Roger, 143, 145, 158
Hill, Craig, 373
Himmelfarb, Gertrude, 407
Hitler, Adolf, 264
Hobbes, Thomas, 8, 35, 221, 315, 319, 320, 347
Holden, Raymond, xi

Holmes, Nathaniel, 101
Holton, Gerald, 142–43, 145, 150, 151–53, 154, 155, 156, 168
Homer, 212, 352
Hooker, Joseph Dalton, 43, 62, 66
Horace, 172, 212, 263, 332
Horney, Karen, 76–77, 344
Howard, John, 374
Howison, George Holmes, 114
Hubble, Edwin, 167–68
Hudnut, Robin, 371
Hull, David L., 66–67
Hulme, T.E., xxiv
Hume, David, 255
Hutton, R. H., 349
Huxley, Aldous, 25, 36, 58, 61, 243–44, 322, 335
Huxley, Henrietta, 57–59, 438
Huxley, Leonard, 57, 59, 60–61, 356, 358, 439
Huxley, Sir Julian, 56, 58–60, 62, 104–5, 283, 285, 287, 288, 291, 293, 294, 335, 350
Huxley, Thomas Henry, 24, 27, 29, 30, 38, 42–44, 46–53, 57, 58, 59–72, 74, 82, 86, 115, 161, 198, 287, 291, 303, 315, 346–60, 362, 363–64, 372, 405–7, 425, 437, 438, 439–40

## I

Icarus, 332
Infeld, Leopold, 141, 418
Ingebretsen, Edward J., 325, 371

## J

Jackson, Andrew, 270
James, Henry, 94
James, William, v, viii, 33, 34–35, 39, 45, 47, 52, 88, 91, 94, 111, 112–13, 115–16, 134, 200–201, 206, 316, 360, 368, 370, 372, 400, 402
James I, King, 173
Jarrell, Randall, 176

# About the Authors

Peter J. Stanlis, a native of New Jersey, earned a B.A. at Middlebury College (1942), an M.A. at The Bread Loaf School of English (1944), and a Ph.D. at the University of Michigan (1951). He taught at various American colleges and universities for over forty years, and was a guest lecturer at four European universities. He published over 100 articles and reviews on political, historical, legal, educational, and literary subjects, and edited a law journal. In over a score of publications on Edmund Burke, including *Edmund Burke and the Natural Law* (1958), he modified how modern scholarship perceives the Whig statesman. In 1969 he was one of six scholars that founded The American Society of Eighteenth-Century Studies. In 1982 President Ronald Reagan appointed him to the National Council for the Humanities. In 1987 he was selected to be a British Academy Research Fellow, and became a member of the Academic Board of the National Humanities Institute. His many articles in *Modern Age* resulted in being appointed as Associate Editor to that journal. Since 1988 he has been retired as Distinguished Professor of Humanities, Emeritus, of Rockford College.

While teaching at the University of Detroit, Stanlis served as a city councilman for six years, and Governor G. Mennen Williams appointed him a member of the Michigan Constitutional Revision Commission, which resulted in a new constitution being adopted by that state.

Stanlis met Robert Frost in June 1939, and remained a friend of the poet for over twenty-three years, until Frost's death. His publications on Frost include a dozen articles, and a long literary memoir on his conversations with the poet at Bread Loaf during the summers of 1939–41.

Timothy Steele, a native of Burlington, Vermont, earned a B.A. at Stanford University (1970), and an M.A. (1972) and Ph.D. at Brandeis University (1977). He was a Guggenheim Fellow, and is currently a President's Distinguished Professor in English at California State University, Los Angeles. Steele's books of poetry include *Uncertainties and Rest* (1979), *The Color Wheel* (1994), *Sapphics and Uncertainties: Poems, 1970–1986* (1995), and *Toward the Winter Solstice* (2006).

Like Robert Frost's original structured and measured verse, Steele's own brand of originality in his poems retains iambic meters, modulated rhythms, rhyme, and intricate stanza forms. Like Frost, he does not write free verse, and is recognized as an outstanding poet in the new formalism. His article "The Meter and Versification of Robert Frost" and his book-length study *All the Fun's in How You Say a Thing* (1999) established him as a foremost authority on the art and thought of Frost, and on versification.